Frommer's®

W9-AHF-880

Colorado

9th Edition

by Don & Barbara Laine & Eric Peterson

Here's what the critics say about Frommer's:

"Amazingly easy to use. Very portable, very complete."

—*Booklist*

"Detailed, accurate, and easy-to-read information for all price ranges."

—*Glamour Magazine*

"Hotel information is close to encyclopedic."

—*Des Moines Sunday Register*

"Frommer's Guides have a way of giving you a real feel for a place."

—*Knight Ridder Newspapers*

Wiley Publishing, Inc.

Published by:

Wiley Publishing, Inc.
111 River St.
Hoboken, NJ 07030-5774

ISBN: 978-0-470-06857-1

Editor: Elizabeth Heath
Production Editor: Katie Robinson
Cartographer: Andrew Dolan
Photo Editor: Richard Fox
Anniversary Logo Design: Richard Pacifico
Production by Wiley Indianapolis Composition Services

Front cover photo: White River National Forest: Maroon Bells Mountains reflecting in Maroon Lake
Back cover photo: Arkansas River, Browns Canyon: Overhead shot of people whitewater rafting

For information on our other products and services or to obtain technical support, please contact our Customer Care Department within the U.S. at 800/762-2974, outside the U.S. at 317/572-3993 or fax 317/572-4002.

Wiley also publishes its books in a variety of electronic formats. Some content that appears in print may not be available in electronic formats.

Manufactured in the United States of America

5 4 3 2 1

Contents

List of Maps

Acknowledgments

The authors wish to thank the many people throughout Colorado who helped provide information for this book, and special thanks to Rich Grant and Shannon Dexheimer with the Denver Metro Convention and Visitors Bureau, the Boulder Convention and Visitors Bureau, Terry Coffey with the Colorado Springs Convention and Visitors Bureau, Suzy Blackhurst with the Estes Park Convention and Visitors Bureau, Irene Carlow with the Grand Junction Visitor & Convention Bureau, Tara Crowe with the Greater Pueblo Chamber of Commerce, and Gaylene Ore with Ore Communications, who helped update the sections on Cortez and Grand Lake.

An Invitation to the Reader

In researching this book, we discovered many wonderful places—hotels, restaurants, shops, and more. We're sure you'll find others. Please tell us about them, so we can share the information with your fellow travelers in upcoming editions. If you were disappointed with a recommendation, we'd love to know that, too. Please write to:

Frommer's Colorado, 9th Edition
Wiley Publishing, Inc. • 111 River St. • Hoboken, NJ 07030-5774

An Additional Note

Please be advised that travel information is subject to change at any time—and this is especially true of prices. We therefore suggest that you write or call ahead for confirmation when making your travel plans. The authors, editors, and publisher cannot be held responsible for the experiences of readers while traveling. Your safety is important to us, however, so we encourage you to stay alert and be aware of your surroundings. Keep a close eye on cameras, purses, and wallets, all favorite targets of thieves and pickpockets.

About the Authors

A Denver-based freelance writer, **Eric Peterson** has contributed to numerous Frommer's guides covering the American West, and written *Frommer's Montana & Wyoming, Frommer's Yellowstone & Grand Teton National Parks,* and *Ramble: A Field Guide to the U.S.A.* (www.speckpress.com). Peterson also writes about travel and other topics for such publications as *ColoradoBiz, United Hemispheres, Delta Sky,* and the *New York Daily News.* In his free time, he's an avid camper and hiker, a lifelong Broncos fan, and part-time rock star (at least in the eyes of his niece Olivia).

Residents of northern New Mexico since 1970, **Don and Barbara Laine** have traveled extensively throughout the Rocky Mountains and the Southwest, spending as much time as possible in the outdoors, and especially in the region's national parks and monuments. They have written Frommer's guides to Utah, Colorado, and the National Parks of the American West. The Laines have also authored *Little-Known Southwest, New Mexico & Arizona State Parks,* and *Best Short Hikes in Arizona* for The Mountaineers; and *The New Mexico Guide* for Fulcrum Publishing.

Other Great Guides for Your Trip:

Frommer's Denver, Boulder & Colorado Springs
Frommer's National Parks of the American West
Frommer's Rocky Mountain National Park
Frommer's Arizona
Frommer's New Mexico

Frommer's Star Ratings, Icons & Abbreviations

Every hotel, restaurant, and attraction listing in this guide has been ranked for quality, value, service, amenities, and special features using a **star-rating system.** In country, state, and regional guides, we also rate towns and regions to help you narrow down your choices and budget your time accordingly. Hotels and restaurants are rated on a scale of zero (recommended) to three stars (exceptional). Attractions, shopping, nightlife, towns, and regions are rated according to the following scale: zero stars (recommended), one star (highly recommended), two stars (very highly recommended), and three stars (must-see).

In addition to the star-rating system, we also use **seven feature icons** that point you to the great deals, in-the-know advice, and unique experiences that separate travelers from tourists. Throughout the book, look for:

Finds	Special finds—those places only insiders know about
Fun Fact	Fun facts—details that make travelers more informed and their trips more fun
Kids	Best bets for kids and advice for the whole family
Moments	Special moments—those experiences that memories are made of
Overrated	Places or experiences not worth your time or money
Tips	Insider tips—great ways to save time and money
Value	Great values—where to get the best deals

The following **abbreviations** are used for credit cards:

AE	American Express	DISC	Discover	V	Visa
DC	Diners Club	MC	MasterCard		

Frommers.com

Now that you have this guidebook to help you plan a great trip, visit our website at **www. frommers.com** for additional travel information on more than 3,500 destinations. We update features regularly to give you instant access to the most current trip-planning information available. At Frommers.com, you'll find scoops on the best airfares, lodging rates, and car rental bargains. You can even book your travel online through our reliable travel booking partners. Other popular features include:

- Online updates of our most popular guidebooks
- Vacation sweepstakes and contest giveaways
- Newsletters highlighting the hottest travel trends
- Online travel message boards with featured travel discussions

What's New in Colorado

Colorado is a rich combination of the old and new, urban and rural, the civilized and the wild. The state's major cities lure us with their museums, galleries, performing arts, and historic sites, but just outside their boundaries await a vast array of outdoor recreation opportunities and some of America's most beautiful mountain scenery.

Growth, which Coloradans see as both a blessing and a curse, continues to be the main change occurring here. And for at least the next few years those who venture into the mountains will see not only the remnants of damage from dozens of forest fires that plagued the state in 2002, but also how quickly the forests begin to regenerate and heal themselves.

One big statewide change went into effect in the summer of 2006—Colorado became the 13th state to **ban smoking** in restaurants, bars, and most places of business. Smoking remains legal in cigar bars and casinos, and a group of bar and restaurant owners have filed suit in an attempt to overturn the law.

SETTLING INTO DENVER **Southwest Airlines** has made a splash in Denver since its first flights touched down at Denver International Airport in 2006. **T-REX,** a major road and light-rail project was completed in 2006, making for a wider highway through the south end of town and a light-rail line alongside I-25 from the Broadway exit south to County Line Road. The first high-rise built in downtown Denver in a quarter-century,

the **Hyatt Regency Denver,** 650 15th St. (© **800/233-1234** or 303/436-1234), rivals Denver's best downtown luxury hotels and has a bar, Altitude, on the 27th floor, with dramatic views. Denver also boasts some fine new restaurants. These include the **Rioja,** 1431 Larimer Sq. (© **303/820-2282**), serving some of the most creative plates in town under the direction of chef-owner Jennifer Jasinski; **Elway's,** 2500 E. First Ave. next to the Cherry Creek Shopping Center Writer Square (© **303/399-5353**), a popular "New West" steakhouse owned by Denver Broncos legend John Elway; **Table 6,** 609 Corona St. (© **303/831-8800**), which melds slick and cozy into a great neighborhood bistro, and has a terrific wine list to boot. See chapter 5 for details.

WHAT TO SEE & DO IN DENVER The **Denver Art Museum,** 100 W. 14th Ave. (© **720/865-5000**), opened its splashy new expansion designed by Daniel Libeskind in 2006, doubling the amount of exhibit space. The expansion is an avant-garde, platinum-clad building that is the most distinctive in town, if not the Rocky Mountain region. After a period of increased security and bureaucracy, it's back to business as usual for visiting the **U.S. Mint,** City Park, 320 W. Colfax Ave. (© **303/405-4757**). Formerly Colorado's Ocean Journey, **Downtown Aquarium,** City Park, 700 Water St. (© **303/561-4444**), remodeled, added several exhibits, and opened a restaurant and lounge. New in 2006, **Lannie's**

Clocktower Cabaret, in the basement of the D&F Tower, 1601 Arapahoe St. (© 303/293-0075), is a funky bordello-inspired theater that sees a wide variety of entertainers on its stage. The **Colorado Rapids** (© 303/405-1100; www.colorado rapids.com) of Major League Soccer play at a new, soccer-only stadium in Commerce City. For more information, see chapter 6.

COLORADO SPRINGS Since opening in January 2006, the **Summit,** at The Broadmoor, 19 Lake Circle. (© 719/577-5896), has been the rage of the Colorado Springs restaurant scene, garnering lots of national acclaim. The strikingly contemporary room is aesthetically matched by the fare. The **Black Sheep,** 2106 E. Platte Ave. (© 710/227-7625), has emerged as a standout local rock club. The shopping scene has extended further north with the **Promenade Shops at Briargate,** 1885 Briargate Pkwy. (© 719/265-5516). See chapter 7 for details.

BOULDER In 2006, the **Colorado Chautauqua,** 900 Baseline Rd. (© 303/442-3282), became the first National Historical Landmark on Colorado's central Front Range. During the late 19th and early 20th centuries, more than 400 Chautauquas—adult education and cultural entertainment centers—sprang up around the United States, and this is one of the few remaining. The **Leanin' Tree Museum of Western Art,** 6055 Longbow Dr. (© 800/777-8716), has a new outdoor sculpture garden. On the culinary side of things, relative newcomers **Frasca,** 1738 Pearl St. (© 303/442-6966), and **The Kitchen,** 1039 Pearl St. (© 303/544-5973), have risen to the top of Boulder's dining scene in recent years. A major new outdoor shopping center, **Twenty Ninth Street,** is centered on the former site of the Crossroads Mall at the intersection of Canyon Blvd. and 29th St. (© 303/440-0722). Open since October 2006, tenants include Wild Oats, MontBell, Borders,

Apple, and Century Theatres. See chapter 8 for details.

NORTHEASTERN COLORADO
Fort Collins The lodging market is evolving here, with the longstanding "Home of the Rams" Holiday Inn becoming the **Hilton Fort Collins,** 425 W. Prospect Ave. (© 800/445-8667 or 970/482-2626) in 2005, and undergoing a slick renovation in the process. The year before marked the opening of the **Armstrong Hotel,** 259 S. College Ave. (© 866/384-3883 or 970/484-3883), a boutique hotel that is the only place to bunk downtown.

See chapter 9 for all the details.

THE NORTHERN ROCKIES Estes Park Shuttered for a quarter-century, **Marys Lake Lodge,** 2625 Mary's Lake Rd. (© 877/443-6279 or 970/586-5958) has reopened in the 21st century and emerged as a local standout for both lodging and dining. New in 2007: an outdoor pool and more modern condo units out front.

Shuttle buses began operating in 2006 throughout the business district of Estes Park and from Estes Park into Rocky Mountain National Park. The buses run daily from July through Labor Day; schedules are available at the Estes Park Visitor Center.

Steamboat Springs At the ski resort, plans for a base area redevelopment are in the works, with the first projects slated for 2007. A new standby for sandwiches to eat on-site or on the trail, **Backcountry Provisions,** 635 Lincoln Ave. (© 970/879-3617) has a great menu that caters to both vegetarians and carnivores.

Winter Park Devil's Thumb Ranch, Grand C.R. 83, Tabernash, 8 miles north of Winter Park (© 800/933-4339 or 970/726-5632), has pegged summer 2007 as the opening date of its new 53-room lodge, as well as a spa/fitness center.

Breckenridge A **new gondola** started connecting the Breckenridge Transportation Center, just off Main Street, and Peak 7 and Peak 8, opened for the 2006–07 ski season.

Vail A billion-dollar redevelopment of Vail Village, **Vail's New Dawn** is underway, a slick makeover consisting of numerous hotel, residential, retail, and infrastructure projects. The first project to be completed was the rebuilt **Tivoli Lodge,** 386 Hanson Ranch Rd. (© **800/ 451-4756** or 970/476-5615), which reopened in 2006 on the same spot of the original Tivoli. West of Vail, **State Bridge Lodge and River Resort** near Bond (© **970/653-4444**) is under new ownership, giving the rowdy music venue a much-needed face-lift as a lodging option.

Beaver Creek To help get you onto the mountain faster, **Beaver Creek Resort** (© **800/404-3535**) is opening a new gondola from Avon for the 2007–08 ski season.

Aspen One of our longstanding affordably priced favorites, the **Limelight Lodge,** 228 E. Cooper Ave. (© **800/433-0832** or 970/925-3025) was bulldozed in 2006 to make way for a killer new "green" motel on the same spot, slated to reopen during the 2007–08 ski season. Nearby **Snowmass Village** is in the midst of a major redevelopment.

See chapter 10 for more information.

THE WESTERN SLOPE   Grand Junction The dinosaur quarry and visitor center at **Dinosaur National Monument,** 4545 E. U.S. 40, Dinosaur (© **970/374-3000**) has been closed indefinitely while much-needed structural repairs are made. There's still plenty to do there, though, and some spectacular scenic views as well.

A wonderful new antique and classic car museum opened in May 2006 about an hour's drive southwest of Grand Junction. The **Gateway Colorado Auto Museum,** 43200 Colo. 141, Gateway (© **866/671-4733** or 970/931-2458), displays about four dozen rare vehicles, all beautifully restored, in a state-of-the-art facility.

Glenwood Springs   Glenwood Caverns Adventure Park, 51000 Two Rivers Plaza Rd. (© **800/530-1635** or 970/945-4228) has added more activities to its already popular tram ride and cave tours—now there is also horseback riding, mechanical bull riding, and rock climbing.

See chapter 11 for more information.

SOUTHWESTERN   COLORADO Durango The **Durango & Silverton Narrow Gauge Railroad,** 479 Main Ave. (© **888/872-4607** or 970/247-2733), has added an upscale Vista Car—offering fantastic views—to its steam train rides.

See chapter 12 for more information.

SOUTHERN   ROCKIES   Alamosa There's a new train in Southern Colorado. The **Rio Grande Scenic Railroad,** 601 State St. (© **877/726-7245**) began offering scenic rides along historic train routes in late spring 2006.

See chapter 13 for details.

1

The Best of Colorado

The old and the new, the rustic and the sophisticated, the wild and the refined—all of these experiences exist practically side by side in Colorado, amid what is arguably the most breathtaking mountain scenery in America.

Colorado's booming cities—Boulder, Colorado Springs, and Denver—and it's admittedly somewhat glitzy resorts—especially Vail and Aspen—offer much of the comfort and culture of New York or Los Angeles but at a slower, more relaxed pace. Throughout the state, you'll also find testaments to another time, when life was simpler but rougher, and only the strong survived: historic Victorian mansions, working turn-of-the-20th-century steam trains, thousand-year-old adobe-and-stone villages, and authentic Old West towns complete with false-fronted saloons and dusty streets.

Colorado truly comes alive for those who venture outdoors—among the towering Rocky Mountains, the western canyons, or the broad eastern plains. Atop Pikes Peak, you'll see what inspired Katharine Lee Bates to pen the lyrics to "America the Beautiful." Climb on a horse or mountain bike, take a hike or raft trip—or simply sit back and gaze at the mountains. Whatever you do, though, don't stay indoors. Enos Mills, an early-20th-century environmentalist and one of the driving forces behind the creation of Rocky Mountain National Park, said that knowledge of nature is the basis of wisdom. For many, that's the essence of Colorado.

The following are what we consider Colorado's best experiences—highlights that will help you begin planning your trip.

1 The Best Ski Resorts

- **Aspen:** Not only does Aspen have predictably superior ski terrain ranging from some of the most expert runs in Colorado to what *Ski* magazine has called the best mountain in America for beginners (Buttermilk), it's also one of the most fun, genuinely historic ski towns in Colorado. Although it might come off at first as somewhat glitzy and certainly expensive, Aspen is a real town, with long-time, year-round residents and a history that goes beyond the slopes. See chapter 10.

- **Breckenridge:** The lure of Breckenridge lies in its fabulous trails for skiers of all abilities, its location in an old gold-prospecting settlement, and its abundance of ski-in/ski-out lodging. It's also less expensive than Aspen or Vail, more rustic in feel, and appealing to families for its variety of après-ski activities. See chapter 10.

- **Vail:** This is it, the big one, America's most popular ski resort, as well as one of its largest, with 5,289 acres of ski-able terrain, 193 trails, and 34 lifts. Every serious skier needs to ski Vail at least once. Its free bus system makes it easy to get around, but be prepared for steep prices, and don't look for Victorian charm—all you'll find are rows of condominiums. See chapter 10.

- **Durango Mountain Resort:** One of Colorado's best-kept skiing secrets, this resort is known for its beautiful sunny days, heavy annual snowfall, and exceptionally friendly, easygoing atmosphere. See chapter 12.

2 The Best Active Vacations

- **Hiking in Rocky Mountain National Park:** There's something for everyone here, from short hikes around a lovely mountain lake to the difficult 8-mile trek to the top of 14,259-foot Longs Peak. Trail heads can be accessed with the park's shuttle bus, from campgrounds, and from stops along Trail Ridge Road. However you do it, getting into the wilds is a treat in this beautiful setting. See chapter 10.

- **Cowpunching on a Cattle Drive:** To really step back into the West of the 1800s, join working cowboys on a genuine cattle drive. The **Saddleback Ranch** near Steamboat Springs (© 970/871-4697) is a working cattle ranch, where you'll become just another cowpuncher, moving stock from one pasture to another, and performing other ranch duties. See p. 267.

- **Skiing the San Juan Hut System:** Ambitious cross-country skiers who want to put a few miles behind them and ski among 14,000-foot alpine peaks love the San Juan Hut System's trail and series of shelters between Telluride and Moab, Utah. Designed for intermediate skiers, the trail can be tackled in small sections or its entirety, with overnight stays in the well-equipped huts. See chapter 12.

3 The Best Hiking Trails

- **The Buttes Trail at Pawnee Buttes:** This easy day hike exposes you to some of the "other" Colorado: the prairie on the state's eastern plains. A 1.5-mile trail leads to Pawnee Buttes, the Rattlesnake Buttes made famous in James Michener's *Centennial.* Keep your eyes open for coyotes, a variety of birds, and other wildlife, and colorful wildflowers in the spring. See p. 230.

- **The Emerald Lake Trail at Rocky Mountain National Park:** If you like mountain lakes, this is the trail for you. Starting at Bear Lake, it's an easy .5-mile to Nymph Lake, then a moderate .5-mile climb to Dream Lake, and the last .8-mile brings you to Emerald Lake. Total elevation change is 605 feet over a little less than 2 miles, with spectacular scenery all along the way. See p. 259.

- **The Colorado Trail at Kenosha Pass:** This easy section of the Colorado Trail near Breckenridge is a fun day's walk or can be the starting point for a serious backpacking trip. Pick up the trail off U.S. 285 where the highway crosses 10,001-foot Kenosha Pass. This access point provides opportunities for short or long hikes through the aspen and bristlecone forest. See p. 292.

- **Hiking the Dunes in Great Sand Dunes National Monument & Preserve:** This isn't a trail at all, but an opportunity to don your best French foreign legion hat and set out into the shifting sands in search of dramatic views from the top of a 750-foot dune. See p. 422.

Colorado

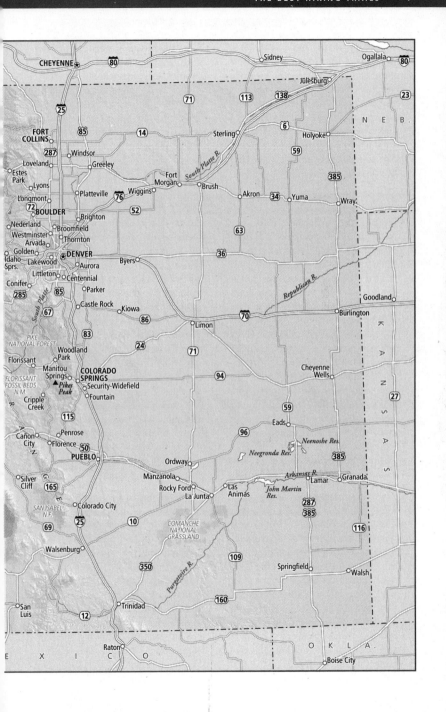

4 The Best Mountain Biking

- **Tipperary Creek Trail:** Considered by many to be Colorado's very best mountain-biking trail, this 30-mile ride from Fraser to Winter Park runs through dense forest and wildflower-covered meadows, offering views of rugged snowcapped peaks. It's also strenuous, rising from an 8,600-foot elevation to more than 10,000 feet. See p. 283.

- **Crested Butte:** Crested Butte vies with Winter Park for the title of mountain-biking capital of Colorado. The highly skilled should try Trail 401, a strenuous single-track loop that combines scenic beauty with steep grades and rough terrain. See p. 415.

5 The Best Wilderness Experiences

- **Hiking the Colorado Trail:** For some 500 miles, this trail winds from Denver to Durango, through some of the state's most spectacular and rugged terrain, crossing the Continental Divide, eight mountain ranges, and six wilderness areas. Just to the west of Leadville, the trail passes through the Collegiate Peaks Wilderness with a view of some of Colorado's most prominent fourteeners (mountains at least 14,000 ft. high) and fields of wildflowers. The hardier might take a side trip up Mount Elbert, the state's tallest peak at 14,433 feet. See chapters 4, 6, 10, and 12.

- **Hiking to Crater Lake in the Maroon Bells National Wilderness Area:** With a number of fourteeners, including the namesake Maroon Bells, this is one of the most scenic mountainscapes in the West. A vision of glaciated rock and lush greenery, the trails here are popular with backpackers, but the hike to Crater Lake is a superb half-day trek. See p. 326.

- **Rafting Glenwood Canyon:** Running the rapids of the Colorado River is one of the best and surely most exciting ways to see one of the most beautiful canyons in the West. Although a bit too popular to provide a genuine wilderness experience, this stretch of river has sections rated for experts during the high spring runoff as well as quieter areas appropriate for everyone. See chapter 11.

6 The Best Places to Discover American Indian Culture

- **Ute Indian Museum (Montrose):** One of Colorado's few museums dedicated to an existing Indian tribe, this excellent collection, run by the Colorado Historical Society, shows how Utes lived in the 19th century, as they were being forced to reconcile their way of life with that of the invading white pioneers. There's a particularly good exhibit of Ute ceremonial items. See p. 362.

- **Mesa Verde National Park:** Home to the most impressive prehistoric cliff dwellings in the Southwest, Mesa Verde (Spanish for "green table") overwhelms you with its size and complexity. The first national park set aside to preserve works created by humans, it covers some 52,000 acres just outside Cortez. Among the most compelling sites are Spruce Tree House, Square Tower House, and

Cliff Palace, a four-story apartment-style dwelling. See p. 388.

- **Ute Mountain Tribal Park:** These ruins differ from others in Colorado because they're located on the Ute Mountain Indian Reservation, and the only way to see it is on a guided tour conducted by members of the Ute tribe. You'll see ruins and petroglyphs similar to those in Mesa Verde, but with an informed personal guide and without the crowds. See p. 391.

7 The Best Places to Recapture the Old West

- **Old Town (Burlington):** On Colorado's eastern plains, right next door to Kansas, is this living-history museum, containing two dozen buildings (many from the 1880s). Watch a cancan, melodrama, or gunfight in a setting more reminiscent of Dodge City than Colorado's Victorian mountain towns. See chapter 9.
- **Creede, Lake City, and Leadville:** With extensive historic districts and false-fronted buildings, these mountain towns take you back to the time when Butch Cassidy, Doc Holliday, and other infamous dudes stalked the saloons in search of the next card game. See chapters 10 (Leadville) and 13 (Creede, Lake City).
- **Bent's Old Fort National Historic Site (La Junta):** Reconstructed to the way it appeared in the 1830s and 1840s, this adobe fort shows life as it really was, when pioneers spent their time either trading peaceably with or fighting off plains warriors. See p. 447.

8 The Most Scenic Views

- **Garden of the Gods:** There's nothing like sunrise at Garden of the Gods in Colorado Springs, with its fantastic and sometimes fanciful red-sandstone formations sculpted by wind and water over hundreds of thousands of years. It's worth spending some foot power to get away from the crowds on one of the park's many trails, to listen to the wind, and imagine the gods cavorting among the formations. See p. 161.
- **Trail Ridge Road:** Transversing Rocky Mountain National Park, Trail Ridge affords expansive and sometimes dizzying views in all directions. There are a dozen stops where you can take a short hike, possibly glimpse the unofficial mascots of the park (bighorn sheep), and get a close-up look at tundra. The drive rises above 12,000 feet and crosses the Continental Divide. See p. 254.
- **The Black Canyon of the Gunnison:** Among the steepest and most narrow canyons in North America, the Black Canyon of the Gunnison, near Montrose, offers breathtaking and sometimes eerie views into the darkness below or, for ambitious hikers, from the canyon depths to daylight above. The sheerness of its 2,500-foot-high walls, the narrowness of its 40-foot-wide base, and the resulting darkness at its core evoke a somber, almost religious mood. See p. 365.
- **Colorado National Monument:** Just west of Grand Junction are stunning vistas of red-rock canyons and sandstone monoliths. The monument's 23-mile Rim Rock Drive offers incredible views, and short walks and backcountry trails afford more solitude. You'll get the best light in the early morning or late afternoon, when the rocks glow red and shadows dance among the stone sculptures. See p. 337.

- **The San Juan Skyway:** This 233-mile circle drive that goes through Durango, Telluride, and Ouray is among the most beautiful scenic drives in America, passing historic mining camps, fields of wildflowers, stately forests, snowcapped peaks, and cascading waterfalls; and crossing five mountain passes. It's not advisable for those who have difficulty with high elevation (Red Mountain Pass has an 11,008-ft. elevation) or steep, winding roads. Except in summer, it's wise to be sure the passes are open before heading out. See p. 384.

9 The Best Family Vacations

- **Playing Cowboy at the Home Ranch and Devil's Thumb Ranch:** Nestled in the mountains near Steamboat Springs and Winter Park, respectively, these are two of the state's standout guest ranches, with luxurious perks. At the Home Ranch, expect food from an expertly trained French chef and adventurous horseback rides; at Devil's Thumb, there are all sorts of outdoor activities and geothermally heated cabins. See chapter 10.
- **Riding an 1880s Narrow Gauge Steam Train:** There are two: the Durango & Silverton follows the Animas River from Durango up through the San Juan Mountains to historic Silverton; the Cumbres & Toltec chugs out of Antonito, Colorado, through the Toltec Gorge of the Los Piños River, over Cumbres Pass into Chama, New Mexico. Scenery is stupendous over both lines, and each fulfills every train buff's greatest dream of smoke in your eyes and cinders in your hair. See chapters 12 (Durango & Silverton) and 13 (Cumbres & Toltec).
- **Exploring Great Sand Dunes National Park and Preserve:** About 40 miles northeast of Alamosa, this huge pile of sand is a great place to explore, camp, hike, or just play in the 750-foot-tall dunes. Rangers provide guided nature walks and campfire programs in the summer, and a hiking/off-road-vehicle trail leads out the back of the monument into the national forest. See chapter 13.

10 The Best Luxury Hotels

- **Brown Palace Hotel** (Denver; ✆ 800/321-2599 or 303/297-3111): Denver's finest hotel, the Brown Palace has been open continuously since 1892, serving high society and celebrities—from President Dwight Eisenhower to the Beatles—with elegance and charm. Although most of the rooms are Victorian in decor, with Tiffany lamps and other accouterments, our favorites are the Art Deco rooms, which have an undeniable feel of the 1920s and 1930s. See p. 82.
- **The Broadmoor** (Colorado Springs; ✆ 800/634-7711 or 719/634-7711): Colorado's top-rated resort hotel has it all—excellent dining, golf courses, pools, tennis courts, a state-of-the-art fitness center, full-service spa, and shopping, plus extraordinary service—in a magnificently restored historic building set in immaculate grounds. Although extremely impressive, The Broadmoor is never pretentious, and it certainly knows how to pamper its guests. See p. 150.

- **The St. Regis Aspen** (Aspen; ⓒ **888/454-9005** or 970/920-3300): At the base of Ajax Mountain, the St. Regis offers great views of the mountains or town, impeccable service, luxurious rooms, and all the services and amenities you'd expect in a fine hotel. Although a bit pricey, especially at Christmas, the hotel is supremely elegant in a comfortable, cozy way. See p. 330.

- **Ritz-Carlton, Bachelor Gulch** (Avon; ⓒ **800/241-3333** or 970/748-6200): A stunning structure modeled after the grand national park lodges, the rock-and-log "parkitechture" exterior sheaths one of the most luxurious hotels in the West. The rooms are also studies in "New West" glitz, complete with mountain and earth tones, decor inspired by wildlife and forests, and jaw-dropping views. See p. 309.

11 The Best Moderately Priced Accommodations

- **Alpine Trail Ridge Inn** (Estes Park; ⓒ **800/223-5023** or 970/586-4585): This is a top-notch independent motel, right next to the entrance to Rocky Mountain National Park. Proprietors Jay and Fran Grooters are also great sources for hiking advice. See p. 247.

- **Boulder Outlook** (Boulder; ⓒ **800/542-0304** or 303/443-3322): The Outlook is fun, fresh, and definitively Boulder, with two bouldering rocks, a huge dog run, and discounts on bike rentals and other activities. The rooms are larger than average and the indoor pool is superb, complete with a waterfall and a mural of a cloud-speckled sky. See p. 191.

- **Hotel Bristol** (Steamboat Springs; ⓒ **800/851-0872** or 970/879-3083): Lodging with character, historic ambience, and unusual room layouts appeal to us at this reasonably priced 1940s hotel in downtown Steamboat. Rooms are small, but the family units easily accommodate four people. See p. 274.

12 The Best Bed & Breakfasts

- **Old Town GuestHouse** (Colorado Springs; ⓒ **888/375-4210** or 719/632-9194): This three-story redbrick building looks like a 19th-century inn but was built in 1997 to offer all the modern amenities in a warm and inviting atmosphere. The overstuffed chairs in the library invite you to kick off your shoes and relax before the fireplace while enjoying a good book, or maybe a nap. See p. 152.

- **Barn on the River** (Breckenridge; ⓒ **800/795-2975** or 970/453-2975): This delightful bed and breakfast is right on the banks of the Blue River, its serene riverside location belying the fact that it's on the edge of downtown. See p. 295.

- **The Bradley** (Boulder; ⓒ **800/858-5811** or 303/545-5200): Built as an upscale inn in 1994, the Bradley nicely blends into the surrounding historic neighborhood, just northeast of the Pearl Street Mall. The striking Great Room and uniquely decorated guest rooms are all adorned with bold contemporary art from local galleries. See p. 190.

2

Planning Your Trip to Colorado

The beauty of a Colorado vacation is that there's truly something for everyone. Depending on where you choose to go, you can have an affordable and fun time, or you can spend a bit more and have a truly world-class experience. The more expensive resorts—Vail, Aspen, Steamboat, and Telluride—tend to fill up quickly, especially during ski season; you'll want to book as far in advance as possible. The same is true for the state's most popular attractions, such as the national parks—especially busy over school vacations. This chapter gives you the information you need to get started.

1 The Regions in Brief

This book is organized primarily geographically, and because this is a big state, many visitors will limit their Colorado vacation to one or two regions.

THE FRONT RANGE The state's three major cities—Denver, Boulder, and Colorado Springs—form a line along the eastern slope of the Rocky Mountains known as the **Front Range.** These cities are a blend of old and new; rustic and sophisticated; urban and rural. Founded in the mid–19th century by both East Coast gold-seekers and European and Asian immigrants in search of a better life, these cities became home to what we might call the more civilized pioneer—the mine owner instead of the prospector, the merchant rather than the gambler.

Today, these modern cities have virtually all the amenities you'd expect to find in a major U.S. metropolis: opera, theater, dance, art, excellent restaurants, and sophisticated hotels and convention centers. You'll also find historic Victorian mansions, working steam trains, and old gold mines. You can go horseback riding, hiking, skiing, or shopping; or spend hours exploring museums, galleries, and shops. See chapters 5 through 8.

NORTHEASTERN COLORADO This region is quite different from the major cities and even more of a departure from the rugged mountain towns to the west. Northeastern Colorado contains the sparsely populated plains, a place where buffalo once roamed and pioneer farmers endured drought, dust, snow, and wind to create farms and ranches.

Here is the college town of Fort Collins, home of the large Anheuser-Busch brewery; the town of Loveland, known primarily for its name and Valentine card remailing; plus smaller communities such as Fort Morgan, the boyhood home of big band leader Glenn Miller. This region is dotted with pioneer homes and museums, frontier forts, and preserved downtown districts, plus a surprising number of lakes and seemingly endless fields of wheat and corn. See chapter 9.

THE NORTHERN ROCKIES For many people, the northern Rockies epitomize Colorado. Here you'll find some of the West's most spectacular and inspiring scenery at Rocky Mountain National Park, as well as America's top ski resorts, including Vail and Aspen, both home and playground to many of Hollywood's beautiful people. But tucked away amid the ski slopes, overpriced boutiques, and towering peaks are delightful historic Old West towns such as Leadville and Steamboat Springs, where you can step back to a simpler, more rugged era. This region is ideal for year-round outdoor activities, from skiing and snowboarding to hiking, mountain biking, fishing, boating, and four-wheeling. See chapter 10.

THE WESTERN SLOPE This region more closely resembles the canyon country of Utah than Colorado's famed Rocky Mountains. The area is defined in large part by its rivers—the Colorado, Gunnison, and Yampa—which over tens of thousands of years have carved ruggedly beautiful canyons. The Black Canyon of the Gunnison National Park encompasses an awe-inspiring narrow chasm, and colorful layers of rock define the canyon walls and unusual formations of the Colorado and Dinosaur national monuments. The latter also boasts one of the best dinosaur quarries you'll see anywhere. In addition, the western slope offers about a dozen wineries near the region's largest city, Grand Junction, and mineral hot springs and eye-opening caves in Glenwood Springs, where Old West gunfighter Doc Holliday is buried. See chapter 11.

SOUTHWESTERN COLORADO Those curious about the prehistoric peoples who once populated the West should head to this part of the state, where Mesa Verde National Park and a number of other sites preserve ancient cliff dwellings and other archaeological sites that help explain what life was like here 1,000 years ago. Also in this region is the historic community of Durango, with its main street (ca. 1880) and narrow-gauge steam railroad. Another Old West town, Telluride, retains its historic charm while emerging as a major ski and summer resort. In addition, the San Juan Mountains rival the vistas in Colorado's northern Rockies. See chapter 12.

THE SOUTHERN ROCKIES An exciting mix of terrain and experiences await visitors to the southern Rockies, which contain 30 peaks soaring over 14,000 feet, as well as white-water rafting near Salida, the historic picturesque mining town of Creede, and the tallest sand dunes in North America at Great Sand Dunes National Monument and Preserve. This area also contains splendid boating and fishing at Curecanti National Recreation Area, plus skiing and mountain biking, and a historic narrow-gauge steam train at Antonito, south of Alamosa. See chapter 13.

SOUTHEASTERN COLORADO History and a scenic stark beauty are the main draws of this region, which is best known for one of the world's most spectacular canyons—the deep, narrow Royal Gorge, which is carved by the Arkansas River as it makes its way down from the Rocky Mountains to the plains. The sector's largest city, Pueblo, offers outdoor recreation, several good museums, and a fine zoo. Boating and fishing opportunities abound on two lakes—Pueblo and Trinidad—both operated as state parks; and Bent's Old Fort is a national historic site that has re-created one of the West's most important frontier trading posts. The towns of Trinidad and La Junta also have a number of historic attractions, and you'll find dinosaur tracks in the Comanche National Grassland. See chapter 14.

2 Visitor Information

Start by contacting the **Colorado Tourism Office,** 1625 Broadway, Denver, CO 80202 (✆ **800/COLORADO;** www.colorado.com), for a free copy of the official state vacation guide, which includes a state map and describes attractions, activities, and lodgings throughout Colorado. Another good source for Colorado information is the website of the *Denver Post,* the state's major daily newspaper, at www.denverpost.com.

The **Colorado Hotel and Lodging Association,** 999 18th St., Suite 1240, Denver, CO 80202 (✆ **303/297-8335;** www.coloradolodging.com), offers a free guide to lodging across the state. The nonprofit **Bed and Breakfast Innkeepers of Colorado,** P.O. Box 38416, Colorado Springs, CO 80937 (✆ **800/265-7696;** www.innsofcolorado.org), distributes a free directory describing about 100 B&Bs across the state.

Hostelling International-USA, 8401 Colesville Rd., Suite 600, Silver Spring, MD 20910 (✆ **301/495-1240;** www. hiayh.org), has a computerized system for making reservations in hostels worldwide, and also has a print directory of U.S. hostels.

A free copy of *Your Guide to Outdoor Adventure,* which contains details on the state's 40 parks, is available from state park offices at 1313 Sherman St., Suite 618, Denver, CO 80203 (✆ **303/866-3437;** www.parks.state.co.us). State park offices can also provide information on boating and snowmobiling.

Destination: Colorado—Pre-Departure Checklist

- Are there any **special requirements** for your destination? Special visas, passports, or IDs? Detailed road maps? Bug repellents? Appropriate attire? If you're flying, are you carrying a current, government-issued ID, such as a driver's license or passport?
- Did you find out your daily ATM withdrawal limit?
- Do you have your credit card PIN numbers? If you have a 5- or 6-digit PIN number, did you obtain a 4-digit number from your bank?
- To check in at a kiosk with an e-ticket, do you have the credit card you bought your ticket with or a frequent-flier card?
- If you purchased traveler's checks, have you recorded the check numbers and stored the documentation separately from the checks?
- Did you bring your ID cards that could entitle you to discounts, such as AAA and AARP cards and student IDs?
- Did you leave a copy of your itinerary with someone at home?
- Do any theater, restaurant, or travel reservations need to be booked in advance?
- If you want to attend a Denver Broncos game, call early—home games sell out months ahead.

3 Entry Requirements & Customs

ENTRY REQUIREMENTS
PASSPORTS

For information on how to get a passport, see **"Passports"** in the **"Fast Facts"** section of this chapter—the websites listed provide passport applications as well as the current fees for processing applications. For an up-to-date, country-by-country listing of passport requirements around the world, go to the "Foreign Entry Requirement" Web page of the U.S. State Department at **http://travel.state.gov**. International visitors can obtain a visa application at the same website.

VISAS

For information on how to get a Visa, go to **"Visas"** in the **"Fast Facts"** section of this chapter.

The U.S. State Department has a **Visa Waiver Program** allowing citizens of the following countries (as of press time) to enter the United States without a visa for stays of up to 90 days: Andorra, Australia, Austria, Belgium, Brunei, Denmark, Finland, France, Germany, Iceland, Ireland, Italy, Japan, Liechtenstein, Luxembourg, Monaco, the Netherlands, New Zealand, Norway, Portugal, San Marino, Singapore, Slovenia, Spain, Sweden, Switzerland, and the United Kingdom. Citizens of these nations need only a valid passport and a round-trip air or cruise ticket upon arrival. If they first enter the United States, they may also visit Mexico, Canada, Bermuda, and/or the Caribbean islands and return to the United States without a visa. Further information is available from any U.S. embassy or consulate. Canadian citizens may enter the United States without visas; they need only proof of residence.

Citizens of all other countries must have (1) a valid passport that expires at least 6 months later than the scheduled end of their visit to the United States, and (2) a tourist visa, which may be obtained without charge from any U.S. consulate.

MEDICAL REQUIREMENTS

Unless you're arriving from an area known to be suffering from an epidemic (particularly cholera or yellow fever), inoculations or vaccinations are not required for entry into the United States. If you have a medical condition that requires **syringe-administered medications,** carry a valid signed prescription from your physician—the Federal Aviation Administration (FAA) no longer allows airline passengers to pack syringes in their carry-on baggage without documented proof of medical need. If you have a disease that requires treatment with **narcotics,** you should also carry documented proof with you—smuggling narcotics aboard a plane is a serious offense that carries severe penalties in the U.S.

For **HIV-positive visitors,** requirements for entering the United States are somewhat vague and change frequently. For up-to-the-minute information, contact **AIDSinfo** (② **800/448-0440** or 301/519-6616 outside the U.S.; http://aidsinfo.nih.gov) or the **Gay Men's Health Crisis** (② **212/367-1000;** www.gmhc.org).

CUSTOMS
WHAT YOU CAN BRING INTO COLORADO

Every visitor more than 21 years of age may bring in, free of duty, the following: (1) 1 liter of wine or hard liquor; (2) 200 cigarettes, 100 cigars (but not from Cuba), or 3 pounds of smoking tobacco; and (3) $100 worth of gifts. These exemptions are offered to travelers who spend at least 72 hours in the United States and who have not claimed them within the preceding 6 months. It is altogether forbidden to bring into the country foodstuffs (particularly fruit, cooked meats, and canned goods) and plants (vegetables, seeds, tropical plants, and the like). Foreign tourists may carry in or out up to $10,000 in U.S. or foreign currency with no formalities; larger sums must be declared to U.S. Customs on entering or leaving, which includes filing form CM 4790. For details regarding U.S. Customs and Border Protection, consult your nearest U.S. embassy or consulate, or **U.S. Customs** (© **202/927-1770;** www.customs.ustreas. gov).

WHAT YOU CAN TAKE HOME FROM COLORADO
Canadian Citizens
For a clear summary of Canadian rules, write for the booklet *I Declare,* issued by the **Canada Border Services Agency** (© **800/461-9999** in Canada, or 204/ 983-3500; **www.cbsa-asfc.gc.ca**).

U.K. Citizens
For information, contact **HM Customs & Excise** at © **0845/010-9000** (from outside the U.K., 020/8929-0152), or consult their website at **www.hmce.gov.uk**.

Australian Citizens
A helpful brochure available from Australian consulates or customs offices is *Know Before You Go.* For more information, call the **Australian Customs Service** at © **1300/363-263,** or log on to **www. customs.gov.au**.

New Zealand Citizens
Most questions are answered in a free pamphlet available at New Zealand consulates and customs offices: *New Zealand Customs Guide for Travellers, Notice no. 4.* For more information, contact **New Zealand Customs,** The Customhouse, 17–21 Whitmore St., Box 2218, Wellington (© **04/473-6099** or 0800/428-786; **www. customs.govt.nz**).

4 Money

Generally, Colorado is not particularly expensive, especially compared to destinations on the East and West coasts. You'll find a wide range of prices for lodging and dining, and admission to most attractions is less than $10 (it's sometimes free, especially in Boulder). Prices in Denver and other major cities are mostly on a par with other Western cities, such as Albuquerque and Salt Lake City. Those traveling outside of the cities will discover that prices in small towns are usually quite reasonable, although ski resorts such as Vail and Aspen can be rather pricey, especially during winter holidays. Traveler's checks and credit cards are accepted at almost all hotels, restaurants, shops, and attractions, plus many grocery stores; and ATMs for all the major national networks are practically everywhere, even in most small towns.

ATMs
Nationwide, the easiest and best way to get cash away from home is from an ATM (automated teller machine). The **Cirrus** (© **800/424-7787;** www.mastercard. com) and **PLUS** (© **800/843-7587;** www. visa.com) networks span the country; you can find them even in remote regions. Look at the back of your bank card to see which network you're on, then call or check online for ATM locations at your destination. Be sure you know your personal identification number (PIN) and daily withdrawal limit before you depart. Also, if you have a 5- or 6-digit PIN, change it to a 4-digit PIN before coming to Colorado. *Note:* Remember that many banks impose a fee every time you use a card at another bank's ATM, and that fee can be higher for international transactions (up to $5 or more) than for domestic ones

(where they're rarely more than $2). In addition, the bank from which you withdraw cash may charge its own fee.

CREDIT CARDS & DEBIT CARDS

Credit cards are the most widely used form of payment in the United States: **Visa** (Barclaycard in Britain), **Master-Card** (EuroCard in Europe, Access in Britain, Chargex in Canada), **American Express, Diners Club,** and **Discover.** They also provide a convenient record of all your expenses, and they generally offer relatively good exchange rates. You can withdraw cash advances from your credit cards at banks or ATMs, provided you know your PIN.

Visitors from outside the U.S. should inquire whether their bank assesses a 1%–3% fee on charges incurred abroad.

It's highly recommended that you travel with at least one major credit card. You must have one to rent a car, and hotels and airlines usually require a credit card imprint as a deposit against expenses.

ATM cards with major credit card backing, known as **debit cards,** are now a commonly acceptable form of payment in most stores and restaurants.

TRAVELER'S CHECKS

Traveler's checks are widely accepted in the U.S., but foreign visitors should make sure that they're denominated in U.S. dollars; foreign-currency checks are often difficult to exchange.

You can buy traveler's checks at most banks. Most are offered in denominations of $20, $50, $100, $500, and sometimes $1,000. Generally, you'll pay a service charge ranging from 1% to 4%.

The most popular traveler's checks are offered by **American Express** (℃ **800/807-6233;** ℃ **800/221-7282** for card holders—this number accepts collect calls, offers service in several foreign languages, and exempts Amex gold and platinum cardholders from the 1% fee.); **Visa** (℃ **800/732-1322**)—AAA members can obtain Visa checks for a $9.95 fee (for checks up to $1,500) at most AAA offices or by calling ℃ **866/339-3378;** and **MasterCard** (℃ **800/223-9920**).

If you do choose to carry traveler's checks, keep a record of their serial numbers separate from your checks in the event that they are stolen or lost. You'll get a refund faster if you know the numbers.

5 When to Go

Colorado has two main tourist seasons: warm and cold. Those who want to see the state's parks and other scenic wonders, by hiking, mountain biking, or rafting, will usually visit from May through October; those who prefer skiing, snowboarding, and snowmobiling will have to wait for winter, usually from late November through March or April, depending on snow levels. Although you can visit most museums year-round, some close in winter.

The best way to avoid crowds at the more popular destinations, such as Rocky Mountain National Park, Garden of the Gods, and Pikes Peak, is to try to visit during the shoulder seasons of March through May and October through mid-December. Generally, those traveling without children will want to avoid visiting during school vacations.

To hear Coloradans tell it, the state has perfect weather all the time. Although they may be exaggerating just a bit, the weather here is usually quite pleasant, with an abundance of sun and relatively mild temperatures in most places—just avoid those winter snowstorms.

Along the Front Range, where Denver and Colorado Springs are located, summer days are hot and dry, and evenings mild. Humidity is low, and temperatures seldom rise above the 90s (30s Celsius). Evenings start to get cooler by mid-September, but even as late as November the days are often warm. Surprisingly, winters here are warmer and less snowy than winters in the Great Lakes or New England.

Most of Colorado is considered semiarid, and overall the state has an average of 296 sunny days a year—more sunshine than San Diego or Miami Beach. The prairies average about 16 inches of precipitation annually; the Front Range, 14 inches; the western slope, only about 8 inches. Rain, when it falls, is commonly a short afternoon thunderstorm. However, if you want to see snow, simply head to the mountains, where snowfall is measured in feet rather than inches, and mountain peaks may still be white in July. Mountain temperatures can be bitterly cold, especially if it's windy, but even at the higher elevations of some of the nation's top ski resorts, you'll find plenty of sunshine.

Average Monthly High/Low Temperatures (°F & °C) & Precipitation (in.):

		Jan	Feb	Mar	Apr	May	June	July	Aug	Sept	Oct	Nov	Dec
Denver	Temp. (°F)	43/16	47/20	52/26	62/35	71/44	81/52	88/59	86/57	77/48	66/36	53/25	45/17
	Temp. (°C)	6/–9	8/–7	11/–3	17/2	22/7	27/11	31/15	30/14	25/9	19/2	12/–4	7/–8
	Precip. (in.)	0.5	0.6	1.3	1.7	2.4	1.8	1.9	1.5	1.2	1.0	0.9	0.6
Elev. 5,280'													
Col. Springs	Temp. (°F)	41/16	45/20	49/24	60/33	69/43	80/52	85/57	82/56	75/47	66/37	50/25	44/19
	Temp. (°C)	5/–9	7/–7	9/–4	16/1	21/6	27/11	29/14	28/13	24/8	19/3	10/–4	7/–7
	Precip. (in.)	0.3	0.4	0.9	1.2	2.2	2.3	2.9	3.0	1.3	0.8	0.5	0.5
Elev. 6,035'													
Grand Junction	Temp. (°F)	36/15	45/24	56/32	66/38	76/48	88/57	94/64	91/62	81/54	68/42	51/39	66/40
	Temp. (°C)	2/–9	7/–4	13/0	19/3	24/9	31/14	34/18	33/17	27/12	20/6	11/4	19/4
	Precip. (in.)	0.6	0.5	0.9	0.8	0.9	0.5	0.7	0.8	0.8	1.0	0.7	0.6
Elev. 4,586'													

CALENDAR OF EVENTS

Below are some of the major annual events in Colorado. You'll find additional events on the Internet at **www.colorado.com** and **www.coloradofestival.com**, as well as on each city's website. We strongly recommend, however, that if a particular event is especially important to you, that you confirm the date by telephone before you leave home.

January

Great Fruitcake Toss, Colorado Springs. This zany event, where contestants compete to see who can throw a fruitcake the farthest, is among the most outlandish and festive spectacles of the year. It takes place in Manitou Springs' Memorial Park, 5 miles west of downtown Colorado Springs. Call ℂ **800/642-2567** or 719/685-5089 for more information. Early January.

Mahlerfest, Boulder. This may be the only festival celebrating the work of composer Gustav Mahler. Attend a full orchestra concert, free chamber concerts, or the free symposium. Call ℂ **303/447-0513** or visit www.mahlerfest.org for more information. Early January.

National Western Stock Show and Rodeo, Denver. This is the world's largest livestock show and indoor rodeo, with about two dozen rodeo performances, a trade exposition, Western food and crafts booths, and livestock auctions. Call ℂ **303/297-1166** for details. Second and third week of January.

Wintersköl Carnival, Aspen and Snowmass. A 4-day event that includes a parade, fireworks, and a torchlight descent. Call ✆ **800/262-7736,** 970/925-1940, or see www.aspenchamber.org. Mid-January.

International Snow Sculpture Championships, Breckenridge. Four-person teams transform 20-ton blocks of snow into works of art. Call ✆ **970/453-6018** or visit www.gobreck.com. Late January.

Boulder Bach Festival, Boulder. Music of the master baroque composer. Call ✆ **303/652-9101** or visit www.boulderbachfest.org for details. Last weekend in January.

February

Loveland Valentine Remailing Program, Loveland. More than 200,000 valentines are remailed annually from Loveland. Call ✆ **970/667-6311** or see www.loveland.org for details. Early February.

Steamboat Springs Winter Carnival, Steamboat Springs. Festivities include races, jumping, broomball, and skijoring—that's horse-powered skiing—street events. Call ✆ **970/879-0695** or visit www.sswsc.org. First full week in February.

Leadville Valentine's Day Wine Tasting, Leadville. Wine tasting, good food, workshops, and related activities cosponsored by the National Mining Hall of Fame and Museum. Call ✆ **888/532-3845** or see www.leadvilleusa.com for information. Mid-February.

Buffalo Bill's Birthday Celebration, Golden. Ceremonies and live entertainment that commemorate the life of the legendary scout and entertainer take place at the Buffalo Bill Memorial Museum. Call ✆ **303/526-0744** or 303/526-0747 or check www.buffalobill.org for further information. Late February.

March

Colorado Springs Dance Theatre Wine Festival, Colorado Springs. Sample the best wines at this 3-day benefit for the Colorado Springs Dance Theatre. Call ✆ **719/630-7434** for further information. Early March.

Pow Wow, Denver. More than 1,500 American Indians (as well as 60 drum groups), representing some 85 tribes from 32 states, perform traditional music and dances. Arts and crafts are also sold. Call ✆ **303/934-8045** for details. Mid-March.

Saint Patrick's Day, Denver. Among the largest Irish holiday parades in the United States, with floats, marching bands, and more than 5,000 horses. Call ✆ **303/892-1112** for further information. Saturday before March 17.

April

Easter Sunrise Service, Colorado Springs and Denver. Worshipers watch the rising sun illuminate red sandstone formations in the Garden of the Gods in Colorado Springs. For details, call ✆ **719/634-3144.** Denver's Easter Sunrise Service takes place at Red Rocks Amphitheatre, also in the midst of stunning geological formations. Call ✆ **303/295-4444** or visit www.redrocksonline.com for further information. Easter Sunday.

Spring Barrel Tasting, Grand Junction. Wine sampling, talks on winemaking, and good food. Call ✆ **970/244-1480** or see www.visitgrandjunction.com for information. Late April.

May

Cinco de Mayo, Denver and Colorado Springs. More than 250,000 people from around the Denver area celebrate this annual event centered on north Federal Boulevard with mariachi bands, dancers, Mexican food, and other activities. Call ✆ **303/534-8342** for information. Memorial Park is the site for the Colorado Springs celebration. Call © **719/635-5001** for information. May 5.

Plant and Book Sale, Denver. The largest volunteer-run plant and book sale in the nation, this event at Denver Botanic Gardens offers more than 250,000 plants, thousands of new and used books, and free gardening advice. Call © **720/865-3500** or visit www. botanicgardens.org for details. Early May.

Boulder Kinetic Fest, Boulder. A wacky event that's a real crowd pleaser. Most years an average of 70 teams race over land and water at Boulder Reservoir in a variety of imaginative human-powered conveyances. Activities include the kinetic parade, kinetic concerts, the kinetic ball, and a hot-air-balloon launch. Call © **303/444-5600** for details. Early May.

Iron Horse Bicycle Classic, Durango. Mountain bikers race against a steam train from Durango to Silverton. Call © **970/259-4621** or see www.ironhorse bicycleclassic.com. Memorial Day weekend.

Taste of Creede, Creede. A festival of fine arts, with live music, artists' demonstrations, food, and an art auction. Call **800/327-2102** or see www. creede.com for information. Memorial Day weekend.

Bolder Boulder, Boulder. This footrace attracts some 40,000 entrants each year, plus numerous spectators. Participants walk, jog, or run the 10K course. Call © **303/444-RACE** or visit www.bolderboulder.com for details. Memorial Day.

June

FIBArk Whitewater Festival, Salida. North America's longest and oldest downriver kayak race highlights this festival, which includes carnival rides, a parade, a white-water rodeo, and live entertainment. Call © **719/539-6918** or visit www.fibark.net. Mid-June.

Strawberry Days, Glenwood Springs. One of Colorado's oldest civic celebrations, with a rodeo, talent show, music, dancing, an arts-and-crafts fair, parade, carnival, and footraces. Call © **970/ 945-6589** or visit www.strawberrydays festival.com. Mid-June.

Glenn Miller Dancin' on the Plains, Fort Morgan. A big-band music extravaganza in the hometown of the legendary big band leader. Call © **800/ 354-8660** or see www.fortmorgan chamber.org for information. Mid-June.

International Buskerfest, Denver. An international street performers' festival featuring amazing shows by world-class jugglers, sword swallowers, magicians, tightrope artists, mimes, and acrobats! Call © **303/478-7878** for more information. Mid-June.

Wool Market, Estes Park. This huge natural-fiber show boasts contests, demonstrations, a children's tent, and sale of animals plus products made from their wool. Kids love it. Call © **970/586-5800** or go to www.estes net.com. Mid-June.

Aspen Music Festival, Aspen. Considered one of the finest summer music festivals in the country, featuring world-renowned artists in classical, chamber, and opera performances. Call © **970/925-9042** or see www.aspen musicfestival.com. Mid-June through mid-August.

Strings in the Mountains Summer Music Festival, Steamboat Springs. Top-notch classical, jazz, country, and pop musicians perform. Call © **970/ 879-5056** or see www.stringsinthe mountains.com. June through mid-August.

Greeley Stampede, Greeley. One of the West's biggest rodeos, with top national entertainers, plus concerts, kids' events, art exhibits, fireworks, and more. Call ✆ **800/982-2855** or go to www.greeleystampede.org for details. Late June to early July.

Colorado Brewers' Festival, Fort Collins. Samples of more than 40 Colorado beers plus food and music. Call ✆ **800/274-3678** or see www.downtownfortcollins.com. Late June.

Telluride Bluegrass Festival, Telluride. This major international music gathering features bluegrass, folk, and country music. Call ✆ **800/624-2422** or see www.telluridebluegrass.com. Late June.

Colorado Shakespeare Festival, Boulder. Considered among the top Shakespeare festivals in the country, with most performances in an outdoor theater. Call ✆ **303/492-0554** for details. Late June through late August.

Garden Concerts, Denver. Jazz, blues, and folk concerts take place in the outdoor amphitheater at **Denver Botanic Gardens.** Call ✆ **720/865-3500** or visit www.botanicgardens.org for information. June through September.

July

Brush Rodeo, Brush. Billed as Colorado's largest professional rodeo, with hundreds of participants, this event offers traditional rodeo competition, children's activities, an art show, a parade, a free barbecue, a footrace, a dance, and fireworks. Call ✆ **800/354-8659** or see www.brushcolo.com. Early July.

Colorado State Mining Championship, Creede. Entrants from six states compete in old-style hand steeling, hand mucking, spike driving, and newer methods of machine drilling and machine mucking. Call ✆ **800/327-2102** or visit www.creede.com. July 4th weekend.

Pikes Peak Auto Hill Climb, Colorado Springs. This "race to the clouds," held annually since 1916, takes drivers to the top of 14,110-foot Pikes Peak. Call ✆ **719/685-4400** for additional information. Saturday close to July 4th.

Woodcarvers Rendezvous, Creede. This weeklong event includes woodcarving classes, demonstrations, and an auction. Call ✆ **800/327-2102** or see www.creedewoodcarvers.com. Early to mid-July.

Rooftop Rodeo & Parade, Estes Park. Award-winning rodeos Tuesday through Sunday evenings. A grand parade kicks it all off on Tuesday morning. Call ✆ **970/586-5800** or visit www.estes net.com for details. Mid-July.

Crested Butte Wild Flower Festival, Crested Butte. This mountain community shows off its spectacular wildflowers with hikes, photo workshops, classes, and other activities. Call ✆ **800/455-1290** or see www.crestedbuttewild flowerfestival.com. Mid-July.

Art Fair, Boulder. Some 150 local and regional artists display their works in downtown Boulder, offering "fine art to fun art" plus live musical performances. Call ✆ **303/449-3774** or visit www.boulderdowntown.com for more information. Third weekend in July.

Buffalo Bill Days, Golden. A parade, kids' rides, burro race, arts and crafts displays, petting zoo, car show, and a pancake breakfast mark Golden's largest event. Call ✆ **303/384-0003** or visit www.buffalobilldays.com for more information. Late July.

August

Boom Days, Leadville. Events celebrate Leadville's mining and Wild West heritage with a parade, carnival, gun-slinger reenactments, mine-drilling competition, and a burro race. Call ✆ **888/532-3845** or see www.leadville

boomdays.com. First weekend in August.

Pikes Peak or Bust Rodeo, Colorado Springs. Colorado's largest outdoor rodeo, and a popular stop on the professional rodeo circuit. Call ✆ 719/635-3547 or visit www.coloradosprings rodeo.com for details. Early August.

Sculpture in the Park, Loveland. This outdoor juried exhibit of sculpture includes works by close to 200 sculptors from around the world. Call ✆ 970/663-2940 or see www.sculptureinthe park.org. Mid-August.

Colorado State Fair, Pueblo. National professional rodeo, carnival rides, food booths, industrial displays, horse shows, animal exhibits, and entertainment by top-name performers. Call ✆ 800/876-4567, ext. 2028, or visit www.coloradostatefair.com for additional information. Mid-August through Labor Day.

September

Telluride Film Festival, Telluride. This influential festival has premiered some of the finest independent films. Call ✆ 603/433-9202 or see www.telluride filmfestival.org. Early September.

Colorado Springs Balloon Classic, Colorado Springs. More than 100 colorful hot-air balloons launch from Memorial Park, making this one of the largest balloon rallies in the country. Call ✆ 719/471-4833 or visit www. balloonclassic.com for more information. Labor Day weekend.

A Taste of Colorado, Denver. This is Denver's largest celebration, with an annual attendance of about 400,000. Local restaurants serve house specialties; there are also crafts exhibits and free concerts. Call ✆ 303/295-6330 or visit www.atasteofcolorado.com for details. Labor Day weekend.

Vail Oktoberfest, Vail. A traditional village-wide weekend celebration, it features street entertainment, German beer and food, dancing, games, and singalongs. Call ✆ 970/476-6797 or go to www.vailoktoberfest.com. Mid-September.

Colorado Performing Arts Festival, Denver. This celebration of performing arts, which takes place at the Denver Performing Arts Complex, includes dance, music, theater, and storytelling. Call ✆ 303/640-6943 or visit www. denvergov.org/performingartsfest for information. Mid-September.

Fall Festival, Boulder. An Oktoberfest celebration, this festival includes polka bands, food, carnival rides, and an art fair. Call ✆ 303/449-3774 or visit www.boulderdowntown.com for more information. Late September or early October.

October

Great American Beer Festival, Denver. Hundreds of American beers are available for sampling, and seminars are presented at what is considered the largest and most prestigious beer event in the United States. Call ✆ 303/447-0816 or visit www.beertown.org for information. Early October.

Cowboy Gathering, Durango. Cowboy poetry, Western art, motorless parade, a dance, historical lectures, and demonstrations. Call ✆ 970/382-7494 or go to www.durangocowboy gathering.org. Early October.

Pumpkin Festival, Denver. This family event, sponsored by Denver Botanic Gardens and held at Chatfield Nature Preserve southwest of town, includes pumpkin picking, food, crafts, hayrides, and other activities. Call ✆ 720/865-3500 or visit www.botanicgardens.org for details. Mid-October.

November

Holiday Gift & Garden Market, Denver. Handmade Christmas ornaments, gifts, dried-flower arrangements, and food items are among the unique merchandise at this annual sale at Denver Botanic Gardens. Call ✆ **720/865-3500** or visit www.botanic gardens.org for information. Mid-November.

Christmas Mountain USA, Salida. More than 3,000 lights outline a huge tree; it also boasts a parade of lights and a visit from Santa Claus. Call ✆ **877/772-5432** or see www.salida chamber.org. Day after Thanksgiving.

December

World's Largest Christmas Lighting Display, Denver. Some 40,000 colored floodlights illuminate the Denver City and County Building. All month.

Blossoms of Light, Denver. Over 12,000 sparkling lights cascade through the Botanic Gardens. Grand topiaries, nightly entertainment, "kissing spots," whimsical displays, and warm treats make for an unforgettable winter evening. Call ✆ **303/865-3500** or visit www.botanicgardens.org for information. All month.

Parade of Lights, Denver. A holiday parade winds through downtown Denver, with floats, balloons, and marching bands. Call ✆ **303/478-7878** or visit www.denverparadeoflights.com for information. Early December.

Festival of Lights Parade, Colorado Springs. A nighttime parade kicks off this month-long celebration of the holidays. Features include decorated live trees and holiday scenes from cultures around the world. Call ✆ **719/634-5581** or visit www.csfineartscenter.org for information. Early December.

Country Christmas Jubilee at Old Town, Burlington. Victorian carolers and Christmas music, historic buildings decorated in individual themes, bell-ringing, plus other Victorian Christmas activities. Call ✆ **800/288-1334** or check www.burlingtoncolo. com. Early December.

Christmas with Cody, Golden. Buffalo Bill Cody playing Santa? He sure did, and a reenactor continues the tradition, with gifts for the kids at the Buffalo Bill Memorial Museum. Call ✆ **303/526-0744** or 303/526-0747 or check www.buffalobill.org for further information. First Sunday in December.

Olde Golden Christmas, Golden. Come to Golden for an old-fashioned candlelight walk on the first Friday in December, and stay for weekend festivities in town. Call ✆ **303/279-3113** or visit www.goldencochamber.org for information. Begins in early December.

Pikes Peak Summit Fireworks, Colorado Springs. A wondrous fireworks display to ring in the New Year. Call (✆ **800/888-4748** or 719/635-7506 or check out www.coloradosprings-travel.com. December 31.

6 Travel Insurance

The cost of travel insurance varies widely, depending on the cost and length of your trip, your age and health, and the type of trip you're taking, but expect to pay between 5% and 8% of the vacation itself. You can get estimates from various providers through **InsureMyTrip.com.**

Enter your trip cost and dates, your age, and other information, for prices from more than a dozen companies.

TRIP-CANCELLATION INSURANCE

Trip-cancellation insurance will help retrieve your money if you have to back

> ### *Tips* Quick ID
>
> Tie a colorful ribbon or piece of yarn around your luggage handle, or slap a distinctive sticker on the side of your bag. This makes it less likely that someone will mistakenly appropriate it. And if your luggage gets lost, it will be easier to find.

out of a trip or depart early, or if your travel supplier goes bankrupt. Permissible reasons for trip cancellation can range from sickness to natural disasters to the State Department declaring a destination unsafe for travel.

For more information, contact one of the following recommended insurers: **Access America** (© 866/807-3982; www.accessamerica.com); **Travel Guard International** (© 800/826-4919; www.travelguard.com); **Travel Insured International** (© 800/243-3174; www.travelinsured.com); and **Travelex Insurance Services** (© 888/457-4602; www.travelexinsurance.com).

MEDICAL INSURANCE

Although it's not required of travelers, health insurance is highly recommended. Most health insurance policies cover you if you get sick away from home—but verify that you're covered before you depart, particularly if you're insured by an HMO.

International visitors should note that unlike many European countries, the United States does not usually offer free or low-cost medical care to its citizens or visitors. Doctors and hospitals are expensive, and in most cases will require advance payment or proof of coverage before they render their services. Good policies will cover the costs of an accident, repatriation, or death. Packages such as **Europ Assistance's "Worldwide Healthcare Plan"** are sold by European automobile clubs and travel agencies at attractive rates. **Worldwide Assistance Services, Inc.** (© 800/777-8710; www.worldwideassistance.com) is the agent for Europ Assistance in the United States.

Though lack of health insurance may prevent you from being admitted to a hospital in nonemergencies, don't worry about being left on a street corner to die: The American way is to fix you now and bill the living daylights out of you later.

INSURANCE FOR BRITISH TRAVELERS Most big travel agents offer their own insurance and will probably try to sell you their package when you book a holiday. Think before you sign. **Britain's Consumers' Association** recommends that you insist on seeing the policy and reading the fine print before buying travel insurance. **The Association of British Insurers** (© 020/7600-3333; www.abi.org.uk) gives advice by phone and publishes *Holiday Insurance,* a free guide to policy provisions and prices. You might also shop around for better deals: Try **Columbus Direct** (© 0870/033-9988; www.columbusdirect.net).

INSURANCE FOR CANADIAN TRAVELERS Canadians should check with their provincial health plan offices or call **Health Canada** (© 866/225-0709; www.hc-sc.gc.ca) to find out the extent of their coverage and what documentation and receipts they must take home in case they are treated in the United States.

LOST-LUGGAGE INSURANCE

On flights within the U.S., checked baggage is covered up to $2,500 per ticketed passenger. On flights outside the U.S. (and on U.S. portions of international trips), baggage coverage is limited to approximately $9.07 per pound, up to approximately $635 per checked bag. If you plan to check items more valuable than what's covered by the standard liability, see if your homeowner's policy covers your valuables, get baggage insurance as part of your comprehensive travel-insurance package, or buy Travel Guard's "BagTrak" product.

If your luggage is lost, immediately file a lost-luggage claim at the airport, detailing the luggage contents. Most airlines require that you report delayed, damaged, or lost baggage within 4 hours of arrival. The airlines are required to deliver luggage, once found, directly to your house or destination free of charge.

7 Health & Safety

STAYING HEALTHY
GENERAL AVAILABILITY OF HEALTHCARE

Contact the **International Association for Medical Assistance to Travelers** (IAMAT) (© **716/754-4883** or, in Canada, 416/652-0137; www.iamat.org) for tips on travel and health concerns in the countries you're visiting, and for lists of local, English-speaking doctors. The United States **Centers for Disease Control and Prevention** (© **800/311-3435;** www.cdc.gov) provides up-to-date information on health hazards by region or country and offers tips on food safety. The website www.tripprep.com, sponsored by a consortium of travel medicine practitioners, may also offer helpful advice on traveling abroad. You can find listings of reliable clinics overseas at the **International Society of Travel Medicine** (www.istm.org).

COMMON AILMENTS

ALTITUDE SICKNESS About two-thirds of Colorado is more than a mile above sea level, which means there is less oxygen and lower humidity than many travelers are accustomed to. This creates a unique set of problems for short-term visitors, such as the possibility of shortness of breath, fatigue, and other physical concerns.

Those not used to higher elevations should get sufficient rest, avoid large meals, and drink plenty of nonalcoholic fluids, especially water. Individuals with heart or respiratory problems should consult their personal physicians before planning a trip to the Colorado mountains. Those in generally good health need not take any special precautions, but it is best to ease the transition to higher elevations by changing altitude gradually. For instance, spend a night or two in Denver

Avoiding "Economy Class Syndrome"

Deep vein thrombosis, or as it's known in the world of flying, "economy-class syndrome," is a blood clot that develops in a deep vein. It's a potentially deadly condition that can be caused by sitting in cramped conditions—such as an airplane cabin—for too long. During a flight (especially a long-haul flight), get up, walk around, and stretch your legs every 60 to 90 minutes to keep your blood flowing. Other preventative measures include frequent flexing of the legs while sitting, drinking lots of water, and avoiding alcohol and sleeping pills. If you have a history of deep vein thrombosis, heart disease, or another condition that puts you at high risk, some experts recommend wearing compression stockings or taking anticoagulants when you fly; always ask your physician about the best course for you. Symptoms of deep vein thrombosis include leg pain or swelling, or even shortness of breath.

(elevation 5,280 ft.) or Colorado Springs (elevation 6,035 ft.) before driving or taking the cog railway to the top of Pikes Peak (elevation 14,110 ft.).

Lowlanders can also help their bodies adjust to higher elevations by taking it easy for their first few days in the mountains, cutting down on cigarettes and alcohol, and avoiding sleeping pills and other drugs. Your doctor can provide prescription drugs to help prevent and relieve symptoms of altitude sickness.

Because the sun's rays are more direct in the thinner atmosphere, they cause sunburn more quickly. The potential for skin damage increases when the sun reflects off snow or water. A good sunblock is strongly recommended, as are good-quality ultraviolet-blocking sunglasses. Remember that children need more protection than adults.

HANTAVIRUS   State health officials warn outdoor enthusiasts to take precautions against the hantavirus, a rare but often fatal respiratory disease first recognized in 1993. About half of the country's confirmed cases have been reported in the Four Corners states of Colorado, New Mexico, Arizona, and Utah. The disease is usually spread by the urine and droppings of deer mice and other rodents, and health officials recommend that campers avoid areas with signs of rodent droppings. Symptoms of hantavirus are similar to flu and lead to breathing difficulties and shock.

WEST NILE VIRUS   Colorado has also had its share of cases of the West Nile virus illness. The best prevention is mosquito repellent and keeping mosquito populations across the state in check. The virus can be fatal, but is typically not.

Symptoms include fever, headache, and body aches.

WHAT TO DO IF YOU GET SICK AWAY FROM HOME

We list **hospitals** and **emergency numbers** under "Fast Facts," p. 44.

If you suffer from a chronic illness, consult your doctor before your departure. Pack **prescription medications** in your carry-on luggage, and carry them in their original containers, with pharmacy labels—otherwise they won't make it through airport security. Visitors from outside the U.S. should carry generic names of prescription drugs. For U.S. travelers, most reliable healthcare plans provide coverage if you get sick away from home. Foreign visitors may have to pay all medical costs upfront and be reimbursed later. See "Medical Insurance," under "Travel Insurance," above.

STAYING SAFE

While there are many reasons to visit Colorado, two of the reasons most often cited are its historic sites and magnificent outdoor activities. However, visiting historic sites and participating in outdoor activities can lead to accidents.

When visiting such historic sites as ghost towns, gold mines, and railroads, keep in mind that they were probably built more than 100 years ago, at a time when safety standards were extremely lax, if they existed at all. Never enter abandoned buildings, mines, or railroad equipment on your own. When you're visiting commercially operated historic tourist attractions, use common sense and don't be afraid to ask questions.

Walkways in mines are often uneven and poorly lit, and are sometimes slippery

---

High & Mighty
Colorado boasts 75% of the land in the contiguous United States above 10,000 feet in elevation.

Healthy Travels to You

The following government websites offer up-to-date health-related travel advice.

- **Australia:** www.dfat.gov.au/travel
- **Canada:** www.hc-sc.gc.ca/index_e.html
- **U.K.:** www.dh.gov.uk/PolicyAndGuidance/HealthAdviceForTravellers/fs/en
- **U.S.:** www.cdc.gov/travel

---

due to seeping groundwater that can also stain your clothing with its high iron content. When entering old buildings, be prepared for steep, narrow stairways; creaky floors; and low ceilings and doorways. Steam trains are a wonderful experience as long as you remember that steam is very hot, and that oil and grease can ruin your clothing.

When heading to the great outdoors, keep in mind that injuries often occur when people fail to follow instructions. Pay attention when the experts tell you to stay on established ski trails, hike only in designated areas, carry rain gear, and wear a life jacket when rafting. Mountain weather can be fickle, and many of the most beautiful spots are in remote areas. Be prepared for extreme changes in temperature at any time of year, and watch out for sudden summer-afternoon thunderstorms that can leave you drenched and shivering in minutes.

8 Specialized Travel Resources

TRAVELERS WITH DISABILITIES

Most disabilities shouldn't stop anyone from traveling in the U.S. There are more options and resources out there than ever before.

The **Golden Access Passport** gives visually impaired or permanently disabled persons (regardless of age) free lifetime entrance to all properties administered by the National Park Service, the U.S. Fish and Wildlife Service, the U.S. Forest Service, the U.S. Army Corps of Engineers, the Bureau of Land Management, and the Tennessee Valley Authority. This may include national parks, monuments, historic sites, recreation areas, and national wildlife refuges.

You may pick up a Golden Access Passport at any NPS entrance fee area by showing proof of medically determined disability and eligibility for benefits under federal law. Besides free entry, the Golden Access Passport also offers a 50% discount on federal-use fees charged for such facilities as camping, swimming, parking, boat launching, and tours. For more information, go to www.nps.gov/fees_passes.htm or call © **888/467-2757.**

Many travel agencies offer customized tours and itineraries for travelers with disabilities. Among them are **Flying Wheels Travel** (© **507/451-5005;** www.flyingwheelstravel.com); **Access-Able Travel Source** (© **303/232-2979;** www.accessable.com); and **Accessible Journeys** (© **800/846-4537** or 610/521-0339; www.disabilitytravel.com). **Avis Rent a Car** has an "Avis Access" program that offers such services as a dedicated 24-hour toll-free number (© **888/879-4273**) for customers with special travel needs; special car features such as swivel seats, spinner knobs, and hand controls; and accessible bus service.

Organizations that offer assistance to disabled travelers include **MossRehab** (www.mossresourcenet.org); the **American Foundation for the Blind (AFB)**

(© **800/232-5463**; www.afb.org); and **SATH** (Society for Accessible Travel & Hospitality) (© **212/447-7284**; www.sath.org). **AirAmbulanceCard.com** is now partnered with SATH and allows you to preselect top-notch hospitals in case of an emergency.

The community website **iCan** (www.icanonline.net/channels/travel) has destination guides and several regular columns on accessible travel. Also check out the quarterly magazine *Emerging Horizons* (www.emerginghorizons.com); and *Open World* magazine, published by SATH.

GAY & LESBIAN TRAVELERS

In general, gay and lesbian travelers will find they are treated just like any other travelers in Colorado. Even cities such as Colorado Springs, home of Focus on the Family and other conservative groups, have become somewhat more open-minded about alternative lifestyles recently. Those with specific concerns can contact **Gay, Lesbian, Bisexual, and Transgender Community Services Center of Colorado** (© **303/733-7743**; www.glbtcolorado.org) in Denver; the organization can also provide information on events and venues of interest to gay and lesbian visitors.

The **International Gay and Lesbian Travel Association (IGLTA)** (© **800/448-8550** or 954/776-2626; www.iglta.org) is the trade association for the gay and lesbian travel industry, and offers an online directory of gay- and lesbian-friendly travel businesses; go to their website and click on "Members."

Many agencies offer tours and travel itineraries specifically for gay and lesbian travelers. Among them are **Above and Beyond Tours** (© **800/397-2681**; www.abovebeyondtours.com); **Now, Voyager** (© **800/255-6951**; www.nowvoyager.com); and Olivia **Cruises & Resorts** (© **800/631-6277**; www.olivia.com).

Gay.com Travel (© **800/929-2268** or 415/644-8044; www.gay.com/travel or

www.outandabout.com), is an excellent online successor to the popular *Out & About* print magazine. It provides regularly updated information about gay-owned, gay-oriented, and gay-friendly lodging, dining, sightseeing, nightlife, and shopping establishments in every important destination worldwide.

The following travel guides are available at many bookstores, or you can order them from any online bookseller: *Spartacus International Gay Guide* (Bruno Gmünder Verlag; www.spartacusworld.com/gayguide) and *Odysseus: The International Gay Travel Planner* (Odysseus Enterprises Ltd.); and the *Damron* guides (www.damron.com), with separate, annual books for gay men and lesbians.

SENIOR TRAVEL

Many Colorado hotels and motels offer special rates to senior citizens, and an increasing number of restaurants, attractions, and public transportation systems offer discounts as well, some for "oldsters" as young as 55.

Members of **AARP** (formerly known as the American Association of Retired Persons), 601 E St. NW, Washington, DC 20049 (© **888/687-2277**; www.aarp.org), get discounts on hotels, airfares, and car rentals. AARP offers members a wide range of benefits, including *AARP: The Magazine* and a monthly newsletter. Anyone over 50 can join.

The **U.S. National Park Service** offers a **Golden Age Passport** that gives seniors 62 years or older lifetime entrance to all properties administered by the National Park Service—national parks, monuments, historic sites, recreation areas, and national wildlife refuges—for a one-time processing fee of $10, which must be purchased in person at any NPS facility that charges an entrance fee. Besides free entry, a Golden Age Passport also offers a 50% discount on federal-use fees charged for such facilities as camping, swimming, parking, boat launching, and tours. For more information, go to www.nps.gov/ fees_passes.htm or call © **888/467-2757.**

Many reliable agencies and organizations target the 50-plus market. **Elderhostel** (© **877/426-8056;** www.elder hostel.org) arranges study programs for those aged 55 and over. **ElderTreks** (© **800/741-7956;** www.eldertreks.com) offers small-group tours to off-the-beaten-path or adventure-travel locations, restricted to travelers 50 and older. **INTRAV** (© **800/456-8100;** www.intrav. com) is a high-end tour operator that caters to the mature, discerning traveler (not specifically seniors), with trips around the world that include guided safaris, polar expeditions, private-jet adventures, and small-boat cruises down jungle rivers.

Recommended publications offering travel resources and discounts for seniors include: the quarterly magazine *Travel 50 & Beyond* (www.travel50andbeyond. com); *Travel Unlimited: Uncommon Adventures for the Mature Traveler* (Avalon); *101 Tips for Mature Travelers,* available from Grand Circle Travel (© **800/221-2610** or 617/350-7500; www.gct.com); and *Unbelievably Good Deals and Great Adventures That You Absolutely Can't Get Unless You're Over 50* (McGraw-Hill), by Joann Rattner Heilman.

FAMILY TRAVEL

Colorado is generally a family-friendly state, with lots of things for all ages to enjoy. Throughout this book you'll find numerous attractions, lodgings, and even restaurants that are especially well suited to kids. These include places such as the Butterfly Pavilion & Insect Center in Denver, North Pole/Santa's Workshop in the Colorado Springs area, Dinosaur Journey Museum in Grand Junction, and Fairy Caves in Glenwood Springs.

Additionally, state and national parks are great places for family vacations, and the national parks usually have excellent children's programs (be sure to ask about Junior Ranger programs). The state's many ski resorts all have special programs for kids.

To locate accommodations, restaurants, and attractions that are particularly kid-friendly, refer to the "Kids" icon throughout this guide.

Recommended family travel websites include **Family Travel Forum** (www. familytravelforum.com), a comprehensive site that offers customized trip planning; **Family Travel Network** (www.family travelnetwork.com), an award-winning site that offers travel features, deals, and tips; **Traveling Internationally with Your Kids** (www.travelwithyourkids.com), a comprehensive site offering sound advice for long-distance and international travel with children; and **Family Travel Files** (www.thefamilytravelfiles.com), which offers an online magazine and a directory of off-the-beaten-path tours and tour operators for families.

Frommer's Family Vacations in the National Parks (Wiley Publishing, Inc.) offers suggestions for family activities on a national park vacation.

STUDENT TRAVEL

A valid student ID will often qualify students for discounts on airfare, accommodations, entry to museums, cultural events, movies, and more. If you're no longer a student but are still under 26, you can get an **International Youth Travel Card (IYTC)** from the same people, which entitles you to some discounts (but not on museum admissions). **Travel CUTS** (© **800/667-2887** or 416/614-2887; www.travelcuts.com) offers similar services for both Canadians and U.S. residents. Irish students may prefer to turn to **USIT** (© **01/602-1600;** www.usit now.ie), an Ireland-based specialist in student, youth, and independent travel.

Tips **The Peripatetic Pet**

Never leave your pet inside a parked car with the windows rolled up. It's never a good idea to leave a pet inside a hot car, even with the windows rolled down, for any length of time.

Make sure your pet is wearing a name tag with the name and phone number of a contact person who can take the call if your pet gets lost while you're away from home.

ECO-TOURISM

You can find eco-friendly travel tips, statistics, and touring companies and associations—listed by destination under "Travel Choice"—at the TIES website, www.ecotourism.org. **Ecotravel.com** is part online magazine and part eco-directory that lets you search for touring companies in several categories (water-based, land-based, spiritually oriented, and so on). Also check out **Conservation International** (www.conservation.org)—which, with *National Geographic Traveler,* annually presents **World Legacy Awards** (www.wlaward.org) to those travel tour operators, businesses, organizations, and places that have made a significant contribution to sustainable tourism.

TRAVELING WITH PETS

Many of us wouldn't dream of going on vacation without our pets. Under the right circumstances, it can be a wonderful experience for both you and your animals. Dogs and cats are accepted at many lodgings in Colorado, but not as universally at resorts and expensive hotels. Throughout this book, we've tried to consistently note those lodgings that take pets. Some properties require you to pay a fee or damage deposit in advance, and most insist they be notified at check in that you have a pet.

Be aware, however, that national parks and monuments and other federal lands administered by the National Park Service are not pet-friendly. Dogs are usually prohibited on all hiking trails, must always be leashed, and in some cases cannot be taken more than 100 feet from established roads. On the other hand, U.S. Forest Service and Bureau of Land Management (BLM) areas and most state parks are pro-pet, allowing dogs on trails and just about everywhere except inside buildings. State parks require that dogs be leashed; regulations in national forests and BLM lands are generally looser.

Aside from regulations, though, you need to be concerned with your pet's well-being. Just as people need extra water in Colorado's dry climate, so do pets. We especially like those clever spill-resistant travel water bowls sold in pet shops. And keep in mind that many trails are rough, and jagged rocks can cut the pads on your dog's feet.

The websites www.petswelcome.com, www.pettravel.com, and www.travelpets. com are all good resources. Also check out *The Portable Petswelcome.com: The Complete Guide to Traveling with Your Pet* (Howell Book House), which features the best selection of pet travel information anywhere. Another resource is *Canine Colorado: Where to Go and What to Do with Your Dog* (Fulcrum Publishing). Also keep in mind that all Motel 6 motels accept pets.

9 Planning Your Trip Online

SURFING FOR AIRFARE

The most popular online travel agencies are **Travelocity** (**www.travelocity.com**, or www.travelocity.co.uk); **Expedia** (**www.expedia.com**, www.expedia.co.uk, or www.expedia.ca); and **Orbitz** (www.orbitz.com).

In addition, most airlines now offer online-only fares that even their phone agents know nothing about. For the websites of airlines that fly to and from your destination, go to "Getting There," p. 33.

Other helpful websites for booking airline tickets online include:

- www.biddingfortravel.com
- www.cheapflights.com
- www.hotwire.com
- www.kayak.com
- www.lastminutetravel.com
- www.opodo.co.uk
- www.priceline.com
- www.sidestep.com
- www.site59.com
- www.smartertravel.com

SURFING FOR HOTELS

In addition to **Travelocity, Expedia, Orbitz, Priceline,** and **Hotwire** (see above), the following websites will help you with booking hotel rooms online:

- www.hotels.com
- www.quickbook.com
- www.travelaxe.net
- www.travelweb.com
- www.tripadvisor.com

It's a good idea to **get a confirmation number** and **make a printout** of any online booking transaction.

And keep in mind that weekend rates in downtown Denver are often heavily discounted from weekday rates. In Boulder and Colorado Springs, special events—namely the graduations of the University of Colorado and the Air Force Academy—cause lodging rates to go through the roof.

SURFING FOR RENTAL CARS

For booking rental cars online, the best deals are usually found at rental-car company websites, although all the major online travel agencies also offer rental-car reservations services. Priceline and Hotwire work well for rental cars, too; the only "mystery" is which major rental company you get, and for most travelers the difference between Hertz, Avis, and Budget is negligible.

10 The 21st-Century Traveler

INTERNET ACCESS AWAY FROM HOME
WITHOUT YOUR OWN COMPUTER

To find cybercafes in your destination check **www.cybercaptive.com** and **www.cybercafe.com**. In Colorado's major cities, most cybercafes are located downtown.

Aside from formal cybercafes, most **youth hostels** and **public libraries** offer Internet access. Avoid **hotel business centers** unless you're willing to pay exorbitant rates.

Most major airports now have **Internet kiosks** scattered throughout their gates. These give you basic Web access for a per-minute fee that's usually higher than cybercafe prices.

WITH YOUR OWN COMPUTER

More and more hotels, cafes, and retailers are signing on as Wi-Fi (wireless fidelity) "hotspots." Mac owners have their own networking technology, Apple AirPort. **T-Mobile Hotspot** (www.t-mobile.com/hotspot) serves up wireless connections at more than 1,000 Starbucks coffee shops nationwide. **Boingo** (www.boingo.com) and **Wayport** (www.wayport.com) have set up networks in airports and high-class hotel lobbies. To locate other hotspots that provide **free wireless networks** in cities around the world, go to **www. personaltelco.net/index.cgi/Wireless Communities**.

For dial-up access, most business-class hotels in the U.S. offer dataports for laptop modems, and a few thousand hotels in the U.S. now offer free high-speed Internet access. In addition, major Internet Service Providers (ISPs) have **local access numbers** around the world, allowing you to go online by placing a local call. Wherever you go, bring a **connection kit** of the right power and phone adapters, a spare phone cord, and a spare Ethernet network cable—or find out whether your hotel supplies them to guests.

For information on electrical currency conversions, see "Electricity," in the "Fast Facts" section at the end of this chapter.

CELLPHONE USE IN THE U.S.

Just because your cellphone works at home doesn't mean it'll work everywhere in the U.S. (thanks to our nation's fragmented cellphone system). It's a good bet that your phone will work in major cities, but take a look at your wireless company's coverage map on its website before heading out; T-Mobile, Sprint, and Nextel are particularly weak in rural areas. If you need to stay in touch at a destination where you know your phone won't work, **rent** a phone that does from **InTouch USA** (© 800/872-7626; www.intouch global.com) or a rental car location, but beware that you'll pay $1 a minute or more for airtime.

If you're venturing deep into national parks, you may want to consider renting a **satellite phone (satphone).** It's different from a cellphone in that it connects to satellites rather than ground-based towers. Unfortunately, you'll pay at least $2 per minute to use the phone, and it only works where you can see the horizon (that is, usually not indoors). In North America, you can rent Iridium satellite phones from **RoadPost** (www.roadpost. com; © 888/290-1606 or 905/272-5665). InTouch USA (see above) offers a wider range of satphones but at higher rates.

Frommers.com: The Complete Travel Resource

For an excellent travel-planning resource, we highly recommend **Frommers. com** (www.frommers.com), voted Best Travel Site by *PC Magazine*. We're a little biased, of course, but we guarantee that you'll find the travel tips, reviews, monthly vacation giveaways, bookstore, and online-booking capabilities to be thoroughly indispensable. Special features include our popular **Destinations** section, where you can access expert travel tips, hotel and dining recommendations, and advice on the sights to see in more than 3,500 destinations around the globe; the **Frommers.com Newsletter,** with the latest deals, travel trends, and money-saving secrets; and our **Travel Talk** area featuring **Message Boards,** where Frommer's readers post queries and share advice, and where our authors sometimes show up to answer questions. Once you finish your research, the **Book a Trip** area can lead you to Frommer's preferred online partners' websites, where you can book your vacation at affordable prices.

Online Traveler's Toolbox

Veteran travelers usually carry some essential items to make their trips easier. Following is a selection of handy online tools to bookmark and use.

- **Airplane Food** (www.airlinemeals.net)
- **Airplane Seating** (www.seatguru.com and www.airlinequality.com)
- **Foreign Languages for Travelers** (www.travlang.com)
- **Local Events, dining reviews** (www.westword.com, www.denverpost.com, and www.rockymountainnews.com)
- **Maps** (www.mapquest.com)
- **MasterCard ATM Locator** (www.mastercard.com)
- **Time and Date** (www.timeanddate.com)
- **Universal Currency Converter** (www.xe.com/ucc)
- **Visa ATM Locator** (www.visa.com)
- **Weather** (www.intellicast.com and www.weather.com)

If you're not from the U.S., you'll be appalled at the poor reach of our **GSM** (Global System for Mobiles) **wireless network,** which is used by much of the rest of the world. Your phone will probably work in most major U.S. cities; it definitely won't work in many rural areas. (To see where GSM phones work in the U.S., check out www.tmobile.com/coverage/national_popup.asp) And you may or may not be able to send SMS (text messaging) home.

11 Getting There

BY PLANE

Those flying to Colorado will probably land at Denver International Airport or Colorado Springs Airport. Both offer car rentals and shuttle services to their city's hotels.

Denver International Airport (DIA) is 23 miles northeast of downtown Denver, about a 35- to 45-minute drive. It is the sixth-busiest airport in the nation, with six runways and 93 gates. An information line (© **800/AIR-2-DEN** or 303/342-2000; www.flydenver.com) provides data on flight schedules and connections, parking, ground transportation, current weather conditions, and local accommodations. The local airport information and paging number is © **303/342-2300.** Airlines serving Denver include **Air Canada** (© 888/247-2262; www.air canada.ca), **Alaska Airlines** (© 800/252-7522; www.alaskaair.com), **American** (© 800/433-7300; www.aa.com), **America West** (© 800/235-9292; www.america west.com), **Continental** (© 800/523-3273; www.continental.com), **Delta** (© 800/221-1212; www.delta.com), **Frontier** (© 800/432-1359; www.frontierairlines. com), **jetBlue Airways** (© 800/538-2583; www.jetblue.com), **Mesa** (© 800/637-2247; www.mesa-air.com), **Mexicana** (© 800/531-7921; www.mexicana. com), **Midwest Airlines** (© 800/452-2022; www.midwestairlines.com), **Northwest** (© 800/225-2525; www.nwa.com), **Southwest** (© 800/435-9792; www. southwest.com), **Sun Country** (© 800/359-6786; www.suncountry.com), **United** (© 800/241-6522; www.ual.com), and **US Airways** (© 800/428-4322; www. usair.com).

Tips   Prepare to Be Fingerprinted

As of January 2004, many international visitors traveling on visas to the United States will be photographed and fingerprinted at Customs in a new program created by the Department of Homeland Security called US-VISIT. Non-U.S. citizens arriving at airports and on cruise ships must undergo an instant background check as part of the government's efforts to deter terrorism by verifying the identity of incoming and outgoing visitors. Exempt from the extra scrutiny are visitors entering by land or those that don't require a visa for short-term visits (mostly visitors from Europe; see p. 15). For more information, go to the Homeland Security website at www.dhs.gov/dhspublic.

Colorado Springs Airport (© 719/550-1900), located in the southeast corner of Colorado Springs, has nearly 100 flights each day, with connections to most major U.S. cities. **American, America West, Continental, Mesa, Northwest,** and **United** serve Colorado Springs.

A good alternative to flying to Denver or Colorado Springs for those heading to western Colorado is Grand Junction's **Walker Field** (© 970/244-9100; www.walkerfield.com), which has direct flights or connections from most major cities on **America West Express, Delta/Skywest, Frontier, Great Lakes,** and **United Express,** and car rentals from most major companies.

FLIGHTS FROM THE UNITED KINGDOM

British Airways (© 800/247-9297, 0845/773-3377 in London; www.british-airways.com) offers one daily nonstop flight between London and Denver. Travelers from the United Kingdom can also take British Airways to other U.S. cities and make connecting flights to Denver or Colorado Springs.

IMMIGRATION & CUSTOMS CLEARANCE   Foreign visitors arriving by air, no matter what the port of entry, should cultivate patience and resignation before setting foot on U.S. soil. Clearing immigration control can take as long as 2 hours. This is especially true in the aftermath of the September 11, 2001, terrorist attacks, when U.S. airports considerably beefed up security clearances. People traveling by air from Canada, Bermuda, and certain Caribbean countries can sometimes clear Customs and Immigration at the point of departure, which is much faster.

FLYING FOR LESS: TIPS FOR GETTING THE BEST AIRFARE

- Passengers who can book their ticket either **long in advance or at the last minute,** or who **fly midweek** or at **less-trafficked hours** may pay a fraction of the full fare. If your schedule is flexible, say so, and ask if you can secure a cheaper fare by changing your flight plans.
- Search **the Internet** for cheap fares (see "Planning Your Trip Online").
- Keep an eye on local newspapers for **promotional specials** or **fare wars,** when airlines lower prices on their most popular routes. You rarely see fare wars offered for peak travel times, but if you can travel in the off months, you may snag a bargain.
- Try to book a ticket **in its country of origin.** If you're planning a one-way flight from Johannesburg to New York, a South Africa–based travel agent will probably have the lowest fares. For foreign travelers on multileg

trips, book in the country of the first leg; for example, book New York–Chicago–Montreal–New York in the U.S.

- Join **frequent-flier clubs.** Frequent-flier membership doesn't cost a cent, but it does entitle you to better seats, faster response to phone inquiries, and prompter service if your luggage is stolen or your flight is canceled or delayed, or if you want to change your seat. And you don't have to fly to earn points; **frequent-flier credit cards** can earn you thousands of miles for doing your everyday shopping. With more than 70 mileage awards programs on the market, consumers have never had more options. Investigate the program details of your favorite airlines before you sink points into any one. Consider which airlines have hubs in the airport nearest you, and, of those carriers, which have the most advantageous alliances, given your most common routes. To play the frequent-flier game to your best advantage, consult Randy Petersen's **Inside Flyer** (www.inside flyer.com). Petersen and friends review all the programs in detail and post regular updates on changes in policies and trends.

LONG-HAUL FLIGHTS: HOW TO STAY COMFORTABLE

- Your choice of airline and airplane will definitely affect your leg room. Find more details about U.S. airlines at **www.seatguru.com**. For international airlines, the research firm Skytrax has posted a list of average seat pitches at **www.airlinequality.com**.
- Emergency exit seats and bulkhead seats typically have the most legroom. Emergency exit seats are usually left unassigned until the day of a flight (to ensure that someone able-bodied fills the seats); it's worth getting to

---

Tips   Getting Through the Airport

- Arrive at the airport 1 hour before a domestic flight and 2 hours before an international flight; if you show up late, tell an airline employee and he or she will probably whisk you to the front of the line.
- Beat the ticket-counter lines by using airport electronic kiosks or even online check in from your home computer, from where you can print out boarding passes in advance. Curbside check in is also a good way to avoid lines.
- Bring a current, government-issued photo ID such as a driver's license or passport. Children under 18 do not need government-issued photo IDs for flights within the U.S., but they do for international flights to most countries.
- Speed up security by removing your jacket and shoes before you're screened. In addition, remove metal objects such as big belt buckles. If you've got metallic body parts, a note from your doctor can prevent a long chat with the security screeners.
- Use a TSA-approved lock for your checked luggage. Look for Travel Sentry certified locks at luggage or travel shops and Brookstone stores (or online at www.brookstone.com).

the ticket counter early to snag one of these spots for a long flight. Many passengers find that bulkhead seating (the row facing the wall at the front of the cabin) offers more legroom, but keep in mind that bulkheads are where airlines often put baby bassinets, so you may be sitting next to an infant.

- To have two seats for yourself in a three-seat row, try for an aisle seat in a center section toward the back of coach. If you're traveling with a companion, book an aisle and a window seat. Middle seats are usually booked last, so chances are good you'll end up with three seats to yourselves. And in the event that a third passenger is assigned the middle seat, he or she will probably be more than happy to trade for a window or an aisle.
- Ask about entertainment options. Many airlines offer seatback video systems where you get to choose your movies or play video games—but only on some of their planes. (Boeing 777s are your best bet.)

- To sleep, avoid the last row of any section or the row in front of an emergency exit, as these seats are the least likely to recline. Avoid seats near highly trafficked toilet areas. Avoid seats in the back of many jets—these can be narrower than those in the rest of coach. You also may want to reserve a window seat so you can rest your head and avoid being bumped in the aisle.
- Get up, walk around, and stretch every 60 to 90 minutes to keep your blood flowing. This helps avoid **deep vein thrombosis,** or "economy-class syndrome." See the box "Avoiding 'Economy Class Syndrome,'" under "Health & Safety," p. 25.
- Drink water before, during, and after your flight to combat the lack of humidity in airplane cabins. Avoid alcohol, which will dehydrate you.
- If you're flying with kids, don't forget to carry on toys, books, pacifiers, and chewing gum to help them relieve ear pressure buildup during ascent and descent.

Tips Coping with Jet Lag

Jet lag is a pitfall of traveling across time zones. If you're flying north-south and you feel sluggish when you touch down, your symptoms will be the result of dehydration and the general stress of air travel. When you travel east-west or vice versa, however, your body becomes thoroughly confused about what time it is, and everything from your digestive system to your brain is knocked for a loop. Traveling east, say from San Francisco to Boston, is more difficult on your internal clock than traveling west, say from Atlanta to Hawaii, because most peoples' bodies are more inclined to stay up late than fall asleep early.

Here are some tips for combating jet lag:

- **Reset your watch** to your destination time before you board the plane.
- **Drink lots of water** before, during, and after your flight. Avoid alcohol.
- **Exercise and sleep well** for a few days before your trip.
- If you have trouble sleeping on planes, **fly eastward on morning flights.**
- **Daylight is the key** to resetting your body clock. At the website for Outside In (www.bodyclock.com), you can get a customized plan of when to seek and avoid light.

Fun Fact Take the High Road

The world's highest automobile tunnel, the Eisenhower Tunnel, crosses the Continental Divide 65 miles west of Denver, at an elevation of 11,000 feet.

BY CAR

An excellent road system, connecting to interstate highways heading in all directions, makes driving in Colorado both a good and an economical choice. This is especially true for those planning excursions away from the major cities, where there is little or no public transportation and a car, either your own or a rental, will be practically mandatory.

Some 1,000 miles of interstate highways form a star on the map of Colorado, with its center at Denver. **I-25** crosses the state from south to north, extending from New Mexico to Wyoming; over its 300 miles, it goes through nearly every major city of the Front Range, including Pueblo, Colorado Springs, Denver, and Fort Collins.

I-70 crosses from west to east, extending from Utah to Baltimore, Maryland. It enters Colorado near Grand Junction, passes through Glenwood Springs, Vail, and Denver, and exits just east of Burlington, a distance of about 450 miles. **I-76** is an additional 190-mile spur that begins in Denver and extends northeast to Nebraska,

joining **I-80** just beyond Julesburg. Visitors entering Colorado from the southwest may take **U.S. 160** (from Flagstaff, Arizona) or **U.S. 550** (from Farmington, New Mexico). Both routes enter the state near Durango.

Denver is about 1,025 miles from Los Angeles, 780 miles from Dallas, 600 miles from Kansas City, 510 miles from Salt Lake City, 440 miles from Albuquerque, 750 miles from Las Vegas, 820 miles from Phoenix, 1,010 miles from Chicago, and 1,800 miles from New York.

GETTING THERE BY TRAIN

Amtrak (✆ **800/USA-RAIL;** www. amtrak.com) has two routes through Colorado. The California Zephyr, which links San Francisco and Chicago, passes through Grand Junction, Glenwood Springs, Granby, Winter Park, Denver, and Fort Morgan en route to Omaha, Nebraska. The Southwest Chief, which runs between Los Angeles and Chicago, travels from Albuquerque, New Mexico, via Trinidad, La Junta, and Lamar before crossing the southeastern Colorado border into Kansas.

---

12 Packages for the Independent Traveler

Package tours are simply a way to buy the airfare, accommodations, and other elements of your trip (such as car rentals, airport transfers, and sometimes even activities) at the same time and often at discounted prices.

One good source of package deals is the airlines themselves. Most major airlines offer air/land packages, including **American Airlines Vacations** (✆ 800/321-2121; www.aavacations.com), **Delta Vacations** (✆ 800/221-6666; www.deltavacations.

com), **Continental Airlines Vacations** (✆ 800/301-3800; www.covacations. com), and **United Vacations** (✆ 888/854-3899; www.unitedvacations.com). Several big **online travel agencies**—Expedia, Travelocity, Orbitz, Site59, and Lastminute.com—also do a brisk business in packages.

One company that puts together packages for trips to several resort communities of Colorado, including Vail, Aspen, Steamboat Springs, and Durango, as well

> ## Tips Ask Before You Go
>
> Before you invest in a package deal or an escorted tour:
>
> - Always ask about the **cancellation policy.** Can you get your money back? Is there a deposit required?
> - Ask about the **accommodations choices and prices** for each. Then look up the hotels' reviews in a Frommer's guide and check their rates online for your specific dates of travel. Also find out what types of rooms are offered.
> - Request a complete **schedule** (escorted tours only).
> - Ask about the **size** and demographics of the group (escorted tours only).
> - Discuss what is included in the **price:** transportation, meals, tips, airport transfers, and so on (escorted tours only).
> - Finally, look for **hidden expenses.** Ask whether airport departure fees and taxes, for example, are included in the total cost—they rarely are.

as Denver (but not Boulder or Colorado Springs), is **Funjet Vacations** (© 888/ 558-6654; www.funjet.com).

Travel packages are also listed in the travel section of your local Sunday newspaper. Or check ads in the national travel magazines such as *Arthur Frommer's Budget Travel Magazine, Travel & Leisure, National Geographic Traveler,* and *Condé Nast Traveler.*

13 Escorted General-Interest Tours

Escorted tours are structured group tours, with a group leader. The price usually includes everything from airfare to hotels, meals, tours, admission costs, and local transportation. Below are some of the better companies that offer escorted tours in Colorado.

Gray Line, 5855 E. 56th Ave. (P.O. Box 646), Denver, CO 80217 (© 303/ 289-2841; www.coloradograyline.com), provides traditional bus and van tours to the U.S. Air Force Academy, Pikes Peak, Rocky Mountain National Park, and historic sites of Denver.

Maupintour, 2688 Rainbow Blvd., Las Vegas, NV 89146 (© 800/255-4266; www.maupintour.com), offers a variety of tours, including well-planned multiday tours of Rocky Mountain National Park and other scenic and historic areas.

Despite the fact that escorted tours require big deposits and predetermine hotels, restaurants, and itineraries, many people derive security and peace of mind from the structure they offer. Escorted tours—whether they're navigated by bus, motor coach, train, or boat—let travelers sit back and enjoy the trip without having to drive or worry about details. They take you to the maximum number of sights in the minimum amount of time with the least amount of hassle. They're particularly convenient for people with limited mobility and they can be a great way to make new friends.

On the downside, you'll have little opportunity for serendipitous interactions with locals. The tours can be jam-packed with activities, leaving little room for individual sightseeing, whim, or adventure—plus they often focus on the heavily touristed sites, so you miss out on many a lesser-known gem.

14 Special-Interest Trips

Hikers, bikers, and other outdoor recreationists can head into the mountains with a variety of companies. See chapter 4, "The Active Vacation Planner," for details.

15 Getting Around Colorado

BY CAR

Cars are not really necessary for those visiting Denver, but for those going practically anywhere else in Colorado they're not only handy but in many cases essential.

Colorado law requires all drivers to carry proof of insurance, as well as a valid driver's license. Safety belts are required for drivers and all front-seat passengers; all children up to age 16 must wear safety belts or be in approved child seats, regardless of where they're seated in the vehicle. The minimum age for drivers is 16. Motorcyclists are not required to wear helmets (but are required to have protective eyewear); radar detectors are permitted.

The maximum speed limit is 75 mph on rural interstate highways and 65 mph on noninterstates, unless otherwise posted.

A state highway map can be obtained from visitor centers or by mail (see "Visitor Information," earlier in this chapter). Otherwise, maps can be purchased at bookstores, gas stations, and most supermarkets and discount stores. Maps are available free to members of the American Automobile Association.

If you're visiting from abroad and plan to rent a car in the United States, you probably won't need the services of an additional automobile organization. If you're planning to buy or borrow a car, automobile association membership is recommended. **AAA, the American Automobile Association** (© **800/222-4357; http://travel.aaa.com**), is the country's largest auto club and supplies its members with maps, insurance, and, most important, emergency road service. *Note:* Foreign driver's licenses are usually recognized in the U.S., but you should get an international one if your home license is not in English.

Each of the chapters that follow contains information on car rentals and public transportation in the individual areas discussed.

ROAD CONDITIONS

A recorded 24-hour hot line (© **303/639-1111; www.cotrip.org**) provides information on road conditions and possible delays due to road construction statewide.

Some of Colorado's roads and highways are closed during winter months. One is U.S. 34, the Trail Ridge Road through Rocky Mountain National Park. It's the highest continuous highway in the world, crossing the Continental Divide at 12,183 feet. Also, Colo. 82, over Independence Pass (elevation 12,095 ft.) east of Aspen, is the main route between Denver and Aspen in the summer months, but it's closed in winter. In addition, the Mount Evans Road (Colo. 103 and Colo. 5) is open from June to September only. It stretches from Idaho Springs (35 miles west of Denver) to the 14,264-foot summit of Mount Evans and is the highest paved road in North America. Among the world's highest tunnels at 11,000 feet, Eisenhower Tunnel carries I-70 beneath Loveland Pass, west of Denver, year-round, though this stretch of interstate is sometimes closed by winter storms. Snow tires or chains are often required when roads are snow covered or icy.

ROAD EMERGENCIES

In case of an accident or road emergency, call © **911.** American Automobile Association members can get free emergency road service wherever they are, 24 hours a day, by calling AAA's emergency number (© **800/AAA-HELP**). In Colorado, AAA headquarters is at 4100 E. Arkansas Ave., Denver, CO 80222, just off S. Colorado Boulevard (© **800/283-5222** or 303/753-8800; www.aaa.com).

BY PLANE

Commuter flights are available from Denver to Grand Junction and several other cities year-round, as well as to some ski resort areas during winter. See the individual town and city listings for details.

While you can fly between Denver and Colorado Springs, it's not nearly as economical as driving, and it's only 70 miles.

Overseas visitors, however, might be able to take advantage of the APEX (Advance Purchase Excursion) reductions offered by all major U.S. and European carriers. In addition, some large airlines offer transatlantic or transpacific passengers special discount tickets under the name **Visit USA,** which allows mostly one-way travel from one U.S. destination to another at very low prices. Unavailable in the U.S., these discount tickets must be purchased abroad in conjunction with your international fare. This system is the easiest, fastest, cheapest way to see the country.

16 Tips on Accommodations

Colorado offers a variety of lodging options, from typical American chain motels to luxury hotels, cozy bed-and-breakfasts to inexpensive mom-and-pop independent motels, cabins to magnificent grande-dame hotels.

The chains here are the same ones you see everywhere else in America: Best Western, Comfort, Days Inn, Embassy Suites, Hampton Inn, Hilton, Holiday Inn, Motel 6, Quality Inn, Sheraton, Super 8, Travelodge, and so on. They look just about the same as those found elsewhere, and have the same levels of service. In most cases their rooms are little more than boring boxes of various sizes, with beds and the appropriate plumbing and heating fixtures, and, if you're lucky, a decent view out the window. These chains, even the high-end ones like Hilton and Sheraton, are fine if you just want a place to sleep and plan to take advantage of their swimming pools, exercise rooms, and other facilities. However, they do very little to enhance your vacation experience, to let you know you're in Colorado.

To make your lodging an integral part of your Colorado experience, we suggest choosing a historic property. We discuss numerous historic bed-and-breakfast inns in the following pages, and—especially when you take into consideration the wonderful breakfasts most of them serve—the rates are fairly reasonable. Why spend $90 for a boring motel room and then another $10 to $15 for breakfast when for just a bit more you can sleep in a handsome, antique-decorated Victorian home and enjoy a home-cooked breakfast?

Colorado also boasts some magnificent but pricey historic hotels, including the absolutely wonderful Brown Palace in Denver and the family-friendly The Broadmoor in Colorado Springs. These hotels are as much attractions as lodgings, and what better way to see them than to book a room for the night, just as others have done for the better part of a century?

Other lodging choices here include cabins and a handful of small independent motels. Both are usually fairly inexpensive, although they often lack the facilities, such as pools, spas, and exercise equipment that you'll find in most chains. We still prefer the cabins and independents, though, because they're often a very good value and the rooms usually have at least some personality (can anybody actually describe the decor of the last Super 8 or Days Inn they stayed at?), and cabins, although sometimes a bit primitive, are often in beautiful settings.

SAVING ON YOUR HOTEL ROOM

The **rack rate** is the maximum rate that a hotel charges for a room. Hardly anybody pays this price, however, except in high season or on holidays. To lower the cost of your room:

- **Ask about special rates or other discounts.** Most rack rates include commissions of 10% to 25% for travel agents, which some hotels may be willing to give you if you make your own reservations and haggle a bit. Always ask whether a room less expensive than the first one quoted is available, or whether any special rates apply to you. You may qualify for corporate, student, military, senior, or other discounts. Be sure to mention membership in AAA, AARP, frequent-flier programs, or trade unions, which may entitle you to special deals as well. Find out the hotel policy on children—do kids stay free in the room or is there a special rate?

- **Watch for coupon books and advertised discounts.** State welcome centers, community visitor centers, and a variety of businesses (but not hotels) distribute free booklets that contain nothing but discount lodging coupons. These are usually for chains, and usually are for walk-ins only, so you won't be able to make a reservation. They also do not usually apply during special events. But if you can use one of these coupons, you can often save 20% to 40% off the rack rate. These coupons are also available online: try www.hotelcoupons.com, and www.roomsaver.com. Also check ads in your local Sunday newspaper travel section, a good source for up-to-the-minute hotel deals, especially for lodging in resort areas.

- **Dial direct.** When booking a room in a chain hotel, you'll often get a better deal by calling the individual hotel's reservation desk rather than the chain's main number.

- **Book online.** Many hotels offer Internet-only discounts, or supply rooms to Priceline, Hotwire, or Expedia at rates much lower than the ones you can get through the hotel itself.

- **Remember the law of supply and demand.** Resort hotels are most crowded and therefore most expensive on weekends, so discounts are usually available for midweek stays. Business hotels in downtown locations are busiest during the week, so you can expect big discounts over the weekend. Many hotels have high-season and low-season prices, and booking even one day after high season ends can mean big discounts.

- **Look into group or long-stay discounts.** If you come as part of a large group, you should be able to negotiate a bargain rate. Likewise, if you're planning a long stay (at least 5 days), you might qualify for a discount. As a general rule, expect 1 night free after a 7-night stay.

- **Avoid excess charges and hidden costs.** When you book a room, ask whether the hotel charges for parking. Use your own cellphone, pay phones, or prepaid phone cards instead of dialing direct from hotel phones, which usually have exorbitant rates. And don't be tempted by the room's minibar offerings: Most hotels charge through the nose for water, soda, and snacks. Finally, ask about local taxes and service charges, which can increase the cost of a room by 15% or more.

- **Book an efficiency.** A room with a kitchenette allows you to shop for groceries and cook your own meals. This is a big money saver, especially for families on long stays.

- **Consider enrolling in hotel "frequent-stay" programs,** which have been upping the ante lately to win the loyalty of repeat customers. Frequent guests can now accumulate points or credits to earn free hotel nights, airline miles, in-room amenities, merchandise, tickets to concerts and events, and discounts on sporting facilities. Perks are awarded not only by many chain hotels and motels (Hilton HHonors, Marriott Rewards, Wyndham ByRequest, to name a few), but individual inns and B&Bs. Many chain hotels partner with other hotel chains, car-rental firms, airlines, and credit card companies to give consumers additional incentive to do repeat business.

LANDING THE BEST ROOM

Somebody has to get the best room in the house. It might as well be you. You can start by joining the hotel's frequent-guest program, which may make you eligible for upgrades. A hotel-branded credit card usually gives its owner "silver" or "gold" status in frequent-guest programs for free. Always ask about a corner room. They're often larger and quieter, with more windows and light, and they often cost the same as standard rooms. When you make your reservation, ask if the hotel is renovating; if it is, request a room away from the construction. Ask about nonsmoking rooms, rooms with views, rooms with twin, queen- or king-size beds. If you're a light sleeper, request a quiet room away from vending machines, elevators, restaurants, bars, and discos. Ask for a room that has been most recently renovated or redecorated.

If you aren't happy with your room when you arrive, ask for another one. Most lodgings will be willing to accommodate you.

17 Tips on Dining

In most parts of Colorado, restaurants tend to close at 9 or 10pm during the week and 11pm on weekends, although there are exceptions. Tipping is standard for the U.S. at 15% to 20%. Local delicacies include Rocky Mountain oysters, Mexican fare, beef, and game. There are also quite a few microbreweries throughout the state, and Denver has been dubbed "the Napa Valley of beer."

18 Recommended Books, Film & Music

Those planning vacations in Colorado can turn to a number of sources for background on the state and its major cities. Among our favorites is *A Lady's Life in the Rocky Mountains,* a fascinating compilation of Isabella L. Bird's letters to her sister; they were written in the late 1800s as she traveled alone through the Rockies, usually on horseback. Those who enjoy lengthy novels will want to get their hands on a copy of James Michener's 1,000-page *Centennial,* inspired by the northeastern plains of Colorado. For a more bohemian point of view, look no further than Jack Kerouac's classic, *On the Road.* Also engrossing is Wallace Stegner's Pulitzer Prize–winning 1971 novel, *Angle of Repose.* Horror fans will surely appreciate a pair of Stephen King classics with Colorado ties: *The Stand* is set in Boulder and *The Shining* was inspired by the writer's stay at the Stanley Hotel in Estes Park.

Travelers interested in seeing wildlife will likely be successful with help from the *Colorado Wildlife Viewing Guide,* by Mary Taylor Gray. You'll likely see a lot of historical sights here, so it's good to first

Tips for Digital Travel Photography

- **Take along a spare camera—or two.** Even if you've been anointed the "official" photographer of your travel group, encourage others in your party to carry their own cameras and provide fresh perspectives—and backup. Your photographic "second unit" may include you in a few shots so you're not the invisible person of the trip.

- **Stock up on digital film cards.** At home, it's easy to copy pictures from your memory cards to your computer as they fill up. During your travels, cards seem to fill up more quickly. Take along enough digital film for your entire trip or, at a minimum, enough for at least a few days of shooting. At intervals, you can copy images to CDs. Many camera stores and souvenir shops offer this service, and a growing number of mass merchandisers have walk-up kiosks you can use to make prints or create CDs while you travel.

- **Share and share alike.** No need to wait until you get home to share your photos. You can upload a gallery's worth to an online photo sharing service. Just find an Internet cafe where the computers have card readers, or connect your camera to the computer with a cable. You can find online photo sharing services that cost little or nothing at **www.clickherefree. com**. You can also use America Online's Your Pictures service, or commercial enterprises that give you free or low-cost photo sharing: Kodak's EasyShare gallery (**www.kodak.com**), Yahoo! Photos (**www.photos.yahoo. com**), Snapfish (**www.snapfish.com**), or Shutterfly (**www.shutterfly.com**).

- **Add voice annotations to your photos.** Many digital cameras allow you to add voice annotations to your shots after they're taken. These serve as excellent reminders and documentation. One castle or cathedral may look like another after a long tour; your voice notes will help you distinguish them.

- **Experiment!** Travel is a great time to try out new techniques. Take photos at night, resting your camera on a handy wall or other support as your self-timer trips the shutter for a long exposure. Try close-ups of flowers, crafts, wildlife, or maybe the exotic cuisine you're about to consume. Discover action photography—shoot the countryside from trains, buses, or cars. With a digital camera, you can experiment and then erase your mistakes.

—From Travel Photography Digital Field Guide,
1st edition (Wiley Publishing, Inc.)

get some background from the short, easy-to-read *Colorado: A History,* by Marshall Sprague.

An excellent video introduction to the state is *Explore Colorado,* a 55-minute video tour that touches on most of the state's scenic and historic highlights. Videos, in both VHS and PAL formats, plus DVDs and interactive CD-ROMs, can be obtained from **Interpark** (© **800/687-5967** or 970/564-9985; www.petroglyph trail.com).

Movies set in Colorado range from numerous westerns—mostly filmed in the state's southwestern corner—such as the John Wayne classic *The Searchers,* as well as *Butch Cassidy and the Sundance Kid* and *City Slickers.* There's also *Things to Do in Denver When You're Dead, About Schmidt,* and *WarGames.* Television shows shot in the state include *Dynasty* (Denver), *Mork & Mindy* (Boulder), and *South Park* (50 miles southwest of Denver).

Musically speaking, the region has a rich heritage and a diverse current scene. John Denver; Judy Collins; Earth, Wind & Fire; Big Head Todd and the Monsters; and the String Cheese Incident are among the bands that broke it big with strong ties to Denver or Boulder. In parts of the world, the "Denver Sound," a roots-based genre that melds gothic and country, has been gaining notoriety, with bands like 16 Horsepower, Munly and the Lee Lewis Harlots, DeVotchKa, and Slim Cessna's Auto Club gaining an international following.

FAST FACTS: Colorado

American Express The American Express travel agency, 555 17th St., Denver (℡ 303/383-5050), is open Monday through Friday from 8am to 5pm. It offers full member services and currency exchange.

Area Codes Colorado uses four telephone area codes. Area codes in the immediate Denver and Boulder area are **303** and **720.** To make local calls in these cities, you will have to dial all 10 digits, starting with 303 or 720. The south-central and southeastern parts of the state, including Colorado Springs, use area code **719;** and the rest (west and north) use **970.** In 719 and 970 areas, local calls are reached by using only the seven-digit number. Long-distance calls in all areas of the state require dialing 1 plus the area code plus the seven-digit number.

ATM Networks See "Money," p. 16.

Automobile Organizations Auto clubs will supply maps, suggested routes, guidebooks, accident and bail-bond insurance, and emergency road service. The **American Automobile Association (AAA)** is the major auto club in the United States. If you belong to an auto club in your home country, inquire about AAA reciprocity before you leave. You may be able to join AAA even if you're not a member of a reciprocal club; to inquire, call AAA (℡ **800/222-4357**). AAA is actually an organization of regional auto clubs, so look under "AAA Automobile Club" in the White Pages of the telephone directory. AAA has a nationwide emergency road service telephone number (℡ 800/AAA-HELP).

Business Hours Generally, business offices are open weekdays from 9am to 5pm and government offices are open from 8am until 4:30 or 5pm. Stores are open 6 days a week, with many also open on Sunday; department stores usually stay open until 9pm at least 1 day a week. Discount stores and supermarkets are often open later than other stores, and some supermarkets are open 24 hours a day.

Banks are usually open weekdays from 9am to 5pm, occasionally a bit later on Friday, and sometimes on Saturday. There's 24-hour access to automated teller machines (ATMs) at most banks, plus in many shopping centers and other outlets.

Car Rentals See "Getting Around," p. 39.

Currency The most common bills are the $1 (a "buck"), $5, $10, and $20 denominations. There are also $2 bills (seldom encountered), $50 bills, and $100 bills (the last two are usually not welcome as payment for small purchases).

Coins come in seven denominations: 1¢ (1 cent, or a penny); 5¢ (5 cents, or a nickel); 10¢ (10 cents, or a dime); 25¢ (25 cents, or a quarter); 50¢ (50 cents, or a half dollar); the gold-colored Sacagawea coin, worth $1; and the rare silver dollar.

For additional information see "Money," p. 16.

Drinking Laws The legal age for purchase and consumption of alcoholic beverages is 21; proof of age is required and often requested at bars, nightclubs, and restaurants, so it's always a good idea to bring ID when you go out.

Colorado is unusual in that its "blue laws" ban the sale of hard alcohol and beer over 3.2% alcohol content on Sundays. Convenience stores and supermarkets sell beer under 3.2% alcohol content on Sundays, and bars sell all their normal wares. By law, all bars in Colorado must close by 2am. Incidentally, 3.2% beer, which is sold only in Colorado, Utah, Oklahoma, and Kansas, does have less alcohol than the same beer sold elsewhere despite what some storekeepers may tell you. According to the Budweiser people, 3.2% beer has about 4% alcohol by volume (which is equivalent to 3.2% alcohol by weight), while full-strength American beers have about 5% alcohol by volume. Some microbrews and specialty beers and ales have higher alcohol content.

Do not carry open containers of alcohol in your car or any public area that isn't zoned for alcohol consumption. The police can fine you on the spot. And nothing will ruin your trip faster than getting a citation for DUI ("driving under the influence"), so don't even think about driving while intoxicated.

Driving Rules See "Getting Around," p. 39.

Electricity Like Canada, the United States uses 110 to 120 volts AC (60 cycles), compared to 220 to 240 volts AC (50 cycles) in most of Europe, Australia, and New Zealand. Downward converters that change 220–240 volts to 110–120 volts are difficult to find in the United States, so bring one with you.

Embassies & Consulates All embassies are located in the nation's capital, Washington, D.C. Some consulates are located in major U.S. cities, and most nations have a mission to the United Nations in New York City. If your country isn't listed below, call for directory information in Washington, D.C. (© **202/555-1212**) or log on to **www.embassy.org/embassies**.

The embassy of **Australia** is at 1601 Massachusetts Ave. NW, Washington, DC 20036 (© **202/797-3000**; www.austemb.org). There are consulates in New York, Honolulu, Houston, Los Angeles, and San Francisco.

The embassy of **Canada** is at 501 Pennsylvania Ave. NW, Washington, DC 20001 (© **202/682-1740**; www.canadianembassy.org). Other Canadian consulates are in Buffalo (New York), Detroit, Los Angeles, New York, and Seattle.

The embassy of **Ireland** is at 2234 Massachusetts Ave. NW, Washington, DC 20008 (© **202/462-3939**; www.irelandemb.org). Irish consulates are in Boston, Chicago, New York, San Francisco, and other cities. See website for complete listing.

The embassy of **New Zealand** is at 37 Observatory Circle NW, Washington, DC 20008 (© **202/328-4800**; www.nzemb.org). New Zealand consulates are in Los Angeles, Salt Lake City, San Francisco, and Seattle.

The embassy of the **United Kingdom** is at 3100 Massachusetts Ave. NW, Washington, DC 20008 (© **202/588-7800**; www.britainusa.com). Other British consulates are in Atlanta, Boston, Chicago, Cleveland, Houston, Los Angeles, New York, San Francisco, and Seattle.

Emergencies Call © **911**. For the **Colorado Poison Center,** call © **303/739-1123**. For the **Rape Crisis and Domestic Violence Hotline,** call © **303/318-9989**.

Gasoline (Petrol) At press time, in the U.S., the cost of gasoline (also known as gas, but never petrol), is high by U.S. standards with most stations in Colorado charging close to $3 per gallon. The lowest prices are usually found in the major city areas (Denver, Boulder, Colorado Springs, Pueblo, Fort Collins, and Grand Junction), and the highest prices are almost always in resort areas such as Vail. You can get current information on the Web at www.fuelgaugereport. com. Taxes are already included in the printed price. One U.S. gallon equals 3.8 liters or .85 imperial gallons. Fill-up locations are known as gas or service stations.

Holidays Banks, government offices, post offices, and many stores, restaurants, and museums are closed on the following legal national holidays: January 1 (New Year's Day), the third Monday in January (Martin Luther King, Jr., Day), the third Monday in February (Presidents' Day), the last Monday in May (Memorial Day), July 4 (Independence Day), the first Monday in September (Labor Day), the second Monday in October (Columbus Day), November 11 (Veterans Day/Armistice Day), the fourth Thursday in November (Thanksgiving Day), and December 25 (Christmas). The Tuesday after the first Monday in November is Election Day, a federal government holiday in presidential-election years (held every 4 years, and next in 2008).

For more information on holidays see "Calendar of Events," earlier in this chapter.

Hospitals Local hospitals are listed throughout this book. Among Denver-area hospitals are **St. Joseph Hospital,** 1835 Franklin St. (© **303/837-7111**), just east of downtown, and **Children's Hospital,** 1056 E. 19th Ave. (© **303/861-8888**). In Boulder, full medical services, including 24-hour emergency treatment, are available at **Boulder Community Hospital,** 1100 Balsam Ave., at North Broadway (© **303/440-2273**). In Colorado Springs, **Memorial Hospital,** 1400 E. Boulder St. (© **719/365-5000**), offers full medical services, including 24-hour emergency treatment, as does **Penrose-St. Francis Hospital,** 2215 N. Cascade Ave. (© **719/776-5000**).

Hotlines For a weather report, time, and temperature, call © **303/337-2500**. Statewide road condition reports are available by calling © **303/639-1111**. For information on possible road construction delays in the Denver area and statewide, see **www.cotrip.org**.

Internet Access See "The 21st-Century Traveler" (p. 31).

Laundromats There are numerous laundromats throughout the state; consult the local phone book.

Legal Aid If you are "pulled over" for a minor infraction (such as speeding), never attempt to pay the fine directly to a police officer; this could be construed as attempted bribery, a much more serious crime. Pay fines by mail, or directly into the hands of the clerk of the court. If accused of a more serious offense, say and do nothing before consulting a lawyer. Here the burden is on the state to prove a person's guilt beyond a reasonable doubt, and everyone has the right to remain silent, whether he or she is suspected of a crime or actually arrested. Once arrested, a person can make one telephone call to a party of his or her choice. International visitors should call their embassy or consulate.

Lost & Found Be sure to tell all of your credit card companies the minute you discover your wallet has been lost or stolen and file a report at the nearest police precinct. Your credit card company or insurer may require a police report number or record of the loss. Most credit card companies have an emergency toll-free number to call if your card is lost or stolen; they may be able to wire you a cash advance immediately or deliver an emergency credit card in a day or two. Visa's U.S. emergency number is ✆ **800/847-2911** or 410/581-9994. American Express cardholders and traveler's check holders should call ✆ **800/ 221-7282**. MasterCard holders should call ✆ **800/307-7309** or 636/722-7111. For other credit cards, call the toll-free number directory at ✆ **800/555-1212**.

If you need emergency cash over the weekend when all banks and American Express offices are closed, you can have money wired to you via **Western Union** (✆ **800/325-6000**; www.westernunion.com).

Mail At press time, domestic postage rates were 24¢ for a postcard and 39¢ for a letter. For international mail, a first-class letter of up to 1 ounce costs 84¢ (63¢ to Canada and Mexico); a first-class postcard costs 75¢ (55¢ to Canada and Mexico); and a preprinted postal aerogramme costs 75¢. For more information go to **www.usps.com** and click on "Calculate Postage."

If you aren't sure what your address will be in the United States, mail can be sent to you, in your name, c/o General Delivery at the main post office of the city or region where you expect to be. (Call ✆ **800/275-8777** for information on the nearest post office.) The addressee must pick up mail in person and must produce proof of identity (driver's license, passport, and so on). Most post offices will hold your mail for up to 1 month. Hours vary considerably throughout the state; for hours and locations go to **www.usps.com**.

Always include zip codes when mailing items in the U.S. If you don't know your zip code, visit www.usps.com/zip4

Maps Denver's largest map store, **Mapsco Map and Travel Center**, 800 Lincoln St., Denver, CO 80203 (✆ **800/718-4627** or 303/830-2373; www.mapsco.com), offers USGS and recreation maps, state maps and travel guides, raised relief maps, and globes.

Measurements See the chart on the inside front cover of this book for details on converting metric measurements to U.S. equivalents.

Newspapers & Magazines The state's largest daily newspaper is the *Denver Post* (www.denverpost.com), which is published in Denver and distributed statewide. Other cities and large towns, especially regional hubs, have daily newspapers, and many smaller towns publish weeklies. National newspapers such as *USA Today* and the *Wall Street Journal* can be purchased in cities and major hotels.

Passports **For Residents of Australia:** You can pick up an application from your local post office or any branch of Passports Australia, but you must schedule an interview at the passport office to present your application materials. Call the **Australian Passport Information Service** at © **131-232,** or visit the government website at www.passports.gov.au.

For Residents of Canada: Passport applications are available at travel agencies throughout Canada or from the central **Passport Office,** Department of Foreign Affairs and International Trade, Ottawa, ON K1A 0G3 (© **800/567-6868;** www.ppt.gc.ca). *Note:* Canadian children who travel must have their own passport. However, if you hold a valid Canadian passport issued before December 11, 2001, that bears the name of your child, the passport remains valid for you and your child until it expires.

For Residents of Ireland: You can apply for a 10-year passport at the **Passport Office,** Setanta Centre, Molesworth Street, Dublin 2 (© **01/671-1633;** www.irl gov.ie/iveagh). Those under age 18 and over 65 must apply for a €12 3-year passport. You can also apply at 1A South Mall, Cork (© **021/272-525**) or at most main post offices.

For Residents of New Zealand: You can pick up a passport application at any New Zealand Passports Office or download it from their website. Contact the **Passports Office** at © **0800/225-050** in New Zealand or 04/474-8100, or log on to www.passports.govt.nz.

For Residents of the United Kingdom: To pick up an application for a standard 10-year passport (5-yr. passport for children under 16), visit your nearest passport office, major post office, or travel agency or contact the **United Kingdom Passport Service** at © **0870/521-0410** or search its website at www.uk pa.gov.uk.

Police Call © **911** for all emergencies.

Safety See "Health & Safety," earlier in this chapter.

Smoking As of July 1, 2006, smoking was banned in all public places in Colorado, including restaurants and bars. The only exceptions are the smoking lounge at Denver International Airport, tobacco shops, and casinos.

Taxes Colorado has a 2.9% state sales tax; local jurisdictions often add another 4% or 5%. Lodging tax is typically 10% to 15%. Overall, the United States has no value-added tax (VAT) or other indirect tax at the national level. Every state, county, and city may levy its own local tax on all purchases, including hotel and restaurant checks and airline tickets. These taxes will not appear on price tags.

Telephone, Telegraph, Telex & Fax Generally, hotel surcharges on long-distance and local calls are astronomical, so you're better off using your **cellphone** or a **public pay telephone.** Many convenience groceries and packaging services sell **prepaid calling cards** in denominations up to $50; for international visitors these can be the least expensive way to call home. Many public phones at airports now accept American Express, MasterCard, and Visa credit cards. **Local calls** made from public pay phones in most locales cost either 25¢ or 35¢. Pay phones do not accept pennies, and few will take anything larger than a quarter.

Most long-distance and international calls can be dialed directly from any phone. **For calls within the United States and to Canada,** dial 1 followed by the area code and the seven-digit number. **For other international calls,** dial 011 followed by the country code, city code, and the number you are calling.

Calls to area codes **800, 888, 877,** and **866** are toll-free. However, calls to area codes **700** and **900** (chat lines, bulletin boards, "dating" services, and so on) can be very expensive—usually a charge of 95¢ to $3 or more per minute, and they sometimes have minimum charges that can run as high as $15 or more.

For **reversed-charge or collect calls,** and for person-to-person calls, dial the number 0 then the area code and number; an operator will come on the line, and you should specify whether you are calling collect, person-to-person, or both. If your operator-assisted call is international, ask for the overseas operator.

For **local directory assistance** ("information"), dial 411; for long-distance information, dial 1, then the appropriate area code and 555-1212.

Telegraph and telex services are provided primarily by Western Union. You can telegraph money, or have it telegraphed to you, very quickly over the Western Union system, but this service can cost as much as 15% to 20% of the amount sent.

Most hotels have **fax machines** available for guest use (be sure to ask about the charge to use it). Many hotel rooms are even wired for guests' fax machines. A less expensive way to send and receive faxes may be at stores such as **The UPS Store** (formerly Mail Boxes Etc.).

Time All of Colorado is in the Mountain Standard Time Zone. The continental United States is divided into **four time zones:** Eastern Standard Time (EST), Central Standard Time (CST), Mountain Standard Time (MST), and Pacific Standard Time (PST). Alaska and Hawaii have their own zones. For example, when it's 9am in Los Angeles (PST), it's 7am in Honolulu (HST), 10am in Denver (MST), 11am in Chicago (CST), noon in New York City (EST), 5pm in London (GMT), and 2am the next day in Sydney.

Daylight saving time takes effect at 2am the first Sunday in April until 2am the last Sunday in October, except in Arizona, Hawaii, the U.S. Virgin Islands, and Puerto Rico. Daylight saving moves the clock 1 hour ahead of standard time. (A new law will extend daylight saving in 2007; clocks will change the second Sunday in March and the first Sunday in November.)

Tipping Tips are a very important part of certain workers' income, and gratuities are the standard way of showing appreciation for services provided. (Tipping is certainly not compulsory if the service is poor!) In hotels, tip **bellhops** at least $1 per bag ($2–$3 if you have a lot of luggage) and tip the **chamber staff** $1 to $2 per day (more if you've left a disaster area for him or her to clean up). Tip the **doorman** or **concierge** only if he or she has provided you with some specific service (for example, calling a cab for you or obtaining difficult-to-get theater tickets). Tip the **valet-parking attendant** $1 every time you get your car.

In restaurants, bars, and nightclubs, tip **service staff** 15% to 20% of the check, tip **bartenders** 10% to 15%, tip **checkroom attendants** $1 per garment, and tip **valet-parking attendants** $1 per vehicle.

As for other service personnel, tip **cab drivers** 15% of the fare; tip **skycaps** at airports at least $1 per bag ($2–$3 if you have a lot of luggage); and tip **hairdressers** and **barbers** 15% to 20%.

Toilets You won't find public toilets or "restrooms" on the streets in most U.S. cities but they can be found in hotel lobbies, bars, restaurants, museums, and department stores. Large hotels, visitor centers, discount stores such as Wal-Mart and Target, and fast-food restaurants are often the best bet for clean facilities. If possible, avoid the toilets at city parks, railway and bus stations, and service stations, which tend to be dirty; some may be unsafe. Restaurants and bars in resorts or heavily visited areas may reserve their restrooms for patrons.

Useful Phone Numbers

Colorado Tourism Office ✆ 800/COLORADO

Colorado State Patrol (nonemergency) ✆ 303/239-4500

Colorado Department of Transportation ✆ 800/999-4997

U.S. Dept. of State Travel Advisory ✆ 202/647-5225 (manned 24 hrs.)

U.S. Passport Agency ✆ 202/647-0518

U.S. Centers for Disease Control International Traveler's Hotline: ✆ 404/332-4559

Visas For information about U.S. visas go to **http://travel.state.gov** and click on "Visas."

3

Suggested Colorado Itineraries

At the risk of oversimplifying, let us suggest that there are essentially three activities for visitors to Colorado—viewing the scenery, visiting historic and cultural sites, and participating in outdoor sports. While there are some visitors whose only goal is to explore prehistoric American Indian sites or historic mining towns, and perhaps hard-core skiers or hikers who are interested solely in pursuing their preferred form of recreation, the vast majority of Colorado visitors want a smorgasbord of experiences: This might include a scenic drive over a mountain pass, a visit to a small-town museum in a Victorian mansion, and a hike to a picturesque lake.

Our suggested itineraries assume that you're looking for a mix of experiences; those interested primarily in outdoor activities should see chapter 4. We'll look at the most efficient routes and the must-see destinations. All of the following start in Denver.

These are all driving tours and, in fact, a motor vehicle is almost mandatory for anyone who wants to explore Colorado. Visitors to Denver don't need a car, and if you're heading to a major resort to ski for a week you can be car-less, but many of the best destinations here require that you drive.

Colorado has a well-maintained network of roadways that will take you to most places you want to visit, although not always directly. Unfortunately, Colorado is a big state, with everything spread out, so you'll end up doing a lot of driving. One consolation is that traffic congestion, even in the cities, is not nearly as bad as many other areas. Services along rural highways are often limited, though, so be careful about checking fuel levels. Also, because of seasonal road closures, the tours that leave the Front Range are for summer use only, although parts of them can be adapted for winter use.

1 Denver, Boulder & Colorado Springs in 1 Week

Colorado's three major Front Range cities are quite different from each other, offering very different experiences, but they are also close and convenient. They are also close to Colorado's famed Rocky Mountains, making it very easy to leave the city lights behind and enjoy the serenity of the great outdoors.

Day ❶: Arrive in Denver ✈✈

Whether you arrive by car or by air, the best place to base yourself is downtown, where you can see all of the attractions on foot and by public transportation. Get acquainted with the lay of the land by walking the **16th Street Mall** (p. 115) and wandering down Wynkoop Street in LoDo. Have dinner at one of the many top dining spots in the area, such as the **Wynkoop Brewing Company** (p. 132) or **Rioja** (p. 93).

Days ❷ & ❸: Explore Denver

Start the next morning at **Larimer Square,** Denver's birthplace, with a self-guided walking tour of the historic sites (p. 106). Then stroll the 16th Street pedestrian mall and head toward the **state capitol** (p. 104), just across Broadway. En route, take a 1-block detour for an early lunch or a cup of tea at the **Brown Palace Hotel** (p. 82). After seeing the capitol, explore other Civic Center sites, especially the **Denver Art Museum** (p. 101). On your third day, explore more of Denver. The city has numerous historic homes, beautiful parks, attractive shopping centers, and several highly touted museums—for example, the **Denver Museum of Nature and Science** (p. 101), the **Botanic Gardens** (p. 110), and the **Black American West Museum** (p. 106).

Day ❹: Boulder 🎯🎯

From Denver, rent a car and make the 30-minute trip to Boulder. Split your time between the **Pearl Street Mall** (p. 198) and an attraction or two: We're particularly fond of the **Celestial Seasonings tour** (p. 200) and the **Boulder Museum of Contemporary Art** (p. 201). Explore a bit of the Boulder Creek Path by foot or bike as well, if time allows, before dinner and a show at one of many venues—Boulder is renowned for its music.

Day ❺: Explore Rocky Mountain National Park 🎯🎯🎯

Boulder is about an hour's drive from Estes Park, the eastern gateway to **Rocky Mountain National Park** (p. 253). Stop for lunch in **Lyons** (p. 211), and then explore the park by car, parking to take a hike. Stay in Estes Park for the night. See p. 240.

Day ❻: Rocky Mountain National Park to Golden 🎯

Drive over **Trail Ridge Road** (p. 254) and south to Berthoud Pass to get back to I-70. This scenic drive gives you the option to hike in the park, or else hightail it back south to Golden for a tour of the **Coors Brewery** (p. 136) or some time to stroll around the pleasant downtown. Either way, it's an ideal overnight stop that lets you avoid the bulk of the traffic in central Denver. See p. 135.

Day ❼: Colorado Springs 🎯🎯

Leave for the 70-mile trip in the morning and you can easily make it to downtown Colorado Springs for lunch. Spend the afternoon in Manitou Springs, or drive or take the train up to the summit of **Pikes Peak** (p. 162). In the evening, if your pocketbook allows, head to **The Broadmoor** (p. 150) for a fitting dinner to cap the trip. From Colorado Springs it's about an hour and a half to Denver International Airport.

---

2 Denver, Boulder & Colorado Springs in 2 Weeks

Taking 2 weeks to explore these cities and surrounding areas provides time for a more in-depth examination of their attractions, and to spend more time in the mountains.

Days ❶, ❷, ❸ & ❹: Denver 🎯🎯

Follow our Denver itinerary above, but take the extra day in Denver to explore a neighborhood by bike and foot. Get a rental and a map from **Campus Cycles** (p. 128), then hop on one of the in-city trails that converges on Confluence Park

for lunch in the vicinity. After lunch, get your rental car and head to one of the attractions farther afield, or if the schedule allows, take in a Rockies game at Coors Field, or another sporting event in this sports-crazy city.

Days ❺, ❻ & ❼: Boulder ✻✻✻
Explore the Pearl Street Mall and a museum on your first day, but take the second day to hike some of the trails in the area (p. 203), packing a lunch before descending for dinner. On your third day in Boulder, visit the **National Center for Atmospheric Research** (p. 199) or the **Redstone Meadery** (p. 200), and take time to do more hiking, biking, or Pearl Street Mall people-watching.

Days ❽ & ❾: Rocky Mountain National Park ✻✻✻
Use Estes Park as a base on night one and camp in the park (or else stay in Grand Lake, the park's western gateway) on night two. Spending 2 full days in the area allows for the second day to be centered on a significant day hike, like the **Mills Lake Trail** or the **Bierstadt Lake Trail.** See p. 259.

Day ❿: Rocky Mountain National Park to Golden ✻✻
As above.

Days ⓫, ⓬, ⓭ & ⓮: Colorado Springs ✻✻
Take your time to explore the Pikes Peak region over 3 unhurried days. Spend your entire first day and night exploring downtown and its attractions, namely the **Fine Art Center** (p. 165) and the **Pioneers Museum** (p. 163). For day two, head to Manitou Springs before ascending **Pikes Peak** (p. 162) by rail or car, then descend for an overnight in Manitou Springs or Old Colorado City. Day three's foci: **Garden of the Gods** (p. 161) and **The Broadmoor** (p. 150), where the trip-capping dinner from above remains our recommendation. From Colorado Springs it's about an hour and a half to Denver International Airport.

---

3 Denver, Boulder & Colorado Springs for Families

Denver, Boulder, and Colorado Springs are all great family vacation destinations, with plenty of museums, kid-friendly restaurants and accommodations, and parks to romp around in—not to mention easy access to the Rocky Mountains.

Day ❶: Arrive in Denver ✻✻
As with the 1-week itinerary earlier in this chapter, start in Denver and base your time there out of downtown. However, kid-friendly destinations are more far-flung, so rent a car from the get-go. See p. 77.

Days ❷ & ❸: Explore Denver ✻✻
Start with a stop at **Confluence Park** before boarding the **Platte River Trolley** (p. 76), then hit the **Children's Museum** (p. 112) and the **Downtown Aquarium** (p. 111). For dinner, **White Fence Farm** (p. 99) and **Casa Bonita** (p. 99) are beloved birthday places. On the third day, hit the **Colorado State Capitol** (p. 104) and the **U.S. Mint** (p. 104) in the morning, and then head

to the southern suburbs to **Wildlife Experience** (p. 109) or to **City Park,** home of the **Denver Zoo** (p. 111) and the **Denver Museum of Nature & Science** (p. 101).

Days ❹ & ❺: Explore Colorado Springs ✻✻
Take your time leaving Denver on the fourth day, but make time to make it to downtown Colorado Springs for lunch at **Michelle's** (p. 160), and perhaps a romp in the water feature at nearby Acacia Park. In the afternoon, visit **Garden of the Gods** (p. 161), before returning downtown for dinner at **Giuseppe's Old Depot Restaurant** (p. 158). Center your next day around Manitou Springs and a trip up **Pikes Peak** (p. 162) by car or rail.

Days ❻ & ❼: Explore Boulder ⟲⟲
and Rocky Mountain National
Park ⟲⟲⟲

Return north on the sixth day of your trip. En route to Boulder, stop off U.S. 36 at the **Butterfly Pavilion** (p. 109) in

Westminster. Visit **Pearl Street Mall** (p. 198) and **Celestial Seasonings** (p. 200) in the afternoon. On the last day of your trip, make a trip up to Estes Park for a quick taste of the Rockies. See p. 240.

4 Colorado in 2 Weeks

Yes, Colorado is a big state with a lot to offer, and we don't pretend that you can actually see and do everything here is only 2 weeks. But this somewhat rushed driving tour hits many of the highlights—what we might call the best of the best—and if nothing else will show you why Colorado is one of America's top vacation destinations.

Days ❶ & ❷: Denver
and Boulder ⟲⟲

Arrive in Denver, preferably in the late morning or early afternoon. Browse **Larimer Square** and the **16th Street Mall** (p. 115). The next morning, visit the **Denver Art Museum** (p. 101), the **Colorado History Museum** (p. 107), and the **state capitol** (p. 104). After lunch, take the short drive to Boulder, browse the **Pearl Street Mall** (p. 198), where you might see a juggler or mime (or just a sleeping University of Colorado student), and settle in for the night.

Day ❸: Estes Park ⟲

Take Canyon Boulevard (Colo. 119) west to Nederland, then follow the foothills north on Colo. 72 and Colo. 7 to Estes Park, where you can visit the **Enos Mills Homestead Cabin** (p. 243), **Estes Park Museum** (p. 243), and take in some spectacular panoramic views on a ride on the **Estes Park Aerial Tramway** (p. 243).

Day ❹: Rocky Mountain National
Park ⟲⟲⟲

In the morning, enjoy spectacular **Trail Ridge Road** through **Rocky Mountain National Park** (p. 253), across the Continental Divide to **Grand Lake** (p. 251). After lunch, proceed south on U.S. 40 to **Winter Park, Berthoud Pass,** and **Georgetown** (p. 279).

Day ❺: Leadville ⟲

I-70 and Colo. 91 will take you up to Leadville, Colorado's 2-mile-high city. See the historic district and **National Mining Hall of Fame and Museum** (p. 316), then continue across **Independence Pass** to the famed resort town of **Aspen** (p. 320).

Day ❻: Aspen ⟲⟲

Give yourself a day in Aspen to shop, sightsee, hike, bike, or just enjoy the clean mountain air.

Day ❼: Montrose ⟲

Drive to Montrose. The route follows the Roaring Fork River west to Carbondale, then south along scenic Colo. 133 over McClure Pass (elevation 8,755 ft.), and through the quaint historic village of **Redstone.** Try to complete the 140-mile drive by early afternoon, leaving time for a visit to the **Ute Indian Museum** (p. 362) and the wondrous deep, dark gorge at **Black Canyon of the Gunnison National Park** (p. 365).

Day ❽: The Million Dollar Highway
to Durango ⟲⟲⟲

It's 98 miles via the **Million Dollar Highway** (p. 385), U.S. 550, to Durango. En route, between the memorable old mining towns of **Ouray** (p. 401) and **Silverton** (p. 382), you'll cross spectacular **Red Mountain Pass** in the San Juan

Mountains. Durango's historic district (p. 369) is one of Colorado's largest and best preserved.

Day ❾: Mesa Verde National Park ✦✦

Visit the **cliff dwellings** of **Mesa Verde National Park** (p. 388), about 40 miles west of Durango.

Day ❿: Great Sand Dunes National Park & Preserve ✦✦

Get an early start for the 150-mile drive across Wolf Creek Pass on U.S. 160 to Alamosa, and continue to northeast to explore **Great Sand Dunes National Park & Preserve** (p. 422), before returning to **Alamosa** (p. 422) for the night.

Day ⓫: Salida and Cañon City ✦

Head north to the rafting capital of Salida, perhaps stopping for a dip in the **hot springs pool** (p. 420), then head east on U.S. 50 to Cañon City. See the **Royal Gorge** (p. 437), the re-created **Old West town of Buckskin Joe** (p. 438), and the **Territorial Prison Museum** (p. 439).

Days ⓬ & ⓭: Colorado Springs ✦✦

Spend 2 full days seeing the attractions in Colorado Springs and nearby Manitou Springs. Choose among the **Pikes Peak Cog Railway** (p. 162), the **U.S. Olympic Training Center** (p. 163), the **Garden of the Gods** (p. 161), and the **Cheyenne Mountain Zoo** (p. 169), among other sights.

Day ⓮: Back to Denver

Stop and visit the **U.S. Air Force Academy** (p. 161) on your way back to Denver, where your flight home awaits.

5 Colorado in 3 Weeks

Three weeks spent exploring this great state provides the opportunity to see many of its top attractions, and get a feel for its cities, towns, and its spectacular scenery. It covers top celebrity-watching centers such as Aspen and Vail, some of Colorado's most picturesque Old West communities, and takes you to four major national parks.

Days ❶ & ❷: Denver ✦✦

Arrive in Denver, preferably in the late morning or early afternoon. Browse **Larimer Square** and the **16th Street Mall** (p. 115). Explore the **state capitol** (p. 104), the **Denver Art Museum** (p. 101), numerous other museums, and **City Park** (p. 110). If there's time, visit nearby **Golden,** home of **Coors Brewery** (p. 136) and the historic buildings from Colorado's territorial days.

Day ❸: Boulder ✦✦

Enjoy a leisurely day in Boulder. Stroll the **Pearl Street Mall** (p. 198) and **University of Colorado campus** (p. 199), or visit the **Celestial Seasonings Tea factory** (p. 200) for a guided tour. (The mint room will knock your socks off!)

Another option is to rent a bike and explore the city's many bike paths.

Day ❹: Estes Park ✦

Take Canyon Boulevard (Colo. 119) west to Nederland, then follow the foothills north on Colo. 72 and Colo. 7 to Estes Park, where you can visit the **Enos Mills Homestead Cabin** (p. 243), **Estes Park Museum** (p. 243), and take in some spectacular panoramic views on a ride on the **Estes Park Aerial Tramway** (p. 243).

Day ❺: Rocky Mountain National Park ✦✦✦

Spend the day in **Rocky Mountain National Park** (p. 253)—perhaps taking a hike in the high country—and crossing the **Continental Divide** on **Trail Ridge**

Road (p. 254) before enjoying the sunset on **Grand Lake** (p. 251).

Day ❻: Georgetown ⚐

Take U.S. 40 south through the Winter Park resort community, over Berthoud Pass, to **Georgetown,** an old Victorian mining town (p. 141).

Day ❼: Breckenridge and Vail ⚐

Follow I-70 to Frisco, seat of Summit County, and detour on a 10-mile spur to **Breckenridge** (p. 286). After lunch and some window shopping, return to I-70 and proceed west to **Vail** (p. 299), America's most popular ski resort (and a booming summer resort as well).

Day ❽: Leadville ⚐

Take U.S. 24 south to Leadville, **the state's highest city** at over 10,000 feet elevation. See the **historic district** (p. 314) and the **National Mining Hall of Fame** (p. 316), then continue across **Independence Pass** to **Aspen** (p. 320).

Day ❾: Aspen ⚐⚐

Shop, hike, bike, or just enjoy Aspen's clean mountain air, and if the timing works, attend a concert at the **Aspen Music Festival** (p. 327).

Day ❿: Black Canyon of the Gunnison National Park

Drive to Montrose via Carbondale, the historic villages of **Redstone, Paonia,** and **Delta.** Leave a few afternoon hours to visit **Black Canyon of the Gunnison National Park** (p. 365).

Days ⓫, ⓬ & ⓭: Durango and Mesa Verde National Park ⚐⚐

The **"Million Dollar Highway,"** U.S. 550 to Durango, where you'll be based for the next few days, passes through the picturesque historic mining towns of **Ouray** (p. 401) and **Silverton** (p. 382) and across **Red Mountain Pass,** an alpine locale worthy of Switzerland. **Durango's historic district** (p. 369) is one of Colorado's

largest and best preserved. Explore **historic downtown Durango** and take a ride on the **Durango & Silverton Narrow Gauge Railroad** (p. 371), which traverses a magnificent route to Silverton and back. Day 13 will be one of archaeological discovery. Spend most of it at **Mesa Verde National Park** (p. 388), some 40 miles west of Durango, or at **Ute Mountain Tribal Mountain Park** (p. 391), south of Cortez.

Day ⓮: Great Sand Dunes National Park & Preserve ⚐⚐

It's 150 miles on U.S. 160 via **Wolf Creek Pass** to **Alamosa** (p. 422), your base while exploring the seemingly misplaced **Great Sand Dunes National Park and Preserve** (p. 422).

Day ⓯: La Junta ⚐⚐

Continue east again on U.S. 160 over La Veta Pass to Walsenburg, then pick up Colo. 10 to La Junta. Visit the **Koshare Indian Museum** (a surprising find with wonderful early-20th-century art) and **Bent's Old Fort National Historic Site,** the reconstructed hub of a trading empire in the 1830s and 1840s. Proceed to **Pueblo** for dinner.

Day ⓰: Pueblo and Cañon City ⚐

Browse Pueblo in the morning, including the impressive Victorian mansion that contains the **Rosemount Museum** (p. 433), and then take a walk at the **Greenway and Nature Center** (p. 432) or along the **Historic Arkansas Riverwalk of Pueblo** (p. 434). Then take U.S. 50 west to Cañon City to see the **Royal Gorge** (p. 437) and the **Western theme village of Buckskin Joe** (p. 438).

Days ⓱, ⓲ & ⓳: Colorado Springs ⚐⚐

Head north on I-25 to Colorado Springs, where there's plenty to do: the **Pikes Peak Cog Railway** (p. 162), the **U.S. Air Force Academy** (p. 161), the **United**

States Olympic Complex (p. 163), Garden of the God's rock formations (p. 161), Cave of the Winds (p. 168), and a variety of museums and historic sites.

Days ⑳ & ㉑: Back to Denver

Return to Denver and catch up on some of the sites you may have missed earlier, or stop at the **Tattered Cover Bookstore** (p. 126) for some reading matter for the trip home.

4

The Active Vacation Planner

The variety and sheer number of active sports and recreational activities Colorado has to offer is staggering. It's a place where you can easily arrange a weeklong, hard-core mountaineering expedition, but it's also a place where you can just as easily take one of the most scenic 2-hour bike rides of your life right in downtown Boulder—not to mention the superb winter activities, from skiing to snowshoeing to snowmobiling. This chapter outlines your choices and offers a few tips for planning everything from a guided, multisport vacation to an afternoon's outing.

1 Preparing for Your Active Vacation

Once you've picked the sport or activities you want to pursue, ask yourself a few questions: How physically fit am I *really*? How much skill in this particular activity do I have? How dangerous is this activity? How much money am I willing to spend? Answering these questions honestly can make the difference between a successful vacation and an unmitigated disaster. Some activities, such as cattle drives, require an outfitter, while others, such as biking, camping, or hiking, you can do on your own. If you're attempting a dangerous sport in which you're inexperienced, such as rock or ice climbing, it's imperative to go with someone who (literally) knows the ropes.

If cost is an issue, prearranged escorted tour packages that include virtually everything can sometimes save you money. On the other hand, you'll be with a group, with limited freedom and flexibility to strike out on your own. Some people enjoy the company of their fellow tour members and the convenience of having everything arranged; others can't stand it. It's your choice.

The best outfitters run well-organized trips and are willing to answer any and all questions, promptly and fully. They should have well-maintained equipment, possess appropriate land-use permits, and be fully insured. If you have any doubts, ask for the name and phone number of a satisfied former customer, and call that person and ask about their experience.

Several government agencies and other organizations provide maps and information that can be extremely useful for a variety of activities. These include **Colorado State Parks** (for state park, boating, RV, and snowmobile regulations), 1313 Sherman St., no. 618, Denver, CO 80203 (© **303/866-3437;** www.parks.state.co.us); the **Colorado Outfitters Association** (for a list of licensed guides and outfitters in the state), P.O. Box 849, Craig, CO 81626 (© **970/824-2468;** www.colorado-outfitters.com); the **U.S. Bureau of Land Management** (for topographical maps and information on activities on the vast amount of BLM land in the state), 2850 Youngfield St., Lakewood, CO 80215 (© **303/239-3600;** www.co.blm.gov); the **U.S. Forest Service,** Rocky Mountain Region (for maps and information about activities and facilities in national forests), 740 Simms St., Golden, CO 80401 (© **303/275-5350;** www.fs.fed. us/r2); and the **National Park Service,** Intermountain Region (for information on national parks, monuments, historic sites, and recreation areas), 12795 Alameda Pkwy., Denver, CO 80225 (© **303/969-2500;** www.nps.gov). Another good online government source for information on outdoor recreation opportunities is www.recreation.gov.

Of the hundreds of commercial outdoor recreation sites on the Internet, we usually like **GORP** (Great Outdoor Recreation Page), www.gorp.com, or you can go right to the Colorado section at www.gorp.com/gorp/location/co/co.htm, which provides detailed information about hiking trails, fishing, watersports, and other activities on Colorado's public lands. Lately, however, that site has been getting a bit too cluttered and too commercial for us, so we've been checking out the very informative and user-friendly **Public Lands Information Center** website, www.publiclands.org.

The *Denver Post,* the state's major daily newspaper, has an especially good website (www.denverpost.com) with quite a bit of outdoor recreation information.

Those looking to buy or rent equipment will find shops practically everywhere in the state, particularly in resort towns. A convenient, statewide resource is **Sports Authority** (formerly Gart Brothers), the state's largest sporting-goods chain. For the location of the store nearest you, check the web—www.sportsauthority.com—or visit the chain's flagship store at 1000 Broadway in Denver (© **303/863-2260**).

2 Visiting Colorado's National Parks & Monuments

Some of the most beautiful parts of Colorado have been preserved within the federal government's national park and monument system.

Rocky Mountain National Park, easily the most popular of the state's national parks in terms of number of visitors, is also the most spectacular. Because photos of its magnificent snowcapped peaks have graced so many calendars and coffee-table books, people often envision Rocky Mountain National Park when they think of Colorado. **Black Canyon of the Gunnison National Park** also offers fine scenery, but it's entirely different from Rocky. Black Canyon is an extremely narrow, rocky river canyon that's wild and beautiful, but difficult to explore because of its steep canyon walls. And then there's **Mesa Verde National Park.** Its reason for being is history, with the best-preserved ancient cliff dwellings in the Southwest.

The state's national monuments may not be as well-known as Rocky Mountain National Park, but each has its own charm and is well worth a visit. For instance, **Colorado National Monument** is similar to the national parks of southern Utah—somewhat barren, with marvelous red-rock formations; and **Dinosaur National Monument** is really two parks—arid yet scenic canyons in Colorado and its namesake dinosaur quarry just across the border in Utah.

To get the most from your visit, try to avoid school-vacation periods and the dead of winter, when Rocky's high country and parts of Mesa Verde and Black Canyon of the Gunnison may be inaccessible. Although the parks are beautiful under a frosting of snow, you won't be able to see as much.

If you can, take a hike. Most park visitors tend to stay on the beaten track, stopping at the same scenic vistas before rushing to the next one. If you can spend even an hour or two on the trail, it's often possible to simply walk away from the crowds.

American parks and monuments are some of the biggest travel bargains in the world. If you plan to visit a number of national parks and monuments within a year, a **National Parks Pass,** which costs $50, will save you a bundle. The pass is good at all properties under the jurisdiction of the National Park Service, but not at sites administered by the Bureau of Land Management, U.S. Forest Service, or other federal or state agencies. The National Parks Pass provides free entrance for the pass holder and all vehicle occupants to National Park Service properties that charge vehicle entrance fees, and the pass holder, spouse, parents, and children for sites that charge per-person fees. The pass can be purchased at park entrance stations and visitor centers, or by mail order (© **888/GO-PARKS;** www.nationalparks.org).

Available in person at park service properties, as well as other federal recreation sites that charge entrance fees, is the **Golden Age Passport,** for those 62 and older, which has a one-time fee of $10 and provides free admission to all national parks and monuments, plus a 50% discount on camping fees. Be sure you have a photo ID with your date of birth. The **Golden Access Passport,** free for U.S. citizens who are blind or have permanent disabilities, has the same benefits as the Golden Age Passport, and is available at all federal recreation sites that charge entrance fees. You'll need written proof of your disability.

Available from U.S. Forest Service, Bureau of Land Management, and Fish and Wildlife areas (such as wildlife refuges) is the **Golden Eagle Pass.** At a cost of $65 for 1 year from the date of purchase, the pass allows the bearer, plus everyone traveling with him or her in the same vehicle, free admission to all National Park Service properties plus other federal recreation sites that charge fees. The National Parks Pass discussed above can be upgraded to Golden Eagle status for $15.

3 Outdoor Activities A to Z

Throughout this book we recommend outfitters and guides that will help you enjoy the great outdoors in their particular areas. One highly regarded company that offers trips throughout the West, including several areas in Colorado, is the **World Outdoors,** 2840 Wilderness Place, Suite F, Boulder, CO 80301 (© **800/488-8483** or 303/413-0938; www.theworldoutdoors.com), which leads a variety of hiking and multisport adventures. Most trips are 6 days long and include transportation, lodging, and dining.

BALLOONING   You can take a hot-air balloon ride virtually anywhere in the state, but the most awe-inspiring scenery is in the mountains. Hot-air ballooning is expensive, and it's one sport where you don't want to cut corners. Choose an experienced and well-established balloon company, and if you have any qualms, ask about their safety record. And of course, you'll pay the highest rates at resorts.

BICYCLING   Road biking is popular throughout Colorado, but especially in Boulder, which has just as many bikes as it has people; in Fort Collins, public buses have bike racks. Our favorite city path is the **Boulder Creek Path,** which meanders through miles of Boulder parklands, with no motor vehicle intrusion of any kind.

Fun Fact **Elk, Elk, and More Elk**

There are more elk in Colorado than in any other state or Canadian province.

BOATING   Those who take their powerboats along on their visit to Colorado will find lakes scattered across the state. Most have boat ramps, some have fuel and supplies, and some of the larger lakes offer boat rentals. Popular choices include Bonny Lake near Burlington (known for water-skiing), Lake Pueblo, and Trinidad Lake. Because Colorado has been experiencing drought conditions in recent years, it's a good idea to call ahead to check on water conditions. In several instances lake levels have dropped well below the boat ramps, leaving boaters literally "high and dry."

CAMPING   With so many acres of public land, Colorado offers practically unlimited opportunities for camping, especially in the mountains. There are over 400 public campgrounds in the national forests alone, plus sites in Bureau of Land Management areas, national parks, national monuments, and state parks. In addition, most communities have commercially operated campgrounds with RV hookups. If you plan to drive an RV in Colorado, a word of advice: Have the mechanical systems checked out first, as there are some extremely steep grades in the mountains.

One of the best places to camp in the state is Rocky Mountain National Park, but it can be crowded, especially in summer. Visit in late September or early October, if possible. Backpackers will find numerous camping opportunities along the Colorado Trail and in State Forest State Park west of Fort Collins. Mueller State Park, west of Colorado Springs, is tops for RV camping.

The **Colorado Directory, Inc.,** 5101 Pennsylvania Ave., Boulder, CO 80303-2799 (C **888/222-4641** or 303/499-9343; fax 303/499-9333; www.coloradodirectory. com), publishes a free booklet that describes commercial campgrounds, cabin facilities, and resorts throughout the state. For a free copy of *Colorado State Parks,* which contains details on the state's 40-plus parks, contact state park offices (see "Preparing for Your Active Vacation," above).

CATTLE DRIVES   As elsewhere in the West, opportunities abound for city slickers to play cowboy by riding and roping cattle on actual drives that last from a day to a week or more. Each drive is different, so ask very specific questions about food, sleeping arrangements, and other conditions before plunking down your money. The best places for joining a drive are Steamboat Springs and Durango, with their beautiful mountain scenery and fun towns—perfect for relaxing at the end of the trail.

CROSS-COUNTRY SKIING   Practically every major downhill ski area also offers cross-country skiing, and there are thousands of miles of trails throughout Colorado's national forests—often over old mining and logging roads—that are perfect for cross-country skiing. Among top choices are Breckenridge, with trails winding through open meadows and a spruce forest, and the beautiful San Juan Mountains near Durango and Telluride. Information is available from the **Colorado Cross Country Ski Association** (www.colorado-xc.org), and from the **U.S. Forest Service** (see "Preparing for Your Active Vacation," above).

DOG SLEDDING   If your fantasy is to be a Canadian Mountie mushing across the frozen Yukon, save the airfare and head to the mountains of Colorado instead. Dog-sled rides are offered at several ski resorts, but we like Aspen best, where dog-power takes you far from the crowds into the rugged backcountry; some rides end with a fancy dinner.

FISHING   Many cold-water species of fish live in the state's mountains, lakes, and streams, including seven kinds of trout (native cutthroat, rainbow, brown, brook, lake,

> (Fun Fact **A Wimpy State Fish**
>
> Mistakenly believed to be extinct in 1937 and listed as an endangered species in the early 1970s, the greenback cutthroat trout has made a comeback, and in 1994 was named the official Colorado State Fish by the state legislature. It replaced the rainbow trout, a California transplant that had been listed on maps and other documents as the state fish, although state Division of Wildlife officials couldn't say why.
>
> Part of the greenback's problem is that it fails to live up to its cutthroat name, letting other trout invade its waters and practically jumping on any hook dropped into the water. But rumors of its demise were premature, and two native populations were discovered just outside Rocky Mountain National Park in 1973. Efforts were begun to reintroduce the fish to its native waters, as government agencies and Trout Unlimited provided it with places to live that are free from more aggressive newcomers. By 1978 its status had improved from "endangered" to "threatened." State wildlife officials hope that if the greenback continues to prosper it can eventually be removed from the "threatened" list.
>
> Today, the greenback cutthroat can be found in some four dozen bodies of water around the state, including several lakes in Rocky Mountain National Park. A good place in the national park to see the greenback cutthroat close-up is from the boardwalks through the Beaver Ponds on Trail Ridge Road.
>
> Although the greenback's designation as official state fish does not provide any additional protection, Division of Wildlife officials say it strengthens the public's willingness to protect the fish, and encourages anglers to throw it back if they catch it, as should be the rule with any threatened species.

kokanee, and whitefish), walleye, yellow perch, northern pike, tiger muskie, and bluegill. Warm-water sport fish (especially in eastern Colorado and in large rivers) include catfish, crappie, and bass (largemouth, smallmouth, white, and wiper). The best fishing spots are the Arkansas River near Salida, the Roaring Fork River near Aspen, and the numerous streams and lakes in the mountains surrounding Steamboat Springs.

The fishing season is year-round, except in certain specified waters, and licenses are required for all anglers 16 and older. A 1-year license costs $56 for a nonresident, and $26 for a resident. A 5-day license for nonresidents costs $21, and 1-day license costs $9 for both residents and nonresidents. The **Colorado Division of Wildlife,** 6060 Broadway, Denver, CO 80216 (© **303/297-1192;** www.wildlife.state.co.us), can answer your questions; for a recorded fishing statewide report call © **303/291-7534.**

FOUR-WHEELING   For years, skiers have known that four-wheel-drive vehicles make getting to and from the slopes easier. But SUVs and 4WD trucks are also popular for exploring Colorado's backcountry in summer, especially its miles upon miles of old logging and mining roads. Top locations for four-wheeling include the San Juan Mountains around Ouray and Telluride. You can get information on events and tips on places to go from the **Colorado Off Highway Vehicle Coalition,** P.O. Box 620523, Littleton, CO 80162 (℃ **303/539-5010;** www.cohvco.org).

GOLF   Clear blue skies and beautiful scenery are hallmarks of Colorado golf courses, but don't think they're merely pretty faces; these courses can be as challenging as any in the country. Balls travel farther here than at sea level, and golfers tend to tire more quickly, at least until they've adapted to the higher elevation. Be prepared for cool mornings and afternoon thunderstorms even at the height of summer. High-elevation courses, such as those in Steamboat Springs and Vail, are shut down by snow in winter, but those at lower elevations, such as along the western slope, in the southwest corner, and around Denver, are often open year-round.

Good golf resorts can be found in Crested Butte, Winter Park, Pueblo, and Alamosa; for high-altitude putting, try Leadville. For what we think is the absolutely best golf resort in the state, go to The Broadmoor in Colorado Springs. For information on the state's major golf courses, check with the **Colorado Golf Association,** 5990 Greenwood Plaza Blvd., Suite 130, Greenwood Village, CO 80111 (℃ **800/228-4675** or 303/366-4653; www.cogolf.org). Another information resource is *Colorado Golf,* an annual magazine published jointly by several statewide golf organizations and available free at state welcome centers, or check its website, www.golfcolorado.com.

HIKING, BACKPACKING & MOUNTAINEERING   Colorado is literally crisscrossed with hiking trails and dotted with mountains begging to be climbed. We especially like Rocky Mountain National Park's trails, but they can be crowded. The highly respected **Colorado Mountain School,** 341 Moraine Ave., Estes Park, CO 80517 (℃ **800/836-4008;** www.totalclimbing.com), leads climbs up Longs Peak in the national park and provides advice on mountaineering in other parts of the state.

The 500-mile **Colorado Trail** ★★, which winds from Denver to Durango, crosses seven national forests and six designated wilderness areas, and is open to hikers, bikers, and equestrians. Scenery and terrain are varied, from grassy plains to snowcapped

---

⟨Tips⟩ Lightning—A Potential Killer

Colorado is a wonderful place to explore the great outdoors, with some of America's most spectacular scenery and rugged terrain. But like most other places, outdoor activities here are not without risk. The National Weather Service says that although the number of deaths from lightning is not high—an average of 67 each year in the U.S.—lightning does kill more people than either tornadoes or hurricanes, and injures hundreds more. The agency says that most people struck by lightning are not in the rain, and that lightning can travel sideways for up to 10 miles. It recommends that whenever people hear thunder they should immediately seek shelter in a building, cave, or hard-topped vehicle; if trapped by a thunderstorm, people should go to the lowest point in the area, stay out of the water, and avoid metal by dropping metal-frame backpacks and not leaning against cars. Of course, lightning is not the only outdoor hazard in Colorado. Also see "Health & Safety" in chapter 2.

Impressions

You can't see anything from your car. You've got to get out of the damn thing and walk!

—author Edward Abbey

---

mountains. Although those in excellent physical condition can hike the entire trail in 6 to 8 weeks, most hikers make shorter excursions, and many enjoy day hikes. Most of the trail is above 10,000 feet elevation (the highest point is at 13,334 ft.), and hikes of more than a day or two will inevitably include some steep climbs. However, most of the trail has grades of no more than 10%. You'll find the easiest sections of the trail in the first 90 miles from Denver, but other sections, such as one 20-mile stretch near Salida, are also easy to moderate. In the Breckenridge and Winter Park areas, the trail is fairly rugged, and most sections below U.S. 50 are mountainous and at least somewhat strenuous. South of U.S. 50, where the trail winds through the San Juan Mountains, is serenely peaceful, but there are also fewer services, and if you're injured, it could be a long wait for help.

If it's serenity you seek, consider climbing one of the fourteeners—peaks over 14,000 feet—just off the Colorado Trail. Among the easiest is the climb to the summit of 14,420-foot Mount Harvard, the state's third-highest peak. The trail branches off the Colorado Trail about 8 miles north of Buena Vista.

Those planning multiday hikes on the Colorado Trail should carry maps or the official guidebook, which includes maps and details of the entire trail—elevation changes, trail conditions, vehicle access points, closest services, and general descriptions. Contact the **Colorado Trail Foundation,** 710 10th St. #210, Golden, CO 80401-5843 (© **303/384-3729;** www.coloradotrail.org).

Although the Colorado Trail may be the state's most famous hike, there are plenty of other opportunities. We particularly like the hike to **Long Lake** in the **Routt National Forest** outside Steamboat Springs, a moderately difficult 12-mile round-trip hike that leads through a forest and past several waterfalls to a peaceful alpine lake. Another pleasant hike in the Denver area is the easy 9-mile walk around **Barr Lake,** 18 miles northeast of the city, which offers excellent viewing of wildlife and birds. For the best city hike, try the **Boulder Creek Path,** a 16-mile trail leading from downtown Boulder into the nearby mountains, offering wildlife and bird-watching and good views of the mountains and city. Those in Colorado Springs can hike among the beautiful red sandstone formations in the **Garden of the Gods,** or head west 30 miles to **Mueller State Park,** with 75 miles of trails through magnificent mountain scenery.

The **Continental Divide Trail Alliance (CDTA),** P.O. Box 628, Pine, CO 80470 (© **888/909-2382** or 303/838-3760; www.cdtrail.org), is building a trail—using volunteers—along the mountains of the Great Divide from Canada to Mexico, and that means it shoots right through the middle of Colorado. Each year, the CDTA publishes a schedule for the next summer, complete with volunteer needs, project descriptions, and difficulty ratings. This is an opportunity to experience some incredible backcountry, and to help create something your grandchildren will enjoy as well.

HORSEBACK RIDING   It's fun to see the Old West the way 19th-century pioneers did: from a horse's saddle. Plenty of stables and outfitters lead rides lasting from 1 hour to several days, but we recommend those near Estes Park, Steamboat Springs,

Grand Junction, and Telluride. If you'd like to spend your entire vacation on horseback, the **Sylvan Dale Guest Ranch** (© **877/667-3999** or 970/667-3915; www.sylvandale.com) just outside of Loveland is among our top choices.

MOUNTAIN BIKING   The town of Crested Butte claims to be the mountain-biking capital of Colorado, but Telluride, Vail, and Durango are also top spots for fat-tire explorations. Those planning to go mountain biking in western Colorado can get current trail information from the **Colorado Plateau Mountain-Bike Trail Association,** P.O. Box 4602, Grand Junction, CO 81502 (© **970/244-8877;** www.copmoba.com).

The **Colorado Trail** (see above) is also open to mountain bikers. Riding the entire 500 miles—it takes at least 4 weeks—is easily the state's top mountain-bike adventure, but you can join or leave the trail at almost any point. One easily accessible stretch runs 24 miles from Copper Mountain Ski Resort to Tennessee Pass, crossing 12,280-foot Elk Ridge and descending into the ghost town of Camp Hale. On the trail, bikers yield to hikers and equestrians, and detour around designated wilderness areas. Contact the **Colorado Trail Foundation** (see "Hiking, Backpacking & Mountaineering," above).

RAFTING & KAYAKING   Rivers swollen with melted snow lure rafters and kayakers from spring through midsummer, when rivers are at their fullest. Salida has become a famous rafting center; other popular destinations include Fort Collins, Estes Park, Grand Junction, and Glenwood Springs.

Rivers are classified from Class I to VI, depending on the roughness of their rapids. Class I is an easy float trip, practically calm; class II has some rapids alternating with calm; class III has some difficult rapids, with waves and boulders, and can be narrow in spots; class IV is considered very difficult, with long stretches of rough, raft-flipping rapids; class V is extremely difficult with violent rapids and steep drops; and class VI is considered unrunnable. The Arkansas River near Salida offers a variety of rapids from easy to almost unrunnable, and the Colorado River through Glenwood Canyon is a particularly scenic class II to III river, wild enough for some thrills but with enough calm stretches to let you catch your breath and enjoy the view.

You'll find a range of trips from numerous reliable outfitters. For a free directory of licensed river outfitters and tips on choosing a rafting company, contact the **Colorado River Outfitters Association,** P.O. Box 1662, Buena Vista, CO 81211 (© **303/280-2554;** www.croa.org).

ROCK CLIMBING   Although rock climbing is not as big here as in other parts of the West, Colorado does attract its share of climbers. One of the best spots is the Black Canyon of the Gunnison near Montrose, an extremely narrow chasm that sees little daylight; there are also several good spots near Durango. You can get information from the **Colorado Mountain Club,** American Mountaineering Center, 710 10th St., #200, Golden, CO 80401 (© **303/279-3080;** www.cmc.org).

ROCKHOUNDING & GOLD PANNING   The state's mining heritage continues in many areas among rockhounders, who search for semiprecious gemstones, petrified woods, and agatized fossil bones. The Salida area has some of the best rockhounding opportunities in the state, and amateur gold panners should visit Idaho Springs (near Denver), Silverton, and Country Boy Mine in Breckenridge. Contact the **Colorado Geological Survey,** 1313 Sherman St., Room 715, Denver, CO 80203 (© **303/866-2611** or 303/866-4762 for publications; www.geosurvey.state.co.us), for information, maps, and a list of locations.

SKIING & SNOWBOARDING   The most popular winter sport in Colorado is, of course, downhill skiing. Since the state's first resort (Howelsen Hill in Steamboat Springs) opened in 1915, Colorado has been synonymous with skiing in the western United States: It attracts more skiers per day than other Western states, and its resorts continue to win accolades.

The snowboarding craze hit Colorado just as hard as other winter-sports destinations, and after some initial resistance, has been welcomed with open arms. Many resorts have opened snowboarding parks and offer lessons and rentals.

For **current ski conditions** and general information, call **Colorado Ski Country USA,** 1507 Blake St., Denver, CO 80202 (© **303/837-0793** or 303/825-7669 for snow conditions; www.coloradoski.com), or check *Ski* magazine's website (www.ski mag.com). Colorado's slopes are most crowded over Christmas and New Year's, and on the Martin Luther King, Jr., and Presidents' Day weekends, when lodging rates are at their highest. Those who can ski midweek will find more room on the slopes, and the beginning and end of the season are the best times to avoid crowds—assuming snow conditions are good.

Colorado's ski areas range from predominately day-use areas, with little beyond a mountain with trails and a few lifts, to full-fledged resorts, with a variety of accommodations, restaurants, and nightlife all within a half-hour of the slopes. The overview that follows describes the key mountains at these ski areas and resorts.

Arapahoe Basin (Summit County)   Arapahoe Basin, called "A-Basin" by its loyal fans, is the highest ski area in the state, and one of the oldest. Because of its elevation, it gets a bit more snow than elsewhere, so some prefer to ski it during spring's warmer temperatures.

Aspen Highlands (Aspen)   An intense mountain for only the most skilled and athletic of skiers. The views from the top are stupendous.

Tips **A Word About Rates**
_____

In the write-ups for each ski area in the regional chapters, we give the daily lift-ticket rates. Although handy for comparison, few people actually pay these prices. Most skiers buy packages that include lift tickets for a given number of days, and may also include transportation, rental equipment, lessons, lodging, meals, and lift tickets for nearby ski areas. The possibilities are almost endless.

Some resorts charge more for lift tickets at busy times, and offer discounts at slow times, so it's impossible for us to guarantee the accuracy of even the daily lift-ticket prices. Certainly, the most expensive time to ski is between December 20 and January 1, as well as the Martin Luther King, Jr., and Presidents' Day weekends. February through March is next; nonholiday times in January are generally cheaper; and the least expensive time is from Thanksgiving until mid-December and April until ski areas close. We generally prefer the last few weeks of the season—the snow's still great, the weather's nice, and the slopes are less crowded, because many skiers are turning their thoughts to golf and tennis.

Aspen Mountain (Aspen)   With more than 100 restaurants and bars, Aspen is one of Colorado's most sophisticated resorts. Aspen Mountain was designed for advanced skiers and is the second most challenging of Aspen's four slopes.

Beaver Creek (Vail)   Beaver Creek is probably the most refined ski community in Colorado. The mountain has a good mix of runs for everyone but the super expert, and lift lines are usually shorter than at Vail Mountain, especially on weekends.

Breckenridge (Summit County)   Colorado's second most popular resort, Breckenridge is the crown jewel of Summit County's ski areas. There's something for all levels of skiers, and it makes a great base camp for those who want to ski a different Summit County mountain every day.

Buttermilk (Aspen)   The usually uncrowded Buttermilk is a great place for affluent novices to practice their moves. It's located just outside the main village and is known for its great ski school.

Copper Mountain (Summit County)   With its four superb bowls and variety of trails for all levels, Copper is a fun place to ski, and the village is less expensive than nearby Breckenridge.

Crested Butte (Crested Butte)   Dependable snow, good beginner and intermediate trails, and lots of extreme skiing—but very little expert terrain—mark this area.

Durango Mountain (Durango)   This small, low-key ski area offers mostly intermediate, narrow, hilly trails meandering through the trees amid the breathtakingly beautiful San Juan Mountains.

Eldora (Nederland)   Just 21 miles from Boulder, Eldora is one of the state's smaller resorts, but has a good mix of terrain and is the closest ski area to the Denver-Boulder metropolitan area.

Howelsen Hill (Steamboat Springs)   The oldest ski area in continuous use in Colorado—it opened in 1915—Howelsen Hill is a fun little downtown ski area as well as a training facility for ski jumpers.

Keystone (Summit County)   Of Summit County's ski areas, Keystone is the closest to Denver, about 90 miles west of the airport. Its three separate mountains make it a good place for cruising, and night skiing draws locals from miles around.

Loveland (North of Denver)   Less than an hour from Denver by car, Loveland is an old-fashioned day-ski area: There's no village, but enough beginner and advanced trails to satisfy the average skier. If you're staying in Denver in winter, give it a whirl.

Monarch (Salida)   This family-oriented resort in southern Colorado has among the lowest rates, with good terrain and fewer crowds.

Powderhorn (Grand Junction)   This is a good mountain for groups of varying abilities, with half its slopes intermediate, and another 30% advanced or expert.

Silverton Mountain (Silverton)   This new ski/snowboard area plans to be less expensive than most of Colorado's resorts, and is geared to expert/advanced skiers and snowboarders only.

Ski Cooper (Leadville)   A small, inexpensive resort at a high elevation, Ski Cooper is known for its all-natural snow and beautiful mountain scenery. There's a good balance of trails for beginners, intermediates, and experts.

(Tips Ski Packages & Tours

While many skiers enjoy planning their trips, others prefer making one phone call or sending an e-mail, and then letting someone else handle the details. Packages not only save time, but are sometimes cheaper than doing it yourself. The key is to make sure you get all the features you want, without paying for things you don't want. Packages often include air and ground transportation, lodging, and lift tickets, and some include trip-cancellation insurance and meals.

A good first step is to check with a ski club in your hometown. These non-profit organizations often offer some of the best deals if they happen to be planning a trip to where you want to ski at a time you want to go. Many travel agents can arrange ski vacations, and the central reservations service for a particular resort and the reservations desks of nearby lodgings can give you the scoop on the latest packages. Good bets among the well-established companies that offer ski packages throughout Colorado are **Ski.com** (© **800/778-8589**; www.ski.com) and **Ski the Rockies** (© **800/291-2588**; www.skitherockies.com).

Snowmass (Aspen)   The highlight of Aspen, with plenty of wide-open spaces and trails for absolutely every level of ability. This is, by far, the largest mountain at Aspen. The base village has plenty of beds, but not much nightlife—most night owls hop the free shuttle bus to Aspen, 20 minutes down the road.

Solvista Golf & Ski Ranch (Near Winter Park)   Created by the merging of several smaller ski areas, Solvista is an all-season resort comprising two interconnected mountains, with mostly beginner and intermediate runs, and just 20% expert.

Steamboat (Steamboat Springs)   One of Colorado's three largest mountains (the other two are Vail and Snowmass), Steamboat offers near-perfect skiing. It's well laid out and has gorgeous valley views, and the base village offers a wide choice of accommodations and restaurants. Another draw is the authentic old ranching town of Steamboat Springs, just a few miles away. Most of the mountain's trails are for intermediates, but there are beginner and expert trails as well.

Sunlight Mountain (Glenwood Springs)   Sunlight is family oriented, geared to intermediate skiers, and very affordable.

Telluride (Telluride)   Set at the top of a lovely box canyon, Telluride caters mainly to intermediate skiers, but also has novice trails some 2½ miles long and a number of steep expert trails.

Vail (Vail Valley)   Colorado's most popular resort, Vail mountain has a top-notch ski school and trails for everyone. The completely self-contained village at its base was created for skiers and is serviced by free shuttle buses.

Winter Park (Winter Park)   Young and athletic in spirit, Winter Park is unique—the focus is on value, with a variety of trails for all levels, plus well-regarded programs for children and skiers with disabilities.

Wolf Creek (Near Pagosa Springs)   One of the state's oldest ski areas, Wolf Creek is famous for consistently having the most snow in the state—an annual average of 465 inches (almost 39 ft.). There is terrain for skiers of all ability levels, but especially intermediates.

SNOWMOBILING   If you've never been snowmobiling, the best places for a guided snowmobile tour are Steamboat Springs and Aspen. If you're an experienced snowmobiler and you plan to bring your rig with you, national forest trails are prime snowmobiling spots. Some of the state's best and most scenic rides are in Roosevelt National Forest, about 50 miles west of Fort Collins (via U.S. 287 and Colo. 14) at Chambers Lake. Because many of these trails are multiuse, snowmobilers should watch out for cross-country skiers and snowshoers, and slow down when passing. Colorado's light, dry snow is usually suitable for snowmobiling all winter long, although warm spring days can result in sticky snow, especially at lower elevations, which can gum up the works and make the going rough.

Information on snowmobiling in the state, include current trail conditions, is available online from **SledCity** (formerly the Colorado Snowmobile Association) at www.coloradosledcity.com. For information on snowmobile regulations, contact **Colorado State Parks** (see "Preparing for Your Active Vacation," earlier in this chapter).

WILDLIFE & BIRD-WATCHING   There are numerous locations in Colorado to see animals and birds in the wild, including some that are close to the state's major cities. The South Platte River Greenway near Denver is a good spot to see ducks and other waterfowl, songbirds, deer, and beaver; and if you head to the prairie in southeastern Colorado, the Comanche National Grasslands is the place to see the rare lesser prairie chicken. Other top spots for wildlife include Durango, Glenwood Springs, Fort Collins, Vail, Rocky Mountain National Park, and Colorado National Monument.

5

Settling into Denver

It's no accident that Denver is called "the Mile High City": When you climb up to the State Capitol, you're precisely 5,280 feet above sea level when you reach the 13th step. Denver's location at this altitude was purely coincidental; Denver is one of the few cities not built on an ocean, lake, navigable river, or even (at the time) an existing road or railroad.

In the summer of 1858, eager prospectors discovered a few flecks of gold where Cherry Creek empties into the shallow South Platte River, and a tent camp quickly sprang up on the site. (The first permanent structure was a saloon.) When militia Gen. William H. Larimer arrived in 1859, he claim-jumped the land on the east side of the Platte, laid out a city, and, hoping to gain political favors, named it after James Denver, governor of the Kansas Territory, which included this area. Larimer was not aware that Denver had recently resigned.

Larimer's was one of several settlements on the South Platte. Three others also sought recognition, but Larimer had a solution. For the price of a barrel of whisky, he bought out the other would-be town fathers, and the name "Denver" caught on.

Although the gold found in Denver was but a teaser for much larger strikes in the nearby mountains, the community grew as a shipping and trade center, in part because it had a milder climate than the mining towns it served. A devastating fire in 1863, a deadly flash flood in 1864, and American Indian hostilities in the late 1860s created many hardships. But the establishment of rail links to the east and the influx of silver from the rich mines to the west kept Denver going. Silver from Leadville and gold from Cripple Creek made Denver a showcase city in the late 19th and early 20th centuries. The U.S. Mint, built in 1906, established Denver as a banking and financial center.

In the years following World War II, Denver became the largest city between the Great Plains and the Pacific Coast, with about 550,000 residents within the city limits and over 3 million in the metropolitan area. Today, it's a big, growing city, extending from the Rocky Mountain foothills on the west far into the plains to the south and east. Denver is noted for its tree-lined boulevards, 200 city parks, and architecture ranging from Victorian to postmodern.

1 Orientation

ARRIVING
BY PLANE

Denver International Airport (DIA) is 23 miles northeast of downtown, usually a 35- to 45-minute drive. Covering 53 square miles (twice the size of Manhattan), DIA boasts one of the tallest flight-control towers in the world, at 327 feet. The airport, which has 94 gates and six full-service runways, can handle around 33 million passengers annually.

Major national airlines serving Denver include American, Continental, Delta, Frontier, Northwest, Sun Country, jetBlue, Southwest, United, and US Airways. **International airlines** include Air Canada, British Airways, Lufthansa, and Mexicana.

Regional and **commuter airlines** connecting Denver with other points in the Rockies and Southwest include Alaska Airlines, Great Lakes Airlines, and Mesa.

For airlines' national reservations phone numbers and websites, see "Getting There," in chapter 2. For other information, call the Denver International Airport **information line** (© **800/AIR-2-DEN** or 303/342-2000; TDD 800/688-1333; www.flydenver.com). Other important airport phone numbers include: **ground transportation,** © 303/342-4059; **vehicle assistance,** including emergency car-start, © 303/342-4650; **paging,** © 303/342-2300; **parking,** © 303/342-7275; **police,** © 303/342-4212; and **security wait times,** © 303/342-8477.

GETTING TO & FROM THE AIRPORT   Bus, taxi, and limousine services shuttle travelers between the airport and downtown, and most major car-rental companies have outlets at the airport. Because many major hotels are some distance from the airport, travelers should check on the availability and cost of hotel shuttle services when making reservations.

The **city bus** fare from the airport to downtown Denver is $8; from the airport to Boulder and suburban Park-n-Ride lots, it is about $10. The **SuperShuttle** (© **800/525-3177** or 303/370-1300; www.supershuttledenver.com) provides transportation to and from a number of hotels downtown and in the Denver Tech Center. The SuperShuttle has frequent scheduled service between the airport and downtown hotels for $18 per person each way; door-to-door service is also available. **Taxi** companies (see "Getting Around," later in this chapter) are another option, with fares generally in the $30-to-$50 range, and you can often share a cab and split the fare by calling the cab company ahead of time. For instance, **Yellow Cab** (© **303/777-7777**) will take up to five people from DIA to most downtown hotels for a flat rate of $45.

Those who prefer a bit of luxury may call **White Dove Limousine** (© **800/910-7433** or 303/399-3683; www.whitedovelimo.com). Rates to the Denver metro area start around $75 but vary, so call for prices. The company operates sedan, stretch, and Hummer limousines, as well as a minibus. Charter services are also available.

BY CAR

The principal highway routes into Denver are **I-25** from the north (Fort Collins and Wyoming) and south (Colorado Springs and New Mexico); **I-70** from the east (Burlington and Kansas) and west (Grand Junction and Utah); and **I-76** from the northeast (Nebraska). If you're driving into Denver from Boulder, take **U.S. 36;** from Salida and southwest, **U.S. 285.**

BY TRAIN

Amtrak serves Union Station, 17th and Wynkoop streets (© **800/USA-RAIL** or 303/825-2583; www.amtrak.com), in the lower downtown historic district.

BY BUS

Greyhound, 19th and Arapahoe streets (© **800/231-2222;** www.greyhound.com), is the major bus service in Colorado, with about 60 daily arrivals and departures to communities in and out of the state.

VISITOR INFORMATION

The **Denver Metro Convention and Visitors Bureau** operates a visitor center on the 16th Street Mall at 1600 California St. (© **800/233-6837**, 303/892-1505; www. denver.org). It's open Monday through Friday from 9am to 5pm. In summer, it is open until 6pm on weekdays, as well as on Saturday from 9am to 5pm and Sunday from 11am to 3pm. Visitor information is also available at Denver International Airport. Ask for the *Official Visitors Guide,* a 150-plus-page full-color booklet with a comprehensive listing of accommodations, restaurants, and other visitor services in Denver and surrounding areas.

CITY LAYOUT

It's tough to get lost in Denver—just remember that the mountains, nearly always visible, are to the west. Nonetheless, getting around a city of half a million people can be perplexing. One element of confusion is that Denver has both an older grid system downtown, which is oriented northeast-southwest to parallel the South Platte River, and a newer north-south grid system that surrounds the older one.

The *Official Visitors Guide,* available free from the Denver Metro Convention and Visitors Bureau (see "Visitor Information," above), contains a good map.

MAIN ARTERIES & STREETS

It's probably easiest to get your bearings from Civic Center Park. From here, Colfax Avenue (U.S. 40) extends east and west as far as the eye can see. The same is true for Broadway, which reaches north and south.

DOWNTOWN DENVER   North of Colfax and west of Broadway is the center of downtown, where the streets follow the old grid pattern. A mile-long pedestrian mall, **16th Street,** cuts northwest off Broadway just above this intersection. (The numbered streets parallel 16th to the northeast, extending to 44th; and to the southwest, as far as 5th.) Intersecting the numbered streets at right angles are **Lawrence Street** (which runs one-way northeast) and **Larimer Street** (which runs one-way southwest), 12 and 13 blocks north, respectively, of the Colfax-Broadway intersection.

I-25 skirts downtown Denver to the west, with access from Colfax or **Speer Boulevard,** which winds diagonally along Cherry Creek past Larimer Square.

OUTSIDE DOWNTOWN   Outside the downtown sector, the pattern is a little less confusing. But keep in mind that the numbered *avenues* that parallel Colfax to the north and south (Colfax is equivalent to 15th Ave.) have nothing in common with the numbered *streets* of the downtown grid.

FINDING AN ADDRESS

NORTH-SOUTH ARTERIES   The thoroughfare that divides avenues into east and west is **Broadway,** which runs one-way south between 19th Street and I-25. Each block east or west adds 100 to the avenue address; thus, if you wanted to find 2115 E. 17th Ave., it would be 21 blocks east of Broadway, just beyond Vine Street.

Main thoroughfares that parallel Broadway to the east include **Downing Street** (1200 block), **York Street** (2300 block; it becomes **University Blvd.** south of 6th), **Colorado Boulevard** (4000 block), **Monaco Street Parkway** (6500 block), and **Quebec Street** (7300 block). Colorado Boulevard (Colo. 2) is the busiest street in the whole state, intersecting I-25 on the south and I-70 on the north. North-south streets that parallel Broadway to the west include **Santa Fe Drive** (U.S. 85; 1000 block); west of I-25 are **Federal Boulevard** (U.S. 287 North; 3000 block), and **Sheridan Boulevard** (Colo. 95; 5200 block), the boundary between Denver and Lakewood.

EAST-WEST ARTERIES Denver streets are divided into north and south at **Ellsworth Avenue,** about 2 miles south of Colfax. Ellsworth is a relatively minor street, but it's a convenient dividing point because it's just a block south of **1st Avenue.** With building numbers increasing by 100 each block, that puts an address like 1710 Downing St. at the corner of East 17th Avenue. **First, 6th, Colfax** (1500 block), and **26th** avenues, and **Martin Luther King Jr. Boulevard** (3200 block) are the principal east-west thoroughfares. There are no numbered avenues south of Ellsworth. Major east-west byways south of Ellsworth are **Alameda** (Colo. 26; 300 block), **Mississippi** (1100 block), **Louisiana** (1300 block), **Evans** (2100 block), **Yale** (2700 block), and **Hampden** avenues (U.S. 285; 3500 block).

NEIGHBORHOODS IN BRIEF

Lower Downtown (LoDo) A 25-block area around Union Station, and encompassing **Wynkoop Street** southeast to **Market Street** and **20th Street** southwest to **Speer Boulevard,** this delightful historic district was until recently a somewhat seedy neighborhood of deteriorating Victorian houses and redbrick warehouses. A major restoration effort has brought it back to life. Today it is home to chic shops, art galleries, nightclubs, and restaurants. Listed as both a city and county historic district, it boasts numerous National Historic Landmarks; skyscrapers are prohibited by law. Coors Field, the 50,000-seat home of the Rockies baseball team, opened here in 1995.

Central Business District This extends along **16th, 17th, and 18th streets between Lawrence Street and Broadway.** The ban on skyscrapers certainly does not apply here. In this area you'll find the Brown Palace Hotel, the Westin Hotel at Tabor Center, and other upscale lodgings; numerous restaurants and bars; plus the popular 16th Street Mall.

Far East Center Denver's Asian community is concentrated along this strip of **Federal Boulevard,** between **West Alameda** and **West Mississippi** avenues. It grew in the aftermath of the Vietnam War to accommodate throngs of refugees, especially Thai and Vietnamese. Look for authentic restaurants, bakeries, groceries, gift shops, and clothing stores. The Far East Center Building at Federal and Alameda is built in Japanese pagoda style.

Five Points The "five points" actually meet at 23rd Street and Broadway, but the cultural and commercial hub of Denver's black community, from **23rd** to **38th** streets, northeast of downtown, covers a much larger area and incorporates four historic districts. Restaurants offer soul food, barbecued ribs, and Caribbean cuisine, while jazz and blues musicians and contemporary dance troupes perform in theaters and nightclubs. The Black American West Museum and Heritage Center is also in this area.

Highlands Perched northwest of downtown from **32nd** to **38th** avenues between **Federal** and **Zuni** streets, the historic, increasingly chic Highland neighborhood is the most densely populated neighborhood in the city outside of Capitol Hill. Mexican and Italian eateries brush elbows with boutiques and galleries. In the nearby West Highlands neighborhood, the eclectic retail district centered on 32nd Avenue and Lowell Boulevard is one of the most vibrant in the city.

La Alma Lincoln Park/Auraria Hispanic culture, art, food, and entertainment predominate along this strip of **Santa Fe Drive,** between **West Colfax** and **West 6th** avenues. It's notable for its Southwestern character and architecture. This neighborhood is well worth a visit for its numerous restaurants, art galleries, and crafts shops. Denver's annual Cinco de Mayo celebration takes place here.

Uptown Denver's oldest residential neighborhood, from **Broadway** east to **York Street** (City Park) and **23rd Avenue** south to **Colfax Avenue,** is best known today for two things: It's bisected by 17th Avenue, home to many of the city's finest restaurants, and several of its classic Victorian and Queen Anne–style homes have been converted to captivating bed-and-breakfasts (see "Where to Stay," later in this chapter).

Washington Park A grand Victorian neighborhood centered on the lush park of its namesake, "Wash Park" is one of Denver's trendiest neighborhoods. Bounded by **Broadway** east to **University Boulevard,** and **Alameda Avenue** south to **Evans Avenue,** it features a good deal of dining and recreational opportunities, but little in the way of lodging. It is a great place, however, for architecture and history buffs to drive or walk past the grand rows of houses.

Denver Neighborhoods

Capitol Hill One of Denver's most diverse and oldest neighborhoods lies just southeast of downtown. Capitol Hill centers on the gold-domed Capitol Building, encompassing **Broadway** east to **York,** and **Colfax Avenue** south to **6th Avenue.** The north edge is improving after years of neglect and now features such attractions as the Fillmore Auditorium and a lively restaurant and bar scene. There are several commercial and retail districts in the area, nestled amidst Victorian houses and modern lofts and apartments. Also here are the Molly Brown House Museum (see chapter 6) and several lodging options, ranging from B&Bs to luxury hotels (see "Where to Stay," below). You'll notice that there are no old wooden buildings here. After a disastrous fire in 1863, the government forbade the construction of wooden structures, a ban that stood until after World War II.

Cherry Creek Home of the Cherry Creek Shopping Center and Denver Country Club, this area extends north from **East 1st Avenue** to **East 8th Avenue,** and from **Downing Street** east to **Steele Street.** You'll find huge, ostentatious stone mansions here, especially around Circle Drive (southwest of 6th and University), where many of Denver's wealthiest families have lived for generations.

Glendale Denver surrounds Glendale, an incorporated city. The center of a lively entertainment district that is home to a slew of topless clubs, Glendale straddles Cherry Creek on South Colorado Boulevard south of East Alameda Avenue.

Tech Center At the southern end of the metropolitan area is the Denver Tech Center, along **I-25** between **Belleview Avenue** and **Arapahoe Road.** In this district, about a 25-minute drive from downtown, you will find the headquarters of several international and national companies, high-tech businesses, and a handful of upscale hotels heavily oriented toward business travelers.

2 Getting Around

BY PUBLIC TRANSPORTATION

The **Regional Transportation District,** or **RTD** (℡ **800/366-7433,** 303/299-6000, or TDD 303/299-6089 for route and schedule information; 303/299-6700 for other business; www.rtd-denver.com) calls itself "The Ride." It operates bus routes and a light-rail system, with free transfer tickets available. It provides good service within Denver and its suburbs and outlying communities (including Boulder, Longmont, and Evergreen), as well as free parking at 65 Park-n-Ride locations throughout the Denver-Boulder metropolitan area. The light-rail service is designed to get buses and cars out of congested downtown Denver; many of the bus routes from outlying areas deliver passengers to light-rail stations rather than downtown.

The local one-way fare is $1.50; seniors and passengers with disabilities pay 75¢, and children age 5 and under travel free. Regional bus fares vary (for example, Denver to Boulder costs $3.75). Exact change is required for buses, and train tickets can be purchased at vending machines beneath light-rail station awnings.

Depending on the route, the departure time of the last bus or train varies from 9pm to 2am. Maps for all routes are available at any time at the RTD **Civic Center Station,** 16th Street and Broadway; and the **Market Street Station,** Market and 16th streets. RTD also provides special service to Colorado Rockies (baseball) and Denver Broncos (football) games. All RTD buses and trains are completely wheelchair accessible.

Free buses run up and down the 16th Street Mall between the Civic Center and Market Street, daily from 6am to 1am.

The light rail is also useful for exploring downtown and the greater metro area. The **C Line** diverts from the main north-south **D Line** at Colfax Avenue, it veers west and stops at Invesco Field at Mile High, the Pepsi Center, and Six Flags Elitch Gardens before chugging into Union Station at 17th and Wynkoop streets in lower downtown. The D Line continues along northeast through the east side of downtown before its terminus at 30th Avenue and Downing Street. At the end of 2006, a new train began running along I-25 from Broadway to Mineral Avenue in the south suburbs.

The open-air **Platte Valley Trolley** (℡ **303/458-6255;** www.denvertrolley.org) operates year-round. From April through October between 12:30 and 4pm Friday through Sunday, there's a half-hour "Denver Sightseeing Route" ride ($3 adults, $2 seniors and children), which operates from 15th Street at Confluence Park, south to the Denver Children's Museum along the west bank of the Platte River. From Memorial Day to Labor Day, the ride is also available on Wednesdays and Thursdays. Different routes are offered at other times.

BY TAXI

The main companies are **Yellow Cab** (*©* **303/777-7777**) and **Metro Taxi** (*©* **303/333-3333**). Taxis can be hailed on the street, though it's preferable to telephone for a taxi or wait for one at a taxi stand outside a major hotel. On weekends, however, hailing a taxi can be difficult when the bars close down for the night.

BY CAR

Because cars are not necessary downtown, visitors can save money by staying downtown while in Denver, then renting a car to leave the area.

The Denver office of the **American Automobile Association (AAA)** is at 4100 E. Arkansas Ave., Denver, CO 80222-3405 (*©* **800/222-4357** or 303/753-8800); there are several other locations in the Denver area.

CAR RENTALS   Most major car-rental agencies have outlets in or near downtown Denver, as well as at Denver International Airport. These include **Alamo,** 24530 E. 78th Ave. (*©* **800/462-5266** or 303/342-7373); **Avis,** 1900 Broadway (*©* **800/331-1212** or 303/839-1280; 303/342-5500 at DIA); **Dollar,** 10343 N. Federal Blvd., Westminster (*©* **800/800-4000** or 866/434-3336; 303/342-9678 at DIA); **Enterprise,** 5179 S. Broadway (*©* **800/736-8222** or 303/794-3333; 303/342-7350 at DIA); **Hertz,** 2001 Welton St. (*©* **800/654-3131** or 303/297-9400; 303/342-3800 at DIA); **National,** at Denver International Airport (*©* **800/227-7368** or 303/342-0717); and **Thrifty,** 8006 E. Arapahoe Ave. (*©* **800/847-4389** or 303/220-1020; 303/342-9400 at DIA). You can rent campers, travel trailers, motor homes, and motorcycles from **Cruise America** (*©* **800/671-8042**; www.cruiseamerica.com).

Per-day rentals for midsize cars range from $35 to $70, although AAA and other discounts are often available, and weekend and multiday rates can also save money. Four-wheel-drive vehicles, trucks, and campers cost more.

PARKING   Downtown parking-lot rates vary from 75¢ per half-hour to $20 or more per full day. Rates are higher near the 16th Street Mall, in the central business district, and in hotel lots. Keep a handful of quarters if you plan to use on-street parking meters.

FAST FACTS: Denver

American Express The American Express travel agency, 555 17th St. (*©* **303/383-5050**), is open Monday through Friday from 8am to 5pm. It offers full member services and currency exchange. To report a lost card, call *©* **800/528-4800**; to report lost traveler's checks, call *©* **800/221-7282**.

Area Code Area codes are **303** and **720**, and local calls require 10-digit dialing. See the "Telephone, Telegraph, Telex & Fax" section under "Fast Facts," in chapter 2.

Babysitters Front desks at major hotels can often arrange for babysitters for their guests.

Business Hours Generally, business offices are open weekdays from 9am to 5pm and government offices are open from 8am until 4:30 or 5pm. Stores are open 6 days a week, with many also open on Sunday; department stores usually stay open until 9pm at least 1 day a week. Discount stores and supermarkets are often open later than other stores, and some supermarkets are open 24 hours a day.

Banks are usually open weekdays from 9am to 5pm, occasionally later on Friday, and sometimes on Saturday. There's 24-hour access to automated teller machines (ATMs) at most banks, plus in many shopping centers and other outlets.

Car Rentals See "Getting Around," above.

Doctors & Dentists Doctor and dentist referrals are available by calling ℂ **800/ DOCTORS. Ask-A-Nurse Centura** (ℂ **800/327-6877** or 303/777-6877) provides free physician referrals and answers health questions; the **Parent Smart Health Line** (ℂ **303/861-0123**) specializes in referrals to children's doctors and dentists, and also has staff on hand to provide advice.

Drugstores Throughout the metropolitan area, you will find Walgreens and other chain pharmacies, as well as Safeway and King Soopers grocery stores (which also have drugstores). The **Walgreens** at 2000 E. Colfax Ave. (ℂ **303/331-0917**) is open 24 hours a day. For the locations of other Walgreens, call ℂ **800/ WALGREENS.**

Emergencies Call ℂ **911.** For the **Colorado Poison Center,** call ℂ **303/739-1123.** For the **Rape Crisis and Domestic Violence Hotline,** call ℂ **303/318-9989.**

Eyeglasses One-hour replacements and repairs are usually available at **Pearle Vision,** 2720 S. Colorado Blvd. at Yale Avenue (ℂ **303/758-1292**), and **LensCrafters,** in Cherry Creek Shopping Center (ℂ **303/321-8331**).

Hospitals Among Denver-area hospitals are **St. Joseph Hospital,** 1835 Franklin St. (ℂ **303/837-7111**), just east of downtown, and **Children's Hospital,** 1056 E. 19th Ave. (ℂ **303/861-8888**), which expects to move east to the Fitzsimons area by year's end 2007.

Maps Denver's largest map store, **Mapsco Map and Travel Center,** 800 Lincoln St., Denver, CO 80203 (ℂ **800/718-4627** or 303/830-2373; www.mapsco.com), offers USGS and recreation maps, state maps and travel guides, raised relief maps, and globes.

Newspapers & Magazines The *Denver Post* (www.denverpost.com) is Colorado's largest daily newspaper. The *Rocky Mountain News* (www.rockymountain news.com) also covers the metropolitan area. Under a joint operating agreement, each publishes a separate weekday edition, only the *News* prints on Saturday, and only the *Post* appears on Sunday. A widely read free weekly, *Westword* (www.westword.com), is known as much for its controversial jibes at local politicians and celebrities as it is for its entertainment listings.

Photographic Needs For photographic supplies, equipment, 1-hour processing, and repairs, visit **Wolf Camera** at one of its 18 Denver locations; its downtown branch, at 1545 California St. (ℂ **303/623-1155**; www.wolfcamera.com), claims to be the biggest single-floor camera store in the world. Another good source for photo supplies and film processing is **Mike's Camera,** 759 S. Colorado Blvd. (© **303/733-2121;** www.mikescamera.com).

Post Office The main downtown post office, 951 20th St., is open Monday through Friday from 7am to 10:30pm, Saturday and Sunday from 8:30am to 10:30pm. For full 24-hour postal service, go to the General Mail Facility, 7500 E. 53rd Place. For other post office locations and hours, call the U.S. Postal Service (© **800/275-8777;** www.usps.com).

Safety Denver is a relatively safe city, but it is not crime free. Safety is seldom a problem on the 16th Street Mall, but even streetwise Denverites avoid late-night walks along certain sections of Colfax Avenue, just a few blocks away. If you are unsure of a particular area you wish to visit, ask your hotel concierge or desk clerk.

Taxes State and local sales tax in Denver is about 7% (it varies slightly in neighboring counties and suburbs). The hotel tax is about 8%, bringing the total tax on accommodations to nearly 15%.

Useful Telephone Numbers For a weather report, time, and temperature, call © **303/337-2500.** Statewide road condition reports are available by calling © **303/639-1111.** For information on possible road construction delays in the Denver area and statewide, see **www.cotrip.org.**

3 Where to Stay

Although most hotels and motels in the Denver area do not have seasonal rates (as you'll find in many other parts of Colorado), hotels that cater to business travelers, such as the **Brown Palace** and the **Warwick** (see below), often offer substantial weekend discounts, sometimes as much as 50% off the regular rates. Rates listed below do not include the 14.85% accommodations tax.

The lodging industry is catching up with the construction of Denver International Airport, and you'll find that many of the major chains and franchises have built or are in the process of constructing facilities near the airport—there's also a proposed hotel at the terminal itself. Among those now open are **Courtyard by Marriott at DIA,** 6901 Tower Rd., Denver, CO 80249 (© **800/321-2211** or 303/371-0300), with rates of $119 to $199 for a double; and **Hampton Inn DIA,** 6290 Tower Rd., Denver CO 80249 (© **800/426-7866** or 303/371-0200), with rates of $99 to $115 for a double.

Reliable chain hotels in the downtown area include: **Comfort Inn,** 401 17th St., Denver, CO 80202 (© **800/228-5150** or 303/296-0400), with a convenient location and rates of $139 double and $189 to $289 suite; **La Quinta Inn Downtown,** 3500 Park Ave. W. (at I-25 exit 213), Denver, CO 80216 (© **800/531-5900** or 303/458-1222), charging $90 to $100 for a double; and **Red Lion Hotel at Invesco Field,** 1975 Bryant St. (at I-25 exit 210B), Denver, CO 80204 (© **800/388-5381** or 303/433-8331), with rates of $79 to $129 double.

These official, or "rack," rates do not take into consideration any discounts, such as those offered to members of AAA or AARP. Be sure to ask if you qualify for a reduced rate. Because a chain hotel's national reservation service may not be able to offer discounts, your best bet may be to call the hotel directly.

Denver Accommodations

Brown Palace Hotel **7**
Burnsley All Suite Hotel **10**
Cameron Motel **16**
Capitol Hill Mansion B&B **11**
Castle Marne B&B **13**
Hotel Monaco **6**
Hotel Teatro **4**
Hyatt Regency Denver **5**
Innkeeper of the Rockies **12**
Jet Hotel **3**
JW Marriott **14**
Loews Denver Hotel **15**
Lumber Baron **1**
Oxford Hotel **2**
Queen Anne B&B Inn **8**
Renaissance Denver **17**
The Warwick **9**

DOWNTOWN

Hotels in downtown Denver generally cater to businesspeople, with high-tech amenities and locations convenient to the Convention Center or the financial district. These properties are more than adequate for leisure travelers, and especially enticing on weekends when they lower their rates.

VERY EXPENSIVE

Brown Palace Hotel *Moments*   For more than 100 years, the city's finest hotel has been the place to stay for anyone who is anyone. It combines great rooms and amenities with interesting history, romantic atmosphere, regional personality, and impeccable service. A National Historic Landmark, the Brown Palace has operated continuously since it opened in 1892. Designed with an odd triangular shape by the renowned architect Frank Edbrooke, it was built of Colorado red granite and Arizona sandstone. The lobby's walls are paneled with Mexican onyx, and elaborate cast-iron grillwork surrounds six tiers of balconies up to the stained-glass ceiling. Every president since 1905 (except Calvin Coolidge) has visited the hotel, and Dwight Eisenhower made the Brown his home away from the White House. His former room, now known as the Eisenhower Suite, is a vision of stately elegance, with a preserved dent in the fireplace trim that is the alleged result of an errant golf swing. There are also lavish, unique suites named after Teddy Roosevelt, Ronald Reagan, and the Beatles.

Standard rooms are also lush and comfortable, either Victorian or Art Deco in style with reproduction furnishings and fixtures. Each has a desk, a duvet, and individual climate control. The clientele is a mix of leisure travelers and businesspeople with a taste—and a budget—for luxury. The staterooms on the ninth floor are especially enticing, with cordless phones, big-screen TVs, fridges, fax/printers, and safes. The water's great here: The Brown Palace has its own artesian wells!

321 17th St., Denver, CO 80202. ⓒ 800/321-2599 or 303/297-3111. Fax 303/312-5900. www.brownpalace.com. 241 units. $280–$350 double; $350–$1,190 suite. Lower weekend rates. AE, DC, DISC, MC, V. Valet parking $24 overnight. Pets up to 20 lb. accepted. **Amenities:** 3 restaurants (all American; see "Where to Dine," later in this chapter); 2 lounges; exercise room; concierge, courtesy car; business center; 24-hr. room service; in-room massage (for an extra charge). *In room:* A/C, cable TV w/pay movies, hair dryer, iron, 2-line phone w/dataport, voice mail, and complimentary wireless Internet access.

Hotel Monaco *Kids*   Billing itself as "Denver's hippest high-style luxury hotel," the Hotel Monaco is a standout. With eye-catching interiors inspired equally by Art Deco and French design, the hotel occupies a pair of renovated historic buildings in the heart of the central business district. This is one of the few downtown hotels that is 100% pet-friendly—the staff even delivers guests a named goldfish upon request. (The establishment also has a "Director of Pet Relations," a Jack Russell terrier named Lily Sopris.) Rooms have a rich style, with perks such as CD stereos, plush robes, and Starbucks coffee. With jetted tubs, wet bars, and VCRs, the generously sized suites are even more luxurious. You might bump into a celebrity here—the Monaco is a favorite

---

Fun Fact **On the Hoof**

If you're in town for the National Western Stock Show, make sure to visit the Brown Palace Hotel for a study in contrasts—the champion steer is traditionally corralled in the lobby during one of the event's final mornings.

of pro sports teams, rock bands, and Hollywood types, who often stay in the "music suites," named for and decorated after John Lennon, Grace Slick, and Miles Davis. Another perk is the nightly "Altitude Adjustment Hour" in the lobby, where guests enjoy complimentary wine and munchies along with 5-minute massages from the employees of the on-site Aveda Spa.

1717 Champa St. (at 17th St.), Denver, CO 80202. (℃) **800/397-5380** or 303/296-1717. Fax 303/296-1818. www. monaco-denver.com. 189 units. $295 double; $295–$1,300 suite; call for weekend rates. AE, DC, DISC, MC, V. Valet parking $21. Pets accepted. **Amenities:** Restaurant (Panzano; see "Where to Dine," later in this chapter); lounge; exercise room; spa; concierge; 24-hr. room service; in-room massage (for an extra charge); laundry service. *In room:* A/C, cable TV w/pay movies, fax, minibar, fridge, coffeemaker, hair dryer, iron, safe, complimentary high-speed wireless Internet access.

Hotel Teatro 🐨🐨 *(Finds)*   Hotel Teatro is one of Denver's most luxurious hotels. It's also the most dramatic: The Denver Center for the Performing Arts (across the street) inspired the decor, which features masks, playbills, and wardrobe from past productions of its resident theater company. The hotel caters to both business and leisure travelers with exquisitely furnished guest rooms that hold Indonesian marble, cherry-wood desks and fixtures, and Frette linens and towels. The nine-story building is a historic landmark, constructed as the Denver Tramway Building in 1911. Cutting-edge perks include free high-speed Wi-Fi access throughout the property and a combination fax/scanner/copier/printer in each room. Each room also features Aveda amenities and a rainforest showerhead. Kevin Taylor, one of Denver's best-known chefs, runs both restaurants and the room service.

1100 14th St. (at Arapahoe St.), Denver, CO 80202. (℃) **303/228-1100.** Fax 303/228-1101. www.hotelteatro.com. 111 units. $225 double; $345–$1,400 suite. AE, DC, DISC, MC, V. Valet parking $24 overnight. Pets accepted. **Amenities:** 2 restaurants (Italian, French); lounge; concierge; courtesy car; 24-hr. room service; massage; laundry service; dry cleaning. *In room:* A/C, cable TV w/pay movies, fax, dataport, minibar, fridge, coffeemaker, hair dryer, iron, high-speed Internet access.

Hyatt Regency Denver 🐨🐨   Opening in late 2005, the 37-story Hyatt Regency is the city's crisp new convention center hotel, one of the biggest and best such properties in the Rockies and the first skyscraper to rise in downtown Denver since the early 1980s. With an ideal location—adjacent to the newly expanded Colorado Convention Center—and a thorough, modern list of amenities, the Hyatt immediately emerged as the top convention hotel in the Rockies. Showcasing a terrific contemporary art collection with a local bent, the sleek lobby features automated check-in kiosks and the Strata bar. On the 27th floor, another bar, Altitude, offers the best views downtown. In between, the hotel's guest rooms are contemporary but comfortable, with plush furnishings and an ergonomic work station. The suites are the biggest downtown, ranging from 500 all the way up to 5,000 square feet.

650 15th St., Denver, CO 80202. (℃) **800/233-1234** or 303/436-1234. Fax 303/436-9102. www.denverregency.hyatt. com. 1,100 units, including 72 suites. $165–$319 double; $550–$5,000 suite. AE, DC, DISC, MC, V. Underground valet parking $24, self-parking $20. **Amenities:** Restaurant (steaks/seafood); 2 lounges; heated indoor pool; health club (weight room, cardiovascular machines); spa; outdoor Jacuzzi; sauna; concierge; car-rental desk; business center; room service (6am to midnight); dry cleaning; executive level. *In room:* A/C, cable TV w/pay movies, fridge, coffeemaker, hair dryer, iron, safe, high-speed Internet access.

EXPENSIVE

Burnsley All Suite Hotel 🐨🐨   This small, elegant hotel offers suites with private balconies and separate living, bedroom, dining, and fully stocked kitchen areas. The units are handsomely furnished, featuring marble entrance floors and antiques. The suites are expansive (averaging 700 sq. ft.) and popular with travelers who prefer to be a bit away from the hubbub of downtown. The hotel sits on a relatively quiet one-way street a few blocks southeast of the state capitol.

The restaurant serves breakfast, lunch, and dinner on weekdays, and breakfast and dinner on weekends. The lounge is a local favorite, a swank space with live piano Tuesday to Saturday. The hotel is conveniently situated near the Cherry Creek shopping areas and is only 5 blocks from downtown.

1000 Grant St. (at E. 10th Ave.), Denver, CO 80203. ✆ 800/231-3915 or 303/830-1000. Fax 303/830-7676. www.burnsley.com. 80 suites. $119–$219 double. Weekend rates available. AE, DC, MC, V. Free covered parking. **Amenities:** Restaurant (Continental); lounge; seasonal outdoor pool; courtesy car; business center; room service until 10pm; laundry service. *In room:* A/C, cable TV, dataport, kitchen, coffeemaker, hair dryer, iron.

Jet Hotel ✮

This contemporary boutique hotel is one of the few lodging options in the lively LoDo neighborhood. Formerly the LoDo Inn, the property changed hands and underwent a metamorphosis to the Luna Hotel in 2002, then a re-branding to the Jet in 2006. It remains sleek and smart, combining the personal service of a B&B with the conveniences of a full-service hotel. The guest rooms are spare studies in efficiency, with perks like CD and DVD players, unique art prints, and large armoires. Some rooms have private balconies and others have jetted tubs; the suite has a copper-topped table and a small kitchen. The hotel is entirely nonsmoking.

1612 Wazee St., Denver, CO 80202. ✆ **303/572-3300.** Fax 303/623-0773. www.thejethotel.com. 19 units. $129–$189 double; $249–$299 suite. AE, DC, DISC, MC, V. Parking $10. **Amenities:** 2 restaurants (cafe, eclectic); lounge; exercise room; concierge. *In room:* A/C, TV/DVD, kitchenette, coffeemaker, hair dryer, iron, complimentary Wi-Fi network.

Oxford Hotel ✮ *Finds*

Designed by the architect Frank Edbrooke, this is one of Denver's few hotels to have survived from the 19th century (another being the Brown Palace, described earlier in this chapter). The facade is simple red sandstone, but the interior boasts marble walls, stained-glass windows, frescoes, and silver chandeliers, all of which were restored between 1979 and 1983 using Edbrooke's original drawings. The hotel is listed on the National Register of Historic Places.

Antique pieces imported from England and France furnish the large rooms, which were created by combining smaller rooms during the restoration. No two units are alike (they're either Art Deco or Victorian in style), but all are equipped with one king or queen bed, individual thermostats, dressing tables, and large closets.

An Art Deco gem, the Cruise Room Bar boasts perhaps the swankest cocktail atmosphere in Denver, and the spa is the largest in the area.

1600 17th St. (at Wazee St.), Denver, CO 80202. ✆ 800/228-5838 or 303/628-5400. Fax 303/628-5413. www.theoxfordhotel.com. 80 units. $189–$229 double; $369 suite. Children under 18 stay free in parent's room. AE, DC, DISC, MC, V. Valet parking $21. **Amenities:** Restaurant (McCormick's Fish House & Bar; see "Where to Dine," below); 2 lounges; exercise room; spa (w/Jacuzzi and sauna); concierge; courtesy car; salon; 24-hr. room service; massage; laundry service; dry cleaning. *In room:* A/C, TV, minibar, hair dryer, iron, complimentary Wi-Fi network.

The Warwick ✮✮

One of four Warwicks in the United States (the others are in New York, San Francisco, and Seattle), this handsome midsize choice boasts an exterior and rooms reminiscent of hotels in Paris, where the corporate office is located. In contrast, the earth-tone lobby stylishly reflects the region, with classic European design, contemporary Western furnishings, and slate and red-stone stonework.

Every room features a full private balcony with a great city view, and most are equipped with a fridge and wet bar. Each has one king- or two full-size beds, contemporary mahogany furniture, floral prints on the walls, cable TV (with pay-per-view movies), and two incoming phone lines—as well as wireless high-speed Internet access. There's also a phone in each bathroom. The standard rooms are very spacious, averaging 450 square feet each, and the 60 suites, which range from two-room parlor suites to grand luxury suites, are even more so.

1776 Grant St. (at E. 18th Ave.), Denver, CO 80203. © **800/525-2888** or 303/861-2000. Fax 303/832-0320. www.warwick denver.com. 220 units, including 60 suites. $139–$210 double; $129–$650 suite. Weekend rates $79–$99 double; from $129 suite. Children under 18 stay free in parent's room. AE, DC, DISC, MC, V. Valet parking $15 per day, self-parking $12 per day, both underground. **Amenities:** Restaurant (contemporary); lounge; rooftop heated pool; exercise room; concierge; courtesy town car; business center; limited room service; laundry service. *In room:* A/C, cable TV w/pay movies, dataport, coffeemaker, hair dryer, iron, safe.

INEXPENSIVE

Innkeeper of the Rockies *(Value)*   This centrally located hostel moved to spiffy new digs in 2005, about 2 miles east of downtown. Now housed in a converted 1905 apartment building—along with private rooms at a nearby house—the hostel is a clean and convenient choice. Facilities include a community kitchen, laundry machines, Internet access, and barbecue grills. There are two men's rooms, two women's rooms, and two co-ed rooms, each with six bunks.

1717 Race St., Denver, CO 80206. © **303/861-7777.** Fax 720/225-9321. www.innkeeperrockies.com. 36 beds, 4 private units. $20 per person; $43 private double. AE, DISC, MC, V. **Amenities:** Complimentary Internet access; coin-op laundry. *In room:* No phone.

BED & BREAKFASTS

Those seeking an alternative to a hotel or motel might consider one of Denver's many bed-and-breakfast inns. Often located in historic 19th-century homes, bed-and-breakfasts offer a more personalized lodging experience than you could expect in all but the very best hotels, because you rarely find more than 10 rooms in a B&B, and you are, literally, a guest in someone's home.

Capitol Hill Mansion Bed & Breakfast *(★★)*   Located on Denver's "Mansion Row" just southeast of downtown and the state capitol, this turreted B&B exemplifies Richardsonian Romanesque design with its ruby sandstone exterior and curving front porch. The mansion, built in 1891, is listed on the National Register of Historic Places and boasts the original woodwork and stained glass.

The inn is outfitted for the 21st century, with refrigerators, color TVs, and wireless high-speed Web access. Each individually decorated room is named after a Colorado wildflower; some feature two-person Jacuzzi tubs, fireplaces, and private balconies. The elegant Elk Thistle Suite on the third floor features a panoramic view of the Rockies, a claw-foot tub, and a kitchen. Honeymooners might enjoy the second floor Shooting Star Balcony Room, which has a separate whirlpool tub and shower, and a private balcony with a city view.

Breakfasts include such items as crème brûlée French toast and pecan bread pudding. Smoking is not permitted inside the inn.

1207 Pennsylvania St., Denver, CO 80203. © **800/839-9329** or 303/839-5221. Fax 303/839-8046. www.capitolhill mansion.com. 8 units. $99–$179 double; $149–$179 suite. Rates include full breakfast and evening wine and refreshments. AE, DC, DISC, MC, V. Free off-street parking. *In room:* A/C, cable TV, dataport, fridge, coffeemaker, hair dryer, iron.

Castle Marne Bed & Breakfast *(★★)*   A National Historic Landmark, Castle Marne is an impressive stone fortress designed and built in 1889 by the renowned architect William Lang for a contemporary silver baron. It was so named because a subsequent owner's son fought in the Battle of the Marne during World War I.

The inn is furnished with antiques, fine reproductions, and family heirlooms. Three rooms have private balconies with hot tubs, and 2006 saw the addition of a fourth suite. Three rooms have old-fashioned bathrooms with pedestal sinks and cast-iron claw-foot tubs. A gourmet breakfast (two seatings) is served in the original formal dining room, and a proper afternoon tea is served daily in the parlor. Smoking is not permitted, but well-behaved kids over 10 are welcome.

1572 Race St., Denver, CO 80206. © 800/92-MARNE or 303/331-0621 for reservations. Fax 303/331-0623. www.castle marne.com. 9 units. $105–$185 double; $205–$260 suite. Rates include full breakfast and afternoon tea. AE, DC, DISC, MC, V. Free off-street parking. *In room:* A/C, Wi-Fi network.

Lumber Baron *Finds*   After buying this turreted mansion in Denver's Highlands neighborhood on April Fool's Day 1991, Walt Keller began a 4-year, $1.5-million renovation. Built in 1890 by lumber baron John Mouat (hence the name), the 8,500-square-foot house held many surprises: a myriad of ornate wood fixtures (cherry, poplar, maple, and oak, to name a few) and a once-hidden third-story ballroom under an ornate pyramidal dome. The rooms feature antique furnishings from around the world and unique themes: the Honeymoon Suite has a neoclassical bent, a four-poster mahogany queen bed, and a gargantuan mirror; and the Helen Keller Suite (named for Walt's distant relative) has a garden motif with historic photos and intricate Anglo-Japanese wallpapering. For those seeking entertainment, the Lumber Baron hosts 50 "murder mystery parties" annually for $37 (dinner included; two-for-one pricing for guests); comedic events with a handful of actors amongst the 50 to 100 partygoers.

2555 W. 37th Ave., Denver, CO 80211. © 303/477-8205. Fax 303/477-0269. www.lumberbaron.com. 5 units. $145 double; $195–$235 suite. Much lower weekday rates. Rates include full breakfast. AE, DISC, MC, V. *In room:* A/C, hair dryer, iron.

Queen Anne Bed & Breakfast Inn ★★   A favorite of both business travelers and couples, the Queen Anne might be considered the perfect bed-and-breakfast in the perfect home. It consists of two Victorian houses: one built by the well-known architect Frank Edbrooke in 1879, and the other built in 1886. Innkeeper extraordinaire Tom King provides piped-in chamber music, fresh flowers, and high-speed wireless Internet access. Each of the 10 double rooms in the 1879 Pierce-Tabor House is decorated with period antiques. Three rooms boast original murals: All four walls of the Aspen Room are filled with (what else?) aspen trees; the third-floor Park Room overlooks a park and has a mural depicting the view that visitors would have seen in 1879; and the Rooftop Room has an outdoor hot-tub deck with a superb skyline view. Each of the four two-room suites in the adjacent 1886 Roberts house is dedicated to a famous artist (Norman Rockwell, Frederic Remington, John Audubon, and Alexander Calder). The suites have deep soaking tubs, and the Remington suite has a hot tub. Half of the rooms have cable television.

Located in the Clements Historic District, the Queen Anne borders downtown Denver and is within easy walking distance of the major attractions. Smoking is not permitted.

2147–51 Tremont Place, Denver, CO 80205. © 800/432-4667 or 303/296-6666. Fax 303/296-2151. www.queenanne bnb.com. 14 units. $85–$185 double; $175–$185 suite. Rates include hot breakfast and Colorado wine each evening. AE, DC, DISC, MC, V. Free off-street parking. *In room:* A/C, dataport.

Kids Family-Friendly Hotels

Hotel Monaco (p. 82)   Kids get a kick out of the colorful decor, the complimentary goldfish, and the house mascot, a Jack Russell terrier named Lily Sopris.

Loews Denver Hotel (see below)   Kids get a teddy bear and coloring books when they arrive; the Tuscany Restaurant has a special children's menu.

OUTSIDE DOWNTOWN
VERY EXPENSIVE

JW Marriott 𝒢𝒢   Opened in 2004, the high-end JW Marriott was the first hotel in the Cherry Creek neighborhood, and it was well worth the wait. Sumptuous interiors and bold primary colors make for a distinctive ambience, and the attention to detail is excellent. The little touches are what this hotel is all about: jumbo flatscreen TVs with DVD players, spectacular views, big bathrooms with granite aplenty, user-friendly thermostats, and excellent service. For shoppers, it's beyond ideal, a block from the Cherry Creek Mall and surrounded by chic retailers of all stripes. The standout amenities: Mirepoix, the sleek eatery; a huge exercise room; a 9,300-square-foot day spa; and an upscale shopping arcade. The hotel is also very close to the Cherry Creek bike path.

150 Clayton Lane, Denver, CO 80206. ⓒ **800/372-0064** or 303/316-2700. Fax 303/316-4697. www.jwmarriott denver.com. 196 units. $269–$359 double; $549–$1,200 suite; weekend rates from $189. AE, DC, DISC, MC, V. Pets accepted. **Amenities:** Restaurant (Mirepoix; see "Where to Dine," later in this chapter); lounge; exercise room; spa; 2 outdoor Jacuzzis; concierge; courtesy car; business center; shopping arcade; salon; 24-hr. room service; massage; coin-op washers and dryers; dry cleaning; executive level. *In room:* A/C, cable TV/DVD w/pay movies, dataport, mini-bar, coffeemaker, hair dryer, iron, safe, high-speed Internet access.

EXPENSIVE

Loews Denver Hotel 𝒢 *Kids*   Located just east of Colorado Boulevard and south of Cherry Creek, the Loews Denver's sleek, towering exterior is black steel with a reflecting glass tower. Inside, it's bella Italia, with columns finished in imitation marble, and Renaissance-style murals and paintings that look 500 years old. The location, about a 15-minute drive from downtown, is good for those who want access to scattered attractions or the Denver Tech Center. Throughout the hotel, much use has been made of floral patterns, Italian silk wall coverings, and marble-top furnishings. All of the spacious rooms have elegant decor, along with all of the business perks any traveler could want: at least three phones, high-speed Internet access, and a fax machine. The resident eatery, the Tuscany, is also excellent.

4150 E. Mississippi Ave., Denver, CO 80246. ⓒ **800/345-9172** or 303/782-9300. Fax 303/758-6542. www.loewshotels. com. 200 units. $109–$189 double; $209–$1,000 suite; weekend rates from $89. Children under 18 stay free in parent's room. AE, DC, DISC, MC, V. Free valet and self-parking. Pets accepted. **Amenities:** Restaurant (Mediterranean); lounge; exercise room; access to nearby health club; concierge; courtesy van; business center; secretarial services; 24-hr. room service; massage; laundry service; dry cleaning; business-traveler rooms. *In room:* A/C, cable TV w/pay movies, dataport, minibar, coffeemaker, hair dryer, iron, safe, high-speed Internet access.

MODERATE

Renaissance Denver   About midway between downtown and Denver International Airport, the Renaissance is our pick for a comfortable but still somewhat elegant hotel that offers all the amenities we might want. Particularly impressive is the architecture—a white double pyramid 12 stories high. The 10-story atrium lobby has tropical palms and fig trees growing beneath the central skylight, fountains, lots of marble and brass, and plants draping down from the balconies. Each spacious room—among the largest you'll find in Denver—is decorated in a contemporary style and includes an easy chair and ottoman, two phones, and a private balcony. The hotel is adjacent to now-closed Stapleton Airport, which is now the site of a bustling residential/retail redevelopment. It's also a good choice for budget-minded tourists looking for a convenient stopover between the mountains and DIA, with lower rates than comparable downtown properties.

3801 Quebec St., Denver, CO 80207. ℂ 800/HOTELS-1 or 303/399-7500. Fax 303/321-1966. www.renaissance hotels.com. 400 units. $139 double; $195–$650 suite. Weekend rates from $79 double. AE, DC, DISC, MC, V. Valet parking $5; self-parking free. **Amenities:** Restaurant (American); lounge; indoor and outdoor pools; exercise room; 2 Jacuzzis; sauna; car-rental desk; courtesy car; business center; 24-hr. room service; complimentary washers and dryers; dry cleaning; executive level. *In room:* A/C, cable TV w/pay movies, minibar, coffeemaker, hair dryer, iron, complimentary Wi-Fi network.

INEXPENSIVE

Cameron Motel *Value*   A small mom-and-pop motel located about 10 minutes south of downtown, the Cameron provides a quiet alternative to some of the more expensive chains. Built in the 1940s, the property has been completely renovated. The walls of the average-size rooms are glazed brick; remote-control cable TVs offer 60 channels. Three rooms are equipped with kitchenettes, and some also have dataports. The owners live on-site, and their pride of ownership shows.

4500 E. Evans Ave. (I-25 exit 203), Denver, CO 80222. ℂ 303/757-2100. Fax 303/757-0974. 35 units (14 with shower only). $45–$58 double; $72 suite. AE, DISC, MC, V. Free off-street parking. Pets accepted with $5 nightly fee. *In room:* A/C, cable TV, dataport (some rooms), kitchenettes (some rooms), complimentary Wi-Fi network.

CAMPING

Chatfield State Park *⚡*   On the south side of Denver, 1 mile south of the intersection of Colo. 121 (Wadsworth) and Colo. 470, Chatfield has a 1,550-acre reservoir with ample opportunities for boating, water-skiing, fishing, and swimming, plus around 20 miles of trails for horseback riding, mountain biking, and hiking. Facilities include hot showers, picnic areas, a dump station, boat ramps and rentals, and full hookups.

11500 N. Roxborough Park Rd., Littleton, CO 80125. ℂ 303/791-7275 or 800/678-2267 for state park reservation service. www.parks.state.co.us. 197 sites. $16–$20, plus $5–$6 day-use fee. MC, V only for advance reservations.

Delux R.V. Park   The only RV campground actually in Denver city limits, this campground's main attraction is its location, and it's convenient to buses (no. 31 RTD), shopping, and recreational facilities. There are shaded sites, hot showers, a laundry, a dumpsite, and full hookups. Open year-round, the campground is 5 blocks north of I-70 exit 272, and 2 blocks south of I-76 exit 3, on the east side of Federal Boulevard.

5520 N. Federal Blvd., Denver, CO 80221. ℂ 303/433-0452. www.deluxrvpark.com. 51 sites. $31. MC, V.

Chief Hosa Campground   Those seeking the amenities and easy accessibility of a commercial campground close to Denver will find a nice (but often quite busy) campground at this longstanding establishment 20 miles west of Denver. There are tent and

RV sites, and most of the latter have electric and water hookups. When it opened in 1913, the south campground here was dubbed "America's First Motor-Camping Area." The campground is open year-round. The amenities include showers, grills, and a volleyball court.

27661 Genesee Dr., Golden, CO 80401. ⓒ **800/244-3346** or 303/526-1324. 87 sites. $22–$26. AE, DC, DISC, MC, V. Just off I-70 exit 253, 20 miles west of Denver.

4 Where to Dine

Denver abounds with Mexican hole-in-the-walls, chain eateries, steak joints, and even a few bison joints, and the restaurants in LoDo and Cherry Creek become more like those in Los Angeles and Manhattan every year. The restaurants we've listed here are mostly independent, unique to this area, and a cut above others in their price ranges.

DOWNTOWN
VERY EXPENSIVE
Buckhorn Exchange 𝒜𝒜𝒜 ROCKY MOUNTAIN   In the same rickety premises where it was established in 1893, this landmark restaurant displays its Colorado Liquor License No. 1 above the 140-year-old bar in the upstairs saloon. On the first level, the densely decorated dining room, dominated by a daunting menagerie of taxidermy, will alarm vegetarians, but meat lovers will not be disappointed one bit. The Buckhorn's game dishes (slow-roasted buffalo prime rib, lean and served medium rare, elk, pheasant, and quail) are the best in the city. The beefsteaks, ranging from 8-ounce tenderloins to 64-ounce table steaks for five, are also quite good. With fried alligator tail, Rocky Mountain oysters, and smoked buffalo sausage among the options, the appetizers will surely broaden one's palate. Our recommendation: rattlesnake, served in cream cheese–chipotle dip with tricolor tortilla chips. For dessert, try a slab of hot Dutch apple pie—if you have room. Lunch is lighter and more affordable, with an assortment of charbroiled meat entrees, sandwiches, and hearty homemade soups. A mile southwest of the state capitol, the Buckhorn has its own light-rail stop, making it a fun and easy trip from downtown.

1000 Osage St. (at W. 10th Ave.). ⓒ **303/534-9505.** www.buckhorn.com. Reservations recommended. Main courses $8–$16 lunch, $18–$44 dinner. AE, DC, DISC, MC, V. Mon–Thurs 11am–2pm and 5:30–9pm; Fri 11am–2pm and 5:30–10pm; Sat 5–10pm; Sun 5–9pm. Bar open all day. Light-rail: Osage.

Palace Arms 𝒜𝒜 CONTINENTAL/REGIONAL Despite its dramatic Napoleonic decor—antiques dating from 1700s include a dispatch case and a pair of dueling pistols that may have belonged to Napoleon—the Palace Arms offers cuisine that is a combination of traditional American, new American, and classical French. To begin, the sherry-braised rabbit loin is a special treat, or maybe you'd rather have the superb Caesar salad, prepared tableside for two. For an excellent main course, try the Kobe New York Strip, butter-poached Maine lobster, or pan-seared loin of Colorado lamb. There are a number of tasty "heart healthy" items on the menu, and the wine list has received *Wine Spectator*'s "Best of" award.

If you're short a dinner jacket, try the **Ship Tavern,** also in the Brown Palace Hotel (ⓒ **303/297-3111**), with a similar, less expensive menu. The lunch menu at the Brown's third restaurant, **Ellyngton's,** has some great gourmet sandwiches, and is also the site of the Brown's luxuriant Sunday brunch.

In the Brown Palace Hotel, 321 17th St. ⓒ **303/297-3111.** www.brownpalace.com. Reservations recommended. Jacket requested at dinner. Main courses $27–$50 dinner. AE, DC, DISC, MC, V. Daily 6–10pm.

Denver Dining

EXPENSIVE

Bistro Vendome ⚜ FRENCH BISTRO Chef-owner Eric Roeder serves up splendid interpretations of Gallic standbys (dubbing it "French soul food") at his intimate space on Larimer Square. The steak tartare, which we loved for its spicy kick and flavors of beef, onions, cumin, and sweet soy, is the perfect starting point. The menu changes regularly, but you can expect excellent seafood—say, slow-roasted salmon with French lentils—as well as a succulent seared duck breast and some creative game dishes. The salty-sweet steak frites (also known as french fries) are also beloved by locals, and the side dishes and desserts don't disappoint. The patio is one of the best in Denver.

1424-H Larimer Square. ℂ 303/825-3232. www.bistrovendome.com. Reservations accepted. Main courses $7–$14 brunch, $15–$23 dinner. AE, DC, DISC, MC, V. Sun and Tues–Thurs 5–10pm; Fri–Sat 5–11pm; brunch Fri–Sun 10am–2pm. Closed Mon.

Denver ChopHouse & Brewery ⚜ STEAKS A LoDo mainstay since it opened alongside Coors Field in 1995, this is one of the Mile High City's best places for carnivores. Set in the steeped brick-and-wood atmosphere of a restored early-19th-century train depot, the ChopHouse does classic meat and potatoes (not to mention microbrews) as well as anybody in town. Our picks are always juicy steaks, from filet mignon to New York strip, and the other hearty classics, such as huge, cheese-stuffed pork chops and herb-crusted racks of lamb; white cheddar mashers are our side of choice. The restaurant also serves a nice selection of fresh seafood and some less expensive sandwiches and pizzas, and even a few vegetarian items.

1735 19th St. ℂ 303/296-0800. www.chophouse.com. Reservations recommended for dinner. Main courses $10–$30. AE, DC, MC, V. Mon–Thurs 11am–2:30pm and 5–11pm; Fri 4:30pm–midnight; Sat 11am–2:30pm, 11am–3:30pm (brunch available), and 4:30pm–midnight; Sun 11am–3:30pm (brunch) and 4:30–10pm.

Panzano ⚜ CONTEMPORARY ITALIAN The Hotel Monaco's resident eatery is one of the best Italian restaurants in town. Served in a densely decorated dining room with a busy open kitchen, the menu changes every 3 months, but you'll likely find the signature *buridda,* a Genovese seafood stew with mussels, calamari, and shrimp in a savory lobster broth; *gamberi alla carbonara,* shrimp fettuccine, served with pancetta cream sauce and fried egg; and an array of pastas prepared fresh in-house daily. There are also innovative variations on steak, seafood, soups, and salads, which change according to available ingredients: In the summer, for example, a sweet corn soup

---

⟮Kids⟯ Family-Friendly Restaurants

Casa Bonita (p. 99) If the kids aren't concentrating on the tacos, the puppet shows, high divers, fun house, and video arcade will enthrall them.

White Fence Farm (p. 99) Meals are served family style, with Mom or Dad doling out the vegetables to live musical entertainment, but the best part is outside, with live farm animals and a playground.

Wynkoop Brewing Company (p. 95) With a dining area separate from the bar, this pub and restaurant has a loud, bustling atmosphere and plenty of kid-friendly menu options.

appears on the menu. For dessert, don't pass on the tiramisu, which manages to be heavenly and sinful at once. With lighter, similar fare (including killer salads), lunch attracts power meetings.

In Hotel Monaco, 909 17th St. ℰ 303/296-3525. www.panzano-denver.com. Reservations recommended. Main courses $6–$12 breakfast, $9–$23 lunch, $16–$30 dinner. AE, DC, DISC, MC, V. Mon–Thurs 7–10am, 11am–2:30pm, and 5–10pm; Fri 7–10am, 11am–2:30pm, and 5–11pm; Sat 5–11pm; Sun 4:30–9:30pm. Closed Thanksgiving and Dec 25.

Rioja 🏵🏵🏵 CONTEMPORARY MEDITERRANEAN Chef-owner Jennifer Jasinski (formerly of Panzano at the Hotel Monaco) has emerged as Denver's most creatively inspired restaurateur since opening Rioja in 2004. In two short years, the slick Larimer Square eatery has emerged as a national standout, a critical darling, and our pick for dinner in downtown Denver. With a copper-topped bar and an atmosphere that's formal without being stuffy, Rioja is the perfect vehicle for Jasinski's menu of contrasting flavors and textures. Offerings range from curried cauliflower soup served with fresh apple salad to expertly grilled leg of Colorado lamb on a bed of goat-cheese polenta. Jasinski keeps the menu fresh, but you'll always get a selection of her delectable handmade pastas for dinner—the artichoke tortellini is our pick—and truly transcendent beignets for dessert.

1431 Larimer Sq. ℰ 303/820-2282. www.riojadenver.com. Reservations recommended. Main courses $9.50–$18 brunch and lunch, $16–$30 dinner. AE, DISC, MC, V. Mon–Tues 5–10pm; Wed–Thurs 11:30am–2:30pm and 5–10pm; Fri 11:30am–2:30pm and 5–11pm; Sat 11am–2:30pm and 5–11pm; Sun 11am–2:30pm and 5–10pm.

Strings 🏵🏵 CONTEMPORARY Open for 20 years in Denver's Uptown neighborhood, Strings attracts a hip crowd of loyal locals, as well as visiting celebrities who contribute to a wall of autographed photos. Popular and typically crowded, the restaurant welcomes guests in T-shirts as well as tuxedos; it's especially busy during the before- and after-theater hours. The menu focuses on "New American" cuisine, creative noodle dishes, and fresh seafood—such as cashew-crusted sea bass with saffron couscous and vanilla bean butter. Lunch and dinner specials change weekly to match the season and the mood of the chef. Strings has an outdoor patio for summer dining.

1700 Humboldt St. (at E. 17th Ave.). ℰ 303/831-7310. www.stringsrestaurant.com. Reservations recommended. Main courses $11–$18 lunch, $14–$30 dinner. AE, DISC, MC, V. Mon–Thurs 11am–10pm; Fri 11am–11pm; Sat 5–11pm; Sun 5–9pm.

The Palm 🏵 ITALIAN/STEAK/SEAFOOD Pio Bozzi and John Ganzi opened the first Palm restaurant in New York City in 1926. It originally specialized in cuisine from their hometown of Parma, Italy, but whenever a customer requested steak, Ganzi ran to a nearby butcher shop, bought a steak, and cooked it to order. This eventually led to the Palm's having its own meat wholesale company to ensure the quality of its steaks. The current third-generation owners introduced seafood to the menu and expanded the business by opening a dozen more restaurants across the country. Most famous for its prime cuts of beef and live Nova Scotia lobsters, the Palm celebrates tradition, with some of Ganzi's original Italian dishes still popular (and cheaper) menu items. The dining room is plastered with caricatures of local celebrities; customers are seated at either booths or tables.

In the Westin at Tabor Center, 1672 Lawrence St. ℰ 303/825-7256. www.thepalm.com. Reservations recommended. Main courses $8.50–$18 lunch, $17–$40 dinner. AE, DC, DISC, MC, V. Mon–Fri 11am–11pm; Sat 5–11pm; Sun 5–10pm.

Zengo 🏵 LATIN/ASIAN With a menu that runs the gamut from dim sum and sushi to empanadas and ceviche, Zengo—Japanese for "give and take"—is the standout eatery in the booming Riverfront area just west of LoDo. Under the guidance of Chef Richard Sandoval (who also owns restaurants in New York, San Francisco, and Las Vegas, as well as Tamayo in Denver), the restaurant is a favorite of the young and hip, and just the place to see and be seen. The colorful contemporary decor matches the lively social scene and the vibrant dishes. Entrees are often Latin-Asian fusions, such as wok-seared salmon with Peruvian corn, or the *unagi* sushi roll, with barbecued eel and chile serrano.

1610 Little Raven St. ✆ 720/904-0965. www.modernmexican.com. Reservations recommended. Main courses $16–$30 dinner. AE, DISC, MC, V. Sun–Thurs 5–10:30pm; Fri–Sat 5–11pm. Bar open later.

MODERATE

Appaloosa Grill   CONTEMPORARY/ECLECTIC   The employee-owned Appaloosa features an eclectic menu, merging Asian, Southwestern, and bar grub. The ribs are a good bet, as are the tamales, and the all-natural Highland Heritage steaks, originating in the Rockies. The lunch menu includes salads, sandwiches, and assorted lighter entrees. With a casual, semi-intimate atmosphere and a handsome antique bar, this is a good place for dinner to morph into a night on the town. There is live musical entertainment nightly.

535 16th St. Mall (at Welton St.). ✆ **720/932-1700**. Main courses $7–$10 lunch, $9–$25 dinner. AE, DISC, MC, V. Daily 11am–1am. Bar open later.

Le Central ✯ *Value* FRENCH   Seven blocks south of the Colorado State Capitol, Le Central is a romantic restaurant that prides itself on creating French dishes that are both top quality and affordable. Housed in an aged urban structure with a distinctive European vibe, the restaurant changes its menus daily, but you can always expect to find a selection of fresh chicken, pork, beef, lamb, and seafood. They're available grilled, sautéed, or roasted and finished with some of the tastiest sauces this side of Provence. Bouillabaisse and paella are usually available, and every menu features a vegetarian dish. Shellfish fanatics, take note: Le Central's mussel menu is legendary, and served with all the french fries you can eat.

112 E. 8th Ave. (at Lincoln St.). ✆ **303/863-8094**. www.lecentral.com. Reservations recommended. Main courses $7–$9 lunch, $14–$22 dinner. AE, DC, DISC, MC, V. Mon–Thurs 11:30am–2:15pm and 5:30–10pm; Fri 11:30am–2:15pm and 5–10pm; Sat 11am–2pm and 5–10pm; Sun 11am–2pm and 5–9pm.

McCormick's Fish House & Bar ✯ SEAFOOD   In lower downtown's historic Oxford Hotel, McCormick's maintains a late-19th-century feel with stained-glass windows, oak booths, and a fine polished-wood bar. Come here for the best seafood in town—it's flown in daily, and might include Alaskan salmon and halibut, mussels from Florida, lobsters from Maine, Hawaiian mahimahi, red rockfish from Oregon, and trout from Idaho. The menu also offers pasta, chicken, and a full line of prime beef. Across the hall, the Corner Bar's happy hour (served 3–6pm every day and 10pm–midnight on Fri and Sat) is legendary, featuring $1.95 crab cakes, cheeseburgers, and steamed mussels. There's another McCormick's in the Denver Tech Center (8100 E. Union Ave., ✆ **720/200-9339**).

In the Oxford Hotel, 1659 Wazee St. ✆ **303/825-1107**. www.msmg.com. Reservations recommended. Lunch and light dishes $6–$12; dinner $12–$24. AE, DC, DISC, MC, V. Mon–Thurs 11am–2pm and 5–10pm; Fri 11am–2pm and 5–11pm; Sat 5–11pm; Sun 11am–2pm (brunch) and 5–10pm.

Red Square Euro Bistro ✯✯ RUSSIAN/CONTEMPORARY   After the Little Russian Café closed in 2003, its all-Russian staff reunited under owner Steve Ryan and opened Red Square. They did their old place one better, with a rich red interior, contemporary

Russian art, and a vodka bar stocked with infusions made in-house (ranging from raspberry to garlic) and about 100 brands from 17 countries, including Russia, Holland, Poland, Sweden, and even Mexico. Chef Maxim Ionikh's excellent entrees are not purely Russian: the steak stroganoff has a salmon counterpart, the menu has Asian and French influences, and the appetizers include pâté and Dungeness crab ravioli. But there is cold borscht, a roasted Russian wild boar chop, and, of course, the vodka. Lots and lots of vodka.

1512 Larimer St. at Writer Square. ✆ 303/595-8600. www.redsquarebistro.com. Main courses $13–$20. AE, DC, DISC, MC, V. Daily 5–10pm. Bar open later.

Tosh's Hacienda ✪ *(Finds* MEXICAN   In a city brimming with Mexican restaurants, the food here stands out. Open for more than half a century in the Five Points neighborhood, Tosh's has an easygoing atmosphere, and tile and redbrick decor. The reasonably priced combination plates feature one or two main dishes with rice and beans. You can't go wrong with enchiladas, burritos, or rellenos, and the margaritas are both tart and strong.

3090 Downing St. ✆ 303/295-1861. Main courses $7–$15. AE, DC, DISC, MC, V. Sun–Thurs 11am–9pm; Fri–Sat 11am–10pm.

Wynkoop Brewing Company ✪ *(Kids* REGIONAL AMERICAN/PUB   Denver's biggest and best brewpub took on an even more esteemed significance in 2003 when owner John Hickenlooper took office as the mayor of Denver. Occupying a renovated warehouse across from Union Station and close to Coors Field, the Wynkoop is one of the country's model microbreweries, and even served as a catalyst for the rebirth of surrounding LoDo. The menu offers pub fare, sandwiches, soups, and salads, plus dinners of steak, Denver-cut elk medallions, and buffalo steak—not to mention a nice variety of beers on tap. See also "Denver After Dark," in chapter 6.

1634 18th St. (at Wynkoop St.). ✆ 303/297-2700. www.wynkoop.com. Reservations recommended for large parties. Main courses $8–$20. AE, DC, DISC, MC, V. Mon–Thurs 11am–11pm; Fri–Sat 11am–midnight; Sun 11am–10pm. Bar open later.

INEXPENSIVE

In addition to the options listed below, there are a number of great breakfast spots in the downtown area. **Dozens,** 236 W. 13th Ave. (✆ **303/572-0066**), is a local favorite of everyone from plumbers to politicians with a beloved breakfast menu. Established in 1942, **Pete's Kitchen,** 1962 E. Colfax Ave. (✆ **303/321-3139**), is a prototypical urban diner, with checkerboard floors, a breakfast bar, booths, plenty of local color, and killer breakfast burritos. The menu has a nice selection of Greek, Mexican, and American standbys. Pete's is open 24 hours on weekends, making it a favorite of the barhopping crowd. For burrito aficionados, the world's first **Chipotle** is located near the University of Denver, at 1644 E. Evans Ave. (✆ **303/777-4121**).

Bayou Bob's CAJUN   Fishnets, street signs, and Southern-tinged bric-a-brac cover the walls of Bayou Bob's, which serves Denverites reasonably priced Cajun food in its bar and dining room. Gumbo, red beans and rice, fresh crawfish étouffée, and jambalaya are all favorites, as are the huge Mardi Gras–style Hurricanes. The spicy fried alligator is a great starter, and the many combination plates are a good bet for almost any taste. Catfish, po' boys, and hamburgers are also available.

1635 Glenarm St. (in the Paramount Theatre Building). ✆ 303/573-6828. Main courses $6–$14. AE, DC, DISC, MC, V. Mon–Sat 11am–10pm.

Tips   A Good City for Green Chile Fiends

Green chile (green *chil*-ee) n. a fiery-sweet stew made of chile peppers and other ingredients, often but not always including chunks of pork, tomato, and onion. Denver's eateries serve bowl after bowl of good green chile, stuff that ranges from merely spicy to flat-out nuclear. If you—like us—have a serious weakness for a bowl of green, here are six hotspots in the Mile High City, in no particular order.

1. **Las Delicias,** 439 E. 19th Ave. (☎ **303/839-5675**): A Denver tradition, Las Delicias serves up some of the city's best green chile from its downtown location among its four metro-area eateries.
2. **Brewery Bar II,** 150 Kalamath St. (☎ **303/893-0971**): Inconspicuously nestled in a warehouse district, the Brewery Bar serves up some of the hottest green chile in Denver. It also happens to be some of the tastiest.
3. **Jack-N-Grill,** 2524 N. Federal Blvd. (☎ **303/964-9544**): Sweet and typically served in a bowl with beans, Jack Martinez's green chile is excellent, as is his red.
4. **Little Anita's,** 1550 S. Colorado Blvd. (☎ **303/691-3337**): Relatively new in Denver, this longtime Albuquerque eatery cooks up wicked green chile from a strip mall in southeast Denver.
5. **Lime,** 1424 Larimer St. (☎ **303/893-5463**): Almost too hip for its own good, Larimer Square's Lime eschews pork for chicken and dresses up the bowl with tortilla strips. Defying tradition tastes pretty good.
6. **Campus Lounge,** 701 S. University Blvd. (☎ **303/722-9696**): Near the University of Denver, this first-rate hockey bar also serves a mean green that is good by itself or for quesadilla dipping.

Duffy's Shamrock ☆ *Finds* AMERICAN   This traditional Irish bar and restaurant with fast, cheerful service has been thriving since the late 1950s. Drink specialties include Irish coffees and imported Irish beers, but the food is mostly American. Daily specials may include prime rib, fried Louisiana prawns, low-carb plates, or grilled liver and onions. Sandwiches, on practically every kind of bread imaginable, include corned beef, Reuben, roast beef with gravy, and BLT.

1635 Court Place. ☎ 303/534-4935. Main courses $2–$6 breakfast, $5–$9 lunch, $5–$11 dinner. AE, DC, DISC, MC, V. Mon–Fri 7am–1:30am; Sat 7:30am–1:30am.

Paramount Cafe AMERICAN   Housed in the restored lobby of Denver's historic Paramount Theatre on the 16th Street Mall, this bar and grill is popular, lively, and a bit noisy. It's got a plethora of televisions, a poolroom with five tables plus satellite trivia games, and a year-round patio on the mall makes this a good choice for people-watching. The menu features exotic subs, excellent burgers, large salads, and some Tex-Mex fare.

519 16th St. (at Glenarm St.). ☎ 303/893-2000. Main courses $6–$10. AE, DC, DISC, MC, V. Daily 11am–1am. Bar open later.

Wazee Supper Club ✿ *(Finds)* PIZZA/SANDWICHES   A former plumbing-supply store in lower downtown, the Wazee is a Depression-era relic with a black-and-white tile floor and a bleached mahogany burl bar—a magnificent example of 1930s Art Deco. It's been popular for more than 30 years with artists, architects, theatergoers, entertainers, businesspeople, and just about everybody else. Pizza lovers throng to the place (some believe the pizza here is the best in town, if not the world), but you'll also find an array of overstuffed sandwiches, from New York Reubens to Philly cheese steaks, plus buffalo burgers, and over 20 draft beers. Don't miss the dumbwaiter used to shuttle food and drinks to the mezzanine floor—it's a converted 1937 garage-door opener.

1600 15th St. (at Wazee St.). © 303/623-9518. Most menu items $6.50–$9; large pizzas $20 and up. AE, MC, V. Mon–Sat 11am–2am; Sun noon–midnight.

OUTSIDE DOWNTOWN
VERY EXPENSIVE

Elway's ✿✿ STEAKS/SEAFOOD   Owned by retired Denver Broncos quarterback John Elway, this popular Cherry Creek eatery—unlike many celebrity restaurants—is no flash in the pan. Dim but lively, the restaurant is a model of "New West" design, with a menu that melds swank and comfortable. On the swank side: crab cakes, hand-cut USDA prime steaks, bone-in swordfish chops, and veggies served a la carte. And the comfy: creamed corn, steak loaf, and a dessert menu that includes Ding Dongs and warm chocolate-chip cookies and cold milk. But it's the little details, such as buttonholes in the napkins, milk bottles full of water, and tiramisu cones, that won us over in the end. Service is smooth and business is brisk, in both the cavernous dining room and the bustling bar. If you're lucky, you might bump into Elway himself here—he's not just the owner, but a regular, too.

2500 E. 1st Ave. (immediately west of the Cherry Creek Shopping Center). © 303/399-5353. www.elways.com. Reservations recommended. Main courses $9–$24 lunch and brunch, $19–$40 dinner. AE, DC, DISC, MC, V. Daily 11am–2pm; Mon–Thurs 5–10pm; Fri–Sat 5–11pm; Sun 5–9pm.

The Fort ✿✿✿ *(Moments)* ROCKY MOUNTAIN   There are several reasons to drive 18 miles southwest (and 800 ft. up) from downtown to the Fort in Denver's foothills. First, the atmosphere: The building was hand constructed of adobe bricks in 1962 as a full-scale reproduction of Bent's Fort, Colorado's first fur-trading post. The equally authentic interior boasts striking views of Denver's city lights. Second: the continuing vision of late owner Sam Arnold, the gregarious master chef who was known to open champagne bottles with a tomahawk. Third: The Fort's impeccable, gracious service might just be the best in town.

The fourth and best reason to go is the food. The Fort built its reputation on high-quality, low-cholesterol buffalo, of which it claims to serve the largest variety and greatest quantity of any restaurant in the world. There's steak, roast marrow, tongue, and even "bison eggs"—hard-boiled quail eggs wrapped in buffalo sausage. Our pick is the game plate, with elk chop, teriyaki-style quail, and buffalo filet, served with a salad (and extraordinary homemade dressings), rice, and vegetables. Other house specialties include Rocky Mountain oysters and elk medallions with wild-huckleberry sauce. Diehards can get good ol' beefsteak.

19192 Colo. 8 (just north of the intersection of Colo. 8 and W. Hampden Ave./U.S. 285), Morrison. © 303/697-4771. www.thefort.com. Reservations recommended. Main courses $20–$46. AE, DC, DISC, MC, V. Mon–Fri 5:30–9:30pm; Sat 5–9:30pm; Sun 5–9pm. Call for special holiday hours.

Mirepoix ✦ CONTEMPORARY AMERICAN   Located in the JW Marriott in Cherry Creek, Mirepoix is dark, intimate, and stunningly contemporary. The eye-catching back wall is adorned with purple neon and displays the restaurant's impressive wine racks. But the food is the real centerpiece: Chef Gabe Valenzuela directs a skilled staff that delivers such dishes as a dry-aged New York steak, artichoke-stuffed ravioli, and a "black and blue" ahi served with smoky ham sauce and shrimp paella. Many of the items on the menu are "small plates"; entrees are on the small side and beg for an order of several to be shared.

In JW Marriott Hotel, 150 Clayton Lane. ✆ 303/253-3000. Reservations recommended. Breakfast $9–$15, lunch $9–$13, dinner $21–$28. AE, DC, DISC, MC, V. Daily 6am–2pm and 5–10pm.

EXPENSIVE

Lola ✦✦ MEXICAN SEAFOOD   Moving from south Denver to the hip Highlands neighborhood in 2006 quadrupled this popular eatery's floor space, and it still fills to the rafters. It's easy to see why: Lola has oodles of pizzazz, in terms of both its art and airy design—complete with a killer patio with an indoor/outdoor bar and great city views—and the savory dishes on its menu. Start off with some guacamole, prepared fresh tableside, before moving onto a bowl of caldo, a succulent seafood stew, or grouper crusted with Brazil nuts. Served Saturday and Sunday from 10am to 2pm, the brunch favorite is chicken-fried steak smothered in chorizo gravy. Lola's margaritas and *caipirinhas*, sweet Brazilian cocktails with entire quartered limes, are also hard to beat.

1575 Boulder St. ✆ 720/570-8686. www.loladenver.com. Main courses $15–$23. AE, DC, MC, V. Mon–Fri 4–10pm; Sat 10am–11pm; Sun 10am–9pm.

Sushi Den ✦✦ SUSHI/JAPANESE   The longstanding Sushi Den is not only the best sushi restaurant in Denver, but on the short list of the top sushi restaurants in the country. Owned by three Kizaki brothers—one of whom is based in Japan and sends a daily shipment of ingredients—the Sushi Den's landlocked location is incidental: This is some of the freshest fish you'll find anywhere. The formidable sushi menu, running the gamut from squid and salmon to smoked trout, is complemented by lunch and dinner menus with a wide variety of Japanese fare and sushi and sashimi combination plates. Located in south Denver in the charming Old South Pearl Street retail district, the Sushi Den is one of two locations worldwide—its sister restaurant is in Fukuoka, Japan.

1487 S. Pearl St. ✆ 303/777-0826. www.sushiden.net. Main courses $8–$13 lunch, $10–$22 dinner; sushi rolls $4–$10. AE, DC, MC, V. Mon–Thurs 11am–2:30pm and 4:30–10:30pm; Fri 11am–2:30pm and 4:30pm–midnight; Sat 4:30pm–midnight; Sun 5–10:30pm.

Table 6 ✦✦ *Finds* CONTEMPORARY MEDITERRANEAN   A bistro with a bit of southern comfort, Table 6 balances a hip but unpretentious sensibility, great food, and one of the best wine lists in town, offered on a tableside stand in an antique photo album. Directed by Chef Scott Parker, the open kitchen plates up such tantalizing dishes as roasted mushroom pot pie, crisp duck confit, and grilled lamb sirloin with yogurt smashed red potatoes. The atmosphere is lived-in and homey, with rough hardwood floors, brick walls, and ceiling fans, with a blackboard showcasing the day's specials. The desserts are hard to turn down, especially the Nutella beignets and margarita nachos.

609 Corona St. ✆ 303/831-8800. www.table6denver.com. Reservations recommended. Main courses $15–$24. AE, MC, V. Daily 5–10pm.

MODERATE

Trail Dust Steak House STEAK   Country-music lovers flock to the Trail Dust, which serves up live dance music along with mesquite-grilled steaks and ribs. Steaks range from 7 to 30 ounces and come with salad, beans, and bread. Chicken, fish, pasta, and a smattering of Mexican dishes are also available. The decor is made up of necktie tips and Western antiques interspersed with large photos of Hollywood western heroes. The necktie tips are the result of a Trail Dust tradition: Wear a tie and the staff will snip it off with scissors, then buy you a drink.

7101 S. Clinton St., Tech Center, Englewood. © 303/790-2420. www.traildust.com. Reservations accepted. Main courses $6–$16 lunch, $9–$30 dinner. AE, DC, DISC, MC, V. Mon–Fri 11am–10pm; Sat noon–11pm; Sun noon–10pm. Exit I-25 south at Dry Creek Rd., drive 1 block east, and turn left onto Clinton St.

White Fence Farm ☆ *Kids* AMERICAN   Locals come to this seemingly rural spot in suburban Lakewood for family-style fried-chicken dinners—a delicately fried half chicken per person, plus heaping bowls of potatoes, corn fritters, homemade gravy, coleslaw, cottage cheese, pickled beets, and bean salad. Also available are T-bone steaks, pork chops, deep-fried shrimp, roast turkey, and liver and onions. For dessert, try the fresh pies. A children's menu is available, as are a children's playground, farm animals, carriage rides, and a unique gift shop, all in a beautiful country setting a 20-minute drive from downtown Denver.

6263 W. Jewell Ave., Lakewood. © 303/935-5945. www.whitefencefarm.com. Reservations accepted for parties of 15 or more. Complete meals $13–$20. DISC, MC, V. Tues–Sat 4:30–8:30pm; Sun 11:30am–8pm. Closed Jan.

INEXPENSIVE

Casa Bonita *Kids* MEXICAN/AMERICAN   A west Denver landmark, Casa Bonita is more of a theme park than a restaurant. A pink Spanish cathedral-type bell tower greets visitors, who discover nonstop action inside: divers plummeting into a pool below a 30-foot waterfall, puppet shows, a video arcade, "Black Bart's Cave," and strolling mariachi bands. The 52,000-square-foot restaurant is said to be the largest restaurant in the Western Hemisphere. There's standard Mexican fare—enchiladas, tacos, and fajitas—along with country-fried steak and fried chicken dinners. While the food is average at best, many plates are all-you-can-eat, and patrons need only raise a miniature flag to get another round of tacos. Meals include hot *sopaipillas* (deep-fried sweet dough), served with honey.

In the JCRS Shopping Center, 6715 W. Colfax Ave., Lakewood. © 303/232-5115. www.casabonitadenver.com. Reservations not accepted. Main courses $7–$13; children's meals around $3. DISC, MC, V. Mon–Thurs 11am–9:30pm; Fri–Sat 11am–10pm.

Jack-N-Grill ☆ *Finds* NEW MEXICAN   "We are not fast food," reads a sign at Jack-N-Grill, and it's spot on: This is clearly a restaurant that takes its time, and its food is worth the wait. Named for Jack Martinez and his ever-present grill, the food reflects Jack's father's motto: "Comida sin chile, no es comida," or "A meal without chile is not a meal." Not surprisingly, just about everything at Jack-N-Grill has chile in it, roasted by the Martinez family on-site. Both the green and red chile are top notch, as are the Mexican dishes and the fresh homemade salsa. Also popular: Frito pies and cal-abacitas, bowls with squash, zucchini, corn, green chile, and onions. Don't expect Jack to add any chile-free dishes to the menu. "What's the use?" he says.

2524 N. Federal Blvd. © 303/964-9544. Plates $5–$12, a la carte dishes $2–$5. AE, MC, V. Mon–Thurs 7am–9pm; Fri–Sat 7am–10pm; Sun 7am–9pm.

Govinda's Spiritual Food *(Finds)* VEGETARIAN   Attached to—and operated by—a Hare Krishna temple, Govinda's is a surprising gem of a restaurant and a godsend to vegetarians and vegans. With a different all-you-can-eat buffet every day, patrons can select from one of the city's best salad bars, great soups, fresh-baked bread, and an array of meatless main dishes, from enchiladas to casseroles to stir-fry dishes, with a good deal of Indian and Middle Eastern fare. The atmosphere is basic, and the seasonal patio is a pleasant, breezy spot for a meal. There are free Sunday dinners in the attached temple at 6pm, if you're on an extremely tight budget.

1400 N. Cherry St. ⓒ 303/333-5461. Buffet $5–$8. MC, V. Mon–Fri 11:30am–2:30pm and 5–8pm; Sat 5–8pm.

T-Wa Inn *(Finds)* VIETNAMESE   Denver's oldest Vietnamese restaurant is still the best. With simple, pleasant decor and relics from the Far East on display, it looks the part, but the food is what makes it work. Everything is excellent, but we especially like the succulent shrimp, perfect pork tenderloin, and the attention to authentic Vietnamese flavors. T-Wa also serves several spicy Thai dishes, as well as Asian beers and a whole rainbow of neon-colored specialty drinks.

555 S. Federal Blvd. (2 blocks south of Alameda Ave.) ⓒ 303/922-2378. Most main courses $6–$13. AE, DISC, MC, V. Sun–Thurs 11am–9:30pm; Fri–Sat 11am–10pm.

6

What to See & Do in Denver

Denver, an intriguing combination of modern American city and overgrown Old West town, offers a wide variety of attractions, activities, and events. Thanks to its geographic isolation, it's a true cultural hub for a significant chunk of the country: You'll discover art, history, sports, recreation, shopping, and plenty of nightlife. It is quite easy to spend an entire week of vacation in the city, but Denver also makes a convenient base for trips to Boulder, Colorado Springs, or the mountains.

1 The Top Attractions

Denver Art Museum 🌟🌟   Founded in 1893, this seven-story museum has two distinct buildings. The main 1972 building is wrapped by a thin 28-sided wall faced with one million sparkling tiles. The second, a jagged, avant-garde addition, designed by renowned architect Daniel Libeskind, was finished in fall 2006, doubling the size of the museum and giving Denver a unique architectural highlight in the process.

The museum's collection of Western and regional works is its cornerstone. Included are Frederic Remington's bronze *The Cheyenne,* Charles Russell's painting *In the Enemy's Country,* plus 19th-century photography, historical pieces, and works by Georgia O'Keeffe. In 2001, Dorothy and William Harmsen, longtime Colorado residents and founders of the Jolly Rancher Candy Company, donated their Western art collection to the museum, which immediately made the museum's inventory of Western art one of the most impressive in the nation.

The American Indian collection is excellent, consisting of more than 18,000 pieces from 150 tribes of North America, spanning nearly 2,000 years. The collection is growing through the acquisition of historic pieces as well as the commissioning of works by contemporary artists. Other collections include architecture and design; graphics; and Asian, African, Oceanic, pre-Columbian, and Spanish Colonial art.

Overview tours are available Tuesday through Sunday at 1:30pm, plus 11am on Saturday; an in-depth tour of a different area of the museum is offered each Wednesday and Friday at noon and 1pm; and a variety of child-oriented and family programs are scheduled regularly. There is also a gift shop. Allow 2 to 3 hours.

100 W. 14th Ave. (at Civic Center Park). ✆ **720/865-5000.** www.denverartmuseum.org. Admission $8 adults, $6 students and seniors, free for children under 12, free for Colorado residents Sat. Tues–Sat 10am–5pm (Wed until 9pm); Sun noon–5pm. Bus: 5, 7, 8, 9, or 50.

Denver Museum of Nature & Science 🌟🌟 *Kids*   The largest museum of its kind in the Rocky Mountain region, the Denver Museum of Nature & Science features scores of world-renowned dioramas, an extensive gems and minerals display, a pair of Egyptian mummies, a terrific fossil collection, and several other award-winning exhibitions.

Denver Attractions

E 37th Ave.
E 36th Ave.
E 35th Ave.
Randolph Ave.
E 33rd Ave.
M.L.K. Jr. Blvd.
E 31st Ave.   W H I T T I E R
E 29th Ave.
E 27th St.
E 26th Ave.
E 25th Ave.
E 24th Ave.
E 23rd Ave.
E 22nd Ave.
E 21st Ave.
U P T O W N
E 18th Ave.
E 17th Ave.
E 16th Ave.
E. Colfax Ave.
E 14th Ave.
E 13th Ave.
E 12th Ave.
CHEESMAN PARK   BOTANICAL GARDENS
CONGRESS PARK
C O N G R E S S
P A R K
E 9th Ave.
H A L E
E 8th Ave.
E 7th Ave.
E 6th Ave.
E 5th Ave.
E 4th Ave.
E 3rd Ave.
C H E R R Y
C R E E K
E 1st Ave.
DENVER COUNTRY CLUB (PRIVATE)
Cherry Creek Shopping Ctr.

CITY PARK MUNICIPAL GOLF COURSE
CITY PARK
Duck L.
Denver Museum of Nature & Science
City Park Lake
Montview Blvd.
E 19th Ave.
CRANMER PARK

Westminster
Thornton
Federal Heights
Arvada
Wheat Ridge
DENVER
Lakewood
Glendale
Englewood
Greenwood Village
Littleton
Centennial
Aurora
DIA
area of main map

Larimer St.
Downing St.
Franklin St.
Josephine St.
Elizabeth St.
Marion St.
Vine St.
High St.
Columbine St.
Humboldt St.
Lafayette St.
Gilpin St.
Gaylord St.
York St.
Race St.
Williams St.
Detroit St.
Colorado Blvd.
Cherry St.
Dahlia St.
Clermont St.
Bellaire St.
Albion St.
Ash St.
Birch St.
Dexter St.
Cherry St.
Bellaire St.
Jackson St.
Madison St.
Monroe St.
Harrison St.
Adams St.
Steele St.
Fillmore St.
Clayton St.
Detroit St.
Vine St.
Gilpin St.
Lafayette St.
Humboldt St.
Ogden St.
Downing St.
Clarkson St.
Washington St.
Emerson St.
Corona St.
Park Ave.
St. Paul St.
Cook St.
Milwaukee St.
Garfield St.
Steele St.
Hale Pkwy.
Clarkson St.
Washington St.
Emerson St.
Ogden St.
32nd St.
33rd St.
30th St.

103

The museum focuses on six areas of science: anthropology, health science, geology, paleontology, space science, and zoology.

At "Space Odyssey," visitors experience a carefully crafted mix of exhibits, live programming, digital multimedia, and interactive modules that engage them in contemporary stories of space exploration. The state-of-the-art Gates Planetarium has an advanced computer graphics and video system, unlike any other in the world. "Prehistoric Journey" traces the history of life on earth through 3.5 billion years with dinosaur skeletons, fossils, interactive exhibits, and dioramas of ancient ecologies. The "Hall of Life" focuses on the science of the human body. Using a magnetic card, visitors gather information on themselves as they move through the interactive exhibits, and then receive a printout about their own physical condition at the end.

An **IMAX theater** (© 303/322-7009) presents science, nature, and technology-oriented films with surround sound on a screen that measures four and a half stories tall. Allow 2 to 4 hours.

City Park, 2001 Colorado Blvd. © 800/925-2250 or 303/322-7009; 303/370-8257 for the hearing impaired. www. dmns.org. Admission to museum $10 adults, $6 children 3–18 and seniors 65 and older; IMAX $8 adults, $6 children and seniors; planetarium $5 additional adults, $4 additional children and seniors. Daily 9am–5pm. Closed Dec 25. Bus: 24, 32, or 40.

U.S. Mint ★★ There are four mints in the United States, but the Denver Mint is one of only two (the other is the Philadelphia Mint) where we can actually watch the process of turning lumps of metal into shiny coins. Opened in 1863, the Mint originally melted gold dust and nuggets into bars. In 1904 the office moved to this site, and 2 years later began making gold and silver coins. Copper pennies were added a few years later. The last silver dollars (containing 90% silver) were coined in 1935. In 1970, all silver was eliminated from dollars and half dollars (today they're made of a copper-nickel alloy). The Denver Mint stamps billions of coins each year, and each has a small D on it.

Although visitors today can't get as close as previous visitors did, a self-guided tour along the visitors' gallery provides a good look at the process, with a bird's-eye view from the mezzanine of the actual coin-minting process. A variety of displays help explain the minting process, and an adjacent **gift shop** on Cherokee Street (© 303/572-9500) offers a variety of souvenirs. Allow 1 hour.

320 W. Colfax Ave. (between Cherokee and Delaware sts.). © 303/405-4757 or 303/405-4761. www.usmint.gov. Free admission. Tours Mon–Fri 8am–3pm. Gift shop 8am–3:30pm. Reservations recommended. Closed 1–2 weeks in summer for audit; call for exact date. Bus: 7.

Colorado State Capitol ★★ Built to last 1,000 years, the capitol was constructed in 1886 of granite from a Colorado quarry. The dome, which rises 272 feet above the ground, was first sheathed in copper, then replaced with gold leaf after a public outcry: Copper was not a Colorado product.

Murals depicting the history of water in the state adorn the walls of the first-floor rotunda, which offers a splendid view upward to the underside of the dome. The

---

Impressions

. . . Cash! Why, they create it here.

—Walt Whitman, on Denver in *Specimen Days,* 1879

Fun Fact Robbery at the Mint

A daring armed robbery took place at the Denver Mint in 1922, and although police were certain they knew who the culprits were, no one ever served a day in jail for the crime. The most secure building in Denver, the Mint seemed an unlikely target for a robbery. In fact, the thieves did not rob the Mint itself—they simply waited for guards to carry the money out the front door.

A Federal Reserve Bank truck was parked outside the Mint on West Colfax Avenue at about 10:30am on December 18. It was being loaded with $200,000 worth of brand-new $5 bills, to be taken to a bank about 12 blocks away, when a black Buick touring car pulled up. Two men jumped out and began firing sawed-off shotguns, killing one guard and spraying the Mint and nearby buildings, while a third robber grabbed the bags of money. Guards inside the Mint quickly pulled their guns and returned fire, but within a minute and a half the robbers were gone—$200,000 richer.

Mint guards were certain they had hit one of the thieves, and 4 weeks later the Buick turned up in a Denver garage. Lying in the front seat was the frozen, bloody body of Nick Trainor, a convicted criminal who had recently been released on parole from the Nebraska State Penitentiary. Trainor had been shot several times.

Secret Service agents recovered $80,000 of the missing loot the following year in St. Paul, Minnesota, but no arrests were made, and little more was mentioned until 1934, when Denver police announced that they knew the identities of the other men involved. Still, no charges were filed. Two of the suspects were already serving life sentences for other crimes.

At the time, police said a Midwest gang had pulled off the robbery and immediately fled to the Minneapolis–St. Paul area. The robbers gave the money to a prominent Minneapolis attorney, who also was never charged.

rotunda resembles the layout of the U.S. Capitol in Washington, D.C. South of the rotunda is the governor's office, paneled in walnut and lit by a massive chandelier.

On the first floor, the west lobby hosts revolving temporary exhibits. To the right of the main lobby is the governor's reception room. The second floor has main entrances to the House, Senate, and old Supreme Court chambers. On the third floor are entrances to the public and visitor galleries for the House and Senate (open to the public during legislative session from Jan through early May).

Lincoln St. and Colfax Ave. ✆ 303/866-2604. Free admission. 1-hr. tours offered year-round (more frequently in summer), Memorial Day to Labor Day Mon–Fri 9am–3:30pm; rest of year Mon–Fri 9:15am–2:30pm. Bus: 2, 7, 8, 12, or 15.

2 More Attractions

HISTORIC BUILDINGS

Denver encompasses 17 recognized historic districts, including Capitol Hill, the Clements District (around 21st St. and Tremont St., just east of downtown), and 9th

Street Park in Auraria (off 9th St. and West Colfax Ave.). **Historic Denver** (© 303/ 534-5288; www.historicdenver.org), offers publications covering many of these areas and organizes several annual events. The **Colorado Historical Society** (© 303/866- 3682; www.coloradohistory.org) also arranges free tours of historic mansions in July and August. For additional information on some of Denver's historic areas, see the "Neighborhoods in Brief" section in chapter 5.

Byers-Evans House   This elaborate Victorian home, built by *Rocky Mountain News* founding editor William Byers in 1883, has been restored to its appearance of 1912–24, when it was owned by William Gray Evans, son of Colorado's second territorial governor. (The Evans family continued to reside here until 1981.) Guided tours describe the architecture and explain the fascinating lives of these prominent Denver families. There is a gift shop. Allow 45 minutes.

1310 Bannock St. (in front of the Denver Art Museum). © 303/620-4933. Admission $5 adults, $4 seniors, $3 children 6–16, free for children under 6. Tues–Sun 11am–3pm. Closed state holidays. Bus: 8.

Larimer Square   This is where Denver began. Larimer Street between 14th and 15th streets was the entire community of Denver City in 1858, with false-fronted stores, hotels, and saloons to serve gold seekers and other pioneers. In the mid-1870s it was the main street of the city and the site of Denver's first post office, bank, theater, and streetcar line. By the 1930s, however, this part of Larimer Street had become a skid row of pawnshops, gin mills, and flophouses. Plans had been made to tear these structures down, when a group of investors purchased the entire block in 1965.

The Larimer Square project became Denver's first major historic preservation effort. All 16 of the block's commercial buildings, constructed in the 1870s and 1880s, were renovated, providing space for retail shops, restaurants, and nightclubs, as well as upper-story offices. A series of courtyards and open spaces was created, and in 1973 the entire block was added to the National Register of Historic Places. Allow at least a half-hour.

1400 block of Larimer St. © 303/534-2367 or 303/685-8143 (events line). www.larimersquare.com. Bus: 2, 7, 12, 15, 16, 28, 31, 32, 38, or 44.

Molly Brown House Museum   Built in 1889 of Colorado rhyolite with sandstone trim, this was the residence of J. J. and Margaret (Molly) Brown from 1894 to 1932. The "unsinkable" Molly Brown became a national heroine in 1912 when the *Titanic* sank. She took charge of a group of immigrant women in a lifeboat and later raised money for their benefit.

Restored to its 1910 appearance, the Molly Brown House has a large collection of early-20th-century furnishings and art objects, many of which belonged to the Brown family. There are also temporary exhibits (recent ones detailed the lives of servants in Brown's day and trends in Victorian undergarments), and a carriage house with a museum store at the rear is open to visitors. The house can be seen on guided tours. Allow 1 hour.

1340 Pennsylvania St. © 303/832-4092. www.mollybrown.org. Guided tour $6.50 adults, $5 seniors over 65, $3 children 6–12, free for children under 6. June–Aug Mon–Sat 10am–4pm, Sun noon–4pm; Sept–May Tues–Sat 10am–4pm, Sun noon–4pm. Guided tours every 30 min.; last tour of the day begins at 3:30pm. Closed major holidays. Bus: 2 on Logan St. to E. 13th, then 1 block east to Pennsylvania.

MUSEUMS & GALLERIES

Black American West Museum & Heritage Center   Nearly one-third of the cowboys in the Old West were black, and this museum chronicles their little-known history, along with that of black doctors, teachers, miners, farmers, newspaper reporters, and state legislators. The extensive collection occupies the Victorian home of Dr. Justina Ford, the first black woman licensed to practice medicine in Denver. Known locally as the "Lady Doctor," Ford (1871–1951) delivered more than 7,000 babies—most of them at home because she was denied hospital privileges—and consistently served the disadvantaged and underprivileged of Denver.

The museum's founder and curator emeritus, Paul Stewart, loved to play cowboys and Indians as a boy, but his playmates always chose him to be an Indian because "There was no such thing as a black cowboy." He began researching the history of blacks in the West after meeting a black cowboy who had led cattle drives in the early 20th century. Stewart explored almost every corner of the American West, gathering artifacts, memorabilia, photographs, oral histories—anything to document the existence of black cowboys—and his collection served as the nucleus for this museum when it opened in 1971. Allow 1 hour.

3091 California St. (at 31st St.). (C) 303/292-2566. www.blackamericanwestmuseum.com. Admission $6 adults, $5 seniors, $4 children 5–12, free for children under 5. June–Aug Tues–Sat 10am–5pm; Sept–May Wed–Fri 10am–2pm, Sat–Sun 10am–5pm. Light Rail: 30th and Downing.

Colorado History Museum *ac* The Colorado Historical Society's permanent exhibits include "The Colorado Chronicle," an 1800-to-1949 timeline that uses biographical plaques and a remarkable collection of photographs, news clippings, and paraphernalia to illustrate Colorado's past. Dozens of dioramas portray episodes in state history, including an intricate re-creation of 19th-century Denver. There's also a life-size display on early transportation and industry.

The first major new permanent exhibits at the museum in some time, "Ancient Voices" and "Confluence of Cultures," are multimedia gems dedicated to the history of Colorado's native tribes and the state's pioneer era, respectively. The museum offers a series of lectures and statewide historical and archaeological tours. Allow 1 hour.

1300 Broadway. (C) 303/866-3682. www.coloradohistory.org. Admission $7 adults, $6 seniors and students, $5 children 6–12, free for children under 6. Mon–Sat 10am–5pm; Sun noon–5pm. Bus: 8.

Denver Firefighters Museum *Kids* The history of the Denver Fire Department is preserved and displayed here, in historic Fire Station No. 1. Built in 1909 for Engine Company No. 1, it was one of the largest firehouses in Denver, occupying 11,000 square feet on two floors. In its early years, it lodged men, fire engines, and horses. Motorized equipment replaced horse-drawn engines by 1923, and in 1932 the firehouse was "modernized." Concrete replaced the wooden floor, the stables and hayloft were removed, and the plumbing was improved. Visitors today see firefighting equipment dating to 1866, as well as historic photos and newspaper clippings. Allow 45 minutes.

1326 Tremont Place. (C) 303/892-1436. www.denverfirefightersmuseum.org. Admission $4 adults, $3 seniors, $2 children under 15. Mon–Sat 10am–4pm. Closed major holidays. Located 2 blocks west of Civic Center Park on the north side of Colfax.

Denver Museum of Miniatures, Dolls & Toys *Finds* This late-19th-century property is home to an intriguing collection of antique and collectible dolls, from rag and wood to exquisite German and French bisque. Also on display are dollhouses, from a Santa Fe adobe with hand-carved furniture to a replica of a 16-room home in Newport, Rhode Island. The museum also displays wonderful old toys, from teddy bears to model cars. The gift shop is equally delightful. Allow 45 to 60 minutes.

1880 Gaylord St. (just west of City Park). ℂ **303/322-1053**. www.dmmdt.com. Admission $5 adults, $4 seniors and children 5–16, free for children under 5. Tues–Sat 10am–4pm; Sun 1–4pm.

Four Mile Historic Park ✿   Four miles southeast of downtown Denver—thus the name—the oldest log home (1859) still standing in Denver serves as the centerpiece for this 12-acre open-air museum. Everything is authentic to the period from 1859 to 1883, including the house (a former stagecoach stop), its furnishings, outbuildings, and farm equipment. There are draft horses and chickens in the barn, and crops in the garden. Weekend visitors can enjoy horse-drawn carriage rides ($2), weather permitting. Seasonal "Heritage Events" feature pioneer-era musicians and actors as well as many food and craft demonstrations. Big events include July 4th and an outdoor theater series. Allow 1 hour.

715 S. Forest St. (at Exposition Ave.). ℂ **303/399-1859**. www.fourmilepark.org. Free admission; museum tours $3.50 adults, $2 seniors and children 6–15, free for children under 6. Apr–Sept Wed–Fri noon–4pm, Sat–Sun 10am–4pm; Oct–Mar Sat–Sun noon–4pm.

Lakewood's Heritage Center at Belmar Park   In Denver's early days, many wealthy residents maintained summer estates in the rural Lakewood area, and this historic village tells their story as well as that of others who lived and worked here. The visitor center provides an introduction to the museum, and you can begin a personalized guided or self-guided tour here. The village includes an 1870s farmhouse, a 1920s one-room school, a 1950s variety store, and the Barn Gallery. There's an exhibit on "Lakewood People and Places," antique farm machinery, self-guided history walks through the surrounding 127-acre park, changing art exhibits, and a picnic area. Onsite are also an amphitheater and festival area, hosting a summer concert series and a slate of seasonal celebrations. Allow 1 to 2 hours.

801 S. Yarrow Blvd. (near Wadsworth and Ohio), Lakewood. ℂ **303/987-7850**. Admission $3 adults, $2 children 4–18, free for children under 4. Mon–Fri 10am–4pm; Sat noon–4pm. Closed Sun. Bus: 76.

Museo de las Americas ✿ *Finds*   Billed as the only museum in the Rocky Mountains focusing exclusively on the art, culture, and history of Latinos, the Museo is worth a stop, as is a stroll through the surrounding gallery-laden neighborhood. The exhibits here change regularly, and a semipermanent exhibit tells the story of pre-Colombian Latin America, with a replica of an ornate sunstone and exhibits on Tenochtitlán, the Aztec metropolis (on the site of present-day Mexico City) destroyed by invading Spaniards in the 16th century. Allow 1 to 2 hours.

861 Santa Fe Dr. ℂ **303/571-4401**. www.museo.org. Admission $4 adults, $3 seniors and students, free for children under 13. Tues–Fri 10am–5pm; Sat–Sun noon–5pm.

Museum of Contemporary Art/Denver   Rotating avant-garde exhibitions by numerous local and national artists are the main attraction at this downtown museum. Temporary exhibits in the two floors of exhibition space rotate every 5 months. The museum is slated to move into a new LoDo location in mid-2007. Allow 1 hour.

1275 19th St. at Sakura Sq. (19th and Larimer sts.). ℂ **303/298-7554**. www.mcartdenver.org. Admission $5 adults, $3 seniors and students, free for children under 12. Tues–Sat 11am–5:30pm; Sun noon–5:30pm.

Kirkland Museum of Fine & Decorative Art ✿✿ *Finds*   This relatively new museum covers Colorado's most illustrious artist, Vance Kirkland (1904–81), in grand fashion, while also presenting a world-class collection of decorative arts. Kirkland was a watercolor painter focused on Western landscapes when he started experimenting and combined oils and watercolors on one canvas. The traditional arts establishment dropped his modern ideas like a bad habit, but he later won accolades for creating his own artistic universe in his stunning paintings, about 60 of which are on display here. His preserved brick studio (first built in 1911) has an unusual harness he used for painting on flat canvases face down (dating from his "dot" period). The decorative arts collection includes over 3,300 pieces ranging from teacups to armchairs, and there are also over 700 works by notable Colorado artists other than Kirkland.

1311 Pearl St. (C) 303/832-8576. www.kirklandmuseum.org. Admission $6 adults; $5 seniors, students, and teachers. No one under 13 permitted due to the fragile nature of the collection. Children 13 to 17 must be accompanied by an adult. Tues–Sun 1–5pm. Guided tour Wed–Sat at 1:30pm. Closed major holidays.

The Wildlife Experience ⓖ Opened in 2002 near the Denver Technological Center, this impressive $40 million museum has three foci: natural history, nature films, and wildlife art, with nine galleries of paintings, sculptures, and photography. The museum's aim is to educate visitors about conservation and the delicate balance between people and the environment, and do it in an aesthetically pleasing fashion. They accomplish the task, with such highlights as a National Geographic Channel screening room and an interactive Children's Gallery. Also here are a 315-seat Iwerks Extreme Screen Theater, a restaurant, and a gift shop. Allow 1 hour.

10035 S. Peoria St. (C) 720/488-3300. www.thewildlifeexperience.org. Admission or theater tickets $7.95 adults, $6.95 seniors, $4.95 children; combination museum/theater tickets $12 adults, $11 seniors, $6.95 children. Tues–Sun 9am–5pm. Closed major holidays. Located 1 mile east of I-25 via Lincoln Ave. (exit 193).

Wings Over the Rockies Air & Space Museum ⓖ *Kids* More than 40 planes and spacecraft occupy cavernous Hangar No. 1, which became a museum when Lowry Air Force Base closed in 1995; now it's a burgeoning residential area about 6 miles southeast of downtown. On display are antique biplanes, a search-and-rescue helicopter, an F-14 Tomcat, a massive B-1A bomber—one of only two in existence—and most of the F-100 fighter series. You can also see a World War II uniform collection, a Norden bombsight, U3A Blue Canoe, and a mock-up of the space station module, plus seasonal exhibits. On each month's second Saturday the museum hosts "Demo Cockpit Day," when visitors get to climb into the planes' cockpits. Sci-fi fans take note: A full-size X-Wing prop used in the filming of *Star Wars* is on permanent display. Allow 1½ hours.

7711 E. Academy Blvd., Hangar No. 1. (C) 303/360-5360. www.wingsmuseum.org. Admission $7 adults, $6 seniors, $5 children 6–17, free for children under 6. Mon–Sat 10am–5pm; Sun noon–5pm. Bus: 6.

PARKS, GARDENS & ZOOS

Butterfly Pavilion & Insect Center ⓖⓖ *Kids* A walk through the butterfly conservatory introduces the visitor to a world of grace and beauty. The constant mist creates a hazy habitat to support the lush green plants that are both food and home to the 1,200 butterfly inhabitants. If you stand still for a few minutes, a butterfly might land on you, but don't try to pick them up—the oils on your hands contaminate their senses, interfering with their ability to find food. One display describes the differences among butterflies, moths, and skippers, and color charts help with identification.

In the insect room you'll discover that honeybees beat their wings some 200 times per second, and beetles make up one-fifth of all living things on earth. Meet arthropods (the scientific name for insects) that are native to Colorado, and see exotic species from around the world. A fascinating "touch cart" allows you to get up close to a cockroach or tarantula, assuming that you really want to. "Shrunk!" features giant animatronic insects (it can be scary for little ones) and nifty interactive exhibits about the biomechanics of bugs. Also on the premises are a large gift shop and snack bar. Outside, a .5-mile nature trail meanders amidst cacti and other desert-friendly plants. Allow 2 to 3 hours.

6252 W. 104th Ave., Westminster. ✆ 303/469-5441. www.butterflies.org. Admission $7.95 adults, $5.95 seniors, $4.95 children 4–12, free for children under 4. Memorial Day–Labor Day daily 9am–6pm; rest of year 9am–5pm. Take the Denver-Boulder Turnpike (U.S. 36) to W. 104th Ave. and go east for about a block. The pavilion is on your right.

City Park   Denver's largest urban park covers 330 acres (96 sq. blocks) on the east side of uptown. Established in 1881, it retains Victorian touches. The park encompasses two lakes (with boat rentals and fishing), athletic fields, jogging and walking trails, a free children's water feature, playgrounds, tennis courts, picnic areas, and an 18-hole municipal golf course. In summer, there are concerts. The park is also the site of the Denver Zoo and the Denver Museum of Nature & Science (including its IMAX Theater), discussed earlier in this chapter.

E. 17th to E. 26th aves., between York St. and Colorado Blvd. Free admission to park. Separate admission to zoo, museum, golf course, and other sites. Daily 24 hr. Bus: 24 or 32.

Denver Botanic Gardens 🐾🐾   Twenty-three acres of outdoor and indoor gardens display plants native to the desert, plains, mountain foothills, and alpine zones. There's also a traditional Japanese garden, herb garden, water garden, fragrance garden, and a garden inspired by the art of Monet. Even in the cold of winter, the dome-shaped Tropical Conservatory houses thousands of species of tropical and subtropical plants. Huge, colorful orchids and bromeliads share space with a collection of plants used for food, fibers, dyes, building materials, and medicines. The Botanic Gardens also have a gift shop, library, and auditorium. Special events are scheduled throughout the year; offerings range from garden concerts in summer to a spring plant sale to a cornfield maze southwest of Denver in the fall. Allow 1 to 2 hours.

1005 York St. ✆ 720/865-3500. www.botanicgardens.org. Admission May to mid-Sept $8.50 adults, $5.50 seniors, $5 children 4–15; mid-Sept to Apr $7.50 adults, $4.50 seniors, $4 children 4–15; free for children under 4 year-round. May to mid-Sept Sat–Tues 9am–8pm, Wed–Fri 9am–5pm; mid-Sept to Apr daily 9am–5pm. Bus: 2, 6, or 10.

Denver Mountain Parks 🐾🐾   Formally established in 1913, the city's mountain parks system began acquiring land in the mountains near Denver to be set aside for recreational use. Today it includes more than 14,000 acres, with 31 developed mountain parks and 16 unnamed wilderness areas that are wonderful places for hiking, picnicking, bird-watching, golfing, or lazing in the grass and sun.

The first and largest, **Genesee Park,** is 20 miles west of Denver off I-70 exit 254; its 2,341 acres contain the Chief Hosa Lodge and Campground (the only overnight camping available in the system), picnic areas with fireplaces, a softball field, a scenic overlook, and an elk-and-buffalo enclosure.

Echo Lake is about 45 minutes from downtown Denver on Colo. 103. At 10,600 feet elevation on Mount Evans, the park has good fishing, hiking, and picnicking, plus a restaurant and curio shop. Other parks include 1,000-acre **Daniels Park** (23 miles south of Denver; take I-25 to Castle Pines Parkway, then go west to the park), which offers picnic areas, a bison enclosure, and a scenic overlook; and **Dedisse Park** (2 miles west of Evergreen on Colo. 74), which provides picnic facilities, golf course, restaurant, clubhouse, ice-skating, fishing, and volleyball.

Dept. of Parks and Recreation. ✆ 303/697-4545. www.denvergov.org. Free admission.

Denver Zoo ★★ (Kids)   More than 700 species of animals (nearly 4,000 individuals) live in this spacious zoological park, home to the rare deerlike okapi as well as endangered cheetahs, Komodo dragons, and western lowland gorillas. The newest (and most ambitious) habitat here is Predator Ridge, a re-created African savannah with lions, hyenas, and other African predators. The exhibit is modeled after a Kenyan preserve, complete with artificial termite mounds that disperse insects for the banded mongoose that live here. The zoo has long been an innovator in re-creating realistic habitats: Bear Mountain, built in 1918, was the first animal exhibit in the United States constructed of simulated concrete rockwork.

The zoo is home to the nation's first natural gas-powered train ($1). The electric Safari Shuttle ($2.50 adults, $1.50 children) tours all zoo paths from spring through fall. An especially kid-friendly attraction is the Conversation Carousel ($1), featuring wood-carved renditions of such endangered species as okapi, polar bears, Komodo dragons, and hippos. The Hungry Elephant cafeteria serves full meals, and picnicking is popular, too. Feeding times are posted near the zoo entrance so you can time your visit to see the animals at their most active. Allow from 2 hours to a whole day.

City Park, 23rd Ave. and Steele St. (main entrance between Colorado Blvd. and York St.). ✆ 303/376-4800. www. denverzoo.org. Admission summer $11 adults, $9 seniors 62 and over, $7 children 3–12; winter $9 adults, $7 seniors 62 and over, $5 children; free year-round for children under 3. Children must be accompanied by an adult. Apr–Sept daily 9am–5pm; Oct–Mar daily 10am–4pm. Bus: 24 or 32.

Downtown Aquarium   Denver's state-of-the-art aquarium—the largest between Chicago and Monterey, California—opened in 1999 as a nonprofit, and in 2003 was sold to the for-profit Landry's seafood restaurant chain. The sale brought the aquarium stability, not to mention new exhibits and a theme restaurant and lounge on-site. Residents include greenback cutthroat trout (the Colorado state fish), river otters, tigers, nurse sharks, sea turtles, and moray eels. Among the other exhibits: a flash-flood simulation, a gold-panning and mining display, "Stingray Reef" (visitors can pet and feed the slippery denizens), and a lifelike animatronic orangutan. On Saturdays, licensed divers and novice snorkelers can swim in the big tanks for a fee ($175 for divers, $75 for snorkelers). Allow 2 hours.

700 Water St., just east of I-25 via 23rd Ave. (exit 211). ✆ 303/561-4444. www.aquariumrestaurants.com. Admission before 6pm $13 adults, $9.95 seniors, $7.95 children 4–12; after 6pm $9.95 adults, $8.95 seniors, $6.95 children 4–12; always free for children under 4. Mon–Fri 10am–10pm; Sat–Sun 10am–11pm. Closed Dec 25.

Rocky Mountain Arsenal National Wildlife Refuge   Once a site where the U.S. Army manufactured chemical weapons such as mustard gas and GB nerve agent, and later leased to a private enterprise to produce pesticides, the Rocky Mountain Arsenal has become an environmental success story. The 27-square-mile Superfund cleanup site, an area of open grasslands and wetlands just west of Denver International Airport, is home to more than 330 species, including deer, coyotes, prairie dogs, and birds of prey. An estimated 100 bald eagles make this one of the country's largest eagle-roosting locales during the winter.

The Rocky Mountain Arsenal Wildlife Society Bookstore is at the visitor center, and there are 10 miles of hiking trails and catch-and-release fishing. For a guided tour, it's best to call a day or two in advance. Allow at least an hour.

56th Ave. at Quebec St. ✆ 303/289-0930. www.fws.gov/rockymountainarsenal. Free admission. Sat–Sun 8am–4:30pm. Bus: 48.

3 Amusement Parks & Places Especially for Kids

Denver abounds in child-oriented activities, and the listings below will probably appeal to young travelers of any age. In addition, some sights listed in other sections may appeal to families. They include the Butterfly Pavilion and Insect Center; Colorado History Museum; Downtown Aquarium; Denver Art Museum; Denver Museum of Miniatures, Dolls & Toys; Denver Museum of Nature & Science; Denver Zoo; Four Mile Historic Park; and the U.S. Mint.

Children's Museum of Denver *Kids*   Denver's best hands-on experience for children, this intriguing museum is both educational and just plain fun. Focusing on the zero-to-8 age bracket, the museum uses "playscapes" to entertain and activate young minds. These exhibits include "Fire Station No. 1," which teaches fire safety, and "Community Market," a faux supermarket that allows kids to role-play as shoppers and clerks. There are several other playscapes with themes ranging from biology to engineering. A cafe serves sandwiches, snacks, and beverages. Allow at least 2 hours.

2121 Children's Museum Dr. © 303/433-7444. www.mychildsmuseum.org. Admission $7 ages 1–59, $5 seniors 60 and over, free for children under 1. Mon–Fri 9am–4pm; Sat–Sun 10am–5pm. Take exit 211 (23rd Ave.) east off I-25; turn right on 7th St., and again on Children's Museum Dr.

Fat City *Kids*   This 3.5-acre indoor entertainment mall boasts that it offers "fun for everyone." That's not much of an exaggeration—inside are 40 lanes of bowling, small thrill rides, minigolf, laser tag, roller-skating, and a large video arcade for the kids; for the more mature crowd, there are scads of TVs, billiards, a restaurant, and a 50-foot martini bar. Allow 1 to 4 hours.

9670 W. Coal Mine Ave. (at Kipling St.), Littleton. © 303/972-4344. www.fatcityinfo.com. Free admission; activities $2.50–$7; multiactivity tickets available. Mon–Thurs 11am–11pm; Fri 11am–2am; Sat 10am–2am; Sun 10am–1am; call for activity availability. About 15 miles southwest of downtown Denver. Bus: 67 or 76.

Lakeside Amusement Park *Kids*   Among the largest and most historic amusement parks in the Rocky Mountains, Lakeside has about 40 rides, including a Cyclone roller coaster, a midway with carnival and arcade games, and a rare steam-powered miniature train that circles the lake. There are also food stands and picnic facilities, plus a separate Kiddie's Playland with 15 rides. Allow 3 hours.

Fun Fact   The Big Blue Bear

Denver has a new face to the world, and it's peering into the second floor of the Colorado Convention Center. Known popularly as "The Big Blue Bear," the 40-foot blue ursine immediately became Denver's most photogenic piece of public art when it was installed in 2005. Sculptor Lawrence Argent designed the big fella—officially named *I See What You Mean*—then a California-based fabricator shaped him out of five tons of steel, fiberglass, and cement; transported him to Colorado in sections; and bolted him into place.

The sculpture is located right by the convention center's 14th Street entrance, and can be photographed from inside or out.

4601 Sheridan Blvd. (just south of I-70, exit 271). ✆ **303/477-1621**. www.lakesideamusementpark.com. Admission $2. Ride coupons 50¢ (rides require 1–4 coupons each); unlimited rides $13 Mon–Fri, $18 Sat–Sun and holidays. May Sat–Sun and holidays noon–11pm; June to Labor Day Mon–Fri 6–11pm, Sat–Sun and holidays noon–11pm. Kiddie's Playland Mon–Fri 1–10pm, Sat–Sun and holidays noon–10pm. Closed from the day after Labor Day to Apr.

Six Flags Elitch Gardens Theme Park ⍟ (Kids)

A Denver tradition established in 1889, this amusement park moved to its present downtown site in 1995. The 45-plus rides include Twister II, an unbelievable 10-story roller coaster with a 90-foot drop and dark tunnel; the Flying Coaster, a one-of-a-kind "hang gliding" experience where passengers lie facedown; the Halfpipe, a snowboarding-themed thrill ride that involves 16 passengers on a 39-foot board; the 220-foot, free-fall Tower of Doom; and a fully restored 1925 carousel with 67 hand-carved horses and chariots. Patrons of all ages can enjoy the Island Kingdom Water Park while the little ones have fun on pint-sized rides in the Looney Tunes MovieTown. There are also musical revues and stunt shows, games and arcades, food, shopping, and beautiful flower gardens. Allow 3 hours.

Speer Blvd., at I-25 exit 212A. ✆ **303/595-4386**. www.sixflags.com/elitchgardens. Gate admission with unlimited rides $45 for those taller than 4 ft., $22 for seniors 55–69 and those 4 ft. and under, free for seniors over 69 and children under 4. Memorial Day to Labor Day daily 10am–10pm; Apr to late May and early Sept to Oct weekends, call for hours.

Tiny Town and Railroad (Kids) (Finds)

Originally built in 1915 at the site of a Denver-Leadville stagecoach stop, Tiny Town is exactly what its name implies—a one-sixth scale Western village. Nestled in a scenic mountain canyon about 20 miles southeast of downtown Denver, Tiny Town is made up of 100 colorful buildings and a steam-powered locomotive visitors can ride for an additional $1. Allow 1 hour.

6249 S. Turkey Creek Rd., Tiny Town. ✆ **303/697-6829**. www.tinytownrailroad.com. Admission $3 adults, $2 children 2–12, free for children under 2. Memorial Day to Labor Day daily 10am–5pm; early to mid-May and early Sept to Oct Sat–Sun 10am–5pm. Closed Nov–Apr. Located 20 miles southeast of downtown via U.S. 285 (Hampden Ave.).

Water World ⍟ (Kids)

This 64-acre complex, billed as America's largest family water park, has two oceanlike wave pools, river rapids for inner-tubing, twisting water slides, several kids' play areas, plus other attractions—more than 40 in all. Allow at least 4 hours.

88th Ave. and Pecos St., Federal Heights. ✆ **303/427-SURF**. www.waterworldcolorado.com. Admission $29 for those 48 in. and taller, $24 for those under 48 in., free for seniors and children under 4. Memorial Day to Labor Day daily 10am–6pm. Closed rest of year and some school days in Aug. Take the Thornton exit (exit 219, 84th Ave.) off I-25 north.

WALKING TOUR | **DOWNTOWN DENVER**

Start:	Denver Information Center, Civic Center Park.
Finish:	State capitol, Civic Center Park.
Time:	2 to 8 hours, depending on how much time you spend shopping, eating, and sightseeing.
Best Times:	Any Tuesday through Friday in late spring.
Worst Times:	Monday and holidays, when the museums are closed.

Start your tour of the downtown area at Civic Center Park, on West Colfax Avenue at 14th Street.

❶ Civic Center Park

This 2-square-block oasis features a Greek amphitheater, fountains, statues, flower gardens, and 30 different species of trees, 2 of which (it is said) were originally planted by Abraham Lincoln at his Illinois home.

Overlooking the park on its east side is the state capitol. On its south side is the:

❷ Colorado History Museum

The staircaselike building houses exhibits that make the state's colorful history come to life.

Also on the south side of the park are the Denver Public Library and the:

❸ Denver Art Museum

With buildings designed by Gio Ponti of Italy and Daniel Libeskind of Germany, the art museum is an architectural wonder. Inside are more than 35,000 works of art, including renowned Western and American Indian collections.

On the west side of Civic Center Park is the:

❹ City and County Building

During the Christmas season, a rainbow of colored lights decorates it in spectacular fashion.

A block farther west is the:

❺ U.S. Mint

Modeled in Italian Renaissance style, the building resembles the Palazzo Riccardi in Florence. More than 60,000 cubic feet of granite and 1,000 tons of steel went into its construction in 1904.

Cross over Colfax and go diagonally northwest up Court Place. Two blocks ahead is the:

❻ Denver Pavilions

The city's newest retail hot spot sits at the south end of the 16th Street Mall, featuring a Hard Rock Cafe, a 15-screen movie theater, and a Barnes & Noble Superstore.

Three blocks up the 16th Street Mall, head southwest 2 blocks on California Street past the Colorado Convention Center and turn right on 14th Street. Walk 2 blocks to the:

❼ Denver Center for the Performing Arts

The complex covers 4 square blocks between 14th Street and Cherry Creek, Champa Street and Arapahoe Street. The entrance is under a block-long, 80-foot-high glass archway. The center includes seven theaters, a symphony hall in the round, a voice research laboratory, and a smoking solar fountain. Free tours are offered.

Two more blocks up 14th past the arts center is:

❽ Larimer Square

This is Denver's oldest commercial district. Restored late-19th-century Victorian buildings accommodate more than 30 shops and a dozen restaurants and clubs. Colorful awnings, hanging flower baskets, and quiet open courtyards accent the square, once home to such notables as Buffalo Bill Cody and Bat Masterson. Horse-drawn carriage rides originate here for trips up the 16th Street Mall or through lower downtown.

 TAKE A BREAK
Stop at **Rioja,** 1431 Larimer Sq., between 14th and 15th sts. (© **303/820-2282**), for some of Denver's best food. (See full review on p. 93.)

A walkway at the east corner of Larimer and 15th leads through:

❾ Writer Square

Quaint gas lamps, brick walkways, and outdoor cafes dot this shopping-and-dining complex.

At 16th Street, cross to the:

❿ Tabor Center

The glass-enclosed shopping and entertainment complex spreads over three levels, in effect a 2-block-long greenhouse.

Walking Tour: Downtown Denver

1 Civic Center Park
2 Colorado History Museum
3 Denver Art Museum
4 City & County Building
5 U.S. Mint
6 Denver Pavilions
7 Denver Performing Arts Complex
8 Larimer Square
☕ Rioja
9 Writer Square
10 Tabor Center
11 D & F Tower
12 16th Street Mall
13 Brown Palace Hotel
☕ Brown Palace Hotel
14 State Capitol

To the east, the Tabor Center is anchored by the:

⓫ D&F Tower

The city landmark was patterned after the campanile of St. Mark's Basilica in Venice, Italy, in 1910. In the basement is a performing arts venue, Lannie's Clocktower Cabaret.

Here, with the state capitol building to the southeast, begin a leisurely stroll down the:

⓬ 16th Street Mall

The $76-million pedestrian path affords the finest people-watching spot in the city. You'll see everyone from street entertainers to lunching office workers to travelers like yourself. Built of red and gray granite, it is lined with 200 red oak trees, a dozen fountains, and a lighting system straight out of *Star Wars*. You'll also see outdoor cafes, restored Victorian buildings, modern skyscrapers, and hundreds of shops—with an emphasis on sports—plus restaurants and department stores. Sleek European-built shuttle buses run through, offering free transportation up and down the mall as often as every 90 seconds.

You'll walk 7 blocks down 16th Street from the Tabor Center before reaching Tremont Place. Turn left, go 1 block farther, and across the street, on your right, you'll see the:

⑬ Brown Palace Hotel

One of the most beautiful grande-dame hotels in the United States, it was built in 1892 and features a nine-story atrium lobby topped by a Tiffany stained glass ceiling. Step into the lobby for a look, and if you're hungry . . .

TAKE A BREAK
The **Brown Palace Hotel,** 321 17th St. (© **303/297-3111),** serves lunch in several restaurants and also offers afternoon tea in its elegant lobby. Reservations are recommended for the English tea, which includes sandwiches and pastries from the Brown Palace bakery. (See full review on p. 82.)

Continue across Broadway on East 17th Avenue. Go 2 blocks to Sherman Street, turn right, and proceed 2 blocks south on Sherman to East Colfax Avenue. You're back overlooking Civic Center Park, but this time you're at the:

⑭ Colorado State Capitol

If you stand on the 13th step on the west side of the building, you're exactly 5,280 feet (1 mile) above sea level. Architects modeled the Colorado capitol after the U.S. Capitol in Washington, D.C., and used the world's entire known supply of rare rose onyx in its interior wainscoting.

4 Organized Tours

Visitors who want to be personally guided to the attractions of Denver and the surrounding areas by those in the know have a variety of choices. In addition to the following, see the section "Escorted General-Interest Tours" in chapter 2 and chapter 4, "The Active Vacation Planner."

Half- and full-day bus tours of Denver and the nearby Rockies are offered by the ubiquitous **Gray Line,** P.O. Box 17646, Denver, CO 80217 (© **800/348-6877** for information only; 303/289-2841 for reservations and information; www.colorado grayline.com). Fares for children 12 and under are half the adult prices listed below. Prices include entry fees but usually no food. Tours depart the Cherry Creek Shopping Center at 1st Avenue and Milwaukee Street, as well as local hotels and hostels on a reservation basis.

A 4-hour tour (no. 27), leaving at 1:30pm, takes in Denver's mountain parks: Red Rocks Park, Bergen Park, and Buffalo Bill's grave atop Lookout Mountain. It costs $35 for adults. The Denver city tour (no. 28), which departs daily at 8:30am and takes about 3½ hours, gives you a taste of both old Denver—through Larimer Square and other historic buildings—and the modern-day city. It's $30 for adults. The city tour combined with the mountain-parks tour costs $60. Gray Line also offers tours of Rocky Mountain National Park and the Colorado Springs area; call or check the website for information.

The Colorado Sightseer, 6780 W. 84th Circle, Suite 60, Arvada, CO 80003 (© **303/423-8200;** www.coloradosightseer.com), offers guided tours of Denver and environs. The Historic Denver tour includes a visit to LoDo and some of the city's earliest buildings, the state capitol, the Molly Brown House, and Four Mile Historic Park. It lasts about 4 hours and costs $45 for adults, $35 for children 5 to 12. A Rocky Mountain National Park tour, lasting about 9½ hours, costs $85 for adults and $65 for children 5 to 12, including a box lunch. The 4½-hour Foothills Tour includes stops at Coors Brewery, the Buffalo Bill memorial, and scenic Red Rocks Park. The costs are $45 for adults, $35 for children 5 to 12, and free for children 4 and younger.

The **LoDo District** (© 303/628-5428; www.lodo.org) leads guided walking tours of the storied area from June to October. Tours depart from Union Station (17th and Wynkoop sts.) on Saturday at 10am; the cost is $10 adults, $5 students, and free for those under 13. They also offer different walking tours on Thursday and Saturday afternoons. Take advantage of your cellphone with **Rocky Mountain Audio Guides** (© **303/898-7073;** www.rmaguides.com), which delivers 40- and 80-minute walking tours of downtown Denver. Call 24 hours before your tour to buy the tours; then you simply dial a number and walk around town, guided via satellite.

BICYCLING & MULTISPORT TOURS

A few companies operate bicycling and hiking tours out of the Denver area. In and around town, give **RMP&E Bike Tours** (© **720/641-3166;** www.mountainbike tours.us) a holler. They offer 3-hour custom tours of Denver and the foothills west of town for $100 per person. They also offer custom rides.

The World Outdoors (© **800/488-8483** or 303/413-0938; www.theworldoutdoors. com) offers a 6-day, 5-night multisport hut-to-hut tour that begins and ends in Vail (100 miles west of Denver). The huts, described by *Mountain Bike Magazine* as "luxurious backcountry accommodations," act as recreational headquarters for guests, who have plenty of hiking, rafting, and sightseeing opportunities between mountain-biking treks.

The trips aren't cheap, running $1,395 per person, but this might be the best way for the outdoors enthusiast to enjoy the Rockies west of Denver. The trip runs twice each summer, in June and August. Meals are included, biking and camping gear are not.

Colorado Mountain Expeditions (© **877/600-2656;** www.coloradotrailhiking. com) offers supported weeklong treks on the Colorado Trail (which runs 483 miles from Denver to Durango) for about $800 per person, all meals included. The beauty of these trips: You only carry a day pack. A support crew sets up your camp and makes your meals while you focus on the trail, not the campsite.

Another company that offers weeklong tours in the area is **Bicycle Tour of Colorado** (© **303/985-1180;** www.bicycletourcolorado.com). For about $300, a biker can join a tour involving more than 1,000 riders and 70 volunteers—including medical and bike-tech support as well as guiding services—on a 400-mile journey that hits six different cities each year, crossing the Continental Divide several times in the process. While accommodations can be prearranged at hotels, most riders elect to stay at facilities provided by the city (for example, the local high school). All meals are provided for about $300 for the week.

A good resource for bicyclists is the **Denver Bicycle Touring Club** (www.dbtc.org), which organizes local rides and publishes a monthly newsletter. See "Bicycling & Skateboarding," below.

5 Outdoor Activities

Denver's proximity to the Rocky Mountains makes it possible to spend a day skiing, snowmobiling, horseback riding, hiking, river running, sailing, fishing, hunting, mountain climbing, or rock-hounding and return to the city by nightfall. Within the city limits and nearby, visitors will find more than 200 miles of jogging and bicycle paths, over 100 free tennis courts, and several dozen public golf courses.

The city has an excellent system of **mountain parks** (© 303/697-4545), covering more than 14,000 acres, which are discussed earlier in this chapter in the "Parks, Gardens & Zoos" section.

Campsites are easy to reach from Denver, as are suitable sites for hang gliding and hot-air ballooning. Sailing is popular within the city at Sloan's Lake and in Washington Park (both Denver City Parks), and the Platte River is clear for many miles of river running in rafts, kayaks, and canoes.

The Denver Metro Convention and Visitors Bureau (see "Visitor Information," in chapter 5) can supply detailed information about activities in the city. Information on nearby outdoor activities is available from: **Colorado State Parks,** 1313 Sherman St., Suite 618, Denver, CO 80203 (© **303/866-3437;** www.parks.state.co.us); the **U.S. Forest Service,** Rocky Mountain Region, 740 Simms St., Golden, CO 80401 (© **303/275-5350;** www.fs.fed.us/r2); the **U.S. Bureau of Land Management,** 2850 Youngfield St., Lakewood, CO 80215 (© **303/239-3600;** www.co.blm.gov); and the **National Park Service,** 12795 W. Alameda Pkwy., Lakewood, CO 80228 (© **303/969-2000;** www.nps.gov).

The Skinny on Denver

According to a federal study, Denver has the highest proportion of thin people of any city in the country. A 2002 study showed Colorado to be the only state where less than half of the population is overweight.

Visitors who don't bring the necessary equipment should hit the **REI** Flagship store, 1416 Platte St. (© **303/756-3100**); its rental department is stocked with tents, backpacks, stoves, mountaineering equipment, kayaks, and other gear.

BALLOONING   You can't beat a hot-air balloon ride for viewing the magnificent Rocky Mountain scenery. **Life Cycle Balloon Adventures, Ltd.** (© **800/980-9272** or 303/216-1990; www.lifecycleballoons.com), and **Colorado Rocky Ballooning** (© **888/468-9280** or 970/468-9280; www.coloradoballoonrides.com) both offer sunrise flights daily. The cost at both companies is usually $175 to $225 per person.

BICYCLING & SKATEBOARDING   The paved bicycle paths that crisscross Denver include a 12-mile scenic stretch along the bank of the South Platte River and along Cherry Creek beside Speer Boulevard. All told, the city has 85 miles of off-road trails for bikers and runners, and is *Bicycle Magazine*'s top city for bicyclists. Bike paths link the city's 205 parks, and many streets have bike lanes. In all, the city has more than 130 miles of designated bike paths and lanes. For more information, contact **Bike Denver** (www.bikedenver.org) or **Bicycle Colorado** (© **303/417-1544;** www.bicycle colo.org). Bike tours are available from several companies and clubs (see "Organized Tours," above). The **Cherry Creek Bike Rack,** 171 Detroit St. (© **303/388-1630;** www.cherrycreekbikerack.com), offers rentals, service, and free parking for bikes.

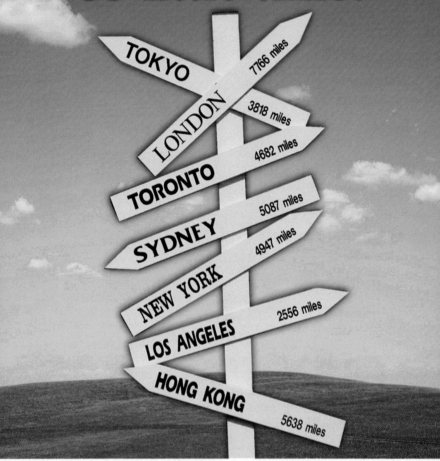

Denver also has the largest free skateboarding park (3 acres) in the country, the **Denver Skatepark,** 19th and Little Raven streets. (© **720/913-0696;** www.denver skatepark.com). It is quite popular and open between the hours of 5am and 11pm.

BOATING A quiet way to view some of downtown Denver is from a punt on scenic Cherry Creek. **Venice on the Creek** (© **303/893-0750;** www.veniceonthecreek. com) operates from June to August, Tuesday through Thursday by reservation, Thursday and to Sunday from 5 to 10pm. On weekdays it accommodates only groups of 12 or more; smaller groups are taken on weekends. Guides describe the history of the city while pointing out landmarks. Tickets are available at the kiosk at Creekfront Plaza, at the intersection of Speer Boulevard and Larimer Street. A 1-hour trip costs $25 to $35 per bench (each accommodates two).

You'll find powerboat marinas at **Cherry Creek State Park,** 4201 S. Parker Rd., Aurora (© **303/699-3860**), 11 miles from downtown off I-225; and **Chatfield State Park,** 11500 N. Roxborough Park Rd., Littleton (© **303/791-7275**), 16 miles south of downtown Denver. Jet-skiing and sail boarding are also permitted at both parks. Sail boarding, canoeing, and other wakeless boating are popular at **Barr Lake State Park,** 13401 Picadilly Rd., Brighton (© **303/659-6005**), 21 miles northeast of downtown on I-76.

For a different watersports experience, try river boarding with **RipBoard** (© **866/ 311-2627** or 303/904-8367; www.ripboard.com), which entails going down Clear Creek face first with flippers on your feet and a helmet on your head. It's exciting and exhausting, but can be a lot of fun in the right water. Lessons (including equipment) are $55 for 2 hours; rentals and sales are also available.

For information on other boating opportunities, contact Colorado State Parks, the National Park Service, or the U.S. Forest Service (see above).

FISHING A couple of good bets in the metropolitan area are Chatfield State Park, with trout, bass, and panfish, and Cherry Creek State Park, which boasts trout, walleye pike, bass, and crappie (see "Boating," above). In all, there are more than 7,100 miles of streams and 2,000 reservoirs and lakes in Colorado. For information, contact Colorado State Parks, the Colorado Division of Wildlife (© **303/297-1192**), or the U.S. Fish and Wildlife Service (© **303/236-7917**). Within Denver city limits, the **Denver Department of Parks and Recreation** (© **720/913-0696**) stocks 24 lakes with fish.

A number of sporting-goods stores can provide more detailed information. The skilled and experienced staff at **Anglers All,** 5211 S. Santa Fe Dr. (© **303/794-1104;** www.anglersall.com), can help with equipment choices and recommendations for where to go. Anglers All also offers lessons, seminars, clinics, and guided wade and float trips ($400 a day for two people).

GOLF Throughout the Front Range, it's often said that you can play golf at least 320 days a year, because the sun always seems to be shining, and even when it snows, the little snow that sticks melts quickly. There are more than 50 courses in the Denver area, including seven municipal golf courses, with nonresident greens fees up to $24 for 18 holes. City courses are: **City Park Golf Course,** East 25th Avenue and York Street (© 303/295-4420); **Evergreen Golf Course,** 29614 Upper Bear Creek Rd., Evergreen (© 303/674-4128); the par-3 **Harvard Gulch Golf Course,** East Iliff Avenue and South Clarkson Street (© 303/698-4078); **Kennedy Golf Course,** 10500 E. Hampden Ave. (© 303/751-0311); **Overland Park Golf Course,** South

Santa Fe Drive and West Jewell Avenue (© 303/698-4975); **Wellshire Golf Course,** 3333 S. Colorado Blvd. (© 303/692-5636); and **Willis Case Golf Course,** 4999 Vrain St. near West 50th Avenue (© 303/458-4877). Wellshire is the best overall course, but we prefer Willis Case for its spectacular mountain views.

You can make same-day reservations by calling the course; otherwise, nonresident golfers must purchase a $10 card at City Park, Wellshire, or Willis Case, then make reservations through the **automated phone system** (© 303/784-4000). The one exception to this policy is Evergreen Golf Course, where you can call the starter for reservations 3 days in advance. For information on any course, you can also call the **Department of Parks and Recreation** (© 720/913-0696).

An 18-hole Frisbee golf course is located at Lakewood Gulch, near Federal Boulevard and 12th Street Call the **Department of Parks and Recreation** (© 720/913-0696) for more information.

HIKING & BACKPACKING The **Colorado Trail** ⟨ᵃ is a hiking, horse, and mountain-biking route stretching 500 miles from Denver to Durango. The trail is also open to cross-country skiing, snowshoeing, and llama-pack hiking. Opened in 1988, the trail is still being fine-tuned. It took 15 years to establish, using volunteer labor, and crosses eight mountain ranges and five river systems, winding from rugged terrain to pristine meadows. For information, contact the **Colorado Trail Foundation,** 710 10th St., Room 210, Golden, CO 80401-1022 (© 303/384-3729; www.colorado trail.org). Beyond being a source of information, the foundation maintains and improves the trail, publishes relevant guidebooks, and offers supported treks (see "Bicycling & Multisport Tours," earlier in this chapter) and accredited courses.

For hikes in the Denver area, contact the city **Department of Parks and Recreation** (© 720/913-0696) for information on Denver's park system. Or contact any of the following agencies: Colorado State Parks, Colorado Division of Wildlife, National Park Service, U.S. Bureau of Land Management, or U.S. Forest Service (see the introduction to this section and "Fishing," above). A good source for the many published area maps and hiking guides is **Mapsco Map and Travel Center,** 800 Lincoln St., Denver (© 303/623-4299).

Mount Falcon Park ⟨ᵃ offers excellent trails that are easy to moderate, making this a good place for families with children. There are also picnic areas, shelters, and ruins of an old castlelike home. From Denver, go west on U.S. 285, north on Parmalee Gulch Road, and follow the signs; the park is open daily from dawn to dusk, and admission is free. Mountain bikes and horseback riding are permitted, as are leashed dogs.

Other relatively easy trails near Denver are in **Roxborough State Park** (© 303/973-3959), 10 miles south of Littleton—the 1-mile **Willow Creek Trail** and the 2.3-mile **Fountain Valley Trail** ⟨ᵃ. There are several more strenuous trails at Roxborough, but worth the effort if you enjoy beautiful red rocks and the chance to see wildlife. To get to Roxborough Park, exit Colo. 470 south onto U.S. 85 and turn west onto Titan Road, then south again at Roxborough Park Road to the main entrance. Admission costs $5 per passenger vehicle. The park is open daily from 8am to 8pm in summer, with shorter hours the rest of the year. Dogs, bikes, and horseback riding are not permitted.

HORSEBACK RIDING Equestrians can find a mount year-round at **Stockton's Plum Creek Stables,** 7479 W. Titan Rd., Littleton (© 303/791-1966; www.stocktons plumcreek.com), near Chatfield State Park, 15 miles south of downtown. Stockton's offers hayrides and barbecue picnics, as well as lessons ($50 an hour). **Paint Horse Stables,** 4201 S. Parker Rd., Aurora (© 303/690-8235; www.painthorsestables.net),

---

Tips **Denver's Dog Parks**

New in 2004, Denver allows canines to roam free at five parks within city limits, and there are dozens of off-leash parks in the metropolitan area as a whole.
Contact the Department of Parks and Recreation (℗ **720/913-0696**) for more
information or visit **www.denvergov.org.**

---

at Cherry Creek State Park, also rents horses, boards horses, and provides riding lessons, hayrides, and pony rides for kids.

RECREATION CENTERS   The **Denver Department of Parks and Recreation**
(℗ **720/913-0696**) operates about 30 recreation centers around the city, several of
which have facilities oriented to seniors. Daily guest passes for all facilities, including
swimming pools, cost $5 for adults, $2 for children under 18. Facilities vary but may
include basketball courts, indoor or outdoor pools, gyms, and weight rooms. The centers offer fitness classes and other recreation programs, including programs for those
with special needs. Call ℗ **720/913-0693** for current program information.

Among the city's recreation centers are the following: **Scheitler Recreation Center,**
5031 W. 46th Ave. (℗ **303/458-4898**), which has an indoor pool and a weight room;
Martin Luther King, Jr. Recreation Center, 3880 Newport St. (℗ **303/331-4034**),
which is the nearest full-service center to Denver International Airport and has an
indoor pool, large gym, and racquetball court; **20th Street Recreation Center,** downtown at 1011 20th St., between Arapahoe and Curtis streets (℗ **303/295-4430**), with
an indoor pool and weight room; and **Washington Park Recreation Center,** 701 S.
Franklin St. (℗ **303/698-4962**), with an indoor pool, advanced weight room, large
gym, and walking and jogging trails.

SKIING   Several ski resorts are close to Denver. They include **Eldora Mountain
Resort,** 45 miles west (℗ **303/440-8700;** www.eldora.com), which covers almost 700
acres and has 53 trails, with skiing rated 20% beginner, 50% intermediate, and 30%
advanced. **Loveland Basin and Valley,** 56 miles west on I-70, exit 216 (℗ **800/736-
3754** or 303/569-3203; www.skiloveland.com), covers 1,365 acres and has 70 trails,
rated 13% beginner, 41% intermediate, and 46% advanced. **Winter Park Resort** ⋆,
73 miles west of Denver on I-70 and U.S. 40 (℗ **800/979-0332** or 970/726-1564;
www.winterparkresort.com), boasts 2,762 skiable acres with 134 trails, rated 9%
beginner, 21% intermediate, and 70% advanced.

Eldora and Winter Park offer Nordic as well as alpine terrain.

Full information on statewide skiing is available from **Colorado Ski Country USA**
(℗ **303/837-0793;** www.coloradoski.com), and the **Colorado Cross Country Ski
Association** (www.colorado-xc.org).

Some useful Denver telephone numbers for skiers include: **ski-area information
and snow report** (℗ 303/825-7669), **weather report** (℗ 303/337-2500), and **road
conditions** (℗ 303/639-1111).

SWIMMING   The Denver Department of Parks and Recreation (℗ **303/458-
4795**) operates 17 outdoor swimming pools (open daily mid-June to mid-Aug) and
12 indoor pools (open Mon–Sat year-round). Nonresident fees are $3 for adults and
$2 for children. See "Recreation Centers," above.

TENNIS   The Denver Department of Parks and Recreation (© **720/913-0696**) manages or owns close to 150 tennis courts, more than one-third of them lit for night play. Among the most popular courts are those in City Park (York St. and E. 17th Ave.), Berkeley Park (Tennyson St. and W. 17th Ave.), Green Valley East Ranch Park (Jebel St. and E. 45th Ave.), Washington Park (S. Downing St. and E. Louisiana Ave.), and Sloan's Lake Park (Sheridan Blvd. and W. 17th Ave.). The public courts are free. For more information, contact the **Colorado Tennis Association** (© **303/695-4116;** www.coloradotennis.com).

GREAT NEARBY STATE PARKS

Colorado has a number of excellent state parks offering a wide range of activities and scenery. Information on the state's parks is available at **www.parks.state.co.us**.

BARR LAKE STATE PARK   About 25 miles northeast of Denver on I-76 in Brighton, this wildlife sanctuary of almost 2,800 acres comprises a prairie reservoir and surrounding wetlands and uplands. Boats with motors exceeding 10 horsepower are not allowed, but you can sail, paddle, row, and fish. A 9-mile hiking and biking trail circles the lake. A boardwalk from the nature center at the south parking lot leads to a good view of a heron rookery, and bird blinds along this trail allow wildlife observation and photography. Three picnic areas provide tables and grills; there's a commercial campground opposite the park on the west side. The entrance is at 13401 Picadilly Rd. Admission costs $5 per vehicle. Call © **303/659-6005** for more information.

CASTLEWOOD CANYON STATE PARK 🦌   Steep canyons, a meandering stream, a waterfall, lush vegetation, and considerable wildlife distinguish this 2,000-acre park. You can see the remains of Castlewood Canyon Dam, which was built for irrigation in 1890; it collapsed in 1933, killing two people and flooding the streets of Denver. The park, 30 miles south of Denver on Colo. 83, east of Castle Rock in Franktown, provides picnic facilities and hiking trails. The entrance is at 2989 S. State Hwy. 83; admission is $5 per vehicle. Call © **303/688-5242** for more information.

CHATFIELD STATE PARK 🦌   Sixteen miles south of downtown Denver on U.S. 85 in Littleton, this park occupies 5,600 acres of prairie against a backdrop of the steeply rising Rocky Mountains. Chatfield Reservoir, with a 26-mile shoreline, invites swimming, boating, fishing, and other watersports. The area also has 18 miles of paved bicycle trails, plus hiking and horseback-riding paths. In winter, there's ice fishing and cross-country skiing. The park also has a hot-air-balloon launch pad, a radio-controlled model aircraft field, and a 21-acre man-made wetlands area.

Facilities include 197 pull-through campsites, showers, laundry, and a dump station. Admission is $5 to $6 per vehicle; the camping fee is $16 to $20 daily. The entrance is 1 mile south of C-470 on Wadsworth Boulevard (© **303/791-7275**).

CHERRY CREEK STATE PARK   The 880-acre Cherry Creek Reservoir, created for flood control by the construction of a dam in 1950, is the central attraction of this popular park, which draws 1.5 million visitors each year. Located at the southeast Denver city limits (off Parker Rd. and I-225) about 12 miles from downtown, the park encompasses 4,200 acres in all.

Watersports include swimming, water-skiing, boating, and fishing. There's a nature trail, dog-training area, model-airplane field with paved runways, jet ski rental facility, rifle range, pistol range, and trap-shooting area. Twelve miles of paved bicycle paths and 12 miles of bridle trails circle the reservoir (horse rentals are available).

Rangers offer guided walks by appointment, as well as evening campfire programs in an amphitheater. In winter, there's skating, ice fishing, and ice boating.

Each of the park's 102 campsites has access to showers, laundry, and a dump station. Most sites have full hookups with water and electric. Many lakeshore day-use sites have picnic tables and grills.

Admission costs $6 to $7 per vehicle; the camping fee is $12 to $20 daily. Campgrounds are open year-round. The entrance is at 4201 S. Parker Rd. in Aurora. Call © **303/699-3860** for general information or © **800/678-2267** for camping reservations.

GOLDEN GATE STATE PARK 🛱   One hour west of Denver, this 14,000-acre park ranges in elevation from 7,400 to 10,400 feet and offers camping, picnicking, hiking, biking, fishing, hunting, and horseback-riding opportunities. A daily vehicle pass costs $5, and camping fees range from $12 to $18 in developed campgrounds, $7 for backcountry camping. There are around 160 developed campsites, with a limited number of electrical hookups. Reverend's Ridge, the park's largest campground, has coin-operated showers and laundry facilities.

To get to Golden Gate, take Colo. 93 north from Golden 1 mile to Golden Gate Canyon Road. Turn left and continue 13 miles to the park. For more information, call © **303/582-3707.**

6 Spectator Sports

Tickets to many sporting events can be obtained from **Ticketmaster** (© **303/830-TIXS**), with several outlets in the Denver area.

AUTO RACING   The **Grand Prix of Denver** (© **877/772-5425** for tickets or 303/825-0300 for information; www.gpdenver.com) is held over Labor Day weekend in the streets surrounding the Pepsi Center (Speer Blvd. and Chopper Circle). General-admission tickets run $27 to $49 per day for adults, less for children; grandstand seats are more expensive.

For drag racing, head to **Bandimere Speedway,** 3051 S. Rooney Rd., Morrison (© **303/697-6001** or 303/697-4870 for a 24-hr. recording; www.bandimere.com). Races are scheduled from April through October. There are motorcycles, pickup trucks, street cars, and sports cars, plus car shows, swap meets, and other special events.

BASEBALL   The **Colorado Rockies** (© **800/388-7625** or 303/762-5437; www.coloradorockies.com), who began as a National League expansion team in 1993, initially enjoyed record-breaking fan support, but attendance has fallen recently. The team plays at the attractive Coors Field, in historic lower downtown. The 50,000-seat stadium, with a redbrick exterior and on-site microbrewery, was designed in the style of baseball stadiums of old. Tickets are easy to come by, from either the box office or the gaggle of scalpers on the street.

BASKETBALL   The traditionally floundering **Denver Nuggets** (© **303/405-1212** for ticket information; www.nuggets.com) of the National Basketball Association have skyrocketed in popularity thanks to new superstar Carmelo Anthony. The Nuggets play their home games at the handsome Pepsi Center (downtown at Speer Blvd. and Auraria Pkwy.). There are 41 home games a year between November and April, with playoffs continuing into June.

The **University of Denver** (© **303/871-2336** for ticket office) plays a competitive college basketball schedule from late November through March.

FOOTBALL   The **Denver Broncos** (✆ 720/258-3333 for tickets; www.denver broncos.com) of the National Football League make their home at the new Invesco Field at Mile High, after abandoning the legendary Mile High Stadium in 2001. Home games are sold out months in advance, so call early; there are also a few tickets sold on game day. Your best bet may be to find someone hawking tickets outside the stadium entrance on game day. Pricing tickets above face value is technically illegal, but the law is rarely enforced.

You might have better luck getting into a college game. The **University of Colorado Buffaloes** (✆ 303/492-8337; www.cubuffs.com) of the Big Twelve Conference play in Boulder. Other top college football teams in the area are Colorado State University, in Fort Collins, and the Air Force Academy, in Colorado Springs.

GREYHOUND RACING   **Mile High Greyhound Park,** 6200 Dahlia St., Commerce City (✆ 303/288-1591), has parimutuel dog races from June to February, as well as simulcast horse racing year-round. Call for the schedule.

HOCKEY   Denver's National Hockey League team, the **Colorado Avalanche** (✆ 303/405-1212 for ticket information; www.coloradoavalanche.com), plays in front of sellout crowds at the Pepsi Center (Speer Blvd. and Auraria Pkwy.). The season runs from October through April. Tickets are typically expensive and hard to come by.

For a cheaper ticket (and a fun atmosphere), the **University of Denver** (✆ 303/871-2336 for ticket office) men's hockey team (the 2004 and 2005 back-to-back National Champions) plays a competitive schedule between October and mid-March.

HORSE RACING   **Arapahoe Park,** 26000 E. Quincy Ave., Aurora (✆ 303/690-2400), offers horse racing each summer, with simulcast wagering the rest of the year.

RODEO   The **National Western Stock Show, Rodeo and Horse Show** (✆ 303/297-1166; www.nationalwestern.com) is held the second and third week of January. The rodeo takes place at the Denver Coliseum, and other activities at the National Western Complex and the Event Center. With more than $500,000 available in prize money and 600,000 people in attendance, this is one of the world's richest and largest rodeos.

SOCCER   The **Colorado Rapids** (✆ 303/405-1100; www.coloradorapids.com) of Major League Soccer play home games at a new, soccer-only stadium in Commerce City.

7 Shopping

If you're in Denver on foot, you'll find that most visitors do their shopping along the **16th Street Mall** (the mile-long pedestrian walkway between Market St. and Tremont Place), and adjacent areas, including **Larimer Square, the Shops at Tabor Center, Writer Square,** and the newest retail development downtown, **Denver Pavilions.**

Outside the downtown area there are more options, primarily the huge **Cherry Creek Shopping Center**—a shopper's dream—south of downtown. There are also numerous funky urban retail areas within city limits, as well as suburban shopping malls.

Business hours vary from store to store and from mall to mall. Generally, stores are open 6 days a week, with many open on Sunday, too; department stores usually stay open until 9pm at least 1 evening a week. Discount stores and supermarkets are often open later than other stores, and some supermarkets are open 24 hours a day.

SHOPPING A TO Z
ANTIQUES

Denver's main antiques area is **Antique Row,** along **South Broadway** between Mississippi and Iowa streets, with some 400 dealers selling all sorts of fine antiques, collectibles, and junk. Wandering through the gigantic rooms, where each dealer has his or her own little space, is great fun. Just remember that prices are often negotiable; unless you're quite knowledgeable about antiques, it wouldn't hurt to do some comparison shopping before making a major purchase.

Serious antiques hunters will also want to explore the **Antique Mall of Lakewood,** 9635 W. Colfax Ave. (© **303/238-6940**), where about 60 dealers display a wide variety of items from the 18th and 19th centuries, as well as more recent collectibles.

ART & FINE CRAFTS

The renaissance of Denver's lower downtown (LoDo) has resulted in the creation of the **Lower Downtown Arts District,** where you can explore more than two dozen galleries. The district runs from Larimer to Wynkoop streets between 14th and 20th streets. Call © **303/628-5424** or browse **www.lodo.org** for additional information.

A mile to the southeast, the Golden Triangle neighborhood, bordered by Lincoln Street, Speer Boulevard, and Colfax Avenue, has over 25 galleries and a number of museums. The **Golden Triangle Museum District** (© **303/534-0771;** www.gtmd. org) puts together an open gallery event the first Friday night of every month, complete with a free shuttle.

Andenken   Open weekends, this hip LoDo gallery shows the work of contemporary young artists working in every medium under the sun, usually outside the boundaries of tradition. 2110 Market St. © **303/292-3281.**

Camera Obscura *(Finds*   This highly respected gallery exhibits vintage and contemporary photographs, including works by internationally renowned photographers. Closed Monday. 1309 Bannock St. © **303/623-4059.**

Dori Quilts & Lodge Furniture   This 10,000 square foot gallery, which calls itself the largest quilt gallery in America, has some 3,000 to 5,000 handmade quilts on display at any given time. It also sells handmade red cedar log and dried cactus furniture and accessories. Colorado Mills Mall, 14500 W. Colfax Ave., Lakewood © **303/590-1490.**

Native American Trading Company   Older weavings, pottery, baskets, jewelry, and other American Indian works from the Rocky Mountain region are the focus at this fine gallery. Appropriately, it's across the street from the Denver Art Museum. 213 W. 13th Ave. © **303/534-0771.**

Pirate   Denver's oldest arts co-op, Pirate has showcased the work of cutting-edge contemporary artists of all kinds for more than 20 years. It's in a funky north Denver neighborhood with several dining options and a theater. 3655 Navajo St. © **303/458-6058.**

Pismo Contemporary Art Glass   Nationally renowned glass artists, as well as emerging stars, are represented in this gallery, located in Cherry Creek North. 2770 E. 2nd Ave. © **303/333-2879.**

Sandy Carson Gallery   Established regional artists are represented at this respected gallery in a burgeoning gallery area on Santa Fe Drive, which is known for showing contemporary works in traditional media. 760 Santa Fe Dr. © **303/573-8585.**

BOOKS

Barnes & Noble   This two-story location is in the Denver Pavilions retail area on the south side of downtown Denver. There's a particularly good travel section, where you'll find local and regional maps. 500 16th St. (in the Denver Pavilions). ⓒ **303/825-9166.**

Mile High Comics Megastore *(Kids*   One of five Mile High Comics locations in the Denver area, this is the largest comic-book store in the nation. Its 11,000 square feet are packed with comics of all descriptions, plus games, toys, posters, and other books. 9201 N. Washington St., Thornton (10 miles north of downtown Denver). ⓒ **303/457-2612.**

Tattered Cover *ⓡⓡ*   One of the country's largest bookstores, the locally beloved Tattered Cover moved to new digs on East Colfax Avenue in 2006 after more than 30 years in Cherry Creek. Taking over the old Lowenstein Theater, the store remains a bibliophile's paradise, with comprehensive selections on every subject and a design that incorporates elements of the old theater. Also in the development: Twist & Shout, Denver's top indie record store; an art-house movie theater and eatery, the Denver Folklore Center, and a coffee shop. 2526 E. Colfax Ave. (opposite East High School). ⓒ **800/833-9327** or 303/322-7727. www.tatteredcover.com. There are also locations at Denver's LoDo at 16th and Wynkoop sts. (ⓒ **303/436-1070**) and in the Town Center development in Highlands Ranch (ⓒ **303/470-7050**).

FASHION

Eddie Bauer   This is the place to come for good deals on the famous Eddie Bauer line of upscale outdoor clothing. This extra-large store features a wide variety of men's and women's fashions alongside outdoor-oriented gadgetry. 3000 E. Cherry Creek Ave. (in the Cherry Creek Mall). ⓒ **303/377-2100.**

Lawrence Covell   This renowned upscale shop, established in 1967 by Lawrence and Cathy Covell, offers the finest men's and women's fashions, including designer clothing by Kiton, John Lobb, Etro, and Paul Smith. 225 Steele St. (in Cherry Creek N.). ⓒ **303/320-1023.**

Rockmount Ranch Wear *ⓡⓡ*   Founded in 1946 by Jack A. Weil—who is well into his 100s and still serves as CEO—Rockmount is one of the last real Western landmarks in town. The three-generation family business—which was the first company to put a snap on a shirt!—recently turned its landmark warehouse into a retail store, and it's even got a museum of Western wear and memorabilia. The place sells hats, shirts, scarves, and everything else anyone might need to dud up like a cowboy or cowgirl. Rock bands and movie stars love the brand, and even stop by the store on a regular basis. 1626 Wazee St. ⓒ **303/629-7777.**

FOOD & DRINK

King Soopers, Safeway, and **Albertson's** are the main grocery-store chains.

Applejack Liquors *(Value*   This huge store, which covers some 40,000 square feet and claims to be America's largest beer, wine, and liquor supermarket, offers some of the best prices in the area. It also delivers. The store has a wide choice of single-malt scotches; an extensive wine section, which includes a number of Colorado wines; and a good selection of cigars. 3320 Youngfield St. (in the Applewood Shopping Center), Wheat Ridge (I-70 exit 264). ⓒ **303/233-3331.**

Corks/Wine Complements   Side by side near Confluence Park, these two stores offer oenophiles a nice selection of reasonably priced bottles (Corks) and every wine gadget and edible wine accompaniment imaginable (Wine Complements). 1600 Platte St. ⓒ **303/477-5799.**

The Market at Larimer Square   A combination deli/gourmet market/coffee shop right downtown, the Market is something of a community hub for all of downtown Denver. Its location on Larimer Square is ideal for people-watching and convenience. 1445 Larimer Sq. ✆ **303/534-5140.**

Whole Foods   This enormous store helps perpetuate Coloradans' healthy lifestyles. No food sold here contains artificial flavoring or preservatives, nor was any grown using pesticides, chemicals, or other additives. There's sushi, a salad bar, and many to-go lunch and dinner offerings as well. This Cherry Creek–area store, part of the national chain, opened in 2001; others are scattered throughout the metropolitan area. 2375 E. 1st Ave. (at University Blvd.). ✆ **720/941-4100.**

GIFTS & SOUVENIRS
Colorado History Museum Store   This museum shop carries unique made-in-Colorado gifts and souvenirs, including American Indian jewelry and sand paintings, plus an excellent selection of books on Colorado. 1300 Broadway. ✆ **303/866-4993.**

Where the Buffalo Roam   Here you'll find the gamut of traditional Denver and Colorado souvenirs, from T-shirts to buttons to hats to mugs. 535 16th St. ✆ **303/260-7347.**

JEWELRY
Atlantis Gems   This store features unique custom jewelry plus a large selection of loose gemstones and exotic minerals. It also stocks fossils, estate jewelry, and vintage watches; a gemologist is on site. 910 16th St. Mall. ✆ **303/825-3366.**

Jeweler's Center at the University Building   Here you'll find about a dozen retail and wholesale outlets in what is billed as Denver's largest concentration of jewelers. 910 16th St. ✆ **303/534-6270.**

John Atencio   A highly regarded Colorado artist, John Atencio has received several awards for his unique jewelry designs. Located on historic Larimer Square, his store offers 14- and 18-karat gold jewelry accented with high-quality stones, plus special collections such as "Elements," which features unusual combinations of gold, sterling silver, and stones. 1440 Larimer St. (on Larimer Sq.). ✆ **303/534-4277.**

MALLS & SHOPPING CENTERS
Cherry Creek Shopping Center   Saks Fifth Avenue, Neiman Marcus, and Foley's anchor this deluxe million-square-foot mall, with more than 160 shops, restaurants, and services, including an eight-screen movie theater. Across the street is Cherry Creek North, an upscale retail neighborhood. The mall is open Monday through Friday from 10am to 9pm, Saturday from 10am to 8pm, and Sunday from 11am to 6pm. 3000 E. 1st Ave. (between University Blvd. and Steele St.). ✆ **303/388-3900.**

Denver Pavilions   Located on the southern end of the 16th Street Mall., this three-level complex jammed with entertainment and dining options features Denver's Hard Rock Cafe, a movie-plex, Nike Town, a bowling alley, Virgin Records, and Barnes & Noble (see "Books," above). Store hours are Monday through Thursday from 10am to 9pm, Friday and Saturday from 10am to 10pm, and Sunday from 11am to 6pm; the restaurants and movie theaters are open later. 500 16th St. (between Welton and Tremont sts.). ✆ **303/260-6000.**

Larimer Square   This restored quarter of old Denver (see "More Attractions," earlier in this chapter) includes numerous art galleries, boutiques, restaurants, and nightclubs. Most shops are open Monday through Thursday from 10am to 7pm, Friday and Saturday from 10am to 6pm, and Sunday from noon to 5pm. Restaurant and nightclub hours vary, and hours are slightly shorter during the winter. 1400 block of Larimer St. © 303/534-2367.

Mile High Flea Market   Just 10 minutes northeast of downtown Denver, this huge market attracts more than 1.5 million shoppers a year to its 80 paved acres. Besides closeouts, garage sales, and seasonal merchandise, it has more than a dozen places to eat and snack, plus family rides. It's open year-round on Wednesday, Saturday, and Sunday from 7am to 5pm. Admission is $2 Saturday, $3 Sunday, $1 Wednesday, and always free for children under 12. 7007 E. 88th Ave. (at I-76), Henderson. © 303/289-4656.

The Outlets at Castle Rock   This outlet mall between Denver and Colorado Springs, about 30 minutes south of Denver, has about 100 stores, including Levi's, Van Heusen, Eddie Bauer, Bass, Nike, Big Dog, Gap, and Coleman, plus a food court. Open Monday through Saturday from 10am to 8pm and Sunday from 11am to 6pm. I-25 exit 184. © 303/688-4494.

Park Meadows Retail Resort   Located at the C-470/I-25 interchange south of Denver, this is the largest shopping center in Colorado, and now the heart of a mind-boggling retail area. Very posh and upscale—the interior is reminiscent of a luxurious mountain lodge—Park Meadows features Nordstrom, Dillard's, Foley's, and 160 specialty shops and restaurants. Stores are open Monday through Saturday from 10am to 9:30pm, Sunday from 11am to 6pm. 8401 Park Meadows Center Dr. (south of C-470 on Yosemite St.), Littleton. © 303/792-2533.

SPORTING GOODS

Those in need of a bike should talk to the experts at **Campus Cycles,** 2102 S. Washington St. (© **303/698-2811**), which carries the Gary Fisher, Trek, and Giant brands. Sports fans looking for that Rockies cap or Broncos shirt will have no trouble finding it at the appropriately named **Sportsfan,** 1962 Blake St., across from Coors Field (© **303/295-3460**). There are several other locations in the Denver area, and mail orders are accepted.

For information on where to rent sporting-goods equipment, see the "Outdoor Activities" section, earlier in this chapter.

Gart Sports Castle   Active travelers will be pleased to discover that Denver has the world's largest sporting-goods store—this five-story monster. With everything from footballs to golf clubs to tents, the selection is comprehensive. Extras include a driving cage for golfers, ball courts on the roof, and the annual Sniagrab (that's bargains spelled backwards), featuring rock-bottom prices on ski equipment every Labor Day weekend. 1000 Broadway. © **303/861-1122.** www.gartsports.com.

REI 🏃🏃   While the Seattle-based co-op has several stores in the metro area, its flagship store, a beautifully restored redbrick just west of downtown, is one of the country's best and biggest outdoor-oriented retailers. (It is one of only three flagship stores; the others are in Seattle and the Minneapolis area.) This is the place to go before heading for an excursion in the Rockies. The gargantuan store features a climbing wall, an outdoor bike-testing area, a kayaking area on adjacent Cherry Creek, and a "cold room" to try out outerwear and sleeping bags. 1416 Platte St. © **303/756-3100.** www.rei.com.

TOYS & HOBBIES

Caboose Hobbies   Model-train buffs should plan to spend at least half a day here. Billed as the world's largest train store, it stocks electric trains, accessories, books, and so much train-related stuff that it's hard to know where to start. The knowledgeable employees seem just as happy to talk about trains as to sell them. Naturally, there are model trains of every scale winding through the store, as well as test tracks so that you can check out a locomotive before purchasing it. There are also mugs, patches, and decals from just about every railroad line that ever existed in North America. 500 S. Broadway. ℂ **303/777-6766.** www.caboosehobbies.com.

Wizard's Chest *(Kids)* This store's magical design—a castle with drawbridge and moat—and legendary wizard out front are worth the trip alone, but be sure to go inside. The Wizard's Chest is paradise for kids of all ages, specializing in games, toys, and puzzles. The costume department is fully stocked with attire, wigs, masks, and professional makeup. 230 Fillmore St. in Cherry Creek N. ℂ **303/321-4304.** www.wizardschest.com.

8 Denver After Dark

The anchor of Denver's performing arts scene, an important part of this increasingly sophisticated city, is the 4-square-block **Denver Performing Arts Complex,** located downtown just a few blocks from major hotels. The complex houses nine theaters, a concert hall, and what may be the nation's first symphony hall in the round. It is home to the Colorado Symphony, Colorado Ballet, Opera Colorado, and the Denver Center for the Performing Arts (an umbrella organization for resident and touring theater companies).

Denver has some 30 theaters, more than 100 cinemas, and dozens of concert halls, nightclubs, discos, and bars. Clubs offer country-and-western music, jazz, rock, and comedy.

Current entertainment listings appear in special Friday-morning sections of the two daily newspapers, the *Denver Post* and the *Rocky Mountain News. Westword,* a weekly newspaper distributed free throughout the city every Wednesday, has perhaps the best listings: It focuses on the arts, entertainment, and local politics.

You can get tickets for nearly all major entertainment and sporting events from **Ticketmaster** (ℂ **303/830-TIXS**), which has several outlets in the Denver area.

THE CLUB & MUSIC SCENE
ROCK, JAZZ & BLUES

3 Kings Tavern A hard rock venue in the up-and-coming Baker neighborhood, 3 Kings offers a hip vibe, a nice dose of Elvis paraphernalia, and plenty of rockabilly, punk, metal, and country. 60 S. Broadway. ℂ **303/777-7352.** www.myspace.com/3kingstavern.

Bluebird Theater This historic theater, built in 1913 to show silent movies, has been restored and now offers a diverse selection of rock, alternative, and other live music, as well as films. The performers generally target teens and 20-somethings. Tickets usually run $7 to $20. 3317 E. Colfax Ave. (at Adams St.). ℂ **303/322-2308.** www.nipp.com.

The Church Located just a few blocks southeast of downtown, this cavernous and historic former church features three dance floors and several bars, including wine and sushi bars. One of Denver's most popular dance clubs, it attracts celebrity DJs and a throng of beautiful people on a regular basis. The semireligious decor and diverse crowd, in conjunction with the loud music, make for near sensory overload. 1160 Lincoln St. ℂ **303/832-3528.**

El Chapultepec Denver's oldest jazz club, the "Pec" offers live jazz nightly in a noisy, friendly atmosphere. You'll often find standing room only, not to mention a hearty helping of local color—young and old, poor and rich, in equal measure. A small burrito kitchen and poolroom adjoin the club. 1962 Market St. (℃ 303/295-9126.

Gothic Theatre   One of metro Denver's best-looking (and best-sounding) midsize venues, the Gothic is light-years beyond the heavy-metal dive it was in the 1980s. Both local and national acts play the stage here. Tickets usually cost $7 to $30. 3263 S. Broadway, Englewood. (℃ 303/380-2333. www.nipp.com.

Larimer Lounge   This bar on old Larimer Street has been serving drinks since 1892 and serving loud punk rock and alternative music since 2003. The place is out of the hustle and bustle of LoDo, in an old neighborhood east of Broadway, and has seen such national acts as J. Mascis and Black Rebel Motorcycle Club take the stage. The average patron is young, tattooed, and a bit rough around the edges. 2721 Larimer St. (℃ 303/291-1007.

Mercury Cafe   It's hard to classify the Mercury as specializing in any genre of music, but there's always something exciting happening, even on poetry night. It attracts a casual, eclectic clientele. Offerings usually range from avant-garde jazz to classical violin and harp to big band to progressive rock. A healthful-oriented restaurant is also here. 2199 California St. (at 22nd St.). (℃ 303/294-9258. www.mercurycafe.com. Cover free to $10.

COUNTRY MUSIC

Grizzly Rose ℛ   Known to locals as "the Griz" or "the Rose," its 5,000-square-foot dance floor beneath a 1-acre roof has drawn such national acts such as George Thorogood, Garth Brooks, Willie Nelson, Don Williams, LeAnn Rimes, Tanya Tucker, and Johnny Paycheck. There's live music Tuesday through Saturday; Sunday is family night. The cafe serves a full-service menu, and dance lessons are available. 5450 N. Valley Hwy., at I-25 exit 215. (℃ 303/295-1330 or 303/295-2353. www.grizzlyrose.com.

Stampede   This colossal nightclub offers free country-and-western dance lessons on Friday and Saturday, a huge solid oak dance floor, pool tables, a restaurant, and seven bars. It's off I-225 exit 4 (north on Parker Rd. about 2 miles to Havana St.). Closed Sunday through Tuesday. 2430 S. Havana St. (at Parker Rd.), Aurora. (℃ 303/337-6909.

THE BAR SCENE

The first permanent structure on the site of modern Denver was supposedly a saloon, and the city has built on that tradition ever since. Today, there are sports bars, dance bars, lots of brewpubs, outdoor cafe bars, English pubs, Old West saloons, city-overlook bars, Art Deco bars, gay bars, and a few bars we don't want to discuss here.

Appropriately, the newest Denver "in" spot for bar-hopping is also the oldest part of the city—LoDo—which has been renovated and upgraded, and now attracts all the smart Generation Xers and other young professionals. Its trendy nightspots are often noisy and crowded, but if you're looking for action, this is where you'll find it.

Other popular "strips" are along Broadway (centered on 10th and Ellsworth aves., respectively), and along East Colfax Avenue from about Ogden to York streets. For

---

Bottoms Up!

More beer is brewed in metropolitan Denver than in any other city in the United States.

Finds **Brewery Tours**

Whether or not you drink beer, it can be fun to look behind the scenes and see how beer is made. Denver's first modern microbrewery, the **Wynkoop Brewing Co.,** 1634 18th St., at Wynkoop Street (© 303/297-2700), offers tours every Saturday between 1 and 5pm. Housed in the renovated 1898 J. S. Brown Mercantile Building across from Union Station, the Wynkoop is also a popular restaurant (see "Where to Dine," in chapter 5). At least 10 beers are always on tap, including a few exotic recipes—the spicy chili beer is our favorite. If you can't decide which one to try, the "taster set" provides a nice sampling: nine 4-ounce glasses of different brews. For non–beer drinkers, the Wynkoop offers some of the best root beer in town. On the second floor is a top-notch pool hall with billiards, snooker, and darts.

Also downtown, **Flying Dog Brewery,** 2401 Blake St. (© 303/292-5027), offers tours Monday through Friday at 4pm and Saturday at 3pm. The brewery is perhaps best known for its labels, featuring art by Ralph Steadman, an illustrator favored by the late Hunter S. Thompson. Next door and also available for public tour is the distillery for Stranahan's Colorado Whiskey, which has the same ownership.

Since it opened in 1991, **Rock Bottom Brewery,** 1001 16th St. (© 303/534-7616), has been one of the leading brewpubs in the area. Tours, which are given upon request, offer great views of the brewing process, plus a sampling of the product.

Breckenridge Brewery, 471 Kalamath St. (© 303/623-BREW), a mile south of downtown, also lets you see the brewing process. Free brewery tours are given by appointment. In addition to its award-winning ales, the brewery serves traditional pub fare. Breckenridge also has a brew pub at 2220 Blake St., across from Coors Field (© 303/297-3644).

In Cherry Creek, **Bull & Bush Pub & Brewery,** 4700 Cherry Creek Dr. S. (© 303/759-0333), produces about 10 handcrafted ales and will give tours of its facilities upon request. Northwest of Denver, the **Cheshire Cat,** 7803 Ralston Rd., Arvada (© 303/431-9000), is an authentic English pub in a historic building (1891) that offers tours on request.

For a look at the other side of the coin, take a trip to nearby Golden for a look at **Coors,** the world's largest single-site brewery (see "A Side Trip to Colorado's Gold Circle Towns," below).

those who prefer caffeine to alcohol, there are also a number of good coffee bars throughout downtown Denver, as well as the Capitol Hill and Uptown neighborhoods.

The following are among the popular bars and pubs, but there are plenty more, so be sure to check out the publications mentioned at the beginning of this section.

Bull & Bush Pub & Brewery   A neighborhood hangout in Cherry Creek, this re-creation of a famous London pub always has about 10 of its own award-winning beers on tap. On Sunday evening, there's traditional jazz by regional groups. A full brewhouse menu is available. 4700 Cherry Creek Dr. S., Glendale. © 303/759-0333.

Charlie Brown's   Just south of downtown, Charlie Brown's is a piano bar, some version of which has been in existence since 1927. The atmosphere is casual, with a baby grand piano and a diverse crowd. The grill serves three meals a day, inside and outside on a great patio. 980 Grant St. (at 10th Ave.). ℭ **303/860-1655.**

Churchill Bar   You'll find an excellent selection of fine cigars, single-malt Scotch, and after-dinner drinks at this refined cigar bar, which caters to older, well-to-do Establishment types. In the Brown Palace Hotel, 321 17th St. ℭ **303/297-3111.**

Cruise Room Bar   Modeled after a 1930s-era bar aboard the *Queen Mary,* the Cruise Room opened in 1933 on the day Prohibition ended. Recently restored to its Art Deco best, it draws a sophisticated, fairly young crowd with a free jukebox and one of the best martinis in town. In the Oxford Hotel, 1600 17th St. (at Wazee St.). ℭ **303/628-5400.**

Falling Rock Tap House   Comfy, woody, and just down the street from Coors Field, this LoDo pub has 69 beers on tap—the best selection of good beer in Denver. You'll also find darts and pool, happy hours, and occasional live music. 1919 Blake St. ℭ **303/293-8338.**

JR's   A cavernous gay bar with a little bit of country, JR's is centered on a horseshoe-shaped bar and known for its drink specials and busy dance floor. 777 E. 17th Ave. ℭ **303/831-0459.**

Meadowlark   This slick subterranean bar oozes style, featuring plenty of industrial chic, great margaritas, and an eclectic music calendar that's both live and prerecorded. 2721 Larimer St. ℭ **303/293-0251.**

My Brother's Bar   A Platte Valley fixture since the Beat Generation (this was one of Jack Kerouac's favorite Denver hangouts), this is the locals' choice for big, juicy burgers, wrapped in wax paper and served with an array of condiments and a side helping of friendly, unpretentious vibes. 2376 15th St. ℭ **303/455-9991.**

Old Curtis Street Bar   A classic family-owned bar, complete with vinyl booths and a Mexican menu, Old Curtis Street is our pick for a low-key evening downtown. There is an eclectic entertainment calendar featuring punk bands, DJs, and stand-up comedy nights. 2100 Curtis St. ℭ **303/292-2083.**

Samba Room   The atmosphere at the Samba Room—Cuban murals, booming Latin music, a fashionable young clientele—is right up there with Denver's flashiest nightclubs. The menu of Latin-Caribbean fusion, albeit a bit pricey and uneven, adds to the theme. 1460 Larimer St. ℭ **720/956-1701.**

Sing Sing   A noisy, eclectic crowd dominates the scene at this LoDo hot spot, located beneath the Denver ChopHouse & Brewery (see "Where to Dine" in chapter 5). You'll often find low-priced beer specials, which encourage the hard-partying college types to sing along (loudly and badly) with the dueling pianos. A fun place, but hang on tight. Closed Sunday. 1735 19th St. ℭ **303/291-0880.**

Wynkoop Brewing Company   Owned by Denver Mayor John Hickenlooper, Denver's first modern brewpub is still the city's best. Among its most interesting offerings are India pale ale, chile beer, and Scotch ale, but you really can't go wrong with any of the selections. An added attraction is a large upstairs pool hall, which generally attracts a more party-hearty crowd than the restaurant and bar. 1634 18th St. (at Wynkoop St.). ℭ **303/297-2700.**

THE PERFORMING ARTS
CLASSICAL MUSIC & OPERA
Colorado Symphony Orchestra   This international-caliber orchestra performs more than 100 classical, pops, and family concerts each year at locations throughout the metropolitan area, mostly at the Denver Center for the Performing Arts. Tickets run $15 to $70. 1000 14th St., #15. ℂ **303/623-7876.** www.coloradosymphony.org.

Opera Colorado   The company stages three operas (four performances each) with English supertitles each season at the new Ellie Caulkins Opera House at the Denver Performing Arts Complex. Internationally renowned singers and local favorites sing the lead roles. The typical schedule is three evening performances and one matinee each week from February through May. Tickets usually cost $30 to $120. 695 S. Colorado Blvd., #20. ℂ **877/475-4833** for tickets or 303/468-2030. www.operacolorado.org.

THEATER & COMEDY
Buntport Theater   Injecting a fresh dose of originality and zaniness into the Denver theater scene, the Buntport plays host to a number of original productions and touring shows at its black-box-style theater south of downtown. 717 Lipan St. ℂ **720/946-1388.** www.rattlebraintheater.com.

Comedy Works   Considered one of the region's top comedy clubs for more than 20 years, this is your best bet for seeing America's hot comics at work—Dave Chappelle and Lewis Black recently took the stage. Admission is $7 to $10 on weekdays, more on weekends and for marquee performers. Several shows a week are nonsmoking. 1226 15th St. ℂ **303/595-3637.** www.comedyworks.com.

Denver Center for the Performing Arts   An umbrella organization for resident and touring theater, youth outreach, and conservatory training, the DCPA includes the **Denver Center Theatre Company,** the largest professional resident theater company in the Rockies. With 40 artists on its payroll, the troupe performs about 10 plays in repertory from October through June, including classical and contemporary dramas, musicals, and premieres of new plays. Tickets cost roughly $30 to $60. **Denver Center Attractions** brings in over 10 touring Broadway productions annually. Tickets run $20 to $80. For both companies, many shows sell out well in advance. 14th and Curtis sts. ℂ **800/641-1222** or 303/893-4100. www.denvercenter.org.

Denver Civic Theatre   A recently restored 1921 gem, the Denver Civic Theatre is a burgeoning outlet for touring productions, typically a bit edgy. Tickets usually cost $30 to $50. 721 Santa Fe Dr. ℂ **303/309-3773.** www.denvercivic.com.

El Centro Su Teatro   A Hispanic theater and cultural center, El Centro presents bilingual productions on a regular basis. Tickets cost $10 to $20. 4725 High St. ℂ **303/296-0219.** www.suteatro.org.

Lannie's Clocktower Cabaret   In the basement of the landmark D&F Tower on the 16th Street Mall, Lannie's is a funky bordello-inspired theater that sees a wide variety of entertainers on its stage, including hostess/singer Lannie Garrett (known for her portrayal of "Patsy DeCline") as well as burlesque, comedy, and music. In the D&F Tower, 1601 Arapahoe St. ℂ **303/293-0075.** www.lannies.com.

DANCE
Cleo Parker Robinson Dance   A highly acclaimed multicultural modern-dance ensemble and school, the Cleo Parker Robinson group performs a varied selection of

programs each year, both on tour around the world and at several Denver locations. Tickets usually run $25 to $40. 119 Park Ave. W. ℂ 303/295-1759. www.cleoparkerdance.org.

Colorado Ballet   The state's premier professional resident ballet company performs at various theaters downtown. The company presents five productions during its fall-through-spring season—a balance of classical and contemporary works that always includes *The Nutcracker* at Christmastime. Tickets range from $25 to $150. 1278 Lincoln St. ℂ 303/837-8888. www.coloradoballet.org.

MAJOR CONCERT HALLS & AUDITORIUMS

Arvada Center for the Arts & Humanities   This multidisciplinary arts center is in use almost every day of the year for performances by internationally known artists and its own theater companies, its historical museum and art gallery exhibitions, and hands-on education programs for all ages. In addition, the children's theater program performs in front of an annual audience of 60,000. A new, fully accessible playground features a 343-foot sea creature by the name of Squiggles. 6901 Wadsworth Blvd., Arvada (2½ miles north of I-70). ℂ 720/898-7200. www.arvadacenter.org.

Coors Amphitheatre   Formerly Fiddler's Green, alfresco summer concerts here feature national and international stars of rock, jazz, classical, and country music. The amphitheater has about 6,500 reserved seats and room for 10,000 more on its spacious lawn. Located in the southwestern section of the metropolitan area, just west of I-25 between Arapahoe and Orchard roads, it's open from May through September. 6350 Greenwood Plaza Blvd., Englewood. ℂ 303/220-7000.

Denver Performing Arts Complex   Covering 4 square downtown blocks, from Speer Boulevard to 14th Street and Champa to Arapahoe streets, the Center for the Performing Arts (called the "Plex" by locals) is impressive even to those not attending a performance. Its numerous theaters seat from 157 to 2,800, and there's also a restaurant. 14th and Curtis sts. ℂ 800/641-1222 or 303/893-4100. www.denvercenter.org.

Fillmore Auditorium   The 3,600-seat Fillmore is the former Mammoth Gardens, which was recently renovated by proprietors of the legendary Fillmore in San Francisco. The slickly remodeled venue is now one of Denver's best, loaded with bars and countless vintage rock photos. It attracts national rock acts from Ween to Bob Dylan. Tickets generally cost $20 to $100. 1510 Clarkson St. ℂ 303/837-0360. www.fillmoreauditorium.com.

Paramount Theatre   A performing-arts center since 1929, this restored 2,000-seat downtown theater is a wonderful place to enjoy jazz, pop, and folk performances, as well as comedy, lectures, and theater. Recent bookings have included Burt Bacharach and Dwight Yoakam. 1621 Glenarm Place. ℂ 303/623-0106. www.paramountdenver.com.

Red Rocks Amphitheatre 🏚️🏚️🏚️   Quite possibly the country's best and most beautiful venue for top-name outdoor summer concerts, Red Rocks is in the foothills of the Rocky Mountains, 15 miles southwest of the city. Four-hundred-foot-high red sandstone rocks flank the 9,000-seat amphitheater, a product of the Civilian Conservation Corps. At night, with the lights of Denver spread across the horizon, the atmosphere is magical.

The Beatles performed here, as have Jimi Hendrix, Paul Simon, the Grateful Dead, Sting, Bonnie Raitt, Lyle Lovett, and Willie Nelson and top symphony orchestras from around the world. The venue has a sparkling new **visitor center** at the amphitheater's apex, which affords amazing views and displays detailing the varied performances that have taken place here since it opened in 1941. There's also a restaurant. The

trading post carries a good selection of American Indian jewelry and pottery, plus a variety of other curios and souvenirs. I-70 exit 259 S., 16351 County Rd. 93, Morrison. (C) 303/295-4444. www.redrocksonline.com.

9 A Side Trip to Colorado's Gold Circle Towns

Golden, Idaho Springs, and **Georgetown** make up most of the fabled Gold Circle—those towns that boomed with the first strikes of the gold rush in 1859. Central City, once the richest of the four towns but now the least attractive, completes the circle. Central City is trying to relive its glory days with a return to gambling, largely supported by locals from Denver, and although the exteriors of its historic buildings remain appealing, the rows of electronic slot machines and other gambling devices inside are a turnoff. Visitors to the area might like to make a brief stop and then move on to Idaho Springs.

GOLDEN ✦✦

Golden, 15 miles west of downtown Denver by way of U.S. 6 or Colo. 58 off I-70, is better known for the Coors Brewery (founded in 1873) and the Colorado School of Mines (established in 1874) than for its years as territorial capital.

For tourist information, contact the **Greater Golden Area Chamber of Commerce,** 1010 Washington Ave., Golden, CO 80402 ((C) **303/279-3113;** www.golden cochamber.org).

WHAT TO SEE & DO

Historic downtown Golden centers on the **Territorial Capitol** in the **Loveland Building,** 12th Street and Washington Avenue. Built in 1861, it housed the first state legislature from 1862 to 1867, when the capital was moved to Denver. Today it contains offices and a restaurant. The **Armory,** 13th and Arapahoe streets, is probably the largest cobblestone structure in the United States; 3,300 wagonloads of stone and quartz went into its construction. **The Rock Flour Mill Warehouse,** 8th and Cheyenne streets, dates from 1863; it was built with red granite from nearby Golden Gate Canyon and still has its original cedar beams and wooden floors.

In addition to the attractions listed below, see the section on Golden Gate State Park in the Denver "Outdoor Activities" section, earlier in this chapter.

Astor House Museum   This handsome native stone structure, believed to be the first stone hotel built west of the Mississippi River, was constructed in 1867 to house legislators when Golden was the territorial capital. Scheduled for demolition to make space for a parking lot, the Astor House was instead restored in the 1970s and is now listed on the National Register of Historic Places. Today the Western-style Victorian hotel offers glimpses into life in Golden during the town's heyday in the late 19th century. Allow 30 to 60 minutes.

While there, you can obtain a walking-tour guide for the 12th Street Historic District or visit the Victorian Gift Shop, whose proceeds benefit the museum.

822 12th St. (C) 303/278-3557. www.astorhousemuseum.org. Admission $3 adults ($4.50 for combo ticket that also includes Clear Creek History Park), $2 children under 13 ($3 combo ticket). Tues–Sat 10am–4:30pm.

Boettcher Mansion   This historic Jefferson County estate was built by Charles Boettcher in 1917 as a summer home and hunting lodge. It contains displays of furnishings and other items from the American Arts and Crafts period of the late 1800s and early 1900s. Other exhibits explore the history of Golden and the Boettcher family. Allow 1 hour.

900 Colorow Rd. (on Lookout Mountain). (C) 303/526-0855. http://jeffco.us/boettcher/index.htm. Free admission, donations accepted. Mon–Fri 8am–5pm, or by appointment.

Buffalo Bill Museum & Grave (*R* (*Kids*) William Frederick Cody, the famous Western scout, is buried atop Lookout Mountain, south of Golden. (Some folks claim that friends stole Cody's body after his sister sold it to the City of Denver and the *Denver Post,* hightailed it north, and buried it in Wyoming, but we were assured that this was the real McCoy.) The museum contains memorabilia from the life and legend of Buffalo Bill, who rode for the Pony Express, organized buffalo hunts for foreign royalty, and toured the world with his Wild West Show. There are also displays of American Indian artifacts, guns, and Western art; an observation deck provides a great view of Denver. The museum is in 66-acre **Lookout Mountain Park,** a Denver municipal park popular for picnicking. Allow 1 to 1½ hours.

987½ Lookout Mountain Rd. (C) 303/526-0747. www.buffalobill.org. Admission $3 adults, $2 seniors, $1 children 6–15, free for children under 6. May–Oct daily 9am–5pm; Nov–Apr Tues–Sun 9am–4pm. Closed Dec 25. I-70 exit 256.

Clear Creek History Park This 3-acre creek-side park illustrates the history of the area's ranching, with two log cabins, several animal barns, a blacksmith's shop, and a one-room schoolhouse from the 1870s. The buildings were moved to this site to save them from development in nearby Golden Gate Canyon, their original location. Allow about an hour.

11th and Arapahoe sts. in downtown Golden. (C) 303/278-3557. www.clearcreekhistorypark.org. Admission $3 adults ($4.50 for combo ticket that also includes the Astor House Museum), $2 children under 13 ($3 combo ticket). June–Aug Tues–Sat 10am–4:30pm, Sun 1–4pm; May and Sept Sat 10am–4:30pm. Closed Oct–Apr.

Colorado Railroad Museum (*R* Housed in a replica of an 1880 railroad depot, this museum 2 miles east of Golden is a must-see for railroad buffs. On display are more than four dozen narrow- and standard-gauge locomotives and cars, plus other historic equipment, artifacts, photos, documents, and model trains. The exhibits cover 12 acres, including the two-story depot and a working roundhouse. You can climb into many of the old locomotives and wander through the parlor cars. The excellent gift-and-souvenir shop sells hundreds of railroad-related items, from coffee mugs to posters to T-shirts. Allow 1 to 2 hours.

17155 W. 44th Ave. (C) 800/365-6263 or 303/279-4591. www.crrm.org. Admission $8 adults, $7 seniors over 60, $5 children under 16, free for children under 2, $18 families. June–Aug daily 9am–6pm; Sept–May daily 9am–5pm. Closed Jan 1, Thanksgiving, and Dec 25. Follow signs from I-70 exit 265 westbound, exit 266 eastbound.

Colorado School of Mines Geology Museum (*R* Exhibits here help explain the history of mining in Colorado with a replica of a uranium mine and other displays. On exhibit are some 50,000 minerals, gems, fossils, and artifacts from around the world, plus displays on geology, earth history, and paleontology. There's also a kids' corner. The Colorado School of Mines, founded in 1874, has an enrollment of about 3,000. Allow 1 hour.

13th and Maple sts. (C) 303/273-3815. Free admission. School year Mon–Sat 9am–4pm, Sun 1–4pm; summer Mon–Sat 9am–4pm. Call for holiday closures.

Coors Brewing Company Reputedly the world's largest single-site brewery, this facility produces 1.5 million gallons of beer each day. Coors conducts free public tours, followed by free samples of the various beers produced. The entire presentation lasts about 1½ hours. Tours leave a central parking lot at 13th and Ford streets, where visitors board a bus for a short drive through historic Golden before arriving at the brewery. There, a 30-minute walking tour covers the history of the Coors family and

Golden

ATTRACTIONS●
Armory **11**
Astor House Museum **6**
Boettcher Mansion **16**
Buffalo Bill Museum & Grave **18**
Clear Creek History Park **4**
Colorado School of Mines
   Geology Museum **12**
Colorado Railroad Museum **15**
Coors Brewing Company **9**
Foothills Art Center **13**
Golden Pioneer Museum **2**
Heritage Square **20**
Lookout Mountain Nature Center **17**

Loveland Building **6**
Mother Cabrini Shrine **19**
National Earthquake Information Center **14**
Rock Flour Mill Warehouse **1**
Rocky Mountain Quilt Museum **8**

ACCOMMODATIONS■
Golden Hotel **3**
La Quinta Inn–Golden **5**
Table Mountain Inn **10**

DINING◆
The Bridgewater Grill **3**
Old Capitol Grill **7**

company, the barley malting process, the 13,640-gallon gleaming copper kettles, and the entire production process all the way to packaging. Children are welcome, and arrangements can be made for visitors with disabilities and non–English speakers. There's also a gift shop and an interactive time line in the reception area. Allow about 2 hours. *Note:* Visitors 18 and younger must be accompanied by an adult.

13th and Ford sts. ℂ **866/812-2337** or 303/277-2337. www.coors.com. Free admission. Tours Mon–Sat 10am–4pm; gift shop Mon–Sat 10am–5pm. Closed holidays. Visitors under 18 must be accompanied by an adult.

Foothills Art Center   Housed in an 1872 Gothic-style Presbyterian church (which is on the National Register of Historic Places), this exhibition center evolved from the annual Golden Sidewalk Art Show and features changing national and regional exhibits. A gift shop sells crafts by local artisans. Allow 30 minutes.

809 15th St. ℂ **303/279-3922.** www.foothillsartcenter.org. Admission $3 adults, $2 seniors. Mon–Sat 10am–5pm; Sun 1–5pm.

Golden Pioneer Museum   This museum exhibits an impressive collection of furniture, household articles, photographs, and other items, including a re-created 19th-century parlor and boudoir. Especially impressive is its collection of 200 American Indian dolls, representing 39 different tribes from all around North America. There are also a genealogical and historic research library and a small gift shop. Allow 1 hour.

923 10th St. ℂ **303/278-7151.** www.goldenpioneermuseum.com. Admission $3 adults, $2 seniors and children 6–18, free for children under 6, $10 families. Mon–Sat 10am–4:30pm; Memorial Day to Labor Day also Sun 11am–5pm. Closed major holidays.

Heritage Square *Kids*   A family-oriented shopping, dining, and entertainment village with a Wild West theme, Heritage Square features some Victorian specialty shops, a Ferris wheel, a stocked fishing pond, and a dinner theater. Warm-weather activities include go-carts, bumper boats, and a 2,350-foot alpine slide with bobsled-style carts. Heritage Square Music Hall offers shows for adults and children, and there's a nostalgic ice-cream parlor. Allow 1 to 2 hours.

18301 Colfax Ave. (U.S. 40). ℂ **303/279-2789.** www.heritagesquare.info. Free admission; separate charges for individual activities. Memorial Day to Labor Day Mon–Sat 10am–8pm, Sun noon–8pm; rest of year Mon–Sat 10am–6pm, Sun noon–6pm. I-70, exit 259.

Lookout Mountain Nature Center *Kids*   A 1.5-mile self-guided nature trail winds through this 110-acre preserve among ponderosa pines and pretty mountain meadows. A free trail guide is available at the Nature Center when it's open, and a map is on display at a kiosk for those walking the trail at other times. The nonprofit Nature Center has displays on the pine beetle, pollination, and Colorado wildlife, plus an interactive exhibit on the ponderosa pine forest. The building is also worth a look—it's constructed of used and recycled materials such as ground-up plastic soda containers and the pulp of aspen trees. The center schedules free naturalist-guided environmental education activities year-round. Topics vary, but could include the flowers, butterflies, or wildlife of the area, or a look at the night sky. Advance registration is required for most programs, and age restrictions may apply. Call for details. Allow at least 1 hour.

910 Colorow Rd. (on Lookout Mountain). ℂ **303/526-0594.** Free admission. Trail daily 8am–dusk; Nature Center Tues–Sun 10am–4pm in winter; Tues–Fri 10am–4pm and Sat–Sun 9am–5pm in summer.

Mother Cabrini Shrine   A 22-foot statue of Jesus stands at the top of a 373-step stairway adorned by carvings representing the stations of the cross and mysteries of the rosary. Terra-cotta benches provide rest stops along the way. The shrine is dedicated to the country's first citizen saint, St. Frances Xavier Cabrini, who founded the Order of the Missionary Sisters of the Sacred Heart. The order has a convent here with a gift shop that's open from 9am to 5pm daily. Allow 45 to 90 minutes.

20189 Cabrini Blvd. (I-70 exit 259), Lookout Mountain. ℂ **303/526-0758**. www.den-cabrini-shrine.org. Free admission, donations welcome. Daily 7am–5pm; Mass Mon–Sat 7:30am, Sun 7:30am and 11am.

National Earthquake Information Center   The U.S. Geological Survey operates this facility to collect rapid earthquake information, transmit warnings over the Earthquake Early Alerting Service, and publish and disseminate earthquake data. Tours of 30 to 45 minutes can be scheduled by appointment when a guide is available. They include information about the NEIC, the Earthquake Early Alerting Service, and earthquakes in general.

1711 Illinois St. ℂ **303/273-8500** or 303/273-8420. http://neic.usgs.gov. Free admission. Tues–Thurs 9–11am and 1–3pm, by appointment only.

Rocky Mountain Quilt Museum   This museum presents changing exhibits, including works from its permanent collection of over 300 quilts. Consigned works are for sale in the gift shop. Allow 30 minutes.

1111 Washington Ave. ℂ **303/277-0377**. www.rmqm.org. Admission $5 adults, $4 seniors, $3 children 6–12, free for children under 6. Mon–Sat 10am–4pm.

WHERE TO STAY & DINE
La Quinta Inn—Golden, just off I-70 exit 264, at 3301 Youngfield Service Rd. (ℂ **800/531-5900** or 303/279-5565), is a dependable choice, with 129 units and rates of $89 for a double room. **Table Mountain Inn,** 1310 Washington Ave. (ℂ **800/ 762-9898** or 303/277-9898; www.tablemountaininn.com), is a smaller, slightly more expensive alternative. Rates are $120 to $160 double, $175 to $225 suite. Completely renovated in 2004, the **Golden Hotel,** 800 11th St. (ℂ **800/233-7214** or 303/279-0100, www.thegoldenhotel.com), offers the best of the West, old and new, in its attractive guest rooms. Doubles run $149 to $169 and suites $259 to $289.

For a good meal in a historic setting, try the **Old Capitol Grill** in downtown Golden, 1122 Washington Ave. at 12th Street (ℂ **303/279-6390**), offering steak and burgers plus a good selection of sandwiches. Located in the Territorial Capitol Building constructed in 1862, the restaurant is open daily for lunch and dinner, with dinner prices in the $8-to-$18 range. A more upscale dinner choice is **the Bridgewater Grill,** in the Golden Hotel, 800 11th St. (ℂ **303/279-2010**). It serves creative regional fare in the $16-to-$23 range.

IDAHO SPRINGS ⓕ
For visitor information, contact the **Idaho Springs Chamber of Commerce,** P.O. Box 97, Idaho Springs, CO 80452 (ℂ **303/567-4382**). Information on Idaho Springs and the nearby towns of Empire, Georgetown, and Silver Plume is available from the **Clear Creek County Tourism Board,** P.O. Box 100, Idaho Springs, CO 80452 (ℂ **800/88-BLAST** or 303/567-4660; www.clearcreekcounty.org).

WHAT TO SEE & DO
The scenic "Oh My God" dirt road, a steep, winding thoroughfare, runs from Central City through Virginia Canyon to Idaho Springs, although most visitors prefer to take I-70 directly to this community 35 miles west of Denver. The site of a major gold strike in 1859, today Idaho Springs beckons visitors to try their luck at panning for

any gold that may remain. The quaint Victorian downtown is worth a look; don't miss the Bridal Veil Falls tumbling through the largest waterwheel in Colorado, right across from City Hall.

The **Argo Gold Mine, Mill, and Museum,** 2350 Riverside Dr. (*©* **303/567-2421;** www.historicargotours.com), is listed on the National Register of Historic Places, and offers tours daily from mid-April through October from 9am to 6pm. Visitors can see the Double Eagle Gold Mine, relatively unchanged since the early miners first worked it more than 100 years ago, and the mill, where ore was processed into gold. Everyone is welcome to take part in gold- and gemstone-panning. Admission is $15 for adults, $7.50 for children 7 to 12, and free for kids under 7. Allow at least 45 minutes.

At the **Phoenix Gold Mine** *⋒*, on Trail Creek Road (*©* **303/567-0422;** www. phoenixgoldmine.com), you can don a hard hat and follow a working miner through narrow tunnels to see what mining 100 years ago was all about. You can also pan for gold on the property and relax in the picnic area. Weather permitting, the mine is open daily from 10am to 6pm in the summer (call ahead in the winter); the tours are informal and entertaining. Cost is $10 for adults, $8 for seniors, $5 for children 6 to 11, and free for children under 6. Allow about 1 hour.

Just outside Idaho Springs is **Indian Springs Resort,** 302 Soda Creek Rd. (*©* **303/ 989-6666;** www.indianspringsresort.com), a fine spot for a relaxing soak in the hot springs after a long day of skiing or hiking. The resort has a covered swimming pool, indoor and outdoor private baths, and a vapor cave with soaking pools. Rates are $18 to $24 per person for an hour in the private baths or all-day use of the vapor cave, $14 to $16 for all-day use of the pool, and $10 for a mud bath in "Club Mud." Lodging ($78–$120 for two), meals, and weekend entertainment are also offered. The resort is open daily from 7:30am to 10:30pm year-round.

Idaho Springs is the starting point for a 28-mile drive to the summit of 14,260-foot **Mount Evans** *⋒⋒*. From I-70 exit 240, follow Colo. 103—also called Mount Evans Highway—as it winds along Chicago Creek through Arapahoe National Forest to **Echo Lake Park,** another Denver mountain park with fireplaces, hiking trails, and fishing. From here, Colo. 5—the highest paved auto road in North America—climbs to the Mount Evans summit. Views along this highway are of spectacular snowcapped peaks even in June, and you're likely to see mountain goats, bighorn sheep, marmots, eagles, and other wildlife. The road is generally open from Memorial Day to Labor Day. Allow at least 4 hours.

Another way to see this area's great scenery is by horseback. **A&A Historical Trails Stables,** 5 miles up Virginia Canyon from Idaho Springs (*©* **303/567-4808;** www. aastables.com), offers a variety of trail rides, including breakfast and moonlight rides. Rides are usually offered from May through November, weather permitting. A 1-hour ride costs $30 per person, and a 2-hour ride costs $45.

WHERE TO STAY & DINE
H&H Motor Lodge, 2445 Colorado Blvd. (P.O. Box 1359), Idaho Springs, CO 80452 (*©* **800/445-2893** or 303/567-2838; www.hhlodge.com), is a mom-and-pop motel on the east side of town. It offers bright and cheery rooms, TVs with HBO, a hot tub, and a sauna. The 34 rooms and suites include several larger family units. Rates are $59 double for a standard room, kitchenettes $10 to $20 extra; two-bedroom suites start at $69.

Beau Jo's Colorado Style Pizza, 1517 Miner St. (*©* **303/567-4376**), offers a wide variety of so-called mountain pizzas, including standard pepperoni; "Skier Mike's," with Canadian bacon, green peppers, and chicken breast; and a roasted garlic and veggie combo. Sandwiches are also available, plus a salad bar set up in a pair of old clawfoot bathtubs. The bill usually comes out to $10 to $15 per person. Smoking is not permitted.

GEORGETOWN ⚑

A pretty village of Victorian-era houses and stores, Georgetown, 45 miles west of Denver on I-70 at an elevation of 8,500 feet, is named for an 1860 gold camp. Among the best preserved of the foothill mining towns, Georgetown is one of the few that didn't suffer a major fire during its formative years. Perhaps to acknowledge their blessings, townspeople built eye-catching steeples on top of their firehouses, not their churches.

For information on attractions and travel services, drop by or contact the **Georgetown Visitors Center,** 613 6th St. (P.O. Box 444), Georgetown, CO 80444 (✆ **800/ 472-8230** or 303/569-2888), which runs a visitor information center at 6th and Argentine streets across from the Georgetown post office; or **Historic Georgetown, Inc.,** 15th and Argentine streets, P.O. Box 667, Georgetown, CO 80444 (✆ **303/ 569-2840;** www.historicgeorgetown.org).

WHAT TO SEE & DO

The Georgetown–Silver Plume Mining Area was declared a National Historic Landmark District in 1966, and more than 200 of its buildings have been restored.

A convenient place to begin a **walking tour** is the Old County Courthouse, 6th and Argentine streets. Now the community center and tourist information office, it was built in 1867. Across Argentine Street is the Old Stone Jail (1868); 3 blocks south, at 3rd and Argentine, is the Hamill House (see below).

Sixth Street is Georgetown's main commercial strip. Walk east from the Old Courthouse. On your left are the Masonic Hall (1891), the Fish Block (1886), the Monti and Guanella Building (1868), and the Cushman Block (1874); on your right, the Hamill Block (1881) and the Kneisel & Anderson Building (1893). The Hotel de Paris (see below) is at the corner of 6th and Taos. Nearly opposite, at 6th and Griffith, is the Star Hook and Ladder Building (1886), along with the town hall and marshal's office.

If you turn south on Taos Street, you'll find Grace Episcopal Church (1869) at 5th Street, and the Maxwell House (1890) a couple of steps east on 4th. Glance west on 5th to see Alpine Hose Company No. 2 (1874) and the Courier Building (1875). North on Taos Street from the Hotel de Paris are the Old Georgetown School (1874) at 8th Street, First Presbyterian Church (1874) at 9th, Our Lady of Lourdes Catholic Church (1918) at 9th, and the Old Missouri Firehouse (1870) at 10th and Taos.

If you turn west on 9th at the Catholic church, you'll find two more historic structures: the Bowman-White House (1892) at Rose and 9th, and the Tucker-Rutherford House (ca. 1860), a miner's log cabin with four small rooms and a trapper's cabin in back, on 9th Street at Clear Creek.

Georgetown Energy Museum   This small museum is dedicated to educating people about the history of hydropower in Georgetown and Colorado. Located at Georgetown's power plant—built in 1900 and still operating—the museum allows visitors an up-close look at a pair of hydroelectric-generating units in action. The museum also features photographic and text displays detailing the history of similar plants in the region, as well as a collection of antiques: washing machines, stoves, and generator meters. Allow 30 minutes.

600 Griffith St. ⓒ **303/569-3557.** www.georgetownenergymuseum.org. Free admission, donations accepted. June–Sept Mon–Sat 10am–4pm, Sun noon–4pm; Oct–May by appointment only.

Hamill House   Built in Country Gothic Revival style, this house dates from 1867, when silver speculator William Hamill owned it. When Historic Georgetown, Inc., acquired it in 1971, the house had its original woodwork, fireplaces, and wallpaper. A delicately carved outhouse had two sections: one with walnut seats for the family; the other with pine seats for servants. Allow 30 to 60 minutes.

305 Argentine St. ⓒ **303/569-2840.** Admission $5 adults, $4 seniors 60 and older, $4 students, free for children under 6. Memorial Day to Sept daily 10am–4pm; Oct–Dec Sat–Sun noon–4pm. Closed Jan to late May except for pre-arranged tours.

Hotel de Paris ⚘   The builder of the hotel, Louis Dupuy, once explained his desire to build a French inn so far away from his homeland: "I love these mountains and I love America, but you will pardon me if I bring into this community a remembrance of my youth and my country." The hotel opened in 1875 and soon became famous for its French provincial luxury.

Today it's a historic museum run by the National Society of Colonial Dames of America, embellished with many of its original furnishings, including Haviland china, a big pendulum clock, paintings and etchings, photographs by William Henry Jackson, and carved walnut furniture. The kitchen contains an antique stove and other cooking equipment, and the wine cellar houses early wine barrels, with their labels still in place. Allow 45 to 60 minutes.

409 6th St. (at Taos St.). ⓒ **303/569-2311.** www.hoteldeparismuseum.org. Admission $4 adults, $3 seniors 60 and older, $2 children 6–16, free for children under 6. Memorial Day to Labor Day daily 10am–4:30pm; early Sept to Dec and Apr Sat–Sun noon–4pm, weather permitting. Closed Jan–Apr and major holidays.

WHERE TO STAY & DINE

Colorado's oldest continuously operating hotel, about 5 minutes from Georgetown, is the **Peck House Hotel and Restaurant,** 83 Sunny Ave. (P.O. Box 428), on U.S. 40 off I-70 exit 232, Empire, CO 80438 (ⓒ **303/569-9870;** fax 303/569-2743; www. thepeckhouse.com). Established in 1862 as a stagecoach stop for travelers and immigrants from the East Coast, the hotel has an antique-filled parlor lined with photos of the Peck family and their late-19th- and early-20th-century guests. The rooms are comfortable and quaint (claw-foot tubs grace many bathrooms). One of the best parts of a stay here is the fine panoramic view of the Empire Valley afforded by the wide veranda. There are 11 rooms (9 with private bathroom), and rates for two are in the $60-to-$125 range. The hotel's excellent **restaurant** serves fish and steak entrees and seriously delicious hot-fudge cake and raspberries Romanoff. The restaurant serves dinner daily year-round; prices for entrees are $20 to $30.

Back in Georgetown, the **Happy Cooker,** 412 6th St. (ⓒ **303/569-3166**), serves unusual soups, sandwiches on homemade breads, crepes, quiches, and more substantial fare such as frittatas and eggs Benedict, in a converted home in Georgetown's historic business district. It's open Monday through Friday from 7am to 4pm, Saturday and Sunday from 7am to 5pm. Prices are in the $4-to-$8 range, and breakfast is served all day. For a beer, a burger, and a dose of local color, head to the **Red Ram Restaurant & Saloon,** 606 6th St. (ⓒ **303/569-2300**). The menu also has Mexican plates and slow-cooked baby back ribs; prices run $6 to $15 for a main course.

7

Colorado Springs

M agnificent scenic beauty, a favorable climate, and dreams of gold have lured visitors to Colorado Springs and neighboring Pikes Peak Country for well over 100 years.

In 1806, army Lt. Zebulon Pike led a company of soldiers on a trek around the base of an enormous mountain. He called it "Grand Peak," declared it unconquerable, and moved on. Today, the 14,110-foot mountain we know as Pikes Peak has been conquered so often that an auto highway and a cog railway take visitors to the top.

Unlike many Colorado towns, neither mineral wealth nor ranching was the cornerstone of Colorado Springs' economy during the 19th century—tourism was. In fact, Colorado Springs, founded in 1871, was the first genuine resort community west of Chicago. Gen. William J. Palmer, builder of the Denver & Rio Grande Railroad, established the resort on his rail line, at an elevation of 6,035 feet. The state's growing reputation as a health center, with its high mountains and mineral springs, convinced him to build at the foot of Pikes Peak. In an attempt to lure affluent easterners, he named the resort Colorado Springs, because most fashionable eastern resorts were called "springs." The mineral waters at Manitou Springs were only 5 miles away, and soon Palmer exploited them by installing a resident physician, Dr. Samuel Solly, who exuberantly trumpeted the benefits of Manitou's springs both in print and in person.

The 1890s gold strikes at Cripple Creek, on the southwestern slope of Pikes Peak, added a new dimension to life in Colorado Springs. Among those who cashed in on the boom was Spencer Penrose, a middle-aged Philadelphian and Harvard graduate who arrived in 1892, made some astute investments, and became quite rich. Penrose, who believed that the automobile would revolutionize life in the United States, promoted the creation of new highways. To show the effectiveness of motorcars in the mountains, he built (from 1913–15) the Pikes Peak highway, using more than $250,000 of his own money. Then, during World War I, at a cost of more than $2 million, he built the luxurious hotel The Broadmoor at the foot of Cheyenne Mountain. World War II brought the military and defense industry to this area, and in 1958 the $200-million U.S. Air Force Academy opened.

Modern Colorado Springs is a growing city of around 380,000, with over half a million people in the metropolitan area. The majority of its residents are conservative, and the city is also home to some of the country's largest nondenominational churches and conservative groups.

To many visitors, the city retains the feel and mood of a small Western town. Most tourists come to see the Air Force Academy, marvel at the scenery at Garden of the Gods and Pikes Peak, and explore the history of America's West. We're pleased to report that Colorado Springs also has some of the best lodging and dining in the state.

1 Orientation

ARRIVING

BY PLANE

Major airlines offer nearly 100 flights a day to **Colorado Springs Airport,** located north of Drennan Road and east of Powers Boulevard in the southeastern part of the city (© **719/550-1972;** www.flycos.com).

Airlines serving Colorado Springs include **Allegiant** (© 888/594-6937), **American** (© 800/433-7300; www.aa.com), **America West** (© 800/235-9292; www.america west.com), **Continental** (© 800/525-0280; www.flycontinental.com), **Delta** (© 800/221-1212; www.delta.com), **Mesa** (© 800/637-2247; www.mesa-air.com), **Northwest** (© 800/225-2525; www.nwa.com), and **United** (© 800/864-8331; www.united.com).

GETTING TO & FROM THE AIRPORT   Several companies provide airport shuttle services; call © **719/550-1930** for information.

BY CAR

The principal artery to and from the north and south, I-25, bisects Colorado Springs. Denver is 70 miles north; Pueblo, 42 miles south. U.S. 24 is the principal east-west route through the city.

Visitors arriving on I-70 from the east can take exit 359 at Limon and follow U.S. 24 into Colorado Springs. Arriving on I-70 from the west, the most direct route is exit 201 at Frisco, then Colo. 9 through Breckenridge 53 miles to U.S. 24 (at Hartsel), and then east 66 miles to Colorado Springs. This route is mountainous, so check road conditions before setting out in winter.

VISITOR INFORMATION

The **Colorado Springs Convention and Visitors Bureau** is at 515 S. Cascade Ave., Colorado Springs, CO 80903 (© **800/888-4748** or 719/635-7506; fax 719/635-4968; www.experiencecoloradosprings.com). Ask for the free *Official Visitor Guide to Colorado Springs and the Pikes Peak Region,* a colorful booklet with a comprehensive listing of accommodations, restaurants, and other area visitor services, as well as a basic but efficient map. Inquire at the Visitor Information Center or local bookstores for more detailed maps. An excellent one is the Pierson Graphics Corporation's *Colorado Springs and Monument Valley Street Map.* The **Visitor Information Center,** at the south-

---

Heads Up

At an elevation of 6,035 feet, Colorado Springs has two-thirds the oxygen found at sea level; Pikes Peak, at 14,110 feet, has only one-half the oxygen.

---

east corner of Cascade Avenue and Cimarron Street, is open from 8:30am to 5pm daily in summer, Monday through Friday in winter. From I-25, take the Cimarron Street exit (exit 141), and head east about 4 blocks.

Visitors to Manitou Springs—every Colorado Springs visitor should also get to Manitou Springs—can get information from the **Manitou Springs Chamber of Commerce & Visitors Bureau,** 354 Manitou Ave., Manitou Springs, CO 80829 (© **800/642-2567** or 719/685-5089; www.manitousprings.org). You can also contact the **Pikes Peak Country Attractions Association** at the same address (© **800/525-2250;** www.pikes-peak.com).

CITY LAYOUT

It's easy to get around central Colorado Springs, which is laid out on a classic grid pattern.

If you focus on the intersection of I-25 and U.S. 24, downtown Colorado Springs lies in the northeast quadrant, bounded on the west by I-25 and on the south by U.S. 24 (Cimarron St.). Boulder Street to the north and Wahsatch Avenue to the east complete the downtown frame. Nevada Avenue (Bus. 25 and Colo. 115) parallels the freeway for 15 miles through the city, intersecting it twice; Tejon Street and Cascade Avenue also run north-south through downtown between Nevada Avenue and the freeway. **Colorado Avenue** and **Platte Avenue** are the busiest east-west downtown cross streets.

West of downtown, Colorado Avenue extends through the historic Old Colorado City district and the quaint foothill community of **Manitou Springs,** rejoining U.S. 24—a busy but less interesting artery—as it enters Pike National Forest.

South of downtown, **Nevada Avenue** intersects **Lake Avenue,** the principal boulevard into The Broadmoor hotel, and proceeds south as Colo. 115 past Fort Carson.

North and east of downtown, **Academy Boulevard** (Colo. 83) is the street name to remember. From the south gate of the Air Force Academy north of Colorado Springs, it winds through residential hills, crosses Austin Bluff Parkway, then runs without a curve 8 miles due south, finally bending west to intersect I-25 and Colo. 115 at Fort Carson. U.S. 24, which exits downtown east as Platte Avenue, and Fountain Boulevard, which leads to the airport, are among its cross streets. Austin Bluffs Parkway extends west of I-25 as **Garden of the Gods Road,** leading to that natural wonder.

City street addresses are divided by Pikes Peak Avenue into north and south; by Nevada Avenue into east and west.

2 Getting Around

Although Colorado Springs has public transportation, most visitors prefer to drive. Parking and roads are good, and some of the best attractions, such as the Garden of the Gods, are accessible only by car (or foot or bike for the truly ambitious).

BY CAR

For regulations and advice on driving in Colorado, see "Getting Around Colorado" in chapter 2. The **American Automobile Association (AAA)** maintains an office in Colorado Springs at 3525 N. Carefree Circle (© **800/283-5222** or 719/591-2222; www. aaa.com), open Monday through Friday from 8:30am to 5:30pm and Saturday from 9am to 1pm.

CAR RENTALS   Car-rental agencies in Colorado Springs, some of which have offices in or near downtown as well as at the airport, include **Advantage** (© 800/777-5500 or 719/574-1144), **Alamo** (© 800/462-5366 or 719/574-8579), **Avis** (© 800/831-2847 or 719/596-2751), **Budget** (© 800/527-7000 or 719/473-6535), **Enterprise** (© 800/736-8222 or 719/636-3900), **Hertz** (© 800/654-3131 or 719/596-1863), **National** (© 800/227-7368 or 719/596-1519), and **Thrifty** (© 800/847-4389 or 719/390-9800).

PARKING   Most downtown streets have parking meters; the rate is 25¢ for a half-hour. Look for city-run parking lots, which charge 25¢ per half-hour and also offer day rates. Outside of downtown, free parking is generally available on side streets.

BY BUS

Mountain Metropolitan Transit (© 719/385-7433; www.springsgov.com) provides city bus service. Buses operate Monday through Friday from 5:10am to 10:40pm, Saturday from 5:30am to 10:45pm, and Sunday from 7:30am to 5:35pm, except major holidays. Fares on in-city routes are $1.25 for adults; 95¢ students; 60¢ for children 6 to 11, seniors, and passengers with disabilities; and free for children under 6. There is also a free downtown shuttle and free seasonal trolley service in Manitou Springs. Bus schedules can be obtained at terminals, city libraries, and the Colorado Springs Convention and Visitors Bureau.

BY TAXI

Call **Yellow Cab** (© 719/634-5000) for taxi service.

ON FOOT

Each of the main sections of town can easily be explored without a vehicle. It's fun, for instance, to wander the winding streets of Manitou Springs or explore the Old Colorado City "strip." Between neighborhoods, however, distances are considerable. Unless you're particularly fit, it's wise to drive or take a bus or taxi.

FAST FACTS: Colorado Springs

American Express To report a lost card, call © **800/528-4800;** to report lost traveler's checks, call © **800/221-7282.**

Area Code The telephone area code is **719.**

Babysitters Front desks at major hotels often can make arrangements.

Business Hours Most banks are open Monday through Friday from 9am to 5pm, and some have Saturday hours. Major stores are open Monday through Saturday from 9 or 10am until 5 or 6pm (sometimes until 9pm Fri), and often Sunday from noon until 5pm. Stores that cater to tourists are usually open longer in the summer, with shorter hours in winter.

Car Rentals See "Getting Around," above.

Dentists For referrals for dentists who accept emergency patients, contact the **Colorado Springs Dental Society** (© **719/598-5161).**

Doctors For referrals and other health information, call **HealthLink** (© **719/444-2273).**

Drugstores Walgreens, 920 N. Circle Dr. (© **719/473-9090),** has a 24-hour prescription service.

Emergencies For police, fire, or medical emergencies, dial © **911.** To reach **Poison Control,** call © **800/332-3073.**

Eyeglasses You can get 1-hour replacement of lost or broken glasses at **Pearle Vision** in the Citadel Mall (© **719/597-0757)** and **LensCrafters,** in Erindale Centre on North Academy Boulevard (© **719/548-8650).**

Hospitals Memorial Hospital, 1400 E. Boulder St. (© **719/365-5000),** offers full medical services, including 24-hour emergency treatment, as does **Penrose–St. Francis Hospital,** 2215 N. Cascade Ave. (© **719/776-5000).**

Newspapers & Magazines The *Gazette* (www.gazette.com), published daily in Colorado Springs, is the city's most widely read newspaper. The *Denver Post* is also available at newsstands throughout the city. The glossy *Springs* magazine and the politically oriented *Independent* are other free local periodicals. *USA Today* and the *Wall Street Journal* can be purchased on the street and at major hotels.

Photographic Needs There are dozens of photo-finishing outlets throughout the city, including **Walgreens** and **Shewmaker's Camera Shop,** in the Woodmen Valley Shopping Center, 6902 N. Academy Blvd. (℃ **719/598-6412**). For camera and video supplies and repairs as well as photo finishing, go to the downtown location of **Shewmaker's,** 30 N. Tejon St. (℃ **719/636-1696**).

Post Office The main post office is downtown at 201 E. Pikes Peak Ave. Contact the U.S. Postal Service (℃ **800/275-8777**; www.usps.com) for hours and locations of other post offices.

Safety Although Colorado Springs is generally a safe city, it is not crime free. Try to be aware of your surroundings at all times, and ask at your hotel or the visitor center about the safety of neighborhoods you plan to explore, especially after dark.

Taxes Total taxes on retail sales in Colorado Springs amount to about 6.4%; room taxes total about 9%. Rates in Manitou Springs are a bit higher.

Useful Telephone Numbers For **weather and road conditions,** including road construction, throughout the state, call ℃ **303/639-1111** or visit www.cotrip.org.

3 Where to Stay

You'll find a wide range of lodging possibilities here, from Colorado's ritziest resort—The Broadmoor—to basic budget motels. There are also several particularly nice bed-and-breakfasts. The rates listed here are the officially quoted prices ("rack rates") and don't take into account individual or group discounts. Generally, rates are highest from Memorial Day to Labor Day, and lowest in the spring. During graduation and other special events at the Air Force Academy, rates can increase markedly, and you may have trouble finding a room at any price. Rates listed below do not include the lodging tax (about 9% in Colorado Springs, almost 10% in Manitou Springs).

In addition to the accommodations described below, a number of moderately priced chain and franchise motels offer reliable lodging. These include the economical **Best Western Pikes Peak Inn,** 3010 N. Chestnut St., Colorado Springs, CO 80907 (℃ **800/223-9127** or 719/636-5201), which charges $59 to $89 double; **Econo Lodge Downtown,** 714 N. Nevada Ave., Colorado Springs, CO 80903 (℃ **800/553-2666** or 719/636-3385), with rates from $35 to $85 double; the attractive and well-maintained **Rodeway Inn & Suites Garden of the Gods,** 555 W. Garden of the Gods Rd., Colorado Springs, CO 80907 (℃ **800/828-4347** or 719/593-9119), with rates for two of $61 to $106; and **Super 8,** near Garden of the Gods at 4604 Rusina Rd., Colorado Springs, CO 80907 (℃ **800/800-8000** or 719/594-0964), which charges $45 to $65 double.

Colorado Springs

DINING ◆
Adam's Mountain Café **52**
Amanda's Fonda **45**
The Blue Star **23**
Charles Court **31**
Cliff House Dining Room **51**
Craftwood Inn **47**
Dutch Kitchen **55**
Edelweiss Restaurant **24**
The Famous **15**
Giuseppe's Old Depot Restaurant **12**
La Petite Maison **5**
Margarita at PineCreek **39**
Marigold Café & Bakery **42**
Meadow Muffins **2**
Michelle's **11**
Phantom Canyon Brewing Co. **14**
Ritz Grill **16**
Summit **28**
The Tavern **29**
Walter's Bistro **25**
The Warehouse **18**

ACCOMMODATIONS ■
Antlers Hilton Hotel **13**
Best Value Inn Villa Motel **48**
Best Western Pikes Peak Inn **43**
The Broadmoor **30**
Cheyenne Mountain Resort **26**
Cliff House at Pikes Peak **51**
Doubletree Hotel
 World Arena **22**
Eastholme in the Rockies **58**
Econo Lodge Downtown **8**
Holden House 1902 B&B Inn **4**
Old Town GuestHouse **1**
Rodeway Inn & Suites
 Garden of the Gods **41**
Sheraton Colorado Springs
 Hotel **22**
Super 8 **41**
Travel Inn **19**
Two Sisters Inn **54**

ATTRACTIONS●

Arcade Amusements, Inc. **53**
Cave of the Winds **50**
Cheyenne Mountain Zoo **33**
Colorado Springs Fine Arts Center **6**
Colorado Springs Pioneers Museum **17**
Garden of the Gods **46**
Ghost Town **3**
Manitou Cliff Dwellings Preserve & Museums **49**
May Natural History Museum of the Tropics **34**
McAllister House **10**
Memorial Park **21**
Miramont Castle Museum **56**

Money Museum **7**
Monument Valley Park **9**
North Cheyenne Cañon Park & Starsmore Discovery Center **60**
North Pole/Santa's Workshop **59**
Palmer Park **36**
Peterson Air & Space Museum **35**
Pikes Peak Cog Railway **57**
ProRodeo Hall of Fame & American Cowboy Museum **40**
Rock Ledge Ranch Historic Site **44**
Seven Falls **32**
United States Air Force Academy **38**
United States Olympic Complex **20**
Western Museum of Mining & Industry **37**
World Figure Skating Museum & Hall of Fame **27**

Those looking for a more upscale chain won't go wrong with the **Doubletree Hotel World Arena,** 1775 E. Cheyenne Mountain Blvd. (I-25 exit 138), Colorado Springs, CO 80906 (✆ **800/222-TREE** or 719/576-8900); or the **Sheraton Colorado Springs Hotel,** 2886 S. Circle Dr. (I-25 exit 138), Colorado Springs, CO 80906 (✆ **800/981-4012** or 719/576-5900).

VERY EXPENSIVE

The Broadmoor ✸✸✸ *(Kids)*   We thought The Broadmoor couldn't get much better, but it continues to reinvest in itself. The storied resort keeps itself on the forefront of luxury, where it's been since Spencer Penrose originally opened it in 1918. (The first names entered on the guest register were those of John D. Rockefeller, Jr., and his party.) Today The Broadmoor is an enormous resort complex of historic pink Mediterranean-style buildings with modern additions, set at the foot of Cheyenne Mountain on magnificently landscaped 3,000-acre grounds about 3½ miles southwest of downtown Colorado Springs. The original Italian Renaissance–style main building features a marble staircase, chandeliers, Italian tile, hand-painted beams and ceilings, and a carved-marble fountain, not to mention a priceless art collection with original work by Toulouse-Lautrec and Ming dynasty ceramicists.

Behind the main building is lovely Cheyenne Lake; a swimming pool almost seamlessly attached to the west end looks like a part of the lake. This swimming complex will make you think you're at an ocean-side beach resort, with water slides, two outdoor hot tubs, 13 cabanas, and an outdoor cafe. The guest rooms occupy a series of separate buildings centered on the lake and pool area. The spacious, luxurious rooms are beautifully decorated in European style, with chandeliers, Italian fabrics, rich wood, and limited-edition works of art. Most units hold two double beds or one king-size bed, desks and tables, plush seating, two-line portable phones, and wireless Internet access. Many rooms contain large soaking tubs and separate marble showers; some in the South Tower have high-tech touch screens that control the lights, drapes, and even the "Privacy" and "Do Not Disturb" lights in the hall. The service is impeccable: The hotel averages two employees for every guest.

Lake Circle, at Lake Ave. (P.O. Box 1439), Colorado Springs, CO 80901. ✆ 800/634-7711 or 719/634-7711. Fax 719/577-5700. www.broadmoor.com. 700 units. May–Oct $385–$550 double, $550–$900 standard suite; Nov–Apr $280–$425 double, $420–$740 standard suite; year-round up to $3,500 large suite. AE, DC, DISC, MC, V. Valet parking $15, self-parking $12. **Amenities:** 12 restaurants (all Continental, American, or Contemporary); 4 lounges; outdoor pool cafe; 3 swimming pools (indoor, outdoor with water slide, outdoor lap pool); 2 outdoor hot tubs; 3 18-hole golf courses; 9 all-weather tennis courts; state-of-the-art fitness center and full-service spa with aerobics classes, saunas, and whirlpool tubs; paddleboats; bicycle rentals; children's programs (summer); riding concierge; car-rental agency; shopping arcade; 24-hr. room service; in-room massage; valet laundry; stables; fly-fishing school; movie theater; shuttle bus between buildings; service station. *In room:* A/C, cable TV, dataport, minibar, coffeemaker, hair dryer, iron, safe.

EXPENSIVE

Antlers Hilton Hotel ✸   The Antlers has been a Colorado Springs landmark for more than a century. Although it is in many ways geared to business travelers, for vacationers it offers the best accommodations within a short walking distance of many of downtown Colorado Springs' major attractions and restaurants. There have been three different Antlers on this site. The first, a turreted Victorian showcase built in 1883, was named for General William Palmer's collection of deer and elk trophies. After it was destroyed by fire in 1898, Palmer built an extravagant Italian Renaissance–style building that survived until 1964, when it was leveled to make room for the more contemporary Antlers Plaza. Antique black-walnut nightstands from the previous incarnation provide a touch of historic continuity to the spacious guest rooms, which are handsomely decorated in earth tones with rich wood furnishings. The corner rooms are larger, and we prefer the west-side rooms, which provide great views of Pikes Peak.

4 S. Cascade Ave., Colorado Springs, CO 80903. ℂ **877/754-9940** or 719/473-5600. Fax 719/389-0259. www.antlers. com. 292 units. Summer $139–$300 double; $250–$1,000 suite. AE, DC, DISC, MC, V. Valet parking $12, self-parking $8. **Amenities:** 2 restaurants (American); indoor pool; fitness center; whirlpool; salon; room service (6:30am–11pm); laundry. *In room:* A/C, cable TV, coffeemaker, hair dryer, iron.

Cheyenne Mountain Resort ℛℛ   Set at the foot of Cheyenne Mountain, this resort was built at a preexisting country club with a Pete Dye–designed golf course in 1985, and is something of a less expensive alternative to The Broadmoor, just a few miles uphill. With a stunning view of the mountain from the lobby, the Cheyenne Mountain Resort features top-notch recreational facilities and attracts numerous conferences and meetings, but is an outstanding choice for tourists as well. The rooms—which are in a series of buildings set off from the main lodge—are rich and masculine, and have either one king or two queens (or both in some suites). The bathrooms are a cut above, with granite counters and shower/tub combos, as well as jetted soakers in the executive suites. All rooms have a private balcony, and most of them have great views.

3225 Broadmoor Valley Rd. Colorado Springs, CO 80906. ℂ **800/428-8886** or 719/538-4000. Fax 719/540-5779. www. cheyennemountain.com. 321 units, including 5 suites. Summer $129–$209 double; $485–$650 suite. AE, DC, DISC, MC, V. Free parking. **Amenities:** 2 restaurants (American); 2 lounges; indoor pool; 18-hole golf course; 18 indoor tennis courts; health club; Jacuzzi; sauna; bike rental; children's programs; concierge; business center; room service (7am–11pm); massage; dry cleaning. *In room:* A/C, cable TV w/pay movies, coffeemaker, hair dryer, iron, Wi-Fi network.

Cliff House at Pikes Peak ℛℛ *Finds*   Striving to compete with the best that Colorado has to offer (and doing a pretty good job), the Cliff House is an old yet new facility. Built in 1874, it was designated a National Historic Landmark in 1980, and has hosted such eminent guests as Theodore Roosevelt, Clark Gable, and Thomas Edison. A major fire forced the Cliff House to close in 1982, and it remained closed until a massive reconstruction in 1997. The project incorporated several pieces of the hotel's original decor, including ornate woodwork and a tile fireplace, and what the fire destroyed was replicated with an emphasis on attention to detail. Once again a grand and luxurious hotel, the Cliff House reopened in 1999.

Today, the lovely, uniquely decorated accommodations vary in size and personality, although the overall decor is Queen Anne–Victorian. Units range from average-size, relatively simple studios to large, luxurious celebrity suites named for former guests. Some units have gas fireplaces, two-person spas, steam showers, and terrific views of the mountains. All have live flowering plants, robes, heated toilet seats, working desks, and high-speed Internet access. We wouldn't turn down any room at the Cliff House, but our favorite is definitely the Clark Gable Suite ($475 double in summer), which is decorated in subdued Hollywood style—if you can call leopard-print wallpaper subdued—and contains a shower for two, a jetted tub, a wet bar and refrigerator, two TVs, a gas fireplace, and photos of Clark, who stayed at the hotel in the early 1940s.

There's a fine dining restaurant (see "Where to Dine," below), and the entire property is nonsmoking.

306 Cañon Ave., Manitou Springs, CO 80829. ℂ **888/212-7000** or 719/685-3000. Fax 719/685-3913. www.thecliff house.com. 55 units. $145–$200 double; $189–$475 suite. Children under 13 stay free in parent's room. Rates include breakfast buffet. AE, DC, MC, V. **Amenities:** Restaurant (American); bar; small fitness center; concierge; activities

desk; airport pickup; room service 7am–11pm; on-call massage; valet laundry service. *In room:* A/C, cable TV/VCR, dataport, coffeemaker, hair dryer, iron, safe, CD player.

Old Town GuestHouse 🎔🎔   Just a half-block south of the main street of Colorado Springs' historic Old Colorado City stands this three-story redbrick inn. It may appear to be from the 1890s, but it actually dates from the 1990s. As a result, it features all the modern amenities, not to mention great service from innkeepers Don and Shirley Wick, who've owned the inn since 2005.

All eight of the individually decorated rooms are named for flowers: for example, Colorado Columbine, with a mountain mural above the king bed; Moroccan Jasmine, with a Sahara Desert theme; Oriental Poppy, decorated with collectibles from the Orient; and romantic Victorian Rose. Each room has individual climate control, robes, and a queen or king bed. Several have gas-log fireplaces, seven have a private porch or balcony, and some have steam showers for two or private outdoor hot tubs. There's an elevator, and one room is ADA compliant.

The attractive library has a fireplace, music, and overstuffed chairs. Downstairs is a game room with pool table and exercise equipment, plus wireless Web access throughout the inn.

115 S. 26th St., Colorado Springs, CO 80904. ✆ **888/375-4210** or 719/632-9194. Fax 719/632-9026. www.oldtown-guesthouse.com. 8 units. $99–$210 double. AE, DISC, MC, V. Off-street parking. Children under 12 not accepted. *In room:* A/C, cable TV/VCR/DVD, fridge, coffeemaker, hair dryer, iron.

MODERATE

Eastholme in the Rockies 🎔   Nestled in the quaint Pikes Peak mountain village of Cascade, 10 miles west of downtown Colorado Springs, this Victorian B&B gives guests an opportunity to see the city and get away from it all in the same day. Originally built in 1885 as a resort hotel, this property has a storied history that includes a stint as a boarding house before becoming a guest inn in 1988. Today it is a favorite of vacationers who want to be within striking distance of city attractions, but whose main interests lay in the Rockies.

The parlor holds a bay window, fireplace, and antiques. Most of the inn's large rooms feature 10-foot ceilings, and all provide plush quilts and remarkable views. The Marriott and Eisenhower suites feature original furnishings and a plethora of antiques, and the cottages offer VCRs, fireplaces, and spacious bathrooms with whirlpool tubs.

Breakfasts include freshly baked breads, pastries, and entrees such as soufflés or frittatas; gourmet dinners are available with advance reservations. The mountainous pine scenery of the Pike National Forest surrounds Eastholme, and stargazers love the views from the second-floor balcony, free of the light pollution of Colorado Springs. Guest amenities include a wedding gazebo, shared kitchen, and library. Smoking is not permitted.

4445 Hagerman Ave. (P.O. Box 98), Cascade, CO 80809. ✆ **800/672-9901** or 719/684-9901. www.eastholme.com. 8 units (6 with bathroom), including 2 cottages. $85–$135 double; $135 suite; $150 cottage. Rates include full breakfast. AE, DISC, MC, V. Free parking. 10 miles west of I-25, about 1 mile off U.S. 24. **Amenities:** Hot tub. *In room:* Cable TV/VCR, fridge, coffeemaker, hair dryer.

Holden House 1902 Bed & Breakfast Inn 🎔🎔   Innkeepers Sallie and Welling Clark restored this storybook 1902 Colonial Revival–style Victorian house, adjacent carriage house, and the 1898 house next door, filling the rooms with antiques and family heirlooms. Located near Old Colorado City, the inn has a living room with a

<Kids> **Family-Friendly Hotels**

The Broadmoor (p. 150)   A lake and pool area with a terrific water slide, plus tennis, golf, riding stables, and a great summer kids' program that includes a visit to the Cheyenne Mountain Zoo all add up to a wonderful family experience.

Sheraton Colorado Springs Hotel (p. 150)   Two swimming pools, a separate children's pool, shuffleboard, and a putting green should keep most kids occupied.

tile fireplace, a front parlor with a bay window, verandas, and a lovely garden out back. Guests enjoy 24-hour coffee and tea service with a bottomless cookie jar, an afternoon wine social, and a gourmet breakfast in the formal dining room. Smoking is not allowed and pets are not permitted—except the two resident cats, Mingtoy and Muffin.

Two suites are in the main house, two are in the adjacent carriage house, and one is in the second home. Each guest room bears the name of a Colorado mining area and contains memorabilia of that district. All have sitting areas, queen-size beds, fireplaces, CD/DVD players, and tubs for two. The Cripple Creek suite features Victorian fretwork in the sitting area, a mahogany fireplace, and a magnificent Roman marble tub. The Independence Suite is accessible to guests with disabilities and is located in the house next door.

1102 W. Pikes Peak Ave., Colorado Springs, CO 80904. © 888/565-3980 or 719/471-3980. Fax 719/471-4740. www. holdenhouse.com. 5 suites. $140–$150 double. Rates include full breakfast. AE, DC, DISC, MC, V. Children not accepted. *In room:* A/C, TV/DVD, fridge, hair dryer, iron, wireless Internet access.

Two Sisters Inn 🕸🕸   Built by two sisters in 1919 as a boarding house, this splendid bed-and-breakfast has been owned and operated by two women—sisters in spirit if not in blood—since 1990. Wendy Goldstein and Sharon Smith have furnished the four bedrooms and separate honeymoon cottage with family heirlooms and photographs, in a style best described as informal elegance. The rooms in the main house feature Victorian frills and furnishings, such as quilts and claw-foot bathtubs. The two rooms that share a bathroom are only rented together ($75 for the second bedroom), which is a great choice for two couples or for parents traveling with teenagers. Across a splendid garden area, the small cottage, with a separate bedroom and living room, has a feather bed, gas-log fireplace, refrigerator, and shower with skylight. Fresh flowers adorn each room, and homemade chocolates and baked goods are served upon arrival.

The rooms are great, but we especially like the breakfasts, which the proprietors describe as "healthy decadence." They often cook with herbs and vegetables from their garden, and do some marvelous things with fruit. In the summer, Wendy and Sharon's lemonade, made fresh with naturally sparkling Manitou Springs water, is the perfect refreshment. Smoking is not permitted.

10 Otoe Place, Manitou Springs, CO 80829. © 800/2SISINN or 719/685-9684. www.twosisinn.com. 5 units. $120 double; $135 cottage. Rates include full breakfast. DISC, MC, V. Children under 10 not accepted. Located 1 block south of the town clock on Manitou Ave.

INEXPENSIVE

Best Value Inn Villa Motel A solid option right off the main drag in Manitou Springs, the Villa offers well-kept rooms and reasonable rates within walking distance of all of Manitou's restaurants and shops, as well as some older cottages that are the least expensive rooms on-site. While the cottages have two double beds, the newer motel rooms have two queens or a king, and deluxe rooms have a jetted tub and a kitchenette to boot.

481 Manitou Ave., Manitou Springs, CO 80829. (©) **888/315-2378** or 719/685-5492. www.villamotel.com. 47 units. $55–$105 double. AE, DC, DISC, MC, V. Free parking. **Amenities:** Large outdoor pool. *In room:* A/C, cable TV, fridge, coffeemaker, hair dryer, iron, wireless Internet access, microwave.

Travel Inn *(Value)* Popular with both business travelers and vacationers on a budget, the Travel Inn offers a comfortable place to sleep at very reasonable rates. The two-story motel with bright turquoise trim is conveniently located near downtown Colorado Springs, with easy access to all the area attractions on I-25 and U.S. 24. The recently remodeled rooms are simple and comfortable, with white stucco walls and dark-wood furnishings. There is one apartment with a kitchenette that is designed for longer stays.

512 S. Nevada Ave., Colorado Springs, CO 80903. (©) **719/636-3986.** Fax 719/636-3980. 34 units (most with shower only). Summer $49–$69 double; winter $35–$45 double. Rates include continental breakfast. AE, DC, DISC, MC, V. Free parking. **Amenities:** Outdoor heated pool (seasonal); coin-op washers and dryers. *In room:* A/C, cable TV.

CAMPING

Also see the section on **Mueller State Park** under "Parks & Zoos," later in this chapter.

Garden of the Gods Campground Located near Garden of the Gods (see "Attractions," p. 161), this large, tree-shaded campground offers 250 full RV hookups (30- and 50-amp service, some with modems and phones), and additional tent sites. Facilities include tables, barbecue grills, bathhouses, a grocery store, Internet cafe, laundry, heated swimming pool, whirlpool tub, playground, and clubhouse with pool tables and game room. The 12 camping cabins, which share the campground's bathhouse, rent for $45 to $50 double. There are also motel-style rooms for $60 to $120 double.

3704 W. Colorado Ave., Colorado Springs, CO 80904. (©) **800/248-9451** or 719/475-9450. www.coloradocampground. com. $28–$40 for 2 people. Extra person $3. DISC, MC, V. Take I-25 exit 141, head west on U.S. 24, then north (right) on 31st St., then left on Colorado Ave. for 6 blocks (keep right), and turn right to gate.

4 Where to Dine

Colorado Springs has an excellent variety of above-average restaurants, with a good sampling of continental cuisine, Mexican restaurants, and steak joints. See also the section on dinner theaters in "Colorado Springs After Dark," later in this chapter. A good online resource for information on area restaurants and nightlife is www.scene inthesprings.com.

VERY EXPENSIVE

Charles Court *(★★)* PROGRESSIVE AMERICAN The English country-manor atmosphere of this outstanding restaurant at The Broadmoor resort, with picture windows looking across Cheyenne Lake to the renowned hotel, lends itself to a fine dining experience. The creative American menu, which changes seasonally, has a decidedly Rocky Mountain emphasis. You'll usually find such delicacies as a Colorado lamb rib-eye, beef tenderloin, wild king salmon, honey-lacquered duck, and a wild-game selection such as prime rib of venison. The wine list includes more than 600 selections, service is superlative, and the desserts are extraordinary. A seasonal outdoor patio provides splendid views of the mountains across the lake.

Broadmoor W., in The Broadmoor, Lake Circle. ℂ **719/634-7711**. Reservations recommended. Breakfast $7.75–$16; dinner main courses $22–$38. AE, DC, DISC, MC, V. Daily 7–11am and 6–10pm.

Cliff House Dining Room ☆☆ AMERICAN   The Cliff House Dining Room is an excellent choice for a romantic occasion. The Villeroy & Boch china, damask linen, crystal glassware, and 19th-century tiled fireplace evoke the charm of the Victorian era. Dinners are the main event; old favorites expertly prepared in new ways. We recommend the filet mignon, charbroiled with roasted garlic pepper, and the seafood (trout to scallops and prawns), but everything is quite good. As would be expected, service is impeccable. The breakfast menu offers traditional American selections, plus a nifty wild-mushroom Florentine with smoked bacon, and lunches are upscale sandwiches and entrees like quiche du jour and blackened ruby red trout. The excellent wine list includes some 600 selections.

Cliff House Inn, 306 Cañon Ave., Manitou Springs. ℂ **719/785-2415**. Reservations recommended. Lunch main courses $7–$24; fixed-price lunch $18; dinner main courses $24–$32. AE, DC, DISC, MC, V. Daily 6:30–10:30am, 11:30am–2:30pm, and 5:30–9:30pm.

Craftwood Inn ☆☆☆ *Finds* COLORADO CUISINE   Ensconced in an English Tudor building with beamed ceilings, stained-glass windows, and a copper-hooded fireplace, the casually elegant Craftwood Inn, built in 1912, was originally a coppersmith's shop. Today this excellent restaurant specializes in regional game and also offers steak, seafood, and vegetarian dishes. The extensive selection of game—elk, venison, pheasant, quail, caribou, antelope, wild boar, ostrich, and buffalo—attracts the most acclaim. We especially recommend grilled Rocky Mountain elk steak (when available), marinated in herb and smoke-infused oil, and served with a cabernet sauvignon hunter's sauce. The adventurous might opt for the wild grill: elk, antelope, and venison, each accompanied by a distinctive sauce. Be sure to save room for one of the superb—and somewhat unusual—desserts, such as jalapeño white-chocolate mousse with raspberry sauce, or prickly pear sorbet. The outdoor patio provides wonderful views of Pikes Peak.

404 El Paso Blvd., Manitou Springs. ℂ **719/685-9000**. Reservations recommended. Main courses $18–$38. AE, DC, DISC, MC, V. Daily 5:30–8:30pm. Turn north off Manitou Ave. onto Mayfair Ave., go uphill 1 block, and turn left onto El Paso Blvd.; the Craftwood is on your right.

The Famous ☆☆ STEAK   A swank urban steakhouse, the Famous is a magnet for beefeaters, serving up choice cuts of U.S. Prime. It's hard to go wrong here, but bring an appetite: No steak is less than a pound, outside of two filets. We like the Kansas City Bone-In Strip, but everything is top-shelf here, even the nonbeef fare, like salmon, Colorado lamb, and chicken Oscar. The lunch menu is similarly carnivorous, with a few salads for good measure. There are shiny booths and jet black tables, as well as a full bar and live piano every night.

31 N. Tejon St. ℂ **719/227-7333**. Reservations recommended. Main courses $8–$16 lunch, $22–$40 dinner. AE, DISC, MC, V. Sun–Thurs 11am–3pm and 5–10pm; Fri–Sat 11am–3pm and 5–11pm.

Summit ☆☆☆ CONTEMPORARY AMERICAN   Flashy, modern, and brand-new in 2006, Summit is a departure from The Broadmoor's typical eatery formula—Continental has long ruled the roost here—but it quickly rose to the top of the local

culinary stratosphere. Designed by acclaimed architect Adam Tihany, the strikingly contemporary room is at once slick and romantic, with cloth chandeliers, contemporary metalwork on the windows and walls, and a glassed-in, rotating turret holding 432 bottles of wine behind the bar. The visual spectacle is aesthetically matched by the fare, which is innovative and adventurous—the seasonal menu might have a terrific roasted beet salad or monkfish *osso bucco,* but it depends on what's currently domestically available. The service is impeccable, and the sommelier is skilled at wine pairings from the 2,000-bottle inventory.

In The Broadmoor, 19 Lake Circle. ℰ 719/577-5896. www.summitatbroadmoor.com. Reservations recommended. Main courses $18–$32. AE, DC, DISC, MC, V. Daily 5:30–9pm.

Walter's Bistro ✿✿ CONTINENTAL   Slick but not stuffy, Walter's manages to be classy, casual, and classic, all at once. Proprietor Walter Iser, a native of Salzburg, Austria, has long worked the front of the house in various upscale properties in Colorado Springs and environs, but he's truly hit his stride with Walter's, which opened in 1999 and relocated to a handsome new location in 2004. Watching over four dining areas—including a richly decorated "red room" and a chef's table beneath windows into the kitchen—Iser's gracious style and steady direction leads right into an expertly prepared menu of continental staples that manage to simultaneously taste traditional and completely original. The menu changes regularly, but our visit included a terrific rack of lamb, herb-roasted and served with a creamy English pea risotto, pan-roasted Chilean sea bass, and a truly phenomenal bone-in filet mignon with an equally superlative bread pudding with wild mushrooms and andouille sausage. Desserts are decadent, including a chocolate "bag" filled with tiramisu, and the wine list is long and varied.

136 E. Cheyenne Mountain Blvd. ℰ 719/630-0201. Reservations recommended. Lunch main courses $7–$24; fixed-price lunch $18; dinner main courses $24–$32. AE, DC, DISC, MC, V. Mon–Fri 11am–2pm and 5:30–9pm; Sat 5:30–9pm.

EXPENSIVE

The Blue Star ✿✿ INTERNATIONAL FUSION   In a quiet area just south of downtown, the Blue Star is one of the most popular eateries in Colorado Springs, and deservedly so. The menu changes monthly, but it always includes filet mignon, fresh fish (flown in daily), pork, and chicken, prepared with a nose for invention. The culinary inspiration comes from both Mediterranean and Pacific Rim cultures; the restaurant might serve Thai chile beef tips with avocado sorbet one week and beef bourguignon the next. Social and colorful, the bar features sleek wood and metal decor and walls adorned with well-lit artwork, while the dining room's atmosphere is milder with an open kitchen. Each room serves its own menu: The bar room is "eating" (that is, lunch, dinner, tapas, live jazz Monday, dancing on weekends) and the main room is serious "dining" (dinner only, as the proprietors say). Blue Star has won *Wine Spectator*'s "Best of" award with its 8,500-bottle cellar since 2003.

1645 S. Tejon St. ℰ 719/632-1086. www.thebluestar.net. Reservations recommended. Main courses $6–$14 lunch, $9–$25 dinner. AE, MC, V. Dining room Sun–Thurs 5:30–9pm; Fri–Sat 5:30–10pm. Bar open during restaurant hours; bar food service Mon–Wed 11:30am–10:30pm, Thurs–Fri 11:30am–midnight, Sat 3pm–midnight, Sun 3–10:30pm.

La Petite Maison ✿✿ FRENCH/CONTEMPORARY   This delightful 1894 Victorian cottage houses a gem of a restaurant, chef-owned by Henri Chaperont. Since 1978, it has served a blend of classic French and eclectic modern cuisine in a friendly, intimate setting with jazz playing in the background. The food is innovative, interesting, and well presented; service is impeccable. The menus change monthly; if they're available, we suggest curried chicken salad with cashews and grapes, and crab cakes with corn pico de gallo. Being beefeaters, we especially like the grilled Black Angus filet with fresh horseradish and peppercorn crust and shallot jus. Another good dinner item is nut-crusted duck breast with brandy-infused cherries. There's also usually a hand-made vegetarian pasta of the day. Desserts, all made in-house, might include white-chocolate mousse with fresh berries, fresh fruit tart with almond paste, or crème brûlée.

1015 W. Colorado Ave. ℂ 719/632-4887. Reservations recommended. Main courses $8–$16 patio/lunch, $19–$30 dinner. AE, DC, DISC, MC, V. Tues–Fri 11am–2pm and 5–10pm; Sat–Sun 5–10pm.

Margarita at PineCreek ⊛⊛ ECLECTIC   A delightful spot to sit and watch the sun setting over Pikes Peak, the Margarita is tucked away above two creeks on the north side of the city. The decor is attractively simple, with tile floors and stucco walls; a tree-shaded outdoor patio is open in summer. Saturday evenings bring live harpsi-chord music in the dining room, and Friday nights often feature live acoustic music—bluegrass to Celtic.

Although the style of cooking may vary, depending on the chef's whim, the empha-sis is on fresh ingredients, and everything is prepared from scratch, including breads and stocks. Lunches feature a choice of two homemade soups, salad, and fresh bread; there are also Southwestern and weekly specials. Six-course dinners offer three entree choices, usually fresh fish, veal, steak, pasta, lamb, or duckling.

7350 Pine Creek Rd. ℂ 719/598-8667. Reservations recommended. Fixed-price lunch $9.50; fixed-price dinner $25–$35; brunch $10–$15. AE, DISC, MC, V. Tues–Fri 11:30am–2pm and 5:30–9pm; Sat 5:30–9pm; Sun 10:30am–2pm.

The Tavern ⊛⊛ STEAK/SEAFOOD   Authentic Toulouse-Lautrec lithographs on the walls and knotty pine furniture and paneling mark the Tavern, open since 1939, as a restaurant with unusual ambience. In the front dining room, a four-piece ensemble fol-lows piano music nightly—guests are welcome to take a turn around the dance floor between courses. The quieter garden room, with luxuriant tropical foliage, gives the feel-ing of outdoor dining without being outdoors. Service in both rooms is impeccable.

Many selections are prepared in the restaurant's stone grill, and the emphasis is on fresh ingredients and classic cuisine. The lunch menu features changes seasonally, but typically includes steaks, gourmet burgers, crab cakes, and a variety of sandwiches and salads. Dinners are more elaborate: Choose from slow-roasted prime rib, filet mignon, Colorado brown trout, or roast chicken. All entrees come with a selection of home-made breads.

Broadmoor Main, at The Broadmoor, Lake Circle. ℂ 719/634-7711. Reservations recommended. Main courses $9–$25 lunch, $18–$36 dinner. AE, DC, DISC, MC, V. Daily 11am–11pm.

The Warehouse ⊛⊛ CONTEMPORARY/FUSION   This stalwart locals' joint has a style that helped launch a revitalization of the south side of downtown Colorado Springs when it opened in 1997, and it's as strong as ever today. Home to the Palmer Lake Brewing Company, The Warehouse is located in, yes, a converted century-old warehouse, a mixed-use building that's one of the most stylish addresses in the city. One side of the restaurant is the main dining area, with an array of tables centered on a cop-per-topped bar; across the hall is a gallery with couches where many people enjoy liba-tions or wait for a table. The attractive industrial chic atmosphere is a nice match for the diverse menu, which is known for a superb beef tenderloin and a locally beloved grilled vegetarian fusilli, with forest mushrooms, asparagus tips, and fresh spinach. Lunch is lighter, mainly unique sandwiches and wraps, and the house beers are excellent.

25 W. Cimarron St. ℂ 719475-8880. www.thewarehouserestaurant.com. Reservations recommended. Main courses $9–$15 lunch, $15–29 dinner. AE, DISC, MC, V. Mon–Fri 11:30am–10pm; Sat 6–10pm.

Kids Family-Friendly Restaurants

Edelweiss Restaurant (see below) Kids will enjoy the strolling musicians who play German folk music on weekends, and they'll love the apple and cherry strudels.

Giuseppe's Old Depot Restaurant (see below) An original locomotive stands outside this old Denver & Rio Grande Railroad station. Most kids will adore the spaghetti and pizza.

Meadow Muffins (p. 160) The junk-store appearance and kid-friendly food (like a burger with peanut butter) make this place a hit with the younger set.

MODERATE

Edelweiss Restaurant ★ *Kids* GERMAN   The Edelweiss occupies an impressive stone building with a trio of fireplaces and an outdoor *biergarten*. It underscores its Bavarian atmosphere with strolling folk musicians on weekends, which gives it a party feel that makes this a fun place for kids. It offers a hearty menu of Jägerschnitzel, Wiener schnitzel, sauerbraten, bratwurst, and other old-country specials, as well as New York strip steak, fresh fish, and chicken. The fruit strudels are excellent, and there are some great German beers.

34 E. Ramona Ave. (southwest of I-25, 1 block west of Nevada Ave.). ✆ **719/633-2220.** Reservations recommended. Main courses $6–$8.25 lunch, $10–$20 dinner. AE, DC, DISC, MC, V. Daily 11:30am–9pm.

Giuseppe's Old Depot Restaurant ★ *Kids* ITALIAN/AMERICAN   Located in a restored Denver & Rio Grande train station with glass ticket windows lining the walls, Giuseppe's is a fun place with a lot of historic ambience. You can see freight trains going by just outside the windows. The same extensive menu is served all day. Spaghetti, lasagna (vegetarian spinach or spicy sausage and ground beef), and stone-baked pizza are house specialties. American dishes include our favorite—baby back pork ribs, smothered in Giuseppe's secret sauce—plus prime rib, grilled salmon filet, and fried chicken.

10 S. Sierra Madre St. ✆ **719/635-3111.** Menu items $7–$25; pizzas $10–$18. AE, DC, DISC, MC, V. Sun–Thurs 11am–9pm; Fri–Sat 11am–10pm.

Marigold Café and Bakery ★ INTERNATIONAL   This bustling restaurant and bakery is known for its fresh ingredients and homemade breads and pastries. A low wall separates the bakery counter from the cafelike dining area. Breakfast and lunch are casual, featuring traditional menus and gourmet-savvy items such as Greek pizzas and innovative sandwiches served on fresh breads. The restaurant takes on a more refined atmosphere at dinner, when the menu reflects a wide range of international influences. Favorites include flat iron steak, served with a balsamic and red wine reduction, salmon with sautéed spinach and goat cheese and dried tomato pesto, and fresh pasta dishes. The bakery counter bustles through the early afternoon, offering splendid breads, pastries, and sandwiches. Box lunches, coffee, lattes, and cappuccinos are also available.

4605 Centennial Blvd. (at Garden of the Gods Rd.). ✆ **719/599-4776.** Main courses $5.50–$10 lunch, $9.25–$23 dinner. AE, DC, DISC, MC, V. Restaurant Mon–Sat 7–10:30am, 11am–2:30pm, and 5–9pm. Coffee bar and bakery Mon–Fri 6am–9pm; Sat 7am–9pm. Closed Sun.

Phantom Canyon Brewing Co. ⚘ CONTEMPORARY AMERICAN   This popular, busy brewpub is in the Cheyenne Building, home to the Chicago Rock Island &
Pacific Railroad in the early 1900s. On any given day, 8 to 10 of Phantom Canyon's
specialty beers are on tap, including homemade root beer. The signature beer is the
Phantom, a traditional India pale ale; others include the Cascade Amber and a light
ale called Queen's Blonde.

The dining room is large and wide open, with ceiling fans, hardwood floors, and
the large brewing vats, visible in the corner. Lunch is typical but well-prepared brewpub fare: wood-fired pizzas, hearty salads, half-pound burgers, fish and chips, and the
like. The dinner menu is varied and more innovative, with choices such as sesame
chicken stir-fry, spice-crusted pork tenderloin, or macaroni and cheese with lobster
and crab. The menus change periodically. On the second floor is a billiard hall with
TVs and foosball. See also "Colorado Springs After Dark," later in this chapter.

2 E. Pikes Peak Ave. ⓒ 719/635-2800. Main courses $7.50–$11 lunch, $9.95–$20 dinner. AE, DC, DISC, MC, V.
Mon–Thurs 11am–10pm; Fri–Sat 11am–midnight; Sun 9am–10pm.

Ritz Grill ⚘ NEW AMERICAN   This lively restaurant-lounge with a large central
bar is where it's at for many of the city's young professionals. The decor is Art Deco,
the service fast and friendly. The varied, trendy menu offers such specialties as Garden
Ritz veggie pizza, with fresh spinach, sun-dried tomatoes, bell peppers, onions, mushrooms, fresh pesto, and three cheeses; and Siamese tuna salad—served rare with wild
greens, mango salsa, radish sprouts, pickled ginger chestnuts, and wasabi peas. For
beefeaters, we recommend the mesquite-grilled 8-ounce center-cut filet mignon,
served on a bed of raspberry-chipotle demi-glace, or the semolina-crusted salmon
topped with balsamic jus and tart cherry chutney. See also "Colorado Springs After
Dark," later in this chapter.

15 S. Tejon St. ⓒ 719/635-8484. www.ritzgrill.com. Main courses $6–$12 brunch and lunch, $10–$25 dinner. AE,
MC, V. Mon–Thurs 11am–midnight; Fri–Sat 11am–1am; Sun 9:30am–midnight. Bar open later with a limited menu.

INEXPENSIVE

Adam's Mountain Cafe ⚘⚘ *Finds* AMERICAN/VEGETARIAN   Not strictly vegetarian, Adam's Mountain Cafe is one of the best restaurants in the area for those seeking vegetarian or what we might call health food. Exposed brick and stone, antique
tables and chairs, fresh flowers, and original works by a local artist create a country
French–Victorian appearance. The menu includes grilled items, fresh fish, and many
Mediterranean-style entrees. Breakfast specialties include orange-almond French toast,
our top choice, and the P. W. Busboy Special, consisting of two whole-grain pancakes,
two scrambled eggs, and slices of fresh fruit. Lunch offerings include sandwiches,
soups, salads, fresh pasta, and Southwestern plates. Come dinner, we recommend the
harvest crepes, packed with roasted butternut squash and finished with a vegetarian
red chili, and the Caribbean jerked chicken.

110 Cañon Ave., Manitou Springs. ⓒ 719/685-1430. www.adamsmountain.com. Main courses $4.50–$9 breakfast
and lunch, $8–$19 dinner. AE, DISC, MC, V. Sun–Mon 8am–3pm; Tues–Sat 8am–3pm and 5–9pm. Closed Mon Oct–Apr.

Amanda's Fonda ⚘ *Finds* AMERICAN   Our pick for Mexican food in Colorado
Springs, Amanda's Fonda is the handiwork of a family that has owned Mexican restaurants for five generations. Clearly they've honed the art of making remarkable chile in
that time: Both the chile Colorado and the green chile are excellent; the former is red
with big hunks of steak, the latter spicier with pork. The burritos, spinach-and-mush-
room enchiladas, and seafood are also quite tasty, and the menu includes both *menudo*

and *pozole* (soups) on weekends. The interior of the place is a funky maze, one part log cabin, one part family restaurant, and one part Mexican bar and grill.

3625 W. Colorado Ave. ℂ 719/227-1975. Main courses $6–$14. AE, DISC, MC, V. Mon–Sat 11:30–9pm; Sun noon–9pm.

Dutch Kitchen ⍟ (Value) AMERICAN   Good homemade food served in a casual, friendly atmosphere is the draw at this relatively small restaurant, which the Flynn family has owned and operated since 1959. We especially like the corned beef, pastrami, and ham sandwiches, and if you're there in summer, be sure to try the fresh rhubarb pie. Other house specialties include buttermilk pie and homemade soups.

1025 Manitou Ave., Manitou Springs. ℂ 719/685-9962. Main courses $4–$8 lunch, $7–$13 dinner. No credit cards. Sat–Thurs 11:30am–3:30pm and 4:30–8pm. Closed Thurs in spring and fall. Closed Dec–Feb.

Meadow Muffins ⍟ (Value) (Kids) AMERICAN   A fun spot for a good, inexpensive meal in a lively atmosphere, Meadow Muffins is a boisterous bar packed with movie memorabilia and assorted oddities. The decorations range from two buckboard wagons (hung from the ceiling near the front door) that were supposedly used in *Gone With the Wind* to a 5-ton cannon used in a number of war movies. The menu includes chicken wings, onion rings, sandwiches, salads, and the like. The burgers are especially good—just ask anyone in Colorado Springs—but we have to admit that we couldn't bring ourselves to try the Jiffy Burger: a large ground-beef burger topped with bacon, provolone cheese, and—believe it or not—peanut butter. On most days, there are great food and drink specials. See also "Colorado Springs After Dark," later in this chapter.

2432 W. Colorado Ave., in Old Colorado City. ℂ 719/633-0583. Most menu items $4.25–$6.75. AE, DISC, MC, V. Daily 11am–2am (or earlier, depending on business).

Michelle's ⍟ (Value) AMERICAN/GREEK/SOUTHWESTERN   The menu is eclectic, but it's amazing how many different dishes Michelle's prepares well—and at such reasonable prices. Since it opened in 1952, this charming little diner and candy store hasn't changed much: It's long been known for its excellent handmade chocolates, fresh-churned ice cream, and Greek specialties such as gyros and spanakopita. It also serves good burgers, croissant sandwiches, a half-dozen salads, numerous omelets, and a delicious breakfast burrito. A three-page ice-cream menu includes everything from a single scoop of vanilla to the "Believe It or Not Sundae" featured in *Life* magazine in November 1959: It weighs 42 pounds and includes every flavor of ice cream Michelle's makes!

122 N. Tejon St. ℂ 719/633-5089. Reservations not accepted. Lunch and dinner $5–$8.50. AE, DC, DISC, MC, V. Mon–Thurs 9am–11pm; Fri–Sat 9am–midnight; Sun 10am–11pm.

5 Attractions

Most of the attractions of the Pikes Peak region fit in two general categories: natural, such as Pikes Peak, Garden of the Gods, and Cave of the Winds, and historic/educational, including the Air Force Academy, Olympic Complex training center, museums, historic homes, and art galleries. There are also gambling houses in Cripple Creek.

If you visit Colorado from a sea-level area, you might want to schedule mountain excursions, such as the cog railway to the top of Pikes Peak, at the end of your stay. This will give your body time to adapt to the lower oxygen level at these higher elevations. See also "Health & Safety," in chapter 2.

THE TOP ATTRACTIONS

United States Air Force Academy *𝓡𝓡*   Colorado Springs' pride and joy got its start in 1954 when Congress authorized the establishment of a U.S. Air Force Academy and chose this 18,000-acre site from among 400 prospective locations. The first class of cadets enrolled in 1959, and each year since, about 4,000 cadets have enrolled for the 4 years of rigorous training required to become Air Force officers.

The academy is 12 miles north of downtown; enter at the North Gate, off I-25 exit 156B. Soon after entering the grounds, at the intersection of North Gate Boulevard and Stadium Boulevard, you'll see an impressive outdoor B-52 bomber display. Where North Gate Boulevard becomes Academy Drive (in another mile or so), look to your left to see the Cadet Field House, where the basketball and ice hockey teams play (see "Spectator Sports," later in this chapter), and the Parade Ground, where you can sometimes spot cadets marching.

Academy Drive soon curves to the left. Six miles from the North Gate, signs mark the turnoff to the Barry Goldwater Air Force Academy Visitor Center. Open daily, it offers a variety of exhibits and films on the academy's history and cadet life, extensive literature and self-guided tour maps, and the latest information and schedules on academy activities. There's also a large gift shop and coffee shop.

A short trail from the visitor center leads to the Cadet Chapel. Its 17 gleaming aluminum spires soar 150 feet, and within the building are separate chapels for the major Western faiths as well as an "all-faiths" room. The public can visit Monday through Saturday from 9am to 5pm; Sunday services at 10am are open to the public. The chapel is closed for 5 days around graduation and during special events.

Also within easy walking distance of the visitor center is Arnold Hall, the social center that houses historical exhibits, a cafeteria, and a theater featuring a variety of public shows and lectures.

Off I-25 exit 156B. ☎ 719/333-2025. www.usafa.af.mil. Free admission. Daily 9am–5pm; additional hours for special events.

Garden of the Gods *𝓡𝓡𝓡* *(Value*   One of the West's unique geological sites, the 1,300-acre Garden of the Gods is a giant rock garden composed of spectacular red sandstone formations sculpted by rain and wind over millions of years. Located where

---

Fun Fact **Fit for the Gods**

In 1859 large numbers of pioneers were arriving in Colorado hoping to find gold (their motto: "Pikes Peak or Bust"). Many of them established communities along what is now called the Front Range, including Colorado City, which was later incorporated within Colorado Springs.

Legend has it that certain pioneers who explored the remarkable sandstone formations in the area wanted to establish a beer garden there. However, one Rufus Cable objected: "Beer Garden! Why this is a fit place for a Garden of the Gods!"

Fortunately for posterity, Charles Elliott Perkins (head of the Burlington Railroad) bought the area some 20 years later and kept it in its natural state. Upon Perkins's death in 1907, his heirs gave the remarkable area to Colorado Springs on the condition that it be preserved as a park and open to the public. The park was dedicated in 1909 and is now a Registered National Landmark.

---

several life zones and ecosystems converge, the beautiful city-run park harbors a variety of plant and animal communities. The oldest survivors are the ancient, twisted junipers, some 1,000 years old. The strangest animals are the honey ants, which gorge themselves on honey in the summer and fall, becoming living honey pots to feed their colonies during winter hibernation.

The park has a number of hiking trails—mostly easy to moderate—that offer great scenery and an opportunity to get away from the crowds. Leashed dogs are permitted on trails (owners should clean up after their pets). Many trails are also open to horseback riding and mountain biking. You can get trail maps for the park at the **Visitor Center,** which also offers exhibits on the history, geology, plants, and wildlife of the area; a cafeteria; and other conveniences.

A 12-minute multimedia theater presentation, *How Did Those Red Rocks Get There?* ($2 adults, $1 children 5–12, free for children under 5), is a fast-paced exploration of the geologic history of the area. In summer, park naturalists lead free 45-minute walks through the park and conduct free afternoon interpretive programs. You can also take a 20-minute bus tour of the park ($5 adults, $2.50 children under 13). You may spot technical rock climbers on some of the park spires; they are required to register at the Visitor Center.

Also in the park is the **Rock Ledge Ranch Historic Site** (see "More Attractions," below).

1805 N. 30th St. © 719/634-6666. www.gardenofgods.com. Free admission. Park May–Oct daily 5am–11pm; Nov–Apr daily 5am–9pm. Visitor Center Memorial Day–Labor Day daily 8am–8pm; Labor Day–Memorial Day 9am–5pm. Take Garden of the Gods Rd. west from I-25 exit 146 and turn south on 30th St.

Pikes Peak Cog Railway 🌟🌟   For those who enjoy rail travel, spectacular scenery, and the thrill of mountain climbing without all the work, this is the trip to take. The first passenger train climbed Pikes Peak on June 30, 1891, and diesel slowly replaced steam power between 1939 and 1955. Four custom-built Swiss twin-unit rail cars, each seating 216 passengers, went into service in 1989. The 9-mile route, with grades up to 25%, takes 75 minutes to reach the top of 14,110-foot Pikes Peak; the round trip requires 3 hours and 10 minutes (including a 40-min. stopover at the top). Runs depart between 8am and 5pm in midsummer, with shorter hours at other times.

The journey is exciting from the start, but passengers really begin to ooh and aah when the track leaves the forest, creeping above timberline at about 11,500 feet. The view from the summit takes in Denver, 75 miles north; New Mexico's Sangre de Cristo range, 100 miles south; the Cripple Creek mining district, on the mountain's western flank; wave after wave of Rocky Mountain subranges to the west; and the seemingly endless sea of Great Plains to the east. This is also where you'll want to watch for Rocky Mountain bighorn sheep and yellow-bellied marmots. The Summit House at the top of Pikes Peak has a restaurant (sandwiches, snacks, beverages, and box lunches), a gift shop, and even a flavored oxygen bar.

Take a jacket or sweater—it can be cold and windy on top, even on warm summer days. This trip is not recommended if you have cardiac or respiratory problems. Even those in good health may feel faint or light-headed.

515 Ruxton Ave., Manitou Springs. ⓒ **719/685-5401.** www.cograilway.com. $29–$31 adults, $16–$17 children under 12, free for children under 3 held on an adult's lap. Mid-Apr to mid-Nov, with 2 to 8 departures daily; call or check schedules online. Closed mid-Nov to mid-Apr, except for special events. Reservations required (available online). Take I-25 exit 141 west on U.S. 24 for 4 miles, turn onto Manitou Ave. west and go 1½ miles to Ruxton Ave., turn left and go about ½ mile.

Pikes Peak Highway ⚘   Perhaps no view in Colorado equals the 360-degree panorama from the 14,110-foot summit of Pikes Peak. Whether you go by cog railway (see above) or private vehicle, the ascent is a spectacular, exciting experience—although not for those with heart or breathing problems or a fear of heights. The 19-mile toll highway (paved for 10 miles, all-weather gravel thereafter) starts at 7,400 feet, some 4 miles west of Manitou Springs. There are numerous photo stops as you head up the mountain, and deer, mountain sheep, marmots, and other animals often appear on the slopes, especially above timberline (around 11,500 ft.). This 156-curve road is the site of the annual Pikes Peak International Hill Climb (see "Spectator Sports," later in this chapter). Allow 3 hours minimum.

Off U.S. 24 at Cascade Ave. ⓒ **800/318-9505** or 719/385-7325. www.pikespeakcolorado.com. Admission $10 adults, $5 children 6–15, free for children under 6, $35 maximum per car. Memorial Day–Labor Day daily 7am–7pm; Labor Day to late Sept daily 7am–5pm; Oct to Memorial Day daily 9am–3pm, weather permitting. Take I-25 exit 141 west on U.S. 24 about 10 miles.

Colorado Springs Pioneers Museum ⚘⚘ *Value*   Housed in the former El Paso County Courthouse (1903), which is on the National Register of Historic Places, this museum is an excellent place to begin your visit to Colorado Springs. Exhibits depict the community's rich history, including its beginning as a fashionable resort, the railroad and mining eras, and its growth and development in the 20th century. Also here is the Victorian home of writer Helen Hunt Jackson.

You can ride an Otis birdcage elevator, which dates to the early 1900s, to the restored original courtroom, where several *Perry Mason* episodes were filmed. A recent renovation uncovered intriguing gold and silver images of goddesses, painted on the courtroom walls in part to represent the two key resources of the state's economy at the time. However, it's believed that they were also painted as a subtle protest when the country was changing from a gold and silver standard to a gold-only monetary standard. Another series of murals depict over 400 years of Pikes Peak region history.

Changing exhibit areas house traveling shows such as quilts, historic photographs, aviation, American Indian culture, and art pottery. The museum has hosted a wide range of events, including lectures on the American cowboy, antique auto shows, jazz concerts, and Hispanic celebrations. The historic reference library and archives are available by appointment. Allow 1 to 3 hours.

215 S. Tejon St. ⓒ **719/385-5990.** www.cspm.org. Free admission, donations accepted. Year-round Tues–Sat 10am–5pm; Jun–Aug Sun 1–5pm. Take I-25 exit 141 east to Tejon St., turn right and go 4 blocks.

United States Olympic Complex   So you think your local fitness center is state-of-the-art? Check out the 37-acre United States Olympic Complex, a sophisticated center where thousands of athletes train each year in a variety of Olympic sports. Free guided tours, available daily, take about an hour, and include a film depicting the U.S. Olympic effort. Visitors may also see athletes in training. The visitor center includes the U.S. Olympic Hall of Fame, interactive kiosks on Olympics subjects, various other displays, and a gift shop that sells Olympic-logo merchandise.

The complex includes the **Olympic Sports Center I,** with five gymnasiums and a weight-training room; **Sports Center II,** which accommodates 14 sports; the **Indoor Shooting Center,** the largest facility of its kind in the Western Hemisphere, with areas for rifle and pistol shooting, rapid-fire and women's sport pistol bays, running-target rifle ranges, and air-rifle and pistol-fire points; and the **Aquatics Center,** which contains a 50-by-25-meter pool with two movable bulkheads, 10 50m and 20 25m lanes, and more than 800,000 gallons of water. The U.S. Olympic Committee also operates the **7-Eleven Velodrome,** with a banked track for bicycle and roller speed skating, about 1 mile south of the Olympic Complex, in Memorial Park (see "Parks & Zoos," later in this chapter) off Union Boulevard. Olympic figure skaters train at the **World Arena,** southwest of downtown. Allow 1 to 2 hours.

1 Olympic Plaza, corner of Boulder St. (entrance) and Union Blvd. (**888/659-8687** or 719/866-4618. www.usolympic team.com. Free admission. Complex daily 9am–6pm. Guided tours begin every half-hour 9am–4pm; reservations required for groups of 10 or more ((719/866-4656). From I-25, take exit 143.

MORE ATTRACTIONS
ARCHITECTURAL HIGHLIGHTS
The Broadmoor   This famous Italian Renaissance–style resort hotel has been a Colorado Springs landmark since Spencer Penrose built it in 1918. (See "Where to Stay," earlier in this chapter.)

Lake Circle, at Lake Ave. (**719/634-7711.** www.broadmoor.com. Free admission. Daily year-round.

Miramont Castle Museum   Architecture buffs will love this place. Built into a hillside by a wealthy French priest as a private home in 1895 and converted by the Sisters of Mercy into a sanatorium in 1907, this unique Victorian mansion has always aroused curiosity. The structure incorporates at least nine identifiable architectural styles in its 4 stories, 46 rooms, 14,000 square feet of floor space, and 2-foot-thick stone walls. If you like tiny stuff, don't miss the room housing the miniatures museum. In summer, light meals and tea are served Tuesday through Saturday from 11am to 4pm in the Queen's Parlor. The museum lies on the route from Manitou Avenue to the Pikes Peak Cog Railway. Allow at least 1 hour.

9 Capitol Hill Ave., Manitou Springs. (**888/685-1011** or 719/685-1011. www.miramontcastle.org. Admission $6 adults, $2 children 6–15, free for children under 6. Tues–Sun 10am–4pm. Located 1 block west of the intersection of Manitou and Ruxton aves.

HISTORIC BUILDINGS
McAllister House   This Gothic cottage, listed on the National Register of Historic Places, is a good place for a quick look at the Colorado of the late 19th century. It was built in 1873, and the builder, an army major named Henry McAllister, decided to construct the house with brick when he learned that the local wind was so strong it had blown a train off the tracks nearby. The house has many original furnishings, including three marble fireplaces. It is now owned by the Colonial Dames of America, whose knowledgeable volunteers lead guided tours. Allow about 1 hour.

423 N. Cascade Ave. (at St. Vrain St.). (**719/635-7925.** Admission $5 adults, $4 seniors 62 and older, $3 children 6–12, free for children under 6. Summer Wed–Sat 10am–4pm, Sun noon–4pm; winter Thurs–Sat 10am–4pm. Take I-25 exit 141 east to Cascade Ave., go left and continue for about 6 blocks.

Rock Ledge Ranch Historic Site   Visitors can explore the history of three pioneer eras at this living-history farm at the east entrance to Garden of the Gods Park. Listed on the National Register of Historic Places, the ranch presents the rigors of the homestead era at the 1860s Galloway Homestead, the agricultural difficulties of the working-ranch era at the 1880s Chambers Farm and Blacksmith Shop, and the more sophisticated estate period at the 1907 Orchard House. Special events, which take place frequently, include an old-fashioned Fourth of July celebration, an 1860s vintage baseball game in late summer, a Victorian Halloween party, and holiday celebrations from Thanksgiving through Christmas. The General Store stocks a wide selection of historic reproductions, books, and gift items, and the proceeds help with preservation and restoration of the ranch. Allow 1 to 2 hours.

N. 30th St. and Gateway Rd., Garden of the Gods. *©* **719/578-6777**. www.rockledgeranch.com. Admission $5 adults, $3 seniors 55 and older and students 13–18, $1 children 6–12, free for children under 6. June to Labor Day Wed–Sun 10am–5pm; early Sept to Dec Sat 10am–4pm, Sun noon–4pm. Closed Jan–May. Take I-25 exit 146, then follow signs west to Garden of the Gods.

HISTORIC NEIGHBORHOODS

Manitou Springs, which centers on Manitou Avenue off U.S. 24 West, is a separate town with its own government. It is one of the country's largest National Historic Districts. Legend has it that Utes named the springs Manitou, their word for "Great Spirit," because they believed that the Great Spirit had breathed into the waters to create the natural effervescence of the springs. Pikes Peak soars above the town nestled at its base.

Today, the community offers visitors a chance to step back to a slower and quieter time. It boasts numerous elegant Victorian buildings, many of which house delightful shops, galleries, restaurants, and lodgings. Manitou Springs is also home to many fine artists and artisans, whom you might spot painting or sketching about town. A small group of sculptors began the Manitou Art Project in 1992; it installed over 20 sculptures in various locations downtown and in the parks, creating a large sculpture garden for all to enjoy. The works, which stay on display for a year, are for sale, with 25% of the proceeds used to purchase permanent sculpture for the city.

Visitors are encouraged to take the self-guided tour of the nine restored mineral springs of Manitou. Pick up the *Manitou Springs Visitor's Guide,* which contains a map and descriptions to help you find each spring. It's available at the Manitou Springs Chamber of Commerce & Visitors Bureau, 354 Manitou Ave. (*©* **800/642-2567** or 719/685-5089; www.manitousprings.org), which is open daily.

Old Colorado City, Colorado Avenue between 21st and 31st streets, was founded in 1859, 12 years before Colorado Springs. The town boomed in the 1880s after General Palmer's railroad came through. Tunnels led from the respectable side of town to this saloon and red-light district so that the city fathers could carouse without being seen coming or going—or so the legend goes. Today this historic district has an interesting assortment of shops, galleries, and restaurants.

MUSEUMS & GALLERIES

Colorado Springs Fine Arts Center *ℱ*   The center's permanent collection includes works by Georgia O'Keeffe, John James Audubon, John Singer Sargent, Charles Russell, Albert Bierstadt, Nicolai Fechin, and other famed painters and sculptors, as well as a world-class collection of American Indian and Hispanic works.

Opened in 1936, the center also houses a 450-seat performing-arts theater, a 32,000-volume art-research library, the Bemis School of Art, a tactile gallery for those who are visually impaired, and a delightful sculpture garden. Changing exhibits showcase local collections as well as touring international exhibits. Designed by renowned Santa Fe architect John Gaw Meem, the Art Deco–style building reflects Southwestern mission and Pueblo influences. Allow 1 to 3 hours.

30 W. Dale St. (west of N. Cascade Ave.). **©** **719/634-5581.** www.csfineartscenter.org. Admission to galleries and museum $5 adults, $4 seniors and students, $3 children 3–12, free for children under 3. Separate admission for performing-arts events. Galleries and museum Mon–Sat 9am–5pm, Sun 10–5pm. Open the 1st Thurs of every month until 9pm for a wine tasting. Closed federal holidays. Take I-25 exit 143 east to Cascade St., turn right to Dale St., and then turn right again.

Ghost Town *(Kids)*   A fun place to take the family, Ghost Town is part historic attraction, part theme park. Made up of authentic 19th-century buildings relocated from other parts of Colorado, this "town" is sheltered from the elements in Old Colorado City. There's a sheriff's office, jail, saloon, general store, livery stable, blacksmith shop, rooming house, and assay office. Animated frontier characters tell stories of the Old West, while a shooting gallery, antique arcade machines, and nickelodeons provide additional entertainment. During the summer you can even pan for real gold. Allow about 2 hours.

400 S. 21st St. (on U.S. 24). **©** **719/634-0696.** www.ghosttownmuseum.com. Admission $6.50 adults, $3.50 children 6–16, free for children under 6. June–Aug Mon–Sat 9am–6pm, Sun 11am–6pm; Sept–May Mon–Sat 10am–5pm, Sun 11am–5pm. Take I-25 exit 141; town is just west of exit.

Manitou Cliff Dwellings Preserve & Museums *★ (Kids)*   The cliff dwelling ruins here are real, although originally they were located elsewhere. This put us off at first—they would be more authentic if they were in their original location—but the move here may have saved them. In the early 1900s, archaeologists, who saw such dwellings being plundered by treasure hunters, dismantled some of the ancient buildings, gathered artifacts found there, and hauled them away. Some of these ruins, constructed from 1200 to 1300 A.D., can be seen here in a village reconstructed by archaeologists, with no "Don't Touch" signs to be seen. There are also two museums with exhibits on prehistoric American Indian life, and several gift shops that sell Indian-made jewelry, pottery, and other crafts, plus Colorado souvenirs. American Indian dancers perform during the summer. Allow 2 hours.

U.S. 24, Manitou Springs. **©** **800/354-9971** or 719/685-5242. www.cliffdwellingsmuseum.com. Admission $8.50 adults, $7.50 seniors 60 and over, $6.50 children 7–11, free for children under 7. May–Sept daily 9am–6pm; Oct–Nov and Mar–Apr daily 9am–5pm; Dec–Feb daily 10am–4pm. Closed Thanksgiving and Dec 25. Take I-25 exit 141, go west on U.S. 24 about 5 miles.

May Natural History Museum of the Tropics *(Kids)*   Here you'll find one of the world's best public collections of giant insects and other tropical invertebrates, not to mention a statue out front touted to be the world's largest Hercules beetle. James F. W. May (1884–1956) spent more than half a century exploring the world's jungles while compiling his illustrious collection, which has grown to more than 100,000 invertebrates, about 8,000 of which are on display at any given time. The specimens are irreplaceable, because many came from areas that are now so politically unstable that no one is willing or able to explore the backcountry to collect them again. Exhibits change periodically.

Also on the grounds is the **Museum of Space Exploration,** where you can take a pictorial trip through the history of space exploration, beginning with man's first attempts to fly and continuing through the most recent photos from NASA. Also on display are numerous models of early aircraft, World War II planes, and spacecraft. Take time to view one or more of the NASA space films, which include the first moon landing. Allow 2 to 3 hours for both museums. There's also a 500-site campground ($20–$22 for campsites) with hiking trails, fishing, and a playground area.

710 Rock Creek Canyon Rd. © 719/576-0450. www.maymuseum-camp-rvpark.com. Admission (includes Museum of Space Exploration) $4.50 adults, $3.50 seniors 60 and older, $2.50 children 6–12, free for children under 6. May–Sept daily 9am–6pm. Closed Oct–Apr except for groups of 10 or more. Take Colo. 115 and drive southwest out of Colorado Springs for 9 miles; watch for signs and the Hercules Beetle of the West Indies that mark the turnoff to the museum.

Money Museum *Finds*   Operated by the American Numismatic Association, this museum is the largest collection of its kind west of the Smithsonian Institution, consisting of four galleries of coins, tokens, medals, and paper money from around the world. Of special note is the earliest *reale* (Spanish coin) struck in the New World, struck in Mexico in 1536. There's also an 1804 dollar, a 1913 "V" nickel, and a nice collectors' library. Allow 1 hour.

818 N. Cascade Ave., on the campus of Colorado College. © 800/367-9723 or 719/482-9823. www.money.org. Free admission, donations welcome. Tues–Fri 9am–5pm; Sat 10am–5pm; Sun noon–5pm. Take I-25 exit 143 east to Cascade Ave., then turn right and go about 6 blocks.

Peterson Air & Space Museum   Through its exhibits, this museum traces the history of Peterson Air Force Base, NORAD, the Air Defense Command, and Air Force Space Command. Of special interest are 17 historic aircraft, including P-47 Thunderbolt and P-40 Warhawk fighters from World War II, plus four missiles and jets from the Korean War to the present. To mark the 50th anniversary of the U.S. Air Force, a memorial grove of 58 conifer trees honoring the USAF Medal of Honor recipients was planted. There's also a small gift shop. Allow 1 to 2 hours. *Note:* Visitors must have a military ID or give administration at least 24 hours' advance notice to get on the base.

Peterson Air Force Base main gate, off U.S. 24. © 719/556-4915. www.petemuseum.org. Free admission. Tues–Sat 8:30am–4:30pm. Closed holidays and occasionally during military exercises; call ahead. Take I-25 exit 141, then follow U.S. 24 east about 7½ miles.

ProRodeo Hall of Fame & American Cowboy Museum *Kids*   No rhinestone cowboys here. This is the real thing, with exhibits on the development of rodeo, from its origins in early ranch work to major professional sport. You'll learn about historic and modern cowboys, including those brave (or crazy) enough to climb onto bucking broncos and wild bulls, in Heritage Hall. The Hall of Champions displays photos, gear, personal memorabilia, and trophies honoring rodeo greats. There are two multimedia presentations, and the museum features changing exhibits of Western art. Outside you'll find a replica rodeo arena, live rodeo animals, and a sculpture garden. Allow 2 hours.

101 ProRodeo Dr. (off Rockrimmon Blvd.). © 719/528-4764. www.prorodeo.com. Admission $6 adults, $5 seniors 55 and older, $3 children 6–12, free for children under 6. Daily 9am–5pm. Closed Jan 1, Easter, Thanksgiving, and Dec 25. Take I-25 to exit 147.

Western Museum of Mining & Industry   Machines are fun, and the bigger the better. Historic hard-rock mining machinery and other equipment from Cripple Creek and other late-19th-century Colorado gold camps form the basis of this museum's 4,000-plus-item collection. Visitors can see an operating Corliss steam

engine with an enormous 17-ton flywheel, a life-size underground mine reconstruction, and an exhibit on mining-town life showing how early Western miners and their
families lived. You can also pan for gold—there's a wheelchair-accessible trough—and
view a 23-minute video presentation on life in the early mining camps. Various hands-
on family activities focus on themes such as life in a mining town, minerals in everyday products, and recycled art. Free guided tours are available; call for information
and times. Allow at least 2 hours.

1025 North Gate Rd., at I-25 exit 156A (off Gleneagle Dr. just east of the north gate of the U.S. Air Force Academy).
© 800/752-6558 or 719/488-0880. www.wmmi.org. Admission $7 adults, $5 seniors 60 and older and students
13–17, $3 children 3–12, free for children under 3. June–Aug Mon–Sat 9am–5pm Sept–May Mon–Sat 9am–4pm.
Guided tours begin at 10am and 1pm. Located just east of I-25 via Gleneagle Dr.

World Figure Skating Museum & Hall of Fame   This is the only museum of its
kind in the world, exhibiting 1,200 years of ice skates—from early versions of carved
bone to highly decorated cast-iron examples and finally the steel blades of today. There
are also skating costumes, medals, and other memorabilia, changing exhibits, films, a
library, and a gift shop. A gallery displays skating-related paintings, including works
by the 17th-century Dutch artist Pieter Bruegel and Americans Winslow Homer and
Andy Warhol. The museum is recognized by the International Skating Union, the
international governing body, as the repository for the history and official records of
figure skating and the sport's official hall of fame. Here also are the U.S. national,
regional, sectional, and international trophies. Allow 1 to 2 hours.

20 1st St. © 719/635-5200. www.worldskatingmuseum.org. Admission $3 adults, $2 seniors 60 and over and children 6–12, free for children under 6. Year-round Mon–Sat 10am–4pm. Closed major holidays. Take I-25 exit 138, west
on Lake Ave.; just before The Broadmoor, turn right onto 1st St.

NATURAL ATTRACTIONS

Cave of the Winds ☞   Discovered by two boys on a church outing in the 1880s,
this impressive underground cavern has offered public tours for well over a century. It
provides a good opportunity to see the beauty of the underworld. The 45-minute Discovery Tour takes visitors along a well-lit ¾-mile passageway through 20 subterranean
chambers, complete with classic stalagmites, stalactites, crystal flowers, and limestone
canopies. In the Adventure Room, modern lighting techniques return visitors to an
era when spelunking was done by candle and lantern. The 1½-hour Lantern Tour follows unpaved and unlighted passageways and corridors. This tour is rather strenuous,
with some stooping required in areas with low ceilings; it might muddy your shoes,
but not your clothes.

Kids especially like the outdoor laser shows (with stereophonic sound) presented
nightly during the summer at 9pm ($10 adults, $5 children 6–15, free for children
under 6).

U.S. 24, Manitou Springs. © 719/685-5444. www.caveofthewinds.com. Discovery Tour $16 adults, $8 children 6–15,
free for children under 6. Tours depart every 15–30 min. Lantern Tour $20 adults, $12 children 6–15, not recommended
for children under 6. Tour offered 3 times daily in summer and on weekends; other times by reservation. Visitors with
heart conditions, visual impairment, or other physical limitations are advised not to take Lantern Tour. Memorial Day
to Labor Day daily 9am–9pm; early Sept to Apr daily 10am–5pm. Take I-25 exit 141, go 6 miles west on U.S. 24.

Seven Falls   This is a good choice for those who have not yet gotten their fill of Colorado's spectacular mountain scenery. A picturesque 1-mile drive through a box canyon
takes you between the Pillars of Hercules, where the canyon narrows to just 42 feet, end-
ing at these cascading falls. Seven separate waterfalls dance down a granite cliff, cascading

Impressions

The air is so refined that you can live without much lungs.
                              —Shane Leslie, *American Wonderland*, 1936

some 181 feet. A free elevator takes visitors to the Eagle Nest viewing platform. A mile-long trail atop the plateau passes the grave of 19th-century novelist Helen Hunt Jackson, the author of *Ramona,* and ends at a panoramic view of Colorado Springs. Watch for birds and other wildlife along the way. Allow 2 hours.

At the end of S. Cheyenne Canyon Rd. *©* **719/632-0765.** www.sevenfalls.com. Day admission $8.75 adults, $7.75 seniors, $5.50 children 6–15, free for children under 6; night admission $10 adults, $9.25 seniors, $6.50 children 6–15, free for children under 6; lower rates in winter. Mid-May to early June and mid-Aug to early Sept daily 8:30am–9:30pm; early June to mid-Aug daily 8:30am–10:30pm; early Sept to mid-May daily 9am–5:15pm. Christmas lighting Dec 16–26 5–9:30pm. Closed major holidays. Take I-25 exit 141, head west on U.S. 24, turn south on 21st St. for about 3 miles, turn west on Cheyenne Blvd., and then left onto S. Cheyenne Canyon Rd.

PARKS & ZOOS

Cheyenne Mountain Zoo *☆* *Kids*   On the lower slopes of Cheyenne Mountain at 6,800 feet above sea level, this medium-size zoological park is our top choice for a family outing. The zoo's 650-plus animals, many in "natural" environments, include wolves, lions, leopards, red pandas, elephants, hippos, monkeys, giraffes, reptiles, snakes, and lots of birds. Rocky cliffs have been created for the mountain goats; there's a pebbled beach for penguins and a new animal-contact area for children. The zoo is home to more than 30 endangered species, including the Siberian tiger, Amur leopard, and black-footed ferret. The zoo's giraffes are the most prolific captive herd in the world; there have been 185 live births since the 1950s. Visitors can actually feed the long-necked beasts.

There's also a colorful antique carousel, built in 1926, the year the zoo was founded. A stroller- and wheelchair-accessible tram makes a full loop of the zoo in about 15 minutes; it operates from Memorial Day to Labor Day. Admission to the zoo includes road access to the nearby **Will Rogers Shrine of the Sun,** a granite tower built in 1937, with photos and information on the American humorist. The tower also affords great views of the city and surrounding countryside. Strollers, double strollers, wheelchairs, and wagons are available for rent at Thundergod Gift and Snack Shop. Allow 2 to 4 hours for the zoo and an extra 45 minutes for the shrine.

4250 Cheyenne Mountain Zoo Rd. *©* **719/633-9925.** www.cmzoo.org. Admission $12 adults, $10 seniors 65 and over, $6 children 3–11, free for children under 3. Summer daily 9am–6pm; off season daily 9am–5pm. Take I-25 exit 138, drive west to The Broadmoor hotel and follow signs.

Memorial Park   One of the largest parks in the city, Memorial is home to the Mark "Pa" Sertich Ice Center and the Aquatics and Fitness Center, as well as the famed 7-Eleven Velodrome, which is used for world-class bicycling events. Other facilities include baseball and softball fields, volleyball courts, tennis courts, a bicycle criterium, and jogging trails. The park also stages a terrific fireworks display on Independence Day. See the sections on ice-skating, swimming, and tennis under "Outdoor Activities," below.

1605 E. Pikes Peak Ave. (between Hancock Ave. and Union Blvd.). *©* **719/385-5940.** www.springsgov.com. Free admission. Daily year-round. Located 1 mile east of downtown.

Monument Valley Park This long, slender park follows Monument Creek through downtown Colorado Springs. At its south end are formal zinnia, begonia, and rose gardens, and in the middle are demonstration gardens of the Horticultural Art Society. Facilities include softball and baseball fields, a swimming pool (open daily in summer; $4 adults, $2.50 children), volleyball and tennis courts, children's playgrounds, and picnic shelters. Also in the park are the 4.3-mile Monument Creek Trail for walkers, runners, and cyclists, and the 1-mile Monument Valley Fitness Trail at the north end, beside Bodington Field.

170 W. Cache La Poudre Blvd. © 719/385-5940. www.springsgov.com. Free admission. Daily year-round.

Mueller State Park ★★★ *(Finds)* Somewhat like a junior version of Rocky Mountain National Park, Mueller contains over 5,000 acres of prime scenic beauty along the west slope of Pikes Peak. The 55 miles of trails, designated for hikers, horseback riders, and mountain bikers, afford opportunities to observe elk, bighorn sheep, black bear, and the park's other wildlife. The best times to spot wildlife are spring and fall, just after sunrise and just before sunset. In the summer, rangers lead hikes and offer campfire programs in a 100-seat amphitheater. The park has 132 campsites (© **800/ 678-2267** for reservations), with fees ranging from $14 for walk-in sites to $18 for drive-in sites with electricity; coin-operated pay showers are available from mid-May to mid-October.

P.O. Box 39, Divide, CO 80814. © **719/687-2366.** www.parks.state.co.us. Admission $5 per vehicle. Take U.S. 24 west from Colorado Springs to Divide (25 miles), then go 3½ miles south on Colo. 67.

North Cheyenne Cañon Park and Starsmore Discovery Center ★★ A delightful escape on a hot summer day, this 1,600-acre park includes North Cheyenne Creek, which drops 1,800 feet over the course of 5 miles in a series of cascades and waterfalls. The heavily wooded park contains picnic areas and hiking/biking/horseback riding trails. The small visitor center at the foot of scenic Helen Hunt Falls has exhibits on history, geology, flora, and fauna. The **Starsmore Discovery Center,** at the entrance to the park, offers maps, information, and interactive exhibits for both kids and adults, including audiovisual programs and a climbing wall where you can learn about rock climbing. Call for current climbing-wall hours. During the summer, the center schedules a series of free programs on subjects such as rock climbing, butterflies, and hummingbirds, and guided walks and hikes (call for the current schedule). The park also has excellent rock-climbing areas for experienced climbers; pick up information at the Starsmore Discovery Center or Helen Hunt Falls Visitor Center.

2120 S. Cheyenne Cañon Rd. (west of 21st St.). © **719/578-6146.** www.springsgov.com. Free admission. Park May–Oct daily 5am–11pm; Nov–Apr daily 5am–9pm. Starsmore Discovery Center summer daily 9am–5pm; call for hours at other times. Helen Hunt Falls Visitor Center Memorial Day to Labor Day daily 9am–5pm; closed rest of year. Located just west of The Broadmoor Golf Club via Cheyenne Blvd.

Palmer Park Deeded to the city in 1899 by Colorado Springs founder Gen. William Jackson Palmer, this 737-acre preserve offers hiking, biking, and horseback riding across a mesa overlooking the city. It boasts a variety of minerals (including quartz, topaz, jasper, and tourmaline), rich vegetation (including a yucca preservation area), and considerable wildlife. The Edna Mae Bennet Nature Trail is a self-guided excursion, and there are numerous other trails. Other facilities include 12 separate picnic areas, softball and baseball fields, and volleyball courts.

3650 Maizeland Rd. off Academy Blvd. © **719/385-5940.** www.springsgov.com. Free admission. Daily year-round. Located 3 miles east of I-25 via Austin Bluffs Pkwy (exit 146).

ESPECIALLY FOR KIDS

In addition to the listings below, children will probably enjoy the **Cheyenne Mountain Zoo, May Natural History Museum,** and **Ghost Town,** described above.

Arcade Amusements, Inc ✦ *Kids*   Among the West's oldest and largest amusement arcades, this game complex just might be considered a hands-on arcade museum as well as a fun place for kids of all ages. Some 250 machines range from original working penny pinball machines to modern video games, Skee-Ball, and 12-player horse racing.

930 Block Manitou Ave., Manitou Springs. © **719/685-9815.** Free admission; arcade games from 1¢. Early May to Labor Day daily 10am–midnight. Call for winter hours. Located in downtown Manitou Springs.

North Pole/Santa's Workshop *Kids*   A good spot for young kids, Santa's workshop is busy from mid-May right up until Christmas Eve. Not only can kids visit shops where elves have some early Christmas gifts for sale, but they can also see Santa and whisper their requests in his ear. This 26-acre village features numerous rides; including a miniature train, a 60-foot Ferris wheel, and a space shuttle replica that swings to and fro; as well as magic shows and musical entertainment, snack shops, and an ice-cream parlor.

At the foot of Pikes Peak Hwy. off U.S. 24, 5 miles west of Manitou Springs. © **719/684-9432.** www.santascolo.com. Admission (includes all rides, shows, and attractions) $16 ages 2–59, $5.95 seniors 60 and over, free for children under 2. Mid-May to Mid-June and one week in Aug daily 10am–5pm; mid-June to mid-Aug daily 10am–6pm; mid-Aug to Dec 24 (weather permitting) Fri–Tues 10am–5pm. Closed Dec 25 to mid-May. Take I-25 exit 141, go west on U.S. 24 about 10 miles.

ORGANIZED TOURS

Half- and full-day bus tours of Colorado Springs, Pikes Peak, the Air Force Academy, and other nearby attractions are offered by **Gray Line of Colorado Springs,** 3704 W. Colorado Ave. (© **800/348-6877;** www.coloradograyline.com). From May through October, it offers a variety of other tours, including an excursion to Royal Gorge and white-water rafting trips. Prices range from $30 to $75 per person.

A free downtown **walking tour** brochure, with a map and descriptions of more than 30 historic buildings, is available at the Colorado Springs Convention and Visitors Bureau, as well as at local businesses.

Another free brochure, *Old Colorado City,* shows the location of more than a dozen historic buildings and lists shops, galleries, and other businesses.

The **Manitou Springs Chamber of Commerce & Visitors Bureau** (see "Visitor Information," earlier in this chapter) distributes the free *Manitou Springs Visitor's Guide,* which includes a self-guided walking-tour map of Mineral Springs, as well as information on where to find a variety of outdoor sculptures. See "Historic Neighborhoods," earlier in this chapter.

6 Outdoor Activities

For information on the city's parks and programs, contact the **Colorado Springs Parks and Recreation Department** (© **719/385-5940;** www.springsgov.com). Most of the state and federal agencies concerned with outdoor recreation are headquartered in Denver. There are branch offices in Colorado Springs for **Colorado State Parks,** 2128 N. Weber St. (© **719/471-0900;** www.parks.state.co.us); the **Colorado Division of Wildlife,** 2126 N. Weber St. (© **719/227-5200;** www.wildlife.state.co.us); and the **U.S. Forest Service,** Pikes Peak Ranger District of the Pike National Forest, 601 S. Weber St. (© **719/636-1602;** www.fs.fed.us/r2/psicc/pp).

You can get hunting and fishing licenses at many sporting-goods stores, as well as at the Colorado Division of Wildlife office listed above.

AERIAL SPORTS The **Black Forest Soaring Society,** 24566 David C. Johnson Loop, Elbert, CO 80106 (✆ **303/648-3623;** www.soarbfss.org), some 50 miles northeast of Colorado Springs, offers glider rides, rentals, and instruction. Rides start at about $100 for a 15-minute ride; rentals (to those with gliding licenses) and instruction are also available. Advance reservations are required.

The area's commercial ballooning companies include **High But Dry Balloons,** 4164 Austin Bluffs Pkwy., #146, Colorado Springs, CO 80918 (✆ **719/260-0011;** www.highbutdryballoons.com), for tours, champagne flights, and weddings. Sunrise flights are scheduled daily year-round, weather permitting. Cost depends on the number of passengers, locations, and type of flight, but averages about $175 per person. Generally, flights last 2 or 3 hours, with a minimum of 1 hour. On Labor Day weekend, the **Colorado Springs Balloon Classic** ✺✺ (✆ **719/471-4833;** www.balloon classic.com) sees more than 100 hot-air balloons launched from the city's Memorial Park. Admission is free.

BICYCLING Aside from the 4.3-mile loop trail around Monument Valley Park (see "Parks & Zoos" under "Attractions," above), there are numerous other urban trails for bikers. You can get information at the city's Visitor Information Center (see "Visitor Information," earlier in this chapter). For guided tours and rentals ($25/day), contact **Challenge Unlimited** (see "Mountain Biking," below).

FISHING Most serious Colorado Springs anglers drive south 40 miles to the Arkansas River or west to the Rocky Mountain streams and lakes, such as those found in Eleven Mile State Park and Spinney Mountain State Park on the South Platte River west of Florissant. Bass, catfish, walleye pike, and panfish are found in the streams of eastern Colorado; trout is the preferred sport fish of the mountain regions.

Angler's Covey, 295 S. 21st St. (✆ **719/471-2984;** www.anglerscovey.com), is a specialty fly-fishing shop and a good source of general fishing information for southern Colorado. It offers guided half- and full-day trips ($195–$345 for one to three persons), as well as state fishing licenses, rentals, flies, tackle, and so forth.

GOLF Public courses include the **Patty Jewett Golf Course,** 900 E. Española St. (✆ **719/385-6950); Pine Creek Golf Club,** 9850 Divot Trail (✆ **719/594-9999);** and **Valley Hi Golf Course,** 610 S. Chelton Rd. (✆ **719/385-6917).** Nonresident greens fees range from $32 to $42 for 18 holes (not including a cart).

The finest golf courses in the Colorado Springs area are private. Guests of The Broadmoor hotel can play the 54-hole **The Broadmoor Golf Club** (✆ **719/577-5790).**

HIKING Opportunities abound in municipal parks (see "Parks & Zoos" under "Attractions," above) and Pike National Forest, which borders Colorado Springs to the west. The U.S. Forest Service district office can provide maps and general information (see address and phone number in the introduction to this section).

Impressions

Could one live in constant view of these grand mountains without being elevated by them into a lofty plane of thought and purpose?
—General William J. Palmer, founder of Colorado Springs, 1871

Especially popular are the 7.5-mile **Waldo Canyon Trail,** with its trailhead just east of Cascade Avenue off U.S. 24; the 6-mile **Mount Manitou Trail,** starting in Ruxton Canyon above the hydroelectric plant; and the 12-mile **Barr Trail** to the summit of Pikes Peak. **Mueller State Park** (© 719/687-2366), 3½ miles south of Divide en route to Cripple Creek, has 55 miles of trails. See "Parks & Zoos" under "Attractions," above.

HORSEBACK RIDING You'll find good opportunities at city parks, including Garden of the Gods, North Cheyenne Cañon Park, and Palmer Park, plus Mueller State Park (see "Attractions," earlier in this chapter). The **Academy Riding Stables,** 4 El Paso Blvd., near Garden of the Gods (© 888/700-0410 or 719/633-5667; www. academyridingstables.com), offers guided trail rides for children and adults by reservation ($35 for 1 hour, $51 for 2).

ICE-SKATING The **Mark "Pa" Sertich Ice Center** at Memorial Park (© 719/385-5983) is open daily, offering prearranged instruction and rentals. The U.S. Olympic Complex operates the **Colorado Springs World Arena Ice Hall,** 3185 Venetucci Blvd. (© 719/477-2100; www.worldarena.com), with public sessions daily. Admission is $1 to $4, skate rentals $2. If you have hockey equipment, you can join a pickup game ($7); call for times. To get there, take I-25 exit 138, go west on Circle Drive to Venetucci Boulevard, and south to the arena.

MOUNTAIN BIKING There are abundant mountain-biking opportunities in the Colorado Springs area; contact the U.S. Forest Service for details (see address and phone number, in the introduction to this section). From May through early October, **Challenge Unlimited,** 204 S. 24th St. (© 800/798-5954 or 719/633-6399; www.bikithikit.com), hosts fully equipped, guided rides for every level of experience. Your guide on the 19-mile ride down the Pikes Peak Highway, from the summit at 14,110 feet to the tollgate at 7,000 feet, presents an interpretation of the nature, history, and beauty of the mountain. Participants must be at least 10 years old; advance reservations are advised. Rates are $75 to $105 per person. Challenge Unlimited also rents bikes and guides multiday excursions.

RIVER RAFTING Colorado Springs is 40 miles from the Arkansas River near Cañon City. Several licensed white-water outfitters tackle the Royal Gorge. **Echo Canyon River Expeditions,** 45000 U.S. 50 West, Cañon City, CO 81212 (© 800/755-3246 or 719/275-3154; www.raftecho.com), offers half-day to 3-day trips on "mild to wild" stretches of river. The company uses state-of-the-art equipment, including self-bailing rafts. Costs range from $44 (half-day, adult) to $135 for a daylong rental of an inflatable kayak. **Arkansas River Tours,** P.O. Box 337, Cotopaxi, CO 81223 (© 800/321-4352 or 719/942-4362; www.arkansasrivertours.com), offers white-water trips of lengths from a quarter of a day to all day for $32 to $105, and 2-day trips for about $240.

SWIMMING & TENNIS Many city parks have pool or lake swimming, for which they charge a small fee, and free tennis courts. Contact the Colorado Springs Parks and Recreation Department (© 719/385-5940) for locations and hours.

7 Spectator Sports

The **Air Force Academy Falcons** football team dominates the sports scene, and there are also competitive baseball, basketball, hockey, and soccer teams. Call for schedules and ticket information (© 800/666-USAF or 719/472-1895; www.goairforcefalcons. com).

AUTO RACING   The **Pikes Peak International Hill Climb** (© 719/685-4400; www.ppihc.com), known as the "Race to the Clouds," takes place annually in late June or early July. An international field of drivers negotiates the hairpin turns of the final 12⅓ miles of the Pikes Peak Highway to the top of the 14,110-foot mountain. On the way to the top, there are 156 turns (many of them of the hairpin variety), 2,000-foot cliffs, and no guardrails.

BASEBALL   The **Colorado Springs Sky Sox** of the Pacific Coast League, the AAA farm team for the Colorado Rockies of Denver, play a full 144-game season, with 72 home games at Sky Sox Stadium, 4385 Tutt Blvd., off Barnes Road east of Powers Boulevard (© 719/597-1449; www.skysox.com). The season runs from April through Labor Day. Tickets cost $7 to $9.

HOCKEY   In addition to Air Force Academy Hockey (see above), the **World Arena,** 3185 Venetucci Blvd. (© 719/477-2100; www.worldarena.com), is home to the Colorado College Tigers (© 719/389-6324; www.cctigers.com).

RODEO   Held annually since 1941, the **Pikes Peak or Bust Rodeo** (© 719/635-3547; www.coloradospringsrodeo.com), takes place in mid-July, and is a major stop on the Professional Rodeo Cowboys Association circuit. Its purse of more than $150,000 makes it the second-largest rodeo in Colorado, after Denver's National Western Stock Show. Events are at the **Norris-Penrose Events Center,** 945 W. Rio Grande St. Various events around the city, including a parade and a street breakfast, mark the rodeo.

8 Shopping

Five principal areas attract shoppers in Colorado Springs. The Manitou Springs and Old Colorado City neighborhoods are excellent places to browse for art, jewelry, arts and crafts, books, antiques, and other specialty items. The Chapel Hills and Citadel malls combine major department stores with a variety of national chain outlets. Downtown Colorado Springs also has numerous fine shops.

SHOPPING A TO Z
ANTIQUES
Antique Emporium at Manitou Springs   The shop's 4,000 square feet of floor space provides ample room for displaying its collection of antique furniture, china, glassware, books, collectibles, and primitives. 719 Manitou Ave., Manitou Springs. © 719/685-9195.

Nevada Avenue Antiques   This well-established multidealer mall, covering some 7,000 square feet, is filled with a wide variety of antiques and collectibles, including a good selection of lower-priced items. 405 S. Nevada Ave. © 719/473-3351.

The Villagers   Here you will find a diverse array of quality antiques and collectibles. Volunteers run the shop, and all proceeds go to Cheyenne Village, a community of adults with developmental disabilities. 2514 W. Colorado Ave., Old Colorado City. © 719/632-1400.

ART GALLERIES
Business of Art Center   Primarily an educational facility to help artists learn the business end of their profession, the center also has workshops, classes, and lectures, plus numerous artists' studios (open for viewing), six exhibition galleries, and a gift shop. Featured are renowned Colorado artists and juried exhibits of regional art. The shop offers a varied selection of regional artwork, including prints, photographs, jewelry, sculpture,

ceramics, wearable art, handblown glass, and carved-wood objects. Theater, music, and dance performances are occasionally staged. 513 Manitou Ave., Manitou Springs. ℭ **719/685-1861.**

Commonwheel Artists Co-op   Original art and fine crafts by area artists fill this excellent gallery, where you'll find a good selection of paintings, photography, sculpture, jewelry, textiles, and other items. 102 Cañon Ave., Manitou Springs. ℭ **719/685-1008.** www.commonwheel.com.

Flute Player Gallery   This gallery offers contemporary and traditional American Indian silver and turquoise jewelry, Pueblo pottery, Navajo weavings, and Hopi kachina dolls. 2511 W. Colorado Ave., Old Colorado City. ℭ **719/632-7702.**

Michael Garman's Gallery *(Kids*   A showcase for Garman's sculptures and casts depicting urban and Western life, this gallery also holds "Magic Town," a large model of an old-time inner city, with sculptures and holographic actors. Admission to Magic Town is $3 for adults, $1.50 for children 7 to 12, and free for children under 7. 2418 W. Colorado Ave., Old Colorado City. ℭ **800/731-3908** or 719/471-9391. www.michaelgarman.com.

BOOKS

There are numerous chain bookstores around the city, including **Barnes & Noble,** 795 Citadel Dr. E. (ℭ **719/637-8282**).

Book Sleuth *(Finds*   For all your mystery needs, visit this bookstore. In addition to a wide selection of mystery novels (including a good stock of out-of-print books), the shop offers numerous puzzles and games. 2501 W. Colorado Ave. #105, Old Colorado City. ℭ **719/632-2727.**

CRAFTS

Van Briggle Art Pottery   Founded in 1899 by Artus Van Briggle, who applied Chinese matte glaze to Rocky Mountain clays molded into imaginative Art Nouveau shapes, this is one of the oldest active art potteries in the United States. Artisans demonstrate their craft, from throwing on the wheel to glazing and firing. Free tours are available, and finished works are sold in the showroom. 600 S. 21st St., Old Colorado City. ℭ **800/847-6341** or 719/633-7729. www.vanbriggle.com.

JEWELRY

Manitou Jack's Jewelry & Gifts   Black Hills gold, 10- and 14-karat, is the specialty here. There's also an extensive collection of American Indian jewelry, pottery, sand paintings, and other art. The shop will create custom jewelry and make repairs. 814 Manitou Ave., Manitou Springs. ℭ **719/685-5004.**

Zerbe Jewelers   This well-established downtown Colorado Springs jeweler is known for beautiful custom work and one-of-a-kind designer jewelry. 26 N. Tejon St. ℭ **719/635-3521.**

MALLS & SHOPPING CENTERS

Chapel Hills Mall   Foley's, Sears, JCPenney, and Dillard's are among the 150 stores at this mall, which also houses an ice-skating arena, 40-foot climbing wall, children's play area, 15-screen movie theater, and about two dozen food outlets. 1710 Briargate Blvd. (N. Academy Blvd., at I-25 exit 150A). ℭ **719/594-0111.** www.chapelhillsmall.com.

The Citadel   This is southern Colorado's largest regional shopping mall, with Dillard's, Foley's, JCPenney, and more than 170 specialty shops and restaurants. 750 Citadel Dr. E. (N. Academy Blvd. at E. Platte Ave.). ℭ **719/591-5516.** www.shopthecitadel.com.

The Promenade Shops at Briargate Among the shops and restaurants at this chic outdoor shopping center on the city's northern suburban fringe are Pottery Barn, Ann Taylor, P.F. Chang's China Bistro, and Ted's Montana Grill. 1885 Briargate Pkwy., ⓒ 719/265-5516, www.thepromenadeshopsatbriargate.com.

SPORTING GOODS

In business since 1968, the independent **Mountain Chalet,** 226 N. Tejon St. (ⓒ 719/ 633-0732; www.mtnchalet.com), sells camping gear, outdoor clothing, hiking and climbing gear, and winter sports equipment. Another good source for all sorts of outdoor clothing and equipment is **Sports Authority,** with stores at 7730 N. Academy Blvd. (ⓒ 719/532-1020), and 1409 N. Academy Blvd. (ⓒ 719/574-1400).

WESTERN WEAR

Lorig's Western Wear ⚮ This Colorado Springs institution is where real cowboys get their hats, boots, jeans, and those fancy belts with the big buckles. 15 N. Union Blvd. ⓒ 719/633-4695.

WINE & LIQUOR

Cheers Liquor Mart This liquor supermarket has a huge selection of beer and wine, including Colorado wines, at good prices. 1105 N. Circle Dr. ⓒ 719/574-2244.

The Wines of Colorado This tasting room and sales outlet offers the greatest number of Colorado wines available for tasting under one roof. There are also gift items, and the restaurant offers a grill menu. 8045 W. U.S. 24, Cascade (about 10 miles west of Colorado Springs). ⓒ 719/684-0900.

9 Colorado Springs After Dark

The Colorado Springs entertainment scene spreads throughout the metropolitan area. Pikes Peak Center, the Colorado Springs Fine Arts Center, City Auditorium, Colorado College, and various facilities at the U.S. Air Force Academy are all outstanding venues for the performing arts. The city also supports dozens of cinemas, nightclubs, bars, and other after-dark attractions. Downtown is the major nightlife hub, but Old Colorado City and Manitou Springs also have their fair share of interesting establishments.

Weekly entertainment schedules appear in the Friday *Gazette.* Also look at the listings in *Springs* magazine and *The Independent,* free entertainment tabloids. A good online resource for information on events and nightlife, as well as restaurants, is www.sceneinthesprings.com.

Tickets for many major entertainment and sporting events can be obtained from **Ticketmaster** (ⓒ 719/520-9090; www.ticketmaster.com).

THE CLUB & MUSIC SCENE

Black Sheep A good bet for punk and indie rock, the Black Sheep features graffiti art on the walls and an edgy vibe throughout. 2106 E. Platte Ave. ⓒ 719/227-7625.

Cowboys Two-steppers and country-and-western music lovers flock to this east-side club, which boasts the largest dance floor in the area. It's open Wednesday to Sunday, and dance lessons are available. 3910 Palmer Park Blvd. ⓒ 719/596-1212.

Poor Richard's Restaurant An eclectic variety of performers appears at this bohemian landmark 1 or 2 nights a week, presenting everything from acoustic folk to

Celtic melodies to jazz to bluegrass. The menu includes pizza, sandwiches, and the area's best nachos (blue corn chips and mozzarella) as well as beer and wine. Adjacent are Poor Richard's Bookstore and Little Richard's Toy Store, all owned by local politico Richard Skorman. 324½ N. Tejon St. © **719/632-7721.**

Rum Bay   Located in the renovated Woolworth Building downtown, the lively Rum Bay is a massive nightclub sporting a wall full of rum bottles and a tropical theme. Disc jockeys spin records for two dance floors; there's also a piano bar featuring dueling players. The entire block contains six additional bars under the same management, ranging from "the world's smallest bar" to Rum Bay–like clubs focusing on tequila and bourbon. 20 N. Tejon St. © **719/634-3522.**

Underground Pub   This popular hangout attracts a diverse crowd, from college students and other young people to baby boomers and retirees. Patrons come to dance or just listen to the equally eclectic music (live or recorded), which ranges from rock to jazz to reggae, with some occasional folk. 110 N. Nevada Ave. © **719/633-0590.**

THE BAR SCENE

15C   An unmarked speakeasy-style joint with an alley entrance, 15C is a slick martini and cigar bar with an upscale ambience accented by dim lighting and leather couches. Located just off Bijou St. in the alley between Cascade Ave. and Tejon St. © **719/635-8303.**

Bijou Bar and Grill   Southern Colorado's longest-standing gay and lesbian bar, the Bijou Bar has a Mexican menu, regular drink specials, Wednesday karaoke nights, and DJs spinning dance music on Friday and Saturday. 2510 W. Bijou Ave. © **719/473-5718.**

Golden Bee *(Moments*   An opulent 19th-century English pub was disassembled, shipped from Great Britain, and reassembled piece by piece to create this delightful drinking establishment. You can have imported English ale by the yard or half-yard while enjoying steak-and-potato pie, Devonshire cheddar-cheese soup, sandwiches, or other British specialties. Evenings bring a ragtime pianist to enliven the atmosphere; interested guests are given songbooks so they can sing along. Lower level entrance of The Broadmoor International Center, Lake Circle. © **719/634-7711.**

Meadow Muffins   A boisterous barroom packed to the gills with movie memorabilia and assorted knickknacks, Meadow Muffins certainly doesn't lack personality. It features DJs or live music several nights a week. The food is standard bar fare, but the burgers are great. On most days, there are several specials, with happy hour from 4 to 7pm daily and 4pm until closing on Friday. There are also pool tables, a pair of big-screen TVs, and arcade games. See also the restaurant listing on p. 160. 2432 W. Colorado Ave., in Old Colorado City. © **719/633-0583.**

Oscar's   Featuring aquariums above the bar, this downtown hangout shucks more oysters than anyplace in the area, including The Broadmoor's eateries. The menu here is Cajun, the crowd eclectic, the music tending towards jazz and blues. 333 S. Tejon St. © **719/471-8070.**

Phantom Canyon Brewing Co.   This popular brewpub generally offers 8 to 10 of its specialty beers, including homemade root beer. The beers are unfiltered and unpasteurized, served at the traditional temperature for the style. We recommend Railyard Ale, a light amber ale with a smooth, malty taste; Hefeweizen, a traditional German wheat beer; and a very hoppy India pale ale. A billiard hall is on the second floor. See also the restaurant listing on p. 159. 2 E. Pikes Peak Ave. © **719/635-2800.**

Ritz Grill Especially popular with young professionals after work and the chic clique later in the evening, this noisy restaurant-lounge, known for its martinis and large central bar, brings an Art Deco feel to downtown Colorado Springs. There's live music (usually rock) starting at 9pm Thursday through Saturday. See also the restaurant listing on p. 159. 15 S. Tejon St. ℂ **719/635-8484.**

Tony's Laden with plenty of brick and sports memorabilia, this neighborhood bar just north of Acacia Park has a laid-back vibe, Wisconsin roots, and the best fried cheese curds in the state. 311 N. Tejon St. ℂ **719/228-6566.**

THE PERFORMING ARTS

Among the major venues for performing arts is the 8,000-seat **Colorado Springs World Arena,** 3185 Venetucci Blvd., at I-25 exit 138 (ℂ **719/477-2100;** www.world arena.com). The area's newest entertainment center, it presents big-name country and rock concerts and a wide variety of sporting events. Other major facilities include the handsome **Pikes Peak Center,** 190 S. Cascade Ave. (ℂ **719/520-7453** for general information, or 719/520-7469 for the ticket office; www.pikespeakcenter.org), a 2,000-seat concert hall in the heart of downtown that has been acclaimed for its outstanding acoustics. The city's symphony orchestra and dance theater call the Pikes Peak Center home, and top-flight touring entertainers, Broadway musicals, and symphony orchestras appear here as well. The **Colorado Springs Fine Arts Center,** 30 W. Dale St. (ℂ **719/634-5581** for general information, or 719/634-5583 for the box office; www.csfineartscenter.org), is a historic facility (see "Museums & Galleries" under "Attractions," earlier in this chapter) that includes a children's theater program, a repertory theater company, dance programs and concerts, and classic films. Recent productions have included *Annie* and *Oklahoma.* At the historic **City Auditorium,** 221 E. Kiowa St. (ℂ **719/578-6652;** www.springsgov.com), you can often attend a trade show or big-name concert—Willie Nelson performed recently—or drop in at the Lon Chaney Theatre, with its resident Star Bar Players (see below) and Pikes Peak Youth Theatre.

THEATER & DANCE

BlueBards The Air Force Academy's cadet theater group performs Broadway and other productions; it recently staged Shakespeare's *As You Like It.* Arnold Hall Theater, U.S. Air Force Academy. ℂ **719/333-4497.**

Colorado Springs Dance Theatre This nonprofit organization presents international dance companies from September to May at Pikes Peak Center, Colorado College's Armstrong Hall, and other venues. Notable productions have included Mikhail Baryshnikov, Alvin Ailey Repertory Ensemble, Ballet Folklorico of Mexico, and other traditional, modern, ethnic, and jazz dance programs. Each year, three to five performances are scheduled, and master classes, lectures, and other programs often coincide with the performances. Tickets typically run $20 to $35. 7 E. Bijou St., Suite 209. ℂ **719/630-7434.** www.csdance.org.

Star Bar Players Each year, this resident theater company presents several full-length plays, ranging from Greek comedies to modern murder mysteries. Recent productions have included *Dancing at Lughnasa* and *Bell, Book and Candle.* Tickets are typically $10 to $20. Lon Chaney Theatre, City Auditorium, 221 E. Kiowa St. ℂ **719/573-7411.** www.starbarplayers.org.

DINNER THEATERS

Flying W Ranch ☞   This working cattle and horse ranch just north of the Garden of the Gods encompasses a Western village of more than a dozen restored buildings and a mine train. There are also demonstrations of Navajo weaving and horse shoeing. A Western stage show features bunkhouse comedy, cowboy balladry, and footstompin' fiddle, mandolin, and guitar music. From mid-May through September the town opens each afternoon at 4:30pm; a chuck-wagon dinner (barbecued beef or chicken, potatoes, beans, biscuits, and cake) is served ranch-style at 7:15pm, and the show begins at 8:30pm. The winter steakhouse is open October to December and March to May on Friday and Saturday, with seatings at 5 and 8pm and a Western stage show at each seating.

3330 Chuckwagon Rd. ℭ **800/232-FLYW** or 719/598-4000. www.flyingw.com. Reservations recommended. Chuck-wagon dinner $20 adults, $9.50 children under 9; winter steakhouse $21–$24 adults, $12 children under 9.

Iron Springs Chateau Melodrama ☞   Located near the foot of the Pikes Peak Cog Railway, this popular comedy and drama dinner theater urges patrons to boo the villain and cheer the hero. Past productions have included *Farther North to Laughter or Buck of the Yukon, Part Two,* and *When the Halibut Start Running or Don't Slam the Door on Davy Jones' Locker.* A family-style dinner, with free seconds, includes ovenbaked chicken and barbecued beef brisket, mashed potatoes, green beans almandine, pineapple coleslaw, and buttermilk biscuits. A singalong and a vaudeville-style olio show follow the performance. Iron Springs Chateau is open from April through mid-October and in December. Dinner is served on Tuesday, Wednesday, Friday, and Saturday between 6 and 6:45pm; the show follows at 8pm.

444 Ruxton Ave., Manitou Springs. ℭ **719/685-5104** or 719/685-5572. www.pikes-peak.com. Reservations required. Dinner and show $25 adults, $24 seniors, $15 children; show only $14 adults, $14 seniors, $9.50 children.

---

10 Side Trips to Florissant Fossil Beds National Monument & Cripple Creek

FLORISSANT FOSSIL BEDS NATIONAL MONUMENT ☞☞

Approximately 35 miles west of Colorado Springs on U.S. 24 is the small village of Florissant, which means "flowering" in French. It couldn't be more aptly named—every spring its hillsides virtually blaze with wildflowers. Just 2 miles south is one of the most spectacular, yet relatively unknown, fossil deposits in the world, Florissant Fossil Beds National Monument. From Florissant, follow the signs along Teller County Road 1.

The fossils in this 6,000-acre National Park Service property are preserved in the rocks of ancient Lake Florissant, which existed 34 million years ago. Volcanic eruptions spanning half a million years trapped plants and animals under layers of ash and dust; the creatures were fossilized as the sediment settled and became shale.

The detailed impressions, first discovered in 1873, offer the most extensive record of its kind in the world. Scientists have removed thousands of specimens, including 1,100 separate species of insects. Dragonflies, beetles, and ants; more fossil butterflies than anywhere else in the world; plus spiders, fish, some mammals, and birds are all perfectly preserved from 34 to 35 million years ago. Leaves from willows, maples, and hickories; extinct relatives of birches, elms, and beeches; and needles of pines and sequoias are also plentiful. These fossil plants, very different from those living in the area today, show how the climate has changed over the centuries.

Mudflows also buried forests during this long period, petrifying the trees where they stood. Nature trails pass petrified tree stumps; one sequoia stump is 10 feet in diameter and 11 feet high. There's a display of carbonized fossils at the visitor center, which also offers interpretive programs. An added attraction within the monument is the homestead of Adeline Hornbek, who pioneered the area with her children in 1878. The national monument also has some 14 miles of hiking trails.

Nearby, about ½ mile north of the monument, there's superb fishing for German browns and cutthroats at Spinney Mountain Reservoir.

Admission to the monument is $3 per adult and free for children under 15, making a visit here an incredibly affordable outing. It's open from 9am to 5pm daily, closed January 1, Thanksgiving, and December 25. Contact Florissant Fossil Beds National Monument, P.O. Box 185, Florissant, CO 80816-0185 (© **719/748-3253;** www.nps.gov/flfo).

CRIPPLE CREEK

This old mining town on the southwestern flank of Pikes Peak was known as the world's greatest gold camp after the precious metal was first discovered here in 1890. During its heyday at the beginning of the 20th century, Cripple Creek (elevation 9,494 ft.) had a stock exchange, 2 opera houses, 5 daily newspapers, 16 churches, 19 schools, and 73 saloons, plus an elaborate streetcar system and a railroad depot that saw 18 arrivals and departures a day. By the time mining ceased in 1961, more than $800 million worth of ore had been taken from the surrounding hills.

Today Cripple Creek has several dozen limited-stakes gambling casinos, most lining Bennett Avenue. They cash in not only on the lure of gambling but also on the nostalgia for the gambling houses that were once prominent throughout the Old West. Although gamblers must be at least 21 years old, some casinos offer special children's areas, along with other family activities. Among the more interesting of the many casinos in town is the **Imperial Casino Hotel,** 123 N. 3rd St. at Bennett Ave. (P.O. Box 869), Cripple Creek, CO 80813 (© **800/235-2922** or 719/689-7777; www.imperialcasinohotel.com). Built in 1896 following a disastrous fire that razed most of the city, the fully renovated Imperial offers Victorian accommodations in a handsome historic building, a casino, and several restaurants and bars.

One of the town's unique attractions is a herd of wild donkeys, descendants of the miners' runaways, that roam freely through the hills and into the streets. The year's biggest celebration, **Donkey Derby Days** in late June, culminates with a donkey race.

Although gambling takes place year-round, many of the historic attractions are open in summer only or have limited winter hours. Among those you'll want to check out is the 1891 **Mollie Kathleen Gold Mine,** 1 mile north of Cripple Creek on Colo. 67 (© **719/689-2466;** www.goldminetours.com). It offers visitors a rare chance to join hard-rock miners on a 1,050-foot underground descent into a genuine gold mine and take home a gold-ore specimen as a souvenir. Tours last about 40 minutes; temperatures in the mine are 45°F to 50°F (7°C–10°C), and jackets are provided. Admission is $15 for adults, $7 for children 5 to 14, and free for children under 5. The mine is open from early April through October daily from 9am to 5pm, and usually open Friday through Sunday in winter; call ahead.

The **Cripple Creek District Museum,** at the east end of Bennett Avenue (© **719/689-2634;** www.cripple-creek.org), includes three historic buildings packed with late-19th-century relics, including mining and railroad memorabilia. There's a gold-ore exhibit, Victorian fashions and furniture, exhibits on local wildlife, historic photos, a fully restored Victorian-era flat, and an assay office where fire testing of local ores took place. The museum is open daily from 10am to 5pm Memorial Day through September, and Friday through Sunday from 10am to 4pm the rest of the year.

The **Cripple Creek & Victor Narrow Gauge Railroad Co.** ﷼﷼, at the Midland Terminal Depot, east end of Bennett Avenue at 5th St. (© **719/689-2640;** www.cripple creekrailroad.com), takes visitors on a 4-mile narrated tour. The route runs past abandoned mines and over a reconstructed trestle to the ghost town of Anaconda, powered by a 15-ton "iron horse" steam locomotive. The train operates daily from mid-June to mid-October. The first train leaves the station at 10am and subsequent trains leave every 45 minutes, give or take, until 5pm. Tickets are $11 for adults, $9.50 seniors, $6 children 3 to 12, and free for kids under 3.

Cripple Creek is 45 miles west of Colorado Springs; take U.S. 24 west and Colo. 67 south. For additional information, contact the **Cripple Creek Chamber of Commerce,** P.O. Box 430, Cripple Creek, CO 80813 (© **877/858-4653** or 719/689-3461; www.cripple-creek.co.us).

NEARBY SCENIC DRIVES

When you leave Cripple Creek, two drives of particular beauty offer alternatives to Colo. 67. Neither is paved and both are narrow and winding, but both are usually acceptable for everyday vehicles under dry conditions. Each is roughly 30 miles long but requires about 90 minutes to negotiate. First, take Colo. 67 south out of Cripple Creek for 6 miles to the historic mining town of **Victor,** a delightful, picturesque destination.

The **Gold Camp Road** leads east from Victor to Colorado Springs via the North Cheyenne Cañon. Teddy Roosevelt said that this trip up the old Short Line Railroad bed had "scenery that bankrupts the English language." The **Phantom Canyon Road** leads south from Victor to Florence, following another old narrow-gauge railroad bed known as the Gold Belt Line. A number of ghost towns and fossil areas mark this route.

8

Boulder

Although Boulder is known primarily as a college town (the University of Colorado is here), it would be inaccurate to begin and end the description there. Sophisticated and artsy, Boulder is home to numerous high-tech companies and research concerns; it also attracts countless outdoor sports enthusiasts with its delightful climate, vast open spaces, and proximity to Rocky Mountain National Park.

Set at the foot of the Flatirons of the Rocky Mountains, just 30 miles northwest of downtown Denver and only 74 feet higher than the Mile High City, Boulder was settled by hopeful miners in 1858 and named for the large rocks in the area. Welcomed by Chief Niwot and the resident southern Arapaho, the miners struck gold in the nearby hills the following year. By the 1870s, Boulder had become a regional rail and trade center for mining and farming. The university, founded in 1877, became the economic mainstay of the community after mining collapsed around the beginning of the 20th century.

In the 1950s, Boulder emerged as a national hub for scientific and environmental research. The National Center for Atmospheric Research and the National Institute of Standards and Technology are located here, as are dozens of high-tech and aerospace companies. Alongside the ongoing high-tech boom, the university and attendant vibrant culture have attracted a diverse mix of intellectuals, individualists, and eccentrics. Writers William S. Burroughs, Jr., Stephen King, and Allen Ginsberg, cofounder of the city's Naropa Institute, all called Boulder home at one time or another.

Today's residents are a mix of students attending the University of Colorado (called CU by locals); employees of the many computer, biotech, and research firms; and others attracted by the casual, bohemian, environmentally aware, and otherwise hip lifestyles that prevail here. Whatever differences exist among the residents, they are united by a common love of the outdoors. Boulder has 30,000 acres of open space within its city limits, 56 parks, and 200 miles of trails. On any given day, seemingly three-quarters of the population is outside making great use of this land, generally from the vantage point of a bicycle seat, the preferred mode of transport—there are about 100,000 bicycles in Boulder, one for each of the city's 100,000 residents.

1 Orientation

ARRIVING

BY PLANE

Boulder doesn't have a commercial airport. Air travelers must fly into Denver International Airport, then make ground connections to Boulder, a trip of about an hour.

GETTING TO & FROM THE AIRPORT   The **SuperShuttle Boulder** (© 303/227-0000; www.supershuttle.com) leaves Denver International Airport hourly from

8am to 11pm, and Boulder hourly between 3:30am and 9:30pm, with fewer departures on holidays. Scheduled pickups in Boulder are at the University of Colorado
campus and area hotels; pickups from other locations are made on call. The one-way
fare from a scheduled pickup point to the airport is $20 per person, or $26 for residential pickup service from other points; children 8 and under ride free.

Boulder Yellow Cab (© **303/777-7777**) charges $70 one-way to the airport for
up to five passengers.

Buses operated by the **Regional Transportation District,** known locally as **RTD**
(© **800/366-7433** or 303/299-6000, TDD 303/299-6089; www.rtd-denver.com),
charge $10 for a one-way trip to the airport (exact change required). Buses leave from,
and return to, the main terminal at 14th and Walnut streets daily every hour from
before 4am to after midnight.

Boulder Limousine Service (© **303/449-5466**) charges $100 to $250 to take up
to three people from Boulder to DIA in a limousine.

BY CAR

The Boulder Turnpike (U.S. 36) branches off I-25 north of Denver and passes
through the suburbs of Westminster, Broomfield, and Louisville before reaching Boulder. The trip takes about 30 minutes. If you are coming from Denver International
Airport, E-470 west to I-25 south is the best route to U.S. 36.

If you're arriving from the north, take the Longmont exit from I-25 and follow
Colo. 119 all the way. Longmont is 7 miles due west of the freeway; Boulder is
another 15 miles southwest on the Longmont Diagonal Highway.

VISITOR INFORMATION

The **Boulder Convention and Visitors Bureau,** 2440 Pearl St. (at Folsom St.), Boulder, CO 80302 (© **800/444-0447** or 303/442-2911; www.bouldercoloradousa.com),
is open Monday through Thursday from 8:30am to 5pm, Friday from 8:30am to 4pm,
and can provide excellent maps, brochures, and general information on the city.

There are also visitor information kiosks on **Pearl Street Mall** and at the **Davidson
Mesa overlook,** several miles southeast of Boulder on U.S. 36. Brochures are available
at both sites year-round.

CITY LAYOUT

The north-south streets increase in number going from west to east, beginning with
3rd Street. (The eastern city limit is at 61st St., although the numbers continue to the
Boulder County line at 124th St. in Broomfield.) Where U.S. 36 enters Boulder (and
does a 45-degree turn to the north), it becomes 28th Street, a major commercial
artery. The Longmont Diagonal Highway (Colo. 119) enters Boulder from the northeast and intersects 28th Street at the north end of the city.

To reach downtown Boulder from U.S. 36, turn west on Canyon Boulevard (Colo.
119 west) and north on Broadway, which would be 12th Street if it had a number. It's

---

Fun Fact **A Job Well Done**

The National Trust for Historic Preservation has named Boulder one of the
nation's "dozen distinctive destinations" for preserving historic sites, managing
growth, and maintaining a vibrant downtown.

2 blocks to the Pearl Street Mall, a 4-block, east-west pedestrian-only strip from 11th to 15th streets that constitutes the historic downtown district. Boulder's few one-way streets circle the mall: 13th and 15th streets are one-way north, 11th and 14th one-way south, Walnut Street (a block south of the mall) one-way east, and Spruce Street (a block north) one-way west.

Broadway continues across the mall, eventually joining U.S. 36 north of the city. South of Arapahoe Avenue, Broadway turns southeast, skirting the University of Colorado campus and becoming Colo. 93 (the Foothills Hwy. to Golden) after crossing Baseline Road. Baseline follows a straight line from east Boulder, across U.S. 36 and Broadway, past Chautauqua Park and up the mountain slopes. To the south, Table Mesa Drive takes a similar course.

The Foothills Parkway (not to be confused with the Foothills Hwy.) is the principal north-south route on the east side of Boulder, extending from U.S. 36 at Table Mesa Drive to the Longmont Diagonal; Arapahoe Avenue, a block south of Canyon Boulevard, continues east across 28th Street as Arapahoe Road.

2 Getting Around

BY PUBLIC TRANSPORTATION

The **Regional Transportation District,** known as the **RTD** (✆ **800/366-7433** or 303/299-6000; www.rtd-denver.com), provides bus service throughout Boulder as well as the Denver greater metropolitan area. The Boulder Transit Center, 14th and Walnut streets, is open Monday through Friday from 5am to midnight and Saturday and Sunday from 6am to midnight. Fares within the city are $1.50 for adults and children, 75¢ for seniors and passengers with disabilities, children under 6 ride free. Schedules are available at the Transit Center, the Chamber of Commerce, and other locations. Buses are wheelchair accessible.

The city of Boulder runs a shuttle bus service called the **HOP** (✆ **303/447-8282**), connecting downtown, University Hill, the University of Colorado, and 30th and Pearl. The HOP operates Monday through Thursday from 7am to 10pm, Friday and Saturday from 9am to 10pm, and Sunday from 10am to 6pm. While the University of Colorado is in session, the night HOP runs Friday and Saturday from 10pm to 3am. Buses run about every 8 to 15 minutes during the day, every 15 to 20 minutes at night; the fare is $1.50 (75¢ for seniors).

The RTD runs a complementary local shuttle, the **SKIP,** Monday through Friday from 5:09am to 12:30am, Saturday from 7:30am to 12:30am, and Sunday from 7:18am to 11pm. Buses run north and south along Broadway, with a loop through the west Table Mesa neighborhood, every 6 to 10 minutes during peak weekday times and less frequently in the evenings and on weekends.

BY CAR

The **American Automobile Association (AAA)** has an office at 1933 28th St., #200 (✆ **303/753-8800**). It's open Monday through Friday from 8:30am to 5:30pm, Saturday from 9am to 1pm.

CAR RENTALS   Most people who fly to Colorado land at Denver International Airport and rent a car there. To rent a car in Boulder, contact **Avis** (✆ 800/331-1212), **Dollar** (✆ 800/800-4000), **Enterprise** (✆ 800/736-8222), **Hertz** (✆ 800/654-3131), or **National** (✆ 888/227-7368).

PARKING   Most downtown streets have parking meters, with rates of about 25¢ per 20 minutes. Downtown parking lots cost $1 to $3 for 3 hours. Parking can be hard to find around the Pearl Street Mall, but new lots have eased the pain. Outside downtown, free parking is generally available on side streets.

BY BICYCLE

Boulder is a wonderful place for bicycling; there are bike paths throughout the city and an extensive trail system leading for miles beyond Boulder's borders (see "Bicycling" under "Sports & Outdoor Activities," later in this chapter).

You can rent and repair mountain bikes and buy trail and city maps at **University Bicycles,** 839 Pearl St., about 2 blocks west of the Pearl Street Mall (© 303/444-4196; www.ubikes.com), and **Full Cycle,** 1211 13th St., near the campus (© 303/440-7771; www.fullcyclebikes.com). Bike rentals cost $20 to $80 daily. Maps and other information are also available at the **Boulder Convention and Visitors Bureau,** 2440 Pearl St. (© 303/442-2911).

BY TAXI

Boulder Yellow Cab (© 303/777-7777) operates 24 hours, but you need to call for service—there are no taxi stands, and taxis won't stop for you on the street. Another company that serves Boulder is **Metro Taxi** (© 303/333-3333).

ON FOOT

You can walk to most of what's worth seeing in downtown Boulder, especially around the Pearl Street Mall and University of Colorado campus. **Historic Boulder, Inc.,** 4735 Walnut St. (© 303/444-5192; www.historicboulder.org), can provide advice about exploring the city's historic neighborhoods on foot. It prints a brochure, *Walking Tours of Boulder,* that's available for $3.50 at the Convention and Visitors Bureau, 2440 Pearl St.

FAST FACTS: Boulder

Area Code Area codes are **303** and **720,** and local calls require 10-digit dialing. See the "Telephone, Telegraph, Telex & Fax" section under "Fast Facts," in chapter 2.

Babysitters The front desk at a major hotel often can make arrangements on your behalf. Boulder's **Child Care Referral Service** (© 303/441-3180) can also help if you call in advance.

Business Hours Most banks are open Monday through Friday from 9am to 5pm, and some have Saturday hours, too. Major stores are open Monday through Saturday from 9 or 10am until 5 or 6pm, and often Sunday from noon until 5pm. Department and discount stores often have later closing times.

Car Rentals See "Getting Around," above.

Drugstores Reliable prescription services are available at the Medical Center Pharmacy in the **Boulder Medical Center,** 2750 N. Broadway (© 303/440-3111). The pharmacy at **King Soopers Supermarket,** 1650 30th St., in Sunrise Plaza (© 303/444-0164), is open from 8am to 9pm weekdays, 9am to 6pm Saturdays, and 10am to 6pm Sundays.

Emergencies For police, fire, or medical emergencies, call 🕿 **911**. For the **Poison Control Center,** call 🕿 **800/332-3073** or 303/739-1123. For the **Rape Crisis Hotline,** call 🕿 **303/443-7300.**

Eyeglasses You can get fast repair or replacement of your glasses at **Boulder Optical,** 1928 14th St. (🕿 **303/442-4521**).

Hospitals Full medical services, including 24-hour emergency treatment, are available at **Boulder Community Hospital,** 1100 Balsam Ave., at North Broadway (🕿 **303/440-2273**).

Newspapers & Magazines Newspaper options include the *Daily Camera* and the *Boulder Weekly.* Many Boulderites also read the campus paper, the *Colorado Daily,* available all over town. Both Denver dailies—the *Denver Post* and the *Rocky Mountain News*—are available at newsstands throughout the city. You can also find the *New York Times, Wall Street Journal,* and *Christian Science Monitor* at many newsstands.

Photographic Needs For standard processing requirements (including 2-hr. slide processing), as well as custom lab work, contact **Photo Craft,** 3550 Arapahoe Ave. (🕿 **303/442-6410**). For equipment, supplies, and repairs, visit **Mike's Camera,** 2500 Pearl St. (🕿 **303/443-1715;** www.mikescamera.com).

Post Office The main downtown post office is at 15th and Walnut streets. Contact the U.S. Postal Service (🕿 **800/275-8777;** www.usps.com) for hours and other locations.

Safety Although Boulder is generally a safe city, it is not crime free. Many locals avoid walking alone late at night along the Boulder Creek Path because of the transients who tend to hang out there.

Taxes State and city sales taxes total almost 7%.

Useful Telephone Numbers Call 🕿 **303/639-1111** for **road conditions;** 🕿 **303/825-7669** for **ski reports;** and 🕿 **303/494-4221** for **weather reports.**

3 Where to Stay

You'll find a good selection of comfortable lodgings in Boulder, with a wide range of rates to suit almost every budget. Be aware, though, that the town literally fills up during the popular summer season, making advance reservations essential. It's also almost impossible to find a place to sleep during any major event at the University of Colorado, particularly graduation. Those who do find themselves in Boulder without lodging can check with the Boulder Convention and Visitors Bureau (see "Visitor Information," under "Orientation," above), which keeps track of availability. You can usually find a room in Denver, a half-hour or so away. Rates listed below do not include the 10.25% accommodations tax. Parking is free unless otherwise specified.

Major chains and franchises that provide reasonably priced lodging in Boulder include **Best Western Boulder Inn,** 770 28th St., Boulder, CO 80303 (🕿 **800/223-8469** or 303/449-3800), with rates of $79 to $144 double; **Boulder Creek Quality Inn and Suites,** 2020 Arapahoe Ave., Boulder, CO 80302 (🕿 **888/449-7550** or 303/449-7550; www.qualityinnboulder.com), with rates of $79 to $149 double; and

Days Inn, 5397 S. Boulder Rd., Boulder, CO 80303 (✆ **800/329-7466** or 303/499-4422), with rates of $69 to $109 double. Among the nonchains, **Boulder University Inn,** just south of downtown at 1632 Broadway (✆ **303/417-1700;** www.boulder universityinn.com), is a solid option, with reasonable double rates of $79 to $119.

VERY EXPENSIVE

St. Julien ⚘⚘⚘   The first new hotel in downtown Boulder since the Boulderado opened in 1909, the $24 million St. Julien instantly raised the bar for lodging in Boulder when it opened in 2005. The flagstone and Norman brick exterior (accented by patina copper and red roof tiles) sheaths a sumptuous lobby and exquisite guest rooms, averaging a healthy 400 square feet each. Everything from the luxurious linens to the premium bath amenities to the artistic Boulder photographs on the wall is first rate. Honeyed tones and French doors accent the guest rooms, which feature either one California king or two queens. The bathrooms are the best in town; there are separate tubs and showers in every granite-laden one. Perks include guided hikes on weekends ($10 for about 3 hours), a two-lane lap pool, and a spa that offers "indigenous therapies" using local minerals and plants. Expect to be wowed.

900 Walnut St., Boulder, CO 80302. ✆ **877/303-0900** or 720/406-9696. Fax 720/406-9668. www.stjulien.com. 201 units, including 15 suites. $285 double; $499–$599 suite. Lower weekend rates. AE, DC, DISC, MC, V. Valet parking $15 per night. **Amenities:** Restaurant (American); lounge; indoor heated pool; outdoor heated pool; fitness center; spa; complimentary bikes; concierge; business center; dry cleaning. *In room:* A/C, cable TV w/pay movies, coffeemaker, hair dryer, iron, safe, high-speed wireless Internet.

EXPENSIVE

The Alps ⚘⚘ *(Finds)*   A stage stop in the late 1800s, this historic log lodge sits on a mountainside about 7 minutes west of downtown Boulder. Converted into a beautiful bed-and-breakfast decorated with Arts and Crafts and Mission furnishing by owners Jeannine and John Vanderhart, the Alps is ideal for travelers planning to split time between Boulder and its outlying wilderness and scenery. Each room here is different and named after a Colorado mining town, including Magnolia, Salina, and Wall Street. All have functional fireplaces with Victorian mantels, king or queen beds with down comforters, and individual thermostats. Most are spacious, with a claw-foot or double whirlpool tub plus a double shower, and many have private porches. Shared spaces include a beautiful lounge with a huge rock fireplace, plus delightful gardens and patio areas. The entrance is the original log cabin built in the 1870s. Smoking is not permitted.

38619 Boulder Canyon Dr., Boulder, CO 80302. ✆ **800/414-2577** or 303/444-5445. Fax 303/444-5522. www.alps inn.com. 12 units. $139–$260 double. Rates include full breakfast. AE, DC, DISC, MC, V. **Amenities:** Jacuzzi; concierge; activities desk; in-room massage. *In room:* A/C, cable TV, dataport, hair dryer, iron.

Boulder Marriott ⚘   Until the St. Julien came along (see above), the Marriott was the newest full-service hotel in the city. It is conveniently located just a block off 28th Street (U.S. 36), providing great access to everything in town. Furnished with Southwestern touches, the rooms are geared to the business traveler, with multiline phones, large work desks, and ergonomic chairs. Local and toll-free calls cost $1. The concierge level has a private lounge, and rates include continental breakfast, happy hour, and hors d'oeuvres. Three-quarters of the rooms feature mountain views.

2660 Canyon Blvd., Boulder, CO 80302 (1 block west of Canyon and 28th St.). ✆ **303/440-8877.** Fax 303/440-3377. www.marriott.com/denbo. 157 units. $139–$219 double; $259–$279 suite. AE, DC, DISC, MC, V. Free valet and self-parking. **Amenities:** Restaurant (steakhouse); lounge; indoor heated pool; exercise room; spa; Jacuzzi; 24-hr. business

Boulder

center; shopping arcade; limited room service; massage; laundry service; dry cleaning; executive level. *In room:* A/C, cable TV w/pay movies, dataport, coffeemaker, hair dryer, iron, safe, complimentary wireless Internet access.

The Bradley 🐾🐾   Built as an upscale inn in 1994, the Bradley nicely blends into the surrounding historic neighborhood, just northeast of the Pearl Street Mall. The striking Great Room and uniquely decorated guest rooms are all adorned with bold contemporary art from local galleries, and it's all for sale. Some of the rooms have hot tubs and balconies; all of them have standout Bob Timberlake furnishings from North Carolina, rainforest showerheads, and tiny sleeping cat sculptures at the foot of the bed. The eclectic inn has a very homey feel, and the breakfasts—featuring huge fresh fruit salads and bread that is baked on-site—and the nightly wine and cheese are big events.

2040 16th St., Boulder, CO 80302. ✆ **800/858-5811** or 303/545-5200. Fax 303/440-6740. www.thebradley boulder.com. 12 units. $150–$200 double. Rates include full breakfast. AE, DC, DISC, MC, V. **Amenities:** Complimentary access to a nearby health club; concierge; business center; dry cleaning. *In room:* A/C, cable TV/DVD, hair dryer, iron, complimentary wireless Internet access.

Briar Rose 🐾   A country-style brick home built in the 1890s, this midcity bed-and-breakfast might remind you of Grandma's place. Every room is furnished with antiques, from the bedrooms to the parlor to the sunny back porch, and the lovely gardens offer a quiet escape. Two of the six units in the main house have fireplaces; four in a separate cottage come with either a patio or a balcony. All are furnished with feather comforters. The full organic breakfast is gourmet quality: homemade granola, fresh nut breads, yogurt with fruit, and much more. Refreshments are available in the lobby from 8am to 9pm. Smoking is permitted only in the outside garden areas.

2151 Arapahoe Ave., Boulder, CO 80302. ✆ **303/442-3007**. Fax 303/786-8440. www.briarrosebb.com. 10 units (6 with shower only). $149–$179 double. Rates include full breakfast. AE, MC, V. *In room:* A/C, cable TV, dataport, hair dryer.

Hotel Boulderado 🐾🐾   Opened on January 1, 1909, this elegant and historic hotel still has the same Otis elevator that wowed visiting dignitaries that day. The colorful stained-glass ceiling and cantilevered cherrywood staircase are other reminders of days past, along with the rich woodwork of the balusters around the mezzanine and the handsome armchairs and settees in the main-floor lobby. The hotel's Christmas tree, a 28 footer with over 1,000 white lights, is a Boulder tradition, and the setting for afternoon tea on the mezzanine in December.

Five stories tall and just a block off the Pearl Street Mall, this contemporary of Denver's Brown Palace has 42 original guest rooms, all bright and cozy, individually decorated with panache. Although the rooms are continuously renovated and refurbished, they retain a Victorian flavor, with lush floral wallpapering, custom bedspreads, and furnishings alternately stately and plush. The construction of a spacious North Wing in 1989 almost quadrupled the number of rooms; while these are larger and more typical of a modern hotel, they also embody the early-20th-century theme. All have a few high-tech touches: electronic locks and two-line phones with voicemail; most rooms have refrigerators, and a few have jetted tubs.

2115 13th St. (at Spruce St.), Boulder, CO 80302. ✆ **800/433-4344** or 303/442-4344. Fax 303/442-4378. www. boulderado.com. 160 units. $150–$280 double; $275–$375 suite. AE, DC, DISC, MC, V. **Amenities:** 2 restaurants (contemporary American, see "Where to Dine," below); 3 lounges; access to nearby health club; business center; laundry service. *In room:* A/C, cable TV w/pay movies, dataport, coffeemaker, hair dryer, iron, high-speed wireless Internet access.

Millennium Harvest House *(Kids)*   The Harvest House is a full-service hotel with spacious and lovely grounds. Located on the west side of U.S. 36 on the south side of

(Kids) Family-Friendly Hotels

Boulder Outlook (p. see below)   At this former "Holidome," kids can use the pool and play inside even when the weather is bad, and the diversions are many (bouldering rocks, game room, dog park).

Foot of the Mountain Motel (p. 192)   There's lots of space here where the kids can expend their energy. Across the street is a lovely park with a play-ground, as well as the Boulder Creek Path.

Millennium Harvest House (p. 190)   A good place to stay with the kids, especially in the summer. The Harvest House has a nice swimming pool and lots of nearby green space; it's also next to the Boulder Creek Path and within walking distance of the Crossroads Mall.

Boulder, the former Regal Harvest House looks like almost any other four-story hotel from the front—but its backyard melts into a park that surrounds the east end of the 10-mile Boulder Creek Path (see "Attractions," later in this chapter), where bike rentals are available. All rooms hold one king-size or two double beds, a lounge chair and ottoman, remote-control cable TV, and direct-dial phone. Our favorite rooms here are those that look out on the Boulder Creek Path.

1345 28th St., Boulder, CO 80302. (C) 800/545-6285 or 303/443-3850. Fax 303/443-1480. www.millenniumhotels. com. 269 units. $89–$245 double; $164–$420 suite. AE, DC, DISC, MC, V. **Amenities:** Restaurant (American); 2 lounges; indoor lap pool; outdoor heated swimming pool; 15 tennis courts (5 indoor); fitness center; 2 Jacuzzis (indoor and outdoor); bike rental, game room; courtesy shuttle (local); limited room service; on-call masseur; valet and self-service laundry; Internet-access kiosks (for a fee). *In room:* A/C, cable TV w/pay movies, coffeemaker, hair dryer, iron.

MODERATE

Boulder Outlook (Kids) (Value)   The proprietors of this former Ramada and Holidome have outdone every chain motel in town. The Outlook is fun, fresh, and definitively Boulder, with such unique perks as two bouldering rocks (one is 11 ft. high, the other 4 ft.), a fenced, 4,000 square foot dog run, and an ecologically con-scious approach and comprehensive recycling program. The brightly painted motel has 40 rooms which have an outdoor entrance; the rest are accessed indoors. Overall, the rooms are larger than average and contemporary; the bathrooms are nicely tiled. In-room recycling containers and all-natural bath amenities are two more distinctly Boulder touches. The indoor pool is superb, complete with a waterfall and a mural of a cloud-speckled sky, and the bar and grill here features live music Thursday, Satur-day, and Sunday nights, as well as Wednesday during the school year.

800 28th St., Boulder, CO 80303. (C) 800/542-0304 or 303/443-3322. Fax 303/449-5130. www.boulderoutlook.com. 162 units. $69–159 double. Rates include continental breakfast. AE, DC, DISC, MC, V. Pets accepted, $10/night. **Amenities:** Restaurant (American); lounge; indoor heated pool; exercise room; Jacuzzi; men's and women's saunas; game room; activities desk; 24-hr. business center; limited room service; massage; coin-op washers and dryers; dry cleaning, executive level. *In room:* A/C, cable TV, dataport, coffeemaker, hair dryer, iron, safe.

Colorado Chautauqua (Finds)   During the late 19th and early 20th centuries, more than 400 Chautauquas—adult education and cultural entertainment centers—sprang up around the United States. This 26-acre park, at the foot of the Flatiron Mountains, is one of the few remaining and a National Historic Landmark. In summer, it hosts a wide-ranging arts program, including the Colorado Music Festival (see "Boulder After Dark," later in this chapter).

Lodging is in attractive cottages and in rooms and apartments in two historic lodges. All units were outfitted with new furnishings in recent years and come with linens and towels. They have balconies or porches, and either private or shared kitchens. Cottages range from efficiencies to three-bedroom, two-bathroom units. Larger groups might take the newly restored Mission House, which has eight bedrooms, a kitchen, and a screened-in porch and rents for $967 a night. From September to May, many cottages and apartments are rented by the month or longer, but nightly accommodations are generally available.

Guests have access to the park's playgrounds, picnic grounds, and hiking trailheads. The historic Chautauqua Dining Hall, which opened on July 4, 1898, serves three moderately priced meals a day year-round.

900 Baseline Rd. (at 9th St.), Boulder, CO 80302. (© **303/442-3282**, ext. 11 for lodging, 303/440-3776 for restaurant. Fax 303/449-0790. www.chautauqua.com. 87 units. $69–$114 lodge room; $89–$104 efficiency cottage; $114–$124 1-bedroom cottage; $129–$169 2- or 3-bedroom cottage. MC, V. Bus: 203. Pets accepted in cottages for a nonrefundable $100 fee. Pets not accepted in lodges. **Amenities:** Restaurant (creative American); 4 tennis courts; children's programs during summer; self-service laundry. *In room:* Kitchen, coffeemaker, no phone.

Foot of the Mountain Motel *(Kids* *(Value*   This motel, a series of connected, cabin-style units with bright red trim near the east gate of Boulder Canyon, dates from 1930 but has been fully modernized. The location is inspiring, on the west edge of town where city meets mountains, and right across the street is the top end of the Boulder Creek Path and the trailhead that leads to the summit of Flagstaff Mountain. The pleasant pine-walled cabins are furnished with queen or double beds and individual water heaters; two suites are big enough for families and outfitted with full kitchens and a shared hot tub.

200 Arapahoe Ave., Boulder, CO 80302. (© **866/773-5489** or 303/442-5688. www.footofthemountainmotel.com. 20 units (2 with shower only), including 2 suites. $85 double; $105–$175 suite. AE, DISC, MC, V. Pets accepted for $5 nightly fee and a $50 refundable deposit. *In room:* Cable TV, kitchen, fridge.

INEXPENSIVE

Boulder International Hostel *(Value*   Established in 1961, this hostel, spread over 12 buildings with a maximum occupancy of 400, has a little something for everybody: communal dorm rooms, private rooms, and even extended-stay apartments. Wonderfully international, the hostel has a social and intellectual vibe you won't find at the hotels. The toilets, showers, kitchen, laundry, and TV room are communal. Just 2 blocks from the University of Colorado campus, the hostel is open for registration daily from 8am to 11pm. To stay in a bunk, you must present identification proving you are not a resident of Colorado.

1107 12th St., Boulder, CO 80302-7029. (© **888/442-0522** or 303/442-0522. Fax 303/442-0523. www.boulder hostel.com. 250 units. $19 dorm bed; $35–$45 private unit. AE, DISC, MC, V. **Amenities:** Coin-op washers and dryers. *In room:* No phone.

4 Where to Dine

Partly because Boulder is a young, hip community, it has attracted a variety of small, with-it restaurants. At these chef-owned and operated establishments, innovative and often-changing cuisine is the rule. You'll find a lot of California influences here, as well as a number of top-notch chefs doing their own thing.

A Boulder city ordinance prohibits smoking inside restaurants.

VERY EXPENSIVE

Flagstaff House Restaurant ★★ *(Moments* NEW AMERICAN/REGIONAL
Named for its perch on Flagstaff Mountain, this restaurant attracts patrons from
across the state and nation with excellent cuisine and service, and the spectacular
nighttime view of the lights of Boulder spread out 1,000 feet below. A local institution since 1951, this family-owned and operated restaurant has an elegant, candlelit
dining room with glass walls that maximize the view. The prices aren't for the budget
minded, but those seeking a romantic setting and superlative food can't miss with the
Flagstaff House.

The menu, which changes daily, offers an excellent selection of fresh fish, flown in
from the source, and Rocky Mountain game, all prepared with a creative flair. Typical
appetizers include pancetta-wrapped rabbit loin or pheasant breast, oysters, morel
mushrooms, and caviar. Entrees, many of which are seasonal, might include Colorado
buffalo, ahi tuna, Canadian halibut, and soft-shell crabs. The restaurant also boasts
dessert soufflés, a world-renowned wine cellar (at, 20,000 bottles, undoubtedly the
best in Colorado), and an impressive selection of after-dinner drinks.

1138 Flagstaff Rd. (west up Baseline Rd.). ✆ 303/442-4640. www.flagstaffhouse.com. Reservations recommended.
Main courses $25–$60. AE, DC, MC, V. Sun–Fri 6–10pm; Sat 5–10pm.

EXPENSIVE

Frasca ★★★ ITALIAN   Winning raves since its 2004 opening, Frasca is the critical
darling in Boulder for its impeccable service and peerless cuisine, drawn exclusively
from the culinary traditions of Friuli–Venezia Giulia, a subalpine region in northeastern Italy. Using fresh ingredients, with a special emphasis on terrific seafood, cheese,
and wine, the masterful kitchen delivers some of the best fare in the West. The menu
changes daily, but always includes a vast selection of small plates leading up to pasta,
seafood, pork loin, and other specialties of the region. Every year the staff takes a trip
to Italy for a refresher course in Italian culinary appreciation, and it shows.

1738 Pearl St ✆ 303/442-6966. www.frascafoodandwine.com. Reservations recommended. Main courses
$19–$31. AE, DC, MC, V. Mon–Thurs 5:30–9pm, Fri–Sat 5:30–10pm. Closed Sun and two weeks in early June.

John's Restaurant ★★ *(Finds* CONTINENTAL/MEDITERRANEAN   This
funky but elegant converted house has set the pace for the Boulder dining scene for
nearly 30 years. The emphasis here is squarely on the food. Chef-owner Corey Buck
(who bought the place from founder John Bizzarro in 2003) starts with the classic cuisine of southern Europe, but adds his own creative signature spin to each dish; compared to Bizzarro, Buck prepares bigger plates and is more fond of game dishes. For
starters, apple Stilton pecan salad and ricotta-and-spinach gnocchi verde set the stage
for the continually changing main-course offerings. Menu mainstays include filet
mignon with Stilton ale sauce, surrounded by grilled Bermuda onions; chile-crusted
pork tenderloin with cranberry-orange sauce; and a variety of fresh seafood dishes.
The menu also includes vegetarian items, and near-transcendent homemade desserts.

2328 Pearl St. ✆ 303/444-5232. www.johnsrestaurantboulder.com. Reservations recommended. Main courses
$20–$40. AE, DISC, MC, V. Tues–Sat from 5:30pm.

The Kitchen ★★ ECLECTIC   Since it opened in 2004, The Kitchen has emerged
as a standout in a competitive dining market. Locals flock here for the fresh, often
organic food, expert service, and the casual atmosphere that melds metropolitan flair
with Boulder funkiness. The lunch menu changes seasonally, often depending on

what ingredients are locally available, but the buttery, melt-in-your-mouth slow-roasted pork sandwich, topped with a mellow salsa verde, and lamb burger are always available. The daily-evolving dinner slate might include chargrilled pork chops, crab gnocchi, Maine oysters, and a vegetarian selection or two, once again with an emphasis on local and organic ingredients. On Monday "Community Nights," food is presented family style for $35; reservations are necessary. Upstairs is the aptly named, swank wine bar that serves a light menu and libations from the 4,500-bottle cellar, staying open into the wee hours.

1039 Pearl St. (✆ 303/544-5973. www.thekitchencafe.com. Reservations recommended. Main courses $8.50–$16 lunch ($17 for a prix-fixe lunch that includes a tarter or dessert), $19–$27 dinner. AE, MC, V. Mon–Thurs 8am–9pm; Fri 8am–10pm; Sat 5:30–10pm; Sun 5:30–9pm. Bar open later.

Q's Restaurant *Ƭ Ƭ* CONTEMPORARY AMERICAN   The historic ambience that makes the Hotel Boulderado such a delightful place to stay also makes its way into Q's, the hotel's main restaurant. The dining room combines the old—rich polished wood and stained glass—with the comfortable, casually elegant feel of today. Of course, the important thing is the food, and chef-owner John Platt does an excellent job, using locally grown organic vegetables whenever possible.

Platt, who claims seafood as his specialty after years on Cape Cod, always includes several fresh fish selections on the menu, such as grilled ahi tuna served with potato-leek purée with roasted cauliflower, apple-smoked bacon, and a sweet pepper salad. Rotisseried meats often include allspice-cured pork loin served with shoestring onions, whipped potatoes, and BBQ jus. Other specialties: grilled scallop risotto, gnocchi in pesto broth, and harissa-marinated chicken.

In the Hotel Boulderado, 2115 13th St. (at Spruce St.). (✆ 303/442-4880. Reservations recommended. Main courses $5–$10 breakfast, $8–$16 lunch, $16–$27 dinner. AE, DC, DISC, MC, V. Mon–Fri 6:30–11am, 11:30am–2pm, and 5–10pm; Sat–Sun 7am–2pm and 5–10pm.

Sushi Zanmai *Ƭ Ƭ* *Kids* SUSHI/JAPANESE   Boulder is a hot spot for great sushi: Zanmai is a go-to stalwart but faces stiff competition from a number of like-minded upstarts. We still prefer the place for its festive atmosphere, impeccable service, and traditional sushi. Prepared while you watch—at the sushi bar or table side—the options include everything from tuna and trout to sea urchin and octopus, with such exotic rolls as Colorado (raw filet mignon), Z-No. 9 (shrimp tempura, avocado, salmon, and eel sauce), and LSD (lettuce shrimp deluxe). There are lunch specials as well as sushi happy-hour specials during lunch and dinner. Karaoke singalong takes place every Saturday from 10pm to midnight. Under the same ownership next door is **Amu** ((✆ 303/440-0807), a traditional sake bar with its own menu of artfully prepared sashimi and other Japanese staples. Amu, which translates approximately to "everything/nothing," requires patrons to leave their shoes at the door.

1221 Spruce St. (at Broadway). (✆ 303/440-0733. Reservations recommended for groups of 4 or more. Main courses $7.50–$13 lunch, $15–$26 dinner; sushi rolls $2–$12. AE, DC, MC, V. Mon–Fri 11:30am–2pm and 5–10pm; Sat 5pm–midnight; Sun 5–10pm.

MODERATE

Boulder Dushanbe Teahouse *Ƭ* *Finds* ETHNIC WORLD CUISINE   In 1990, 200 crates were shipped to Colorado as a gift from Dushanbe, Tajikistan, Boulder's sister city. From the ornately hand-carved and painted pieces of a Persian teahouse in the crates, the building was assembled at its present site with help from four Tajik artisans. It's the only teahouse of its kind in the Western Hemisphere. Lavishly and

Family-Friendly Restaurants

Sushi Zanmai (p. 194)   Flashing knives and table-side cooking keep kids fully entertained.

Tom's Tavern (p. 197)   The big burgers and low-key atmosphere are a great match for kids' appetites and attitudes.

authentically decorated, the teahouse holds 14 pillars carved from Siberian cedar, and a grand central fountain. The cuisine includes traditional ethnic dishes from the Middle East, Asia, and elsewhere, including several noodle and vegetarian options. There are even a few Tajik specialties, often a lamb dish. Pastries, coffees, and more than 70 teas are also available. There is a full bar on-site as well.

1770 13th St. ✆ 303/442-4993. Main courses $6–$13 lunch, $8–$18 dinner. www.boulderteahouse.com. AE, DISC, MC, V. Mon–Fri 8am–10:30am, 11am–3pm, and 5–10pm; Sat–Sun 8am–3pm and 5–10pm. Tea and coffee bar daily 8am–10pm.

14th Street Bar & Grill ✶ CONTEMPORARY AMERICAN   An open restaurant with large windows facing the street, this is a great spot for people-watching as well as dining. The open wood grill and pizza oven, the long, crowded full-service bar, and a changing display of abstract art let you know that this is a fun place. The menu centers around what chef-owner Kathy Andrade calls "American grill" cuisine, which includes grilled sandwiches, Southwestern chicken salads, and unusual homemade pizzas, such as a pie topped with chorizo sausage, garlic, and roasted green chiles. A variety of pasta dishes are also offered, plus fantastic food and drink specials during the daily social hour (3–6pm).

1400 Pearl St. (at 14th St.). ✆ 303/444-5854. www.14thstreetbarandgrill.com. Main courses $9–$22. AE, MC, V. Daily 11:30am–10pm.

Jax Fish House ✶ SEAFOOD   Fresh seafood is flown in daily from the East and West coasts to supply this restaurant, a lively space with colored chalk graffiti and oceanic art on its brick walls, social patrons, and a booming stereo system. At patio, bar, and table seating, you can order one of the house specialties—the Mississippi catfish skillet is a good bet—or simply slurp down raw oysters and martinis to your heart's content. Entrees usually include scallops, New Zealand bluenose, wild King salmon, and halibut, along with soft-shell crab when in season. Or try a seafood po' boy, with slaw or fresh mussels or clams in mango-lemongrass broth or white wine and garlic. Those who prefer beef can choose from a filet and all-natural burgers.

928 Pearl St. (1 block west of the mall). ✆ 303/444-1811. www.jaxfishhouseboulder.com. Main courses $8–$24. AE, DC, MC, V. Mon–Thurs 4–10pm; Fri–Sat 4–11pm; Sun 4–9pm.

The Mediterranean ✶ MEDITERRANEAN/TAPAS   Known as "The Med," this local favorite is designed as an homage to the casual eateries of Spain and Italy. With a multihued tile interior and an enjoyable breezy patio, the Med draws a bustling after-work drinking crowd for its weekday tapas hour (3–6:30pm), which includes such delicacies as fried artichoke hearts, Moroccan spiced BBQ pork, and hummus for reasonable prices. For a full dinner, the selection is extensive, ranging from pasta to poultry, steaks to gourmet wood-fired pizzas, with several vegetarian dishes to please the health-conscious Boulder crowd. The lunch menu is similar, with a nice selection of panini sandwiches (including lamb, salmon, and vegetarian). There are also several daily specials.

1002 Walnut St. (303/444-5335. www.themedboulder.com. Main courses $9–$26; most tapas $3–$5. AE, DC, DISC, MC, V. Sun–Wed 11am–10pm; Thurs–Sat 11am–11pm.

Rhumba ℱ CARIBBEAN   A loud and lively Caribbean cafe, Rhumba has a loyal local following. With a curved bar that abuts a popular patio and plenty of plants, sun, and original art, this hip eatery dishes out plates of jerked pork and chicken, noodle bowls, and curried dishes, served with such sides as black beans, sweet potato hash browns, and grilled flatbread. More exotic offerings include the ceviche of the day, grilled ahi with guava coulis, and chile-glazed tofu over couscous. Even the cheeseburgers have an island flavor when doused with Rhumba's banana-guava ketchup. There is spice aplenty for fiery-food fanatics, but there are also plenty of dishes that won't set meeker mouths afire. The cocktail of choice is the mojito: silver rum, fresh mint and lime, sugar, and soda water. There is live music (reggae, Latin, jazz, and funk) on a regular basis.

950 Pearl St. (303/442-7771. www.rhumbarestaurant.com. Main courses $10–$25. AE, MC, V. Mon–Fri 11:30am–10pm; Sat–Sun 1–10pm.

Sunflower ℱℱ *Finds* CONTEMPORARY/ORGANIC   This pleasant contemporary eatery, eclectically decorated with murals, rotating local art, and a flagstone floor, touts itself as "Boulder's most unique restaurant," based on its dedication to healthy cuisine. The ingredients include certified organic produce, fresh seafood, and free-range, hormone-free poultry and game. Owner-chef Jon Pell takes a multicultural approach: Sunflower features a diverse selection of dinner entrees, including *shiso* (Japanese herb) grilled ahi tuna served with lemon-soy watercress and jicama salad; seared elk tenderloin with wild mushroom demi-glace; and tempeh scaloppine with wine, lemon, and fresh herbs. Lunch includes fresh variations on sandwiches—such as a blackened salmon burger—as well as specialties like pad Thai and farfalle with saffron creme. An all-you-can-eat organic salad buffet is served daily until 4pm, organic juices and wines are available, and there's a popular weekend brunch.

1701 Pearl St. (2 blocks east of the mall). (303/440-0220. Main courses $9–$15 lunch, $15–$27 dinner. AE, MC, V. Tues–Fri 11am–2:30pm and 5–10pm; Sat–Sun 10am–3pm (brunch) and 5–10pm.

INEXPENSIVE

In addition to the choices below, try a slice of Boulder's best New York–style pie at any **Abo's Pizza** location: 1110 13th St. ((**303/443-3199**), 1911 Broadway ((**303/443-9113**), 2761 Iris Ave. ((**303/443-1921**), and 637 S. Broadway ((**303/494-1274**). **Lucile's,** 2124 14th St. ((**303/442-4743**) is a Boulder breakfast mainstay, serving beignets, buttermilk biscuits, and other morning delicacies that take inspiration from the Big Easy.

Corner Bar ℱ CONTEMPORARY AMERICAN   With the same kitchen as the highly rated Q's Restaurant (see above), the Hotel Boulderado's Corner Bar is far above your average sandwich shop, although sandwiches and burgers are on the menu, too. Here you can savor a grilled-salmon sandwich, served with red-onion marmalade, spinach, and horseradish aioli. Or you might try a roast turkey BLT with herbed mayo, a grilled New York Strip, or pan-roasted halibut with potato/corn/shiitake risotto. Those not in search of a full meal can opt for an appetizer, such as fried oysters or chipotle-tomato soup.

In the Hotel Boulderado, 2115 13th St. (at Spruce St.). (303/442-4560. Main courses $7–$14. AE, DC, DISC, MC, V. Daily 11am–midnight.

Illegal Pete's _(Value_ MEXICAN Located at the far east end of the Pearl Street Mall, Illegal Pete's is renowned locally for its creative, healthy burritos, packed with chicken, steak, veggies, or fish. The menu also includes a similar range of tacos, as well as salads, quesadillas, and chili. There's a full bar you can belly up to in the back, and a patio out front. Another Illegal Pete's is on the Hill at 1320 College Ave. (✆ **303/444-3055**).

1447 Pearl St. ✆ **303/440-3955**. www.illegalpetes.com. Menu items $4–$6. AE, DISC, MC, V. Mon–Thurs 7:30am–10:30pm; Fri 7:30am–2:30am; Sat 10am–2:30am; Sun 10am–10:30pm.

Rio Grande MEXICAN This popular neighborhood restaurant and bar, just south of the Pearl Street Mall, is probably best known for its huge, award-winning margaritas—so potent that the staff enforces a strict limit of three. Frequented by college students and Boulder's under-30 crowd, the Rio is bustling for reasons beyond its alcoholic concoctions—the loud, social atmosphere and the food, a good variety of oversize Mexican entrees and combos. Our favorites are hearty fajitas (steak or veggie, with handmade tortillas), zesty Yucatan shrimp, and creative chiles rellenos.

1101 Walnut St. ✆ **303/444-3690**. www.riograndemexican.com. Meals $6–$14. AE, MC, V. Mon–Wed 11am–2pm and 5–10pm; Thurs 11am–2pm and 5–10:30pm; Fri–Sun 11am–10:30pm.

Sherpa's _(Finds_ TIBETAN/NEPALI Owned by Pemba Sherpa—a native of Nepal who in fact is a Sherpa, or Himalayan mountain guide—Sherpa's is located in a converted Victorian house just southwest of the Pearl Street Mall. Decorated with Himalayan relics and photography of the peaks of Nepal and Tibet, the restaurant serves up food to match: Tibetan dishes like _thupka_ (noodle bowls) and Sherpa stew as well as spicier Nepali and Indian cuisine, including _saag_ (creamed spinach with garlic, cumin, ginger, and your choice of veggie or meat) and curry dishes. There are lunch specials daily, as well as a comfortable bar with a library full of climbing tomes.

825 Walnut St. ✆ **303/440-7151**. Reservations accepted. Main courses $5–$9 lunch, $6–$13 dinner. AE, DISC, MC, V. Sun–Thurs 11am–3pm and 5–9:30pm; Fri–Sat 11am–3pm and 5–10pm.

Tom's Tavern _(Kids_ AMERICAN Boulder's most popular place for a good hamburger, Tom's has been a neighborhood institution owned by local politician Tom Eldridge for almost 40 years. Located in an early-20th-century building that once housed an undertaker, the tavern has vinyl-upholstered booths and patio seating. Besides the ⅓-pound burgers (made from all-organic Coleman beef) and other sandwiches, you can get a 10-ounce steak, fried chicken, or a veggie burger, not to mention a variety of BBQ plates. Tom's serves dinner anytime.

1047 Pearl St. ✆ **303/443-3893**. Menu items $6–$12. AE, DC, DISC, MC, V. Mon–Thurs 10am–10pm; Fri–Sat 10am–11pm; Sun 12:30–8:30pm.

ESPRESSO BARS, COFFEEHOUSES & RELATED ESTABLISHMENTS

Espresso fans will have no problem finding a decent espresso, cappuccino, or latte: Boulder has a number of **Starbucks** establishments, as well as many more interesting independent coffeehouses. Many of the independents, located near the Pearl Street Mall, provide outdoor seating in nice weather. Attached to the Boulder Book Store, the **Bookend Cafe,** 1115 Pearl St. (✆ **303/440-6699**), offers a variety of coffee drinks and a delightful array of baked goods, soups, and pies. **Trident Booksellers & Café,** 940 Pearl St. (✆ **303/443-3133**), features indoor and outdoor seating as well as a comprehensive selection of used books. The **Boulder Dushanbe Teahouse,** 1770 13th St. (✆ **303/442-4993;** p. 194), offers an authentic Persian setting for quaffing more than 70 varieties of tea and a good selection of coffees from 8am to 10pm daily. Homemade baked goods are also available.

5 Attractions

THE TOP ATTRACTIONS

Boulder Creek Path *Kids* Following Boulder Creek, this nature corridor provides about a 16-mile-long oasis and recreation area through the city and west into the mountains. With no street crossings (there are bridges and underpasses instead), the path is popular with Boulder residents, especially on weekends, when you'll see numerous walkers, runners, bicyclists, and in-line skaters. (Walkers should stay to the right; the left lane is for faster traffic.) The path links the CU campus, several city parks, and office buildings. Near the east end, watch for deer, prairie dog colonies, and wetlands, where some 150 species of birds have been spotted. You might see Canada geese, mallard ducks, spotted sandpipers, owls, and woodpeckers.

At 30th Street, south of Arapahoe Road, the path cuts through **Scott Carpenter Park** (named for the astronaut and Colorado native), where you can enjoy swimming in summer and sledding in winter. Just west of Scott Carpenter Park, you'll find **Boulder Creek Stream Observatory,** which is adjacent to the Millennium Harvest House. In addition to observing trout and other aquatic wildlife, you're invited to feed the fish with trout food purchased from a vending machine (25¢). **Central Park,** at Broadway and Canyon Boulevard, preserves some of Boulder's history with a restored steam locomotive. The **Boulder Public Library** is also in this area.

Traveling west, watch for the **Charles A. Heartling Sculpture Garden** (with the stone image of local Indian chief Niwot) and the **Kids' Fishing Ponds;** the Boulder Fish and Game Club stocks the ponds, which are open only to children under 12, who can fish for free and keep what they catch. Near 3rd Street and Canyon Boulevard, you'll find the **Xeriscape Garden,** where drought-tolerant plants are tested for reduced water intake.

The **Eben G. Fine Park** is named for the Boulder pharmacist who discovered Arapahoe Glacier on nearby Arapahoe Peak. To the west, **Red Rocks Settlers' Park** marks the beginning of the **Boulder Canyon Pioneer Trail,** which leads to a continuation of Boulder Creek Path. The park is named for Missouri gold seekers who camped at this spot in 1858 and later found gold about 12 miles farther west. Watch for explanatory signs along the 1.3-mile path. The **Whitewater Kayak Course** has 20 slalom gates for kayakers and canoeists to use free; to the west, **Elephant Buttresses** is one of Boulder's more popular rock-climbing areas. The path ends at **Four Mile Canyon,** the old town site of Orodell.

Note: Although the path is generally well populated and quite safe, Boulderites warn against using it late at night if you are alone; one of the problems is the number of transients who take refuge there.

55th St. and Pearl Pkwy., to the mouth of Boulder Canyon. ✆ 303/413-7200. Free admission. Daily 24 hr. Bus: HOP.

Pearl Street Mall *Kids* This 4-block-long tree-lined pedestrian mall marks Boulder's downtown core and its center for dining, shopping, strolling, and people-watching. Musicians, mimes, jugglers, and other street entertainers hold court on the landscaped mall day and night, year-round. Buy your lunch from one of the many vendors and sprawl on the grass in front of the courthouse to relax and eat. Locally owned businesses and galleries share the mall with trendy boutiques, sidewalk cafes, and major chains including Peppercorn, Banana Republic, and Abercrombie & Fitch. There's a wonderful play area for youngsters, with climbable boulders set in gravel. Don't miss the bronze bust of Chief Niwot (of the southern Arapaho) in front of the

Impressions

If heaven has a college town, it's probably as beautiful as Boulder.
—*Sunset Magazine*

Boulder County Courthouse between 13th and 14th streets. Niwot, who welcomed the first Boulder settlers, was killed in southeastern Colorado during the Sand Creek Massacre of 1864.

Pearl St. from 11th to 15th sts. Bus: HOP.

University of Colorado ⚐   The largest university in the state, with nearly 29,000 students (including about 4,600 graduate students), CU dominates the city. Its student population, cultural and sports events, and intellectual atmosphere have helped shape Boulder into the city it is today. The school boasts 16 alumni astronauts who have flown in space and three Nobel laureates on the faculty.

Old Main, on the Norlin Quadrangle, was the first building erected after the university was established in 1876; at that time, it housed the entire school. Later, pink-sandstone Italian Renaissance–style buildings came to dominate the campus. Visitors may want to take in the university's **Heritage Center,** on the third floor of Old Main; the **University of Colorado Museum** (see "More Attractions," below), a natural history museum in the Henderson Building on Broadway; the **Mary Rippon Outdoor Theatre,** behind the Henderson Building, site of the annual Colorado Shakespeare Festival; **Fiske Planetarium,** between Kittredge Loop Drive and Regent Drive on the south side of campus; and the **Norlin Library,** on the Norlin Quadrangle, the largest research library in the state, with extensive holdings of American and English literature. Other attractions include the CU Art Museum, the University Memorial Center (the student center), and the Integrated Teaching and Learning Laboratory in the College of Engineering. Prospective students and their parents can arrange campus tours by contacting the admissions office (✆ **303/492-6301**).

The **Sommers-Bausch Observatory** (✆ **303/492-6732** during the day, 303/492-2020 at night) offers tours and Friday-evening open houses. Among the telescopes there are 16-, 18-, and 24-inch Cassegrain reflectors and a 10-inch aperture heliostat.

East side of Broadway, between Arapahoe Ave. and Baseline Rd. ✆ 303/492-1411. www.colorado.edu. Bus: HOP, SKIP, STAMPEDE, and Denver buses.

National Center for Atmospheric Research ⚐ *Finds*   Inspired by the cliff dwellings at Mesa Verde National Park, I. M. Pei designed this striking pink-sandstone building, which overlooks Boulder from high atop Table Mesa in the southwestern foothills. (You might recognize the center from Woody Allen's *Sleeper;* scenes were shot here.) Scientists study such phenomena as the greenhouse effect, wind shear, and ozone depletion to gain a better understanding of the earth's atmosphere. Among the technological tools on display are satellites, weather balloons, interactive computer monitors, robots, and supercomputers that can simulate the world's climate. There are also hands-on, weather-oriented exhibits and a theater. The **Walter Orr Roberts Weather Trail** outside the building's west doors takes visitors on a .4-mile, wheelchair-accessible loop along a path with interpretive signs describing various aspects of weather and climate plus the plants and animals of the area. The center also houses a changing art exhibit and a science-oriented gift shop. Allow 1 to 2 hours.

1850 Table Mesa Dr. (C) 303/497-1174. www.ncar.ucar.edu. Free admission. Self-guided tours weekdays 8am–5pm; weekends and holidays 9am–4pm. 1-hr. guided tours daily at noon; there is also a self-guided audio tour. Take Broadway heading southwest out of town to Table Mesa Dr., and follow it west to the center.

MORE ATTRACTIONS

Beyond the attractions listed below, the **Boulder Creek Winery,** 6440 Odell Place ((C) **303/516-9031;** www.bouldercreekwine.com) offers a complimentary tasting on Thursday through Sunday from 1 to 5:30pm in summer and 1 to 5pm Saturday and Sunday spring and fall, but is closed in winter.

Banjo Billy's Bus Tours   A rollicking journey through Boulder and its storied history, Banjo Billy's Bus Tours utilize one of the funkiest vehicles you've ever seen. Featuring armchairs for guests inside, the exterior looks like the offspring of a log cabin and a school bus. The 90-minute tours delve into ghost stories and lurid tales of crime, but the tone is tongue-in-cheek and entertaining.

Tours depart from the Hotel Boulderado, 13th and Spruce sts. (C) 720/771-0087. www.banjobilly.com. Tickets $16 adult, $14 seniors, $10 children 5 to 12, and free for children under 5. Tours depart daily at noon, 2pm, and 6pm in the summer, less frequently at other times of year.

Celestial Seasonings ✸ (Value)   The nation's leading producer of herbal teas, housed in a modern building in northeastern Boulder, offers tours that are an experience for the senses. The company, which began in a Boulder garage in the 1970s, now produces more than 50 varieties of tea from more than 75 different herbs and spices imported from 35 foreign countries. You'll understand why the company invites you to "see, taste, and smell the world of Celestial Seasonings" as you move from a consumer taste test in the lobby to marketing displays, and finally into the production plant where 9 million tea bags roll off the line daily. The overpowering "Mint Room" is a highlight. The tour lasts about 45 minutes, and there is a cafe on-site.

4600 Sleepytime Dr. (C) 303/581-1202. www.celestialseasonings.com. Free admission. Mon–Sat 10am–3pm; Sun 11am–3pm; tours on the hour. Reservations required for groups of 8 or more. Exit Colo. 119, Longmont Diagonal, at Jay Rd. and go east to Spine, then north on Spine. Bus: J.

Redstone Meadery ✸ (Finds)   Drunk by Beowulf and Shakespeare, mead is the original fermented beverage. There are about 60 active meaderies in the United States, including this standout in Boulder. Founded by David Myers in 2000, the meadery crafts several beverages (ranging from sparkling to portlike) that quickly demonstrate why this amateur mead maker turned pro. The meadery offers free 30-minute tours and tasting, and sells its wares ($10–$25 a bottle) and other regional foods and gifts. The meadery is the host of the International Mead Festival, held annually on Valentine's Day.

4700 Old Pearl St., #2A. (C) 720/406-1125. www.redstonemeadery.com. Free admission. Tours Mon–Fri 1pm and 3pm, Sat 12:30pm; tasting room Mon–Fri noon–6:30pm, Sat noon–5pm. Located 1 block northeast of the Pearl St. exit off Foothills Pkwy.

Rockies Brewing Company   From the grinding of the grain to the bottling of the beer, the 25-minute tour of this attractive "designer" microbrewery ends as all brewery tours should: in the pub. Tours pass by glistening copper vats that turn out hundreds of kegs of Boulder Beer a day. The pub overlooks the bottling area, so even if you visit without taking a tour, you still get a good view of the brewing process. The menu includes burgers, burritos, salads, and appetizers; entrees run $6 to $8.

2880 Wilderness Place. ✆ 303/444-8448. www.boulderbeer.com. Free admission. Tours Mon–Sat 2pm; pub Mon–Fri 11am–9pm. Take U.S. 36 north to Valmont Rd., then head east to Wilderness Place.

MUSEUMS & GALLERIES

There are three art galleries on the University of Colorado campus, all with free admission. The **CU Art Galleries,** in the Sibell-Wolle Fine Arts Building near Euclid Avenue and Broadway (✆ **303/492-8300**), displays the work of CU students and faculty as well as pieces from the Colorado Collection, about 5,000 works by international artists including Warhol, Dürer, Rembrandt, Tiepolo, Hogarth, Hiroshige, Matisse, and Picasso. There are also rotating exhibits. The gallery is open Monday to Friday from 10am to 5pm, Tuesday 10am to 7pm, and Saturday from noon to 4pm. Bus: HOP, SKIP.

At the University Memorial Center, the **UMC Art Gallery** (✆ **303/492-7465**) organizes and hosts a variety of exhibitions featuring regional and national artists. In the music-listening rooms, visitors can peruse current periodicals while listening to modern and classical music. The gallery is on the second floor of the center, just left of the information desk; it's open Monday to Friday from 9am to 6pm. Bus: HOP, SKIP, STAMPEDE.

The **Andrew J. Macky Gallery** (✆ **303/492-8423**), at the main entrance of Macky Auditorium, shows touring exhibits and works by local artists. It's open Wednesday from 9am to 4pm. Bus: HOP, SKIP, STAMPEDE.

There are also studios and a gallery at the **Dairy Center for the Arts,** 2590 Walnut St. (✆ **303/440-7826;** www.thedairy.org), which also houses two theaters, classrooms, and several dance, theater, and arts organizations. See "Theater & Dance," later in this chapter.

Boulder Museum of Contemporary Art   This multidisciplinary art museum, created in 1972 to exhibit the work of contemporary artists, has evolved into an exciting venue where one can expect to see almost anything art related, from the lighthearted to the elegant, political to religious, by regional and international contemporary artists. There are special programs for young children and a variety of other events throughout the year. Performing arts—from poetry and dance to music and drama—are presented in the museum's award-winning "black box" performance venue, featuring local, national, and international performers. Allow 30 to 45 minutes. In addition, on Saturday evenings in summer, classic movies such as *Citizen Kane* and cult classics are shown outside ($5 per person). Take a lawn chair or blanket.

1750 13th St. ✆ 303/443-2122. www.bmoca.org. Admission $4 adults, $3 seniors and students, free for children under 12. Tues–Sat 11am–6pm (Sat 9am–4pm in summer). Hours change seasonally; call ahead for current information. Closed Sun–Mon and major holidays. Bus: HOP, SKIP.

Boulder History Museum   Ensconced on University Hill in the 1899–1900 Harbeck-Bergheim House, a Victorian mansion with a Dutch-style front door and Italian tile fireplaces, the museum houses one of the most comprehensive local history collections in the region. There are more than 30,000 artifacts (from snake oil to sidesaddles), plus hundreds of thousands of photographs and historical documents from Colorado's early days to the present.

Permanent exhibits include "Storymakers: A Boulder History," featuring a rich collection of oral histories and late-19th-to-early-20th-century photographs. There are also rotating exhibits that stay up for 6 to 10 months. The museum also hosts numerous lectures, programs, tours, and community events, including the Great Boulder Pie

Festival and Quilt Raffle in July, Northern Arapaho Pow Wow in June, and Boulder History Day in May. Allow 1 to 2 hours.

1206 Euclid Ave. © 303/449-3464. www.boulderhistorymuseum.org. Admission $5 adults, $3 seniors, $2 students and children, free for children under 5. Tues–Fri 10am–5pm; Sat–Sun noon–4pm. Guided tours by appointment. Closed Mon and major holidays. Bus: HOP.

CU Heritage Center   Located in the oldest building on campus, this museum reflects the history of the university. Its seven galleries hold exhibits on early student life (together with a complete set of yearbooks), CU's contributions to space exploration, campus architecture, distinguished alumni, and an overview of the university's history. Allow 30 minutes; a lot more if you're an alum.

3rd floor of Old Main, University of Colorado. © 303/492-6329. Free admission. Mon–Fri 10am–4pm. Bus: HOP, SKIP, STAMPEDE.

CU Museum of Natural History 𝕽 *Kids*   The natural history and anthropology of the Rocky Mountains and Southwest are the focus of this campus museum, founded in 1902 and one of the best of its kind. Featured exhibits include Ancestral Puebloan pottery and collections pertaining to dinosaurs, geology, paleontology, botany, entomology, and zoology. A children's area has interactive exhibits, and one gallery is devoted to special displays that change throughout the year. Allow 1 to 3 hours.

University of Colorado, Henderson Bldg., Broadway at 15th St. © 303/492-6892. Admission $3 adults, $1 seniors and children 6–18, free for children under 6. Mon–Fri 9am–5pm; Sat 9am–4pm; Sun 10am–4pm. Bus: HOP.

Leanin' Tree Museum of Western Art   You may know Leanin' Tree as the world's largest publisher of Western-art greeting cards. What's not so well-known is that the company's headquarters houses an outstanding 400-piece collection of original paintings and bronze sculptures by contemporary artists. All depict scenes from the Old or New West, including a collection of humorous cowboy art. There is also an outdoor sculpture garden of likenesses of human and animal Western icons. Free guided tours are available. Allow 1 hour.

6055 Longbow Dr. (exit Jay Rd. and Longmont Diagonal). © 800/777-8716 or 303/530-1442, ext. 4299. www.leanintreemuseum.com. Free admission. Mon–Fri 8am–5pm; Sat–Sun 10am–5pm. Closed major holidays. Bus: 205.

ESPECIALLY FOR KIDS

City parks (see "Sports & Outdoor Activities," below) offer the best diversions for children.

On the **Boulder Creek Path** (see "The Top Attractions," earlier in this chapter), the underwater fish observatory behind the Millennium Harvest House fascinates youngsters. They can feed the huge trout swimming behind a glass barrier on the creek (machines cough up handfuls of fish food for 25¢). Farther up the path, on the south bank around 6th Street, Kids' Fishing Ponds, stocked by the Boulder Fish and Game Club, are open to children under 12. There's no charge for either activity.

The **Fiske Planetarium** (© 303/492-5001) offers visitors a walk through the solar system. Dedicated to the memory of CU alumnus Ellison Onizuka and the six other astronauts who died in the space shuttle *Challenger* explosion, the outdoor scale model begins at the entrance to the planetarium with the sun and inner planets, and continues across Regent Drive to the outer planets, located along the walkway to the Engineering Center. Admission is free; allow at least a half-hour. The planetarium offers after-school and summer discovery programs for kids, star shows, and other programs where you get a chance to look at the sky through the planetarium's telescopes. Admission for these events is usually $3 to $6; call for the latest schedule. Bus: HOP.

6 Sports & Outdoor Activities

Boulder is one of the leading spots for outdoor sports in North America. The city manages over 38,000 acres of parklands, including more than 200 miles of hiking trails and bicycle paths. Several canyons lead down from the Rockies directly into Boulder, attracting mountaineers and rock climbers. Families enjoy picnicking and camping in the beautiful surroundings. It seems that everywhere you look, people of all ages are running, walking, biking, skiing, or engaged in other active sports.

The **Boulder Parks and Recreation Department** (© **303/413-7200;** www.ci. boulder.co.us/parks-recreation) manages many of the outdoor facilities and schedules a variety of year-round activities for children as well as adults. Seasonal booklets on activities and city parks are available free from the Chamber of Commerce office and through the parks and recreation department's website (see above). Although many of the programs last for several weeks or months, some are half- or full-day activities that visiting children can join, usually at a slightly higher price than that for city residents. The department sponsors hikes, fitness programs, ski trips, watersports, special holiday events, and performances in local parks, and even operates a skate park and a pottery lab. (TV trivia buffs, take note: Mork of *Mork and Mindy* first touched down on planet Earth in Chautauqua Park, on the city's south side, and the house used as their residence's exterior is at 1619 Pine St.)

One destination where you can enjoy several kinds of outdoor activities is **Eldorado Canyon State Park** ✦. This mountain park, just 5 miles southwest of Boulder in Eldorado Springs, is a favorite of technical rock climbers, but the 850-foot-high canyon's beauty makes it just as popular with hikers, picnickers, and others who want to get away from it all. The 1,448-acre park features 9 miles of hiking and horseback-riding trails, plus 7.5 miles of trails suitable for mountain bikes; fishing is permitted, but camping is not. An exhibit at the brand-new visitor center describes the history of the park; there's also a bookstore and rotating displays covering topics from wildflowers to climbing. Admission is $5 to $6 per vehicle and $2 to $3 per pedestrian; the park is open daily from dawn to dusk. For further information, contact Eldorado Canyon State Park, Box B, Eldorado Springs, CO 80025 (© **303/494-3943;** www.parks.state.co.us).

BALLOONING Float above the majestic Rocky Mountains in a hot-air balloon, watching as the early morning light gradually brightens to full day. Flights often include champagne and an elaborate continental breakfast or brunch. **Fair Winds Hot Air Balloon Flights** (© **303/939-9323;** www.fairwindsinc.com) flies 7 days a week year-round, weather permitting. Prices are $145 to $245 per person, and include a certificate, T-shirt, and photograph.

BICYCLING On some days, you can see more bikes than cars in Boulder. Paths run along many of the city's major arteries, and local racing and touring events are scheduled year-round. Bicyclists riding at night are required to have lights; perhaps because of the large number of bicyclists in Boulder, the local police actively enforce traffic regulations that apply to them. Generally, bicyclists must obey the same laws that apply to operators of motor vehicles.

Impressions

This is Mork from Ork signing off from Boulder, Colorado. Nanu, Nanu!
—Mork from Ork (Robin Williams), on TV's *Mork & Mindy,* 1978–82

For current information on biking events, tips on the best places to ride, and equipment sales and repairs, check with **University Bicycles,** 839 Pearl St., about 2 blocks west of the Pearl Street Mall (© **303/444-4196;** www.ubikes.com), and **Full Cycle,** 1211 13th St., near the campus (© **303/440-7771;** www.fullcyclebikes.com). University Bikes rents bikes for $20 to $80 per day, and has maps of the city's 90 miles of bike lanes, paths, and routes. See also "By Bicycle" under "Getting Around," earlier in this chapter.

CLIMBING & BOULDERING   If you would like to tackle the nearby mountains and cliffs with ropes and pitons, contact **Mountain Sports,** 2835 Pearl St. (© **303/442-8355**), which sells clothing and technical equipment, and can also provide maps and advice on climbing and trail running. Other good information sources are **Colorado Athletic Training School,** 2800 30th St. (© **303/939-9699**), and the **Boulder Rock Club,** 2829 Mapleton Ave. (© **800/447-4008;** www.boulderrock.com). The latter houses 10,000 square feet of indoor climbing surfaces and offers guide services.

Boulderers (those who climb without ropes) flock to **The Spot,** billed as the country's largest bouldering gym, at 3240 Prairie Ave. (© **303/379-8806;** www.thespotgym.com). Lessons and guiding service are available, and there is a cafe and a yoga studio on-site.

The Flatiron Range (easily visible from downtown Boulder) and nearby Eldorado Canyon are two favorite destinations for expert rock scalers. The Third Flatiron is 1,400 feet high, taller than the Empire State Building, and has been climbed by people without using their hands, on roller skates, naked, and in a record 8 minutes (by separate climbers). For bouldering, Carter Lake (30 miles north on U.S. 36) and Boulder Canyon (west of the city on Canyon Blvd.) are two of the top spots.

FISHING   Favored fishing areas near Boulder include **Boulder Reservoir,** North 51st Street, northeast of the city off the Longmont Diagonal, where you can try your luck at walleye, catfish, largemouth bass, bluegill, crappie, and carp. The Boulder Parks and Recreation Department (© **303/441-3461**) manages the reservoir. Other favorite fishing holes include **Lagerman Reservoir,** west of North 73rd Street off Pike Road, about 15 miles northeast of the city, where only nonmotorized boats can be used; **Barker Reservoir,** just east of Nederland on the Boulder Canyon Drive (Colo. 119), for bank fishing; and **Walden Ponds Wildlife Habitat,** about 6 miles east of downtown on North 75th Street. Fly-fishing is also popular in the area; guide service is available through **Kinsley Outfitters,** 2070 Broadway (© **800/442-7420** or 303/442-6204; www.kinsleyoutfitters.com), for $225 for one person for a full day or $295 for two. Kinsley's fly shop offers a good selection of supplies.

GLIDER FLYING & SOARING   The atmospheric conditions generated by the peaks of the Front Range are ideal for year-round soaring and gliding. **Mile High Gliding,** 5534 Independence Rd. (© **303/527-1122;** www.milehighskyride.com), offers rides and lessons on the north side of Boulder Municipal Airport, 2 miles northeast of downtown. Rides for one person range from $140 to $295 and last from 15 minutes to an hour or more; a 25-minute ride for two costs $210.

GOLF   Local courses include the 18-hole **Flatirons Golf Course** (run by Boulder Parks and Recreation), 5706 E. Arapahoe Ave. (© **303/442-7851**), and the 9-hole **Haystack Mountain Golf Course,** 5877 Niwot Rd. in Niwot., 5 miles north of Boulder (© **303/530-1400**). Nonresident greens fees range from $15 to $30.

HIKING & BACKPACKING   There are plenty of opportunities in the Boulder area—the Boulder Mountain Parks system includes 4,625 acres bordering the city limits, including the Flatirons and Flagstaff Mountain. You can obtain a map with descriptions of more than 60 trails from the **Boulder Convention and Visitors Bureau,** 2440 Pearl St. (© **303/442-2911**).

Numerous Roosevelt National Forest trailheads leave the Peak-to-Peak Scenic Byway (Colo. 72) west of Boulder. Check with the **U.S. Forest Service,** Boulder Ranger District, 2140 Yarmouth Ave. (© **303/541-2500**), for hiking and backpacking information. During dry weather, check on possible fire and smoking restrictions before heading into the forest. The trailheads leading to Long, Mitchell, and Brainard lakes are among the most popular, as is the 2-mile hike to Isabel Glacier.

About 70 miles west of Boulder, on the Continental Divide, is the **Indian Peaks Wilderness Area** (© **303/541-2500**). More than half of the area is fragile alpine tundra; a $5 permit is required for camping from June 1 to September 15. North of Boulder, via Estes Park, is **Rocky Mountain National Park** (© **970/586-1206**), one of the state's prime destinations for hikers and those seeking beautiful mountain scenery. The 2.5-mile **Mills Lake Trail** ⊛, one of our favorites, is here. Another good hike is the 6-mile Mesa Trail, which departs from the Bluebell Shelter in Chautauqua Park.

RUNNING   The Boulder Creek Path (see "The Top Attractions," earlier in this chapter) is one of the most popular routes for runners in Boulder. A good resource for the traveling runner is **Boulder Road Runners** (© **303/499-2061;** www.boulderroad runners.org). They organize group runs in the area and can provide information. The **Bolder Boulder** (© **303/444-RACE;** www.bolderboulder.com), held every Memorial Day, attracts about 50,000 runners who circle its 6.3-mile course. The **Boulder Running Company,** 2775 Pearl St. (© **303/786-9255**), sells a wide variety of running shoes and gear, going as far as analyzing customers' strides on a treadmill to find the perfect shoe.

SKIING   Friendly **Eldora Mountain Resort,** P.O. Box 1697, Nederland, CO 80466 (© **888/235-3672** or 303/440-8700; fax 303/440/8797; www.eldora.com), is just 21 miles west of downtown Boulder. It's about a 40-minute drive on Colo. 119 through Nederland. RTD buses leave Boulder for Eldora four times daily during ski season. For downhill skiers and snowboarders, Eldora has 53 trails, rated 30% novice, 50% intermediate, and 20% expert terrain on 680 acres. It has snowmaking on 320 acres and a terrain park with a 600-foot superpipe. The area has two quad lifts, two triple and four double chairlifts, four surface lifts, and a vertical rise of 1,500 feet. Lift tickets (2005–06 rates) are $53 for adults, $35 for seniors 65 to 74, $33 for children 6 to 15, and just $5 for those under 6 and over 74. There are also discount packages that include lessons and rental equipment for both skiers and snowboarders. Snowshoeing is also gaining popularity in the area. The season runs from mid-November to mid-April, snow permitting.

For cross-country skiers, Eldora has 28 miles of groomed and backcountry trails, and an overnight hut available by reservation. About 15% of the trails are rated easy, 50% intermediate, and 35% difficult. The trail fee is $16, or $10 for children 6 to 12 and seniors 65 to 69.

You can rent all your ski, snowboard, and snowshoeing equipment at the ski-rental center, and Nordic equipment at the Eldora Nordic Center. A free base-area shuttle runs throughout the day from the lodge to the Little Hawk area and the Nordic Center.

In Boulder, you can rent or buy telemark and alpine touring equipment from **Mountain Sports,** 2835 Pearl St. (© **303/442-8355**) or **Eldora Mountain Sports,** 2775 Canyon Blvd. (© **303/447-2017**).

SWIMMING Five public pools are located within the city. Indoor pools, all open daily year-round, are at the newly renovated **North Boulder Recreation Center,** 3170 N. Broadway (© **303/413-7260**); the **East Boulder Community Center,** 5660 Sioux Dr. (© **303/441-4400**); and the **South Boulder Recreation Center,** 1360 Gillaspie Dr. (© **303/441-3448**). The two outdoor pools (both open daily from Memorial Day to Labor Day) are **Scott Carpenter Pool,** 30th Street and Arapahoe Avenue (© **303/441-3427**), and **Spruce Pool,** 2102 Spruce St. (© **303/441-3426**). Swimming fees for all municipal pools are $5.50 adults, $3.50 seniors, $3 teens, $2.75 children 4 to 12.

TENNIS There are more than 30 public courts in the city. The North and South Boulder Recreation centers (see "Swimming," above) each have four lighted courts and accept reservations ($8 an hour). The North Boulder Recreation Center also has two platform tennis courts. Play is free if you arrive and there's no one using the courts or with a reservation. For locations of other public tennis courts, contact the Boulder Parks and Recreation Department (© **303/413-7200**).

WATERSPORTS For both motorboating and human-powered boating, sailboard instruction, or swimming at a sandy beach, head for the square-mile **Boulder Reservoir** (© **303/441-3461**), on North 51st Street off the Longmont Diagonal northeast of the city. Human-powered boats and canoes (no personal watercraft) can be rented at the **boathouse** (© **303/441-3456**). Rates start at $35 per full day, with sailboards at $65 per full day. There's also a boat ramp and other facilities.

SPECTATOR SPORTS

The major attractions are **University of Colorado football, women's volleyball,** and **men's and women's basketball.** For tickets, contact the Ticket Office, Campus Box 372, Boulder, CO 80309 (© **303/49-BUFFS;** www.cubuffs.com). Football tickets sometimes sell out early, particularly for homecoming and games against Nebraska and Oklahoma.

7 Shopping

For the best shopping in Boulder, head to the **Pearl Street Mall** (see "The Top Attractions," earlier in this chapter), where you'll find not only shops and galleries galore but also street entertainers.

Twenty Ninth Street, centered on the former site of the Crossroads Mall at the intersection of Canyon Blvd. and 29th St. (© **303/440-0722;** www.twentyninth. com) is a major new multi-use development featuring an outdoor shopping center. Open since October 2006, tenants include Wild Oats, MontBell, Borders, Apple, and Century Theatres. Hours are 10am to 9pm Monday through Saturday and 10am to 6pm on Sunday.

The indoor-outdoor, 1½-million-square-foot **FlatIron Crossing** (© **720/887-9900;** www.flatironcrossing.com), an upscale mall featuring Nordstrom, Dillard's, and Lord & Taylor among its 200 shops, is a more comprehensive option for the devout shopper. It's 9 miles southeast of Boulder off U.S. 36 in Broomfield. Hours are 10am to 9pm Monday through Saturday and 11am to 6pm on Sunday.

SHOPPING A TO Z
ARTS & CRAFTS

Art Source International   Natural history prints, maps, and other items relevant to Western Americana, mainly from the 18th and 19th centuries, are the specialty here, along with collections of hundred-year-old Colorado photographs, maps, and prints. The store also features a great selection of new globes, as well as a few reproductions. 1237 Pearl St. ✆ 303/444-4080.

Boulder Arts & Crafts Cooperative   This is a good place to find a unique gift or souvenir. The shop, owned and operated by its artist members since 1971, features a wide variety of original handcrafted works. Pieces range from watercolors, serigraphs, and other fine art to top-quality crafts, including blown glass, stained glass, handmade jewelry, and functional pottery. Many of the items are made in Colorado or the Rocky Mountain region. 1421 Pearl St. ✆ 303/443-3683.

Niwot Antiques *(Finds*   With dozens of dealers (including New England antiques specialist Elysian Fields), this antiques mall, in business since the 1950s, is the area's best, and a good excuse to make a trip to Niwot, 5 miles north of Boulder on the Longmont Diagonal. 136 2nd Ave., Niwot. ✆ 303/652-2587.

BOOKS

Being a college town, Boulder is one of the best cities in the world for a browsing bookworm. It reportedly has more used-book stores per capita than any other U.S. city. Chain outlets include **Barnes & Noble,** 2915 Pearl St. (✆ 303/442-1665). The independents run the gamut from the Kerouac and Burroughs specialists at **Beat Bookshop,** 1713 Pearl St. (✆ 303/444-7111), to the lesbian/feminist/gay selection at **Word Is Out,** 2015 10th St. (✆ 303/449-1415). **Trident Booksellers,** 940 Pearl St. (✆ 303/443-3133), is a good used-book shop with a coffeehouse attached.

Boulder Book Store   This meandering, four-story, 20,000-square-foot bookstore has been locally owned and operated since the 1970s. It attracts students, bohemians, and businesspeople alike with its homey vibe, and features great selections of Buddhism tomes and travel guides. It is attached to a coffeehouse with patio seating on the Pearl Street Mall, The Bookend Cafe (see "Espresso Bars, Coffeehouses & Related Establishments," earlier in this chapter). 1107 Pearl St. ✆ 303/447-2074. www.boulderbookstore.com.

FASHION

Alpaca Connection   Come here for natural-fiber clothing from around the world, including alpaca-and-wool sweaters from South America. 1326 Pearl St. ✆ 303/447-2047.

Rocky Mountain Kids *(Kids*   Offering clothing for newborns to 12-year-olds, this bright store specializes in quality brands and is known for its kid-friendliness: complimentary animal crackers and plenty of toys in the box. 2525 Arapahoe Ave. ✆ 303/447-2267.

Weekends   The selection of men's and women's fashions is somewhat pricey but chosen for comfort and style—and it shows. 1101 Pearl St. ✆ 303/444-4231.

FOOD & DRINK

Boulder Wine Merchant   This store has a solid selection of wines from around the world, plus knowledgeable salespeople (and more than one master sommelier) who can help you make the right choice. 2690 Broadway. ✆ 303/443-6761.

Liquor Mart   Here you'll find a huge choice of discounted wine and liquor, with more than 5,000 wines and 900 beers, including a wide selection of imported and microbrewed beers. 1750 15th St. (at Canyon Blvd.). ℂ **303/449-3374.**

Whole Foods   The latest and greatest of Boulder's organic supermarkets, this huge store—part of the national chain—has a wide-ranging, fresh inventory, and is a favorite lunch spot of locals. Offerings include a deli, soup and salad bar, sushi, and more free samples than you could possibly eat. It's also 100% wind-powered. 2301 30th St. ℂ **303/545-6611.**

GIFTS & SOUVENIRS

The best stops for T-shirts, University of Colorado paraphernalia, and other Boulder souvenirs are **Jackalope and Company,** 1126 Pearl St. (ℂ **303/939-8434**); **Where the Buffalo Roam,** 1320 Pearl St. (ℂ **303/938-1424**); and the **CU Bookstore,** 1111 Broadway (ℂ **303/442-5051**). Long a hub for Eastern religion, Boulder also has a plethora of Tibetan gift shops—**Old Tibet,** 948 Pearl St. (ℂ **303/440-0323**) is the longest standing—and other meditative retailers, like **Now & Zen,** 1638 Pearl St. (ℂ **303/530-9028**).

HARDWARE

McGuckin Hardware   McGuckin's claims to have the world's largest hardware selection, with more than 200,000 items in stock. In addition to the nuts, bolts, brackets, paints, tools, and assorted whatchamacallits that most hardware stores carry, you'll also find sporting goods, kitchen gizmos, automotive supplies, stationery, some clothing, electronics, outdoor furniture, fresh flowers, and a whole lot of other stuff. 2525 Arapahoe Ave. ℂ **303/443-1822** or 86-MCGUCKIN. www.mcguckin.com.

JEWELRY

Angie Star Jewelry   A gallery for some of the area's top jewelry designers, Angie Star's store is a showcase for one-of-a-kind pieces. 1807 Pearl St. ℂ **720/565-0288.**

El Loro   Distinctively Boulder, this bohemian jewelry shop has been a Pearl Street Mall resident for more than 25 years. Aside from a nice selection of sterling silver items with semiprecious stones, El Loro also sells clogs and incense. 1416 Pearl St. ℂ **303/449-3162.**

KITCHENWARE

Peppercorn   From cookbooks to pasta makers, you can find anything and everything for the kitchen here at "the Smithsonian of cookstores." In business since 1977, this vast store (12,000 sq. ft.!) has hundreds of kitchen gadgets and appliances—everything you might need to prepare, serve, and consume the simplest or most exotic meal. 1235 Pearl St. ℂ **800/447-6905** or 303/449-5847.

SPORTING GOODS

Gart Sports, 3320 N. 28th St. (ℂ **303/449-9021**), is a good all-purpose source, while the following are more specialized—and interesting—retail outlets.

Boulder Army Store   Just east of the Pearl Street Mall, this shop has the best inventory of camping gear in the city, along with a limited amount of fishing equipment. There is also a good supply of outdoor clothing and military surplus items such as fatigues, helmets, and that disarmed hand grenade you've always wanted. 1545 Pearl St. ℂ **303/442-7616.**

Mountain Sports This shop, which opened in 1958, boasts of being Boulder's oldest mountaineering shop. It specializes in equipment, clothing, and accessories for backpacking, camping, rock and ice climbing, mountaineering, backcountry skiing, and snowshoeing. Equipment rentals include sleeping bags, tents, backpacks, and snowshoes; backcountry and telemark ski packages are available. Mountain Sports also sells maps and guidebooks, and the knowledgeable staff—which includes several trained guides—can help you plan your trip. 2835 Pearl St. © 303/442-8355.

8 Boulder After Dark

As a cultured and well-educated community (59% of adult residents have at least one college degree), Boulder is especially noted for its summer music, dance, and Shakespeare festivals. Major entertainment events take place year-round, both downtown and on the University of Colorado campus. There's also a wide choice of nightclubs and bars, but it hasn't always been so: Boulder was dry for 60 years, from 1907 (13 years before national Prohibition) to 1967. The first new bar in the city opened in 1969, in the Hotel Boulderado. The notoriously healthy city banned smoking in 1995; only a few establishments allow patrons to ignore the policy.

Entertainment schedules can be found in the *Daily Camera*'s weekly *Friday Magazine;* in either of the Denver dailies, the *Denver Post* or the *Rocky Mountain News;* in *Westword,* the Denver weekly; or in the free *Boulder Weekly.*

THE CLUB & MUSIC SCENE

Boulder Theater *(finds* Rock, folk, bluegrass, jazz, hip-hop, comedy, and who knows what else—performed by musicians such as Lou Reed, Bill Maher, Herbie Hancock, and Norah Jones—take the stage here. During the week, you'll also find independent and otherwise alternative films; there are also annual film festivals here. 14th and Pearl sts. © 303/786-7030. www.bouldertheater.com.

The Catacombs This popular bar books live blues and jazz by local and regional performers. The loud, somewhat raucous atmosphere (and smoking room) draws a crowd of CU students and an eclectic mix of locals and traveling businesspeople. A limited pub menu is served. In the basement of the Hotel Boulderado, 13th and Spruce sts. © 303/443-0486.

Fox Theatre and Cafe *(finds* A variety of live music (including, but not limited to, bluegrass, funk, blues, hip-hop, reggae, and punk) is presented here 5 or 6 nights a week, featuring a mix of local, regional, and national talent. You'll find three bars at this converted movie theater, which is revered for its great acoustics. 1135 13th St. © 303/443-3399 or 303/447-0095. www.foxtheatre.com.

'Round Midnight A hip basement joint on the Pearl Street Mall, 'Round Midnight specializes in malt scotch, good beer, and dancing. An eclectic array of performers (hip-hop, techno, jazz, rock) takes the stage here on weekends and DJs during the week. 1005 Pearl St. © 303/442-2176.

Trilogy Wine Bar Owned and operated by the Emich triplets (Jill, Jessica, and Jennifer), his hip venue is tucked in the back of a stylish restaurant with a diverse international menu and a great wine list. Performers include reggae bands, acid and Latin jazz acts, DJs, and hip-hop acts. 2017 13th St. © 303/473-WINE. www.trilogywinebar.com.

THE BAR SCENE

Conor O'Neill's *(Finds)*   Everything in this pub—from the bar to the art to the timber floors—was designed and built in Ireland. The atmosphere is rich, with a "shop pub" up front and two back rooms centered on a pair of fireplaces that were constructed by visiting Irish stonemasons. There are over a dozen beers on tap, primarily from (where else?) Ireland, and the pub menu features fish and chips, burgers, and a mean shepherd's pie. There is regular live music (surf to Celtic), and an Irish jam session Sunday afternoons. 1922 13th St. *(C)* **303/449-1922.** www.conoroneills.com.

Lazy Dog   With a great rooftop deck and a plethora of TVs tuned into games of all kinds, the Lazy Dog has emerged as the best sports bar in Boulder, especially after its recent relocation to the Pearl Street Mall. 1346 Pearl St. *(C)* **303/440-3355.** www.thelazydog.com.

Mountain Sun Pub & Brewery   An English-style neighborhood pub and microbrewery, Mountain Sun produces dozens of barrels of beer each week and provides tours on request during the day. The mostly made-from-scratch menu features soups, salads, burgers, sandwiches, and a few Mexican dishes. There's live folk, acoustic, and bluegrass music on Sunday night. There is also the **Southern Sun** in south Boulder at 627 S. Broadway (*(C)* **303/543-0886**). 1535 Pearl St. (east of the mall). *(C)* **303/546-0886.** www.mountainsunpub.com.

The Republic of Boulder   Subtitled "The People's Pub," the former Oasis has been rethought to reflect the passions and quirks of its home city—in the form of hemp fan blades, a large dance floor, and creative but affordable eats. The cavernous pub also produces its own beer and has a full array of bar games: pool, darts, and retro video games like Ms. Pac-Man. 1095 Canyon Blvd. *(C)* **303/443-1460.** www.republicofboulder.com.

The Sink *(Finds)*   This off-campus establishment opened in 1923 (CU dropout Robert Redford was once the janitor) but has been updated with new spacey wall murals that help make it one of Boulder's funniest—and most fun—nightspots. There's a full bar with more than a dozen regional microbrews, live music, and fare such as Sinkburgers and "ugly crust" pizza. 1165 13th St. *(C)* **303/444-SINK.** www.thesink.com.

Sundown Saloon   This raucous dive is a CU institution. In a spacious basement on the west end of the Pearl Street Mall, pool is the pastime of choice and the drinks are reasonably priced. 1136 Pearl St. **303/449-4987.** www.thesundownsaloon.com.

Walnut Brewery   In a historic brick warehouse a block from the Pearl Street Mall, this large restaurant/bar/microbrewery is popular with the after-work crowd, both young and old. 1123 Walnut St. (near Broadway). *(C)* **303/447-1345.**

West End Tavern   A 2004 makeover of this popular neighborhood bar left the brick walls and the classic bar intact, but gave the rest of the joint a contemporary shot in the arm and a slick look. Beyond the 48 bourbons stocked by the bar, fare includes a different specialty burger every day, barbecue, and more upscale items. The tavern's roof garden is an ideal spot to unwind and enjoy some of the best views in town and outdoor cinema on certain summer nights. 926 Pearl St. *(C)* **303/444-3535.**

THE PERFORMING ARTS

Music, dance, and theater are important aspects of life for Boulder residents. Many of these activities take place at **Macky Auditorium** at the University of Colorado (*(C)* **303/492-8008;** www.colorado.edu/music) and other campus venues, as well as the

Tips   Lyons: On the Beaten Path

Most tourists driving U.S. 36 to Rocky Mountain National Park from Boulder or Denver blaze through the dinky town of Lyons without even bothering to slow down. They're missing some top-drawer diversions in the process. For beer and music aficionados, **Oskar Blues Grill & Brew,** 303 Main St. (© **303/823-6685;** www.oskarblues.com), is a fun and—to say the least—eclectically decorated place for lunch and a beer, or a blues, rock, or rockabilly show come nighttime. Oskar Blues owns two distinctions in that it's the state's largest brewpub (by beer produced) and that it was the first craft brewery in the country to can its beer (Dale's Pale Ale and our favorite, Old Chub)—visitors can even can a six-pack themselves at certain times. The restaurant is open daily from 11am to 10pm; the bar is open until midnight Sunday through Thursday and 2am on Friday and Saturday. Also worth a look is the **Lyons Pinball Arcade,** 339-A Main St. (© **303/823-6100;** www.lyonspinball.com), with 30 pinball machines dating from the 1970s and more recent decades, including Kiss, Black Knight, and Addams Family. For silverball fiends, it's a real trip down memory lane.

Downtown Lyons is a historic district marked by 16 Victorian sandstones, and just outside of town, the fishing and hiking are excellent. For additional information, contact the **Lyons Chamber of Commerce** 350 Broadway (P.O. Box 426), Lyons, CO 80540 (© **303/823-5215;** www.lyons-colorado.com).

Chautauqua Auditorium, 900 Baseline Rd. (© **303/442-3282;** www.chautauqua.com), and the **Dairy Center for the Arts,** 2590 Walnut St. (© **303/440-7826;** www.thedairy.org).

CLASSICAL MUSIC & OPERA

Boulder Bach Festival   First presented in 1981, this celebration of the music of Johann Sebastian Bach includes not only a late-January festival but also concerts and other events year-round. Tickets run $15 to $30. Series tickets are also available. P.O. Box 1896, Boulder, CO 80306. © 303/776-9666. www.boulderbachfest.org.

Boulder Philharmonic Orchestra   This acclaimed community orchestra performs an annual fall-to-spring season, primarily at Macky Auditorium, with world-class artists who have included singer Marilyn Horne, guitarist Carlos Montoya, cellist Yo-Yo Ma, and violinist Itzhak Perlman. Tickets cost $10 to $65, more for concerts that feature premier performers. 2995 Wilderness Pl., Suite 100, Boulder, CO 80301. © 303/449-1343. www.boulderphil.org.

Colorado Mahlerfest   Begun in 1988, this international festival is the only one of its kind in the world. For a week each January it celebrates the work of Gustav Mahler with a performance of one of his symphonies as well as chamber concerts, films, discussions, seminars, and other musical programs. Most events are free; admission to symphony concerts ranges from $10 to $30. P.O. Box 1314, Boulder, CO 80306. © 303/447-0513. www.mahlerfest.org.

Colorado Music Festival *(Finds)*   Begun in 1976, this series is the single biggest annual arts event in Boulder, with visiting musicians from around the world performing in the acoustically revered Chautauqua Auditorium. The festival presents works of the classical through modern eras, such as Bach, Beethoven, Mozart, Dvorak, and Gershwin, plus living composers. It usually runs from mid-June to mid-August, with symphony orchestra performances Thursday and Friday, chamber-orchestra concerts Sunday, and a chamber-music series Tuesday; all shows start at 7:30pm. There's also a children's concert in late June and a free Independence Day concert at CU's Folsom Field. Adult ticket prices range from $12 to $45. 900 Baseline Rd., Cottage 100, Boulder, CO 80302. (C) **303/449-1397** for general information, 303/440-7666 or visit website for tickets. www.colorado musicfest.org.

CU Concerts   The university's College of Music presents the Artist Series, Music, Theatre, University of Colorado Summer Opera, Takács String Quartet Series, and Holiday Festival at Macky Auditorium and Grusin Music Hall. General admission tickets usually cost between $10 and $40. The Artist Series features an outstanding lineup of classical soloists, jazz artists, dance companies, and multidisciplinary events. Call early for tickets for performances of the renowned Takács String Quartet. The annual Holiday Festival includes the University Symphony Orchestra, university choirs, several smaller ensembles, and soloists from the College of Music's student body and faculty. University of Colorado. (C) **303/492-8008**. www.cuconcerts.org.

THEATER & DANCE

Colorado Shakespeare Festival *(Moments)*   Considered one of the top three Shakespearean festivals in the United States, this 2-month annual event attracts more than 40,000 theatergoers between late June and late August. Held since 1958 in the University of Colorado's Mary Rippon Outdoor Theatre, and indoors at the University Theatre Main Stage, it offers more than a dozen performances of each of four plays. Actors, directors, designers, and everyone associated with the productions are fully schooled Shakespearean professionals. Tickets run from $10 to $52 for single performances, with series packages also available. Campus Box 277, University of Colorado, Boulder, CO 80309. (C) **303/492-0554** for information and the box office. www.coloradoshakes.org.

Nomad Theatre   Boulder's only resident professional theater, the Nomad has presented a mix of classic and contemporary dramas, comedies, and musicals since the curtain first opened in 1951. Tickets cost $18 to $22. 1410 Quince Ave. (C) **720/406-6991** or 303/774-4037 (box office). www.nomadstage.com.

Upstart Crow Theatre Company   Specializing in Shakespeare and more contemporary classics, the Upstart Crow is the resident theater company at the Dairy Center for the Arts. They perform on two stages: a 99-seat theater (where no seat is more than three rows from the stage) and an 86-seat proscenium theater. Tickets are $15 to $18. Dairy Center for the Arts, 2590 Walnut St. (C) **303/442-1415**. www.theupstartcrow.org.

9

Northeastern Colorado

Here are the spacious skies, stretching without interruption hundreds of miles eastward from the foot of the Rocky Mountains. Here also are the golden, rolling, irrigated fields of wheat and corn, spreading along the valleys of the South Platte and Republican rivers and their tributaries.

A different Colorado exists on the sparsely populated plains, one that inspired James Michener's novel *Centennial*. Alive are stories of the prehistoric buffalo hunters who first inhabited the region; trailblazers and railroad crews who opened up the area to Anglo settlement; hardy pioneer farmers who endured drought, economic ruin, and so many other hardships; and ranchers such as John W. Iliff, who carved a feudal empire built on longhorn cattle. Pioneer museums, frontier forts, old battlefields, and preserved downtown districts won't let history die. Vast open stretches—wetlands swollen with migrating waterfowl, the starkly beautiful Pawnee National Grassland—remind us that Colorado is not just the Rocky Mountains.

1 Fort Collins

65 miles N. of Denver, 34 miles S. of Cheyenne, Wyoming

A bustling college town, Fort Collins was founded in 1864 as a military post on the Cache la Poudre (pronounced *Poo*-der) River, named for a powder cache left by French fur traders. The fort, named for Lieutenant Colonel William O. Collins, was abandoned in 1867, but the settlement prospered, first as a center for quarrying and farming, and by 1910 with sugar-beet processing.

Today Fort Collins is among the fastest-growing cities in the United States, with an average annual growth rate of about 3%. Population leaped from 43,000 in 1970 to 65,000 in 1980 to more than 140,000 today, not including the many Colorado State University students. CSU was established in 1870; today it is nationally known for its forestry and veterinary medicine schools, as well as its research advances in space engineering and bone cancer.

Fort Collins, at just under 5,000 feet elevation, makes a good base for fishing, boating, rafting, or exploring Rocky Mountain National Park (see chapter 10). It also has several historic sites and offers a treat for beer lovers, with tours of breweries ranging from micro to the huge facilities operated by Anheuser-Busch.

ESSENTIALS

GETTING THERE **By Car** Coming from south or north, take I-25 to exit 269 (Mulberry St., for downtown Fort Collins), exit 268 (Prospect Rd., for Colorado State University), or exit 265 (Harmony Rd., for south Fort Collins). From Rocky Mountain National Park's Estes Park entrances, follow U.S. 34 to Loveland, then turn north on U.S. 287. The drive takes about 1¼ hours from Denver or Estes Park and about 40 minutes from Cheyenne, Wyoming.

By Plane Many visitors to Fort Collins fly into **Denver International Airport** (see chapter 5). The **Fort Collins/Loveland Airport** (© **970/962-2852;** www.fcgov.com/airport), off I-25 exit 259, 7 miles northeast of downtown Loveland, offers regularly scheduled commercial service with Allegiant Air (© **702/505-8888**); call for the current schedule.

Shamrock Airport Express (© **866/482-0505** or 970/482-0505; www.rideshamrock.com) provides daily shuttle services between Denver and Fort Collins (one-way rates: $26 adults, $8 children 11 and younger, free for children who sit on a parent's lap). Car rentals in Fort Collins are provided by **Advantage** (© **800/574-6000** or 970/224-2211) and **Enterprise** (© **800/736-8222** or 970/224-2592).

VISITOR INFORMATION The **Fort Collins Convention and Visitors Bureau** operates a visitor information center at 19 Old Town Sq., Suite 137, Fort Collins, CO 80524 (© **800/274-3678;** www.ftcollins.com). The state operates a **Colorado Welcome Center,** just east of I-25 at Prospect Road (exit 268); the angular, two-story building's unique architecture makes it hard to miss. Both are open daily from 8am to 6pm Memorial Day to Labor Day, and from 8am to 5pm the rest of the year.

GETTING AROUND Fort Collins is located on the Cache la Poudre River, 4 miles west of I-25. College Avenue (U.S. 287) is the main north-south artery and the city's primary commercial strip; Mulberry Street (Colo. 14) is the main east-west thoroughfare. Downtown Fort Collins extends north of Mulberry Street on College Avenue to Jefferson Street; Old Town is a triangle east of and bounded by College Avenue, 4 blocks north of Mulberry. The main Colorado State University campus covers a square mile on the west side of College Avenue 2 blocks south of Mulberry.

The city bus system, known as **Transfort** (© **970/221-6620;** www.fcgov.com/transfort), operates more than a dozen routes throughout Fort Collins Monday through Saturday, except major holidays. Most routes run from 6:30am to 6:30pm, and additional runs are made when CSU is in session. All buses have bike racks. Fares are $1.25 for adults, 60¢ for seniors 60 and older and those with disabilities; youths 17 and under ride free. Exact change is required. A 10-ride ticket costs $9.

Taxi service is provided 24 hours a day by **Shamrock Yellow Cab** (© **970/224-2222**).

Bicycling is a popular and viable means of transportation in Fort Collins. Just about the only place you can't ride is College Avenue. See "Sports & Outdoor Activities," below, for information about bike rentals.

FAST FACTS The **Poudre Valley Hospital** is at 1024 S. Lemay Ave. (© **800/252-5784** or 970/495-7000), between Prospect Road and Riverside Avenue just east of downtown. The main **post office** is located at 301 E. Boardwalk Dr. Contact the U.S. Postal Service (© **800/275-8777;** www.usps.com) for hours and other post office locations.

SPECIAL EVENTS Gem & Mineral Show, late March; Cinco de Mayo in Old Town, first weekend in May; Colorado Brewers' Festival in Old Town Square, last full weekend in June; Fabric of Legacies Quilt Show, mid-June; New WestFest in Old Town and Library Park, mid-August; Museum of Contemporary Art Studio Tour; and Oktoberfest in Old Town, late September.

Fort Collins

ATTRACTIONS ●
Anheuser-Busch Brewery **16**
Avery House **4**
Big Horn Brewery **1**
Conor O'Neill's **12**
Discovery Science Center **20**
The Farm at Lee Martinez Park **3**
Fort Collins Brewery **16**
Fort Collins Museum **7**
New Belgium Brewing Company **14**
Odell Brewing Company **15**
Swetsville Zoo **23**

ACCOMMODATIONS ■
Armstrong Hotel **6**
Best Western Kiva Inn **17**
Best Western University Inn **18**
Hampton Inn **21**
Hilton Fort Collins **19**
Quality Inn & Suites **21**
Sheldon House B&B **2**
Super 8 Motel **17**

DINING ◆
Bisetti's **8**
Coopersmith's Pub &
  Brewing Co. **9**
Cozzola's Pizza North **11**
Cozzola's Pizza South **22**
The Egg & I **22**
El Burrito **13**
Jay's Bistro **5**
Silver Grill Café **10**

WHAT TO SEE & DO

Families with kids might also want to stop in at the **Discovery Science Center,** 703 E. Prospect Rd. (✆ **970/472-3990;** www.dcsm.org), with interactive exhibits covering everything from dinosaurs to local ecology to electricity.

Anheuser-Busch Brewery ✪✪ One of Fort Collins's leading employers—and its top tourist attraction—this Anheuser-Busch brewery produces some 6 million barrels of beer each year, distributed to 10 Western states. The 1¼-hour tours leave from the visitor center and gift shop, and include exhibits on the history of the Anheuser-Busch company, nostalgic displays of ads from the 1950s and other periods, and a complete look at the brewing process, from the huge brew kettles to the high-speed packaging plant that fills 2,000 cans per minute. The tours end at the tasting room with a free

Finds   The Great Stupa of Dharmakaya and the Shambhala Mountain Center

Founded by Chögyam Trungpa Rinpoche, a Tibetan Buddhist teacher who was a major figure in bringing his religion to the U.S., the **Shambhala Mountain Center** is about an hour's drive northwest of Fort Collins and a world apart. Located in a rocky, forested mountain valley, the center offers a curriculum ranging from meditation and yoga to gardening and storytelling.

Beyond the educational component, the center is also home to a unique structure: **The Great Stupa of Dharmakaya**, dedicated to Shambhala founder Rinpoche, is the largest and most ornate stupa (a spire built in honor of a deceased Buddhist teacher) in the Western Hemisphere. Designed to stand for 1,000 years, nuclear-plant engineers were called in to construct the structure with reinforced concrete and artisans hand-painted every last detail. The stupa is open from 10am to 6pm daily; guided tours are offered at 2pm Saturday and Sunday (donations suggested).

Lodging ranges from tent-cabins with a communal bathhouse to lodge rooms with private bathrooms, with a cafeteria on-site. Many weekend renewal programs are offered, and many programs are open to Buddhists and non-Buddhists alike. There are also 6 miles of hiking paths on the property.

For further information, contact the Shambhala Mountain Center, 4921 CR 68C, Red Feather Lakes, CO 80545 (© **888/788-7221;** www.shambhalamountain.org).

---

sample. You can also visit the barn and see the giant Clydesdale draft horses used to promote Budweiser and other Anheuser-Busch beers since 1933; the first Saturday of each month (year-round) from 1 to 3pm is Clydesdale Camera Day, when the horses are brought out to pose with visitors.

2351 Busch Dr. (I-25 exit 271). © **970/490-4691.** www.budweisertours.com. Free admission. June–Aug daily 9:30am–4:30pm; Sept daily 10am–4pm; Oct–May Thurs–Mon 10am–4pm. Closed some major holidays.

Avery House   Custom-built in 1879 for banker-surveyor Franklin Avery and his wife, Sara, this Victorian home at the corner of Mountain Avenue and Meldrum Street was constructed of red-and-buff sandstone from the quarries west of Fort Collins. The Poudre Landmarks Foundation and the city of Fort Collins purchased the house in 1974, restoring it to its original Victorian splendor—from furniture to wallpaper to wallpapered ceilings. The grounds, with a gazebo, carriage house, and fountain, are popular for weddings and receptions. Allow 30 minutes to 1 hour.

328 W. Mountain Ave. © **970/221-0533.** www.poudrelandmarks.com. Free admission, donations welcome. Wed and Sun 1–3pm except Easter, Christmas, and New Year's Day.

Colorado State University   Fort Collins revolves around this university, with its 25,000 students from every state and close to 100 foreign countries. Founded in 1870 as Colorado Agricultural College, it was renamed Colorado A&M in 1935 and became Colorado State University in 1957. The "A" constructed on the hillside behind Hughes Stadium by students and faculty in 1923 stands for "Aggies" and remains a cherished tradition, even though the school's athletic teams have been called the Rams for decades.

Those wanting to see the campus should stop first at the **visitor center,** at the southwest corner of College Avenue and Pitkin Street (© **970/491-4636**), for information, maps, and parking passes. It's open year-round Monday through Friday from 8am to 5pm. Among suggested stops are the **Administration Building,** on the Oval where the school began, and the **Lory Student Center,** at University and Center avenues, which houses a food court, bookstore, art gallery, floral shop, activities center, ballroom, and other facilities. Allow about an hour for a stroll around campus.

Appointments can be made to visit the renowned **Veterinary Teaching Hospital** and the **Equine Teaching Center.** The **Art Department** has five different galleries with revolving exhibits, and the **University Theatre** in Johnson Hall, on East Drive (© **970/491-5562** or 970/491-5116 for tickets), presents student productions year-round. The university's **Environmental Learning Center** covers some 200 acres, and has 2.5 miles of trails, with opportunities to see wildlife such as golden eagles, muskrats, and white-tail deer, and a variety of plants. Dogs, horses, and bikes are not permitted on the trails.

CSU has all the usual sports teams. For information on who's playing during your visit, check with the Athletic Department (© **970/491-RAMS;** www.csurams.com).

University and College aves. © **970/491-1101.** www.colostate.edu.

The Farm at Lee Martinez Park *(Kids* Early-20th-century farm machinery is on display, crafts are sold in the Silo Store, and oats are available to feed the animals. The Farm Museum has exhibits depicting farming techniques from the late 19th and early 20th centuries. Special programs are scheduled year-round, and kids can take advantage of the weekend pony rides ($5) from mid-March through October; group hayrides and tours can be booked in advance. A gift shop is open from mid-March through October. Allow 1 to 2 hours.

600 N. Sherwood St. © **970/221-6665.** Free admission, donations accepted. June to mid-Aug Tues–Sat 10am–5pm, Sun noon–5pm; mid-Aug to May Wed–Sat 10am–5pm, Sun noon–5pm.

Fort Collins Municipal Railway One of the few remaining original trolley systems in the nation, this restored 1919 Birney streetcar runs on its original route, along Mountain Avenue for 1½ miles from City Park to Howes Street. It's certainly more for fun than practical urban transport. Allow 30 minutes.

Oak and Roosevelt, at City Park. © **970/482-8246.** Admission $1 adults, 75¢ seniors, 50¢ children 12 and under. May–Sept weekends and holidays only, noon–5pm.

Fort Collins Museum Located in the 1903 Carnegie Library Building just a block south of Old Town, this museum boasts the largest collection of Folsom points of any western museum, plus historical artifacts from Fort Collins as well as pioneer and Victorian objects. You can see an 1850s cabin that is among the oldest surviving pioneer buildings in Colorado, an 1864 log officers' mess hall known locally as "Auntie Stone's

---

(Fun Fact **Horsing Around**

Firecracker, the world's first test-tube horse, was born July 2, 1996, at Colorado State University's Animal Reproduction and Biotechnology Laboratory.

Brewery Tours

There's no denying that Fort Collins is a beer town. Not only is it home to the giant **Anheuser-Busch Brewery,** with its famous Clydesdale horses (see above), but the city also boasts several excellent microbreweries.

Coopersmith's Pub & Brewing Co. (see "Where to Dine," later in this chapter) provides patrons a view of the brewing process from inside the restaurant, and offers tours on Saturdays from 1 to 4pm (by appointment only). Using English malted barley and hops from the Pacific Northwest, Coopersmith's brews from 6 to 10 ales. For those averse to beer, the brewery also makes its own root beer, ginger ale, and cream soda.

Just northeast of Old Town, across the railroad tracks, **New Belgium Brewing Company** ★★, 500 Linden St. (© **888/622-4044** or 970/221-0524; www.newbelgium.com), is a "macro" microbrewery—it ranks in the country's top 15 brewers by volume, second only to Coors of Colorado—producing top-quality Belgian-style ales including the very popular Fat Tire. The always-lively brewery is open Monday through Saturday from 10am to 6pm, offering four three-ounce samples to visitors. Tours are offered weekdays at 1pm, 2pm, and 3pm, and Saturdays on the hour from 11am to 4pm, with self-guided tours anytime. Beer can be purchased, along with glasses, caps, T-shirts, and other souvenirs.

You'll find **Odell Brewing Company,** Fort Collins' oldest craft brewery, at 800 E. Lincoln Ave. (© **970/498-9070;** www.odellbrewing.com). Specializing in English-style ales, Odell produces draft and bottled beers, which are available in restaurants and bars throughout the Rocky Mountains and the Southwest. Tours are given Monday through Friday at noon, 2pm, and 4pm and on the hour from 1pm to 4pm on Saturdays. The tasting room is open Monday through Saturday from 11am to 6pm. Beer, which you can sample before making your choice or get a taster of each for $3, plus beer glasses, shirts and other souvenirs are all available.

Also brewing beer in Fort Collins are **Fort Collins Brewery,** 1900 E. Lincoln Ave. #B (© **970/472-1499;** www.fortcollinsbrewery.com), which specializes in lagers; **Big Horn Brewery,** 1415 W. Elizabeth St. (© **970/221-5954**), which brews a variety of beer styles; and **Conor O'Neill's,** 214 Linden St. (© **970/407-0214**), specializing in Irish-style ale. Contact these breweries for tour information.

cabin," and a log one-room schoolhouse built in 1905. Annual events include Rendezvous and Skookum Day in July, a living-history day with blacksmithing, quilting, weaving, branding, and milking demonstrations. Allow 2 hours.

200 Mathews St. © **970/221-6738.** www.fcgov.com/museum. Free admission, $2 suggested donation. Tues–Sat 10am–5pm; Sun noon–5pm.

Old Town   A redbrick pedestrian walkway, flanked by street lamps and surrounding a bubbling fountain, is the focus of this restored historic district, which offers a look at the earliest roots of the city, and has plenty of good shopping opportunities. The main plaza, which covers several square blocks, extends diagonally to the northeast from the intersection of College and Mountain avenues; on either side are shops and galleries, restaurants, and nightspots. Outdoor concerts and a string of special events keep the plaza lively, especially from mid-spring to mid-fall. Self-guided walking-tour maps are available from the Convention and Visitors Bureau, individual merchants, and city offices; and the Fort Collins Museum (see above) conducts guided tours of Old Town during the summer on Saturdays at 11am, 1pm, and 3pm (call the museum for additional information). Allow about an hour, more if you want to do a lot of shopping.

Between College and Mountain aves. and Jefferson St.

Swetsville Zoo *Kids* Don't come to Bill Swets's zoo expecting to find animals—not live ones, that is. The sculpture park is a constantly growing menagerie of more than 150 dinosaurs and other real and imaginary animals, flowers, and windmills—all constructed from car parts, farm machinery, and other scrap metal. The whimsical nature of the sculptures is a delight for kids as well as adults. Several galleries offer works by other local artists, ranging from pottery to paintings to sculptures. Allow at least 1 hour.

4801 E. Harmony Rd. *©* 970/484-9509. Free admission, donations appreciated. Daily, dawn to dusk. The zoo is ¼ mile east of I-25 exit 265.

SPORTS & OUTDOOR ACTIVITIES

With its prime location, nestled in the foothills of the Rockies, Fort Collins is ideally situated for those who want to get out under Colorado's clear blue sky and experience the delights of nature. There are several convenient multiuse trails. The **Poudre River Trail** is an 8.3-mile paved trail that follows the Poudre River from North Taft Hill Road to East Drake Road and the CSU Environmental Learning Center, passing Lee Martinez Park along the way. The paved **Spring Creek Trail** runs 6.5 miles along Spring Creek, passing through several city parks, from West Drake Road to East Prospect Road at the Poudre River, where you can pick up the Poudre River Trail. Both trails are popular with hikers, cyclers, and skaters during warm weather, and cross-country skiers when the snow flies. Contact the Fort Collins Convention and Visitors Bureau (see "Visitor Information," above) for additional information.

There is a vast amount of public land under the jurisdiction of the U.S. Forest Service within easy access of Fort Collins, offering opportunities for hiking, mountain biking, horseback riding, fishing, camping, snowshoeing, and cross-country skiing. For details, check with the information center of the **Arapaho & Roosevelt National Forests and Pawnee Grasslands,** 2150 Centre Ave., Bldg. E, Fort Collins, CO 80526 (*©* **970/295-6600;** www.fs.fed.us/r2/arnf).

Major Fort Collins city parks include: **City Park,** 1500 W. Mulberry St., with a lake, picnic shelters, playgrounds, playing fields, tennis courts, a fitness course, a pottery studio, miniature train rides, a 9-hole golf course, and an outdoor swimming pool; **Edora Park,** 1420 E. Stuart St., with the excellent Edora Pool Ice Center (combination indoor swimming pools and two ice rinks), plus playgrounds, ball fields, tennis courts, a disc golf course, a fitness course, and horseshoe pits; **Rolland Moore Park,** which features an outdoor complex for racquetball and handball players, plus tennis courts, picnic grounds, softball fields, and basketball courts; **Fossil Creek Park,** with playgrounds, a dog park, skate park, and a wetlands interpretation site. For information on these and other city recreation facilities contact the Fort Collins Parks Department (*©* **970/221-6600;** www.fcgov.com/parks).

Among the most popular areas for outdoor recreation is **Horsetooth Reservoir** (© **970/679-4554;** www.larimer.org/parks/horsetooth.htm), about 15 minutes west of downtown, just over the first ridge of the Rocky Mountain foothills. The 6½-mile-long, man-made lake is named for a distinctive tooth-shaped rock that has long been an area landmark. It's reached via C.R. 44E or 42C, both off Overland Trail, or C.R. 38E off Taft Hill Road. At the reservoir and nearby **Horsetooth Mountain Park,** located several miles west via C.R. 38E (same phone as above), you'll find a wide array of outdoor activities from fly-fishing to rock climbing to swimming and water-skiing.

Lory State Park, just west of Fort Collins along the northwest edge of Horsetooth Reservoir (© **970/493-1623**), is known for its scenic beauty and extensive trail system. To get to the park, take U.S. 287 north out of Fort Collins, leaving it to take 54G Road through Laporte, then head west on C.R. 52E for 1 mile, turn left (south) onto C.R. 23N for about 1½ miles to C.R. 25G, where you turn right and drive about 1½ miles to the entrance. **State Forest State Park,** about 75 miles west of Fort Collins via Colo. 14 (© **970/723-8366**), covers 70,000 acres with spectacular mountain scenery, alpine lakes, and an abundance of wildlife, camping, and trails. See below for details on activities at these areas, and check out www.parks.state.co.us on the Web.

BICYCLING   There are more than 75 miles of designated bikeways in Fort Collins, including the Spring Creek and Poudre River trails, both paved (see above). There's also a dirt trail, the 5.8-mile Foothills Trail, parallel to Horsetooth Reservoir from Dixon Reservoir north to Campeau Open Space and Michaud Lane. For rentals of road and mountain bikes (from $25 per day), check with **Recycled Cycles,** 4031 S. Mason St. (© **970/223-1969**); and if you need repairs for your own bike visit **Lee's Cyclery,** 202 W. Laurel St. (© **800/748-2453** or 970/482-6006), or its second location at 931 E. Harmony Rd. (© **970/226-6006**). Also see "Mountain Biking," below.

FLY-FISHING   Guided fly-fishing trips and clinics are available from **Rocky Mountain Adventures,** 1117 N. U.S. 287 (P.O. Box 1989), Fort Collins, CO 80522 (© **800/858-6808** or 970/493-4005; www.shoprma.com). They access the Big Thompson, Cache la Poudre, and North Platte rivers, plus waters on two private ranches and in Rocky Mountain National Park. Half-day guided walk and wade trips cost $125 for one person or $180 for two people, and full-day trips cost $210 and $265, respectively. Those who'd like to strike out on their own might try nearby **Roosevelt National Forest.** For further information, contact the information center of the Arapaho & Roosevelt National Forests and Pawnee Grasslands (see above) and the Colorado Division of Wildlife, 317 W. Prospect Rd. (© **970/472-4300;** http://wildlife.state.co.us). Anglers heading out to State Forest State Park have a good chance of catching a variety of trout species; only artificial flies and lures are permitted in some lakes there.

GOLF   Fort Collins has three municipal courses: **Collindale Golf Course,** 1441 E. Horsetooth Rd. (© **970/221-6651**); **City Park Nine,** 411 S. Bryan Ave. (© **970/221-6650**); and **SouthRidge Golf Club,** 5750 S. Lemay Ave. (© **970/226-2828**). Tee times should be reserved 3 days in advance. Two privately owned courses open to the public are **Link-N-Greens Golf Course,** 777 E. Lincoln Ave. (© **970/221-4818**), and **Mountain Vista Greens Golf Course,** 2808 NE Frontage Rd. (© **970/482-4847**). Courses are open year-round, weather permitting, and greens fees are in the $20 to $25 range for 18 holes.

HIKING   The **Comanche Peak Wilderness area,** 67,500 acres of pine and spruce-fir forests below expanses of alpine tundra, offers scenic hiking trails along the north and east sides of Rocky Mountain National Park. Contact the information center of the **Arapaho & Roosevelt National Forests and Pawnee Grasslands** (see above).

State Forest State Park has miles of hiking trails and even gives overnight visitors the opportunity to stay in a yurt (see "Skiing & Other Winter Sports," below). There are 26 miles of trails at **Horsetooth Mountain Park** that are shared by hikers, mountain bikers, and horseback riders. Finally, **Lory State Park** has about 25 miles of hiking trails, where the top of Arthur's Rock—a hike of 2 miles—offers a marvelous view across Fort Collins and the northeastern Colorado plains. For more information on these parks, see the introduction to the "Sports & Outdoor Activities" section, above.

HORSEBACK RIDING   For the most part, riding is permitted anywhere in the Estes-Poudre District of the Roosevelt National Forest without special permit or license. Horsetooth Mountain Park, State Forest State Park, and Lory State Park have horse trails as well. **Tip Top Guest Ranch,** 22 miles west of Fort Collins in Bellevue (© **970/484-1215;** www.tiptopranch.com), offers a variety of guided rides.

KAYAKING   **Rocky Mountain Adventures** (see "Fly-Fishing," above) offers kayaking classes covering the Eskimo roll, paddling techniques, and white-water skills. Tuition prices are $60 for the roll, $40 for paddling, and $210 for a 2-day "Fast Track" class. Private instruction is also available.

Classes for all levels are also available from **Poudre River Kayaks, Inc.,** a part of the Mountain Shop, 632 S. Mason St., Fort Collins, CO 80524 (© **800/403-5720** or 970/493-5720; www.poudreriverkayaks.com), which also offers kayak rentals ($25 for 2 days, including needed gear).

LLAMA PACKING   Using llamas as pack animals is relatively new in the United States, but they are rapidly becoming the pack animal of choice in the Rocky Mountains. Guided llama trips, overnight pack trips, and llama leasing are the specialty of **Buckhorn Llama Co.** (© **970/667-7411;** www.llamapack.com). Guided pack trips for one to three people cost $350 per person per day.

MOUNTAIN BIKING   A good choice for mountain bikers is the **Foothills Trail,** which runs along the east side of Horsetooth Reservoir from Dixon Dam north to Michaud Lane. Horsetooth Mountain Park, Lory State Park, and State Forest State Park have excellent trails appropriate for mountain biking as well. In addition, there are yurts for overnighting at State Forest State Park (see "Skiing & Other Winter Sports," below). Also see "Bicycling," above.

RIVER RAFTING   River-rafting enthusiasts have ample opportunities for boating the Cache la Poudre, a nationally designated wild-and-scenic river. **Rocky Mountain Adventures** (see "Fly-Fishing," above), offers half-day and full-day trips on the Cache la Poudre and four other regional rivers. Costs range from $42 to $60 for a half-day and $92 for a full day. **A Wanderlust Adventure** (© **800/745-7238** or 970/484-1219; www.awanderlustadventure.com), and **A1 Wildwater** (© **800/369-4165** or 970/ 224-3379; www.a1wildwater.com) offers half-day trips on the Cache la Poudre River for similar prices.

SKIING & OTHER WINTER SPORTS   Cross-country skiers will find plenty of trails and rolling hills at Lory State Park, surrounding national forests, and in State Forest State Park, where they can stay overnight in a backcountry yurt system owned by **Never Summer Nordic** (© **970/723-4070;** www.neversummernordic.com). The yurts, which are circular, tentlike canvas-and-wood structures on a high wood deck, have wood-burning stoves, padded bunks, and complete, albeit nonelectrified, kitchens. Most sleep up to six, and one sleeps at least 10. Winter rates for the entire yurt are $90 to $110. In summer, rates are $60 to $70. Seven yurts (one near Lake Agnes and the other six at North Michigan Reservoir) can be rented by reservation by calling the number above. State Forest State Park also has an extensive system of snowmobile trails, either groomed or packed, that is separate from its cross-country ski trail system.

There's year-round **ice skating** at Edora Pool Ice Center (see "Swimming," below); it costs $4 for adults to age 59, $3 for youths 2 to 17, $3.25 for seniors 60 to 84, and free for infants under 2 and seniors 85 and older. Call for current hours.

SWIMMING   Edora Pool Ice Center (EPIC), at 1801 Riverside Dr. in Edora Park (© **970/221-6683**), offers swimming, water exercise programs, and diving. The indoor **Mulberry Pool,** 424 W. Mulberry St. (© **970/221-6659**), has lap lanes, a diving area, and "Elrog the Frog," a poolside slide. Both have recreational swimming and lap swimming; call for the current schedule or check out **www.fcgov.com/recreation**. The **City Park Outdoor Pool,** 1599 City Park Ave. (© **970/416-2489**), is open afternoons during warm weather (closed in inclement weather). Admission at each of the three above pools costs $4 to $5 for adults to age 59, $3 to $4 for youths 2 to 17, $3.25 to $3.75 for seniors 60 to 84, and is free for infants under 2 and seniors 85 and older.

WILDLIFE WATCHING   Although you'll see some wildlife and water birds at Lory State Park and Horsetooth Reservoir, go to State Forest State Park to try to catch a glimpse of the state's largest moose population, along with elk, mule deer, mountain lions, bighorn sheep, and black bears. State Forest State Park's Moose Visitor Center has wonderful displays and wildlife-viewing information.

SHOPPING

Visitors enjoy shopping in **Old Town Square,** at Mountain and College avenues, with numerous shops, galleries, and restaurants. Old Town is also the site of various events; contact the Downtown Business Association (© **970/484-6500;** www.downtown fortcollins.com). Northern Colorado's largest enclosed shopping mall is the **Foothills Mall,** just north of the intersection of South College Avenue and Horsetooth Road (© **970/226-5555;** www.shopfoothills.com). Anchored by three department stores— Macy's, JCPenney, Sears—it has more than 100 specialty stores and a food court, and is open Monday through Saturday from 10am to 9pm and on Sunday from 11am to 6pm. There is also a small **antiques district** along South College Avenue between Harmony and Trilby roads.

WHERE TO STAY

Lodging rates in Fort Collins are usually higher in summer, and rooms can be especially expensive and hard to find during college graduation and other major college events. The city has numerous chain motels, including the **Best Western Kiva Inn,** 1638 E. Mulberry St., Fort Collins, CO 80524 (© **888/299-5482** or 970/484-2444), with rates of $74 to $109 double; **Best Western University Inn,** 914 S. College Ave., Fort Collins, CO 80524 (© **800/937-8376** or 970/484-1984), with rates of $74 to $125 double; **Hampton Inn,** 1620 Oakridge Dr., Fort Collins, CO 80525 (© **800/ 426-7866** or 970/229-5927), with rates of $99 to $129 double; **Quality Inn & Suites,** 4001 S. Mason St., Fort Collins, CO 80525 (© **800/424-6423** or 970/282-9047), with rates of $89 to $159 double; and **Super 8 Motel,** 409 Centro Way, Fort Collins, CO 80524 (© **800/800-8000** or 970/493-7701), with rates of $45 to $70 double. Rates may be higher during special events, like college graduation. Room taxes add 9.7% to hotel bills.

Armstrong Hotel 🎯 *Finds*   The only downtown lodging in Fort Collins, the boutique Armstrong Hotel is a nice balance of new and old. The historic property opened in 1923 but had gone downhill prior to its renovation and reopening under new ownership in 2004. Now it's a model for a downtown hotel turnaround. Some rooms are furnished with antiques, others with contemporary decor, but all have original art on the walls, hardwood floors, and a sleek, spare style that's quite relaxing. The hotel's website offers real-time reservations so you can see exactly which rooms are available, complete with pictures. Interestingly, every room has a different sink, ranging from vintage to modern, and guests enjoy the use of complimentary cruiser bicycles.

259 S. College Ave., Fort Collins, CO 80524. © **866/384-3883** or 970/484-3883. Fax 970/224-5653. www.thearmstrong hotel.com. 37 units, including 13 suites. $89–$105 double; $115–$130 suite. AE, DISC, MC, V. **Amenities:** Health club access. *In room:* A/C, cable TV w/pay movies, kitchen, wireless Internet access.

Hilton Fort Collins 🎯   Formerly the Holiday Inn, this newly renovated hotel is the official "Home of the CSU Rams," and boasts a location next to campus and the most complete list of facilities and amenities in town. Guest rooms have contemporary decor and queens or two doubles; the 50 rooms on the hotel's west side are bigger, with king beds and great mountain views, but they're also more expensive. The nine-story hotel, centered on an open lobby, also has a restaurant and lounge, indoor pool, and fitness center.

425 W. Prospect Rd., Fort Collins, CO 80526. © **800/445-8667** or 970/482-2626. Fax 970/224-9209. www.hiltonfort-collins.com. 255 units. $89–$239 double. AE, DC, DISC, MC, V. **Amenities:** Restaurant (American); lounge; indoor pool; fitness center; courtesy airport shuttle. *In room:* A/C, cable TV w/pay movies, dataport, coffeemaker, hair dryer, iron.

Sheldon House Bed & Breakfast 🎯🎯   Step back into the early 20th century at this foursquare Victorian home, with golden oak floors and woodwork, leaded windows, and all the ornate furnishings you would expect from the prominent Fort Collins banker who had the home built in 1905. The attractive three-story inn has spacious rooms and an abundance of historic charm. It's an ideal choice for couples intent on exploring downtown Fort Collins or visiting the university (it's just 2 blocks away). Each room is unique—some have four-poster beds—but all have down comforters and attractively appointed private bathrooms with bathrobes. The smallest and least expensive room—Bob's Hideaway—is decorated in Old West style and has one twin bed. Other rooms have queen-size beds, and Miss Olive's Room has a queen and an additional single bed, plus a delightful outdoor balcony.

616 W. Mulberry St., Fort Collins, CO 80521. © **877/221-1918** or 970/221-1917. Fax 970/495-6954. www.theshel-donhouse.com. 4 units. $90–$125 double. Rates include full breakfast. AE, MC, V. Children 10 and older welcome. *In room:* A/C, wireless Internet.

CAMPING

There are several full-service campgrounds in the Fort Collins area. The **Fort Collins Poudre Canyon Kampground of America (KOA)** is about 10 miles northwest of downtown at U.S. 287 and Colo. 14 (© **800/562-2648** for reservations, or 970/493-9758), open May through September, with rates of $27 for tents and $32 to $35 for RVs. A second **KOA,** open year-round, is just off I-25 exit 281, north of Fort Collins at Wellington (© **800/562-8142** for reservations, or 970/568-7486), with rates from $24 per site. Campers looking for a lakeside RV resort might consider

Heron Lake RV Park, northwest of Fort Collins at 1910 N. Taft Rd. (© 877/ 254-4063 or 970/484-9880; www.heronlakerv.com), which is open year-round and has rates of $33 to $43 for RV sites and $23 for tent sites.

Nearby Arapaho and Roosevelt national forests have a number of established camp-grounds, many with restrooms, water, and picnic tables. For rates and other informa-tion, contact the **Arapaho & Roosevelt National Forests and Pawnee Grasslands** office (see "Sports & Outdoor Activities," above).

WHERE TO DINE
EXPENSIVE
Jay's Bistro 🍴🍴 CONTEMPORARY/GAME   Owned and operated by Jay and Jacki Witlen, longtime local favorite Jay's is an intimate eatery with a creative menu centered on innovative game dishes. Served at the inviting bar or one of several small dining areas decorated in earth tones and blonde woods, the menu is interesting to read, from appetizers to dessert, and even better to taste. We like the smoked buffalo carpaccio or a half-dozen fresh oysters to start, before moving on to one of the expertly prepared and presented entrees. We're partial to the seafood and game, especially the ostrich filet, deer loin, and lobster ravioli, but the diverse options also include pasta and vegetarian dishes, poultry, and beef. There is live jazz Wednesday to Saturday, and the crowd is more mature than most restaurants in town. Lunch is served weekdays until 2pm, and an abbreviated menu is served for 2 more hours.

135 W. Oak St. © **970/482-1876.** Reservations recommended. Main courses $16–$33. AE, DC, DISC, MC, V. Mon 11am–4pm and 5–9pm; Tues 11am–4pm and 5–9:30pm; Wed–Fri 11am–4pm and 5–10pm; Sat 5–10pm; Sun 5–8pm.

MODERATE
Bisetti's 🍴🍴 ITALIAN   A delightful atmosphere and good food make Bisetti's one of our favorite dining stops in northeast Colorado. The dining rooms glow with a Tus-can atmosphere and the mahogany bar offers great happy-hour specials. The menu features a variety of homemade pastas, from spaghetti and lasagna to fettuccine and manicotti. Our favorite main course is the basil fettuccine with chicken. If it's a romantic dinner you're looking for, ask about the private cubby for two, and split the mouthwatering tiramisu for dessert.

120 S. College Ave. © **970/493-0086.** www.bisettis.com. Reservations accepted for parties of 5 or more only. Main courses $7–$18. AE, DC, DISC, MC, V. Sun–Thurs 11am–9pm; Fri–Sat 11am–10pm.

Coopersmith's Pub & Brewing Co. MICROBREWPUB   One of the oldest brew-pubs in Colorado, Coopersmith's has been pleasing its customers since 1989. Located in historic Old Town Square, this American brewpub isn't just a place for knocking back a few. Within its brick walls is an open kitchen that prepares such traditional pub specialties as fish and chips, as well as less typical bangers and mash and Highland cot-tage pie, plus fresh fish and steak. You can also get hamburgers, sandwiches, salads, and soups, plus pizzas baked in a wood-fired oven. Portions are generous, and the two out-door patios are popular in good weather. There's also a short children's menu and a great little pool hall with a half-dozen tables, especially popular with university students.

5 Old Town Sq. © **970/498-0483.** www.coopersmithspub.com. Main courses $7–$19. AE, MC, V. Daily 11am–midnight.

INEXPENSIVE
Beyond the restaurants below, we're fans of **The Egg & I,** 2809 S. College Ave. (© **970/223-5271**), for its scrambles and other breakfast favorites; and **El Burrito,**

404 Linden St. (© **970/484-1102**), a family-owned Mexican eatery specializing in the dish of its name.

Cozzola's Pizza North ✿ PIZZA   This is the place to come for the best pizza in Fort Collins. And you don't need to take our word for it: That's been the consensus of the Coloradoan Readers Poll for more than a decade. In addition to offering the traditional chewy white pizza crust, the restaurant offers a whole-wheat poppy-seed or herb crust, and several sauce options: sweet basil, fresh garlic, *salsa del drago* (sauce of the dragon), pesto, or spinach ricotta. The long list of available toppings includes artichoke hearts, feta cheese, sun-dried tomatoes, pineapple, and almonds. If you're not in the mood for pizza, you might try the spinach calzone or stromboli.

   Cozzola's Pizza South (takeout and delivery only) is located at 1112 Oakridge Dr. (© **970/229-5771**).

241 Linden St. © **970/482-3557**. Pizza $6–$15; lunch main courses $4.50–$6. AE, MC, V. Tues–Fri 11am–9pm; Sat 11:30am–9pm; Sun 4–8pm.

Silver Grill Cafe ✿✿ *Finds* AMERICAN   In operation since 1933, this working-man's cafe attracts blue- and white-collar types, as well as seniors, students, and families for tasty, home-style food at very reasonable prices. When there's a line outside, as there often is on weekends, coffee is served to those waiting. You can't go wrong with one of the giant cinnamon rolls, but the rest of the menu is good, too. It's standard American fare: eggs, pancakes, and biscuits 'n' gravy for breakfast (served all day); burgers, sandwiches, and excellent homemade soups for lunch; and "noontime dinners" such as chicken-fried steak and beef pot roast.

218 Walnut St., Old Town. © **970/484-4656**. www.silvergrill.com. Main courses $3.50–$9. DISC, MC, V. Daily 6:30am–2pm.

PERFORMING ARTS & NIGHTLIFE

The college crowd does much of its drinking and partying at **Washington's**, a large, bustling, multilevel dance and drink emporium at 132 Laporte Ave. (© **970/493-1603**), with a variety of recorded music and drink specials. You might try the somewhat bohemian **Avogadro's Number**, 605 S. Mason St. (© **970/493-5555**), which attracts a mixed crowd for live bluegrass and acoustic music. Country-and-western fans head to the big dance floor at the **Sundance Steak House and Country Club**, 2716 E. Mulberry St. (© **970/484-1600**), for live country music and free dance lessons. Sports freaks like the **SportsCaster Bar & Grill**, 165 E. Boardwalk (© **970/223-3553**), which has 50 TV screens and 20 beers on tap. When you just want to quaff a cool beer at the end of the day, **Coopersmith's Pub & Brewing Co.**, 5 Old Town Sq. (© **970/498-0483**), may be the best place in town. Many Fort Collins folk drive 14 miles up the Poudre River to the **Mishawaka Amphitheatre & Restaurant**, 13714 Poudre Canyon (© **970/482-4420**; www.mishawakaconcerts.com), where top regional bands—and occasional national acts—perform during the summer in an outdoor amphitheater on the banks of the Poudre River.

   The principal venue for the performing arts in Fort Collins is **Lincoln Center**, 417 W. Magnolia St., at Meldrum Street (© **970/221-6730** box office or 970/221-6735 administration; www.fcgov.com/lctix). Built in 1978, the center includes the 1,180-seat Performance Hall and the 220-seat Mini Theatre, as well as three art galleries and an outdoor sculpture and performance garden. It's home to the Fort Collins Symphony, Opera Fort Collins, Canyon Concert Ballet, Larimer Chorale, OpenStage Theatre, and the Children's Theater. Concert, dance, children's, and travel film series are presented annually. Ticket prices vary considerably, but children's programs are often free or less than $10, and big name acts and Broadway shows are $20 to $50.

The **Fort Collins Symphony** (© **970/482-4823**; www.fcsymphony.org), established in 1948, performs both classical and pops music plus special events with guest performers. For those who enjoy a casual atmosphere with their classical music, the informal **Cranberry Pops** concert is performed the week after Thanksgiving by the symphony and a sizeable cast of singers and actors.

The **OpenStage Theatre Company** (© **970/484-5237**; www.openstage.com) is the area's leading professional stage group. It offers six productions annually, as well as various popular, classical, and operatic performances. Recent productions have included George Bernard Shaw's *Saint Joan*, Sam Shepard's *True West*, and Bertolt Brecht's *The Threepenny Opera*.

Those who enjoy an intimate theater experience should head to the **Bas Bleu Theatre Company,** 401 Pine St. (© **970/498-8949**; www.basbleu.org), which presents a variety of plays, concerts, poetry readings, and other events.

Broadway musicals are presented year-round at **Carousel Dinner Theatre,** 3509 S. Mason St. (© **970/225-2555**; www.adinnertheatre.com), Thursday through Saturday at 6pm and Sunday at noon. A choice of three entrees is offered, and prices are $34 to $38, which includes dinner, the show, and tax, but not beverages or dessert. Recent productions have included *Jesus Christ Superstar, The Full Monty, The Music Man, Evita,* and *Singin' in the Rain.*

The **Colorado State University Department of Music, Theater, and Dance** (© **970/491-5529**; www.colostate.edu/depts/music) presents a variety of dramas and musicals, plus concerts by music faculty ranging from jazz to classical during the school year. Many of these events are free or very inexpensive.

2 Loveland

13 miles S. of Fort Collins, 52 miles N. of Denver

Named for Colorado Central Railroad President W. A. H. Loveland in the 1870s, this former trading post now calls itself the "Sweetheart City" because every February some 300,000 Valentine's Day cards are remailed from here with a Loveland postmark. Established as a trading post in the late 1850s, this community at the foot of the Rockies grew around a flour mill in the late 1860s, before being platted on a wheat field near the railroad tracks in 1877. Today the city is a shipping and agriculture center with a population of just over 50,000. It also has a growing arts community and several foundries, and, like Fort Collins, its proximity to Rocky Mountain National Park and other outdoor recreation opportunities make this small city a good home base for those exploring the region. Elevation is just under 5,000 feet.

ESSENTIALS

GETTING THERE   By Car   Downtown Loveland is near the junction of U.S. 287 and U.S. 34. Coming from south or north, take I-25 exit 257B. From the west (Rocky Mountain National Park) or east (Greeley), follow U.S. 34 directly to Loveland. The drive takes about 1 hour from Denver.

By Plane   Many visitors to Loveland fly into **Denver International Airport** (see chapter 5). The **Fort Collins/Loveland Airport** (© **970/962-2852**; www.fcgov.com/airport), off I-25 exit 259, 7 miles northeast of downtown Loveland, has service from Allegiant Air (© **702/505-8888**).

Tips **Valentines from Loveland**

To get your Valentine's Day cards remailed with a four-line Valentine cachet from Loveland, address and stamp each one, making sure to leave room in the lower left-hand corner of the envelopes for the special Loveland stamp, and mail them in a large envelope to the Postmaster, Attn.: Valentines, Loveland, CO 80538-9998. To ensure delivery by February 14, mail for the United States must be received in Loveland by February 9, and foreign mail should be received by February 3.

Shamrock Airport Express (© 866/482-0505 or 970/482-0505; www.rideshamrock.com) provides daily shuttle service between Denver and Fort Collins (one-way rates: $26 adults, $8 children 11 and younger, free for children who sit on a parent's lap).

VISITOR INFORMATION   The **Loveland Chamber of Commerce** operates a visitor center at 5400 Stone Creek Circle, Loveland CO 80538, just northwest of the junction of I-25 and U.S. 34 (© 800/258-1278 or 970/667-5728; www.loveland.org).

GETTING AROUND   U.S. 34, Eisenhower Boulevard, is the main east-west thoroughfare and does a slight jog around Lake Loveland, just west of city center. Lincoln Avenue (one-way northbound) and Cleveland Avenue (one-way southbound) make up U.S. 287 through the city. The downtown district is along Lincoln and Cleveland south of Seventh Street, 7 blocks south of Eisenhower.

For a taxi, call **Shamrock Yellow Cab** (© 970/224-2222).

FAST FACTS   The hospital, with a 24-hour emergency room, is **McKee Medical Center,** 2000 N. Boise Ave. (© **970/669-4640**), in the northeastern part of the city. The **post office** is at 446 E. 29th St., just off Lincoln Avenue. Contact the U.S. Postal Service (© **800/275-8777;** www.usps.com) for hours and locations of other nearby post offices.

SPECIAL EVENTS   Larimer County Fair and Rodeo, early August; Loveland Invitational Sculpture Show and Sale and Sculpture in the Park, early August; Corn Roast Festival, mid- to late August.

SPORTS & OUTDOOR ACTIVITIES

Loveland has more than two dozen city parks, a mountain park, three golf courses, and hiking trails, some of which are discussed below. Information on the city-run recreation sites is available from **Loveland Parks and Recreation Department,** 500 E. Third St. (© **970/962-2727;** www.ci.loveland.co.us/parksrec/prmain.htm).

Boyd Lake State Park (© **970/669-1739;** www.parks.state.co.us) is located a mile east of downtown Loveland via Madison Avenue and C.R. 24E. One of the largest lakes in the northern Front Range, with 1,700 surface acres when full, Boyd Lake is geared to watersports, including water-skiing (on the south end of the lake only), sailing, and windsurfing. There are sandy beaches for swimming, 148 campsites ($12–$20), including some with electric hookups, plus showers, a dump station, picnic areas, a children's playground, a paved walking/biking trail that connects to the city's path system, two paved boat ramps, and excellent fishing (especially for walleyes). Visitors often see foxes, beavers, coyotes, great-horned owls, hawks, eagles, and other wildlife. The daily park entrance fee is $5 to $6. A commercially run

marina (② **970/663-2662**) is open in summer, with boat slips and moorings, a full-service gas dock, boat rentals, bait, groceries, and other supplies.

BICYCLING & JOGGING   A combination biking/jogging/walking path that will eventually circle the city, joining with a 3-mile path at Boyd Lake State Park, is gradually being constructed. For a map showing completed sections, stop at the Loveland Chamber of Commerce (see above).

GOLF   Golfers can enjoy two 18-hole municipal golf courses: **Olde Course at Loveland,** 2115 W. 29th St., which charges $28 for 18 holes; and **Marianna Butte,** 701 Clubhouse Dr., with greens fees of $36 for 18 holes. The 9-hole **Cattail Creek Golf Course,** 2116 W. 29th St. (across the street from Olde Course), charges $7 to $10 for 9 holes. For tee times and other information for all three courses, contact the city (② **970/962-2496** or 970/669-5800 for automated reservations; www.ci.loveland.co. us/golf/golfmain.htm).

HIKING   The city-run **Viestenz-Smith Mountain Park,** in Big Thompson Canyon 12 miles west of Loveland along U.S. 34, is one of your best bets for hiking, with two trails. The **Summit Adventure Trail,** a moderately difficult 4.8-mile (one-way) hike, climbs 2,750 feet to offer scenic views of the mountains to the west and plains to the east. Those not interested in that much exercise will enjoy the easy 1-mile (one-way) **Foothills Nature Trail.** The park also has picnic tables, a playground, and a fishing stream, and is open year-round.

SWIMMING   The city-run **Loveland Swim Beach,** at 29th Street and Taft Avenue, has a free swimming beach, fishing, tennis and racquetball courts, a playground, and a miniature narrow-gauge train. There's also swimming at Boyd Lake State Park (see above).

IN-TOWN ATTRACTIONS

Benson Sculpture Garden   More than 60 sculptures are permanently displayed among the trees, plants, and ponds at this city park, and three or four more are added each year. This is also the site of Sculpture in the Park, the largest juried outdoor sculpture show in the United States, which takes place each year over the second weekend in August. The show, with all submissions available for purchase, features over 1,000 works by about 200 different sculptors from across the United States and Canada. Allow 1 hour.

29th St. between Aspen and Beech sts. ② 970/663-2940. www.sculptureinthepark.org. Free admission.

Loveland Museum/Gallery   Changing exhibits of local historical subjects and the work of regional, national, and international artists fill this fine, small museum. A "Life on Main Street" exhibit area depicts Loveland at the turn of the 20th century, and there's an exhibit on the city's Great Western Sugar Factory. The museum also sponsors programs on art and history, workshops, concerts, and poetry readings. Allow an hour.

503 N. Lincoln Ave., at E. Fifth St. ② 970/962-2410. www.ci.loveland.co.us/Cultural_Services/cultural_services_museum.htm. Free admission. Tues–Wed and Fri 10am–5pm; Thurs 10am–9pm; Sat 10am–4pm; Sun noon–4pm.

A FOUNDRY TOUR

For a behind the scenes look at an art foundry, make an appointment to tour **Art Castings of Colorado,** 511 Eighth St. SE (② **970/667-1114;** www.artcastings.com), which gives foundry tours by appointment.

WHERE TO STAY & DINE

Affordable chain motels in Loveland include the **Best Western Crossroads Inn,** 5542 E. U.S. 34 (at I-25 exit 257B), Loveland, CO 80537 (℃ **888/818-6223** or 970/667-7810), with rates of $65 to $95 double; and **Super 8,** 1655 E. Eisenhower Blvd., Loveland, CO 80537 (℃ **800/800-8000** or 970/663-7000), with rates of $50 to $90 double. State and county taxes add about 7% to hotel bills.

For breakfast and lunch we suggest **The Egg & I,** 2525 N. Lincoln Ave. (℃ **970/ 635-0050**), offering numerous egg dishes (isn't that surprising!), plus sandwiches, salads, and Mexican dishes, mostly in the $3.35 to $6.50 range. For dinner, try **Henry's Pub,** 234 E. 4th St. (℃ **970/613-1896**), a swank bar and grill behind a historic storefront downtown. Anytime, veer off I-25 at exit 254 for a bite at truck stop extraordinaire **Johnson's Corner,** 2842 S.E. Frontage Rd. (℃ **970/667-2069**), a Colorado classic that hasn't closed its doors since it first opened in 1954.

Sylvan Dale Guest Ranch ⚲ *Kids*   Owners of a 3,200-acre working cattle and horse ranch on the banks of the Big Thompson River, the Jessup family invites guests to join in with daily ranch chores, horseback riding, and cattle drives, or just kick back, relax, and enjoy the many other available activities. Accommodations here are delightful, quiet, and comfortable; the homey rooms and cabins have a touch of Western charm, and are carpeted and furnished with antiques. Some cabins have fireplaces. A lodge, the Heritage, provides a gathering room with a large stone fireplace, library, gift shop, and exhibits on the history of the ranch, which dates to 1946. Horseback-riding lessons, overnight pack trips, breakfast rides, and adventure rides are included in the summer adult riding package. Other activities offered are fly-fishing, hayrides, and whitewater rafting. There's also a full slate of entertainment, mostly Western in nature. Summer guests must schedule 6-night full-board stays; the rest of the year, overnight guests are welcome for "bunk and breakfast."

2939 N. C.R. 31D, Loveland, CO 80538. ℃ **877/667-3999** or 970/667-3915. Fax 970/635-9336. www.sylvandale.com. 26 units, including 11 cabins. Mid-June to late Aug, 6-night packages only, $1,775 per adult, $1,425 nonriding adult package, $1,195 per youth (ages 6–12), $795 per child (ages 3–5); packages include all meals. Sept to mid-June, $85–$119 double, $95–$379 cabin or guesthouse, $20 extra person; includes full breakfast. MC, V. 7 miles west of Loveland via U.S. 34. **Amenities:** Restaurant; outdoor heated pool; 2 tennis courts; children's program (summer); game room. *In room:* No phone.

3 Greeley

30 miles SE of Fort Collins, 54 miles N. of Denver

Greeley is a good spot to see the "other Colorado," the flatlands to the east of the state's famed mountains, as well as to delve into the area's history at several museums. One of the few cities in the world that owes its existence to a newspaper, Greeley was founded in 1870 as a sort of prairie utopia by Nathan C. Meeker, a farm columnist for the *New York Tribune.* Meeker named the settlement—first known as Union Colony—in honor of his patron, *Tribune* publisher Horace Greeley. Through his widely read column, Meeker recruited more than 100 pioneers from all walks of life and purchased a tract on the Cache la Poudre from the Denver Pacific Railroad. Within a year, the colony's population was 1,000, and it's grown steadily ever since, to around 77,000 today.

Greeley's economy is supported in large part by agriculture, with about 75% of Weld County's 1.9 million acres devoted to farming or the raising of livestock. A combination of irrigated and dry-land farms produce grains, including oats, corn, and wheat, and root vegetables such as sugar beets, onions, potatoes, and carrots. The University of Northern Colorado (UNC), with about 12,000 students, offers undergraduate and graduate degree programs. Elevation is 4,658 feet.

ESSENTIALS

GETTING THERE   By Car   Greeley is located at the crossroads of U.S. 34 (east-west) and U.S. 85 (north-south), midway between Denver and Cheyenne, Wyoming—both of which are more directly reached by U.S. 85 than by I-25. U.S. 34 heads west 17 miles to I-25, beyond which are Loveland and Rocky Mountain National Park. To the east, U.S. 34 connects Greeley to Fort Morgan via I-76, 37 miles away.

By Airport Shuttle   Visitors who fly into Denver International Airport can travel on to Greeley with **Rocky Mountain Shuttle** (© **888/444-3580** or 970/356-3366).

VISITOR INFORMATION   Contact the **Greeley Convention & Visitors Bureau,** 902 7th Ave., Greeley, CO 80631 (© **800/449-3866** or 970/352-3567; www.greeleycvb.com).

GETTING AROUND   Greeley is laid out on a standard grid, and is an easy city to navigate—provided you don't get confused by the numbered streets (which run east-west) and numbered avenues (which run north-south). It helps to know which is which when you're standing at the corner of 10th Street and 10th Avenue. Eighth Avenue (U.S. 85) is the main north-south street through downtown. Ninth Street is U.S. 34 Business, jogging into 10th Street west of 23rd Avenue. The U.S. 34 Bypass joins U.S. 85 in a cloverleaf just south of town.

The city bus system, called simply **The Bus** (© **970/350-9287;** www.greeley gov.com) provides in-town transportation. For a taxi call **Shamrock Yellow Cab** (© **970/686-5555**).

FAST FACTS   The hospital, **North Colorado Medical Center,** is at 1801 16th St. (© **970/352-4121**), just west of downtown. The **post office** is at 925 11th Ave. Contact the U.S. Postal Service (© **800/275-8777;** www.usps.com) for hours and locations of other area post offices.

SPECIAL EVENTS   Colorado Farm Show, late January; the UNC Jazz Festival, April; Semana Latina and Cinco de Mayo, late April and early May; Greeley Stampede, late June and early July; Weld County Fair (second largest county fair in the state), early August; Potato Day celebrates Greeley's heritage, early September; Festival of Trees, early December.

SPORTS & OUTDOOR ACTIVITIES

Beginning about 25 miles northeast of Greeley and extending 60 miles east, the 200,000-acre **Pawnee National Grassland** is a popular destination for hiking, mountain biking, birding, wildlife viewing, and horseback riding. Nomadic tribes lived in this desertlike area until the late 19th century, and farmers subsequently had little success in cultivating the grasslands. Although primarily grassland, the dramatic **Pawnee Buttes,** located in the eastern section, are a pair of sandstone formations that rise some 250 feet. A dirt road leads to an overlook that offers good views of the buttes, and from the overlook a 1.5-mile trail leads to the base of the west butte. The most popular springtime activity is bird-watching, when you're apt to see white-crowned sparrows, lark buntings, meadowlarks, thrushes, orioles, and burrowing owls among the

300-plus species known to frequent the area. Pronghorn, coyotes, mule deer, fox, badger, prairie dogs, and short-horned lizards are among the prolific wildlife.

There are many routes to the grassland; one is to follow U.S. 85 north 11 miles to Ault, then east on Colo. 14 toward Briggsdale, 23 miles away. As much of the grassland is interspersed with private land, those planning to explore the area are advised to stop at the U.S. Forest Service office, 660 O St., Greeley (© **970/346-5000;** www.fs.fed.us/r2/arnf).

In Greeley, the 20-mile **Poudre River Trail** is popular with in-line skaters, bikers, walkers, and runners. For more information, call © **970/336-4044** or visit **www.poudretrail.org**.

SPECTATOR SPORTS

RODEO   Greeley's Rocky Mountain Stampede 👣👣 comes to town for 2 weeks, starting in late June, and boasts the world's largest Fourth of July Rodeo. Hundreds of professional cowboys and cowgirls compete for over $300,000 in prize money at Greeley's Island Grove Regional Park, with bareback bronc riding, calf roping, saddle bronc riding, team roping, steer racing, barrel racing, and bull riding. Festivities include country and classic rock concerts, art shows, a carnival, a children's rodeo, fun-runs, a demolition derby, barbecues, and a parade and fireworks display. For information, call © **800/982-2855** or 970/356-2855 or see **www.rockymountainstampede.com**.

ATTRACTIONS

Cold War history buffs might also want to schedule a tour of the decommissioned Atlas E silo at **Missile Site Park,** 10611 Spur 257 (© **970/381-7451**), which also has basic campsites and a playground.

Centennial Village Museum 👣   A fun step back to times long gone, this collection of more than 30 structures—more are added each year—on 5½ acres depicts life on the High Plains of Colorado from the 1860s to the 1940s. Visit the blacksmith shop, print shop, and fire station of the commercial district, and stroll through Hanna Square, surrounded by elegant Victorian homes, a school, depot, and church. Watch for the exhibit of Rattlesnake Kate's dress, a flapper dress made of rattlesnake skins. Frequent living-history demonstrations and special events bring the past alive. In addition, the gardens here are beautiful, with the most colorful displays from July through September. Allow 2 to 3 hours.

1475 A St. at N. 14th Ave., adjacent to Island Grove Regional Park. © **970/350-9220.** www.greeleymuseums.com. Admission $5 adults, $4 seniors 60 and older, $3 children 6–11, free for children under 6. Tues–Sat 10am–4pm. Closed mid-Oct to mid-Apr.

Greeley History Museum 👣   Opened in 2005, this facility tells the intriguing story of Greeley through its permanent "Utopia: Adaptation of the Great American Desert" exhibit, and it also features several rotating exhibits each year. Housed in the historic former offices of the *Greeley Tribune,* the museum features excellent interpretation of its impressive collection, as well as an interactive children's area. Allow 1 hour.

714 Eighth St. © **970/350-9220.** www.greeleymuseums.com. Free admission. Mon–Fri 8:30am–4:30pm; Sat 10am–4pm; Sun noon–4pm.

Meeker Home Museum   A good place to step back into the 19th century, this impressive two-story adobe home was built in 1870 for Greeley founder Nathan Cook Meeker. Now on the National Register of Historic Places, it is furnished with original family belongings and period antiques, including a 10-foot-tall diamond dust mirror.

Interpretive panels discuss the history of Greeley and vicinity, with an emphasis on the family's struggle for survival after Nathan's death in the 1879 Meeker Massacre. Allow 30 minutes to 1 hour.

1324 Ninth Ave. (C) **970/350-9220.** www.greeleymuseums.com. Free admission. Wed–Fri 1–4pm. Closed Oct–Apr.

WHERE TO STAY

A building boom of chain motels in the past few years has greatly increased lodging choices. Highest rates are during the summer. Options include the **Best Western Regency Hotel,** 701 Eighth St., Greeley, CO 80631 (C) **800/937-8376** or 970/ 353-8444), with double rates of $65 to $105; **Country Inn & Suites,** 2501 W. 29th St., Greeley, CO 80631 (C) **800/456-4000** or 970/330-3404), with rates of $88 to $126 double; and **Days Inn,** 5630 W. 10th St., Greeley, CO 80634 (C) **970/392-1530**), which charges $79 to $99 double. Lodging taxes add about 9% to hotel bills.

Greeley Guest House ⭐   A modern inn—it was built from the ground up and opened in 1996—the Greeley Guest House balances country charm with modern convenience. Centered on a shady courtyard, the brick-and-stucco, ranch-style structure houses two levels of spacious, distinctively furnished rooms, all with gas fireplaces, microwaves, and high-speed Internet access. VCRs and videos are available. The beds are king- and queen-size, and the wooden furnishings and country-style decor are subtly pleasant.

5401 W. Ninth St., Greeley, CO 80634. (C) **800/314-3684** or 970/353-9373. Fax 970/353-9297. www.greeleyguest house.com. 19 units. $114 double; $134–$164 double for units with whirlpool tubs. Rates include full breakfast. AE, MC, V. Located 1 block north of 10th St. (U.S. 34) in west Greeley. **Amenities:** Access to nearby fitness center; business center; laundry service; dry cleaning. *In room:* A/C, cable TV, kitchen, fridge, hair dryer, iron, high-speed Internet access, microwave.

Sod Buster Inn Bed & Breakfast ⭐⭐   This is a great choice for those who love the ambience of a historic lodging but aren't ready to give up modern conveniences. This attractive three-story inn, which immediately stands out for its octagonal shape and wraparound veranda, is located in a historic district and is surrounded by 100-year-old structures. But the Sod Buster was actually built in 1997, designed to blend in with its older neighbors. Innkeepers Mary and Bill Heller offer what may be the best of both worlds—an exceedingly comfortable and attractive modern inn with the look and feel of an historic property, but without the steep staircases, noisy pipes, creaks, groans, and other "charms" you often find in old buildings.

Each guest room is individually decorated with a blend of antiques and country-style furnishings, and all include a king or queen bed, desk, dataport, good reading lamps, CD players, and comfy seating. Several have jetted tubs, while others offer old-fashioned claw-foot ones, and all have separate showers. The gourmet breakfasts might include an egg entree, crepes, fruit, fresh-baked breads, juices, and hot beverages. Smoking is permitted on the veranda only.

1221 Ninth Ave., Greeley, CO 80631. (C) **866/501-8667** or 970/392-1221. Fax 970/392-1222. www.thesodbusterinn. com. 10 units. $99–$129 double. Rates include full breakfast. AE, DC, MC, V. Well-behaved children accepted with advance notification. *In room:* A/C, cable TV, hair dryer, high-speed wireless Internet access.

WHERE TO DINE

The Armadillo *(Finds)* *(Kids)* MEXICAN   There's a fiesta atmosphere at this downtown Mexican restaurant, which is part of a small regional chain started in 1970 by the Lucio family. The Armadillo serves a variety of Mexican food standards, and many of the recipes come from the Lucio family. Especially recommended are the Mexican Turnover (a deep-fried meat pie) and the Burrito Supreme. Fajitas are also popular.

819 Ninth St. ℂ **970/304-9024.** Main courses $5–$12. AE, DISC, MC, V. Mon–Thurs 11am–9:30pm; Fri–Sat 11am–10pm; Sun 10am–9:30pm.

Fat Albert's Food & Drink AMERICAN   A casual and homey family restaurant, this establishment has been in business since 1982. Diners can sit at the bar, tables, or booths bedecked in brick and stained glass, and choose from a lunch menu that includes a good variety of salads, burgers, and sandwiches—ranging from a veggie melt to the perennially popular Monte Cristo. At 5pm, the menu expands to include trout, steak, and several chicken dishes. The award-winning homemade pies and cakes are extra special, and include traditional favorites such as apple crumb pie and carrot cake, as well as more exotic recipes such as chocolate zucchini cake and peanut butter pie.

1717 23rd Ave., in Cottonwood Square shopping center. ℂ **970/356-1999.** Lunch $6–$9; dinner $9–$18. AE, DC, DISC, MC, V. Sun–Thurs 10:30am–9:30pm; Fri–Sat 10:30am–10:30pm.

Potato Brumbaugh's Restaurant & Saloon ℱ AMERICAN   Named for a character in James Michener's *Centennial,* this casually elegant restaurant follows the novel's theme in its Western decor and is a solid if not spectacular choice. Our choice here is the excellent slow-roasted prime rib, and you won't go wrong with the daily fresh fish selection. The menu also features filet mignon, chicken, Colorado lamb and roast duck, plus pastas, such as pasta primavera, which is available with chicken or shrimp and in a marinara or Alfredo sauce.

2400 17th St., in Cottonwood Square shopping center. ℂ **970/356-6340.** Reservations recommended. Lunch $8–$10; dinner $12–$45 (most $16–$22). AE, DC, DISC, MC, V. Mon–Fri 11:30am–2pm and 4:30–10pm; Sat 4:30–10pm.

4 Fort Morgan

51 miles E. of Greeley, 81 miles NE of Denver

A pleasant, laid-back city of just over 11,000 people, Fort Morgan may be best known as the childhood home of famed big-band leader Glenn Miller, who graduated from Fort Morgan High School in 1921 and formed his first band, the Mick-Miller Five, in the city. Established as a military outpost in 1864, the original Fort Morgan housed about 200 troops who protected stagecoaches and pioneers traveling the Overland Trail from marauding Cheyenne and Arapaho warriors. The threat had passed by 1870, and the fort was dismantled, but the name stuck when the city was founded in 1884. Nothing of the fort remains, but a monument on Riverview Avenue marks the fort's site.

The town grew in the 20th century with the establishment of the Great Western Sugar Company for sugar-beet processing, and with a pair of oil discoveries in the 1920s and 1950s. Cattle and sheep ranching remain important today, as well as dairy farming. In addition to sugar beets, the area grows alfalfa, onions, beans, corn, potatoes, sorghum, and wheat. Visitors enjoy the community's historic district and the fine Fort Morgan Museum, and use the town as home base while boating and fishing at Jackson Lake State Park.

About 10 miles east of Fort Morgan is the community of **Brush,** with a population of about 5,000. Also a farming and ranching center, Brush offers food and lodging, easy access to a popular pheasant-hunting area, and a variety of special events. Elevation in the Fort Morgan–Brush area is about 4,300 feet.

ESSENTIALS

GETTING THERE   By Car Fort Morgan is located on U.S. 34 at I-76, the main east-west route between Denver and Omaha, Nebraska. U.S. 34 proceeds west to Greeley and Estes Park, and east to Wray and southern Nebraska. Colo. 52 is the principal north-south route through Fort Morgan.

By Plane   Denver International Airport is less than 90 minutes away (p. 70).

By Train   Amtrak (© **800/872-7245;** www.amtrak.com) trains make daily stops on the Denver-to-Chicago route.

VISITOR INFORMATION Contact the **Fort Morgan Area Chamber of Commerce,** 300 Main St. (P.O. Box 971), Fort Morgan, CO 80701 (© **800/354-8660** or 970/867-6702; www.fortmorganchamber.org). For information on events and activities in the nearby community of Brush, contact the **Brush Chamber of Commerce,** 1215 Edison St., Brush, CO 80723 (© **800/354-8659** or 970/842-2666; www.brushchamber.org).

GETTING AROUND Platte Avenue (U.S. 34) is Fort Morgan's principal east-west thoroughfare. The north-south artery, Main Street, divides it and other streets into east and west designations. I-76 exits onto Main Street north of downtown.

FAST FACTS The **Colorado Plains Medical Center,** with a 24-hour emergency room, is located at 1000 Lincoln St. (© **970/867-3391**). The **Fort Morgan Post Office** is at 300 State St. Contact the U.S. Postal Service (© **800/275-8777;** www.usps.com) for hours and the addresses of other post offices.

SPECIAL EVENTS Glenn Miller Dancin' on the Plains in Fort Morgan, fourth weekend in June; Brush Rodeo, early July; Festival in the Park in Fort Morgan, mid-July.

WHAT TO SEE & DO

In addition to the attractions discussed below, visitors interested in U.S. military history will want to call ahead to arrange a tour of the **U.S. Military Historical Museum,** 404 State St. (© **970/867-5520** or 970/867-8875), where there are about 75 life-size mannequins dressed in authentic military uniforms from the Revolutionary War to the present, plus numerous artifacts from all the wars in which the United States has fought. The museum has no scheduled hours, so appointments are necessary; admission is by donation.

Fort Morgan Museum ★★ *(Finds* Among our favorite small-town museums in Colorado, the Fort Morgan Museum has an impressive collection of northeastern Colorado American Indian artifacts, beginning with a 13,000-year-old tool. Other permanent exhibits cover the history of farming, ranching, the military, and the railroad in Morgan County. Our favorites: a display on the life of native son Glenn Miller and a fully restored 1920s soda fountain. The museum also hosts traveling exhibits and stages temporary shows from its collection, and is a good source for genealogical information in the area. There's a gift shop, and you'll find picnic areas and a playground in the surrounding City Park. Allow about 2 hours.

City Park, 414 Main St. © 970/524-4010. www.ftmorganmus.org. Free admission. Mon, Wed, and Fri 10am–5pm; Tues–Thurs 10am–5pm and 6–8pm; Sat 11am–5pm.

Rainbow Bridge Also called the James Marsh Arch Bridge, this 11-arch concrete bridge was built over the South Platte River in 1923, at a construction cost of

$69,290. Listed on the National Register of Historic Landmarks and the National Register of Engineering Landmarks, the 1,110-foot bridge is the only rainbow-arch design in Colorado. For information, contact the Fort Morgan Museum (see above), and allow 15 to 30 minutes.

At the northwest corner of Riverside Park (I-76 and Colo. 52).

Sherman Street National Historic District Fort Morgan Museum (see above) publishes a walking-tour brochure both for Sherman Street and for the 9-block downtown district, the latter noting 44 buildings that made up the early town. These are available at the chamber of commerce (see "Visitor Information," above) and the museum.

Four Victorian mansions in the Sherman Street District are of special interest. Located around the intersection of Sherman Street and East Platte Avenue, they include the Warner House, an 1886 Queen Anne home; the Curry House, an 1898 Queen Anne with decorative spindle work porches, a barn, carriage house, and water tower; the Graham House, a 1914 American foursquare home; and the Bloedorn House, a 1926 brick Georgian revival–style building. Each is associated with a prominent city pioneer. They are private homes, not open to the public, but it's worth the walk to see the architecture from the sidewalk. For additional information contact the Fort Morgan Museum (see above). Allow at least 2 hours.

400 block of Sherman St.

SPORTS & OUTDOOR ACTIVITIES

The main recreation spot in this area is **Jackson Lake State Park,** located about 25 miles northwest of Fort Morgan (© **970/645-2551;** www.parks.state.co.us). The park offers swimming, boating, fishing, and picnicking in summer; and ice fishing, ice skating, and cross-country skiing in winter ($5 day-use fee).

Water-skiing, sailboarding, and boating are the most popular activities on the park's 2,700-acre reservoir, which has sandy beaches and boat ramps. The **Shoreline Marina** (© **970/645-2628**) has fuel, fishing and boating supplies, propane tank exchange, an ATM, a snack bar, and boat rentals May through September (depending on lake water levels).

Anglers try for walleye, bass, and catfish, except when fishing is prohibited during the migratory waterfowl season. There's also a .5-mile nature trail, plus 260 campsites (some with electric hookups), showers, and a dump station ($12–$18). To get to Jackson Lake, follow Colo. 144 northwest for 22 miles; the park is about 2½ miles north of the community of Goodrich via paved C.R. 3.

One of the nicest city parks in the region is **Riverside Park** ⊕ (© **970/867-3808;** www.cityoffortmorgan.com), located off Main Street between I-76 and the South Platte River. Admission is free, and it has a large children's playground, more than 4 miles of nature trails along the river, tennis and basketball courts, horseshoe pits, an in-line hockey rink, a picnic area, a duck pond where kids can fish, and a swimming pool open in summer. The park offers free tent camping and free overnight RV camping with electrical hookups.

SPECTATOR SPORTS

RODEO The **Brush Rodeo,** billed as the world's largest open rodeo (both amateurs and professionals compete), is held in Brush on the first 4 days of July, with all the usual rodeo events (including the popular wild-cow milking contest), plus a parade, kids' games, a dance, and fireworks. Contact the Brush Chamber of Commerce (see above) or check the Web at **www.brushcolo.com/rodeo.htm**.

STOCK-CAR RACING   Fans head to Fort Morgan's I-76 Speedway (© **970/867-2101;** www.i-76speedway.com), where they can see late-model, street stocks, ministocks, midgets, minisprints, microsprints, dwarf cars, and IMCA modifieds race on a quarter-mile, high-banked dirt oval track from late March through October.

WHERE TO STAY & DINE

Lodging possibilities in Fort Morgan include the well-maintained **Best Western Park Terrace Inn,** 725 Main St. (© **888/593-5793** or 970/867-8256), which charges $60 to $75 double and has a good restaurant on-site (see below); and the **Super 8,** 1220 N. Main St. (© **800/800-8000** or 970/867-9443), charging $52 to $64 double. State and county taxes add just under 8% to hotel bills.

Restaurants in Fort Morgan include **Memories,** at the Best Western Park Terrace Inn (© **970/867-8205;** www.memoriesrestaurant.com), which offers a good selection of well-prepared American standards and Mexican plates daily from 6am to 9pm, with prices for lunch $5 to $10, and for dinner $8 to $16.

Another good dining choice in Fort Morgan is **Country Steak Out,** 19592 E. Eighth Ave. (© **970/867-7887**), which serves steak and seafood (and has a big salad bar), with prices from $5 to $12 at lunch and $7 to $20 at dinner. It's open Tuesday through Saturday from 11am to 9pm and Sunday from 11am to 2pm.

5 Burlington

163 miles E. of Denver, 385 miles W. of Topeka, Kansas

As the first major Colorado community to greet motorists traveling I-70 from the east, Burlington is a good place to overnight at the beginning or end of a Colorado vacation. It's the largest town in east-central Colorado, with a population of about 3,500, and sits at an elevation of 4,165 feet. Those passing through might want to see how the community has preserved its turn-of-the-20th-century heritage with an impressive Old Town and famous carousel. Dry-land farmers established Burlington and other "outback" communities along the Kansas City–Denver rail line in the 1880s, and while wheat is very much the dominant crop today, you'll also find corn, dry beans, and sunflowers.

ESSENTIALS

GETTING THERE   By Car   Burlington is located on east-west I-70, 13 miles from the Kansas border. U.S. 385, which runs the length of Colorado's eastern frontier, makes a north-to-south pass through the town.

VISITOR INFORMATION   The **Colorado Welcome Center** is along I-70 beside Burlington Old Town (© **800/288-1334** or 719/346-5554), and is open daily from 9am to 5pm Monday through Saturday, noon to 5pm Sundays. For information specifically on Burlington, contact the **Burlington Chamber of Commerce,** 420 S. 14th St., Burlington, CO 80807 (© **719/346-8070;** www.burlingtoncolo.com).

GETTING AROUND   The town lies on the north side of I-70. Rose Avenue (U.S. 24) runs east-west through the center of Burlington. Main north-south streets are Eighth Street (U.S. 385 north) on the east side of town, 14th Street (which locals call Main St.), and Lincoln Street (U.S. 385 south) on the west side of town.

FAST FACTS The **Kit Carson County Memorial Hospital** is at 286 16th St. (© 719/346-5311). The **post office** is at 259 14th St. Contact the U.S. Postal Service (© 800/275-8777; www.usps.com) for hours and other information. During inclement weather (but not at other times), you can get a **road condition report** by calling © 719/346-8778.

SPECIAL EVENTS Kit Carson County Fair, August; Old Town Ghost Town, last Saturday in October; Country Christmas Jubilee at Old Town, first Sunday in December; and Storybook Christmas and Parade of Lights, December.

WHAT TO SEE & DO

Kit Carson County Carousel 🎠🎠🎠 *Kids* This is the town's pride and joy, the only National Historic Landmark in eastern Colorado, and a must-see for everyone who stops in Burlington. Carved in 1905 by the Philadelphia Toboggan Company and one of the few wooden carousels left in America that still wears its original coat of paint, it's fully restored and operational. The 46 stationary animals—mostly horses, but also giraffes, zebras, camels, a hippocampus (sea horse), lion, tiger, and others—march counterclockwise around three tiers of oil paintings, representing the lifestyles and interests of the American Victorian middle class. A Wurlitzer Monster Military Band Organ, one of only two of its size and vintage in operation today, provides the music. Allow 1 hour.

County Fairgrounds, 15th St. at Colorado Ave. © 719/346-8070. Admission 25¢ per ride. Memorial Day to Labor Day daily 1–8pm. Private tours given at other times with 2 weeks' advance notice.

Old Town 🎠 *Kids* For a look at the real Old West, take a trip to Old Town. Close to 20 turn-of-the-20th-century-style Old West buildings make up this living-history museum, where you're likely to see a gunfight, or, in the summer months, a cancan show in the Longhorn Saloon. Nine of the buildings are original historic structures, moved to Old Town, and the rest are reproductions, all furnished with genuine Old West artifacts to show what it was like here 100 years ago.

Visit the blacksmith shop, bank, law office, newspaper office and operating print shop, general store, schoolhouse, and barn. The railroad depot, built in 1889 in Bethune, Colorado, is the oldest structure in Old Town. There's the saloon where you're likely to find the piano player tinkling the ivories, or perhaps you'd prefer to stop at the church, built in 1921 and still used for weddings.

The dollhouse is home to a number of unique dolls, and in the wood shop you'll see tools more than 100 years old. The original Burlington town jail cells are also here; and the two-story, six-bedroom Manor house, built in the early 1900s, is magnificent, furnished with splendid antiques of the period. Heritage Hall contains a large collection of 45 wagons, guns, and other exhibits. There's also a 2,000-square-foot gift shop, with handcrafted items and other souvenirs. On summer weekends the horse-drawn "Old Town Express" gives rides from Old Town to the Kit Carson County Carousel (see above). Allow 1 to 3 hours.

420 S. 14th St. © 800/288-1334 or 719/346-7382. Admission $6 adults 19–59, $5 seniors 60 and older, $4 youths 12–18, $2 children 3–11. Mon–Sat 9am–5pm, Sun noon–5pm. Last admission at 4pm.

SPORTS & OUTDOOR ACTIVITIES

As soon as the winter snows are gone, the folks in Burlington and other eastern Colorado communities head to the beach, and that means **Bonny Lake State Park,** 23 miles north of Burlington on U.S. 385, then east on county roads 2 or 3 for about

1½ miles (ⓒ **970/354-7306;** www.parks.state.co.us). Built as a flood control project in 1951, the reservoir contains 1,900 surface acres of relatively warm water, perfect for swimming, water-skiing, windsurfing, and fishing. The 5,000-acre park provides opportunities to see wildlife, with some 250 species of birds, mule and whitetail deer, coyotes, badgers, muskrats, bobcats, beavers, and rabbits. The daily entrance fee is $5 per vehicle.

The lake has two swimming areas (no lifeguards) and four campgrounds with a total of 190 campsites ($12–$22). Some sites have electric hookups, and several are handicapped accessible. Facilities include restrooms, pay showers, picnic areas, a self-guided nature trail (not handicapped accessible), and a fish-cleaning station. Fishing is good for walleye, northern pike, and a variety of bass.

Boat launching ramps are available, and the **Bonny Dam Marina** (ⓒ **970/354-7339**) sells fuel, groceries, and boating and fishing supplies. The marina also rents boats, water level permitting. Call for current rates.

If you're traveling this way in winter, stop by for an afternoon of cross-country ski-ing, ice skating, or ice fishing, but don't forget your long underwear—winter winds are bone chilling out here on the plains. During winter, electric and water are avail-able in the campgrounds, and there are vault toilets, but the showers and flush toilets are shut down.

If you're passing through town and looking for some quick R & R, a good place to take the kids is the **Burlington Swimming Pool,** located at the south end of Mike Lounge Drive. Open afternoons and evenings during the summer, the city-run pool has a new 175-foot flume slide. There's also a wading pool with a sloping entrance and a special slide just for younger kids. Admission costs $2.50 for adults and $1.50 for children 2 to 17. Another good family stop in Burlington is **Outback Territory Park Playground,** which covers a full block between 15th and 16th streets and Railroad and Martin avenues. It's got a marvelous playground (designed by Burlington Elemen-tary School children) and delightful picnic areas with lots of shade. Admission is free. For additional information, contact the Colorado Welcome Center in Burlington or the Burlington Chamber of Commerce (see "Visitor Information," above).

WHERE TO STAY

Because Burlington is simply an overnight stop for many travelers along the interstate highway, you won't have any trouble finding a room here, with all the motels easily accessible from I-70 exits 437 and 438. In addition to the motels discussed below, there's a **Comfort Inn,** 282 S. Lincoln St. (ⓒ **800/228-5150** or 719/346-7676), with double rates of $60 to $120; and a **America's Best Value Inn,** 2100 Fay St. (ⓒ **888/315-2378** or 719/346-5627), charging double rates of $50 to $70. Tax adds about 7% to lodging bills.

Chaparral Motor Inn ⭐ ⓥ𝘢𝘭𝘶𝘦   This conveniently located modern motel is an excel-lent choice for those seeking an exceptionally clean and well-maintained place to spend the night at a reasonable price. The rooms are set back a bit from the road so they're fairly quiet. Rooms and bathrooms are of average size, simply but attractively decorated in a contemporary Southwestern style. All rooms have a small working desk, and a table with two chairs; refrigerators and hair dryers are available on request. An adjacent restaurant serves three meals daily.

405 S. Lincoln St., Burlington, CO 80807. ℂ 800/456-6206 or 719/346-5361. Fax 719/346-8502. 39 units. $45–$60 double; rates include continental breakfast. AE, DISC, MC, V. Small pets accepted ($7 per dog per night; $10 per cat per night). **Amenities:** Outdoor heated pool (seasonal); exercise room. *In room:* A/C, TV, coffeemaker.

Claremont Inn 🌟🌟   One of the few bed-and-breakfasts on Colorado's eastern plains, the striking Claremont Inn is a good choice for those who want more than a clean place to sleep for the night. The three-story inn blends an intimate atmosphere with modern conveniences, and features uniquely decorated rooms such as the flower- and birdhouse-bedecked Waverly Room and the romantic Secret Garden Room, with its own whirlpool for two. The public rooms, which include the domed-ceiling Hearth Room and a theater, are similarly impressive. Innkeeper Dave Dischner, a sea- soned professional chef, prepares the meals, which might include bananas Foster or French toast for breakfast. The restaurant here also serves eclectic dinners, and the inn regularly hosts cooking weekends, often with French and Italian themes. Smoking is not permitted.

800 Claremont Dr., Stratton, CO 80836. ℂ 888/291-8910 or 719/348-5125. Fax 719/348-5948. www.claremont inn.com. 10 units. $169–$249 double; rates include full breakfast. AE, DC, DISC, MC, V. Located 18 miles west of Burlington, off I-70, exit 419. *In room:* A/C. TV/VCR, fridge, coffeemaker, hair dryer, iron.

WHERE TO DINE

Interstate House AMERICAN   A longtime favorite of locals, this family restaurant is popular because of its good home-cooked food, quick service, and low prices. House specialties include the aged, charbroiled steaks that are cut in-house, plus the waffles, which, like many of the other breakfast entrees, are served all day. Tasty burgers, sand- wiches, seafood selections, pork chops, tacos, burritos, chili, and a steak-and-eggs spe- cial round out the menu.

415 S. Lincoln St., at I-70 exit 437. ℂ 719/346-9406. Breakfast $2–$7; lunch and dinner $4–$19. DISC, MC, V. Daily 6am–9pm.

The Route Steakhouse AMERICAN   This family restaurant boasts an especially good salad bar, and a large selection of well-prepared American staples. The large din- ing room is what we might call contemporary Western, with solid wood tables and booth seating. There are various half-pound burgers and sandwiches for lunch—try the Trail Boss sandwich, piled high with brisket, turkey, and ham, and topped with melted Swiss and cheddar. From the dinner menu, we like the 14-ounce rib-eye and the house specialty, chicken-fried steak. Salads here are also very good, especially the Cobb.

218 S. Lincoln St. ℂ 719/346-8790. Lunch items $5–$10; dinner entrees $6–$20. AE, DISC, MC, V. Mon–Thurs 5–9pm; Fri 4–10pm; Sat 11am–10pm; Sun 11am–9pm.

10

The Northern Rockies

Literally and figuratively, this is the mother lode. It's where scrappy silver and gold miners struck it rich time and time again in the late 19th century, yet it's also where Colorado's rugged beauty is shown off to fullest effect.

The northern Rockies begin just outside of Denver and extend on either side of the meandering Continental Divide down sawtooth ridgelines, through precipitous river canyons, and across broad alpine plains. Here, snowfall is measured in feet, not inches; it's where you'll find Colorado's hottest ski resorts—Aspen, Vail, and Steamboat—as well as a few smaller areas that are making headlines, such as Winter Park. And then there's Summit County, with possibly more major ski areas within a half-hour's drive than anywhere else in the country. If you're easily bored, rent a condo or take a

room in Breckenridge and spend your days skiing a different mountain every day. With Copper, Keystone, Arapahoe Basin, and even tiny Loveland all within a few miles' drive, you've got plenty of choices.

When spring's sun finally melts away the walls of white, a whole new world opens up amid the brilliantly colored alpine wildflowers. You can head to any of the area's ski resorts to shop their stores and hike or cycle their trails. Perhaps best of all, though, is a trip to the West's premier mountain vacation spot, and our very favorite mountain destination in Colorado—Rocky Mountain National Park. Here you can enjoy some of the most spectacular scenery in America as well as a broad range of outdoor activities, from hiking to wildlife viewing to cross-country skiing.

1 Estes Park & Grand Lake: Gateways to Rocky Mountain National Park

71 miles NW of Denver, 42 miles SW of Fort Collins, 34 miles NW of Boulder

Estes Park is the eastern gateway to Rocky Mountain National Park, and Grand Lake is the closest town to the park's western entrance. Of the two, Estes Park is more developed. It has more lodging and dining choices, as well as a few noteworthy sights that are worth a visit. If you're driving to Rocky Mountain National Park via Boulder or Denver, you'll want to make Estes Park your base camp.

Grand Lake is a more rustic spot, with plenty of places to camp, a number of motels, and a few guest ranches. If you're coming from Steamboat Springs or Glenwood Springs, Grand Lake is a more convenient base. At any time of year, you can get there via U.S. 34. In summer, you can also get to Grand Lake by taking the Trail Ridge Road through Rocky Mountain National Park from Estes Park. Both routes are scenic, although the national park route (closed in winter) is definitely prettier.

Estes Park

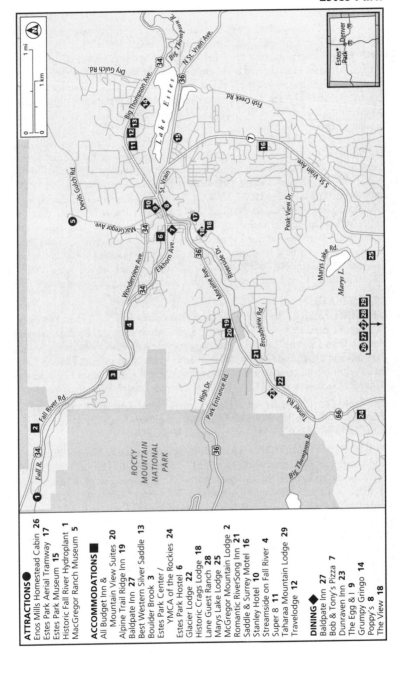

ATTRACTIONS ●
Enos Mills Homestead Cabin **26**
Estes Park Aerial Tramway **17**
Estes Park Museum **15**
Historic Fall River Hydroplant **1**
MacGregor Ranch Museum **5**

ACCOMMODATIONS ■
All Budget Inn &
   Mountain View Suites **20**
Alpine Trail Ridge Inn **19**
Baldpate Inn **27**
Best Western Silver Saddle **13**
Boulder Brook **3**
Estes Park Center /
   YMCA of the Rockies **24**
Estes Park Hostel **6**
Glacier Lodge **22**
Historic Crags Lodge **18**
Lane Guest Ranch **28**
Marys Lake Lodge **25**
McGregor Mountain Lodge **2**
Romantic RiverSong Inn **21**
Saddle & Surrey Motel **16**
Stanley Hotel **10**
Streamside on Fall River **4**
Super 8 **11**
Taharaa Mountain Lodge **29**
Travelodge **12**

DINING ◆
Baldpate Inn **27**
Bob & Tony's Pizza **7**
Dunraven Inn **23**
The Egg & I **9**
Grumpy Gringo **14**
Poppy's **8**
The View **18**

ESTES PARK

Unlike most Colorado mountain communities where mining was the economic bedrock before tourism emerged, Estes Park (elevation 7,522 ft.) has always been a resort town. Long known by Utes and Arapahos, it was "discovered" in 1859 by rancher Joel Estes. He soon sold his homestead to Griff Evans, who built it into a dude ranch. One of Evans' guests, the Welsh Earl of Dunraven, was so taken by the region that he purchased most of the valley and operated it as his private game reserve, until thwarted by such settlers as W. E. James, who built Elkhorn Lodge as a "fish ranch" to supply Denver restaurants.

The growth of Estes Park, however, is inextricably linked with two individuals: Freelan Stanley and Enos Mills. Stanley, who, together with his brother Francis, invented the kerosene-powered Stanley Steamer automobile in 1899, settled in Estes Park in 1907, launched a Stanley Steamer shuttle service from Denver, and in 1909 built the landmark Stanley Hotel. Mills was one of the prime advocates for the establishment of Rocky Mountain National Park. Although less well-known than John Muir, Mills is an equally important figure in the history of the U.S. conservation movement. His efforts increased sentiment nationwide for preserving our wild lands, and resulted in President Woodrow Wilson signing a bill to set aside 400 square miles for Rocky Mountain National Park in 1915. Today the park attracts some 3 million visitors annually. Estes Park, meanwhile, has a year-round population of about 6,000.

ESSENTIALS

GETTING THERE   By Car   The most direct route is U.S. 36 from Denver and Boulder. At Estes Park, U.S. 36 joins U.S. 34, which runs up the Big Thompson Canyon from I-25 and Loveland, and continues through Rocky Mountain National Park to Grand Lake and Granby. An alternative scenic route to Estes Park is Colo. 7, the "Peak-to-Peak Scenic Byway" that traverses Central City (Colo. 119), Nederland (Colo. 72), and Allenspark (Colo. 7) under different designations.

By Plane   The closest airport is Denver International Airport, 80 miles away. The **Estes Park Shuttle** (© 970/586-5151; www.estesparkshuttle.com) connects DIA with Estes Park. Rates are $45 one-way and $85 round-trip.

VISITOR INFORMATION   The **Estes Park Convention & Visitors Bureau,** 500 Big Thompson Ave., Estes Park, CO 80517 (© 800/44-ESTES or 970/577-9900; www.estesparkcvb.com), has a visitor center on U.S. 34, just east of its junction with U.S. 36. In summer, it's open Monday through Saturday from 8am to 9pm and Sunday from 9am to 5pm; winter hours are Monday through Saturday from 9am to 5pm and Sunday from 10am to 4pm.

GETTING AROUND   Shuttle buses began operating in 2006 throughout the business district of Estes Park and from Estes Park into Rocky Mountain National Park. The buses run daily from July through Labor Day; schedules are available at the Estes Park Visitor Center (see "Visitor Information," above).

Local taxi service is provided by **Stanley Brothers Taxi Company** (© 970/577-7433).

FAST FACTS   The hospital, **Estes Park Medical Center,** with a 24-hour emergency room, is at 555 Prospect Ave. (© 970/586-2317). The **post office** is at 215 W. Riverside Dr. Call the U.S. Postal Service (© 800/275-8777; www.usps.com) for hours and locations of other post offices. For statewide **road conditions,** call © 303/639-1111 or check **www.cotrip.org.** For a **current weather report,** call © 970/586-5555.

SPECIAL EVENTS   Jazz Fest and Art Walk, mid-May; the Wool Market, mid-June; the Scandinavian Mid-Summer Festival, on a weekend near summer solstice; the Rooftop Rodeo, mid-July; Longs Peak Scottish Irish Festival, the weekend after Labor Day; and Autumn Gold—A Festival of Brats and Bands, late September.

WHAT TO SEE & DO

In addition to the attractions discussed here, be sure to check out the art galleries and other visual arts venues discussed under "Shopping," below.

Enos Mills Homestead Cabin   This 1885 cabin and homestead belonged to the late-19th- and early-20th-century conservationist, Enos A. Mills, a major force behind the establishment of Rocky Mountain National Park. A short walk down a nature trail brings you to the cabin, with displays of his life and work. Also on the premises are a bookshop and gallery. Allow 30 minutes to 1 hour.

6760 Colo. 7 (opposite Longs Peak Inn). ⓒ 970/586-4706. Admission $5 adults, $3.50 children 6–12. Memorial Day to Labor Day usually Thurs–Fri 11am–3pm, but call to confirm. By appointment in other seasons.

Estes Park Aerial Tramway ⓐ   This tram, which climbs 1,100 vertical feet in less than 5 minutes, offers a great ride up the side of Prospect Mountain and provides spectacular panoramic views of Longs Peak, the Continental Divide, and Estes Park village itself. Its lower terminal is a block south of the post office. You'll find a gift shop, snack bar, and observation deck at the upper terminal, and numerous trails converge atop the mountain. Allow at least 1 hour.

420 E. Riverside Dr. ⓒ 970/586-3675. www.estestram.com. Admission $9 adults, $8 seniors 60 and older, $4 children 6–11, free for children under 6. Late May to mid-Sept daily 9am–6:30pm.

Estes Park Museum ⓐⓐ   The lives of early homesteaders in Estes Park are depicted in this excellent museum, which includes a completely furnished turn-of-the-20th-century log cabin, an original Stanley Steamer car, and a changing exhibit gallery. The museum also features a permanent "Tracks in Time" exhibit that helps visitors see the impact that ordinary people, from the region's American Indians and women pioneers to today's area residents and travelers, have had on Estes Park. You can also see Rocky Mountain National Park's original headquarters building, which has been moved here. In addition, the museum sponsors a variety of programs and distributes a historical walking-tour brochure on downtown Estes Park. Allow 1½ hours.

Under the museum's administration, the **Historic Fall River Hydroplant** at 1754 Fish Hatchery Rd. (ⓒ **970/577-7683**), chronicles the 1909 construction and 1982 destruction of the town's one-time power supply, washed away when a dam inside Rocky Mountain National Park built by F. O. Stanley gave way. It's open Memorial Day through Labor Day, Tuesday through Sunday from 1 to 4pm.

200 Fourth St. at U.S. 36. ⓒ 970/586-6256. www.estesnet.com/museum. Free admission, donations accepted. May–Oct Mon–Sat 10am–5pm, Sun 1–5pm; Nov–Apr Fri–Sat 10am–5pm, Sun 1–5pm.

MacGregor Ranch Museum   Listed on the National Register of Historic Places, the museum is on the one-time domain of the MacGregor family, a big name in local ranching lore. Originally founded in 1873, the ranch today is a lens into life on a cattle ranch in that era. Volunteer-led tours of the restored main house focus on the MacGregor family, but the grounds are full of other historic structures, not to mention a working cattle ranch—beef is for sale at the ranch office. Allow 1 hour.

180 MacGregor Lane. ⓒ 970/586-3749. www.macgregorranch.org. Admission $3 adults, free for those under 18. Jun–Aug Tues–Fri 10am–4pm. Closed rest of year.

SHOPPING

Elkhorn Avenue is the main shopping area in Estes Park, and this is also where you'll find public restrooms and free parking lots. Among the notable galleries and gift shops are those in the **Old Church Shops,** 157 W. Elkhorn Ave. (© **970/586-5860;** www.churchshops.com). Also worth looking for are **The Glassworks,** 323 W. Elkhorn Ave. (© **800/490-6695** or 970/586-8619; www.garthsglassworks.com), a gallery and studio with glass-blowing demonstrations; **Serendipity Trading Company,** 117 E. Elkhorn Ave. (© **800/832-8980** or 970/586-8410; www.serendipity-trading.com), traders in American Indian arts and crafts; and **Trendz,** 100 E. Elkhorn Ave. (© **970/577-0831**), a contemporary home decor shop that gave downtown Estes Park's retail scene a much-needed shot of upscale.

The **Cultural Arts Council of Estes Park,** 304 E. Elkhorn Ave. (P.O. Box 4135), Estes Park, CO 80517 (© **970/586-9203;** www.estesarts.com), has a fine art gallery featuring changing exhibits of works by nationally recognized artists as well as exhibits on loan from private collections and museums. The council sponsors an Art in Public Places series (call for details), and hosts Art Walks—self-guided tours of galleries, artists' studios, special exhibits, and events throughout the area. The Art Walks take place in mid-May, June through Labor Day, late September, and early December; and maps are available. The council also sponsors an outdoor performance series, Thursday nights at 7pm from June through August at Estes Park's Performance Park (west side of downtown). Events, which are free or have a nominal admission fee, start at 7pm and offer classical, jazz, folk, or contemporary music, plus theater and dance.

Established in 1917, **Eagle Plume's,** 9853 S. Colo. 7, Allenspark (© **303/747-2861;** www.eagleplume.com), is a one-of-a-kind museum/gallery that hocks a few souvenirs, but focuses on fine art. Plenty of contemporary Native American arts, crafts, and jewelry are on display.

The **Art Center of Estes Park** in the Stanley Village Shopping Center, 517 Big Thompson Ave. (© **970/586-5882;** www.artcenterofestes.com), is a community visual arts center that features changing exhibits of a wide variety of local and regional art, including paintings, sculpture, photography, textiles, glass work, and wood carvings. Works are for sale, and the center also presents workshops and classes on subjects such as oil painting, sketching, stained glass, and jewelry-making. Cost is usually in the $50 to $100 range, including materials. The Art Center is a bit hard to find; once you get to the shopping center, go up the stairs behind the fountain.

WHERE TO STAY

The highest rates here, sometimes dramatically higher, are in summer. For help in finding accommodations, call the **Estes Park Convention and Visitors Bureau** (© **800/443-7837;** www.estesparkcvb.com). National chains here include **Best Western Silver Saddle,** 1260 Big Thompson Ave. (U.S. 34), Estes Park, CO 80517 (© **800/WEST-ERN** or 970/586-4476), with rates of $99 to $199 double from June to mid-September, $79 to $149 double during the rest of the year; **Super 8,** 1040 Big Thompson Ave., Estes Park, CO 80517 (© **800/800-8000** or 970/586-5338), charging $89 to $120 double in summer, $50 to $99 double during the rest of the year; and **Travelodge,** 1220 Big Thompson Ave., Estes Park, CO 80517 (© **800/578-7878** or 970/586-4421), charging $109 to $220 double in summer, $69 to $107 double during the rest of the year.

Although many lodging facilities in the Estes Park area do not have air-conditioning, it is seldom needed at this elevation. Unless otherwise noted, pets are not permitted. Taxes add 7.7% to hotel bills.

Expensive

Boulder Brook 🎿🎿 It would be hard to find a more beautiful setting for lodging than this. Surrounded by tall pines and cradled in a ruggedly majestic valley 2 miles from the park entrance, all suites face the Fall River, and all have private riverfront decks and full or partial kitchens. The spa suites are equipped with two-person spas, fireplaces, sitting areas with cathedral ceilings, and king-size beds. One-bedroom suites hold king-size beds, window seats, two TVs, and bathrooms with whirlpool tub/shower combinations. The grounds, a serene jumble of forest, rock, and running water, include an outdoor hot tub and barbecue area. Smoking is not allowed.

1900 Fall River Rd., Estes Park, CO 80517. Ⓒ 800/238-0910 or 970/586-0910. Fax 970/586-8067. www.boulder brook.com. 19 units. $109–$225 double. DISC, MC, V. **Amenities:** Year-round outdoor hot tub; large free video and DVD library. *In room:* Cable TV/DVD/VCR, kitchen, fridge, coffeemaker, hair dryer, iron, Wi-Fi network.

Historic Crags Lodge 🎿🎿 Perched above town on the north shoulder of Prospect Mountain, Crags Lodge has a friendly, comfy warmth to it that's removed from the bustle of downtown Estes Park—but only by a few hundred feet. On the National Register of Historic Places, the lodge opened in 1914 as an alternative to the Stanley Hotel, and it is one of the area's standout lodgings today. While the lobby and public areas retain a woodsy elegance, the guest studios and suites are more modern than historic, as several original rooms now make large suite. The decor keeps the Western trappings to a minimum, aside from a few historic photos, instead opting for an upscale condominium feel. All of the rooms have kitchenettes, queen beds, and sitting areas with a hide-a-bed; a few have balconies. The activities list is long and varied, and self-guided tour pamphlets are provided to guests free of charge. The resident restaurant, **The View** (see "Where to Dine," later in this chapter) is excellent.

300 Riverside Dr., Estes Park, CO 80517. Ⓒ 970/586-6066. Fax 970/586-6806. www.ilxresorts.com. 33 units. May–Oct $115–$195 double; Nov–Apr $75–$155 double. AE, DISC, MC, V. **Amenities:** Restaurant; bar; outdoor heated pool (seasonal); outdoor hot tub; activities desk; children's program; concierge. *In room:* A/C, cable TV, kitchenette, coffeemaker, hair dryer, iron.

Marys Lake Lodge 🎿🎿 Open from 1913 and shuttered in 1978, Marys Lake Lodge reopened for the 21st century in grand fashion, renovating its old lodge and building 40 condominium units on the property to boot. The old lodge rooms are funky but nice, with terrific views and some original fixtures and claw-foot tubs. The condo units sleep 2 to 10 people, and feature full kitchens, flat screen TVs, DVD players, and other modern perks. There are two restaurants: **The Tavern,** woodsy and casual, serving top-notch bar fare, beef, and pasta; and upscale **Grandmaison's Chalet Room,** with a menu heavy on Mediterranean influences and fresh seafood.

2625 Mary's Lake Rd., Estes Park, CO 80517. Ⓒ 877/443-6279 or 970/586-5958. Fax 970/586-5308. www.marys lakelodge.com. 16 lodge rooms, 40 condominium units. June–Sept $129–$219 lodge room, $196–$430 condominium; Oct–May $99–$199 lodge room, $157–$350 condominium. AE, DISC, DC, MC, V. **Amenities:** 2 restaurants; lounge; outdoor heated pool; outdoor hot tub; spa. *In room:* A/C, cable TV, kitchen.

Romantic RiverSong Inn 🎿 A 1920 Craftsman mansion on the Big Thompson River, this elegant bed-and-breakfast has 27 forested acres with hiking trails and a trout pond, as well as prolific wildlife and beautiful wildflowers. Very quiet, the inn is at the end of a country lane, the first right off Mary's Lake Road after it branches off U.S. 36 south. The comfortable bedrooms are decorated with a blend of antique and modern country furniture. All have large tubs, separate showers, and fireplaces; six units offer jetted tubs for two. Smoking is not permitted. Gourmet candlelight dinners are available by advance arrangement ($124 per couple), but you must supply your own alcoholic beverages.

1765 Lower Broadview Rd. (P.O. Box 1910), Estes Park, CO 80517. © **970/586-4666.** Fax 970/577-1336. www.romanticriversong.com. 10 units. $150–$295 double. Rates include full breakfast. DISC, MC, V. Not suitable for small children. *In room:* Fridge (in some units), Wi-Fi network.

Stanley Hotel 🌟🌟 F. O. Stanley, inventor of the Stanley Steamer, built this elegant hotel in 1909, and a flurry of recent projects have added a spa and a series of lavish condos. The equal of European resorts the day it opened, the Stanley was constructed in solid rock at an elevation of 7,800 feet on the eastern slope of the Colorado Rockies. Today the hotel and its grounds are listed on the National Register of Historic Places as the Stanley Historic District. Each room differs in size and shape, offering a variety of views of Longs Peak, Lake Estes, and surrounding hillsides. We prefer the deluxe rooms in the front of the building, which provide views of Rocky Mountain National Park.

333 Wonderview Ave. (P.O. Box 1767), Estes Park, CO 80517. © **800/976-1377** or 970/586-3371. Fax 970/586-4964. www.stanleyhotel.com. 140 units. $179–$249 double; $250–$350 suite; $400–$700 condominium; $1,200 presidential cottage. AE, DISC, MC, V. **Amenities:** Restaurant (American); pool (heated outdoor); tennis court (outdoor, unlit); exercise room; spa. *In room:* Cable TV w/pay movies, dataport.

Streamside on Fall River These cabin suites, on 17 acres along the Fall River, about a mile west of Estes Park on U.S. 34, are surrounded by woods and meadows of wildflowers. Deer, elk, and bighorn sheep are such regular visitors that many have been given names. Everything is top drawer inside these cabins: All have king- or queen-size beds, fireplaces, and decks or patios with gas grills. Many have beamed cathedral ceilings, skylights, and whirlpool tubs. Guests can wander the nature trails on the property. A variety of special-occasion packages are offered.

1260 Fall River Rd. (P.O. Box 2930), Estes Park, CO 80517. © **800/321-3303** or 970/586-6464. Fax 970/586-6272. 19 units. June–Sept $155–$295 double; Oct–May $99–$195 double. AE, DISC, MC, V. **Amenities:** Indoor hot tub. *In room:* Cable TV/DVD, kitchen.

Taharaa Mountain Lodge 🌟🌟🌟 A luxurious mountain lodge, Taharaa is named for the French Polynesian word for "beautiful view," and it's a fitting moniker: There are jaw-dropping views of the Mummy Range from just about every room in the house. Built in 1997 and expanded in 2005 by Diane and Ken Harlan, Taharaa melds upscale hotel amenities and service with the intimacy of a B&B. With a contemporary, "New West" feel, the sumptuous interiors are a good match with the sublime panoramas, with individually decorated rooms like the Big Thompson, outfitted with trout art of all kinds, and the two-room Cattle Baron Suite, with an imposing antique headboard and a wet bar. The property has a guest library with Internet access and a phenomenal Great Room, with a 30-foot ceiling and fireplace, a wrought iron chandelier, and picture windows framing the stunning view.

3110 Colo. 7 (P.O. Box 2586), Longs Peak Route, Estes Park, CO 80517. © **800/597-0098** or 970/577-0098. Fax 970/577-0819. www.taharaa.com. 18 units, including 2 suites. May to mid-Oct $170–$240 double, $285–$330 suite; mid-Oct to Apr $145–$220 double, $235–$280 suite. Rates include full breakfast and happy hour. AE, DISC, DC, MC, V. **Amenities:** Indoor Jacuzzi; sauna; exercise room; massage. *In room:* A/C, cable TV/DVD.

Moderate & Inexpensive

In addition to the properties discussed here, we also like the **All Budget Inn & Mountain View Suites,** 945 Moraine Ave. (© **800/628-3438** or 970/586-3485; www.allbudgetinn.com), with doubles for $89 to $130 in summer and suites and condos for $140 to $250; and **Saddle & Surrey Motel,** 1341 S. St. Vrain Ave.

(© 970/586-3326), with queen rooms for $80 and with kitchenettes for $145 in summer. In an attractive stucco building downtown, the **Estes Park Hostel,** 211 Cleave St. (© 877/213-0549 or 970/586-3149; www.estesparkhostel.com), rents bunks for $24 and private rooms for $55 There are also cabins and cottages available at the **Estes Park Campground,** listed under "Camping," below.

Alpine Trail Ridge Inn ⭐ *Value*   This top-notch independent motel, right next to the entrance to Rocky Mountain National Park, offers nicely maintained rooms, many with private balconies, with basic Western decor and plenty of functionality. There are rooms with kings and queens, two doubles, as well as a few two-room family units. Proprietors Jay and Fran Grooters are also great sources for hiking advice—Fran's **Trail Tracks** (www.trailtracks.com) publishes excellent 3-D hiking maps of Rocky Mountain National Park and other hiking meccas.

927 Moraine Ave., Estes Park, CO 80517. © 800/223-5023 or 970/586-4585. Fax 970/586-6249. www.alpinetrail ridgeinn.com. 48 units. Summer $70–$130 double, $130–$192 family unit. Closed mid-Oct to Apr. AE, DISC, DC, MC, V. **Amenities:** Restaurant (American); outdoor heated pool; business center. *In room:* A/C, cable TV, fridge, coffeemaker, hair dryer, complimentary wireless Internet access.

Allenspark Lodge Bed & Breakfast ⭐⭐ *Finds*   We love historic properties, and this one has just the right ambience for a visit to Rocky Mountain National Park. The three-story lodge was built in 1933 of hand-hewn ponderosa pine logs, and includes a large native stone fireplace. Located in a tiny village at the southeast corner of the national park, all lodge rooms offer mountain views and original handmade 1930s pine furniture. At the top end is the Hideaway Room, with a queen-size brass bed, bear-claw-foot tub, fine linens, and a gas-log stove. Guests share the large sunroom, the stone fireplace in the Great Room, videos in the recreation room, and books in the library. A hot family-style breakfast, and afternoon and evening coffee, tea, and cookies are complimentary. There is also a hot tub, espresso coffee shop, and wine and beer bar; horseback riding is available across the street in the summer.

184 Main St., Colo. 7 Business Loop (P.O. Box 247), Allenspark, CO 80510. © 303/747-2552. www.allensparklodge. com. 13 units (7 with bathroom). $75–$145 double. Rates include full breakfast. DISC, MC, V. Children under 14 not accepted. **Amenities:** Bar; hot tub. *In room:* No phone.

Baldpate Inn ⭐ *Finds*   Located 7 miles south of Estes Park, the Baldpate was built in 1917 and named for the novel *Seven Keys to Baldpate,* a murder mystery in which seven visitors believe each possesses the only key to the hotel. Guests today can watch movie versions of the story, read the book, and add to the hotel's collection of more than 30,000 keys. Guests enjoy complimentary refreshments by the handsome stone fireplace in the lobby, relax on the large sun deck, or view free videos on the library VCR. But it might be difficult to stay inside once you experience the spectacular views from the inn's spacious porch and see the nature trails beckoning. Each of the early-20th-century-style rooms is unique, with handmade quilts on the beds. Several of the rooms are a bit small, and although most of the lodge rooms share bathrooms (five bathrooms for nine units), each room does have its own sink. Among our favorites are the Mae West Room (yes, she was a guest here), with a red claw-foot tub and wonderful views of the valley; and the Pinetop Cabin, which has a whirlpool tub, canopy bed, and gas fireplace. In summer, an excellent soup-and-salad buffet is served for lunch and dinner daily.

4900 S. Colo. 7 (P.O. Box 700), Estes Park, CO 80517. © 866/577-5397 or 970/586-6151. www.baldpateinn.com. 14 units (5 with bathroom), 4 cabins. $100 double with shared bathroom; $120 double with private bathroom; $195–$250 cabin. Rates include full breakfast. DISC, MC, V. Closed Nov–Apr. **Amenities:** Restaurant (seasonal). *In room:* No phone.

Estes Park Center/YMCA of the Rockies ⓐ   This extremely popular family resort is an ideal place to get away from it all, and serves as a great home base while exploring the Estes Park area. Lodge units are simply decorated and perfectly adequate, but we prefer the spacious mountain cabins. These have two to four bedrooms (accommodating up to 10), complete kitchens, and some have fireplaces. The center, which occupies 860 wooded acres, offers hiking, horseback riding, miniature golf, fishing, a skate park, and winter activities.

2515 Tunnel Rd., Estes Park, CO 80511-2550. ⓒ 970/586-3341 or 303/448-1616. Fax 970/586-6088. www.ymca rockies.org. 510 lodge rooms (450 with bathroom), 205 cabins. Lodge rooms summer $69–$127, winter $52–$98; cabins year-round $71–$266. YMCA membership required (available at a nominal charge). No credit cards. Pets are permitted in the cabins, but not the lodge rooms. **Amenities:** Indoor heated pool; tennis courts (3 outdoor); bike rentals. *In room:* Kitchen (in the cabins).

Glacier Lodge ⓚⁱᵈˢ   Deer and elk frequently visit these lovely cottages, which spread across 19 acres of woodland along the Big Thompson River. There are poolside chalets; cozy, homey river duplexes with outside decks overlooking the stream; and river triplexes range from earthy to country quaint in decor. All have a porch or patio, and almost all feature kitchens and fireplaces, with a bundle of wood delivered daily. Facilities include a sports court, playground, fishing, gift shop, ice-cream shop, and stables. Breakfast cookouts, barbecues, and special kids' activities take place in summer, at an extra charge. There are also four large lodges available for groups that sleep from 12 to 30 (call for rates).

Colo. 66 (P.O. Box 2656), Estes Park, CO 80517. ⓒ 800/523-3920 or 970/586-4401. www.glacierlodge.com. 26 units. Early June to late Aug $95–$314; mid-May to early June and late Aug to late Sept $75–$246; late Sept to mid-Oct $60–$200. Rates are per unit (2–5 people). Minimum stays of 2–4 nights may be required. DISC, MC, V. Closed mid-Oct to mid-May. **Amenities:** Outdoor pool; children's program; coin-op washers and dryers. *In room:* TV, no phone.

Lane Guest Ranch ⓚⁱᵈˢ   Lloyd Lane opened his guest ranch south of Estes Park in 1953, and built it into a great family resort with a focus on the great outdoors. For this, its location on 30 acres abutting Roosevelt National Forest and Rocky Mountain National Park is ideal. The calendar is pretty packed here, with activities ranging from guided hiking to silversmithing classes and entertainment ranging from Bingo to magic. The horseback rides run the gamut from standard trail rides to wine and cheese rides, overnight rides, and even a shopping-oriented ride! All meals are included, with nightly specials and a standard menu. The cabins here accommodate families up to six, complete with bunk beds, stocked fridges, and knotty pine furnishings. There is also the Doctor's House, a large house that accommodates up to 14.

P.O. Box 1766, Estes Park, CO 80517. ⓒ 303/747-2493. www.laneguestranch.com. 25 cabins. June–Aug $195 per adult per night, $70–$155 per child per night, children under 3 free (childcare packages available for kids). Rates include all meals and activities. 3-night minimum. Pets accepted. MC, V. Closed Sept–May. **Amenities:** Restaurant (American); lounge; outdoor pool; outdoor hot tub; sauna; fitness center; children's program; activities desk. *In room:* TV/DVD/VCR, kitchen, hair dryer, no phone.

McGregor Mountain Lodge ⓐⓚⁱᵈˢ   Our midpriced pick on the east side of Rocky Mountain National Park, this smallish, spread-out property is a stone's throw from the park boundary at the foot of McGregor Mountain, a favorite hangout for bighorn sheep. With efficiencies, cottages, and one- and two-bedroom suites, the 19 rooms here are diverse and uniformly well maintained, and the place has a homey, faraway feel, despite its location off one of the area's main thoroughfares. Many of the rooms have hot tubs and balconies—all of them are great spots to unwind.

2815 Fall River Rd., Estes Park, CO 80517. ⓒ 800/835-8439 or 970/586-3457. Fax 970/586-4040. www.mcgregor mountainlodge.com. 19 units, including 15 cottages and suites. Early June to mid-Aug $142 double, $175–$340 cottage or suite; rest of year $87–$128 double, $109–$281 cottage or suite. AE, DC, DISC, MC, V. **Amenities:** Indoor hot tub; playground. *In room:* Cable TV/VCR, kitchen, Wi-Fi network, no phone.

CAMPING

Elk Meadow Lodge & RV Park   Located close to the national park's Beaver Meadows entrance, this campground boasts 30 open and wooded acres, grand views in all directions, and sites that can handle "big rigs." There are several historic cabins on the property, plus a swimming pool, convenience store, laundry facilities, playgrounds, a dump station, and a recreation room. There are also a number of teepees for rent.

1665 Colo. 66, Estes Park, CO 80517. ⓒ 800/582-5342 or 970/586-5342. www.elkmeadowrv.com. 288 sites. Rates for 2 adults $40 RV, $25 tent; $34 teepee; $76–$122 cabin. DISC, MC, V. Open mid-Apr to mid-Oct.

Estes Park Campground 🏃🏃 *Finds*   Located at the end of the road, 1 mile past the YMCA of the Rockies, and with the national park on two sides, this attractive campground offers glorious views and lots of quiet. Most campsites are nestled among pine trees and are perfect for tenters and pickup campers; only 21 have water and electric (30 amp) hookups. There are modern restrooms with showers, a small playground, a dump station, and a store that stocks supplies including firewood and ice.

3420 Tunnel Rd. (P.O. Box 3517), Estes Park, CO 80517. ⓒ 888/815-2029 or 970/586-4188. www.estesparkcamp ground.com. 68 sites. Rates for 2 adults $24–$28 with no hookups, $28–$32 with hookups. AE, DISC, MC, V. Open mid-May to late Sept.

Mary's Lake Campground   Here you'll find mostly open campsites that can accommodate everything from tents to 45-foot RVs, with full hookups that include cable TV. Facilities include bathhouses, a laundry, a dump station, a playground, a basketball court, a small store, a Wi-Fi network, a heated swimming pool, horseshoe pits, and a game room. Fishing licenses, bait, and tackle for shore fishing at the lake and stream fishing in the national park are available. Pets are welcome.

2120 Mary's Lake Rd. (P.O. Box 2514), Estes Park, CO 80517. ⓒ 800/445-6279 or 970/586-4411. Fax 970/586-4493. www.maryslakecampground.com. 150 sites. Rates for 2 people $36–$39 per RV hookup campsite; $25 for non-hookup site. Extra person (over age 5) $3. Extra fee for A/C or electric heater use. DISC, MC, V. Open May–Sept.

WHERE TO DINE

In addition to the restaurants described here, we also like **Bob & Tony's Pizza,** 124 W. Elkhorn Ave. (ⓒ **970/586-2044**), a busy pizza joint with redbrick walls covered with chalk signatures.

Expensive

Dunraven Inn 🏃🏃 ITALIAN   This is a great spot to celebrate a special occasion in an intimate setting, but not so fancy that you wouldn't want to take the (well-behaved) kids. The decor is eclectic, to say the least: Images of the *Mona Lisa* are scattered about, ranging from a mustachioed lady to opera posters, and autographed dollar bills are posted in the lounge area. House specialties include shrimp scampi, lasagna, and our favorite, the Dunraven Italiano (a 10-oz. charbroiled sirloin steak in a sauce of peppers, onions, and tomatoes). There's a wide choice of pastas, fresh seafood, vegetarian plates, and desserts, plus a children's menu. The full bar is well stocked, and the wine list reasonably priced.

2470 Colo. 66. ⓒ **970/586-6409.** Reservations recommended. Main courses $8–$34. AE, DISC, MC, V. Sun–Thurs 5–10pm; Fri–Sat 5–10pm; closes slightly earlier in winter.

The View &&& *Finds* STEAKS/SEAFOOD   While the restaurant is named for the picture-perfect panorama of the town and surrounding mountainscape, the food is also terrific. Chef Russell Stephens shows an inventive eye for detail with such dishes as the walnut-crusted rainbow trout, served with garlic mashers and a grapefruit beurre blanc sauce, and a pan-seared rib-eye with garlic-bleu cheese crust and merlot sauce. The atmosphere is woodsy but refined, with hardwood floors and red-and-white-checkered tablecloths, and there is often jazz or a Celtic guitarist.

At Historic Crags Lodge (see "Where to Stay," earlier in this chapter), 300 Riverside Dr. ℂ 970/586-6066. Reservations recommended. Main courses $3–$7 breakfast, $5–$8 lunch, $8–$17 dinner. AE, MC, V. Daily 5–9pm. Closed mid-Oct to mid-May.

Moderate

Baldpate Inn & *Finds* SOUP/SALAD   Don't be misled by the simple cuisine—the buffet is deliciously filling and plentiful. Everything is freshly prepared on the premises, with the cooks barely staying one muffin ahead of the guests. Soups—a choice of two is offered each day—include hearty stews, chili, chicken rice, garden vegetable, and classic French onion. The salad bar provides fresh greens and an array of toppings, chunks of cheese, and fruit and vegetable salads. Honey-wheat bread is a staple, plus wonderful rolls, muffins, and corn bread. Topping off the meal are fresh homemade pies and cappuccino.

4900 S. Colo. 7. ℂ **970/586-6151**. www.baldpateinn.com. Reservations recommended. Buffet $12 adults, $4.95 children under 10. DISC, MC, V. Memorial Day to Aug daily 11:30am–8pm. Shorter hours Sept to mid-Oct; call for current schedule.

Grumpy Gringo *Kids* MEXICAN   Dine in style at this classy Mexican restaurant without breaking the bank. The private booths, whitewashed plaster walls, bright poppies, and a few choice sculptures provide a posh atmosphere. And although the food is excellent and portions are large, the prices are surprisingly low. Our choice here is a burrito, but which one to choose? We also recommend the huge enchilada olé. It's actually three enchiladas: one each of cheese, beef, and chicken. The fajitas—either chicken or beef—are delicious. There are six sauces from which to choose, each homemade, and rated mild, semihot, or hot. Burgers and sandwiches are also offered. The house specialty drink is the Gringo Margarita, made with Sauza Gold tequila from a secret recipe, and the signature dessert is deep-fried ice cream.

1560 Big Thompson Ave. (U.S. 34). ℂ **970/586-7705**. www.grumpygringo.com. Main courses $5.95–$18. AE, DISC, MC, V. Daily 11am–10pm summer, 11am–8pm off-season. On U.S. 34, 1 mile east of the junction of U.S. Hwy. 34 and Hwy. 36.

Poppy's *Kids* ITALIAN/AMERICAN   This bright, pleasant, and casual eatery right on the Big Thompson River serves up a menu of gourmet pizzas, sandwiches, and entree salads, and also has a good soup and salad bar. We're partial to some of the Mexican-accented dishes, like the enchilada pizza or the green chile cheeseburger, not to mention the "Adult Italian Sodas," sweet and fizzy drinks that pack a mild punch. You can dine in the family-friendly room or the great riverfront patio.

342 E. Elkhorn Ave. (on the Riverwalk in Barlow Plaza). ℂ **970/586-8282**. www.poppyspizzaandgrill.com. Main courses $6–$20. AE, DC, DISC, MC, V. Summer daily 11am–9pm; rest of year daily 11am–8pm.

Inexpensive

The Egg & I AMERICAN   A bright and cheery place to start your day, the Egg & I is decorated in warm earth tones, with magnificent views of the pristine Rocky Mountains. Breakfast is available at any time, ranging from the simplest fried egg to several variations of eggs Benedict, omelets, frittatas, crepes, and skillet meals—and we do mean meals—plus pancakes and French toast. Those not opting for breakfast can choose among a variety of sandwiches, such as the California croissant, thinly sliced turkey breast, Swiss cheese, alfalfa sprouts, tomato, and avocado on a fresh tender croissant. Soups and a number of salads are also available, and there is takeout.

393 E. Elkhorn at the corner of U.S. Hwy. 34 and 36. © 970/586-1173. Main courses $3.95–$8.95. AE, DISC, MC, V. Summer Mon–Sat 6am–2pm, Sun 7am–2pm; winter daily 7am–2pm.

ARTS & ENTERTAINMENT

It's impossible to get bored in Estes Park, where you'll find a wide variety of performing arts events—many of them free—presented year-round. You'll hear classical music—from small ensembles to symphony orchestras—plus jazz, country, and Christian; and see dance and theater. The community boasts a nice outdoor entertainment venue—Estes Park Performance Park—on West Elkhorn Avenue on the west side of town. For details on what's going on when you plan to be in town, contact the **Cultural Arts Council of Estes Park,** 304 E. Elkhorn Ave. (P.O. Box 4135), Estes Park, CO 80517 (© **970/586-9203;** www.estesarts.com), which represents a number of arts groups and individual artists, and helps coordinate many of the community's arts events. These include a free outdoor concert series (including music, theater, and dance) Thursdays at 7pm June through August at the Estes Park Performance Park; a dance festival in November; and Imagine This, a family-oriented festival of performing and visual arts, each February.

Among individual organizations presenting live productions is the **Fine Arts Guild of the Rockies,** which sponsors musicals and plays; the **Estes Park Music Festival,** which presents a series of classical music concerts each summer; and the **Chamber Music Society of Estes Park,** offering three concerts in early October.

Of local watering holes, we're big fans of the **Wheel Bar,** 132 E. Elkhorn Ave. (© **970/586-9381**), which has been open for a century and owned by the Nagl family since 1945. It's open every day except Christmas, serving as a community hub in more ways than one. The bar is a bit funky, with an excellent steakhouse, **Orlando's,** upstairs, and plenty of wheel decor, including a slowly rotating specimen behind the bar.

Among other bars, the **Rock Inn,** 1675 Colo. 66 (© **970/586-1146**), plates up an eclectic array of dishes and hosts live rock and country music. For live rock music and dancing on weekends, check out **Lonigan's Bar & Grill,** 110 W. Elkhorn Ave. (© **970/586-4346**).

GRAND LAKE

The western entrance to Rocky Mountain National Park is at the picturesque little town of Grand Lake, in the shade of Shadow Mountain at the park's southwestern corner.

Here, in the crisp mountain air at 8,370 feet above sea level, you can stroll down an old-fashioned boardwalk as one of the locals rides by on horseback. In fact, take away the automobiles and electric lights, and this town looks and feels like the late 1800s. Located in the Arapaho National Recreation Area, Grand Lake is surrounded by three lakes—Grand Lake, Shadow Mountain Reservoir, and Lake Granby—each with a marina that offers boating (with rentals), fishing, and other watersports. In the recreation area you'll find miles of trails for hiking, horseback riding, four-wheeling, and mountain biking that become cross-country skiing and snowmobiling trails in winter.

The Grand Lake Yacht Club hosts the **Grand Lake Regatta** in late July and/or early August. The club was organized in 1902, and the regatta began 10 years later.

Sailboats from around the world compete to win the prestigious Lipton Cup, given to the club by Thomas Lipton in 1912. Other summer events include an enormous **Fourth of July fireworks display** over Grand Lake, and **Western Weekend,** with a buffalo barbecue, 5K run, and a pancake breakfast, in mid-July. The **Rocky Mountain Repertory Theatre** (© **970/627-3421** or 970/627-5087; www.rockymountain rep.com) offers a summer program of Broadway shows and other theater, plus programs for children and teens.

Usually open daily from 11am to 5pm in summer, the **Kauffman House,** 407 Pitkin Ave., at Lake Ave. (© **970/627-9644;** www.kauffmanhouse.org), is a log structure that was built as a hotel in 1892. It has been restored and now serves as the museum of the Grand Lake Historical Society, with many of its original furnishings and exhibits on what life was like here back when everyone arrived on horseback or by stagecoach. Admission is free, although donations are welcome.

Golfers may want to test their skills at the 18-hole championship **Grand Lake Golf Course** (© **970/627-8008**), altitude 8,420 feet. Greens fees are $83 for 18 holes.

For further information on what to do in this area, stop at the **Visitor Information Center** on U.S. 34 at the turnoff into town (open daily 9am–5pm in summer, with shorter hours the rest of the year), or contact the **Grand Lake Area Chamber of Commerce,** P.O. Box 429, Grand Lake, CO 80447 (© **800/531-1019** or 970/627-3402; www.grandlakechamber.com). Information is also available from the Forest Service's **Sulphur Ranger District office** (P.O. Box 10, Granby, CO 80446), 9 Ten Mile Dr., off U.S. 40 about a half-mile south of Granby (© **970/887-4100;** www.fs.fed. us/r2), open in summer Monday through Saturday from 8am to 4:30pm (until 6pm Fri), with shorter hours in winter.

WHERE TO STAY

There are plenty of lodging possibilities in Grand Lake. A good source for information is the **Grand Lake Area Chamber of Commerce** (see address above). In addition to the properties below, we like the **Grand Lake Terrace Inn,** 813 Grand Ave. (P.O. Box 1791), Grand Lake, CO 80447 (© **888/627-3001** or 970/627-3000; www. grandlaketerraceinn.com), a quaint mountain inn with three attractively decorated rooms plus a spacious suite, with rates of $50 to $150 double for the rooms and $120 to $240 for the suite. The inn also has a restaurant serving breakfast and lunch daily with dinner main course prices from $8 to $26.

Black Bear Lodge   Located 3 miles south of town across from Shadow Mountain Lake, this comfortable and well-maintained establishment is a great bet if you're looking for is an attractive motel with western ambience. Some units have two rooms and some have kitchenettes. Of the 17 units, bathrooms in eight have showers only; the rest have bathrooms with shower/tub combos. All units are nonsmoking.

12255 U.S. 34 (P.O. Box 609), Grand Lake, CO 80447. © **800/766-1123** or 970/627-3654. www.blackbeargrandlake. com. 17 units. $75–$175 double. DISC, MC, V. **Amenities:** Outdoor pool; 2 whirlpools (1 indoor, 1 outdoor); sauna. In room: TV.

Daven Haven Lodge 🐾🐾   Set among pine trees about a quarter-mile from the lake, this group of cabins is a good choice for those seeking peace and quiet in a secluded mountain resort–type setting. There's a welcoming stone fireplace in the lobby plus old Coke machines and several antique jukeboxes—they actually play 78 rpm records! The cabins vary in size, sleeping from two to eight people; each has its own picnic table and six have stone fireplaces. Decor and furnishings vary, but most have attractive light wood walls and solid wood and upholstered furniture. You'll also find a lovely patio, volleyball court, horseshoes, and a bonfire pit. The Back-Street Steakhouse (see "Where to Dine," below) serves dinner nightly in summer and 4 nights a week in winter. All cabins are nonsmoking.

604 Marina Dr. (P.O. Box 1528), Grand Lake, CO 80447. ℰ 970/627-8144. Fax 970/627-5098. www.davenhaven lodge.com. 16 units. $94–$149 for cabins sleeping 2–4, $138–$215 for cabins sleeping 5–8. DISC, MC, V. 3-night minimum required on reservations during holidays. **Amenities:** Restaurant (steakhouse). *In room:* TV, kitchen.

The Inn at Grand Lake ℱ   For modern lodging with an Old West feel, stay at this handsome historic building, constructed in 1881 as Grand Lake's courthouse and jail. Rooms have a variety of bed combinations, and several sleep up to six. They're equipped with Western-style furniture, ceiling fans, white stucco walls, and Indian-motif draperies and bedspreads. Many units have refrigerators and microwaves. About half of the units have shower-tub combinations, and the rest have showers only. The best views are on the street side of the building. The inn is in the center of town, about a half block from the lake. The Sagebrush BBQ & Grill (see "Where to Dine," below) serves three meals daily. All units are nonsmoking.

1103 Grand Ave. (P.O. Box 2087), Grand Lake, CO 80447. ℰ 800/722-2585 or 970/627-9234. www.innatgrandlake. com. 18 units. $75–$155 double, $115–$170 suite. AE, DISC, MC, V. *In room:* TV, coffeemaker, hair dryer.

WHERE TO DINE
Back-Street Steakhouse ℱ STEAK   This cozy, country inn–style restaurant in the Daven Haven lodge (see above) offers fine dining in a down-home atmosphere. Steaks—from the 8-ounce filet mignon to the 12-ounce New York strip—are all USDA choice beef, cooked to perfection. The house specialty, Jack Daniel's pork chops (breaded, baked, and served with a creamy Jack Daniel's mushroom sauce), has been featured in *Bon Appétit* magazine. Also on the menu are pasta, chicken, and fish dishes, plus slow-roasted prime rib, and children's items. Sandwiches and light entrees, such as the smoked salmon and Creole fried oyster plate, are served in the lounge.

In the Daven Haven Lodge, 604 Marina Dr. ℰ 970/627-8144. www.davenhavenlodge.com. Reservations recommended in summer and on winter weekends. Main courses $13–$32 dining room, $3–$13 lounge. DISC, MC, V. Summer and Christmas holidays daily 5pm–close; winter Thurs–Sun 5pm–close.

Sagebrush BBQ & Grill AMERICAN   Come here to enjoy excellent barbecue plus steaks, sandwiches, and seafood in a historic building that also houses The Inn at Grand Lake. The atmosphere here is definitely Wild West, complete with Grand Lake's original jail doors, and so casual that you're encouraged to munch on peanuts and throw the shells on the floor. The specialty here is barbecue—try the super-tender fall-off-the-bone pork ribs—but we also suggest the New York strip steak, pan-fried rainbow trout, and the elk medallions served with roasted raspberry chipotle sauce. Another good choice is the burrito—pork, chicken, or vegetarian—served with refried beans, green chile, cheese, tomato, and lettuce.

1101 Grand Ave. ℰ 970/627-1404. www.sagebrushbbq.com. Main courses lunch and dinner $5.95–$22. MC, V. Daily 7am–10pm.

2 Rocky Mountain National Park ℱℱℱ

Snow-covered peaks—17 mountains above 13,000 feet—stand over lush valleys and shimmering alpine lakes in the 415 square miles (265,727 acres) that comprise Rocky Mountain National Park. The highest, at 14,259 feet, is Longs Peak.

But what really sets the park apart (after all, this sort of eye-popping beauty is not unusual in the Rockies) is its variety of distinct ecological zones. As you rise and descend in altitude, the landscape of the park changes dramatically. In relatively low areas, from about 7,500 to 9,000 feet, a lush forest of ponderosa pine and juniper cloaks the sunny southern slopes, with Douglas fir on the cooler northern slopes. Thirstier blue spruce and lodgepole pine cling to streamsides, with occasional groves of aspen. Elk and mule deer thrive. On higher slopes, a subalpine ecosystem exists, dominated by forests of Engelmann spruce and subalpine fir, but it's interspersed with wide meadows covered with wildflowers during spring and summer. The park is also home to bighorn sheep, which have become unofficial mascots of the park. Above 11,500 feet, the trees become increasingly gnarled and stunted, until they disappear altogether and alpine tundra predominates. Fully one-third of the park is at this altitude, and in this bleak, rocky world, many of the plants are identical to those found in the Arctic.

Trail Ridge Road 🏕️🏕️, the park's primary east-west roadway, is one of America's great alpine highways. It cuts west through the middle of the park from Estes Park, then south down its western boundary to Grand Lake. Climbing to 12,183 feet near Fall River Pass, it's the highest continuous paved highway in the United States. The road is usually open from Memorial Day into October, depending on snowfall. The 48-mile scenic drive from Estes Park to Grand Lake takes about 3 hours, allowing for stops at numerous scenic outlooks.

Fall River Road, the original park road, leads to Fall River Pass from Estes Park via Horseshoe Park. West of the Endovalley picnic area, the road is one-way uphill, and is closed to trailers and motor homes. As you negotiate its gravelly switchbacks, you get a clear idea of what early auto travel was like in the West. This road, too, is closed in winter. One of the few paved roads in the Rockies that leads into a high mountain basin is **Bear Lake Road;** it is kept open year-round, with occasional half-day closings to clear snow. Numerous trails converge at Bear Lake, southwest of the Park Headquarters/Visitor Center, via Moraine Park.

JUST THE FACTS

ENTRY POINTS   Entry into the park is from either the east (through the town of Estes Park) or the west (through the town of Grand Lake). The east and west sides of the park are connected by Trail Ridge Road, open during summer and early fall, but closed to all motor vehicle traffic by snow the rest of the year. Most visitors enter the park from the Estes Park side. The **Beaver Meadows Entrance,** west of Estes Park via U.S. 36, leads to the Beaver Meadows Visitor Center and park headquarters, and is the most direct route to Trail Ridge Road. U.S. 34 west from Estes Park takes you to the Fall River Visitor Center, just outside the park, and into the park via the **Fall River Entrance,** which is north of the Beaver Meadows Entrance. From there you can access Old Fall River Road or Trail Ridge Road. Those entering the park from the west side should take U.S. 40 to Granby and then follow U.S. 34 north to the **Grand Lake Entrance.**

GETTING AROUND   In summer, a free national park **shuttle bus** runs from Moraine Park Campground, Moraine Park Museum, and the Glacier Basin parking area to Bear Lake, with departures every 10 to 20 minutes. Shuttle buses also began operating in 2006 throughout the business district of Estes Park and from Estes Park into Rocky Mountain National Park. The buses run daily from July through Labor Day; schedules are available at the Estes Park Visitor Center (see "Visitor Centers & Information," below).

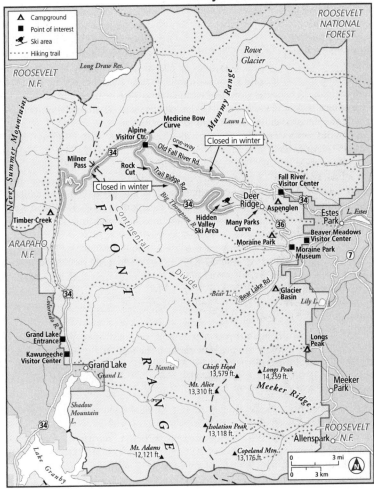

FEES & REGULATIONS Park admission for up to a week costs $20 per vehicle or $10 per person for motorcyclists, bicyclists, and pedestrians.

As is true for most of the national parks, wilderness permits are required for all overnight backpacking trips, and camping is allowed only in specified campsites. Pets must be leashed, aren't permitted on trails or into the backcountry, and may not be left unattended anywhere including vehicles and campsites. Both motor vehicles and bicycles must remain on roads or in parking areas. Do not feed or touch any park animals, and do not pick any wildflowers.

VISITOR CENTERS & INFORMATION Entering the park on U.S. 36 from Estes Park, the **Beaver Meadows Visitor Center** (© **970/586-1206**) has knowledgeable people to answer questions and give advice, a wide choice of books and maps for sale, and interpretive exhibits, including a relief model of the park and an audiovisual program. This center is open daily from 8am to 6pm, year-round.

Just outside the park, on U.S. 34 and just east of the Fall River entrance, is the **Fall River Visitor Center** (© 970/586-1206). Located in a beautiful mountain lodge–style building, it is staffed by park rangers and volunteers from the Rocky Mountain Nature Association. It contains exhibits on park wildlife, including some spectacular full-size bronzes of elk and other animals, plus information and a bookstore. Next door is a large (but somewhat pricey) souvenir and clothing shop plus a cafeteria-style restaurant with snacks and sandwiches. Hours are from 9am to 6pm daily.

Near the park's west side entrance is the **Kawuneeche Visitor Center** (© 970/586-1513), open daily from 8am to 6pm year-round. Located high in the mountains (11,796 ft. above sea level) is the **Alpine Visitor Center** (© 970/586-1206), at Fall River Pass, open from late June to early October, daily from 9am to 5pm, with shorter hours toward the end of the season; exhibits here explain life on the alpine tundra. Visitor facilities are also available at the **Moraine Park Museum** (© 970/586-1206) on Bear Lake Road on the east side of the park, open from mid-April to mid-October, daily from 9am to 5pm.

For more specifics on planning a trip, contact Rocky Mountain National Park, 1000 U.S. 36, Estes Park, CO 80517-8397 (© 970/586-1206 or 970/586-1333 for recorded information; www.nps.gov/romo). You can also get detailed information from the **Rocky Mountain Nature Association,** P.O. Box 3100, Estes Park, CO 80517 (© 800/816-7662 or 970/586-0108; www.rmna.org), which sells a variety of maps, guides, books, and videos.

SEASONS   Even though the park is technically open daily year-round, Trail Ridge Road, the main east-west thoroughfare through the park, is almost always closed in winter. The road is usually open by late May (after the snow has been cleared) and closes between mid- and late October. However, it is not uncommon for snowstorms to close the road for several hours or even a full day at any time, especially in early June and October. The high country is open during the summer and as snow conditions permit in winter.

AVOIDING THE CROWDS   Because large portions of the park are closed in winter, most people visit the park from late spring through early fall. The busiest period, though, is from mid-June to mid-August. In order to avoid the largest crowds, try to visit just before or just after that period. For those who don't mind chilly evenings, late September and early October are less crowded and can be beautiful, although there's always the chance of an early winter storm. Regardless of when you visit, the absolute best way to avoid crowds is by putting on a backpack or climbing onto a horse. Rocky Mountain has some 350 miles of trails leading into all corners of the park (see "Sports & Outdoor Activities," below).

RANGER PROGRAMS   Evening programs take place at campground amphitheaters, and additional talks and programs are offered at visitor centers between June and September. Consult the park's free *High Country Headlines* newspaper for scheduled activities, which vary from photo walks to fly-fishing and orienteering.

SEEING THE HIGHLIGHTS

Although Rocky Mountain National Park is generally considered the domain of hikers and climbers, it's surprisingly easy to thoroughly enjoy this park without working up a sweat. For that we can thank **Trail Ridge Road.** Built in 1932 and undoubtedly one of America's most scenic highways, it provides expansive and sometimes dizzying views in all directions. The drive from Estes Park to Grand Lake covers some 48 miles through the park, rising above 12,000 feet in elevation and crossing the Continental Divide. It offers spectacular vistas of snow-capped peaks, deep forests, and meadows of wildflowers, where bighorn sheep, elk, and deer browse. Allow at least 3 hours for the drive, and more if you'd like to take a short hike from one of the many vista points.

To get a close look at the tundra, pull off Trail Ridge Road into the **Rock Cut** parking area (elevation 12,110 ft.), about halfway along the scenic drive. The views of glacially carved peaks along the Continental Divide are spectacular, and signs on the half-mile Tundra Nature Trail identify the hardy plants and animals that inhabit the region and explain how they have adapted to the harsh environment.

TRAIL RIDGE ROAD ⨭

Along Trail Ridge Road are numbered signs, from 1 to 12, starting on the east side of the park and heading west. These stops are described below, and the route is also discussed in a brochure available at park visitor centers (50¢). Motorists starting from the west side of the park will begin at number 12 and count down.

Stop No. 1: Deer Ridge Junction. This spot offers views of the Mummy Mountain Range to the north. It is the official beginning of Trail Ridge Road, the highest continuous paved road in the United States, reaching an elevation of 12,183 feet. Here you're at a mere 8,940 feet.

Stop No. 2: Hidden Valley. Formerly the site of a downhill ski area, this scenic subalpine valley boasts forests of Engelmann spruce and fir. The elevation is 9,240 feet.

Stop No. 3: Many Parks Curve. This delightfully scenic stop, with one of the best roadside views in the park, is also a good location for birders, who are likely to spot the noisy Steller's jay and Clark's nutcracker. The term "park" is used in the sense of a level valley between mountain ranges (often an open, grassy area), which in this case was carved by glaciers some 10,000 years ago. The elevation is 9,620 feet.

Stop No. 4: Rainbow Curve. Just past a sign announcing your position 2 miles above sea level is Rainbow Curve, an area known for colorful rainbows that are often seen after thunderstorms. It's also famous for ferocious winds and brutal winters. Take a look at the trees that have branches only on their downwind side, where their trunks protect them from the elements. The excellent view from the overlook here extends past Longs Peak and into Hidden Valley and Horseshoe Park, where you can see rock, gravel, and other rubble left by a flood that struck in 1982 after a dam broke. The elevation is 10,829 feet.

Stop No. 5: Forest Canyon Overlook. From this stop's parking area, a short, paved walkway leads to an observation platform offering a beautiful but dizzying view into vast Forest Canyon, where the erosion work of glaciers is clearly evident. The peaks of the Continental Divide appear beyond. Near the overlook, watch for pikas (relatives of rabbits), marmots, and other small mammals. The elevation is 11,716 feet.

Stop No. 6: Rock Cut. Practically the highest point along Trail Ridge Road, this is alpine tundra at its harshest. Winds can reach 150 mph, winter blizzards are frequent, and temperatures in midsummer frequently drop below freezing. You'll have splendid views of the glacially carved peaks along the Continental Divide, and on the .5-mile **Tundra World Nature Trail,** you'll find signs identifying the hardy plants and animals that inhabit this cold and barren region. The elevation is 12,110 feet.

Stop No. 7: Lava Cliffs. Here you'll see a dark cliff, created by the carving action of glacial ice through a thick layer of tuff (volcanic ash and debris) that was deposited here about 28 million years ago during volcanic eruptions in the Never Summer Range, located about 8 miles west. If you look just below the cliff, you'll see a pretty meadow that is a popular grazing spot for elk. The elevation is 12,080 feet.

Stop No. 8: Fall River Pass. At this spot you'll get a good view of a huge amphitheater, and you can take a break at the Alpine Visitor Center. A viewing platform at the rear of the visitor center offers vistas of a wide, glacially carved valley of grasses, wildflowers, shrubs, and small trees where you're practically guaranteed to see elk grazing. This is also the junction of Trail Ridge Road and Old Fall River Road. The elevation is 11,796 feet.

SPORTS & OUTDOOR ACTIVITIES

Rocky Mountain National Park is a fantastic area for a variety of outdoor activities, and many activities also take place just outside the park in the 1,240-square-mile Roosevelt National Forest. In Estes Park, a **Forest Service Information Center** is located at 161 Second St. (© **970/586-3440**); it's usually open daily from 9am to 5pm in summer. For year-round information, contact the **Forest Service Information Center,** 2150 Centre Ave., Building E, Fort Collins, CO 80526 (© **970/295-6700;** www.fs.fed.us/r2).

BICYCLING   Bicyclists share the park roadways with motor vehicles along narrow roads with 5% to 7% grades, and, like most national parks, bikes are not permitted off established roads. However, bicyclists still enjoy the challenge and scenery. One popular 16-mile ride is the **Horseshoe Park/Estes Park Loop,** which goes from Estes Park west on U.S. 34 past Aspenglen Campground and the park's Fall River entrance and visitor center, circles around Horseshoe Park, and then heads east again at the Deer Ridge Junction, following U.S. 36 out through the Beaver Meadows park entrance. There are plenty of beautiful mountain views; allow from 1 to 3 hours. A free park brochure provides information on safety, regulations, and other suggested routes. Tours, rentals, and repairs are available at **Colorado Bicycling Adventures,** 184 E. Elkhorn Ave., Estes Park (© **970/586-4241;** www.coloradobicycling.com). Bike rentals range from $15 to $50 for a half-day and $23 to $90 for a full day, depending on the type of bike, which ranges from very basic to absolutely fantastic. The company offers guided downhill trips in the park for about $75 per person, and also leads a variety of free group bike rides in the Estes Park area from May through September (call or check the website for the current schedule).

CLIMBING & MOUNTAINEERING   **Colorado Mountain School,** 341 Moraine Ave., Estes Park, CO 80517 (© **800/836-4008;** www.totalclimbing.com), is an AMGA (American Mountain Guides Association) accredited year-round guide service, and the sole concessionaire for technical climbing and instruction in Rocky Mountain National Park. The school offers a wide range of programs. Among those we especially recommend are the two-day mountaineering class for $420 and the guided group hike up Longs Peak for $200. The school also offers lodging in a hostel-type setting, at about $35 per night per person in summer with lower rates the rest of the year. (See also "Hiking & Backpacking," below.) Be sure to stop at the ranger station at the Longs Peak trailhead for current trail and weather information before attempting to ascend Longs Peak.

EDUCATIONAL PROGRAMS The **Rocky Mountain Nature Association** (see contact information under "Visitor Centers & Information," above), offers a wide variety of seminars and workshops, ranging from 1 full day to several days. Subjects might include songbirds, flower identification, edible and medicinal herbs, painting, wildlife photography, tracking park animals, and edible mushrooms. Rates are $65 to $75 for full-day programs and $135 and up for multiday programs. There are also kids' programs, including guided children's hikes, from $15 to $20.

FISHING Four species of trout are fished in national park and national forest streams and lakes: brown, rainbow, brook, and cutthroat. A state fishing license is required, and only artificial lures or flies are permitted in the park. A number of lakes and streams in the national park are closed to fishing, including Bear Lake; free park brochures listing open and closed bodies of water plus regulations and other information are available at visitor centers.

HIKING & BACKPACKING The park visitor centers offer topographic maps and hiking guides for sale, and rangers can direct you to lesser-used trails.

One particularly easy park hike is the **Alberta Falls Trail** from the Glacier Gorge Parking Area (a half-mile one-way), which rises in elevation only 160 feet as it follows Glacier Creek to pretty Alberta Falls.

A slightly more difficult option is the **Bierstadt Lake Trail,** accessible from the north side of Bear Lake Road about 6½ miles from Beaver Meadows. This 1.5-mile (one-way) trail climbs 566 feet through an aspen forest to Bierstadt Lake, where you'll find excellent views of Longs Peak.

Starting at Bear Lake, the trail up to **Emerald Lake** ✚ offers spectacular scenery en route, past Nymph and Dream lakes. The half-mile hike to Nymph Lake is easy, climbing 225 feet; from there the trail is rated as moderate to Dream Lake (another half-mile) and then on to Emerald Lake (another .8 mile), which is 605 feet higher than the starting point at Bear Lake. Another moderate hike is the relatively uncrowded **Ouzel Falls Trail,** which leaves from Wild Basin Ranger Station and climbs about 950 feet to a picture-perfect waterfall. The distance one-way is 2.8 miles.

Among our favorite moderate hikes here is the **Mills Lake Trail** ✚✚, a 2.5-mile (one-way) hike, with a rise in elevation of about 700 feet. Starting from Glacier Gorge Junction, the trail goes to a mountain lake nestled in a valley among towering mountain peaks. This lake is an excellent spot for photographing dramatic Longs Peak, especially in late afternoon or early evening, and it's the perfect place for a picnic.

If you prefer a more strenuous adventure, you'll work hard but be amply rewarded with views of timberline lakes and alpine tundra on the **Timber Lake Trail,** in the western part of the park. It's 4.8 miles one-way, with an elevation gain of 2,060 feet. Another strenuous trail, only for experienced mountain hikers and climbers in top physical condition, is the 8-mile (one-way) **East Longs Peak Trail,** which climbs some 4,855 feet along steep ledges and through narrows to the top of Longs Peak.

Backcountry permits (required for all overnight hikes) can be obtained ($20 May–Oct, free Nov–Apr) at park headquarters and ranger stations (in summer); for information call ✆ **970/586-1242.** There is a 7-night backcountry camping limit from June to September, with no more than 3 nights at any one spot.

HORSEBACK RIDING Many of the national park's trails are open to horseback riders. Several outfitters provide guided rides inside and outside the park, including a 1-hour ride (about $30) and the very popular 2-hour rides (about $45). There are also all day rides (from $100 to $125, including lunch) plus breakfast and dinner rides and multiday pack trips. Recommended companies include SK Horses (www.cowpoke cornercorral.com), which operates **National Park Gateway Stables,** at the Fall River entrance of the national park on U.S. 34 (② **970/586-5269**), and the **Cowpoke Corner Corral,** at Glacier Lodge, 3 miles west of town, 2166 Colo. 66 (② **970/586-5890**). **Hi Country Stables** (www.colorado-horses.com) operates two stables inside the park: **Glacier Creek Stables** (② **970/586-3244**) and **Moraine Park Stables** (② **970/586-2327**).

SKIING & SNOWSHOEING During the winter, when deep snow covers roads and trails, much of the park is closed to vehicular travel (including snowmobiles). But this produces ideal conditions for those with cross-country skis or snowshoes to experience the park without the crowds. Snow conditions are usually best January through March. A popular spot for cross-country skiing and snowshoeing in the park is Bear Lake, south of the Beaver Meadows entrance. A lesser-known area of the park is **Wild Basin,** south of the park's east entrances off Colo. 7, about a mile north of the community of Allenspark. A 2-mile road, closed to motor vehicles for the last mile in winter, winds through a subalpine forest to the Wild Basin Trail, from which you follow a picturesque creek to a waterfall, a rustic bridge, and eventually another waterfall. Total distance to the second falls is 2.8 miles. Along the trail, your chances are good for spotting birds such as Clark's nutcrackers, Steller's jays, and the American dipper. On winter weekends, the Colorado Mountain Club often opens a warming hut at the Wild Basin Ranger Station. Before you set forth, stop by park headquarters for maps, information on where the snow is best, and a permit if you plan to stay out overnight. Rangers often lead guided snowshoe walks on winter weekends. Among shops that rent snowshoes is **Estes Park Mountain Shop,** 2050 Big Thompson Ave. (② **866/303-6548** or 970/586-6548; www.estesparkmountainshop.com). Daily rental costs about $6 per pair.

WILDLIFE VIEWING & BIRD-WATCHING Rocky Mountain National Park is a premier wildlife viewing area. Fall, winter, and spring are the best times, although we saw plenty of elk and squirrels, plus a few deer, a marmot, and a coyote during a recent mid-July visit. Large herds of elk and bighorn sheep can often be seen in the meadows and on mountainsides. In addition, you may spot mule deer, beavers, coyotes, and river otters. Watch for moose among the willows on the west side of the park. In the forests are lots of songbirds and small mammals; particularly plentiful are gray and Steller's jays, Clark's nutcrackers, chipmunks, and golden-mantled ground squirrels. There's a good chance of seeing bighorn sheep, marmots, pikas, and ptarmigan along Trail Ridge Road. For current wildlife viewing information, stop by one of the park's visitor centers, and check on the many interpretive programs, including bird walks. Rangers stress that it is both illegal and foolish to feed any wildlife. Not only do you risk personal injury and disease, but you also harm the animals by giving them food that is not good for them and making them dependent on humans.

CAMPING

The best place to camp for those visiting the national park is in the park itself. Although you won't have the modern conveniences of commercial campgrounds (see "Camping," in the "Estes Park & Grand Lake: Gateways to Rocky Mountain National Park" section, earlier in this chapter), you will have plenty of trees, an abundance of wildlife scurrying by your tent or RV, and a true national park experience. The park has five campgrounds with a total of almost 600 sites. Nearly half are at **Moraine Park;** another 150 are at **Glacier Basin.** Moraine Park, **Timber Creek** (98 sites), and **Longs Peak** (26 tent sites) are open year-round; Glacier Basin and **Aspenglen** (54 sites) are seasonal. Camping in summer is limited to 3 days at Longs Peak and 7 days at other campgrounds; the limit is 14 days at all the park's campgrounds in winter. Arrive early in summer if you hope to snare one of these first-come, first-served campsites. Reservations for Moraine Park and Glacier Basin are accepted from Memorial Day through early September and are usually completely booked well in advance. However, any sites not reserved—as well as sites at Timber Creek, Longs Peak, and Aspenglen—are available on a first-come, first-served basis. Make reservations with the **National Park Reservation Service** (© **800/365-2267;** http://reservations.nps.gov). Campsites cost $20 per night during the summer, $14 in the off-season when water is turned off. No showers or RV hookups are available.

3 Steamboat Springs ★★

158 miles NW of Denver, 194 miles E. of Grand Junction, 335 miles E. of Salt Lake City, Utah

One of our favorite Colorado resort towns, in part because it's a real town in addition to being a resort, Steamboat Springs fuses two very different worlds—a state-of-the-art ski village with a genuine Western ranching center. This historic town, with a population of just under 10,000, is a pleasant laid-back community where ranchers still go about their business in cowboy boots and Stetsons, seemingly unaware of the fashion statement they are making to city-slicker visitors.

At an elevation of 6,695 feet, Steamboat Springs's numerous mineral springs and abundant wild game made this a summer retreat for Utes centuries before the arrival of white settlers. Mid-19th-century trappers swore they heard the chugging sound of "a steamboat comin' round the bend" until investigation revealed a bubbling mineral spring. Prospectors never thrived here as they did elsewhere in the Rockies, though coal mining has proven profitable. Ranching and farming were the economic mainstays until tourism arrived, and agriculture remains of key importance today.

This area is perhaps best known as the birthplace of organized skiing in Colorado. Although miners, ranchers, and mail carriers used primitive skis for transportation as early as the 1880s, it wasn't until Norwegian ski-jumping and cross-country champion Carl Howelsen built Howelsen Hill ski jump here in 1914 that skiing began to be considered a recreational sport in Colorado. In 1963, Storm Mountain was developed for skiing, and Steamboat's future as a modern ski resort was ensured. The mountain was renamed Mount Werner after the 1964 avalanche death in Europe of Olympic skier Buddy Werner, a Steamboat Springs native. Today the mountain is managed by the Steamboat Ski & Resort Corporation and, more often than not, is simply called Steamboat. Howelsen Hill, owned by the city of Steamboat Springs, continues to operate as a facility for ski jumpers, as well as a fun little downtown ski area.

ESSENTIALS

GETTING THERE   By Car   The most direct route to Steamboat Springs from Denver is via I-70 west 68 miles to Silverthorne, Colo. 9 north 38 miles to Kremmling, and U.S. 40 west 52 miles to Steamboat. (*Note:* Rabbit Ears Pass, 25 miles east of Steamboat, can be treacherous in winter.) If you're traveling east on I-70, exit at Rifle, proceed 88 miles north on Colo. 13 to Craig, then take U.S. 40 east 42 miles to Steamboat. For statewide **road condition reports,** call © **303/639-1111.**

By Plane The **Yampa Valley Regional Airport,** 22 miles west of Steamboat Springs near Hayden (© **970/276-3669;** www.co.routt.co.us), is served by **United Airlines** (© **800/864-8331**) with year-round commuter service from Denver and **Continental Airlines** (© **800/525-0280**) with summer service to Houston. During the winter, direct flights to major U.S. cities are available from **United** and **Continental** (see above), plus **American Airlines** (© **800/433-7300**), **Delta Airlines** (© **800/221-1212**), and **Northwest Airlines** (© **800/225-2525**). **Delta** also offers service in the fall.

Ground transportation from Yampa Valley Regional Airport is provided by **Alpine Taxi** (© **800/343-7433** or 970/879-2800; www.alpinetaxi.com); the cost is $48 per adult, $24 per child round-trip. The company also offers shuttle service between Steamboat and Denver International Airport. Car-rental agencies at the airport include **Avis** (© **970/276-4377**) and **Hertz** (© **970/276-3304**).

VISITOR INFORMATION The **Steamboat Springs Chamber Resort Association,** 1255 S. Lincoln Ave. (P.O. Box 774408), Steamboat Springs, CO 80477 (© **970/ 879-0880;** www.steamboatchamber.com and www.steamboatsummer.com), operates a visitor center, open in summer from 8am to 5pm Monday through Friday and from 10am to 4pm Saturday.

GETTING AROUND There are really two Steamboats. The ski resort, known as Steamboat Village, is about 2 miles southeast of the historic Steamboat Springs. If you're coming from Denver, U.S. 40 approaches Steamboat from the south and parallels the Yampa River through town. Mount Werner Road, which turns east off U.S. 40, leads directly to the ski resort, centered on Mount Werner Circle and Ski Time Square. U.S. 40 is known as Lincoln Avenue through the town of Steamboat, where it is crossed by 3rd through 13th streets. **Steamboat Springs Transit** (© **970/879-3717**) provides free rides throughout the area. Buses run approximately every 20 to 30 minutes during peak hours; less frequently at other times. **Alpine Taxi** (see above) provides local taxi service.

FAST FACTS The **Yampa Valley Medical Center,** 1024 Central Park Dr. (© **970/ 879-1322;** www.yvmc.org), provides 24-hour medical service, a child-care center, and a sports medicine center. The **post office** is at 200 Lincoln Ave. For hours and other information contact the U.S. Postal Service (© **800/275-8777;** www.usps.com).

SPECIAL EVENTS Winter Carnival, early February; Steamboat Marathon, early June; Cowboy Roundup Days, Fourth of July weekend; Fall Foliage and Brew Festival, mid-September.

SKIING & OTHER WINTER ACTIVITIES

STEAMBOAT ✸✸ When devoted skiers talk about Steamboat, they practically invent adjectives to describe its incredibly light powder.

Six peaks compose the ski area: Mount Werner, Christie, Storm, Sunshine, Pioneer Ridge, and Thunderhead. Christie Peak, the lower mountain area, is ideal for beginners. Thunderhead Peak, served by a high-speed detachable quad chairlift called the Thunderhead Express and the gondola, is great for intermediate and advanced skiers and riders. Arrowhead Glade provides an advanced playground for everybody. The Morningside Park lift accesses the extreme double black diamond terrain—chutes, advanced mogul runs, powder bowls, and one-of-a-kind tree skiing, all from the top of Mount Werner. Buddy's Run, one of the Rockies' great intermediate cruisers, is located on Storm Peak. The most famous tree runs—Shadows, Closet, and Twilight—

ATTRACTIONS ●
Amaze'n Steamboat Maze **12**
Tread of Pioneers Museum **4**
Yampa River Botanic Park **11**

ACCOMMODATIONS ■
Chateau Châmonix **19**
Hotel Bristol **1**
The Lodge at Steamboat **21**
Rabbit Ears Motel **9**
Sheraton Steamboat Resort **16**
Steamboat Bed & Breakfast **7**
Steamboat Grand **17**
Thunderhead Lodge &
   Condominiums **13**
Torian Plum at Steamboat **14**
Trappeur's Crossing Resort **22**

DINING ◆
Backcountry Provisions **5**
Cugino's Pizzeria **3**
Freshies **10**
Harwigs / L'Apogee at
   911 Lincoln Avenue **2**
Hazie's **18**
La Montaña **20**
Mahogany Ridge
   Brewery & Grill **8**
Slopeside Grill (at Torian) **14**
The Tugboat Grill & Pub **15**
Winona's **6**

are on Sunshine Peak, along with more bump runs and cruising slopes. Morningside Park includes 179 acres on the back of Storm Peak, with intermediate to advanced terrain served by a triple chair.

The vertical drop here is one of the highest in Colorado: 3,668 feet from the 10,568-foot summit. Skiable terrain of 2,939 acres (61% groomable) includes 143 named runs, served by 20 lifts—an eight-passenger high-speed gondola, four high-speed quad chairs, one conventional quad, six triple chairs, six double chairs, and two surface lifts. Trails are rated 13% beginner, 56% intermediate, and 31% advanced; the longest run is Why Not, at over 3 miles.

Daily lift tickets cost $64 to $81 for adults, $47 to $63 for teenagers, $36 to $50 for children 6 to 12, $54 to $65 for seniors 65 to 69, $31 for seniors 70 and over, and free for children 5 and younger. The rates are lowest at the beginning of the season, highest during the Christmas–New Year's holidays, and a bit lower the rest of the season. Lessons and rentals are available.

Steamboat is a great mountain for snowboarders, who especially love Mavericks Superpipe, which is 50 feet wide and 650 feet long, with 15-foot walls and a 17-foot transition!

Steamboat is usually open from the third week in November through mid-April, daily from 8:30am to 4pm. For further information, contact **Steamboat Ski & Resort Corporation,** 2305 Mt. Werner Circle, Steamboat Springs, CO 80487 (© **877/237-2628** or 970/879-0740; www.steamboat.com). For daily **ski reports,** check the resort's website (listed above) or dial © **970/879-7300.**

HOWELSEN HILL ✴ In addition to Steamboat, there's Howelsen Hill (© **970/ 879-8499** or 970/879-4300; www.steamboatsprings.net), which has remained open every winter since its first day in 1915, making it the oldest ski area in continuous use in Colorado. The first accredited public-school ski classes in North America were taught on this slope, which is operated by the city of Steamboat Springs. It offers both day and night skiing and snowboarding on its 30 acres of terrain served by a double chair, a Poma lift, and a pony tow. There are 15 trails (the longest is 1 mile) and one half-pipe, and Howelsen Hill rises 440 feet to a 7,136-foot summit elevation.

Tickets are $15 for adults and $8 for children 18 and under and seniors 60 and older, and $5 for everyone for night skiing (5–8pm Tues–Thurs). It's usually open from late November through late March: Monday and Friday noon to 6pm, Tuesday and Thursday noon to 8pm, Wednesday 9am to 8pm, Saturday and Sunday 9am to 4pm.

Howelsen Hill has bred more North American skiers for international competition than any other ski resort—primarily because of its ski-jumping complex. The U.S. ski-jumping team trains each year on the 20m, 30m, 50m, 70m, and 90m jumps. Training and a variety of special events, including a Thursday night race series for adults and a Wednesday youth jumping series, are organized by the **Steamboat Springs Winter Sports Club** (© **970/879-0695;** www.sswsc.org), which was founded in 1914 and claims to be the oldest U.S. ski club west of the Mississippi River.

CROSS-COUNTRY SKIING, TELEMARK SKIING, SNOWSHOEING & ICE CLIMBING   Seasoned cross-country skiers swear by the **Steamboat Ski Touring Center** at the Sheraton Steamboat Resort (© **970/879-8180;** www.nordicski.net). Some 19 miles of groomed cross-country trails are set beside Fish Creek, near the foot of the mountain; there are also 6 miles of snowshoe trails. A full-day adult trail pass costs $15 a day; children 12 and under are $10 and seniors 65 and older are $9. Equipment rentals and lessons are available. Trails are open daily during the ski season from 9am to 4pm. To get to the center follow the signs off Mount Werner Road.

There are also cross-country trails at **Howelsen Hill** (see above). Popular cross-country ski trails in nearby national forest land include **Rabbit Ears Pass,** 25 miles east of Steamboat on U.S. 40, and **Dunkley Pass,** 25 miles south on Colo. 131. For trail maps and information, contact **Medicine Bow–Routt National Forest,** Hahns Peak/Bears Ears Ranger Station, 925 Weiss Dr., Steamboat Springs, CO 80487-9315 (© **970/879-1870;** www.fs.fed.us/r2).

Snowshoeing is gaining in popularity. There are numerous spots ideal for snowshoeing in the surrounding national forests, as well as at Steamboat Ski Touring Center (see above). Snowshoe and cross country ski rentals are available at several outlets, including **Straightline Outdoor Sports** (see "Fishing," below).

ICE DRIVING & Okay all you NASCAR fans, you think you're great drivers? (Almost) any wimp can drive on dry pavement, but how good are you when your car's sliding down a sheet of ice? This is the place to find out. America's first (and only) school of ice driving is based at the foot of Mount Werner. Bridgestone Winter Driving School teaches safe winter driving the smartest way possible—hands-on, on a 1-mile circuit packed with frozen water and snow, and guarded by high snow banks. Classes combine instruction with on-track practice, and are available for average drivers as well as professionals. Classes include a half-day introductory course ($245) and the most popular—a full-day course for $445. There's also a 2-day performance course for $1,550. The school is open daily from mid-December to mid-March, and reservations are recommended. Contact **Bridgestone Winter Driving School,** 1850 Ski Time Sq. Dr. (P.O. Box 774167), Steamboat Springs, CO 80477 (© **800/949-7543** or 970/879-6105; www.winterdrive.com).

ICE SKATING **The Howelsen Ice Arena,** 243 Howelsen Pkwy. (© **970/879-0341** or 970/879-4300; www.steamboatsprings.net), is an enclosed Olympic-size ice arena open year-round that has open skating hours; rents skates; offers lessons in hockey and figure skating; organizes figure-skating, ice-hockey and broom-ball competitions; and hosts birthday parties. Admission is $6 adults, $5 youths 6 to 18, $3 for seniors 50 and older, and free for children 5 and younger. Skate rentals are $3 ($2 for seniors 50 and older), and skate sharpening costs $5. Call for the rink schedule.

SNOWMOBILING Snowmobilers consider the **Continental Divide Trail,** running over 50 miles from Buffalo Pass north of Steamboat to Gore Pass, west of Kremmling, to be one of the finest maintained trails in the Rockies, with some of the most spectacular scenery you'll see anywhere. For information, check with **Medicine Bow–Routt National Forest** (see "**Cross-Country Skiing, Telemark Skiing, Snowshoeing & Ice Climbing**" above).

Among those offering guided snowmobile tours is **High Mountain Tours,** P.O. Box 749, Clark, CO 80428 (© **877/879-6500** or 970/879-6500; www.stmbtsnow mobiletours.com). The cost is $85 for one person plus $50 for a passenger for a 2-hour ride, $145 for one person and $65 for a passenger for a half-day ride with lunch, $215 for one person plus $165 passenger for a full-day tour with lunch. Dinner rides and overnight trips are also offered.

WARM-WEATHER & YEAR-ROUND ACTIVITIES

Most outdoor recreation pursuits are enjoyed in 1.1-million-acre **Routt National Forest,** which virtually surrounds Steamboat Springs and offers opportunities for camping, hiking, backpacking, mountain biking, horseback riding, fishing, and hunting. For trail maps and information, contact **Medicine Bow–Routt National Forest,** Hahns Peak/Bears Ears Ranger Station, 925 Weiss Dr., Steamboat Springs, CO 80477 (© **970/879-1870;** www.fs.fed.us/r2).

Two wilderness areas in the forest are easily reached from Steamboat. Immediately north of town is the **Mount Zirkel Wilderness Area,** a region of rugged peaks approached through 10,800-foot Buffalo Pass, on Forest Road 60 off Strawberry Park Road via Seventh Street. Southwest of Stillwater Reservoir, some 40 miles south of Steamboat via Colo. 131 through Yampa, is the **Flat Tops Wilderness Area,** with picturesque alpine meadows and sheer volcanic cliffs. No motorized vehicles or mountain bikes are allowed in wilderness areas, although horses and dogs are permitted (dogs must be leashed in some areas).

Howelsen Hill (© **970/879-8499** or 970/879-4300; www.steamboatsprings.net) offers several warm-weather activities. You'll find a BMX and skateboard park, tennis, softball, volleyball, horseback riding, and mountain biking, plus the rodeo grounds (see below). In addition, an alpine slide, which operates daily from 10am until dusk during the summer, has a 2,400-foot dual track down the face of Howelsen Hill. For current rates and other information, contact the **Steamboat Springs Winter Sports Club** (© **970/879-0695;** www.sswsc.org).

The **Steamboat Ski Resort** doesn't go into hibernation after the snow melts, it just changes its focus, offering hiking, mountain biking, gondola rides, disc golf, and a multitude of other activities, including many that are great for kids. For information check with **Steamboat Ski & Resort Corporation** (see "Skiing & Other Winter Activities," above).

Some 28 miles north of Steamboat Springs on Routt C.R. 129 is **Steamboat Lake State Park** (© **970/879-3922;** www.parks.state.co.us), encompassing 1,053-acre Steamboat Lake. At an elevation of 8,000 feet, activities include summer camping (198 campsites with fees of $12–$18 plus the $5 park entrance fee; camping reservations are available by calling © **800/678-2267** or through the state park website), picnicking, fishing, hunting, boating, swimming, canoeing, horseback riding, and nature walks. There's an attractive sandy beach (the sand was trucked in) and three boat-launching ramps. In winter, the park offers ice fishing, cross-country skiing, snowmobiling, and snowshoeing. Day-use fee is $5 per vehicle.

Steamboat Lake Marina (© **970/879-7019;** www.steamboatlakemarina.com), open year-round, has a small store with a deli—be sure to sample the especially good homemade fudge—plus groceries, fishing supplies, equipment rentals, boat fuel, and boat rentals. Canoes, kayaks, and paddleboats rent for $15 per hour, small fishing boats are $40 for 2 hours; 20-foot pontoon boats cost $100 for 2 hours; and 24-foot pontoon boats cost $140 for 2 hours. Pontoon boats are either outfitted for fishing or have barbecue grills. (Yes, you can fish from a boat with a grill—then you've got a grill for cooking your catch!) Rates for powerboats include fuel. Boat reservations are strongly recommended.

The marina has 10 cabins that have coffeemakers, small refrigerators, and a shared bathhouse. The nightly rate is $60 for two, and $5 for each additional person or pet.

Stagecoach State Park (© **970/736-2436;** www.parks.state.co.us), south of Steamboat Springs, offers camping, picnicking, fishing, boating, and other watersports. From Steamboat Springs, head 3 miles south on U.S. 40 to Colo. 131, turn southwest (right) and go about 6 miles to Routt C.R. 14, turn south (left) about 5 miles to the park entrance. The main attraction here is a 780-acre reservoir, which is set among rolling hills, interspersed with forests and grasslands. The reservoir is fairly evenly divided for water-skiing and wakeless boating. The park has 92 campsites in four campgrounds, and two campgrounds have electric hookups. Camping fees are $12 to $18, plus the day-use fee of $5 per vehicle that everyone going to the park must pay. Camping reservations are available by calling © **800/678-2267** or through the state park website (above). The elevation at the park is 7,250 feet.

Stagecoach Marina (© **970/736-8342**), usually open from mid-May through mid-September, has a store with fishing and camping supplies, plus boat fuel and boat rentals. Rates are highest Friday through Sunday, when canoes rent for $15 per hour, kayaks and paddleboats cost $13 an hour, small fishing boats are $35 for 2 hours, 20-foot pontoon boats are $83 for 2 hours, and 24-foot pontoon boats cost $100 for

2 hours. There are 30% discounts Monday through Thursday, and also discounts for longer time periods. Reservations are recommended.

The Steamboat Springs Chamber Resort Association produces a **trails map,** available at the information center on Lincoln Avenue, showing which trails are open to what sport: biking, horseback riding, hiking, 4WD, or ATVs. On the reverse side of the map are descriptions of several trails in the area.

ATV TOURS For a quick, fun, and relatively easy way to see this area's beautiful backcountry, consider a guided trip on an all-terrain vehicle. **Steamboat Lake Outfitters,** P.O. Box 749, Clark, CO 80428 (© **800/342-1889** or 970/879-4404; www.steamboatoutfitters.com), leads rides along old mining roads into the mountains, offering splendid views of the Continental Divide and Mount Zirkel Wilderness Area. Rates for a 2-hour ride are $75 for a one-person ATV or $100 for a two-person machine, and half-day, full-day, and overnight rides are also offered.

BIKING & MOUNTAIN BIKING The 5-mile, dual-surface **Yampa River Trail** connects downtown Steamboat Springs with Steamboat Village, and links area parks and national forest trails. The **Mount Werner Trail** links the river to the ski area, which has numerous slopes open to mountain bikers in summer. **Spring Creek Trail** climbs from Yampa River Park into Routt National Forest. Touring enthusiasts can try their road bikes on the 110-mile loop over Rabbit Ears and Gore passes, rated one of the 10 most scenic rides in America by *Bicycling* magazine. Another option, especially for those of us who don't believe that sweating our way up the side of a mountain is fun, is to take the Silver Bullet Gondola (see "Gondola Rides," below) into the mountains and then ride the more than 40 upper mountain trails. Mountain bike rentals are available at the top of the gondola (© **970/871-5252**), with $55 rates for 3 hours for an adult bike and slightly less for kids' bikes. Diggler Mountain Scooters are also available for rent at the same rates. There is also a required mountain bike ticket (beyond the gondola ticket) that is $8 a day.

Stop at **Sore Saddle Cyclery** 🕷🕷, 1136 S. Yampa St. (© **970/879-1675**), for information on the best local trails (maps are on display), accessories, repairs, and rentals. Rentals are also available from **SportStalker,** in Gondola Square at 2305 Mt. Werner Rd. (© **970/879-0371**). Rentals of basic mountain bikes cost $20 to $25 for a half-day and $25 to $35 for a full day.

CATTLE DRIVES 🕷🕷 The **Saddleback Ranch** 🕷, on C.R. 179 about 14 miles southwest of Steamboat Springs (© **970/879-3711;** www.saddlebackranch.net), is a working cattle ranch—not some Hollywood-style dude ranch—that offers a genuine Old West experience. The ranch has some 1,500 head of cattle on its 7,200 acres, and participants join working cowboys in moving cattle from pasture to pasture and performing other ranching tasks that are still done the old-fashioned way. Horses, tack, slickers, and snacks are provided, and cost for a half-day on the trail is $70 for those 8 and older. Children under 8 are not permitted on the rides. The cattle drives are held from June through mid-September.

FISHING The Steamboat Springs area and particularly the Yampa River has some of the best trout fishing in the state. There are nearly 150 lakes and reservoirs and almost 600 miles of streams in Routt County, which surrounds Steamboat Springs. Trout—rainbow, brown, brook, and cutthroat—are prolific, and the Yampa River and Stagecoach Reservoir are known for northern pike as well. Especially popular is the 5-mile stretch of the Yampa in downtown Steamboat Springs that is designated a catch-and-release trout stream; the Yampa's northern pike, whitefish, and small mouth black crappy do not fall under the catch-and-release limitations.

Contact **Straightline Outdoor Sports,** 744 Lincoln Ave. (✆ **800/354-5463** or 970/879-7568; www.straightlinesports.com), for information, licenses, and either rental or purchase of equipment. Straightline also offers guide services (call for details).

GOLF   The golf season here usually runs May through October, or as long as the snow isn't falling. The 18-hole municipal **Haymaker Golf Course,** at the intersection of U.S. 40 and Colo. 131, east of Steamboat Springs (✆ **970/870-1846;** www.hay makergolf.com), is a challenging links-style course with only 110 of its 233 acres used for fairways and greens. It conforms to the open-space philosophy of the Steamboat community, with native grasses, wetlands, and contours mimicking the surrounding valley and mountains. The greens fee during summer is $79 to $89 for 18 holes, and $63 at the beginning and end of the golfing season. Preferred tee times are available with lodging reservations at participating properties through Steamboat Central Reservations (✆ **800/922-2722**).

The course at the **Sheraton Steamboat Resort,** 2200 Village Inn Court (✆ **970/ 879-2220;** www.sheratonsteamboatgolf.com), designed by Robert Trent Jones, Jr., in 1972, is considered one of the Rockies' finest. The 18-hole, 6,906-yard course offers spectacular scenery and challenging fairways. Greens fees, including carts, are $75 to $100 for Sheraton guests, $95 to $140 for the public. The **Steamboat Golf Club,** 6 miles west of downtown Steamboat Springs along U.S. 40 (✆ **970/879-4295;** www.steamboatgolfclub.com), is a picturesque 9-hole course along the Yampa River, with greens fees of $32 for 9 holes and $47 for 18 holes.

GONDOLA RIDES   Summer visitors don't have to work hard to get up into the mountains above Steamboat—simply hop on the Silver Bullet Gondola (✆ **877/ 237-2628** or 970/879-0740; www.steamboat.com), which operates weekends in mid-June and mid-September, and daily from late June through early September. Prices for all-day passes are as follows: adults $18, seniors 65 and older $14, children 6 to 12 $8 (or $20 for one adult and one child 6–12), teens 13 to 17 $13 (or $25 for one adult and one teen 13–17), free for children 5 and younger. From the top of the gondola, hiking and mountain-biking trails can be accessed (see "Biking & Mountain Biking," above).

HIKING, BACKPACKING & MOUNTAINEERING   There are numerous trails in the **Mount Zirkel Wilderness Area,** immediately north of Steamboat, and the **Flat Tops Wilderness Area,** 48 miles southwest. An especially scenic 4-hour hike in the Flat Tops area takes you from Stillwater Reservoir to the Devil's Causeway, with unforgettable views. Contact the U.S. Forest Service (p. 258) for information. There are also hiking trails at Steamboat Ski Area, which are easily reached on the Silver Bullet Gondola (see "Gondola Rides," above).

HORSEBACK RIDING   Located behind the rodeo grounds in town (follow Fifth St. south from Lincoln Ave.) is **Sombrero Ranches** (✆ **970/879-2306;** www.sombrero. com), which offers 1- and 2-hour rides, breakfast rides, and special supervised rides for young children. Prices are $30 for an hour, $40 to $45 for the 2-hour and breakfast rides, and $10 for a half-hour lead-horse ride for kids.

Steamboat Lake Outfitters (see "ATV Tours," above) leads guided horseback tours at Steamboat Lake State Park, ranging from 1- and 2-hour rides ($35 and $55 per person, respectively) to half- and full-day rides, with lunch, for $105 and $195 per person, respectively. This company also offers breakfast and dinner rides plus pack trips and horseback fishing trips into nearby wilderness areas (call for details), and rents rooms and cabins (see "Where to Stay," below).

Dinner rides are offered during the summer by **Saddleback Ranch** (see "Cattle Drives," above), with a choice of New York strip steak, pork tenderloin, salmon, or barbecued chicken, plus all the extras. There's a 35-minute ride to the dinner site (transportation by hay wagon is also available), and the cost is $65 for adults and $45 for kids 6 to 16.

HOT SPRINGS   More than 150 mineral springs are located in and around the Steamboat Springs area. Several are located in city parks. Their healing and restorative qualities were recognized for centuries by Utes, and James Crawford, the area's first white settler, regularly bathed in Heart Spring and helped build the first log bathhouse over it in 1884.

Today, Heart Spring is part of the **Steamboat Springs Health & Recreation complex,** 136 Lincoln Ave. (℃ **970/879-1828;** www.sshra.org), in downtown Steamboat Springs. In addition to the man-made pools into which the spring's waters flow, there's a lap pool, water slide, spa, whirlpool, fitness center, tennis courts, and massage therapy. Pool admission is $8.50 for adults, $5 for youths 13 to 17, and $3.50 for children under 13 and seniors 62 and over. Suit and towel rentals are available. The complex is open year-round, Monday through Friday from 5:30am to 10pm, Saturday 7am to 9pm, and Sunday 8am to 9pm. The slide is open from noon to 6pm in summer and from 4 to 8pm in winter, and, in addition to the pool admission, costs $3 for five rides or $5 for 10 rides.

The **Strawberry Park Hot Springs** ⟨, 44200 C.R. 36 (℃ **970/879-0342;** www. strawberryhotsprings.com), are 7 miles north of downtown (from Seventh St., follow the signs) up a rugged, rocky road navigable by regular cars in summer, but requiring four-wheel-drive in winter, and it's strongly recommended to ride the shuttle. (In summer, you can drive to the Hot Springs trailhead off of C.R. 129 and hike three miles to the park.) The trip may be difficult, but it's a wonderful experience to spend a moonlit evening in a sandy-bottomed, rock-lined soaking pool, kept between 101° and 106°F (38°C–41°C), with snow piled high around you. The hot springs are open Sunday through Thursday from 10am to 10:30pm (no entry after 9:30pm except to shuttles); Friday and Saturday 10am to midnight (no entry after 10:30pm except to shuttles). Admission costs $10 adults, $5 youths 13 to 17, and $3 children 3 to 12. After dark, children under 18 are not permitted and clothing is optional. Massages are available, and rustic cabins ($55 a night) and tent sites ($50 a night) can be rented year-round, as well as a nifty caboose-turned-kitchenette ($105 a night). Overnighters get the pool all to themselves after-hours. There's a picnic area but no restaurant. Pets are not permitted.

RODEO   The **Steamboat Springs PRCA Summer ProRodeo Series** (℃ **970/879-0880;** www.steamboatrodeo.com) takes place each year from mid-June through late August at the Romick Rodeo Arena in Howelsen Park, at the corner of Fifth Street and Howelsen Parkway. Professional rodeo cowboys and cowgirls (or should that be cowpersons?) compete in bull riding, bareback and saddle bronc riding, steer wrestling, calf roping, team roping, and barrel racing. In the Calf Scramble, children are invited to try to pluck a ribbon from the tail of a calf. The rodeo takes place

Friday and Saturday nights starting at 7:30pm. Admission costs $13 for adults, $7 for youths 7 to 15, and is free for children 6 and younger.

SOME GREAT OUTDOOR AREAS

Fish Creek Falls   Just 4 miles from downtown Steamboat in Routt National Forest, a footpath leads to a historic bridge at the base of this breathtaking 283-foot waterfall. There's also an overlook with a short .1-mile trail and ramp designed for those with disabilities, as well as a picnic area and hiking trails. Allow 1 to 2 hours.

Fish Creek Falls Rd. Information: Hahns Peak/Bears Ears Ranger Station, 925 Weiss Dr., Steamboat Springs, CO 80477. ✆ 970/879-1870. www.fs.fed.us/r2. Free admission. Turn right off Lincoln Ave. onto 3rd St., go 1 block, and turn right again onto Fish Creek Falls Rd. Daily 24 hr.

Yampa River Botanic Park 🍂🍂 *Finds*   For a pleasant and relaxing stroll among lovely gardens, stop at this botanic park along the Yampa River, between the ski mountain and downtown. Several picturesque ponds are set among low rolling hills, surrounded by a wide variety of flowering and nonflowering plants and trees of the Yampa River Basin plus many nonnative plants from many areas. A brochure describes the planted areas, with a map to help you navigate the many paths. There are wetlands on each side of the park, and the Yampa River Core trail connects to the park on its west side. The park is not wheelchair accessible, but tours for people with disabilities are offered by appointment. Allow at least an hour.

From late June through August, the Strings in the Mountains Music Festival (see "Musical Mountains," below) presents free 1-hour concerts at the park each Thursday at 12:15pm. Dogs and bikes are not permitted in the park; bike racks and hitching posts for dogs are located at the park entrances.

1000 Pamela Lane (P.O. Box 776269, Steamboat Springs, CO 80477). ✆ 970/879-4300. www.steamboatsprings.net. Free admission, donations welcome. Dawn–dusk spring–Oct (or the first heavy snow). From U.S. 40, turn west toward the river on Trafalgar Dr. (the traffic light north of the Chamber Resort office light), then left on Pamela Lane, and go to the parking lot at the far end.

MORE TO SEE & DO

Amaze'n Steamboat Maze   This intriguing puzzle lets you test your skills, or perhaps luck, in finding your way through a confusing maze. A free observation deck gives a bird's-eye view of the maze, allowing your quicker companions to point and laugh as you stumble into one dead end after another. In addition to the human maze, there is an 18-hole miniature golf course that uses items from Colorado's history, from a mine shaft to a Conestoga wagon, and a bumper car ride. Allow at least 1 hour.

1255 U.S. 40 (behind the chamber office.) ✆ 970/870-8682. www.amazenmazes.com. Admission to the maze $5 adults, $4 children 5–12; golf $7 adults, $6 children; for both maze and golf $10 adults, $9 children; free for children under 5. Additional maze runs $2; additional rounds of golf $3. Memorial Day weekend to mid-Sept daily 10am–9pm; weekends only thereafter, call for hours.

Tread of Pioneers Museum 🍂   This excellent museum combines two beautifully restored Victorian homes and a separate gallery. Exhibits focus on the area's pioneer ranch life, including an extensive firearm collection and a Southwest American Indian collection. A special feature is the 1908 Queen Anne–style Victorian home, furnished with pioneer and turn-of-the-20th-century artifacts. Two permanent displays are particularly interesting: "History of Skiing" (tracing the evolution of skiing from its roots as essential winter transportation to the multimillion-dollar recreational sport of today) and "History of Steamboat Springs" (showing the growth and changes in the

Moments **Musical Mountains**

Summer is a musically magical time in Steamboat Springs. **Strings in the Mountains Music Festival** 🌟🌟🌟 offers an incredible array of musical programs, from classical to jazz, lectures to cabarets, with performances indoors and out. The music directors—husband-and-wife team Katherine Collier, pianist, and Yizhak Schotten, violist—are adept at bringing together fine musicians and crafting superb programs, in addition to being excellent musicians themselves.

If **chamber music** is your choice—as it is ours—don't miss the Wednesday and Saturday evening concerts. The night we were there, the evening began with a gentle Chopin nocturne, progressed to a moving Schumann piano quartet, and finished off with a stupendous performance of Brahms' rich and soaring String Sextet in G, Op. 36. Instead of extensive program notes, nuggets of information about the music and/or composer are presented before each piece by commentators, typically music professors at universities in Colorado.

Should **jazz, country, bluegrass, or pops** be the music that thrills your soul, check the schedule for Friday and Tuesday nights. The 2006 season included performances by folk rocker Rodney Crowell, the folk/pop singing group Trout Fishing in America, and Western swing band Asleep at the Wheel.

Don't forget to pack your lunch for Strings' **"Music on the Green"** at the new **Music Festival Park,** 900 Strings Rd., on 3 acres at the base of Mount Werner, adjacent to the Village at Steamboat—an inspiring location, and the mountains a stirring backdrop—for a concert each Thursday at 12:15pm. The Hyperion Quartet delighted us with a fascinating comparison of two movements from Debussy's Quartet in G Minor, Op. 10 to two from Ravel's Quartet in F Major. You needn't worry about the sound dissipating in the great outdoors: It simply shimmered and filled the clear mountain air. It's a lovely way to spend your lunchtime—and many locals agree, so get there early to snag one of the free umbrellas to keep the scorching sun off your head. There a cafe (5 to 9pm on Wed, Fri, and Sat) that serves light fare and gourmet dinner specials.

What does all this cost, you ask? Surprisingly little for the quality and choices offered, including several free programs. Family concerts Tuesday or Thursday evenings, and youth concerts Tuesday morning, cost $5 to $12 for adults and $1 for those 18 and under; the Wednesday Pre-Concert Talks are free, as are the Thursday Music on the Green lunchtime programs. Chamber music performances, Wednesday and Saturday evenings, cost $20 to $40; the Tuesday and Friday evening programs, which offer a variety of music, have widely varying prices; and there are several special events scattered throughout the summer and during the Christmas season (call for details). Strings also presents musical events at other times of the year, including a series of Christmas holiday concerts and a Winter Concert Series.

For additional information and a complete schedule, contact **Strings in the Mountains,** P.O. Box 774627, Steamboat Springs, CO 80477 (© 970/ 879-5056; www.stringsinthemountains.com).

county from the time of the Ute Indians through the agricultural and tourism growth of the last few decades). The museum also offers guided tours, kids' activities, and an excellent gift shop. Allow about 1½ hours.

800 Oak St. ℂ 970/879-2214. Admission $5 adults, $4 seniors 62 and older, $1 children under 12. May–Nov Tues–Sat 10am–5pm; Oct–Apr Tues–Sat 11am–5pm.

SHOPPING

Lincoln Avenue, between Fifth and Ninth streets, is where most of the more interesting shops and galleries are located. Art lovers will enjoy **Artisans' Market of Steamboat,** 626 Lincoln Ave. (ℂ 970/879-7512; www.rockymountainfun.com/artisans.html), a nonprofit cooperative of local artists; and **Steamboat Art Company,** 903 Lincoln Ave. (ℂ 800/553-7853 or 970/879-3383; www.steamboat-art.com), which offers an eclectic selection of limited-edition prints and other art, plus jewelry and crafts in wood, glass, and pottery. **The Homesteader** 𝕽𝕽, 821 Lincoln Ave. (ℂ 800/321-4702 or 970/879-5880; www.thehomesteader.net), is a delightful kitchen shop with all manner of kitchen gadgets; salsa, chutney, and other Colorado-made food items; plus gourmet coffee beans and an espresso bar.

If you forgot to pack your cowboy hat, there's a tremendous selection of Stetsons, plus just about everything else a Westerner wears, at **F.M. Light & Sons,** 830 Lincoln Ave. (ℂ 970/879-1822; www.fmlight.com), which has been in business since 1905. For books, magazines, card, and gifts—not to mention a coffeehouse and cafe that transforms into a wine bar at night—head to **Off the Beaten Path,** 56 7th St. (ℂ 970/879-6830).

Lyon's Corner Drug & Soda Fountain 𝕽, at the corner of Ninth and Lincoln (ℂ 970/879-1114), isn't just a drugstore and card shop (although it does have an excellent selection of greeting cards); it also has a great old Wurlitzer jukebox spinning golden oldies (no charge!), and an old-time soda fountain where you can get real malts, ice-cream sodas, egg creams, phosphates, sundaes, a variety of gelato flavors, and fresh-squeezed lemonade.

WHERE TO STAY

As at all Colorado ski resorts, rates get progressively higher the closer you get to the slopes. You'll pay the highest rates during the Christmas holiday season (mid-Dec to New Year's Day). Next highest are the rates charged during February and March. Value season is usually January, and the low season runs from Thanksgiving to mid-December and from April until the ski areas close. Rates are normally much lower during the summer, from Memorial Day to mid-October. *Note:* Because vacancy rates are so high during shoulder seasons—April to May and October to November—many accommodations close at these times.

Steamboat Central Reservations (ℂ 877/237-2628 or 970/879-0740; www.steamboat.com) can book your lodging and make virtually all of your travel arrangements. Be sure to ask about special packages and programs. If you're staying in a condo or other unit with kitchen facilities, Steamboat Central Reservations can arrange for **Fridge Fillers** to stock your kitchen the day of your arrival. But it's certainly not a free service: Cost is $40 plus 10% of the total grocery bill.

Resort Quest Steamboat, 1855 Ski Time Sq. Dr., Steamboat Springs, CO 80487 (ℂ 800/228-2458 or 970/879-8811; www.resortqueststeamboat.com), manages over 200 rental units spread among 9 properties. There are both condos and townhomes, with accommodations for 4 to 12 persons; several of the properties are described below.

Steamboat Resorts, 1847 Ski Time Sq. Dr., P.O. Box 772995, Steamboat Springs, CO 80477 (© **800/525-5502** or 970/879-8000; www.steamboatresorts.com), manages 20 properties, offering a variety of possibilities, from small lodge rooms for two to condos that will accommodate up to 10. Several of the properties are described below.

Room tax adds about 9½% to lodging bills, and resort fees at properties at Steamboat Village add another 7½%.

In addition to the properties discussed below, **Steamboat Lake Outfitters,** P.O. Box 749, Clark, CO 80428 (© **800/342-1889** or 970/879-4404; www.steamboat outfitters.com), rents bunkhouse rooms and cabins in the mountains above Steamboat Lake State Park. Although rustic in decor, they have comfortable beds, kitchenettes, and indoor bathrooms, with rates for two starting at $75 per night in the bunkhouse rooms and $115 to $150 per night in the cabins. Call for details.

VERY EXPENSIVE

Château Chamonix 🏨🏨   Made up of three condominium buildings just a few steps from the base of the Silver Bullet Gondola, this is one of the most convenient accommodations at Steamboat Village. Most units have two or three bedrooms—often with two king beds and two twins, with private decks, fireplaces, a whirlpool tub in the master bathroom, wet bars, and attractive wood furnishings. Each unit includes a washer and dryer plus a free high-speed Internet connection. During ski season a free shuttle service into town is offered.

2340 Apres Ski Way, Steamboat Springs, CO 80487. © **800/833-9877** or 970/879-7511. Fax 970/879-9321. www.chateau-chamonix.com. 48 units. 2-bedroom $185–$260 summer, $280–$1,150 winter; 3-bedroom $235–$325 summer, $375–$1,500 winter; 4-bedroom $300–$370 summer, $500–$1,650 winter. Holiday rates higher; discounts possible between seasons. AE, MC, V. Covered parking. **Amenities:** Outdoor heated pool; exercise room; whirlpool; 2 hot tubs; sauna. *In room:* Cable TV/VCR, kitchen.

Steamboat Grand 🏨   Built in 2001, this is Steamboat's big, bold, flagship property, a full-service hotel with plenty of bells and whistles. With upscale, understated interiors, the room configurations are set up to adjoin or not adjoin into one- to three-bedroom suites, as well as a few penthouse suites ranging from three to five bedrooms. Decorated with earth tones and a masculine sensibility, the rooms are some of the nicest and newest on the mountain. The list of amenities and facilities is long and comprehensive. Of special note are the two hot tubs: With maximum capacities of 35 and 45 people, they are said to be the largest in the entire state.

2300 Mt. Werner Cir., Steamboat Springs, CO 80847 © **877/277-1067** or 970/871-5537. Fax 970/871-5559. 327 units. 1- to 3-bedroom units $174–$429 summer and early and late ski season, $285–$930 peak ski season, $115–$420 fall and spring. AE, DISC, MC, V. Underground parking. **Amenities:** 3 restaurants (American); 2 lounges; outdoor heated pool; exercise room; 2 outdoor hot tubs; sauna; children's programs; game room; concierge; ski shuttle; business center; shopping arcade; salon; room service; babysitting. *In room:* A/C, cable TV/DVD, kitchen, coffeemaker, hair dryer, iron, safe, Wi-Fi network.

Torian Plum at Steamboat 🏨🏨   These slope-side ski-in/ski-out condominiums have handsome light-wood furnishings, a tile kitchen complete with microwave and dishwasher, washer/dryer, gas fireplace, private balcony, ski locker, and two phone lines with voice mail and a high-speed Internet connection. The Creekside Tower offers especially opulent master suites and handsome stone fireplaces. The property is scrupulously well maintained and attractive. Numerous free videos and a computer station are available.

1855 Ski Time Sq. Dr. (Resort Quest Steamboat, see above). © **866/634-9618** or 970/879-8811. Fax 970/879-8485. 81 units. 1- to 5-bedroom units $155–$315 summer, $220–$1,095 early and late ski season, $460–$1,700 regular ski season, $725–$2,500 holiday season. AE, DISC, MC, V. Underground parking. **Amenities:** Outdoor heated pool; exercise room; 6 hot tubs (4 outdoor, 2 indoor); sauna; concierge; ski shuttle. *In room:* Cable TV/VCR/DVD, kitchen, Wi-Fi network.

EXPENSIVE

Sheraton Steamboat Resort 🐾🐾　Steamboat Springs's premier hotel is located in the heart of Ski Time Square, at the foot of the Silver Bullet Gondola. The Sheraton opens directly onto the ski slopes, and every room has a view of the mountain, valley, or slopes. There's a great cross-country ski course (p. 264); and in summer, avid golfers enjoy its golf club (p. 268), one of the finest in the Rockies. Most units have one king or two queen beds, humidifiers, and a private balcony. You'll find outdoor hot tubs on a rooftop spa deck, retail shopping space, plus a 23-unit luxury suite tower. Sevens Fine Dining offers magnificent views of the mountain and the Headwall chairlift, along with meals three times a day. The hotel also offers après ski at the casual Western 3 Saddles Bar & Grill and massages and other treatments at the day spa, Sol.

2200 Village Inn Court, Steamboat Springs, CO 80477. 🕐 **800/848-8878** or 970/879-2220. Fax 970/879-7686. www.sheraton.com/steamboat. 315 units. Late May to mid-Oct $109–$169; winter low-season $129–$199; value season $249–$279; regular season $269–$299; holiday $359–$399. AE, DC, MC, V. Underground parking. Closed 1 month in spring and fall. **Amenities:** 3 restaurants; bar; outdoor heated pool; golf club (18-hole); health club; spa; 7 hot tubs; steam room; children's programs; game room; concierge (8am–8pm); shopping arcade; room service (7am–10pm); massage; valet and coin-op laundry service. *In room:* A/C, cable TV/VCR, fridge, coffeemaker.

MODERATE

Hotel Bristol 🐾🐾　Among our top choices in Steamboat Springs, the Hotel Bristol offers lodging with character. Rooms are small (150 sq. ft.), in keeping with the heritage of this historic hotel, built in the 1940s. In fact, the reason we like this place so much is the historic ambience—Zane Grey may not have stayed here, but if he had he would have felt right at home. The standard rooms are what we consider sophisticated Old West, refined but not fancy, with solid dark-wood furnishings, lots of brass, Pendleton wool blankets, and reproduction 1940s-style phones. Rooms have one queen-size bed or two twins, and a bathroom with shower only (no tub). The former caretaker's unit has been converted into two suites with sleeper sofas in the living rooms and TVs with DVD players. The family units, which accommodate four people, are two standard rooms, each with its own toilet and sink, and a shared tub/shower combo. This is an especially quiet downtown lodging choice, in large part because it was built of concrete for fire prevention, a major concern in the 1940s. An on-site restaurant serves dinner daily. High-speed wireless Internet access is available throughout the property.

917 Lincoln Ave. (P.O. Box 774927), Steamboat Springs, CO 80477. 🕐 **800/851-0872** or 970/879-3083. Fax 970/879-8645. 18 units. Late May to mid-Sept $89–$119 double, $139–$159 family unit; mid-Sept to mid-Nov $69 double, $99 family unit; mid-Nov to mid-Apr $89–$129 double, $119–$189 family unit; rates higher Christmas through New Year's. AE, DC, DISC, MC, V. Closed mid-Apr to late May. **Amenities:** Restaurant (Italian); 6-person indoor whirlpool. *In room:* A/C, cable TV.

The Lodge at Steamboat 🐾　These well-maintained condominiums are just 200 yards from the Silver Bullet Gondola, and there's a free shuttle to take you to the mountain village, downtown, or shopping. The individually owned and decorated units have balconies; and upper-floor units have a cathedral ceiling with clerestory windows. A typical average-size unit is simply but pleasantly decorated in what might be termed mountain Western style, and includes an attractive brick fireplace, a sunny dining area, a counter island with high-stool seating between the kitchen and living area, a queen bed in the master bedroom, and twin beds in the second bedroom. Each unit boasts a fireplace and one bathroom per bedroom.

2700 Village Dr. (Steamboat Resorts, see above). ⓒ 800/525-5502 or 970/879-8000. Fax 970/870-8061. 120 units. 1–3 bedrooms winter $105–$650; summer $175–$270. AE, MC, V. **Amenities:** Outdoor heated pool; 2 tennis courts; 5 hot tubs (1 indoor, 4 outdoor); sauna; massage; babysitting; coin-op laundry; free shuttle. *In room:* Cable TV/VCR (video rentals available), kitchen, Wi-Fi network.

Thunderhead Lodge & Condominiums   Known affectionately as "T-head," this ski-in/ski-out property offers a variety of accommodations, from lodge and hotel rooms to one- and two-bedroom condos. Condo units have either full kitchens or kitchenettes, and most have gas fireplaces, but lodge and hotel rooms have neither. Some units have a sleeping loft, all except lodge rooms have balconies, and most boast great views of the ski mountain or valley. Hotel rooms have louvered doors separating the bedroom from the sitting area. The lodge rooms are somewhat small, with a queen bed, a love seat, and no desk. The condos are generally spacious—even the studios, which have a queen bed and queen sofa sleeper. The Thunderhead is located in the heart of the mountain village, close to shopping and dining, and there's a sun deck, free coffee in the lobby, and a complimentary shuttle to grocery stores and downtown.

1965 Ski Time Sq. (Steamboat Resorts, see above). ⓒ 800/525-5502 or 970/879-8000. Fax 970/870-8061. 125 units. Summer $85–$105 double, $130–$235 condo; winter $85–$240 double, $105–$715 condo. AE, MC, V. **Amenities:** Restaurant; lounge; outdoor heated pool; 3 indoor hot tubs; sauna; concierge; massage; babysitting; coin-op laundry; free shuttle. *In room:* Cable TV, kitchen (in condos only), Wi-Fi network.

Trappeur's Crossing Resort *Value*   This is the least expensive of the Resort Quest Steamboat properties, and given its location two blocks from the slopes and its neat, well-maintained condo units, we consider Trappeur's Crossing an especially good value. There are actually three separate properties here, and as with most condominiums, these are individually owned and decorated; all have gas fireplaces, private balconies, washers and dryers, and kitchens. Many units also have whirlpool tubs.

2900 Village Dr. and Medicine Springs Rd. (Resort Quest Steamboat, see above). ⓒ 866/634-9618 or 970/879-8811. Fax 970/879-8485. 102 units. 1- to 4-bedroom units $165–$380 summer; $175–$400 early and late ski season; $237–$640 regular ski season; $545–$1,200 holiday season. AE, DISC, MC, V. **Amenities:** Indoor-outdoor pool; tennis courts (2, summer only); fitness center; hot tubs (indoor, outdoor); sauna; concierge; ski shuttle. *In room:* Cable TV/VCR/DVD, kitchen, iron/ironing board, Wi-Fi network.

INEXPENSIVE
Rabbit Ears Motel 🐇   Owned and operated by the Koehler family since 1970, this comfortable, homey place features a vintage sign with the mug of a grinning bunny, a designated historic landmark that's served as Steamboat's welcome mat for more than a half-century. The motel's original 10 rooms (and the sign) were built in 1952, with additional units added through 1991, some of which overlook the Yampa River. Completely remodeled in the mid-1990s, all rooms are clean and comfortable. Even the smallest rooms (which, at 224 sq. ft., are definitely tiny) have attractive cherry furnishings. The larger rooms are a more-than-comfortable 425 square feet. The motel is conveniently located on the east end of the downtown shopping district, with the river behind, Yampa River Park next door, and the hot springs pool across the street (discount passes are available), and on the local free shuttle bus route. All rooms have a microwave and refrigerator; some have private balconies. A good bargain for families is the meeting room, which doubles as a big suite (albeit a noisy one, being on the street), complete with a full kitchen for $79 a night.

201 Lincoln Ave. (P.O. Box 770573), Steamboat Springs, CO 80477. © **800/828-7702** or 970/879-1150. Fax 970/870-0483. www.rabbitearsmotel.com. 65 units. June–Sept and late Mar to mid-Dec $79–$129 double; early Jan–late Mar $99–$139 double; Christmas holiday $129–$169 double. Children under 12 stay free. Rates include continental breakfast. DC, DISC, MC, V. Pets accepted. **Amenities:** Coin-op laundry. *In room:* A/C, TV, dataport, fridge, coffeemaker, hair dryer, iron/ironing board, Wi-Fi network, microwave.

Steamboat Bed & Breakfast 🏔🏔 Steamboat Springs's first house of worship, an 1891 Congregational Church that lost its steeple and top floor to lightning, is now a fine bed-and-breakfast with many stained-glass windows. There are beautiful European and American Victorian antiques in every room, reproduction antique beds, hardwood floors in the common areas and bathrooms, and carpeting in the bedrooms. Guests share a huge living/dining room with a wood-burning fireplace, where they can enjoy complimentary fresh fruit and baked goods. There's also a 24-hour nonalcoholic-beverage bar and a homemade cookie and biscotti bar. Other facilities include an upstairs library, sun deck, and a music conservatory with piano, TV, and VCR (videos are available). In summer, guests can enjoy an attractive deck, set in a lovely flower garden and lush lawn, or nap in a hammock under shady trees. Smoking is not permitted.

442 Pine St. (P.O. Box 775888), Steamboat Springs, CO 80477. © **877/335-4321** or 970/879-5724. Fax 970/870-8787. www.steamboatb-b.com. 8 units. $109–$209 double. Rates include full breakfast. AE, DISC, MC, V. **Amenities:** Hot tub, sauna.

A GUEST RANCH

The Home Ranch 🏔🏔🏔 One of only two Relais & Châteaux properties in Colorado—the other is the Little Nell in Aspen—the Home Ranch effortlessly balances that French pedigree of culinary excellence with down-home Western hospitality. People come here for the horseback riding, and the 90-horse-strong stable's revered custom program that allows guests to break free of the usual nose-to-tail rides and explore. In winter, riding gives way to cross-country skiing on-site, and the staff also provides transportation to the downhill slopes at Steamboat. The cabins and lodge rooms are beautifully done, with slick tiled bathrooms, wood-burning stoves, and a nice blend of rustic and comfortable that's perfect for the isolated locale. With 1,500 of aspen groves and idyllic woodland crisscrossed with trails, the setting is what ultimately defines Home Ranch, and it's one of the most sublime settings in the Rockies.

P.O. Box 822, Clark, CO 80428. © **970/879-1780.** Fax 970/879-1795. www.homeranch.com. 14 units (8 cabins, 6 lodge rooms). $420–$1,365 per room or cabin; week-long packages only in summer. Rates include all meals and most activities AE, DISC, MC, V. **Amenities:** Restaurant; lounge; hot tub; sauna; horseback riding; cross-country skiing. *In room:* Fridge, coffeemaker, iron, Wi-Fi network, no phone.

WHERE TO DINE

For a killer sandwich to eat on the premises or in the woods, **Backcountry Provisions,** 635 Lincoln Ave. (© **970/879-3617**), is the place, with creative offerings like the Sherpa (Asiago cheese, roasted eggplant, tomato, red peppers, and more) and the Timberline (peanut butter, banana, and local honey). Midway between the slopes and downtown, **Freshies,** 595 S. Lincoln Ave. (© **970/879-8099**), is the local favorite for breakfast and lunch, with omelets, eggs "Benny," and a wide range of sandwiches and wraps. **Winona's,** 617 Lincoln Ave. (© **970/879-2483**) is a locally beloved downtown breakfast and lunch spot.

Many of the restaurants in Steamboat Springs cut back their hours or close completely in the slow seasons—primarily spring and fall—so if you're visiting at those times it's best to call first to confirm hours.

EXPENSIVE

Harwigs/L'Apogée at 911 Lincoln Avenue ☆☆ *Moments* CONTEMPORARY FRENCH   Located in downtown Steamboat Springs in an 1886 building that once housed the Harwigs saddle shop, this fine dining establishment serves French cuisine with an Asian flair in an elegant candlelit atmosphere enhanced by live piano music. Owner-Chef Jamie Jenny, who opened the eatery in 1979, keeps the menu fresh and diverse, but main courses might include selections such as New Orleans jambalaya with chicken, shrimp, duck, and house sausage simmered in a fiery Creole sauce; or two-mushroom veal, medallions of veal sautéed with shallots and shiitake and button mushrooms in a white-wine cream sauce. Our favorite item here is one of the cheapest—the half-pound chargrilled lamb burger with strawberry-green apple chutney and provolone cheese. Service is superb, there's an award-winning wine cellar, and outdoor seating is available.

911 Lincoln Ave. ☏ **970/879-1919.** www.lapogee.com. Reservations recommended. Main courses $12–$35; steaks $5–$6 per ounce. AE, MC, V. Daily 5–11pm.

Hazie's ☆☆ CREATIVE AMERICAN   One of Steamboat Springs's most exciting dining experiences can be found at the top of the gondola, midway up Mount Werner. The views of the upper Yampa River valley are spectacular by day and romantic by night, as the lights of Steamboat Springs spread out at the foot of the mountain. Lunch features a variety of salads and sandwiches, plus a daily chef's special. But it's at dinner that Hazie's really excels. Start with an appetizer such as escargot *au fromage*, then try the soup du jour or Hazie's house salad with caramelized pear vinaigrette. Finally, choose from entrees like grilled mahimahi with roasted pineapple salsa; grilled rack of lamb marinated with roasted shallot and thyme oil; or lobster tail and scallops pasta, sautéed in wine and served over angel-hair pasta in a tarragon-brandy cream sauce. In summer you can enjoy lunch Wednesday through Saturday, overlooking the lush greenery of the Yampa Valley. Sunday brunch is popular with locals and visitors alike.

Steamboat Ski Area, 2305 Mt. Werner Circle, Thunderbird Terminal, top of the Silver Bullet Gondola. ☏ **970/871-5150** or 970/879-6111. www.steamboat.com. Reservations recommended for lunch, required for dinner. Lunch main courses $9–$20; dinner 3-course meal $59 winter, $49 summer. AE, DISC, MC, V. Mid-Dec to early Apr daily 11:30am–2:30pm and 6:00–10pm; mid-June to Labor Day, Fri–Sat 11:30am–2:30pm; Sat 7–10pm; Sun 9:30am–1:30pm (brunch). Closed spring and fall.

La Montaña ☆ SOUTHWESTERN/MEXICAN   This isn't your everyday Mexican restaurant; it's a gourmet experience. The festive decor sets the mood, with greenhouse dining and handsome photos by owner Tom Garrett on the stuccoed walls. Southwestern dishes include unusual combinations such as grilled elk loin with a cilantro pesto crust and ancho chile demi-glace; the chef's award-winning dish of braided sausage, a mesquite-grilled combination of elk, lamb, and chorizo sausage; and enchiladas (which have been featured in *Gourmet* magazine) composed of blue corn tortillas, goat and Monterey Jack cheeses, roasted peppers, and onions.

2500 Village Dr. at Apres Ski Way. ☏ **970/879-5800.** www.la-montana.com. Reservations recommended. Main courses $14–$31. AE, DISC, MC, V. Daily 5–10pm (bar daily 4:30–10pm). Hours vary in spring, summer, and fall; call in advance.

MODERATE

Mahogany Ridge Brewery & Grill ☆ INTERNATIONAL   One of Colorado's slickest brewpubs, this modern restaurant is more than a simple brewpub—it boasts a full bar with an extensive wine list in addition to its own microbrews, and the chef draws from all corners of the globe to offer a unique combination of flavors. Choose your entree—maybe Thai baby back ribs or maple-glazed chicken, or blackened salmon, then choose two sauces ranging from salsa to apple chutney to wasabi cream. Once the order arrives, the dipping begins: The more the tastier, as sharing and double dipping are encouraged. For the less adventuresome, Mahogany Ridge also offers several soups, salads, sandwiches, and burgers; plus fish and chips, fried chicken, and an unusual and delicious chipotle chicken potpie. There's even a kid's menu and live music (see "Performing Arts & Nightlife," below)—ensuring that there's truly something for everybody here.

435 Lincoln Ave. (at Fifth St.). ℭ 970/879-3773. Main courses $6–$19. DISC, MC, V. Daily 4–11pm.

Slopeside Grill ℱ AMERICAN/ITALIAN   This restaurant draws diners with large portions—bring a big appetite—and its views of the slopes. A large U-shaped light-colored wooden bar dominates the dining room, where diners face the ski slopes through large windows, and the walls are decorated with Western and early skiing memorabilia. When the weather cooperates, alfresco dining is popular on the patio under large umbrellas. Grill options (available after 6pm) include the deservedly popular slow-roasted rack of ribs, and we recommend the fresh Gulf mahi blackened and served with raspberry–beurre blanc sauce. We especially like the pizza here, from an Italian-style brick oven, with choices such as "The Chutes" (sweet and hot Italian sausage, fresh tomatoes, red onions, and mushrooms) and the "Vagabond," which combines garlic, feta cheese, sun-dried tomatoes, olive oil, and spinach, and tops it all with mozzarella. Stop in for the late-night happy hour from 10pm to midnight, when you can get pints for $2 and pizzas for $6.

Ski Time Square in Torian Plum Plaza. ℭ 970/879-2916. www.slopesidegrill.com. Reservations suggested. Pizza $8.95–$12; main courses $6.95–$19. AE, DISC, MC, V. Daily 11am–10pm; pizza oven open until midnight; bar open until 2am.

INEXPENSIVE

Cugino's Pizzeria ℱ 𝒱𝒶𝓁𝓊𝑒 ITALIAN   Local families pack this restaurant in downtown Steamboat Springs, and with good reason—it offers great food, generous portions, and low prices. The extensive menu includes pizza, of course, plus hoagies and steak sandwiches, pasta, and calzones. Those with healthy appetites might want to try one of the strombolis—fresh-baked pizza dough stuffed with various ingredients such as mushrooms, onions, peppers, mozzarella and provolone cheeses, plus ham, Genoa salami, and capicola or meatballs, pepperoni, and spicy sausage. A vegetarian version is also served. There is a full bar.

41 8th St. ℭ 970/879-5805. www.cuginosrestaurant.com. Reservations not accepted. Pizzas $6.75–$9.50; sandwiches $5–$6; main courses $7.50–$17. MC, V. Daily 11am–10pm. Delivery available 5–9:30pm.

The Tugboat Grill & Pub AMERICAN   Oak floors and rough barn-wood walls cloaked with game and fishing trophies, sports memorabilia, and celebrity photographs are the trademark of this foot-of-the-slopes establishment, which also boasts a sun deck for great people-watching. The hand-carved cherrywood bar, circa 1850, came from the Log Cabin Saloon in Baggs, Wyoming, a Butch Cassidy hangout; look for the bullet hole in one of the columns. The fare includes a variety of burgers, burritos, deli sandwiches, fish, soups, and huge salads throughout the day, and dinner entrees such as basil chicken, a lightly herbed chicken breast in a creamy vegetable sauce, with black olives, green onions, and tomatoes. Many folks sup on nachos, teriyaki wings, and other generous appetizer plates. There's also live music (see below).

1860 Ski Time Sq. ℭ 970/879-7070. Reservations not accepted. Main courses $4.75–$20. AE, DC, MC, V. Daily 11:30am–9:30pm. Bar open later.

BRECKENRIDGE
COLORADO
Now in season.

Winter in Breckenridge.
Fun. Adventure. History.

What are you waiting for?

PERFORMING ARTS & NIGHTLIFE
The music scene in Steamboat Springs is dominated by the **Strings in the Mountains Music Festival,** which offers a wide variety of musical events almost daily throughout the summer, and with lesser frequency at other times of the year. See the sidebar "Musical Mountains," earlier in this chapter.

The **bar scene** in Steamboat, while never dull, comes especially alive in winter. In fact, like Steamboat's restaurants, its nightlife ranges from quiet to nonexistent in spring. One of the hottest new hangouts is **Level'z Nightclub,** at 1860 Ski Time Sq. (© **970/870-9090**), with live entertainment nightly, 20 beers on tap, pool tables, and video games, and some good happy hour specials. Other popular venues include the rustic **Tugboat Grill & Pub,** 1860 Ski Time Sq. (© **970/879-7070**), which attracts a noisy local crowd for a variety of live music and dancing, starting about 9:30pm.

In downtown Steamboat, **The Tap House,** 729 Lincoln Ave. (© **970/879-2431**), has dozens of TVs (including a couple of huge ones) showing just about any sporting event you'd want to see. There are 21 beers on tap, good fajitas and chicken wings, pool tables, and a video arcade. A riverside bar and grill with New Orleans roots, **Sunpies,** 735 Yampa St. (© **970/870-3360**), is a hp young hangout specializing in po' boy sandwiches and potent rum "Slurricanes." **Mahogany Ridge Brewery & Grill,** 435 Lincoln Ave. (© **970/879-3773**), brews a nice selection of handcrafted ales and a wide variety of musicians grace its stage. **The Old Town Pub,** 600 Lincoln St. (© **970/879-2101**), is a local favorite, a low-key bar in a historic downtown building.

4 Winter Park

67 miles NW of Denver

Originally an Arapaho and Ute hunting ground, Winter Park was first settled by whites in the 1850s. The laying of a rail track over Rollins Pass in 1905 and the completion of the 6¼-mile Moffat Tunnel in 1928 opened forests here to logging, which long supported the economy while providing Denver with raw materials for its growth.

The birth of the Winter Park ski area in January 1940, at the west portal of the Moffat Tunnel, helped give impetus to the Colorado ski boom. Although it hasn't yet achieved the notoriety of Vail or Aspen, the tiny town of Winter Park—population around 700—still manages to attract a million skier visits per season. One of its draws is the Ski Train from Denver to Winter Park, the last of its kind in the West. Elevation here is about 9,400 feet.

ESSENTIALS
GETTING THERE   By Car   From Denver or other points east or west, take I-70 exit 232, at Empire, and climb 24 miles north on U.S. 40 over Berthoud Pass to Winter Park. U.S. 40 links Winter Park directly to Steamboat Springs, 101 miles northwest, and, via U.S. 34 (at Granby) through Rocky Mountain National Park, to Estes Park, 84 miles north.

By Plane   Visitors fly into Denver International Airport and can continue to Winter Park with **Home James Transportation Services** (© **800/359-7503** or 970/726-5060; www.homejamestransportation.com); a one-way trip runs $48.

By Train   Winter Park Resort is the only ski area in the western United States with rail service directly to the slopes. The dramatically scenic **Winter Park Ski Train** (© **303/296-4754;** www.skitrain.com) has been making regular runs between Denver and Winter Park since 1940, stopping just 50 yards from the foot of the lifts. On its 2-hour run, the train climbs almost 4,000 feet and passes through 29 tunnels (including the 6¼-mile Moffat Tunnel). The train operates Saturday and Sunday from late December to early April, plus Friday from late January through the ski season and on Saturday in August. Fees for coach seating are $49 for adults, $39 for seniors 62 and up and kids 3 to 13 (with an adult), and seats are free for children 2 and younger. Rates for the upgraded club cars cost $74 per person, and include a continental breakfast, après-ski snacks, and nonalcoholic beverages.

The **Amtrak California Zephyr** (✆ **800/USA-RAIL;** www.amtrak.com) stops twice daily (once in each direction) in Fraser, 2 miles north of Winter Park, on its Chicago–West Coast run.

VISITOR INFORMATION   Main sources of visitor information are the **Winter Park–Fraser Valley Chamber of Commerce,** P.O. Box 3236, Winter Park, CO 80482 (✆ **800/903-7275** or 970/726-4118 for general information, 800/722-4118 for lodging; www.playwinterpark.com), and the **Winter Park Resort,** P.O. Box 36, Winter Park, CO 80482 (✆ **866/722-5560** or 970/726-5514; www.winterparkresort. com). The chamber of commerce's visitor center, on the east side of U.S. 40 in the center of town, is open year-round, daily from 9am to 5pm.

GETTING AROUND   U.S. 40 (Winter Park Dr.) runs almost directly north-south through the community. Vasquez Road, one of the few side roads with accommodations, is the first major left turn as you arrive from the south. Two miles north on U.S. 40 is Fraser, site of the Amtrak terminal and several condominium developments. **The Lift** (✆ **970/726-4163**), a free local shuttle service, runs between most accommodations and the ski area during the ski season, and from July 4th through Labor Day operates a free "Fun Bus" between Fraser and Winter Park. **Car rentals** are available from **Hertz** (✆ **800/654-3131** or 970/726-8993).

FAST FACTS   The hospital, **Seven Mile Medical Clinic,** at 145 Parsenn Rd. in the Winter Park Resort (✆ **970/726-8066**), can handle most medical emergencies (call for hours). The **post office** is in the heart of Winter Park at 78490 U.S. 40. For hours and other information contact the U.S. Postal Service (✆ **800/275-8777;** www.usps.com).

SPECIAL EVENTS   Women's Ski and Snowboard Weekend, late January or early February; Fat Tire Classic mountain biking and hiking event, late June; Jazz Festival, mid-July; High Country Stampede Rodeo, Saturday nights from early July through August; Rocky Mountain Wine, Beer, and Food Festival, early August; Torchlight Parade, Christmas Eve.

SKIING & OTHER WINTER ACTIVITIES

Winter Park is one of those rare resorts that seem to have something for everyone. Experts rave about the chutes and steep mogul runs on Mary Jane Mountain and the extreme skiing in the Vasquez Cirque, but intermediates and beginners are well served on other slopes. Moreover, Winter Park is noted for wide-ranging programs for children and those with disabilities.

The resort includes three interconnected mountain areas totaling 141 designated trails on 2,770 acres of skiable terrain. There are 25 lifts, including one high-speed six passenger, seven high-speed express quads, five triples, seven double chairs, three surface lifts, two "Magic Carpet" rolling conveyors, and a rope tow. The resort rates its

---

Moments Totally Tubular

The **Fraser Valley Tubing Hill** (behind Kentucky Fried Chicken; © 970/726-5954), offers a return to childhood for many adults, as well as a lot of fun for kids (who must be 7 or older to ride alone). A lift pulls you and your big inner tube to the top of a steep hill, and then you slide down, sometimes reaching speeds of 45 mph. Hours Friday through Sunday are from 10am to 10pm, with slightly shorter hours Monday through Thursday, and the tubing hill is open November to April, snow permitting. Rides run about $12 an hour.

---

trails as 9% beginner, 21% intermediate, 13% advanced, 54% most difficult, and 3% expert only.

Winter Park Resort comprises several distinct areas. **Winter Park Mountain** has mostly beginner and intermediate terrain. **Discovery Park** encompasses more than 25 acres of prime beginner terrain. **Mary Jane Mountain** mainly offers intermediate, most difficult, and expert terrain, best known for its numerous mogul runs. **Vasquez Ridge,** the resort's third mountain area, has primarily intermediate and most difficult terrain. Fans of tree-line skiing will like **Parsenn Bowl,** more than 200 acres of open-bowl and gladed-tree skiing that fan out from the summit at North Cone and merge with Mary Jane's Backside. **Vasquez Cirque** is no place for beginners. It contains steep chutes and gladed pockets for advanced and expert skiers and snowboarders. The five terrain parks at Winter Park are cutting-edge, and there is one for every skill level. **Rail Yard,** consisting of advanced terrain, is considered one of the nation's best.

Annual snowfall at Winter Park averages over 359 inches (almost 30 ft.). The vertical drop is 3,060 feet, from the 12,060-foot summit off North Cone of Parsenn Bowl. There are about a dozen restaurants and several bars, including a mountaintop restaurant.

Winter Park's impressive **Kid's Adventure Junction** ✦ includes a play area, rental shop, restrooms, and a children's instruction hill. The **National Sports Center for the Disabled** ✦✦, founded in 1970, is one of the largest programs of its kind in the world.

Daily lift tickets cost $51 to $77 for adults ages 14 to 64, $31 to $41 for children 6 to 13, $37 to $61 for seniors 65 to 69, and $31 for seniors 70 and older. Kids under 6 ski free. Full rental packages are available, as are alpine, telemark, and snowboard lessons, as well as snowshoe tours.

Winter Park is usually open for skiing from mid-November to mid-April. It's open for summer operations daily from early June until early September. For more information, contact **Winter Park Resort,** P.O. Box 36, Winter Park, CO 80482 (© **970/ 726-5514,** or 303/316-1564; www.winterparkresort.com). For daily ski reports, call © **970/726-7669** or 303/572-7669.

OTHER SKIING NEARBY   Just 78 miles from Denver, **SolVista Basin,** 1000 Village Rd. (P.O. Box 1110), Granby, CO 80446 (© **888/283-7458** or 970/887-3384; www.solvista.com), has long been a favorite with parents and kids for its easy access, affordable prices, and family-friendly atmosphere.

The ski area comprises two separate but interconnected mountains. The resort contains 287 acres of skiable terrain, with 38 trails rated 30% beginner, 50% intermediate, and 20% advanced. The longest run is 1½ miles and the vertical drop is 1,000 feet from the top elevation of 9,202 feet. It's served by one high-speed quad, one fixed-grip quad, one triple, one double, and a surface lift. Average annual snowfall is 220 inches, and 60% of the terrain has snow making, with top-to-bottom coverage on both mountains. Full-day lift tickets are $44 to $46 for adults, $21 to $24 for children 6 to 12, $29 to $31 for seniors 61 to 69, and are free for those under 6 and over 69.

CROSS-COUNTRY SKIING & SNOWSHOEING   The outstanding cross-country skiing in the Winter Park area is highlighted by what the *Denver Post* calls "the best touring center in Colorado." The **Devil's Thumb Nordic Country Center** at Devil's Thumb Ranch Resort (© **970/726-8231;** www.devilsthumbranch.com) has more than 62 miles of groomed trails. Full rentals and instruction are available. Full-day passes are about $15, or free for those staying at the ranch.

There's also cross-country skiing at **SolVista Basin** (see "Other Skiing Nearby," above), with 25 miles of groomed trails. Use of the trails is free, with access at the base of the ski mountain. Those who want to avoid the work of skiing uphill can also access the cross-country trails from the top via a ski lift ($5 per trip).

Snow Mountain Ranch–YMCA Nordic Center, on U.S. 40 between Winter Park and Grand Lake (© **970/887-2152;** www.ymcarockies.org/smrnordic), features 62 miles of groomed trails for all abilities, including a short section of lighted track for night skiing. Trail passes cost $12 for adults and $5 for kids 6 to 12 and seniors 61 to 69. Children under 6 and seniors over 69 ski free, and adults with YMCA membership receive $2 discounts. A 5-day adult trail pass costs $40.

All of the above provide **snowshoeing** opportunities, with rental equipment and guided tours. You can also rent snowshoes and get tips on where to go at **Winter Park Sports Shop** in Kings Crossing Shopping Center, at the intersection of Winter Park Drive and Kings Crossing Road (© **800/222-7547** or 970/726-5554; www.winter parkski.com).

WARM-WEATHER & YEAR-ROUND ACTIVITIES

There are plenty of recreational opportunities in the **Arapaho National Forest** and **Arapaho National Recreation Area.** Maps and brochures on hiking, mountain biking, and other activities are available at the Sulphur Ranger District office, P.O. Box 10, 9 Ten Mile Dr., off U.S. 40 about half a mile south of Granby, CO 80446 (© **970/887-4100;** www.fs.fed.us/r2). The **Devil's Thumb Ranch** (see "Where to Stay," below) is famous for its numerous recreation packages, including rafting, hiking, and fly-fishing.

ALPINE SLIDE   Colorado's longest alpine slide, at 3,030 feet long and with 26 turns, cools summer visitors. Rates are $12 for adults, $10 for children 6 to 13 and for seniors 70 and older on Friday through Sunday. Kids under 6 get in free at all times and seniors 70 and older are admitted free Monday through Thursday. For information, contact the Winter Park Resort (see "Skiing & Other Winter Activities," above).

FISHING   Fraser Valley and surrounding Grand County are renowned among anglers. Head to Williams Fork Reservoir and the Three Lakes District for kokanee salmon, lake trout, brookies, and browns. Fishing ponds stocked with various species are in Fraser, across from the Fraser Valley Center on U.S. 40. The upper pond is reserved for children and people in wheelchairs; the lower pond is open to everyone. Ponds are generally open and stocked by mid-May.

The fly shop at **Devil's Thumb Ranch** (© **970/726-8231**) offers guided fly-fishing trips with rates of $300 for two people for a full day.

GOLF   Local golf courses include **Pole Creek Golf Club,** 10 miles northwest of Winter Park on U.S. 40 (© **970/887-9195**), considered among the finest mountain courses in the state, with greens fees of $50 to $80 for 18 holes; and the **Headwaters Golf Course** (© **970/887-2709**), with fees of $40 to $80.

HIKING & BACKPACKING   The nearby Arapaho National Forest and Arapaho National Recreation Area (see above) offer miles of hiking trails and plenty of back-packing opportunities. Beautiful Rocky Mountain National Park is less than an hour's drive north (see "Rocky Mountain National Park," earlier in this chapter).

MOUNTAIN BIKING   Winter Park and the Fraser Valley have won national recog-nition for their expansive trail system and established race program. Many off-road bike trails connect to the 600 miles of backcountry roads and trails in the adjacent national forest. The King of the Rockies Off-Road Stage Race and Festival, held each year in August, is one of the top professional mountain-bike races in America; part of it is run on the 30-mile **Tipperary Creek Trail** ⚡, among Colorado's best mountain-bike trails. The Fat Tire Classic in late June is another big mountain-biking event and the single largest fundraiser for the American Red Cross. Entrants are recommended to be intermediate or advanced bikers or hikers.

For advice, information, and maps, talk to the knowledgeable folks at **Grand Sports Shop,** in downtown Winter Park at 78786 U.S. 40 (© **970/722-0484;** www.grandsports.net). The shop is open daily year-round, providing mountain sales, repairs, and rentals (starting at $18 per half-day, $24 per day). Ask for a copy of the free trail map, also available from the **Winter Park–Fraser Valley Chamber of Com-merce** (see "Visitor Information," above).

MORE TO SEE & DO
Amaze'n Winter Park   A human maze by Amaze'n Colorado, this two-level labyrinth of twists and turns offers prizes to participants who can "beat the clock." The maze is constructed in such a way that it can be easily changed, which is done weekly to maintain interest for repeat customers. A free observation deck gives a bird's-eye view of the maze, as well as the surrounding scenery. Allow about 1 hour.

At the base of Winter Park Resort. © **970/726-0214.** www.amazenmazes.com. Admission $8 adults, $6 children 5–12, free for children under 5. Additional maze runs $2. Daily Memorial Day weekend to Sept 10am–5:30pm.

Cozens Ranch House Museum   This 1870s homestead is a National Historic Reg-istry site and presents a glimpse into Colorado's pioneer past, with a restored and fur-nished family residence, small hotel, stagecoach stop, and the original Fraser Valley post office. There's also a replica of a stagecoach that traveled roads near here between 1875 and 1905, plus a small gift shop. Allow 30 minutes to an hour.

U.S. 40 between Winter Park and Fraser. © **970/726-5488.** www.grandcountymuseum.com/CozensRanch.htm. Admission $4 adults, $3 seniors 62 and over, $2 students 6–18, free for children under 6. Memorial Day to Sept Tues–Sat 10am–5pm, Sun 1–5pm; rest of year Wed–Sat 11am–4pm.

WHERE TO STAY
There are more than 60 accommodations in the Fraser Valley, including hotels, con-dominiums, family-style mountain inns (serving breakfast and dinner daily), bed-and-breakfasts, lodges, and motels. Bookings can be made through **Winter Park Central Reservations** (© **800/729-5813** or 970/726-5587; www.winterparkresort.com). The agency can also book air and rail tickets, rental cars, airport transfers, lift tickets, ski-school lessons, ski rentals, and other activities.

Another option, for those interested in renting a private, upscale home, town house, or condo, is to contact **Destinations West** (© 800/545-9378; www.mtnlodging.com).

Snow Mountain Ranch–YMCA of the Rockies, on U.S. 40 between Winter Park and Grand Lake, 1101 C.R. 53, Granby, CO 80446 (© **800/777-9622** or 970/887-2152; www.ymcarockies.org), offers a wide range of lodging possibilities, from economical lodge rooms to delightful Western-style cabins with up to five bedrooms. Rates start at about $72 double; up to two pets are accepted in cabins, with a $5 per pet fee. Taxes add about 10% to lodging bills.

The **Rocky Mountain Inn & Hostel,** U.S. 40, Fraser (© **866/467-8351** or 970/726-8256; www.therockymountaininn.com), is a solid budget option, clean and well maintained with a gorgeous valley view, with private rooms from $59 to $119 double and bunks from $19 to $30 a night.

Devil's Thumb Ranch ☆☆   Established in 1937, this guest ranch—8 miles north of Winter Park—has become the standout property in the Fraser Valley, melding charming accommodations, an isolated location, and ecological consciousness into a wonderful whole. Between 1999 and 2001, Bob and Suzanne Fanch bought the ranch and the 4,000 surrounding acres and started nearly from scratch, rebuilding the cabins by 2004 and then starting on a new lodge, which at press time was slated to open in July 2007, with design inspired by the historic lodges of the national parks. The cabins, decorated with antiques in one of four themes (fishing, Nordic, Native American, or Western), are at once rustic, elegant, and cozy, with down pillows, comforters, and warm bathrobes.

But Devil's Thumb Ranch is not all about the indoors: This is just the place to escape the modern world, and it is renowned for cross-country skiing in winter and horseback riding, fly-fishing, and rafting in summer. Winter also offers sleigh rides and ice skating at a rink on-site. Summer 2007 will also see the opening of a new spa and fitness center. The Ranch House Restaurant & Saloon lures Winter Park residents eager for creative country cuisine and seasonal specialties; it's open for dinner nightly and for lunch on weekends.

Beyond the perks and amenities, the Fanches have also embraced sustainability: The cabins utilize geothermal energy to warm the floors, which then radiate heat into the entire cabin; the lodge is being built with the same technology.

Grand County Rd. 83 (P.O. Box 750), Tabernash, CO 80478. © 800/933-4339 or 970/726-5632. Fax 970/726-9038. www.devilsthumbranch.com. 69 units (53 lodge rooms, 16 cabins). $175 double lodge room; $295–$900 cabin. Rates include buffet breakfast. Minimum stay required for some accommodations. MC, V. **Amenities:** Restaurant (American); bar; indoor/outdoor pool; spa; whirlpool; sauna; fitness center; activities desk. *In-room:* A/C, TV/VCR, kitchen, fridge, iron, Wi-Fi network, microwave.

The Vintage Resort Hotel and Conference Center   The châteaulike Vintage rises five stories above the foot of Winter Park's ski slopes, not far from the Mary Jane base facilities. A full-service resort hotel, it offers convenient access to skiing, excellent dining and atmosphere, and luxury accommodations. The units range from average-size rooms with two queen beds to spacious two-bedroom suites with whirlpool tubs. Every room has a view of either the ski slopes or the Continental Divide, and many have kitchenettes and fireplaces. Some rooms also have high-speed Internet available. There are ski lockers and on-site ski rentals, mountain bike storage and work rooms, and a library with a pool table. The entire property is nonsmoking.

100 Winter Park Dr. (P.O. Box 1369), Winter Park, CO 80482. © 800/472-7017 or 970/726-8801. Fax 970/726-9230. www.vintagehotel.com. 118 units. Summer $60–$105 double, $150–$230 suite; winter $75–$205 double, $180–$550 suite. Fri–Sat rates about 10% higher than weekday rates; rates higher during holidays and special

events. AE, DC, DISC, MC, V. Pets accepted (one-time fee of $25). **Amenities:** Restaurant (American); bar; large outdoor heated pool; exercise room; access to a nearby health club; hot tub; sauna; video arcade; concierge; shuttle service; full-service business center; coin-op laundry. *In room:* TV w/pay movies, dataport, fridge (in some units), coffeemaker, hair dryer, iron.

Wild Horse Inn ⌖   Although the Wild Horse Inn was built in 1991, the pine logs used in it are over 400 years old, giving the place a feel of a century-old mountain lodge. With rooms in the main house and a strip of adjacent one-bedroom cabins (with kitchenettes) to choose from, guests are treated to woodsy rooms with pizzazz, complete with jetted tubs and balconies. Innkeepers Chris French and John Cribari are a gourmet chef and a licensed massage therapist, respectively, and both leverage their skills to their utmost: Chris oversees the gourmet breakfasts while John is the prime masseur in the inn's three massage rooms. The couple also owns the **Snowberry Bed & Breakfast** in Fraser (✆ **970/726-5974;** www.thesnowberry.com).

Grand County Rd. 83 (P.O. Box 609), Fraser, CO 80442. ✆ **970/726-0456.** www.wildhorseinn.com. 10 units (7 rooms, 3 cabins). $175–$205 double, $245 cabin. Rates include full breakfast. Children under 12 not accepted. AE, MC, V. **Amenities:** Outdoor hot tub; sauna; massage. *In room:* TV/VCR, kitchenette.

WHERE TO DINE

In addition to the restaurants discussed here, other local standbys include **Fontenot's,** U.S. 40, Winter Park (✆ **970/726-4021**), serving seafood and Cajun dishes; **Hernando's Pizza Pub,** U.S. 40, Winter Park (✆ **970/726-5409**), beloved for its pizzas and Italian fare; and the **Ranch House Restaurant** at Devil's Thumb Ranch (see "Where to Stay," above).

Deno's Mountain Bistro ⌖ CONTEMPORARY AMERICAN   A favorite of locals and visitors alike, this bistro on Winter Park's main street has a casual atmosphere and impressive bar, with an extensive selection of national and international beers and an excellent wine list of more than 300 selections. The restaurant takes up two levels—the upstairs sports pub features copper-topped tables, while downstairs is casually elegant fine dining. Lunch here means excellent sandwiches, burgers, and salads. The gourmet cuisine at dinner includes such dishes as penne pomodoro, with fresh basil, garlic, tomatoes, and sautéed rock shrimp; broiled tenderloin of pork brochette, with mangos, plums, and roasted vegetables; and the absolute favorite of carnivores like us, the grilled aged New York strip steak, served with zesty Tabasco onion strings, roasted vegetables, and potatoes.

78911 U.S. 40 (downtown, across from Copper Creek Sq.). ✆ **970/726-5332.** www.denosmountainbistro.com. Salads and most sandwiches $5.95–$8.95; main courses $11–$30. AE, DC, DISC, MC, V. Daily 11:30am–11pm.

Untamed Steakhouse at Winter Park ⌖⌖ NEW AMERICAN/STEAK   This large Western restaurant, with 30-foot vaulted ceilings, exposed pine beams, and a handsome stone fireplace, offers well-prepared and innovative cuisine. For lunch there are sandwiches and light entrees, and for dinner we suggest the house specialty—wood-fired Angus beef prime rib, slowly roasted with a spicy rub, fresh herbs, and roasted garlic, then lightly grilled and served with crispy horseradish coleslaw and frizzled onions. Other dinner choices include the beef tournedos, roasted with bacon, brie cheese, artichoke bottoms, and a cognac sauce; a tortilla-crusted filet mignon served with portobello "fajitas" and guacamole chèvre; and oven-poached salmon, basted in a tequila sauce, topped with a chipotle-orange beurre blanc, and served with asparagus-tomato hash. There's a very good wine list, plus a nice selection of draft beers and specialty martinis.

78491 U.S. 40 (downtown). ✆ **970/726-1111.** www.untamedsteakhouse.com. Main courses $8–$30. AE, DISC, MC, V. Daily 5–10pm.

5 Breckenridge & Summit County

67 miles W. of Denver, 114 miles NW of Colorado Springs, 23 miles E. of Vail

Breckenridge, and its neighbors throughout Summit County, comprise a major outdoor recreation center, with skiing in winter, and fishing, hiking, and mountain biking in summer. But the area actually offers much more, with a number of historical attractions, good shopping opportunities, a number of fine restaurants, and some interesting places to stay. The town of Breckenridge (elevation 9,603 feet) is a good place to base yourself, as the entire Victorian core of this 19th-century mining town has been carefully preserved, with colorfully painted shops and restaurants occupying the old buildings, most dating from the 1880s and 1890s.

Most of the mountain towns that surround the area's excellent ski resorts—Arapahoe Basin, Breckenridge, Copper, Keystone, and Loveland—were barely on the map in the 1880s, when the rest of the state was laying claim to its stake of history. Breckenridge, however, was a prosperous mining town in 1887 when the largest gold nugget ever found in Colorado, "Tom's Baby," was unearthed there. It weighed 13 pounds, 7 ounces, and is now in the Colorado History Museum in Denver. Today these communities are strictly in the tourism business, and fill to capacity during peak seasons. Breckenridge, for example, has a year-round population of only 2,800 people, but swells to almost 34,000 during its top tourism times.

ESSENTIALS

GETTING THERE   By Car   I-70 runs through the middle of Summit County. For Keystone, exit on U.S. 6 at Dillon; the resort is 6 miles east of the interchange. For Breckenridge, exit on Colo. 9 at Frisco and head south 9 miles to the resort. Copper Mountain is right on I-70 at the Colo. 91 interchange.

By Airport Shuttle   Most visitors fly into Denver International or Colorado Springs and continue to Breckenridge, Frisco, Keystone, and/or Copper Mountain via shuttle. **Colorado Mountain Express** (© 800/525-6363 or 970/926-9800; www.cmex.com) offers shuttles; the cost from Denver starts at about $40 per person, one-way. (For listings of airlines servicing Denver and Colorado Springs, see chapters 2 and 7, respectively.)

VISITOR INFORMATION   For additional information on Breckenridge and other parts of Summit County, contact the **Breckenridge Resort Chamber,** at their new welcome center at 203 S. Main St. (open daily 9am–9pm summer and winter, with shorter hours in spring and fall), and administrative offices at 311 S. Ridge St., Breckenridge, CO 80424 (© 800/221-1091 or 970/453-2913; www.gobreck.com).

A source of visitor information for the entire region is the **Summit Chamber of Commerce,** P.O. Box 2010, Frisco, CO 80443 (© 800/530-3099 or 970/668-2051; www.experiencethesummit.com). The chamber has an information center in Silverthorne just off Colo. 9N. Both are open daily from 9am to 5pm.

Parents traveling with kids can find all sorts of pointers in *The Parents Handbook to Summit County* (© 970/390-3533; www.theparentshandbook.com), available free all over Summit County.

GETTING AROUND   Dillon Reservoir is at the heart of Summit County, and I-70 lies along its northwestern shore, with Frisco at its west end, and Dillon and Silverthorne toward the east. From Dillon take U.S. 6 about 5 miles east to Keystone and another 15 miles to Arapahoe. Breckenridge is about 10 miles south of Frisco on Colo.

ATTRACTIONS●
1875 Edwin Carter Museum **4**
1896 William Harrison Briggle House **6**
Amaze'n Breckenridge **10**
Barney Ford House Museum **7**
Mountain Top Children's Museum **12**

ACCOMMODATIONS■
Allaire Timbers Inn B&B **15**
Barn on the River **1**
Hyatt Main Street Station **13**
Little Mountain Lodge B&B **16**
The Lodge & Spa at Breckenridge **17**

DINING◆
Breckenridge Brewery & Pub **14**
Briar Rose Restaurant **3**
Cafe Alpine **8**
Crepes a la Cart **9**
Giampietro Pizzeria **2**
Hearthstone **5**
Mi Casa **11**

9, and Copper Mountain is just south of I-70 exit 195 (Colo. 91). Loveland is just across the county line at exit 216 on the east side of the Eisenhower Tunnel.

Summit Stage (℃ **970/668-0999;** www.summitstage.com) provides free year-round service between Frisco, Dillon, Silverthorne, Keystone, Breckenridge, and Copper Mountain, daily from 6am to midnight, from late November to mid-April and shorter hours the rest of the year.

You can get around Breckenridge on the **Breckenridge Free Ride** bus system (℃ **970/547-3140**), and there's also free shuttle service at the Keystone Resort (℃ **970/496-4200**).

FAST FACTS Medical facilities here include the **Breckenridge Medical Center,** located in The Village at Breckenridge, 555 S. Park Ave., Plaza II, Breckenridge (℃ **970/453-1010**). **Post offices** are at 305 S. Ridge St., Breckenridge, and 35 W. Main St., Frisco. For hours and other information contact the U.S. Postal Service (℃ **800/275-8777;** www.usps.com). For **weather and road conditions,** call ℃ **970/668-1090.**

SPECIAL EVENTS Ullr Fest, early January, in Breckenridge; International Snow Sculpture Championships, fourth week in January, in Breckenridge; Sunsation, early April, in Copper Mountain; Memorial Day Weekend Beach Party and Festival of the Brewpubs, Memorial Day weekend, in Arapahoe Basin; the Celtic Festival, late June, Keystone; Oktoberfest, mid-September, in Breckenridge. See also "The Festival Scene," later in this chapter.

SKIING & OTHER WINTER ACTIVITIES

Breckenridge and Keystone ski areas are now part of Vail Resorts, and any lift ticket purchased at Vail or Beaver Creek is valid without restriction at Breckenridge and Keystone (and Arapahoe Basin). However, only multiday lift tickets for 3 or more days purchased at Breckenridge or Keystone are also valid at Vail and Beaver Creek.

Snowboarding is permitted at all local resorts.

ARAPAHOE BASIN   Arapahoe Basin, 28194 U.S. 6, between Keystone and Loveland Pass, is one of Colorado's oldest ski areas, having opened in 1946. Several features make Arapahoe exceptional. Most of its 490 skiable acres are intermediate and expert terrain, much of it above timberline. It rates its 69 trails as 15% beginner, 45% intermediate, 20% advanced, and 20% expert. Its longest run is 1½ miles. Arapahoe Basin receives an average of 367 inches of snow a year, and is frequently one of the last Colorado ski areas to close for the season—often not until mid-June. It usually opens in early November. Arapahoe offers a 2,270-foot vertical drop from its summit at 13,050 feet. It is served by two triple and three double chairs plus a conveyor.

Lift tickets during peak season cost $51 for adults, $38 for youths 15 to 19, $22 for children 6 to 14, $41 for seniors 60 to 69, $10 per day for seniors 70 and older, and they're free for children 5 and younger. For information, including a snow report, contact Arapahoe Basin, P.O. Box 8787, Keystone, CO 80435 (② **888/272-7246** or 970/496-0718; www.arapahoebasin.com).

BRECKENRIDGE 🏅🏅   Spread across four large mountains on the west side of the town of Breckenridge, this area ranks third in size among Colorado's ski resorts. Once known for its wealth of open, groomed beginner and intermediate slopes, Breckenridge in recent years has expanded its acreage for expert skiers as well.

Peak 8, the original ski mountain, is the highest of the four at 12,998 feet and has the greatest variety. Peak 9, heavily geared to novices and intermediates, rises above the principal base area. Peak 10, served by a single high-speed quad chair, is predominantly expert territory. The vast bowls of Peak 8 and the North Face of Peak 9 are likewise advanced terrain. There are restaurants high on Peaks 8, 9, and 10 and three cafeterias at the base of the slopes. Peak 7 is a double black-diamond challenge on over 1,200 feet of vertical.

All told, the resort has 2,208 skiable acres, with 146 trails, including Four O'Clock, the longest at 3½ miles! The resort rates its trails as 15% beginner, 33% intermediate, and 52% expert and advanced. There are 28 lifts—two high-speed six passenger chairs, seven high-speed quads, one triple chair, six double chairs, four surface lifts, and eight carpet lifts. A new gondola connecting the north side of town with Peak 7 and Peak 8 is slated to open for the 2007–08 ski season. Vertical drop is 3,398 feet from a summit of 12,998 feet; average annual snowfall is 300 inches (25 ft.).

Lift tickets during peak season cost $75 for adults, $39 for children 5 to 12, $65 for seniors 65 to 69, and are free for children 4 and younger and seniors 70 and older. Tickets purchased at Breckenridge are also valid at Keystone and Arapahoe Basin, and multiday tickets for 3 or more days are also valid at Vail and Beaver Creek.

Among Breckenridge's programs are its women's ski seminars, taught exclusively by women for women skiers of all abilities. Three- and four-day seminars are offered in January, February, March, and April. Women-only ski-school classes are available throughout the ski season. For more information, call ② **888/576-2754.** For snowboarders, the Breckenridge Superpipe is a delight. This half-pipe has a 15-degree slope, 15-foot-high walls, and 17-foot transitions.

Breckenridge is usually open from mid-November to mid-May, daily from 8:30am to 4pm. For further information, contact **Breckenridge Ski Resort,** P.O. Box 1058, Breckenridge, CO 80424 (© **800/789-7669** or 970/453-5000; 970/453-6118 for snow conditions; www.breckenridge.snow.com). From Memorial Day weekend to Labor Day, the alpine slide is in operation, and the trails are open to mountain bikers; minigolf is also available. Call for off-season hours and chairlift schedule.

COPPER MOUNTAIN From Copper Mountain village, the avalanche chutes on the west face of Ten Mile Mountain seem to spell out the word SKI. Though this is a natural coincidence, locals like to say the mountain has terrain created for skiing.

Terrain is about half beginner and intermediate, with the rest ranging from advanced to "you better be really good." The area has a vertical drop of 2,601 feet from a peak elevation of 12,313 feet. There are 2,433 skiable acres and 125 trails served by 22 lifts—one high-speed six-person chair, four high-speed quads, five triple chairs, five double chairs, two surface lifts, four conveyors, and one tubing zone lift. Average annual snowfall is 280 inches. Copper Mountain has two terrain parks. Big floater jumps are spread out across an entire run, with proper takeoff and landing ramps; there's a regulation half-pipe, and several drainage and gladed runs have been thinned to provide challenging tree riding for more advanced snowboarders.

There are three restaurants on the mountain and several more in the base village. Also at the base are 16 miles of cross-country track, a tubing hill, and a full-service racquet and athletic club.

Lift tickets during the peak season cost $69 for adults, $34 for children 6 to 13, and $59 for seniors 65 to 69. Tickets are free for seniors 70 and older and children 5 and under.

Copper Mountain is usually open from early November to mid-April, Monday through Friday from 9am to 4pm, Saturday and Sunday from 8:30am to 4pm. For information, contact **Copper Mountain Resort,** P.O. Box 3001, Copper Mountain, CO 80443 (© **866/841-2481;** www.coppercolorado.com). For reservations, call © **888/219-2441;** for a snow report, call © **800/789-7609.**

KEYSTONE Keystone is actually three separate mountains, offering a variety of terrain. And the resort is one of the best spots for night skiing in America, open daily from 8:30am until 8pm.

From its peak elevation of 12,200 feet, Keystone's vertical drop is 3,128 feet. It's three interconnected mountains offer 2,870 acres of skiing, 117 trails (17 open for night skiing), and 19 lifts—including two connecting high-speed gondolas, a high-speed six-person chair, five high-speed quads, one quad, one triple, four doubles, one surface lift, and four carpets. Average annual snowfall is 230 inches (about 19 ft.). Its trails are rated 12% beginner, 34% intermediate, and 54% expert and advanced.

For snowboarders, Keystone has 66 acres of terrain parks, including two half-pipes, which are lit for night riding.

Lift tickets during the peak season cost $75 for adults, $39 for children 5 to 12, $65 for seniors 65 and older, and are free for children 4 and younger. Tickets purchased at Keystone are also valid at Breckenridge and Arapahoe Basin, and multiday tickets for 3 or more days are also valid at Vail and Beaver Creek.

Excellent on-mountain dining is available at the Alpenglow Stube, located in The Outpost, a log-and-stone lodge atop North Peak (elevation 11,444 ft.). Access is via two scenic gondola rides.

Keystone is usually open from early November through mid-April. For further information, contact **Keystone Resort,** P.O. Box 38, Keystone, CO 80435 (© **800/ 468-5004** or 970/496-4386; www.keystone.snow.com). For snow reports call © **800/ 404-3535** or 970/496-4111.

LOVELAND   Just across the county line, on the east side of I-70's Eisenhower Memorial Tunnel, is **Loveland Ski Area,** P.O. Box 899, Georgetown, CO 80444 (© **800/736-3754** or 303/571-5580; www.skiloveland.com). Comprising Loveland Basin and Loveland Valley, it was created in the late 1930s by a Denver ski club wanting to take advantage of the area's heavy snowfall (400 in., more than 33 ft., annually). You can still see the original rope-tow cabins from 1942, when all-day tickets cost $2. Inflation (and the cost of many improvements) has taken a toll, but this is one of the best deals in the area. Today, tickets during the peak skiing season cost $50 for adults, $39 for seniors 60 to 69, and $22 for children 6 to 14; children under 6 ski free, and seniors 70 and older are offered a season pass for $50.

There's good beginner-intermediate terrain on the 1,365 lift-served acres—17% and 42% respectively, leaving 41% advanced. The vertical drop is 2,410 feet from a top elevation of 13,010 feet, and the longest run is 2 miles. Lifts include three quad chairs, two triples, four doubles, one surface lift, and one tow. Loveland's terrain parks offer natural half-pipes and big powder-filled bowls.

The resort usually opens in mid-October and remains open daily through May.

CROSS-COUNTRY SKIING & SNOWSHOEING   The **Frisco Nordic Center,** at 18454 Colo. 9, south of Frisco (© **970/668-0866;** www.breckenridgenordic.com), sits on the shores of Dillon Reservoir. Its trail network includes 27 miles of groomed cross-country ski trails. The lodge has a snack bar and a shop with rentals and retail sales; instruction and backcountry and snowshoe tours are also offered. From the Frisco Nordic Center you can ski to the **Breckenridge Nordic Center,** on Willow Lane near the foot of Peak 8 (© **970/453-6855;** www.breckenridgenordic.com), with its own series of 19 miles of groomed trails. The two operations share 12 miles of snowshoe trails and 3 miles of snowshoe trails where leashed dogs are welcome. One trail pass ($14 for adults, $10 for seniors and children) covers both Nordic centers, and rental equipment is available. The **Gold Run Nordic Center** at the Breckenridge Golf Club, 200 Club House Dr. (© **970/547-7889**), charges similar rates and features more than 12 miles of groomed trails, from beginner to advanced, in addition to backcountry and snowshoe trails, and also offers rental equipment.

For additional information on these and other cross-country skiing centers check out **www.colorado-xc.org** on the Web. There are also numerous cross-country skiing possibilities in the area's national forests; contact the **Dillon Ranger District** (see below).

WARM-WEATHER & YEAR-ROUND ACTIVITIES

The **White River National Forest** encompasses the boundaries of Summit County. This recreational playground offers opportunities not only for downhill and cross-country skiing and snowmobiling in winter, but also for hiking and backpacking, horseback riding, boating, fishing, hunting, and bicycling in summer. White River National Forest includes the **Eagles Nest Wilderness Area** and **Green Mountain Reservoir,** both in the northern part of the county.

The **U.S. Forest Service's Dillon Ranger District,** located in the town of Silverthorne at 680 River Pkwy. (Colo. 9), Silverthorne, CO 80498, about half a mile north of I-70 exit 205 (© **970/468-5400;** www.fs.fed.us/r2), has an unusually good selection of information on outdoor recreation possibilities, including maps and guides to hiking and mountain-biking trails, jeep roads, cross-country skiing, snowmobiling, fishing, and camping. You can also get information on a wide variety of outdoor activities from the **Breckenridge Resort Chamber Welcome Center,** 203 S. Main St. (© **877/864-0868**).

BICYCLING   There are more than 40 miles of paved bicycle paths in the county, including a path from Breckenridge (with a spur from Keystone) to Frisco and Copper Mountain, continuing across Vail Pass to Vail. This spectacularly beautiful two-lane path is off-limits to motorized vehicles of any kind. Also see "Mountain Biking," below.

BOATING   Dillon Reservoir, a beautiful mountain lake along I-70 between Dillon and Frisco, is the place to go. Also called Lake Dillon, the 3,300-acre reservoir, which provides drinking water to Denver, is more than 200 feet deep in spots. At 9,017 feet elevation, it claims to have America's highest altitude yacht club and holds colorful regattas most summer weekends. The popular Dillon Open, a huge sailboat race, occurs the first weekend in August. Swimming is not permitted.

The full-service **Dillon Marina,** 150 Marina Dr. (© **970/468-5100;** www.dillon marina.com), is open from the last weekend of May through the last weekend of October, offering boats for 2-hour, half-day, or full-day rentals; sailing instruction; and charter cruises. Half-day boat-rental fees run $140 for runabouts, $160 for 22-foot pontoon boats, and $300 for 25-foot pontoons. Fuel is extra. The half-day rate for 18- and 20-foot sailboats is $110, and more upscale 22-foot sailboats rent for $145 to $165 for a half-day. An 8-hour sailing class costs $250 per person, and the "sailing experience" 2-hour sailboat tour for novice sailors costs $45 per person. There's also a small store, repair shop, restaurant, and bar.

FISHING   Major fishing rivers within an hour of Breckenridge include the South Platte, Arkansas, Eagle, Colorado, and Blue rivers, and for lake fishing, try Dillon Reservoir and Spinney Mountain Reservoir. The Blue River, from Lake Dillon Dam to its confluence with the Colorado River at Kremmling, is rated a gold-medal fishing stream. For tips on where they're biting, as well as supplies, fishing licenses, and all the rest, stop at **Mountain Angler** ⚓, 311 S. Main St., Breckenridge, in the Main Street Mall (© **800/453-4669** or 970/453-4665; www.mountainangler.com), which also offers year-round guide service. Guided fly-fishing wading trips, for two anglers, start at $230 for a half-day; $315 for a full day, including lunch. A full-day float-fishing guided trip for two anglers costs $395. Guided fly-fishing trips are also offered by **The Adventure Company** (© **800/497-7238;** www.theadventurecompany.com) at similar rates.

GOLF   Among area golf courses, which all boast wonderful scenery, are the 18-hole **Breckenridge Golf Club,** 200 Clubhouse Dr., Breckenridge (© **970/453-9104**), designed by Jack Nicklaus, with the greens fee of $99 for 18 holes; **Copper Creek Golf Club,** 104 Wheeler Place, Copper Mountain Resort (© **970/968-3333**), among the highest 18-hole courses in North America at 9,752 feet, with fees of $39 to $99, including cart, for 18 holes; **Keystone Ranch Golf Course,** 1239 Keystone Ranch Rd., Keystone (© **970/496-4250**), charging $100 to $140, including a cart, for 18 holes; and the **River Course at Keystone,** 155 River Course Dr., Keystone (© **970/496-4444**), which also charges $100 to $140, including cart, for 18 holes.

HIKING & BACKPACKING The **Colorado Trail** 𝒜𝒜 cuts a swath through Summit County. It enters from the east across Kenosha Pass, follows the Swan River to its confluence with the Blue River, then climbs over Ten Mile Mountain to Copper Mountain. The trail then turns south toward Tennessee Pass, north of Leadville. Contact the **Colorado Trail Foundation,** American Mountaineering Center, 710 10th St. #210, Golden, CO 80401-5843 (© **303/384-3729;** www.coloradotrail.org).

In addition, there are myriad hiking opportunities in the national forests. Consult the U.S. Forest Service, the Breckenridge Resort Chamber Activity Center, or a visitor information center for maps and details.

HORSEBACK RIDING For some spectacular views of this area from atop a horse, take a ride with **Kingdom of Breckenridge Stables,** located just above the Beaver Run ski lift on Village Road (© **970/453-4438;** www.colorado-horses.com/kingdom). The company offers rides of about 90 minutes, plus breakfast rides, for $45 per person (half-price for children 6 and under). Reservations should be made at least 1 day in advance.

MOUNTAIN BIKING Numerous trails are available for mountain bikers. Energetic fat-tire fans can try the Devil's Triangle, a difficult 80-mile loop that begins and ends in Frisco after climbing four mountain passes (including 11,318-ft. Fremont Pass). Check with the U.S. Forest Service or Breckenridge Resort Chamber Activity Center for directions and tips on other trails; for mountain bikers who prefer to not work so hard, check with the Breckenridge Resort Chamber Activity Center on times and costs for taking your bike up the mountain on the Breckenridge chairlift.

Among the companies providing bike rentals and information is **Lone Star Sports,** at 200 W. Washington St., Breckenridge (© **800/621-9733** or 970/453-2003; www.skilonestar.com), which charges full-day rates of $15 to $25.

RIVER RAFTING Trips through the white water of the Blue River—which runs through Breckenridge to Frisco—as well as longer journeys on the Colorado and Arkansas rivers, are offered by various companies, including **Good Times Rafting Company** (© **800/808-0357;** www.goodtimesrafting.com), **Performance Tours Rafting** (© **800/328-7238;** www.performancetours.com), and **The Adventure Company** (© **800/497-7238;** www.theadventurecompany.com), all based in Breckenridge. Rates for half-day trips on the Blue River cost about $40 to $50 for adults and $30 to $40 for children. Full-day trips on other area rivers are about $75 to $100 for adults and $65 to $80 for kids.

THE FESTIVAL SCENE

The **Breckenridge Music Festival** presents dozens of classical and nonclassical music performances, with concerts in the Riverwalk Center from mid-June through mid-August. Tickets cost from $15 to $25; they're only $5 for students under 18. Contact the Breckenridge Music Festival, P.O. Box 1254, Breckenridge, CO 80424 (© **970/453-9142** or 970/547-3100 for the box office; www.breckenridgemusicfestival.com).

Genuine Jazz in Breckenridge, on the last weekend of June, showcases Colorado jazz ensembles with styles ranging from Dixieland to bebop to New Age. Local bars and nightclubs host Friday and Saturday night performances, and there are also free outdoor concerts. Contact Peak Performances, Box 57, Breckenridge, CO 80424 (© **866/464-2626** for tickets; www.genuinejazz.com).

The **Breckenridge Festival of Film,** held in early September, attracts Hollywood directors and actors to town to discuss some two dozen films in all genres. Films that have premiered here include *American Beauty, The Shawshank Redemption, Shark Tale,* and *L.A. Confidential.* For more information contact the Breckenridge Festival of Film, P.O. Box 718, Breckenridge, CO 80424 (© **970/453-6200;** www.breckfilmfest.com).

MORE TO SEE & DO

Families traveling with kids might want to stop at the **Mountain Top Children's Museum,** 605 S. Park Ave. (© **970/453-7878**), with a number of exhibits open daily in summer and winter; and the **Victorian train** at Main Street Station, 505 S. Main St. (© **970/453-RAIL**).

Amaze'n Breckenridge   Quite possibly Colorado's largest human maze, this is Amaze'n Colorado's original creation. The two-level labyrinth of twists and turns offers prizes to participants who can "beat the clock." Like the Amaze'n Winter Park (p. 283), the maze is changed weekly to maintain interest for repeat customers. A free observation deck provides a bird's-eye view of the maze, as well as the surrounding scenery. Allow 1 to 1½ hours.

1579 Ski Hill Rd. at the base of Peak 8, Breckenridge. © 970/453-5000. www.amazenmazes.com. Admission $6 adults, $5 children 5–12, free for children under 5. Additional maze runs $2. Mid-June to Labor Day. Call for hours.

Breckenridge National Historic District   The entire Victorian core of this 19th-century mining town has been carefully preserved, and you can see it on your own (pick up a free walking-tour brochure at the Visitor Information Cabin), or during the summer on guided 1½-hour walking tours conducted by the Summit Historical Society. Colorfully painted shops and restaurants occupy the old buildings, most dating from the 1880s and 1890s. Most of the historic district focuses on Main Street, and extends east on either side of Lincoln Avenue. Among the 254 historic buildings in the district are the **Barney Ford House Museum,** 111 E. Washington Ave., the **1875 Edwin Carter Museum,** 111 N. Ridge St., and the **1896 William Harrison Briggle House,** 104 N. Harris St., in Milne Park. The society also leads tours during the summer to the outskirts of town to visit the underground shaft of the hard-rock **Washington Gold Mine** and the gold-panning operation at **Lomax Placer Gulch.** Allow 2 to 4 hours.

Breckenridge. © 970/453-9022. www.summithistorical.org. Guided tours $3 per person. Tour tickets available at the Breckenridge Resort Chamber Welcome Center, 309 N. Main St. Historic district tours mid-June to Sept Tues–Sat; Edwin Carter Museum tours mid-June to Sept; museum open year-round, call for times; free admission.

Country Boy Mine   At this 100-year-old mine you can take a guided tour 1,000 feet underground, pan for gold in Eureka Creek, explore the mining exhibit and the five-story 75-year-old mill, and listen to the legends. Or take a hay ride up the mountain on old mining trails and enjoy hot chocolate and roasted marshmallows around a campfire. The mine is a constant 45°F (7°C) year-round, so take a jacket even in August. There's also a restored blacksmith shop, indoor gold panning in winter, and sleigh rides are available in the snowy months (www.brecksleighrides.com). Every summer sees the addition of a baby burro. Tours start on the hour. Allow at least an hour.

0542 French Gulch Rd., P.O. Box 8569, Breckenridge. © 970/453-4405. www.countryboymine.com. Mine tour $18 adults, $13 children 4–12, free for kids under 4; hay ride $22 adults, $17 children 4–12, free for kids under 4. Special rates and hours are available for families and groups. MC, V. Summer daily 10am–4pm; winter by reservation. The hours have some other seasonal fluctuations—call for details.

Dillon Schoolhouse Museum   A one-room country school—built in 1883 and filled with such artifacts of early Colorado education as desks with inkwells, McGuffey readers, and scientific teaching apparatus—is the highlight of this historic park.

Also on the site are the 1885 Lula Myers ranch house and the Depression-era Honeymoon Cabin. All buildings were moved from Old Dillon (now beneath the waters of the reservoir) or Keystone. Tours are also conducted (by appointment) of the 1884 Montezuma Schoolhouse, located at 10,400 feet elevation in the 1860s silver-mining camp of Montezuma. Allow about an hour.

403 LaBonte St., Dillon. ✆ 970/453-9022. www.summithistorical.org. Admission/guided tour $6 adults, $3 children 12 and younger. Mid-June to Labor Day Tues–Sat 1–4pm; or by appointment.

Frisco Historic Park ★ Ten historic buildings—including the town's original 1881 jail, a one-room schoolhouse, a log chapel, and homes dating from the 1880s—make up this beautifully maintained historic park. The schoolhouse contains displays and artifacts from Frisco's early days, and a trapper's cabin has a hands-on exhibit of animal pelts. Artisans sell their wares in several buildings, and a variety of events are scheduled during the summer. A self-guided walking tour of historic Frisco can be obtained at the park. Allow 1 hour.

120 Main St. (at Second St.), Frisco. ✆ 970/668-3428. www.townoffrisco.com. Free admission. Tues–Sat 10am–4pm, Sun 10am–2pm.

SHOPPING

Breckenridge is the place to shop in Summit County, with a variety of shops and galleries in the historic buildings along Main Street.

For contemporary art, from realism to Impressionism, check out **Breckenridge Gallery,** 124 S. Main St. (✆ 970/453-2592). Original Western paintings and bronzes, plus historic Navajo weavings and cowboy and Indian collectibles can be found at **Paint Horse Gallery,** 226 S. Main St. (✆ 970/453-6813). A cooperative managed by the Summit Arts Council, **Arts Alive,** in La Cima Mall at 520 S. Main St. (✆ 970/453-0450), is another good gallery that showcases the work of local artists If you're in the market for a unique hat—including some really hilarious ones—try the **Breckenridge Hat Company,** 411 S. Main St. (✆ 970/453-2737). The **Silverthorne Factory Stores** (✆ 970/468-9440) has about 80 outlet shops—from fashion and athletic wear to home accessories; take I-70 to exit 205.

WHERE TO STAY

Thousands of rooms are available here at any given time. Even so, during peak seasons, finding accommodations may be difficult, and rates are dramatically higher from Christmas to New Year's. In many cases it will be best to simply call one of the reservation services, tell them when you plan to visit and how much you want to spend, and ask for their suggestions. Throughout the county, condominiums prevail. While they often offer the best value, they're sometimes short on charm. If you're planning to spend much time in one, it pays to ask about views and fireplaces before booking. Local reservation services include **Summit County Central Reservations** (✆ 800/525-3682; www.skierlodging.com), **Breckenridge Central Reservations** (✆ 877/593-5260; www.gobreck.com), and in Keystone, **Key to the Rockies** (✆ 800/248-1942; www.keytotherockies.com). **ResortQuest Breckenridge** (✆ 800/507-7621; www.resortquestbreckenridge.com) has 440 rooms spread across a number of properties, everything from simple studios to luxurious and spacious three-bedroom units and private luxury homes. Most have mountain views or are nestled among tall pines, have a fireplace, and are within easy strolling distance of historic Main Street, such as the company's flagship

Hyatt Main Street Station (see below). Many units are ski-in/ski-out. Double rates range from $83 to $324 in summer and $115 to $1,238 in ski season.

In addition to the properties discussed below, there's the **Best Western Lake Dillon Lodge,** 1202 Summit Blvd., Frisco (© **800/727-0607** or 970/668-5094), charging $79 to $149 double; **Comfort Suites** in Dillon at I-70 exit 205 (© **800/424-6423** or 970/513-0300), with rates of $69 to $250 double; and **Super 8,** also at I-70 exit 205 (© **800/800-8000** or 970/468-8888), with double rates of $60 to $130. For a hostel bunk or private bed-and-breakfast room, try the funky and eclectic **Fireside Inn,** 114 N. French St. (© **970/453-6456;** www.firesideinn.com), with 18 bunks ($26–$38) and four private rooms ($60–$175 for two). Amenities include free Wi-Fi and one of the oldest hot tubs in Colorado.

Room taxes add about 9.5% to hotel bills.

Allaire Timbers Inn Bed & Breakfast ★★

This romantic mountain hideaway is a lovely contemporary log lodge, with a stone wood-burning fireplace in the living room and magnificent views of the mountains and town. All rooms are named for and decorated around the motif of a Colorado mountain pass. There are hand-painted tiled showers—no tubs—in standard rooms, but the two suites have hot tubs and river-rock gas-burning fireplaces. All units come with private decks, CD players, robes, and fuzzy fleece socks. The homemade gourmet breakfast includes a choice of a meat or vegetarian entree, plus fruit and muffins. In the afternoon, guests can enjoy hot citrus cider (an old family recipe), beer, or wine; and the beverage bar is available 24 hours. Located just outside the town limits, an easy path takes you right into town. The inn is also conveniently located on the free ski shuttle route; children 13 years and older are welcome. Neither smoking nor pets are allowed—the resident dog has prior claim.

9511 Colo. 9 (P.O. Box 4653), Breckenridge, CO 80424. © **800/624-4904** or 970/453-7530. Fax 970/453-8699. www.allairetimbers.com. 10 units. $145–$265 double; $230–$400 suite. Rates include full breakfast. AE, DISC, MC, V. **Amenities:** Outdoor hot tub. *In room:* TV, dataport.

Barn on the River

Built in 1997, this delightful bed-and-breakfast is right on the banks of the Blue River, as was the status quo for barns during Breckenridge's mining heyday. However, its serene riverside location belies the fact that it's on the edge of downtown. With rustic farmhouse decor and antique furnishings and art, the Barn on the River is a refreshing mix of old and new, with satellite TV, cordless phones, and Wi-Fi. Designed for couples, the guest rooms are elegant but not frilly, with gas fireplaces, grand headboards, and a romantic aura. Between the inn and the river is an idyllic garden area with tables and chairs and a hot tub. Innkeepers Fred Kinat and Diane Jaynes are terrific hosts and great sources of advice, and their breakfasts are scrumptious.

303B N. Main St., Breckenridge, CO 80424. © **800/795-2975** or 970/453-2975. www.breckenridge-inn.com. 4 units. $149–$289 double. Rates include full breakfast. AE, DISC, MC, V. **Amenities:** Outdoor hot tub. *In room:* Cable TV, wireless Internet.

Hyatt Main Street Station ★

The flagship property of ResortQuest Breckenridge (see above), Main Street Station is in an enviable location, right on Maggie Pond (which becomes a skating rink in winter), 200 yards from the nearest lift, but on Main Street right downtown. Built in 2001, the property offers an upscale ski lodge ambience and a selection of warmly decorated guest rooms with oversized bathrooms and one to three bedrooms. The units are full-service condos with kitchens, gas fireplaces, and plenty of room to spread out. The amenity list is long and comprehensive, including a shopping arcade, an outdoor Olympic-size pool, and a 24-seat state-of-the-art theater guests can reserve.

505 S. Main St. (P.O. Box 2738), Breckenridge, CO 80424. ☎ 800/506-7621 or 970/547-2700. Fax 970/453-0463. www.hyattmainstreetstation.com. 110 units. Summer $149–$310; winter $379–$806. AE, DISC, MC, V. Underground parking. **Amenities:** 2 restaurants; lounge; outdoor heated pool; fitness center; 7 outdoor hot tubs; concierge; courtesy shuttle. *In room:* Cable TV, kitchen, hair dryer, iron, Wi-Fi network.

Little Mountain Lodge Bed & Breakfast ☞ This handsome, whitewashed log lodge is among our top choices in Breckenridge. Nestled among the trees, the lodge offers breathtaking views of the mountains from the front rooms and the aspen forest from the back. Featuring decor on different themes, all the rooms are open and airy, and boast a balcony or deck, handmade log furnishings, and ceiling fans. Some rooms have whirlpool tubs, one has a steam shower, and most of them feature vaulted ceilings. The living room has a huge river-rock fireplace, with an overstuffed sofa and chairs comfortably arranged around it. A downstairs family room contains a stone fireplace, TV, and VCR and DVD player. There's also a ski and bike storage room and a ski boot dryer. Children of all ages are welcome (rare in B&Bs); smoking is not permitted.

98 Sunbeam Dr. (P.O. Box 2479), Breckenridge, CO 80424. ☎ 800/468-7707 or 970/453-1969. Fax 970/453-1919. www.littlemountainlodge.com. 10 units. $140–$225 double; $170–$270 suite. Lower rates often available in spring and fall. Rates include full breakfast and evening appetizers. AE, DISC, MC, V. **Amenities:** Large hot tub; business center; common refrigerator and microwave. *In room:* Cable TV/VCR (video library available), coffeemaker, hair dryer.

The Lodge & Spa at Breckenridge Nestled on a forested cliff overlooking the ski resort and the Ten Mile mountains, this hotel is upscale, but with a Rocky Mountain atmosphere. The unique rooms have custom furnishings, rustic peeled-log beams, and balconies (or views). Many also have fireplaces, feather duvets, and poster beds, contrasting rustic touches with a contemporary flair. Several suites have kitchenettes, and there's a luxury three-bedroom house with private hot tub. There is a 24-hour front desk, ski and boot storage, and a winter complimentary shuttle (7:30am–11pm) to anywhere in Breckenridge. The on-site Top of the World Restaurant & Bar serves American dinners with a regional influence and has a dramatic mountain view.

112 Overlook Dr. (P.O. Box 1078), Breckenridge, CO 80424. ☎ 800/736-1607 or 970/453-9300. Fax 970/453-0625. www.thelodgeatbreck.com. 46 units. $69–$355 double; $375–$799 house. Rates include continental breakfast. AE, DC, DISC, MC, V. Pets accepted. **Amenities:** Restaurant (American); lounge; indoor heated pool; fitness center; full-service spa; 2 hot tubs; sauna. *In room:* Cable TV, kitchenette (in suites only), coffeemaker, hair dryer, iron.

CAMPING

Tiger Run R.V. & Chalet Resort ☞☞ Named for a historic mine in the area, Tiger Run is both conveniently and beautifully located, with the Swan River running right through the property. Activities in winter include skiing, snowmobiling, cross-country skiing, and snowboarding; in summer there are wine-and-cheese parties, kids' s'mores night, and live music on Saturday. The clubhouse lodge, in the center of the park, is open year-round, with an indoor swimming pool, hot tubs, game room, TV room, laundry facilities, restrooms with showers, and telephones. There's a small no-food convenience store; tennis, volleyball, and basketball courts; a children's playground; and sports equipment available at the office. Pets are welcome in RV sites only. There are also 30 chalet-style cabins on the property, with rates of $70 to $135 for doubles ($10 per extra person); children 3 and under stay free. Smoking and pets are not permitted in the chalets.

85 Tiger Run Rd. (3 miles north of Breckenridge off Colo. 9), Breckenridge, CO 80424. ☎ 800/895-9594 or 970/453-9690. Fax 970/453-6782. www.tigerrunresort.com. 250 sites. $29–$54. Rates include water, sewer, electric, and cable TV hookups. Weekly rates available. AE, DISC, MC, V.

WHERE TO DINE
EXPENSIVE

Briar Rose Restaurant REGIONAL   Located uphill from the Main Street traffic light, the Briar Rose is among the town's most elegant (but still casual) restaurants. Classical paintings, fine music, and linen service underscore Briar Rose's sophisticated atmosphere. The adjoining trophy bar and lounge has big-game heads, sports memorabilia, and a 100-year-old back bar. In fine weather you can dine alfresco while gazing at the surrounding mountains from the new deck outside the lounge. You can start with escargot, crab-stuffed mushrooms, coconut shrimp, wild game sausage, or homemade soup. Dinners feature game—usually elk, buffalo, and caribou. Other popular choices include slow-roasted prime rib, veal, steak, duck, lamb, fresh seafood, and vegetarian and pasta entrees. A children's menu is available, and the extensive wine list offers domestic and imported wines.

109 E. Lincoln St. ℂ 970/453-9948. Reservations recommended. Main courses $15–$30. AE, DISC, MC, V. Ski season daily 5–10pm; rest of year Mon–Sat 6–10pm. Bar opens at 4:30pm.

Cafe Alpine ✺✺ CONTEMPORARY AMERICAN   With a refined, intimate atmosphere and a menu so creative it's a pleasure to read, Cafe Alpine is our pick for a romantic dinner in Breckenridge. Sit in one of several small rooms, upstairs or down, or in the bar, and pick from a seasonally-changing selection that combines traditions from near and far into slick dishes like crispy plantain soft shell crabs with habanero-pineapple upside-down cake, or chicken stuffed with curried crab and mint, and served with hummus potato salad. There is always a selection of fresh seafood and a vegetarian option. The inventive fare is matched by a terrific wine list, and there are tapas served on the deck here from 3pm daily.

106 E. Adams Ave. ℂ 970/453-8218. Reservations recommended. Main courses $16–$26. AE, DC, DISC, MC, V. Daily 5–10pm. Tapas from 3pm.

Hearthstone ✺ REGIONAL   A favorite of locals because of its creative cuisine, the Hearthstone is in a historic home built in 1886. It has a rustic yet elegant interior, with fine mountain views from the upstairs lounge. Start with the house smoked trout, sweet potato gnocchi, or crispy lobster, then choose from fresh seafood such as ginger-crusted scallops or ahi tuna. Other choices include the blackberry elk with a garlic-granola crust, Colorado lamb strip loin with pinot noir reduction, and a local favorite: filet au poivre—an 8-ounce black pepper–encrusted tenderloin with a brandy-Dijon-cream reduction. Come to the smoke-free Victorian Lounge during happy hour (4–6pm) for specials on drinks and appetizers.

130 S. Ridge St. ℂ 970/453-1148. www.stormrestaurants.com/hearthstone. Reservations recommended. Main courses $17–$38. AE, DC, MC, V. Daily 5–10pm.

Keystone Ranch ✺✺ CREATIVE REGIONAL   A working cattle ranch for more than 3 decades until 1972, the Keystone Ranch now boasts riding stables, a golf course, and this outstanding gourmet restaurant, located in a 1940s ranch house with a mountain-lodge decor. Among the area's best restaurants, the Keystone Ranch offers a six-course menu with a choice of appetizer, followed by soup, salad, and fruit sorbet. Main dishes, which vary seasonally, might include roasted rack of Colorado lamb, grilled duck breast, elk or other game, or fresh seafood. An extensive array of desserts is served in the living room in front of a handsome stone fireplace. There's valet parking and a full bar.

Keystone Ranch Rd., Keystone. © **970/496-4386.** Reservations strongly recommended. 6-course dinner $88 adults, $40 children under 13. AE, DC, DISC, MC, V. Summer and winter daily 5:30–8:30pm, 2 seatings; call for spring and fall hours.

MODERATE & INEXPENSIVE

For a quick meal on Main Street—but much better food than the typical fast variety—try **Crepes a la Cart,** 307 S. Main St. (© **970/453-0622**) for crepes packed with everything from broccoli and chicken to ice cream and chocolate.

Breckenridge Brewery and Pub ⭐ AMERICAN/BREWPUB This brewpub was designed around its brewery, giving diners a firsthand view of the brewing process. Of the award-winning beers, try the Trademark Pale or the Avalanche, a local favorite. Like many good brewpubs, lunch choices here include fish and chips, half-pound burgers, and soups and salads (try the mango spinach salad). But the menu also strives to be somewhat more interesting, offering items such as seared ahi tuna and grilled portobello mushroom sandwiches. The dinner menu adds tender tasty baby back ribs, the "Brewer's Top Sirloin," pasta dishes, and charbroiled fajitas for those who like it spicy. The desserts are homemade. Also see "Summit County After Dark," below.

600 S. Main St. © **970/453-1550.** www.breckenridgebrewery.com. Reservations not accepted. Main courses lunch $4.95–$9.95, dinner $7.95–$17. AE, DC, DISC, MC, V. Daily 11am–10pm; bar open later with limited menu.

Giampietro Pizzeria ⭐ *Value* ITALIAN Cozy, busy, and often with a long line out front (reservations are not accepted), Giampietro is worth the wait. The friendly service and red-and-white-checkered tablecloths make for a pleasant, casual atmosphere, but the Italian fare is what keeps people coning back. The pizza is excellent, as is the baked ziti, and the huge calzones—essentially a small pizza folded in half—are a meal that will satisfy just about any appetite, no how many miles biked or runs skied. There is a nice wine list, focused on Italian labels.

115 S. Main St. © **970/453-7463.** Reservations not accepted. Main courses $6.75–$13; pizzas from $13. MC, V. Daily 11am–10pm.

Mi Casa MEXICAN Mi Casa is Breckenridge's best Mexican restaurant. Its newly remodeled cantina is the locals' favorite spot for happy hour, and the margaritas are consistently voted the best in Summit County. In addition to the standard burritos, tostadas, and enchiladas, the restaurant is known for its homemade tamales and chile rellenos and its seafood dishes—fish tacos, chile-encrusted trout, snapper Vera Cruz, and spicy shrimp Diablo. The margaritas and tequila selection are both excellent.

600 Park Ave. © **970/453-2071.** www.stormrestaurants.com. Reservations not accepted. Main courses $7.95–$16. AE, MC, V. Daily 11:30am–3pm and 5–9pm.

SUMMIT COUNTY AFTER DARK

Though every community has its watering holes, Breckenridge has the best nightlife in the area.

The **Backstage Theatre,** 121 S. Ridge St., Breckenridge (© **970/453-0199;** www.backstagetheatre.org), has been presenting a variety of live theater since 1974. Recent productions have included Shakespeare's *Twelfth Night, The Vagina Monologues, Matt & Ben, Nunsense,* and *The Search for Signs of Intelligent Life in the Universe.* Ticket prices vary but most are $15 for adults and $8 for children under 12; reservations are strongly recommended.

Popular bars in Breckenridge include the **Breckenridge Brewery and Pub,** 600 S. Main St. (© **970/453-1550;** www.breckenridgebrewery.com), where the microbrews include Avalanche Ale, a full-bodied amber ale, and our favorite, Trademark Pale, an American-style pale ale loaded with hops. Also see "Where to Dine," above. The **Salt Creek Restaurant and Saloon,** 1101 E. Lincoln Ave. (© **970/453-4949**), is a popular live-music dance club where you'll hear practically everything but country. For everything from live blues to reggae, try **Sherpa & Yeti's,** 318 S. Main St. (© **970/547-9299;** www.sherpaandyetis.com), and the young, hip **Downstairs at Eric's,** a bar and restaurant at 111 S. Main St. (© **970/453-1401;** www.downstairsaterics.com) that is popular with locals and the après-ski crowd alike and boasts 120 types of beer, including 22 on tap. **The Cellar,** 200 S. Ridge St. (© **970/453-4777**), is a slick wine and tapas bar with contemporary art and an attractive red granite bar. Established in the 1870s and said to be the longest continually operating bar west of the Mississippi (local lawmen were afraid to shut it down during Prohibition), the **Gold Pan,** 103 N. Main St. (© **970/ 453-5499**), is a rough-and-tumble, ornery place that's hard not to like.

6 Vail & Beaver Creek

109 miles W. of Denver, 150 miles E. of Grand Junction

Consistently ranked the country's most popular ski resort by skiers and ski magazines almost since its inception, Vail is the big one. It's hard to imagine a more celebrated spot to schuss. Off the slopes, Vail is an incredibly compact Tyrolean village, frequented by almost as many Europeans as Americans, a situation that lends its restaurants, lodgings, and trendy shops a more transatlantic feel than other Colorado resorts. But the size of the mountain and the difficulty and excitement of many of its trails are still what draw the faithful.

Historically speaking, there is very little in the town's past to indicate that Vail would become the megadestination it has. Until U.S. 6 was built through Vail Pass in 1939, the only inhabitants were a handful of sheep ranchers. Dropping farther back into history, it's worth noting that the resort could never have been possible if it weren't for severe droughts in the 1850s and 1860s that resulted in numerous forest fires. The burnings created the wide-open ridges and back bowls that make skiers and snowboarders the world over quiver in their boots.

It was only when veterans of the 10th Mountain Division, who trained during World War II at Camp Hale, 23 miles south of the valley, returned in the 1950s that the reality of skiing was realized. One of them, Peter Siebert (1924–2002), urged development of this mountain land in the White River National Forest, and through his vision, Vail opened to skiers in December 1962, immediately becoming one of the largest ski areas in the United States. Additional ski-lift capacity made Vail America's largest ski resort by 1964.

Beaver Creek, built in 1980, has quickly garnered a reputation as an elegant (and pricey) vacation spot. Like Vail, it is a four-season resort that offers golf (the course was designed by Robert Trent Jones, Jr.), hot-air ballooning, mountain biking, fishing, and horseback riding, in addition to skiing. Its atmosphere is a bit more formal than the surrounding area, and its nightlife tends more toward refined piano bars than rowdy saloons, but the exclusivity of its après-ski spots isn't reflected on the slopes. At Beaver Creek, there's a trail for everyone. Experts are challenged but beginners aren't left out—they too can head straight to the top and then ski all the way down on a trail that matches their skill level.

ESSENTIALS

GETTING THERE   By Car   Vail is right on the I-70 corridor, so it's exceedingly easy to find. Just take exit 176, whether you're coming from the east (Denver) or the west (Grand Junction). A more direct route from the south is U.S. 24 through Leadville; this Tennessee Pass road joins I-70 5 miles west of Vail. Beaver Creek is located 12 miles west of Vail, off I-70 exit 167.

By Plane   Year-round, visitors can fly directly into **Eagle County Airport,** 35 miles west of Vail between I-70 exits 140 and 147 (© 970/524-9490; www.eaglecounty.us/airport), which is served by **American** (© 800/433-7300), **Continental** (© 800/525-0280), **Delta** (© 800/221-1212), **Northwest** (© 800/225-2525), **United** (© 800/864-8331), and **US Airways** (© 800/428-4322).

By Airport Shuttle   Many visitors fly into Denver International Airport and continue to Vail and Beaver Creek aboard a shuttle service such as **Colorado Mountain Express** (© 800/525-6363 or 970/926-9800; www.cmex.com), with one-way rates starting at about $65 per person. There are also shuttle services from the Eagle County Airport to Vail and Beaver Creek; contact **High Mountain Taxi** (© 970/524-5555; www.hmtaxi.com), which charges $95 to $145 for up to six passengers, and also provides regional shuttle services. Both of the above shuttle services offer online reservations. You can also get to the Vail/Beaver Creek area from the regional airport with **Vail Valley Taxi** (© 877/829-8294; www.vailtaxi.com) at similar rates to High Mountain Taxi, but to save a bundle of money, take the **bus** (see "Getting Around," below). Also, see **car rentals** under "Getting Around," below.

VISITOR INFORMATION   For information or reservations in the Vail Valley, contact the **Vail Valley Chamber and Tourism Bureau,** 100 E. Meadow Dr., Suite 34, Vail, CO 81657 (© 800/525-3875 or 970/476-1000; www.visitvailvalley.com), or **Vail Mountain Resort,** P.O. Box 7, Vail, CO 81658 (© 800/525-2257 or 970/476-5601; www.vail.com or www.beavercreek.com). You can also get information on year-round activities and events by calling the **Resort Information and Activities Center** (© 970/476-9090). Information centers are located at the parking structures in Vail and the Lionshead area on South Frontage Road.

Parents traveling with kids can find all sorts of pointers in *The Parents Handbook to the Vail Valley* (© 970/390-3533; www.theparentshandbook.com), available free all over Eagle County.

GETTING AROUND   Vail is one of only a few Colorado communities where you really don't need a car. The town of Vail runs the nation's largest **free shuttle-bus service** between 6am and 2am daily, although hours may be shorter in shoulder seasons. Shuttles in the Vail Village–Lionshead area run every 10 minutes, and there are regularly scheduled trips to West Vail and East Vail (© 970/328-8143). The **Eagle County Regional Transportation Authority,** known locally at ECO Transit © 970/328-3520; www.eaglecounty.us/ecotransit), runs shuttles between Vail and Beaver Creek, a 12-mile trip, plus regional bus service to Avon, Edwards, Minturn, Leadville, and the Eagle County Airport daily ($3–$5 each way). Both **High Mountain Taxi** (© 970/524-5555; www.hmtaxi.com) and **Vail Valley Taxi** (© 877/829-8294; www.vailtaxi.com) operate throughout the area, around the clock.

Car rentals available at the Eagle County Airport, including four-wheel-drive vehicles, include **Avis** (© 800/331-1212 or 970/524-7571), **Budget** (© 800/527-0700

Vail

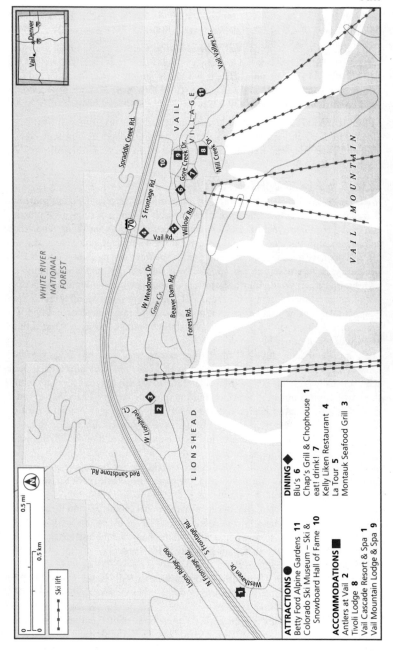

ATTRACTIONS ●
Betty Ford Alpine Gardens **11**
Colorado Ski Museum – Ski &
Snowboard Hall of Fame **10**

ACCOMMODATIONS ■
Antlers at Vail **2**
Tivoli Lodge **8**
Vail Cascade Resort & Spa **1**
Vail Mountain Lodge & Spa **9**

DINING ◆
Blu's **6**
Chap's Grill & Chophouse **1**
eat! drink! **7**
Kelly Liken Restaurant **4**
La Tour **5**
Montauk Seafood Grill **3**

or 970/524-8260), **Dollar** (© **800/800-4000** or 970/524-9429), **Hertz** (© **800/654-3131** or 970/524-7177), and **National** (© **800/227-7368** or 970/524-2277).

FAST FACTS   The hospital, **Vail Valley Medical Center,** with 24-hour emergency care, is at 181 W. Meadow Dr. between Vail Road and East Lionshead Circle (© **970/476-2451**). The **post office** is at 1300 N. Frontage Rd.; for hours and other information contact the U.S. Postal Service (© **800/275-8777;** www.usps.com). For **road conditions,** call © **970/479-2226.**

SPECIAL EVENTS   Taste of Vail, early April; Vail America Days, July 4th; Beaver Creek Arts Festival, early August in Beaver Creek; Oktoberfest, mid-September in Vail; and New Year's Eve Celebration, December 31 in Beaver Creek. Also see "The Festival Scene," below.

SKIING & OTHER WINTER ACTIVITIES

VAIL 🏆🏆🏆   America's top ski resort by practically any standard, Vail is something that all serious skiers must experience at least once. It has fantastic snow, great runs, and everything is so convenient that skiers can concentrate solely on skiing (and related enjoyments, if they so choose). You can arrive at the base village, unload and park your car, and not have to drive again until it's time to go. Your lodging choices offer as much pampering as you want, or can afford. You'll find all the shops, restaurants, and nightlife you could want within a short walk of your hotel or condominium.

In fact, our only real complaint about Vail (aside from the expense) is that it didn't exist before it became a ski resort, and so it lacks the historic ambience and Old West downtown area that you'll find in Aspen, Steamboat Springs, Telluride, Crested Butte, and a number of other Western ski centers.

Ski area boundaries stretch 7 miles from east to west along the ridge top, from Outer Mongolia to Game Creek Bowl, and the skiable terrain is measured at 5,289 acres. Virtually every lift on the front side of the mountain has runs for every level of skier, with a predominance of novice and intermediate terrain. The seven legendary Back Bowls are strictly for advanced and expert skiers; snow and weather conditions determine just how expert you ought to be. One trip down the Slot or Rasputin's Revenge will give you a fair idea of just how good you are. Blue Sky Basin, which opened in 2000 on the next mountain south of Vail, is accessed by three high-speed quad chairlifts, and intermediate to advanced terrain offering backcountry-like conditions. There is a warming hut at the top of the basin with a basic snack bar, water, restroom facilities, and a pair of gas grills.

Vail has a vertical drop of 3,450 feet; average annual snowfall is 346 inches (nearly 29 ft.). All told, there are 193 conventional trails served by 34 lifts—a gondola, 14 high-speed quad chairs, 1 fixed-grip quad, 3 triple chairs, 5 double chairs, and 10 surface lifts. There are also four terrain parks for snowboarders of all skill levels, and a unique log-rail park at Golden Peak.

There are more than 18 **mountain restaurants** at Vail. **Game Creek** (© **970/479-4275**), in a handsome European-style chalet, offers creative regional cuisine and splendid views from its perch overlooking Game Creek Bowl at the top of Vail Mountain. **Two Elk Restaurant** on the top of China Bowl offers Southwestern cuisine, pizza, and pasta, plus baked potato and salad bars. At **Buffalo's** you'll find deli sandwiches, pizza, chili, soup, and a good variety of specialty coffees. **Wildwood** touts an eclectic selection of American dishes; **The Marketplace** serves various ethnic dishes in a cafeteria setting; and a variety of dishes are available at the full-service **Blue Moon Restaurant and Bar.** Mid-Vail has two levels of food courts that serve breakfast, lunch, and après-ski drinks, including **Sarge's Shelter,** which offers great barbecue and burgers and a wonderful outdoor deck.

Vail has a highly respected children's program, and there are daily NASTAR races.

Peak season daily lift tickets are $81 for adults and seniors, $49 for children 5 to 12, and free for children 4 and younger. Any lift ticket purchased at Vail is also valid at Beaver Creek, Keystone, Arapahoe Basin, and Breckenridge ski areas. Vail is usually open from mid-November to late April, daily from 9am to 3:30pm. For further information, contact **Vail Mountain,** P.O. Box 7, Vail, CO 81658 (© **800/404-3535** or 970/476-5601; 970/476-4888 for snow report; www.vail.com or www.snow.com).

BEAVER CREEK 🎿🎿   Also owned by Vail Resorts, Beaver Creek is an outstanding resort in its own right, one with a more secluded atmosphere and maybe even more luxury than its better-known neighbor. Located in a valley 1½ miles off the I-70 corridor, Beaver Creek combines European château-style elegance in its base village with expansive slopes for novice and intermediate skiers. The Grouse Mountain, Birds of Prey, and Cinch lifts reach expert terrain.

The big news here is the opening in 2006 of the new Stone Creek Chutes, an expert terrain area with chutes up to 550 vertical feet long, with pitches up to 44 degrees. On the horizon is a new gondola from Avon, which is scheduled to open for the 2007–08 season. The gondola will connect a new Westin in Avon with the Lower Beaver Creek lift.

From Beaver Creek Village, the Centennial Express lift to Spruce Saddle and Birds of Prey Express lift reach northwest-facing midmountain slopes and the Flattops beginners' area atop the mountain, offering a unique beginner's experience. Opposite, the Strawberry Park Express lift accesses Larkspur Bowl and the McCoy Park cross-country ski and snowshoe area at 9,840 feet. Three other lifts—Larkspur, Grouse Mountain, and Birds of Prey (serving the expert area of the same name, one of the steepest downhill slopes in the world) leave from Red-Tail Camp at midmountain. Arrowhead Mountain is also part of Beaver Creek. The two are connected through Bachelor Gulch, offering village-to-village skiing.

Beaver Creek's vertical drop is 4,040 feet from the 11,440-foot summit. There are 1,805 developed acres, though Vail Associates are licensed to develop up to 5,600. There are 16 lifts (nine high-speed quad chairs, three triple chairs, three doubles, and a surface lift) that serve 162 trails, and the average annual snowfall is 310 inches. There are three terrain parks and a half-pipe. The resort offers a unique **Talons Challenge** every day, awarding a lanyard, pin, and recognition on a "Wall of Fame" to skiers and snowboarders who complete 13 designated runs in one day, a total of 23,722 vertical feet.

There are seven **mountain restaurants,** including the highly praised **Beano's Cabin** (see "Where to Dine," later in this chapter). Among other on-mountain eateries are the **Spruce Saddle Lodge,** a dining court offering burgers, wraps, pizza, and salads; the upscale **Zach's Cabin,** which is reached for dinner via sleigh; the **Red Tail Camp,** a barbecue fast-food stop; and the **Broken Arrow Café,** serving burgers, sandwiches, pizzas, and soups.

Peak season daily lift tickets are $81 for adults and seniors, $49 for children 5 to 12, and free for children 4 and younger. Any lift ticket purchased at Beaver Creek is also valid at Vail, Keystone, Arapahoe Basin, and Breckenridge ski areas.

Beaver Creek is usually open from mid-November to late April, daily from 9am to 4pm. For more information, contact **Beaver Creek Resort,** P.O. Box 7, Vail, CO 81658 (© **800/404-3535** or 970/845-9090, 800/427-8308 for snow reports; www.beavercreek.com).

BACKCOUNTRY SKI TOURS Paragon Guides (© **877/926-5299** or 970/926-5299; www.paragonguides.com), is one of the country's premier winter guide services, offering backcountry ski trips on the 10th Mountain Trail and Hut System between Vail and Aspen (see "Cross-Country Skiing," below). A variety of trips are available, lasting from 3 to 6 days and designed for all ability levels. Costs start around $1,000 per person for the 3-day trip.

CROSS-COUNTRY SKIING Cross-country skiers won't feel left out here, with trails at both resorts as well as a system of trails through the surrounding mountains. **Vail's Nordic Center** (© **970/476-8366**) has 21 miles of trails, part of them on the Vail Golf Course, and offers guided tours, lessons, and snowshoeing. The **Beaver Creek Nordic Center** (© **970/845-5313**), at Beaver Creek Resort, has a 20-mile mountaintop track system with a skating lane in 9,840-foot McCoy Park. Most of the high-altitude terrain here is intermediate, though there's some space for both beginner and advanced cross-country skiers; telemarking lessons are available.

For general information on the network of backcountry trails in the Vail area, contact the **Holy Cross Ranger District Office,** White River National Forest, at 24747 U.S. 24, 2 miles north of Minturn, off I-70 exit 171, Minturn, CO 81645 (© **970/827-5715;** www.fs.fed.us/r2).

Of particular note is the system of trails known as the **10th Mountain Division Hut System,** 1280 Ute Ave., Suite 21, Aspen, CO 81611 (© **970/925-5775;** www. huts.org). Generally following the World War II training network of the Camp Hale militia, the trails cover 300 miles and link Vail with Leadville and Aspen, with huts along the way where cross-country skiers and hikers can find shelter for the night. Huts are basic, with bunk beds, but do have wood stoves, propane burners, photovoltaic lighting, kitchen equipment, mattresses, and pillows. A one-person bed in one of the huts owned by the 10th Mountain Division Hut Association costs $28 per night for adults; huts owned by others but booked through the association cost $20 to $40 per adult. Children under 13 are charged half price.

WARM-WEATHER & OTHER YEAR-ROUND ACTIVITIES

Vail doesn't shut down once the skiers go home. Instead, visitors and locals alike trade their skis for mountain bikes and hiking boots, and hit the trails again. The resort closes parts of the mountain from early May to late June to protect elk-calving habitats, but other than that, warm-weather activities cover the mountains.

Nova Guides in Vail (© **888/949-6682** or 719/486-2656; www.novaguides.com), offers guided fishing, mountain-bike, and off-road tours, plus white-water rafting. The **10th Mountain Division Hut System,** which runs for 300 miles, is open to hikers and mountain bikers (see "Cross-Country Skiing," above).

You'll find many of the companies listed below on the Internet at **www.visitvail valley.com,** and **www.vail.com** is also a good source for information on summer activities. For maps and information on the numerous activities in the White River National Forest, consult the **Holy Cross Ranger District Office** (see "Cross-Country Skiing," above).

FISHING   The streams and mountain lakes surrounding Vail are rich with rainbow, brook, brown, and cutthroat trout, plus mountain whitefish. Gore Creek, which runs through the town of Vail, is a popular anglers' venue, especially toward evening from its banks along the Vail Golf Course. Other prime spots are the Eagle River, joined by Gore Creek 5 miles downstream near Minturn; the Black Lakes near the summit of Vail Pass; and 60-acre Piney Lake (see directions under "Mountain Biking," below). The **Lazy J Ranch** in Wolcott (© **970/926-3472;** www.lazyjranch.net) offers guided fly-fishing trips on four miles of private Eagle River frontage and to stocked lakes; half-day guided wade/float trips cost $275.

Other fishing guides in the area include **Nova Guides** (© **888/949-NOVA** or 719/486-2656; www.novaguides.com), **Piney River Ranch** (© **970/477-1171;** www.pineyriverranch.com), or **Fly Fishing Outfitters, Inc.** (© **800/595-8090** or 970/476-3474; www.flyfishingoutfitters.net), which also has a retail store with fishing supplies and outdoor clothing in Avon, across from the entrance to Beaver Creek.

GOLF   Courses here are usually open from mid-May to mid-October. Both the **Vail Golf Club,** 1778 Vail Valley Dr., Vail (© **970/479-2260**), and the **Eagle-Vail Golf Course,** 6 miles west of Vail at 431 Eagle Dr., Avon (© **970/949-5267**), charge $90 to $100 for 18 holes, with significant discounts after 3pm.

HIKING & BACKPACKING   The surrounding White River National Forest has a plethora of trails leading to pristine lakes and spectacular panoramic views. The Holy Cross Wilderness Area, southwest of Vail, encompasses 14,005-foot Mount of the Holy Cross and is an awesome region with over 100 miles of trails. Eagle's Nest Wilderness Area lies to the north, in the impressive Gore Range. For information and maps for these and other hiking areas, consult the **Holy Cross Ranger District Office** (see "Cross-Country Skiing," above).

HORSEBACK RIDING & CATTLE ROUNDUPS   One of the best ways to explore this beautiful and rugged mountain country is on the back of a horse. **The Ranch at Spraddle Creek,** 100 Spraddle Creek Rd. (© **970/476-6941**), is especially geared to families, with rides for beginners to experts. A 1½-hour ride costs $40. Also providing horseback rides are **Lazy J Ranch** (see above), which offers guided horseback rides starting at $55 for 1 hour. **Triple G Outfitters** at 4 Eagle Ranch, 4 miles north of I-70 exit 157 (© **970/926-1234;** www.tripleg.net), charges $35 and up for horseback rides, and also offers half-day cattle roundups for about $100, lunch included.

LLAMA TREKKING   **Paragon Guides** (see "Backcountry Ski Tours," above) offers llama-trekking trips, from 3 to 6 days, July through September. They are limited to eight persons for camping, or slightly larger groups for hut trips, and start around $1,000 per person for 3 days. Pricier custom treks are also available, from overnight to 1 week.

MOUNTAIN BIKING   Summer visitors can take their bikes up the Eagle Bahn Gondola to Adventure Ridge on Vail Mountain (all-day passes are $30 for adults, $23 for children 5–12) and cruise downhill on a series of trails. There are many other choices for avid bikers, both on backcountry trails and road tours. A popular trip is the 13-mile Lost Lake Trail along Red Sandstone Road to Piney Lake. The 30-mile Vail Pass Bikeway goes to Frisco, with a climb from 8,460 feet up to 10,600 feet. Pick up a trail list (with map) at an information center.

Mountain bike repairs and rentals are available at a number of shops, including **Vail Bike Tech,** 555 E. Lionshead Circle, Vail (© **800/525-5995** or 970/476-5995;

www.vailbiketech.com), which also offers guided tours; and **Wheel Base,** 610 W. Lionshead Circle (© **970/476-5799**). Rental rates are about $10 to $45 for a half day, $15 to $65 for a full day, depending on the type of bike.

RIVER RAFTING The Eagle River, just a few miles west of Vail, offers thrilling white water, especially during the May to June thaw. Families can enjoy the relatively gentle (Class II–IV) lower Eagle, west of Minturn; the upper Eagle, above Minturn, is significantly rougher (Class IV–V rapids). Area rafting companies also take trips on the Colorado River, which they access about 35 miles northwest via Colo. 131, at State Bridge. Rafting companies here include **Timberline Tours** (© **800/831-1414** or 970/476-1414; www.timberlinetours.com); **Nova Guides** (see above); and **Lakota River Guides** (© **800/274-0636** or 970/845-7238; www.lakotariver.com). Rates run $50 to $100 per adult for a half-day trip, with slightly lower rates for youths (young children aren't usually permitted).

THE FESTIVAL SCENE

The summer season's big cultural event is the **Bravo! Vail Valley Music Festival,** from late June through early August. Established in 1988, the festival features a variety of classical music from orchestral to chamber music to vocal, with performers such as the New York Philharmonic, Rochester Philharmonic, and Dallas Symphony. Tickets range from $21 to $82; contact the festival office at P.O. Box 2270, Vail, CO 81658 (© **877/812-5700** or 970/827-5700; www.vailmusicfestival.org).

The **Vail International Dance Festival** features both classes and performances. The World Masters Ballet Academy at Vail teaches the Russian style of artistic expression and other techniques, and presents a series of performances each summer. For information, contact the Vail Valley Foundation, P.O. Box 309, Vail, CO 81658 (© **888/883-8245** or 970/949-1999; www.vvf.org).

The Vail Valley Foundation also hosts **Hot Summer Nights,** free concerts of contemporary rock, jazz, or blues, on Tuesday evenings at 6:30pm from mid-June through early August.

NEARBY MUSEUMS & OTHER ATTRACTIONS

Betty Ford Alpine Gardens ℱ A wonderful place for a relaxing break from the rigors of an active vacation, these peaceful gardens offer a chance to see a variety of flowering alpine plants unique to the Rocky Mountains. At 8,200 feet, these are the highest public botanical gardens in North America. The alpine display, perennial garden, and mountain meditation garden together represent about 2,000 varieties of plants, demonstrating the wide range of choices to be grown at high altitudes. The gardens attract a variety of birds, and there is also a rock garden with a stunning 120-foot waterfall. Allow 1 to 3 hours.

Ford Park, east of Vail Village, Vail. © **970/476-0103.** www.bettyfordalpinegardens.org. Free admission. Snowmelt to snowfall daily dawn–dusk.

Colorado Ski Museum–Ski & Snowboard Hall of Fame The history of more than a century of Colorado skiing—from the boards that mountain miners first strapped on their feet, to the post–World War II resort boom, to Coloradans' success in international racing and the Olympics—is depicted in this popular showcase. Also included is the evolution of snowboarding, plus the role of the U.S. Forest Service. There's one room devoted to the 10th Mountain Division, the only division of the military trained in ski warfare. A theater presents historical and current ski videos. The museum incorporates the Colorado Ski & Snowboard Hall of Fame with plaques and photographs honoring Vail founder Peter Seibert, filmmaker Lowell Thomas, Olympic skier Buddy Werner, and others. Allow 1 hour.

Vail Transportation Center, Level 3. (© **970/476-1876.** www.skimuseum.net. Free admission. Tues–Sun 10am–5pm. Closed May and Oct, except by appointment.

SHOPPING

There are a wide variety of shops and galleries in Vail and Beaver Creek, but this is not a place for bargain hunters. Among art galleries of note are **Vail Fine Art Gallery,** Vail Village Crossroads Center, 141 E. Meadow Dr. (© **970/476-2900**), with beautiful sculptures and fine paintings. **Currents Fine Jewelers,** 285 Bridge St. (© **970/ 476-3322**), offers original designs in platinum, gold, and silver jewelry plus fine Swiss watches. Other interesting shops include **Mountain Dog,** 100 E. Meadow Dr., #33 (© **970/479-8488**), with canine accessories of all kinds; and **Kitchen Collage,** at Riverwalk, the Crystal Building, Edwards (© **970/926-0400;** www.kitchencollage. com), which carries fine cookware, gourmet foods, linens, and a multitude of handy gadgets.

WHERE TO STAY

Like most of Colorado's ski resorts, Vail has an abundance of condominiums. Many are individually owned and available for rent when the owners aren't in town, so you'll find that they have more individuality and homey touches than you often find in a hotel. We discuss some of the better condominium developments below (along with other lodging choices), and there are scores more. Contact the **Vail Valley Chamber and Tourism Bureau** (p. 300), which can provide additional lodging information or make your reservations for you, as well as provide information on skiing and other activities.

As in most ski areas, rates are highest during peak ski season, particularly Christmas, and can sometimes be halved after the lifts close. During ski season, you'll find the lowest rates at the very beginning, from opening to about December 20. Unless otherwise noted, parking is free. Room taxes add almost 12% to lodging bills.

Skiers on a tight budget can probably save a few dollars by staying in the town of Eagle, just south of I-70 exit 147, about 18 miles west of Beaver Creek and 29 miles west of Vail. Here there is a **Comfort Inn,** 285 Market St. (© **970/328-7878**), with rates for two of $79 to $149; and the **Best Western Eagle Lodge,** 200 Loren Lane (© **800/475-4824** or 970/328-6316), which charges double rates of $75 to $165 most of the time and $100 to $275 from December 21 to January 4.

IN VAIL
Expensive
Vail Cascade Resort & Spa ☀☀   A wonderful choice for those who love pampering, the Vail Cascade gets better every time we visit. A $5-million room renovation project has resulted in a decor that we might call "upscale contemporary Rocky Mountain." It includes solid-wood furnishings and woodwork, leather chairs, large desks, granite double-sink vanities, stone tile floors, overstuffed pillows, and pillow-topped mattresses. Both the deluxe rooms (480 sq. ft.), which have the vanity outside the bathing area, and standard rooms (390 sq. ft.) feature bright, bold colors and wooden armoires concealing 27-inch TVs. Suites have 600 to 1,000 square feet in two rooms and most have a king-size bed plus a hide-a-bed. All units boast fabulous mountain or courtyard views; some units have outdoor balconies with tables and chairs.

The courtyard entrance is beautifully landscaped, with tall Colorado blue spruce, aspens, and an abundance of flowers in the summer. There are elevators accessing the four floors, and interior corridors everywhere so you never have to go outside until you're ready to ski—and the Cascade Village chairlift is just outside the door. Of course, there is also a ski concierge on hand to assist.

And here is where the pampering gets really serious: The Aria Spa & Club is a 78,000-square-foot spa and athletic club, offering a complete spa experience with 14 treatment rooms, a couple's spa suite, manicure/pedicure stations, aromatherapy steam rooms, and practically every treatment imaginable.

1300 Westhaven Dr., Vail, CO 81657. ⓒ 800/420-2424 or 970/476-7111. Fax 970/479-7020. www.vailcascade.com. 292 rooms and suites, 72 condos and private residences. Winter $259–$519 double, $879–$1,300 suite, higher at Christmas; summer $129–$299 double, $750 suite. AE, DC, DISC, MC, V. Free underground parking available (7-ft. height limit). Take I-70 exit 173 for West Vail, head east on South Frontage Rd. to Westhaven Dr., and turn right. **Amenities:** Restaurant (Chap's, see "Where to Dine," below); bar; 2 heated outdoor pools; 7 tennis courts (4 indoor, 3 outdoor); state-of-the-art health club and spa; 3 hot tubs (2 outdoor, 1 indoor); sauna; concierge; shopping arcade including sporting-goods stores with rentals and apparel; 24-hr room service; massage; babysitting. *In room:* TV w/pay movies, dataport, minibar, coffeemaker, hair dryer, iron, high-speed Internet access.

Moderate

Antlers at Vail ⓕ This nice condominium property near the foot of the Lionshead Gondola has a well-deserved reputation for friendly service and unobstructed views of Vail Mountain. The comfortable, open, and airy units range in size from studios to four bedrooms, and each has a fireplace, private balcony, high-speed Internet access, and fully equipped kitchen. There's also a great pool and sun deck, a good business center with four computers, and ski storage.

680 W. Lionshead Place, Vail, CO 81657. ⓒ 800/843-8245 or 970/476-2471. Fax 970/476-4146. www.antlersvail.com. 88 units. Winter $265–$2,200; summer $131–$550. AE, DC, DISC, MC, V. Pets accepted in some units, fee $15 per pet per night. **Amenities:** Outdoor heated pool; exercise room; 2 outdoor hot tubs; 2 saunas; basic business center; coin-op laundry; dry cleaning. *In room:* Cable TV/VCR, kitchen, fridge, hair dryer, iron.

Tivoli Lodge ⓕ The first shining ray of light from Vail's New Dawn, a billion-dollar makeover/redevelopment of the base village, the Tivoli Lodge was rebuilt from scratch by the race car–driving Lazier family, who built the original Tivoli on the same spot in 1968. Gone are the small, dated rooms, replaced by large (many are almost 500 sq. ft.) guest quarters decorated with a masculine feel; the corner suite has a commanding view of Vail Mountain from its private balcony. The new lobby, with quartzite floors that sport fossils, features a bar and a breakfast area. Located immediately east of the center of Vail Village, the property offers a great location for skiers and plenty of elbow room for families and large groups.

386 Hanson Ranch Rd., Vail, CO 81657. ⓒ 800/451-4756 or 970/476-5615. Fax 970/476-6601. www.tivolilodge.com. 62 units, including 1 suite. Winter $229–$749 double, $749–$1,299 suite; rest of year $149–$259 double, $599 suite. Rates include full breakfast. AE, DISC, MC, V. **Amenities:** Outdoor heated pool; 2 outdoor hot tubs; concierge; dry cleaning. *In room:* Cable TV, fridge, coffeemaker, hair dryer, iron, Wi-Fi network, microwave.

Vail Mountain Lodge & Spa ⓕⓕ *Finds* Nestled along Gore Creek, this property offers B&B intimacy and hotel service. While the property is relatively small, its 20 rooms are relatively large, and feature a pleasant contemporary decor that doesn't get hung up on Western or ski themes. The property just underwent a $25-million upgrade, and it was money well spent. Located just a few steps from world-class skiing, dining, and shopping, all rooms have gas fireplaces, soaking tubs, and oh-so-comfy feather beds. Beyond the standard rooms, there are a trio of suites with one, two, and three bedrooms, the third of which is a whopping 2,000 square feet. The facilities here are similarly first-rate: Terra Bistro, the resident eatery, offers global fusion cuisine and some of the best tuna tartare in the Rockies, the health club features Vail's only indoor climbing wall, and the spa is frequented by local pros getting ready for ski season.

352 E. Meadow Dr., Vail, CO 81657. © **866/476-0700** or 970/476-0700. Fax 970/476-6451. www.vailmountain lodge.com. 20 units. Winter $350–$600 double; $900–$2,300 suite; rest of year $149–$299 double; $235–$600 suite. Minimum stays required in ski season. Rates include continental breakfast. AE, DC, MC, V. **Amenities:** Restaurant (global fusion); lounge; health club; whirlpool (indoor); spa; concierge; massage; dry cleaning. *In room:* Cable TV, kitchen, coffeemaker, hair dryer, iron. Wi-Fi network.

BEAVER CREEK AREA
Very Expensive
Park Hyatt Beaver Creek Resort and Spa ✶✶ An architecturally unique hotel at the foot of the Beaver Creek lifts, this luxurious ski-in/ski-out Park Hyatt blends features of medieval European alpine monasteries with Rocky Mountain styles and materials. The exterior is native stone, offset with stucco and rough timbers. The interior is of rough-hewn pine and sandstone; wall-size fireplaces enhance numerous cozy alcoves furnished with overstuffed chairs and sofas. Elk-antler chandeliers and works by contemporary artisans lend a Western ambience. Guest rooms have a European country elegance, with knotty-pine furnishings and TVs hidden in armoires. The raised beds have dust ruffles, pillow shams, and quilted comforters; the bathrooms feature a marble-top vanity and heated towel rack; and most rooms have private balconies. Other amenities include high-speed Internet access, bathrobes and slippers, and refrigerators.

The outdoor dining terrace at Bivans, which serves three meals daily, dazzles the eye with spectacular views year-round—wool blankets and heaters keep guests warm when temperatures drop. The Allegria Spa is a state-of-the-art facility that offers an array of treatments, as well as fitness and nutritional counseling.

50 W. Thomas Place (P.O. Box 1595), Avon, CO 81620. © **800/778-7477** or 970/949-1234. Fax 970/949-4164. www.beavercreek.hyatt.com. 190 units. Winter $259–$875 double, $525–$3,300 suite; rest of year $135–$470 double, $575–$1,210 suite. AE, DC, DISC, MC, V. Valet parking $18. **Amenities:** 3 restaurants (American, French, Southwestern); lounge; indoor/outdoor heated pool; 6 outdoor tennis courts; health club; full-service spa; 6 outdoor whirlpools; sauna; children's programs; concierge; limited room service; massage; coin-op laundry; dry cleaning. *In room:* Cable TV w/pay movies, dataport, coffeemaker, hair dryer, iron, safe, wireless Internet access.

Ritz-Carlton, Bachelor Gulch ✶✶✶ A stunning structure modeled after the grand national park lodges, the rock-and-log "parkitechture" exterior sheaths one of the most luxurious hotels in the West. While not your typical Ritz-Carlton at first glance, the property has style and comfort to spare (there are over 100 fireplaces) and a Rocky Mountain style that's all its own. For instance, the property has a "Loan-a-Lab" program for guests who want to hike with the hotel's yellow Labrador, Bachelor, and the staff includes a firepit concierge who tends the coals nightly at the outdoor pit. The rooms are also studies in "New West" glitz, complete with mountain and earth tones, decor inspired by wildlife and forests, and jaw-dropping views. The club level, which includes five courses a day and an open bar, is especially plush. Of the long list of amenities, the spa here is a national standout, featuring 19 treatment rooms centered on a rock-laden, candlelit "Grotto" with an oversized co-ed hot tub. The spa's signature summer treatments include "Mountain Spa Mornings," involving a 90-minute hike to a historic homesteader's cabin and a yoga session and a massage before descending back to the Ritz and its infinite pampering.

0130 Daybreak Ridge (P.O. Box 9190), Avon, CO 81620. (✆) **800/241-3333** or 970/748-6200. Fax 970/343-1070. www.ritzcarlton.com. 237 units, including 29 suites. Winter $495–$1,500 double, $850–$4,400 suite; rest of year $195–$450 double, $340–$1,300 suite. AE, DC, DISC, MC, V. Valet parking $20. **Amenities:** 3 restaurants (American Steakhouse/café/bar); lounge; outdoor heated pool; 4 outdoor tennis courts; health club; full-service spa; indoor and outdoor whirlpools; sauna; children's programs; babysitting; concierge; limited room service; massage; dry cleaning. *In room:* TV w/pay movies, dataport, coffeemaker, hair dryer, iron, safe.

Expensive

The Charter at Beaver Creek ✿   This elegant European-style lodging offers the luxury of a world-class hotel and the convenience of condominiums, set in the magnificent Rocky Mountains. Lodge rooms, simply decorated, can accommodate up to four persons; most have two queen beds, though some have one king. All units have robes, and most have grand views of the valley or surrounding mountains. The one- to five-bedroom condominiums have a full kitchen, fireplace—some of lovely river rock—and balcony or patio. All are decorated by the owners—some in Western motif, some more traditional. The property is ski-in/ski-out, with ski valet service. And there are trails radiating from the property; a walking trail is just 5 minutes from the village center.

The traMonti Restaurant offers northern Tuscan cuisine in an elegant setting for dinner; the more casual Terrace Restaurant serves an American-style breakfast. Wi-Fi is available in common areas.

120 Offerson Rd. (P.O. Box 5310), Beaver Creek, CO 81620. (✆) **800/525-6660** or 970/949-6660. Fax 970/949-6709. www.thecharter.com. Winter $175–$445 double, $225–$2,600 condo; summer $99–$180 double, $169–$695 condo. AE, MC, V. Valet parking; underground parking (7-ft., 6-in. height limit). **Amenities:** 2 restaurants (Italian, American); indoor and outdoor (seasonal) heated pools; separate children's pool (seasonal); 18-hole golf course; large health club and spa; indoor and outdoor hot tubs; sauna; game room; concierge; full-service rental and retail sports shop; limited room service; coin-op laundry; valet laundry and dry cleaning;. *In room:* Cable TV/DVD, dataport (DSL), kitchen (in condos), fridge, coffeemaker, hair dryer, iron, safe.

The Lodge & Spa at Cordillera ✿✿   Reminiscent of a Belgium mountain-style château, this luxurious hideaway nestles in 7,500 acres of private forest just 20 minutes west of Vail and Beaver Creek. Rocky Mountain timber and stone, along with elegant wrought iron, are prominent in the handsome, residential-style guest rooms. More than half the rooms feature wood-burning and gas fireplaces; all have king- or queen-size beds, and most have private balconies or decks with views of the Sawatch Range of the Rockies. Smoking is not permitted. The expanded spa includes two dedicated facial rooms, a hydrotherapy room, a dedicated manicure and pedicure salon, a meditation room, and several multipurpose treatment rooms. The resort offers 15 miles of mountain biking/cross-country ski trails, a Nordic ski center, and golf and ski shuttles.

Restaurant Mirador is one of the Vail Valley's better dining options, with a cuisine that's hard to pin down. The chef draws from flavors around the world, creating dishes that produce an avant garde dining experience. There's also a casual Irish pub, Grouse on the Green.

2205 Cordillera Way (P.O. Box 1110), Edwards, CO 81632. (✆) **800/877-3529** or 970/926-2200. Fax 970/926-2486. www.cordillera.rockresorts.com. 56 units, including 10 suites. $150–$400 double; $275–$750 suite. Extra person $20; children under 12 stay free in parent's room. AE, DC, MC, V. Valet parking. **Amenities:** 2 restaurants (global, pub); 2 pools (outdoor, indoor lap); golf courses (3 18-hole and a 10-hole short course); 2 tennis courts; exercise room; full-service spa; indoor/outdoor whirlpool; steam room; sauna; bicycle rentals; concierge; limited room service (6:30am–10pm); massage; valet laundry and dry cleaning. *In room:* A/C, TV, coffeemaker, hair dryer, iron.

Inexpensive

Inn & Suites at Riverwalk *Value*   Located 10 miles west of Vail at the posh River-walk, a retail/office/entertainment district in Edwards, this is a considerable value in comparison with your options right at the slopes, and access to both Beaver Creek and Vail Mountain is excellent. The rooms are nice, modern hotel rooms with bright colors and attractive spreads; the condos have balconies, gas fireplaces, Jacuzzi tubs, and full kitchens. There are dozens of restaurants and bars within walking distance and, in the off-season, they're typically bustling when the nightlife in Vail Village is sleepy.

27 Main St., Edwards, CO 81632. © **888/926-0606** or 970/926-0606. Fax 970/926-0616. www.innandsuitesatriver walk.com. 75 units, including 16 condos. Winter $105–$230 double, $200–$800 condo; rest of year $64–$99 double, $179–$460 condo. AE, DISC, MC, V. Take I-70 exit 163 to Edwards; the Riverwalk is just south. **Amenities:** Outdoor pool; outdoor hot tub; fitness center; coin-op laundry. *In room:* Cable TV, kitchen (in condos), coffeemaker, hair dryer, iron, wireless high-speed Internet access.

WHERE TO DINE

Vail and Beaver Creek have dozens of excellent restaurants, although few of them are what we would call bargains. We also like **Blu's,** 193 E. Gore Creek Dr. (© **970/4 76-3113**) for its blueberry pancakes and killer creekside patio; and **eat! drink!,** 56 Edwards Village Blvd. at the Corner @ Edwards shopping center (© **970/926-1393**), an establishment with a wine shop on one side and a cafe serving wine, cheese, and small plates on the other.

Beano's Cabin 🏵🏵 AMERICAN CONTINENTAL   A splurge that many Beaver Creek visitors consider one of the highlights of their stay is the sleigh-ride dinner trip (or in summer, on horseback) to Beano's. This isn't the log homestead that Chicago lettuce farmer Frank "Beano" Bienkowski built on Beaver Creek Mountain in 1919—it's far more elegant. Diners board the 42-passenger, Sno-Cat–driven sleighs at the base of the Centennial Lift, arriving 20 minutes later for a candlelit five-course dinner around a crackling fire with musical entertainment. The menu varies, but entree choices might include selections such as grilled Colorado tenderloin of beef, balsamic-marinated ostrich, grilled Atlantic salmon, wood-grilled venison loin chop, and Colorado lamb loin. Vegetarian meals and a lower-priced children's menu are available.

Near Larkspur Bowl, Beaver Creek Resort. © **970/949-9090.** Reservations required. Fixed-price meal $89 and up. AE, DC, DISC, MC, V. Departures from Beaver Creek Chophouse (at Centennial Lift) winter 4:15–9:15pm daily; summer Wed–Sun. Closed several months in spring and fall.

Chap's Grill & Chophouse 🏵🏵 STEAKS/SEAFOOD   Real food for real appetites, expertly prepared and presented in an upscale mountain lodge setting, makes Chap's among our top dining choices in a town that's overflowing with excellent restaurants. The decor is casually elegant, with nicely padded chairs and lots of rich wood, and large windows offering mountain views. The dinner menu includes prime-cut steaks, seafood, Colorado lamb, and game. Among our favorites here are the 12-ounce buffalo rib-eye, grilled with ancho-chile glazes; the grilled Colorado double lamb chops with a cucumber-garlic sauce; and the pepper-herb-crusted ahi tuna. Soups, salads, and sandwiches are served at lunch, and there is a delicious breakfast buffet including made-to-order omelets.

In summer you can dine outside on the patio. The Fireside Bar is a great place to relax in the evenings, with nightly entertainment—usually jazz, folk, country, or contemporary—by local musicians.

In Vail Cascade Resort & Spa, 1300 Westhaven Dr., Vail, CO 81657. © **970/479-7014.** www.vailcascade.com. Reservations recommended. Main courses $7–$14 lunch, $19–$44 dinner. AE, DC, DISC, MC, V. Daily 7–11am, 11:30am–5pm, and 5:30–10pm.

Kelly Liken Restaurant ⭐⭐⭐ SEASONAL AMERICAN   This is our favorite eatery in Vail. Some local chefs grumbled when 20-something Kelly Liken slapped her name on the marquee here when the restaurant opened in 2004, but the fantastic food and stylish room are undeniably Colorado standouts. Liken, who graduated first in her class from the Culinary Institute of America, strove to "raise the bar" in Vail, and she succeeds with such dishes as her signature potato-crusted trout filets or cider-braised organic rabbit with cornmeal crepes. The menu changes with the season, using as much locally grown ingredients as possible. Any time of year, the creative fare is a feast for the senses, with contrasting flavors, sublime sauces, and sensational presentations. The wine list is terrific, the wait staff is sharp (and sharply dressed), and the desserts—especially the "can't be missed" sticky bun sundae—approach otherworldly.

12 Vail Rd., in the Gateway Building. © 970/476-0175. www.kellyliken.com. Reservations recommended. Main courses $30–$40 dinner. AE, DISC, MC, V. Daily 6–10pm. Bar open later.

La Tour ⭐⭐ CONTEMPORARY ITALIAN   La Tour opened in the 1970s, but it sprung to life when chef-owner Paul Ferzacca, known for his high-altitude skills, took it over in 1998. He gave both the room and the menu a needed jolt of creativity, adding contemporary European art and a new bright color scheme to the walls and implementing a metaphorically similar makeover to the menu. The preparations use Italian traditions as a starting point, but Ferzacca loves to mix and match ingredients and preparations from all corners of the globe. The menu is heavy on seafood and steaks, and the pasta dishes are completely unique, such as marinated artichoke and bucatini pasta with asparagus, tomatoes, and scallions in a garlic broth. The soups and desserts are also standouts.

122 E. Meadow Dr. © 970/4764403. Reservations recommended. Main courses $18–$30. AE, DC, DISC, MC, V. Daily 5–9:30pm.

Montauk Seafood Grill ⭐⭐ SEAFOOD   We consider this one of the best seafood restaurants you'll find in landlocked Colorado. Owners Tom Ludwig and Dmitri Souvorin have fresh seafood FedEx-ed from sources in every direction, and it tastes like you're right on the docks, not 1,000 or more miles distant. The busy, high-energy place is decorated in a sort of Colorado casual nautical theme. Chef Souvorin utilizes fresh fish in daily from both coasts, Hawaii, and the Gulf of Mexico; and creates unique specialty presentations. Our top choice here is the Hawaiian ahi, seared rare, with a soy-ginger sauce. Steak, chops, chicken, and pasta are also available.

549 Lionshead Mall. © 970/476-2601. Reservations recommended. Main courses $18–$30. AE, DC, DISC, MC, V. Daily 5–9:30pm.

VAIL AFTER DARK

Vail's greatest concentration of late-night haunts can be found in a 1½-block stretch of Bridge Street from Hanson Ranch Road north to the covered bridge over Gore Creek. From mountainside to creek, they include **The Club** (© 970/479-0556), the **Red Lion** (© 970/476-7676), and **Vendetta's** (© 970/476-5070), reportedly the hangout for Vail's ski patrollers. **The Tap Room,** 333 Bridge St. (© 970/479-0500), not surprisingly, has an extensive selection of beers on tap, plus good pub grub and martinis. **Samana Lounge,** 228 Bridge St. (© 970/479-0500), is a small, sophisticated dance club with a candlelit ambience and world-class DJs.

Another popular hangout is **8,150,** 143 E. Meadow Dr. (© 970/479-0607), so named for Vail's elevation, offering some of Vail's best live music. **Garfinkel's,** 536 E. Lionshead Circle (© 970/476-3789), keeps sports fans busy with tons of TVs and

A Walk on the Wild Side: State Bridge and Rancho Del Rio

Established in 1890, **State Bridge Lodge** has had its share of history. Its location—a stone's throw from the Colorado River and the railroad tracks—means it was a highly trafficked area even before the state built the bridge of the same name here in the late 1800s. Teddy Roosevelt slept here while serving as the country's vice president in 1901. But the lodge has had its share of changes and ups and downs since, emerging as a biker and hippie haven in recent years. The rough edges remain, but new ownership has put a needed polish on the old lodge, with its basic cabins ($79–$169), yurts ($69–$189), and campsites (free). The train still screeches through 20 times a day, there is still live music (primarily jam, reggae, and bluegrass bands) on a great outdoor stage, and the free landing spot for river rafters is right across the street. There's a restaurant and historic bar and a small store that can help arrange rafting trips. Behind the lodge is the State Bridge Anomaly, an interesting red volcanic formation that's worth hiking.

For more information, contact **State Bridge Lodge and River Resort** (© 970/653-4444; www.statebridge.com). The lodge is located at Colorado 131 and Trough Road, 13 miles north of I-70, exit 157.

Beyond the concerts at State Bridge, many visitors come to the area to go rafting from **Rancho Del Rio,** a former hippie commune that's now one of the last remaining river communities of its kind, a haven for river rats who live in the assorted cabins and trailers here. The slow waters of the Upper Colorado River in this area are perfect for beginners and families; even first-timers will be comfortable paddling the river solo. The **Colorado River Center** (© 888/888-7238 or 970/653-7238; www.coloradorivercenter.com), offers rentals, shuttles, lessons, and guided rafting trips. We recommend renting a "duckie" (an inflatable kayak) and paddling it to State Bridge and then getting a shuttle back to Rancho. Then it's time for a bite and a beer at **K.K.'s BBQ,** also known as The Center of the Universe. An outdoor bar and grill with jars of homemade pickles and pots of homemade sauce and slices of homemade pies, this is the most fun you can have at a meal in the Northern Rockies. Eponymous proprietor K. K. is quite the character and a one-woman act, cooking ribs and sausages, making sundaes and change, telling jokes, and generally entertaining everyone within earshot. We love the 4K, a burger with a split Italian sausage on top and a heap of fresh jalapenos under molten cheese. K.K. opens at 11am and closes at 5pm Saturday to Monday between Memorial Day and the last Sunday in September.

For more information, contact **Rancho Del Rio,** 4199 Trough Rd., Bond, CO 80423 (© 970/653-4431; www.ranchodelrio.com). Beyond the rafting and barbecue, there is a campground ($2 per person per night), a pair of rental cabins ($60–$70 a night), and fly-fishing guides.

everybody else happy with a great deck at the foot of the Eagle Bahn gondola. In nearby Minturn, the happy hour at the historic **Minturn Saloon,** 146 N. Main St. (© **970/827-5954**) attracts a party-hearty horde for Vail Valley's best margaritas. In summer, the place to be Friday night is the **Wolcott Yacht Club,** 15 miles west of Vail at 27190 U.S. 6, Wolcott (© **970/926-3444**), and its unbeatable back patio, complete with band shell and live band.

7 Leadville

38 miles S. of Vail, 59 miles E. of Aspen, 113 miles W. of Denver

Not much more than a century ago, Leadville was the most important city between St. Louis and San Francisco. It was the stopping point for Easterners with nothing to lose and everything to gain from the promise of gold and silver. Today, Leadville is one of the best places to rediscover the West's mining heritage.

Founded in 1860 on the gold that glimmered in prospectors' pans, Leadville and nearby Oro City quickly attracted 10,000 miners who dug $5 million in gold out of a 3-mile stretch of the California Gulch by 1865. When the riches were gone, Leadville was deserted, although a smaller lode of gold-bearing quartz kept Oro City alive for another decade. Then in 1875 two prospectors located the California Gulch's first paying silver lode. Over the next 2 decades, Leadville grew to an estimated 30,000 residents—among them "the Unsinkable" Molly Brown, whose husband made his fortune here before moving to Denver, where the family lived at the time of Molly's *Titanic* heroism.

Now a town of about 2,700 residents, this isolated mountain town (elevation 10,152 ft.) has managed to maintain its historic character. Many buildings of the silver boom (which produced $136 million from 1879–89) have been preserved in Leadville's National Historic Landmark District. So for those who want to take a break from playing outdoors to explore Colorado's frontier past, Leadville's just the place to do it.

ESSENTIALS

GETTING THERE   By Car   Coming from Denver, leave I-70 at exit 195 (Copper Mountain), and proceed south 24 miles on Colo. 91. From Grand Junction, depart I-70 at exit 171 (Minturn), and continue south 33 miles on U.S. 24. From Aspen, in the summer take Colo. 82 east 44 miles over Independence Pass (closed in winter), then turn north on U.S. 24 for 15 miles. There's also easy access from the south via U.S. 24.

By Plane   The nearest airport with commercial service is the **Eagle County Regional Airport,** which offers car rentals and bus service to Leadville (see "Essentials," under Vail, earlier in this chapter).

VISITOR INFORMATION   Contact the **Leadville/Lake County Chamber of Commerce,** 809 Harrison Ave. (P.O. Box 861), Leadville, CO 80461 (© **888/532-3845** or 719/486-3900; www.leadvilleusa.com), which operates a visitor center that's usually open daily from 9am to 4pm in summer, and 10am to 4pm Tuesday through Saturday the rest of the year.

GETTING AROUND   U.S. 24 is Leadville's main street. Entering Leadville from the north, it's named Poplar Street; then it turns west on Ninth Street for a block and then south on Harrison Avenue. The next 7 blocks south, to Second Street, are the

Leadville

ATTRACTIONS ●
Baby Doe Tabor Museum **7**
Healy House & Dexter Cabin **3**
The Heritage Museum **4**
Leadville National Fish
   Hatchery **17**
Leadville, Colorado &
   Southern Railroad **5**
Matchless Mine **7**
National Mining Hall of Fame &
   Museum **2**
Tabor Home **12**
Tabor Opera House **14**

ACCOMMODATIONS ■
Apple Blossom Inn **13**
Delaware Hotel **9**
Leadville Hostel **6**
Super 8 **1**

DINING ◆
Columbine Cafe **11**
The Golden Burro Café **8**
The Grill **16**
High Mountain Pies **15**
Quincy's Steakhouse **10**

heart of this historic town. A block north, Seventh Street climbs east to the old train depot and 13,186-foot Mosquito Pass, among America's highest, open to four-wheel-drive vehicles after the snow melts, usually in July.

Dee Hive Tours, 506 Harrison Ave. (© **719/486-2339**), offers **taxi** service.

FAST FACTS There's a 24-hour emergency room at **St. Vincent's General Hospital,** 822 W. Fourth St. (© **719/486-0230**). The **post office** is at 136 W. Fifth St.; for hours and other information contact the U.S. Postal Service (© **800/275-8777;** www.usps.com). The sheriff's office (© **719/486-1249**) provides **road reports.**

EXPERIENCING LEADVILLE'S PAST

A great many residences of successful mining operators, engineers, and financiers are preserved within the **Leadville National Historic Landmark District** ☆☆, which stretches along 7 blocks of Harrison Avenue and part of Chestnut Street, where it intersects Harrison at the south end of downtown. A self-guided walking tour of this district, with map, is available free at the visitor center. An informative 30-minute video, *The Earth Runs Silver: Early Leadville,* is shown at the visitor center (see "Visitor Information," above) on request, with free admission, and provides a good overview of Leadville's place in American mining history.

Leadville has numerous historic buildings open to the public; allow 30 minutes to an hour for each of the following.

You'll discover Leadville's colorful past at **The Heritage Museum,** corner of Ninth Street and Harrison Avenue (© **719/486-1878**), a historical museum loaded with exhibits on and artifacts from Leadville's early days, from mining dioramas to a scale model of the ice palace that Leadville residents created in 1896. There's also an art gallery displaying the work of local artists (most of it is for sale), and a gift shop with a good selection of books and mining-related souvenirs. Admission costs $4 for adults, $3.50 for seniors 62 and older, $3 for students 6 to 16, and free for children 5 and younger. It's open May through October, daily from 10am to 6pm, with slightly shorter hours at the beginning and end of the season.

At the **National Mining Hall of Fame and Museum** ✹✹, 120 W. Ninth St. (© **719/486-1229;** www.mininghalloffame.org), you'll find walk-through replica mines, models of mining machinery, and dioramas depicting the history of Colorado mining from coal to gold. Admission is $6 for adults, $5 for seniors 62 and older, $3 for children 6 to 12, and it's free for children under 6. Open May through October daily from 9am to 5pm, and November through April Monday through Saturday from 10am to 4pm.

Peer into Horace Tabor's **Matchless Mine,** 1¼-mile east up Seventh Street, and tour the **Baby Doe Tabor Museum** (tel] **719/486-1229**), where you'll see the cabin Tabor's widow, Baby Doe, spent the final 36 years of her life, hoping to strike it rich once more. Admission is $6 for adults, $5 for seniors, $3 for children 6 to 12, and free for kids under 6. Open Memorial Day to Labor Day daily from 9am to 5pm. (Combination mining museum/mine tickets run $9 adults, $7 seniors, and $4 kids.)

Built in the 1870s, the **Tabor Home,** 116 E. 5th St. (© **719/486-2092** for information), is where mining magnate Horace Tabor lived with his wife, Augusta, until 1881, when he moved into a local hotel to be closer to his mistress, Baby Doe, whom he eventually married. Here you'll see how a mining king lived in the 1800s, and discover that Horace Tabor did in fact end up paying for his sin. Admission costs $4 for adults, $2 for children 6 to 12, and free for children under 6. It's open from Memorial Day until Labor Day, daily from 11am to 4pm.

To get an up-close look at where a few fortunate miners were able to escape the rough-and-tumble atmosphere of the mines, if only for an evening, visit **Healy House and Dexter Cabin** ✹, 912 Harrison Ave. (© **719/486-0487;** www.coloradohistory. org). Healy House was built by smelter owner August Meyer in 1878, and later converted into a lavish boardinghouse by Daniel Healy. The adjacent rough-hewn log cabin was built by James Dexter and furnished in an elegant style. Admission is $4 for adults, $3.50 for seniors 65 and older, $2.50 for children 6 to 16, and free for children under 6. Open Memorial Day weekend through September, daily from 10am to 4:30pm.

The **Tabor Opera House,** 308 Harrison Ave. (© **719/486-8409;** www.taboroperahouse.net), is where Leadville's mining magnates and their wives kept up with cultural happenings back East. Opened in 1879, over the years it has hosted everything from the Ziegfeld Follies and the Metropolitan Opera to prizefighter Jack Dempsey (a Colorado native) and magician Harry Houdini (whose vanishing square is still evident on the stage floor). Visitors can explore the 880-seat theater, backstage, and dressing rooms, or attend one of the musical or theater performances still held here (check the website for the current schedule and prices). Admission to tour the opera house is $5 for adults, $2.50 for children 12 and under. Open Memorial Day to Labor Day Monday to Saturday from 10am to 5pm.

Although opera and the other refinements of a cultured society may have been on the minds of some early Leadville residents, others were more interested in "pleasures of the flesh," and in the 1870s and 1880s Leadville was a pretty wild place, with a hundred or more saloons and a busy red-light district.

MORE TO SEE & DO

Leadville, Colorado & Southern Railroad ℱ This spectacularly scenic ride, in a 1955 diesel train, departs the 1893 C&S Depot, 3 blocks east of U.S. 24, and follows the old "high line" along the headwaters of the Arkansas River to a splendid view of Fremont Pass. The return takes you to the French Gulch Water Tower for a dramatic look at Mount Elbert, Colorado's tallest mountain, at 14,433 feet. The ride lasts about 2½ hours, and because of the high elevations, jackets or sweaters are recommended even on the hottest summer days.

326 E. Seventh St. at Hazel St. ℂ 719/486-3936. www.leadville-train.com. Admission $27 adults, $15 children 4–12, free for children 3 and under. Daily Memorial Day to early Oct, call for schedule.

Leadville National Fish Hatchery   Established in 1889, this is the second-oldest hatchery operated by the U.S. Fish and Wildlife Service that's in existence today. Rainbow, brown, and cutthroat trout are raised here, at an elevation of 10,000 feet on the east side of Mount Massive. Visitors can also enjoy self-guided nature trails, with breathtaking views of the surrounding mountains and occasionally deer and elk. One trail passes by the remains of the Evergreen Hotel, a late-1800s resort, and several trails connect to the Colorado Trail. In winter, take cross-country skis or snowshoes. There are also picnic tables and two public fishing ponds. Allow 30 to 45 minutes.

2844 Colo. 300 (6 miles southwest of Leadville off U.S. 24). ℂ **719/486-0189.** http://leadville.fws.gov. Free admission. Daily 7am–4pm.

SPORTS & OUTDOOR ACTIVITIES

Much of the outdoor recreation in this area takes place in nearby national forest lands, and you can get information at the **San Isabel National Forest** office, 2015 N. Poplar St. (ℂ **719/486-0749;** www.fs.fed.us/r2), as well as the visitor center. **Bill's Sport Shop,** 225 Harrison Ave. (ℂ **719/486-0739;** www.billsrentals.com), is a good source for gear (rent or buy) and advice.

Adventurous **hikers** can attempt an ascent of Mount Elbert (14,433 ft.) or Mount Massive (14,428 ft.); either can be climbed in a day without technical equipment, though altitude and abruptly changing weather conditions are factors that should be weighed. One popular trail for hiking, walking, and mountain biking is the **Mineral Belt Trail,** a 12-mile loop that circles Leadville, passing through the mining district and the mountains in the process. A good access point for it is near the recreation center at Sixth Street and McWethy Drive.

There's good trout and kokanee **fishing** at Turquoise Lake, Twin Lakes, and other small high-mountain lakes, as well as at beaver ponds located on side streams of the Arkansas River. There's also limited stream fishing in the area.

Golfers head to 9-hole **Mount Massive Golf Course,** 3½ miles west of town at 259 C.R. 5 (ℂ **719/486-2176**), which claims to be North America's highest golf course, at 9,700 feet. Greens fees are $28 to $31 for 18 holes, and views of surrounding mountain peaks are magnificent.

If snow sports are more to your liking, **Ski Cooper,** P.O. Box 896, Leadville, CO 80461 (© **800/707-6114** or 719/486-3684, 719/486-2277 for snow reports; www.skicooper.com), is the place to go, with 400 acres of lift-served skiable terrain and another 2,400 acres accessible by snowcat. It began as a training center for 10th Mountain Division troops from Camp Hale during World War II. Located 10 miles north of Leadville on U.S. 24 near Tennessee Pass, it offers numerous intermediate and novice runs, and hosts backcountry Chicago Ridge Snowcat Tours for experts (call for details). Four lifts serve 26 runs—rated 30% beginner, 40% intermediate, and 30% expert—and the mountain has a 1,200-foot vertical drop from the peak of 11,700 feet. Full-day tickets cost $37 for adults, $18 for children 6 to 14, $26 for seniors 60 to 69, $10 for seniors 70 and older, and are free for kids under 6. The **Tennessee Pass Nordic Center** (© **719/486-1750;** www.tennesseepass.com), at the foot of the mountain, has 15 miles of groomed track and skating trails, plus rentals and lessons. Trail passes cost $10 for adults, $8 for children and seniors.

WHERE TO STAY

In addition to the properties listed below, Leadville has a **Super 8,** 1128 U.S. 24 (© **800/800-8000** or 719/486-3637), with rates of $50 to $100 double. Taxes add just under 9% for lodging bills.

Apple Blossom Inn   An 1879 Victorian on Leadville's historic millionaires' row, this inn features the house's original handcrafted woodwork, detailed mantels, and crystal light fixtures. Rooms range from warm and cozy to large and sunny; the atmosphere is resplendent with mining-era charm. Estelle's Room has a large fireplace, four-poster queen feather bed, and sitting area, while the library features a 14-foot ceiling, five stained-glass windows, a fireplace, parquet floor, and a king-size bed. Tea, coffee, and hot chocolate are provided free, there's a microwave for guest use, and guests have access to a stocked refrigerator of complimentary soft drinks. The hot tub resides in a lovely garden.

120 W. Fourth St., Leadville, CO 80461. © **800/982-9279** or 719/486-2141. Fax 719/486-0994. www.theapple blossominn.com. 6 units. $89–$159 double; from $149 suite. Extra person $20 per night. Rates include full breakfast. MC, V. **Amenities:** Outdoor hot tub.

Delaware Hotel   Built in 1886, this hotel was restored in 1985 and is once again a Victorian gem. The lobby is beautiful in the style of grand old hotels, with a turn-of-the-20th-century player piano, crystal chandeliers, and magnificent Victorian furnishings. Guest rooms have brass or iron beds, quilts, and lace curtains. Rooms have private bathrooms with showers but no tubs; the four suites have full bathrooms with tub/shower combos. There's an eclectic antiques shop in the lobby. Smoking is not permitted.

700 Harrison Ave., Leadville, CO 80461. © **800/748-2004** or 719/486-1418. Fax 719/486-2214. www.delaware hotel.com. 36 units. $70–$119 double; $109–$139 family room or suite. 15%–25% discounts Apr–May and Oct–Nov. Children 12 and younger stay free. Rates include continental breakfast. AE, DC, DISC, MC, V. **Amenities:** Restaurant (American, breakfast only); whirlpool. *In room:* Cable TV, wireless Internet access.

Leadville Hostel *Value*   "Wild Bill" Clower and Cathy Hacking have made this hostel into one of the best in the West. With a convivial atmosphere, an eclectic style, and plenty of amenities (including shuttle service and a massage room), this is a great stopover for outdoors buffs in the midst of a great adventure or anybody looking for a good deal. The dorm rooms—divided into men's and women's—have four to eight bunks each; the more expensive bunk rooms have their own bathrooms. There are also couples rooms with shared bathrooms and family rooms with private bathrooms. There's a big screen TV in the family room, a communal kitchen and dining area, and a picture-perfect backyard. Upkeep is great on this 1970s ranch house, and Cathy and Bill's personable service is second to none. All-you-can-eat breakfasts and dinner are available ($5–$10).

500 E. 7th Ave., Leadville, CO 80461. © 719/486-9334. www.leadvillehostel.com. 32 dorm beds, 5 private rooms (2 with private bathroom). $17–$23 double; $35–$50 private room. MC, V. **Amenities:** Exercise room; massage room; shuttle service; coin-op washers and dryers; Wi-Fi network. *In room:* No phone.

WHERE TO DINE

Besides the establishments listed below, we also like **The Grill,** 715 Elm St. (© **719/ 486-9930**), for Mexican fare and tasty margaritas; and **High Mountain Pies,** 311 Harrison Ave. (© **719/486-5555**), for pizza, sandwiches, and ribs.

Columbine Cafe AMERICAN/VEGETARIAN   This simple, colorful cafe is a local favorite and healthier than the norm. Breakfasts range from traditional eggs and pancakes to more exotic dishes such as malted Belgian waffles and eggs Benedict, which can be prepared with avocados and tomatoes instead of meat. Lunches are sandwiches, burgers, and vegetarian dishes, and down-home dinners include pot roast, fried chicken, and red beans and rice.

612 Harrison Ave. © 719/486-3599. Reservations not accepted. Main courses $5.75–$8.50 breakfast and lunch, $6–$12 dinner. AE, DISC, MC, V. Daily 6am–8pm, with shorter hours fall through spring.

The Golden Burro Café AMERICAN   People have been enjoying good food in a comfortable Western setting at the Golden Burro since it opened in 1938. Old photos and drawings hang on the white walls above the wainscoting, glass-and-brass chandeliers cast a warm glow, and the large front windows provide views of the mountains. The emphasis at the Burro is on food like Grandma used to make, such as a hot meatloaf sandwich (homemade meatloaf, served open-faced with brown gravy, mashed potatoes, and a vegetable), pork chops, chicken-fried steak, and liver and onions, plus burritos with your choice of red or green chile. The freshly baked cinnamon rolls are especially good.

710 Harrison Ave. © 970/486-1239. Main courses $3.95–$9.95. MC, V. Daily 6:30am–9:30pm, with shorter hours fall through spring. Bar open later.

Quincy's Steakhouse *Value* STEAKS   Menus don't get much simpler than this: At Quincy's it's filet mignon Sunday to Thursday and prime rib on Friday and Saturday. That's it. You get a baked potato, too, and bread and a salad, not to mention a helping of historic ambience. But the focus is on the beef, and while you don't have a choice of the kind of steak you want, you do have four sizes to choose from. This is one of the best values in the Northern Rockies, with 6-ounce filets running $6.95 and 8-ounce slices of prime rib for $9.95.

115 E. Seventh St. © 719/486-9765. Reservations accepted for parties for 6 or more only. Main courses $7–$17. MC, V. Daily 4:30–9:30pm (from 5pm fall to spring).

LEADVILLE AFTER DARK

There's occasional entertainment at the **Tabor Opera House** (see "Experiencing Leadville's Past," above), and a handful of historic watering holes. Our picks are the 1878 **Pastime Saloon,** 120 W. 2nd St. (© **719/486-9434**) and the 1879 **Silver Dollar Bar,** 315 Harrison Ave. (© **719/486-9914**), one-time haunts of Doc Holliday.

8 Aspen

172 miles W. of Denver, 130 miles E. of Grand Junction

Like Vail, Aspen's reputation precedes it. Anyone with a pulse knows that it's more than likely to wind up in the tabloids when two celebrities—who are married to other people—are captured on film sharing a chairlift together; and, yes, plenty of Hollywood stars and wannabe stars hang out here.

However, if you take the time to dig beneath the media hype, you may be surprised by what you find. Aspen, at an elevation of 7,908 feet, is a real town with a fascinating history, some great old buildings, and spectacular mountain scenery. If you're a serious skier, you owe yourself at least a few days' worth of hitting the slopes (as if you need us to tell you that); but if you've never strapped on boards and you're thinking of visiting in summer, you'll be doubly pleased: Prices are significantly lower, and the crowds thin out. Many of the fabulous restaurants are still open, the surrounding forests are teeming with great trails for hiking, biking, and horseback riding, and it becomes one of the best destinations in the country for summer music and dance festivals.

Aspen was "discovered" when silver miners from nearby Leadville wandered a bit farther afield. When the Smuggler Mine produced the world's largest silver nugget (1,840 lb.), prospectors started heading to Aspen in droves. The city soon had 12,000 citizens—but just as quickly the population dwindled to one-tenth that number after the 1893 silver crash.

It took almost 50 years for Aspen to begin its comeback, which came as a result of another natural resource—snow. Shortly before World War II, a small ski area was established on the mountain now known as Ajax. During the war, 10th Mountain Division ski-soldiers training near Leadville spent weekends in Aspen and were enthralled with its possibilities. An infusion of money in 1945 by Chicago industrialist Walter Paepcke, who moved to Aspen with his wife, Elizabeth, resulted in the construction of what was then the world's longest chairlift. The Aspen Skiing Corporation (now Company) was founded the following year, and in 1950 Aspen hosted the alpine world skiing championships. Then came the opening in 1958 of Buttermilk Mountain and Highlands, and in 1967, the birth of Snowmass.

The Paepckes' vision of the resort was not exclusively commercial, however. They saw Aspen as a year-round intellectual and artistic community that would nourish the minds and spirits as well as the bodies of those who visited. Chief among their accomplishments was the establishment of the Aspen Music Festival. A love of ideas and high-minded discourse attracted the likes of Thornton Wilder and Albert Schweitzer to the community, and today a wide variety of intellectual types, artists, and writers (and yes, even those annoying Hollywood people) make this town of almost 6,000 their full- or part-time home.

ESSENTIALS

GETTING THERE   By Car   Aspen is located on Colo. 82, halfway between I-70 at Glenwood Springs (42 miles northwest) and U.S. 24 south of Leadville (44 miles east). In summer, it's a scenic 3½-hour drive from Denver: Leave I-70 West at exit 195 (Copper Mountain); follow Colo. 91 south to Leadville, where you pick up U.S. 24; turn west on Colo. 82 through Twin Lakes and over 12,095-foot Independence Pass. In winter, the Independence Pass road is closed, so you'll have to take I-70 to Glenwood Springs, and head east on Colo. 82. In optimal winter driving conditions, it'll take about 4 hours from Denver.

Aspen

ATTRACTIONS ●
Aspen Art Museum **12**
Wheeler/Stallard House
  Museum **1**

ACCOMMODATIONS ■
Hearthstone House **3**
Hotel Jerome **11**
Hotel Lenado **4**
Limelight Lodge **5**
The Little Nell **13**
The Mountain Chalet **7**
Sky Hotel **14**
St. Moritz Lodge &
  Condominiums **2**
St. Regis Resort, Aspen **6**

DINING ◆
Gusto Ristorante **10**
Jimmy's **8**
Piñons **9**

By Plane   Visitors who wish to fly directly into Aspen can arrange to land at **Aspen/ Pitkin County Airport,** 5 miles northwest of Aspen on Colo. 82 (© **970/920-5384;** www.aspenairport.com). Operating year-round flights are **United Airlines** (© 800/ 864-8331), **America West** (© 800/235-9292), and **Delta** (© 800/221-1212). Other airlines sometimes operate during ski season.

Another option is the **Eagle County Regional Airport** near Vail (© 970/524-9490; www.eaglecounty.us/airport). See section 6, earlier in this chapter.

By Airport Shuttle   **Colorado Mountain Express** (© **800/525-6363** or 970/926-9800; www.cmex.com) offers shuttle service from Denver International Airport starting at $109 per person, one-way.

By Train   Coming from San Francisco or Chicago, **Amtrak** (© **800/872-7245;** www.amtrak.com) stops in Glenwood Springs, 42 miles northwest of Aspen.

VISITOR INFORMATION   For information, contact the **Aspen Chamber and Resort Association,** 425 Rio Grande Place, Aspen, CO 81611 (© **800/670-0792** or 970/925-1940; www.aspenchamber.org), which operates a **visitor center** at the same location (open Mon–Fri 8am–5pm), and another at the Wheeler Opera House, located at Hyman Avenue and Mill Street (usually open daily 10am–6pm). You can also get information from the **Snowmass Village Resort Association,** 20 Lower

Moments **Riding in Style: The Ultimate Taxi**

Known in the Aspen Valley as the **Ultimate Taxi,** Jon Barnes' yellow cab is one of the most unusual vehicles on the planet: There's a rainbow of fiber optics on the ceiling, laser projectors, a webcam, a recording studio complete with keyboards and drum machines, a mirror ball, a roller-coaster simulator, and much, much more. Barnes has worked as a cabbie in Aspen since 1984, but started modifying his taxi in the early '90s. Today it's a blast for kids and partiers alike, with rides running $150 per group for 40 minutes. Barnes even takes your picture and posts it on his website (www.ultimatetaxi.com) for posterity—check ours out from June 2006. Call Jon for reservations or a ride at ℭ **970/927-9239.**

Snowmass Mall, Snowmass Village, CO 81615 (ℭ **800/766-9627;** www.snowmass village.com).

GETTING AROUND   Entering town from the northwest on Colo. 82, the artery jogs right (south) 2 blocks on Seventh Street, then left (east) at Main Street. "East" and "West" street numbers are separated by Garmisch Street, the next cross street after First Street. Mill Street is the town's main north-south street. There are several pedestrian malls downtown, which throw a curve into the downtown traffic flow.

By Shuttle Bus   Free bus service is available within the Aspen city limits, beyond which you can get connections west as far as Glenwood Springs, at reasonable rates, usually less than $5. Exact fare is required. Information can be obtained from the Roaring Fork Transportation Authority's **Rubey Park Transit Center,** Durant Avenue between Mill and Galena streets, in Aspen (ℭ **970/925-8484;** www.rfta.com). Schedules, frequency, and routes vary with the seasons; services include free ski shuttles in winter between all four mountains, shuttles to the Aspen Music Festival, and tours to the Maroon Bells scenic area in summer. Free shuttle transportation within Snowmass Village is offered daily during ski season and on a limited schedule in summer, by the **Snowmass Transportation Department** (ℭ **970/923-2543;** www.tosv.com).

By Taxi   Call **High Mountain Taxi** (ℭ **970/925-8294;** www.hmtaxi.com). For a more unusual experience, try the **Ultimate Taxi** (ℭ **970/927-9239;** www.ultimate taxi.com; also see "Riding in Style: The Ultimate Taxi," below).

By Rental Car   Car-rental agencies include **Alamo** (ℭ **800/327-9633** or 970/920-2603), **Budget** (ℭ **800/527-0700** or 970/925-2151), **Eagle** (ℭ **970/925-2128**), and **Thrifty** (ℭ **800/367-2277** or 970/920-2305).

FAST FACTS   The **Aspen Valley Hospital,** 401 Castle Creek Rd., near Aspen Highlands (ℭ **970/925-1120**), has a 24-hour emergency room. The **post office** is at 235 Puppy Smith St., off Mill Street north of Main; there's another in the Snowmass Center. For hours and other information contact the U.S. Postal Service (ℭ **800/275-8777;** www.usps.com). For **road reports,** call ℭ **970/920-5454.**

SPECIAL EVENTS   Wintersköl Carnival, mid-January, in Aspen and Snowmass; Aspen Gay Ski Week, late January; Snowmass Mardi Gras, early March; *Food & Wine* Magazine Classic, in June, in Aspen; Aspen Arts Festival, August; Aspen Filmfest and Aspen Cocktail Classic, late September.

SKIING & OTHER WINTER ACTIVITIES

Skiing Aspen 🎿🎿 really means skiing the four Aspen area resorts—Aspen Mountain, Aspen Highlands, Buttermilk, and Snowmass. All are managed by Aspen Skiing Company, and one ticket gives access to all. Daily lift ticket prices during peak season are $78 for adults 18 to 64, $71 for youths 13 to 17 and seniors 65 and older, and $49 for children 7 to 12. Children 6 and under ski free. For more information, contact **Aspen Skiing Company,** P.O. Box 1248, Aspen, CO 81612 (© **800/525-6200** or 970/925-1220; www.aspensnowmass.com). Call © **888/277-3676** or 970/925-1221 for snow reports.

ASPEN MOUNTAIN   Named for an old miner's claim, Aspen Mountain is not for the timid. This is the American West's original hard-core ski mountain, with no fewer than 23 of its runs named double diamond—for experts only. One-third of the mountain's runs are left forever ungroomed—sheer ecstasy for bump runners. There are mountain-long runs for intermediates as well as advanced skiers, but beginners should look to one of the other Aspen/Snowmass mountains.

From the **Sundeck** restaurant at the mountain's 11,212-foot summit, numerous intermediate runs extend on either side of Bell Mountain—through Copper Bowl and down Spar Gulch. To the east of the gulch, the knob of Bell offers a mecca for mogul mashers, with bump runs down its ridge and its east and west faces. To the west of the gulch, the face of Ruthie's is wonderful for intermediate cruisers, while more mogul runs drop off International. Ruthie's Run extends for over 2 miles down the west ridge of the mountain, with an extension via Magnifico Cut Off and Little Nell to the base, and is accessed by the unique Ruthie's high-speed double chair.

Aspen Mountain has a 3,267-foot vertical drop, with 76 trails on 673 skiable acres. The resort rates its trails as follows: none easiest, 48% more difficult, 26% most difficult, and 26% expert. There are eight lifts—a high-speed gondola, one high-speed quad chair, two quad chairs, one high-speed double, and three double chairs. Average annual snowfall at the 11,212-foot summit is 300 inches (25 ft.). Aspen Mountain is usually open from late November to mid-April.

There are a total of four restaurants.

ASPEN HIGHLANDS   A favorite of locals for its expert and adventure terrain— Highland Bowl—Aspen Highlands also has a good mix of terrain, from novice to expert, with lots of intermediate slopes. It also offers absolutely splendid views of the famed Maroon Bells (see the box "Natural Attractions," below).

It takes two lifts to reach the 11,675-foot Loge Peak summit, where most of the advanced expert runs are found in the Steeplechase area and 199 acres of glades in the Olympic Bowl. Kandahar, Golden Horn, and Thunderbowl give the intermediate skier a long run from top to bottom, and novices are best served midmountain on trails like Red Onion and Apple Strudel. There are also some fantastic opportunities for experts at Highland Bowl, which is a short walk from the top of the Loge Peak lift.

Freestyle Friday, a tradition at Highlands for almost 3 decades, boasts some of the best freestyle-bump and big-air competitors in Colorado every Friday from early January to mid-April. In this technical head-to-head contest, competitors bump their way down Scarlett's Run, and finish with a final jump that lands them within perfect view of lunchtime guests at the Merry-Go-Round Restaurant.

There are 131 trails on 970 acres, served by five lifts (three high-speed quads and two triple chairs). Trails are rated 18% easiest, 30% more difficult, 16% most difficult, and

36% expert. Aspen Highlands also has a terrain park, appropriate for intermediate to expert snowriders.

There are six restaurants, including three on the mountain. Highlands is usually open from mid-December to early April.

BUTTERMILK MOUNTAIN   Buttermilk is a premier beginners' mountain, one of the best places in America to learn how to ski. And it's also the home of the ESPN Winter X Games, at least through 2007.

The smallest of Aspen's four mountains, it has 44 trails, which the resort rates at 35% easiest, 39% more difficult, 26% most difficult, and none expert, plus a great terrain park. There are nine lifts (two high-speed quads, three double chairs, two handle tows, and two school lifts) on 435 acres, with a 2,030-foot vertical drop. Average annual snowfall at the 9,900-foot summit is 200 inches (16 ft., 8 in.). There's a restaurant on top and a cafe at the base. Buttermilk is usually open from mid-December to early April.

SNOWMASS   A huge, mostly intermediate mountain with something for everyone, Snowmass has 33% more skiable acreage than the other three Aspen areas combined! Actually four distinct self-contained areas, each with its own lift system, its terrain varies from easy beginner runs to the pitches of the Cirque and the Hanging Valley Wall, the steepest in the Aspen area.

Big Burn, site of a 19th-century forest fire, boasts wide-open advanced and intermediate slopes and the expert drops of the Cirque. Atop the intermediate Alpine Springs trails is the advanced High Alpine Lift, from which experts can traverse to the formidable Hanging Valley Wall. Elk Camp is ideal for early intermediates who prefer long cruising runs. Sam's Knob has advanced upper trails diving through trees, and a variety of intermediate and novice runs around its northeast face and base. All areas meet in the scattered condominium developments that surround Snowmass Village Mall. All told, there are 3,128 skiable acres at Snowmass, with a 4,406-foot vertical drop from the 12,510-foot summit. The mountain has 87 trails, rated 6% easiest, 50% more difficult, 12% most difficult, and 32% expert. There are 22 lifts (one high-speed six passenger, one six-passenger gondola, six high-speed quad chairs, one triple chair, six double chairs, two platter pulls, two ski/snowboard school lifts, and three Magic Carpets). Average annual snowfall at the summit is 300 inches (25 ft.).

The renowned Snowmass ski school has hundreds of instructors, as well as programs for children 18 months and older. The area also has three terrain parks, one superpipe, and a rail yard. There are 12 restaurants.

Snowmass is usually open from late November to mid-April.

CROSS-COUNTRY SKIING   The Aspen/Snowmass Nordic Council operates a free Nordic trail system with nearly 37 miles of groomed double track extending throughout the Aspen-Snowmass area, and incorporating summer bicycle paths. Instruction and rentals are offered along the trail at the **Aspen Cross-Country Center,** Colo. 82 between Aspen and Buttermilk (© **970/925-2145;** www.utemountaineer.com), and the **Snowmass Cross Country Center,** Snowmass Village (© **970/923-9180**), both of which provide daily condition reports and information regarding the entire trail system.

Independent backcountry skiers should consult **White River National Forest,** 806 W. Hallam St. (© **970/925-3445;** www.fs.fed.us/r2), and two hut systems provide shelter on multiday trips (see "Hiking & Mountaineering," below). Also, see the website **www.aspennordic.com.**

Moments Natural Attractions

The two sheer, pyramidal peaks called **Maroon Bells,** on Maroon Creek Road 10 miles west of Aspen, are probably two of the most photographed mountains in the Rockies. During summer and into early fall, you can take a 20- to 30-minute narrated bus tour from Aspen Highlands up the Maroon Creek Valley (© **970/ 925-8484;** www.rfta.com). Cost for the bus trip is $6 adults, $3 for youths 6 to 16, $4 for seniors, and it's free for children under 6.

DOG SLEDDING   For rides in winter or a kennel tour in summer, call **Krabloonik,** 4250 Divide Rd., Snowmass Village (© **970/923-4342;** www. krabloonik.com). Every day in winter, teams of Alaskan sled dogs pull guests into the Snowmass–Maroon Bells Wilderness Area. Half-day trips, at 8:30am and 12:30pm, include lunch at **Krabloonik** restaurant (see "Where to Dine," later in this chapter) and cost $225 per adult and $170 for children 3 to 8 years of age. Children under 3 are not permitted. One-hour kennel tours run from mid-June to Labor Day, Monday through Saturday, starting at 11am and 2:30pm. Cost is $6 for those over 12, $5 for 12 and under.

WARM-WEATHER & YEAR-ROUND ACTIVITIES

Your best source for information on a wide variety of outdoor activities in the mountains around Aspen, including hiking, mountain biking, horseback riding, four-wheeling, fishing, and camping, is the **White River National Forest** (see "Cross-Country Skiing," above).

There's no lack of guides, outfitters, and sporting-goods shops in Aspen. Among the best one-stop outfitters is **Blazing Adventures** (© **800/282-7238** or 970/923-4544; www.blazingadventures.com), which offers rafting, mountain-biking, hiking, four-wheeling, hot-air ballooning, and horseback-riding excursions.

BICYCLING   There are two bike paths of note. One connects Aspen with Snowmass Village; it covers 13 miles and begins at Seventh Street south of Hopkins Avenue, cuts through the forest to Colo. 82, then follows Owl Creek Road and Brush Creek Road to the Snowmass Mall. Extensions link it with Aspen High School and the Aspen Business Park. The Rio Grande Trail follows the Roaring Fork River from near the Aspen Post Office, on Puppy Smith Street, 2 miles west to Cemetery Lane. See also "Mountain Biking," below.

FISHING   Perhaps the best of a great deal of good trout fishing in the Aspen area is to be found in the Roaring Fork and Frying Pan rivers, both considered gold-medal streams. The Roaring Fork follows Colo. 82 through Aspen from Independence Pass; the Frying Pan starts near Tennessee Pass, northeast of Aspen, and joins the Roaring Fork at Basalt, 18 miles down valley.

Stop at **Taylor Creek Fly Shop** in Basalt at 183 Basalt Circle (© **970/927-4374;** www.taylorcreek.com), for your fishing needs. Guided fishing trips are offered by Taylor Creek and **Blazing Adventures** (see above).

GOLF   Public 18-hole championship courses in the Aspen valley include **Aspen Golf Course,** 9461 Colo. 82, 1 mile west of Aspen (© **970/925-2145**), one of the longer courses in Colorado at 7,165 yards, charging $45 to $90 for 18 holes plus $18 per person for the cart; and **The Snowmass Club,** 239 Snowmass Club Circle (© **970/923-5600**), charging about $175 for 18 holes, including a cart and range balls, with lower rates after 4pm.

HIKING & MOUNTAINEERING   Among the best ways to see the spectacular scenery here is on foot. You can get maps and tips on where to go from **White River National Forest** offices (see above). One popular trail is the route past the Maroon Bells to Crested Butte; the trek would take 175 miles by mountain road, but it's only about 30 miles by foot—14 miles from the end of Aspen's Maroon Creek Road.

Hikers can also make use of two hut systems for multiday trips—the 12-hut **10th Mountain Trail Association's** system toward Vail, and the six-hut **Alfred A. Braun and Friends Hut System** (© **970/925-5775** for both; www.huts.org) toward Crested Butte. Huts are basic, with bunk beds, but do have wood-burning stoves, propane burners, photovoltaic lighting, kitchen equipment, mattresses, and pillows. A bed in one of the huts costs $28 per night. Association offices are at 1280 Ute Ave., Suite 21, in Aspen.

HORSEBACK RIDING   Several stables in the Aspen valley offer a variety of rides, and some outfitters even package gourmet meals and country-and-western serenades with their expeditions. A wide variety of adventures are offered; rates for day trips usually start at about $50 per person for a 1-hour ride or $100 for a half-day. Inquire at **Aspen Wilderness Outfitters** (© **970/963-0211**; www.aspenwilderness.com), **Capitol Peak Outfitters** (© **970/963-4402**; www.capitolpeak.com), and **OutWest Guides** (© **970/984-3801**; www.outwestguides.net).

MOUNTAIN BIKING   There are hundreds of miles of trails through the White River National Forest that are perfect for mountain bikers, offering splendid views of the mountains, meadows, and valleys. Check with the Forest Service (p. 290) and local bike shops for tips on the best trails. Among full-service bike shops offering rentals are **Aspen Velo Bike Shop,** 465 N. Mill St. (© **970/925-1495**; www.aspenvelo.com), and **Aspen Sports,** 408 E. Cooper Ave. (© **970/925-6331**; www.aspensports.com). A half-day rental is $20 to $50.

RIVER RAFTING   Rafting trips are offered on the Roaring Fork, Arkansas, and Colorado rivers with several companies, including **Colorado Riff Raft** (© **800/282-7238** or 970/923-4544; www.riffraft.com), **Up Tha Creek Expeditions** (© **877/982-7335** or 970/947-0030; www.upthacreek.com), and **Blazing Adventures** (see above). Rates are usually about $50 to $90 for a half-day.

MUSEUMS, ART CENTERS & HISTORIC SITES

The **Aspen Historical Society,** 620 W. Bleeker St. (© **970/925-3721**; www.aspen history.org), offers a variety of guided tours of Aspen and the surrounding mining camps during the summer. One 2-hour walking tour of Aspen covers about 1 mile and begins on the grounds of the Wheeler/Stallard House Museum (see below), explores the West End residential area, and ends in the lobby of the historic Hotel Jerome (see "Where to Stay," below). The cost is $10 per person. Guided tours of the **Ashcroft ghost town** are offered daily, at a cost of $3 per person. Call for reservations and specific times. Self-guided tour brochures are also available.

Aspen Art Museum ⚡   This attractive museum presents rotating exhibits highlighting the work of nationally known contemporary artists, and hosts an annual exhibit showcasing local talent. Lectures and art education programs for adults and

Aspen Music

Nestled in the picturesque Roaring Fork Valley is one of the top ski resorts in Colorado, and in summer, when the snows have (mostly) melted, the schussing of skis is replaced with the glorious sound of music.

The **Aspen Music Festival and School** originated in 1949, and is now considered one of America's top summer music programs. Lasting 9 weeks from mid-June to late August, it offers more than 350 events, including symphonic and chamber music, opera, choral, and children's programs. Most concerts take place in the state-of-the-art, 2,050-seat Benedict Music Tent and 500-seat Joan and Irving Harris Concert Hall, both at Third and Gillespie streets. The acoustics in the tent are very good, but in Harris Hall they're awesome.

During the season, ensembles-in-residence—the American and Emerson string quartets, and the American Brass Quintet—give recitals; the Aspen Chamber Symphony and Aspen Festival Orchestra perform; and varied chamber groups are created from amongst the roster of professional musicians that make up the school's faculty. Plus, there are numerous open rehearsals and other programs offered. Events scheduled for 2006 included works by Bartok, Mozart, Beethoven, Chopin, Berlioz, and Frank Zappa, to name a few. Look for the new schedule early in 2007.

On top of Aspen Mountain—you'll have to ride the gondola—student groups perform free 1-hour concerts each Saturday at 1pm. This **"Music on the Mountain"** soars into the backdrop of the Elk Mountain range. Another special experience is the **intimate concerts in private homes,** on various afternoons. The **family events** include several programs geared to youngsters under 10, such as storytelling and music at the Pitkin County Library (free; most Thurs mornings), plus the annual family picnic and concert of short fun classical pieces. Certain **rehearsals** of the Aspen Chamber Symphony and Aspen Festival Orchestra are open to the public, giving visitors an inside look at how a concert is put together. And if you're a visiting musician, check out the master classes while you're in town.

Open rehearsals cost under $20, master classes are $17, and most concert tickets run $20 to $60. Free programs include most of the family events plus the popular Saturday "Music on the Mountain" concerts atop Aspen Mountain. **Free tours** of the tent and concert hall, a historic walking tour from the Hotel Jerome to the tent, and a tour of the music school campus are available. Parking is limited, but there is free bus service from many points in town, Snowmass Village, and down-valley (© **970/925-8484** for schedule information).

For additional information contact **Aspen Music Festival and School,** 2 Music School Rd., Aspen, CO 81611 (© **970/925-9042;** www.aspenmusic festival.com).

children are offered year-round, and there's a free wine-and-cheese reception most Thursdays from 5 to 7pm. Allow 30 minutes.

590 N. Mill St., Aspen. ☎ 970/925-8050. www.aspenartmuseum.org. Admission $5 adults, $3 students and seniors 65 and older, free for children under 12; free general admission Fri. Tues–Sat 10am–6pm (until 7pm most Thurs); Sun noon–6pm.

Wheeler/Stallard House Museum Silver baron Jerome B. Wheeler had this three-story Queen Anne–style brick home built in 1888, and its steeply pitched roofs, dormers, and gables have made it a landmark in Aspen's West End neighborhood. A museum since 1969, the exterior of this handsome house has been restored to its appearance in the heady days of silver mining. Exhibits describe Aspen's history from Ute culture through the mining rush, and from railroads and ranching to the founding of the skiing industry. Allow an hour.

620 W. Bleeker St., Aspen. ☎ 970/925-3721. www.aspenhistory.org. Admission $6 adults, $5 seniors, $3 children 12 and younger. Tues–Sat 1–5pm.

SHOPPING

To truly appreciate the Aspen experience, one must shop Aspen. Note that we say shop (meaning browse) rather than buy, because if you're not careful, you just might blow next month's mortgage payment on some Western fashion accessory. No one ever brags about the great bargain they snagged last season in Aspen.

On the other hand, quality is usually tops, shop clerks are friendly, and your neighbor probably doesn't already have one. Having said all that, we suggest you lock up your credit cards, put on some good walking shoes, and spend a few hours exploring the galleries and shops of Aspen. Following are a few of our favorites, and several are grouped together in a minimall at 525 E. Cooper Ave.

For **original art,** check out: **Aspen Grove Fine Arts,** 525 E. Cooper Ave., upper level (☎ 970/925-5151; www.aspengrovefineart.com), featuring paintings, graphics, and sculpture. When it's time to pick up a gift, we like **Chepita,** 525 E. Cooper Ave. (☎ 970/ 925-2871; www.chipeta.com), an attractive store with jewelry, sculpture, and home accessories; and **Curious George Collectibles,** 426 E. Hyman Ave. (☎ 970/925-3315), for silver buckles, belts, and Western artifacts that (allegedly) used to belong to notorious cowboys. For **clothing,** try **Kemo Sabe,** 434 E. Cooper Ave. (☎ 970/925-7878; www. kemosabe.com), for wonderful hats and other Western wear, and **Gorsuch, Ltd.,** 611 E. Durant Ave. (☎ 800/525-9808 or 970/920-9388; www.gorsuchltd.com), for outdoor clothing.

WHERE TO STAY

Occupancy rates run 90% or higher during peak winter and summer seasons, so it's essential to make reservations as early as possible (or avoid peak seasons, as we try to do). The easiest way to book your lodgings is to call **Stay Aspen Snowmass** central reservations (☎ 888/649-5982; www.stayaspensnowmass.com). You can also find lodging through **Aspen Resort Accommodations** (☎ 800/727-7369; www.aspenreservations.net).

Many accommodations close during the spring and fall; if they're open, rates during those months are typically the lowest of any time during the year. Unless otherwise noted, parking is free. A tax of 9.6% is added to hotel bills.

VERY EXPENSIVE

Hotel Jerome ✦✦✦ The historic ambience and superb service at the Hotel Jerome make it the best place to stay in Aspen—for those who can afford it. Jerome B. Wheeler built the Jerome during the peak of the silver boom. It opened in 1889 as Colorado's first hotel with electricity and indoor plumbing, and the first west of the Mississippi River with an elevator. The silver crash of 1893 ended Aspen's prosperity and the glory years of the Hotel Jerome, but a multimillion-dollar renovation has restored the Jerome to its original splendor. With its original architecture lovingly preserved, and furnished with period antiques, the Jerome is now on the National Register of Historic Places.

Each beautifully appointed guest room is spacious—even the smallest is more than 500 square feet—and unique, containing luxurious furnishings, a desk, comfortable chairs, queen or king beds with down comforters, and plush terry bathrobes. Bathrooms, finished with white Carrara marble and reproduction 19th-century octagonal tiles, boast oversize tubs and separate showers.

The resort's signature Century Room offers savory Alpine-American fare served in comfortable elegance, with main courses in the $20 to $30 range. Guests with lighter appetites can get sandwiches and salads at the historic J-Bar (see "Aspen After Dark," later in this chapter). In summer, the outdoor dining patio is delightful.

Note: The hotel will be closed for renovations from April 2007 until late November 2007.

330 E. Main St., Aspen, CO 81611. © **800/331-7213** or 970/920-1000. Fax 970/925-2784. www.hoteljerome.com. 91 units. Early Apr to late May and late Sept to mid-Nov $265–$430 double, $755–$900 suite; late May to late Sept and late Nov to mid-Dec $475–$640 double, $950–$1,100 suite; early Jan to early Apr $635–$760 double, $1,230–$1,390 suite; Christmas season $885–$1,080 double, $1,375–$1,530 suite. AE, DC, MC, V. Underground valet parking $20. Pets permitted ($75 fee). **Amenities:** 2 restaurants (American); 2 bars; heated outdoor pool; exercise room; 2 whirlpools; concierge; ski concierge; courtesy shuttle; secretarial services; 24-hr. room service; valet laundry. *In room:* A/C, TV/VCR or TV/DVD, dataport, minibar, hair dryer, iron, safe, high-speed Internet.

The Little Nell 🏩🏩   Located just 17 paces (yes, it's been measured) from the base terminal of the Silver Queen Gondola, the Little Nell boasts the virtues of an intimate country inn as well as the personalized service and amenities of a grand hotel. No two guest rooms are alike, but each has a gas fireplace, Belgian-wool carpeting, down-filled lounge chairs or sofa, oversized bed with down comforter, and marble-finished bathroom with two vanities, separate shower and tub, and high-end toiletries. Some suites have separate Jacuzzi tubs and steam showers. All rooms have a view of either the town or the mountain.

The hotel's signature Montagna restaurant serves "farmhouse cooking" by acclaimed chef Ryan Hardy in an artsy atmosphere with large windows looking toward the hotel courtyard and Aspen Mountain. Both the famed living room and the bar were recently redesigned by David Easton, an interior designer of renown. The adjoining Montagna Bar offers a more relaxed atmosphere.

A team of ski concierges are at your beck and call in winter, and there's also a complimentary shuttle.

675 E. Durant Ave., Aspen, CO 81611. © **888/843-6355** or 970/920-4600. Fax 970/920-4670. www.thelittlenell. com. 92 units. Early winter, early spring, and summer $280–$355 double, $600–$1,850 suite; winter $685–$835 double, $1,350–$4,650 suite; spring and fall $360–$385 double, $530–$1,800 suite. Call for holiday rates. AE, DC, DISC, MC, V. Valet parking $21 per day. Pets accepted. **Amenities:** Restaurant (American regional); 2 bars; heated pool; health club and spa; outdoor whirlpool; concierge; shopping arcade; 24-hr. room service; massage; same-day valet laundry. *In room:* A/C, TV/VCR (video rental available), minibar, coffeemaker, hair dryer, iron.

Sky Hotel 🏩🏩   One of the hippest hotels on the planet, the Sky Hotel melds kitsch and class into one satisfying colorful whole. Located slopeside just steps from the Silver Queen Gondola in downtown Aspen, Kimpton Hotels renovated the old Aspen

Club Lodge beyond recognition and reopened the property in 2002. The rooms are a study in color and animal prints, with perks like cordless phones, iPod docking stations, and humidifiers. The only complaint is that the rooms are pretty small—look elsewhere if you need space to spread out. The year-round pool features an outdoor bar, a waterfall, and a pair of fire pits. Walk inside to the ultra-hip bar, **39 degrees,** with an undulating sofa in the center, great burgers, and unusual specialty cocktails like the Botox Martini. The lobby is for the ages, with a 15-foot chandelier shaped like a bright red lampshade, stately wood columns, high-backed white chairs, and an assortment of proudly displayed board games like Sorry! and Yahtzee.

709 E. Durant Ave., Aspen, CO 81611. ℂ 800/882-2582 or 970/925-6760. Fax 970/925-6778. www.theskyhotel.com. 90 units, including 6 suites. $169–$700 double; $400–$1,000 suite. Valet parking $25; self-parking $15. Pets accepted. AE, DISC, MC, V. **Amenities:** Restaurant/lounge; outdoor heated pool; exercise room; outdoor whirlpool; limited watersports rentals; in-room massage; courtesy car; business center; dry cleaning. *In room:* A/C, cable TV w/pay movies, minibar, coffeemaker, hair dryer, iron, wireless Internet access.

St. Regis Resort, Aspen 🌟🌟🌟   Located at the base of Aspen Mountain, between the gondola and Lift 1A, the St. Regis offers luxurious comfort in a casual but definitely upscale Western atmosphere. Decorated with rich wood, muted earth tones, and original paintings by 19th- and 20th-century artists, the lobby offers cozy seating, a large river-rock fireplace, and magnificent views of Aspen Mountain. Most rooms have views of either the mountains or town, and a few on the ground floor offer views of the flower-filled courtyard. Each unit is features "contemporary alpine" decor, with overstuffed leather chairs, leather tabletops, handsome marble bathrooms, and sport such amenities as bathrobes, Bose CD players, 30-inch flat-screen TVs, and portable phones. The Alpine Floor offers key-access service, a dedicated concierge, and five complimentary food and beverage servings throughout the day. The St. Regis recently added new units and constructed a large spa. In winter, a ski concierge coordinates ski rentals, lift tickets, and lessons. Olives Aspen Restaurant serves Mediterranean-inspired cuisine, and in summer the flower-filled courtyard is open to dining.

315 E. Dean St., Aspen, CO 81611. ℂ 888/454-9005 or 970/920-3300. Fax 970/925-8998. www.stregisaspen.com. 179 units. $495–$1,800 double; suites to $4,000. AE, DC, DISC, MC, V. 24-hr. valet parking $26. **Amenities:** Restaurant (Mediterranean); bar; outdoor heated pool; fitness center and spa; 2 whirlpools (1 indoor, 1 outdoor); sauna; steam room; concierge; courtesy airport transportation; business center; 24-hr. room service; concierge-level rooms. *In room:* A/C, TV/DVD, fax (in suites only), dataport, minibar, hair dryer, iron, safe, high-speed Internet.

EXPENSIVE & MODERATE

Hearthstone House   Small and sophisticated, the Hearthstone House is located just 2 blocks west of the Wheeler Opera House. Guests share a large, elegant living room with teak-and-leather furnishings and a wood-burning fireplace, dining room with bright flowers, and an extensive library. Rooms are bright and homey, with queen-size or twin beds, and two rooms have a king-size bed. Four units feature whirlpool tubs. Smoking is not permitted.

134 E. Hyman Ave. (at Aspen St.), Aspen, CO 81611. ℂ 888/925-7632 or 970/925-7632. Fax 970/920-4450. www.hearthstonehouse.com. 16 units. Summer $199–$299 double; winter $259–$359 double. Rates include breakfast plus afternoon wine and cheese. AE, DC, DISC, MC, V. **Amenities:** Access to Aspen Club & Spa; outdoor Jacuzzi; herbal steam room; bikes available (free); wireless Internet access. *In room:* TV/VCR, fridge, coffeemaker.

Hotel Lenado 🌟   This small hotel—best described as a contemporary mountain lodge—feels right at home in this old mining town, with natural wood beams, wood floors, handsome wood furniture, and a comfortable but upscale feel. The Western-style rooms have a rustic appearance, with four-poster hickory or apple-wood beds, down comforters and pillows, excellent sound systems, shared balconies, and twice-daily maid service. Some units have wet bars, refrigerators, and wood-burning stoves. There's a red rock and concrete fireplace in the lobby that stands 28-feet tall, a hot tub on a second-floor deck that offers a spectacular view of Aspen Mountain, ski storage, and a heated locker for ski boots. An excellent gourmet breakfast is served daily.

200 S. Aspen St., Aspen, CO 81611. © **800/321-3457** or 970/925-6246. Fax 970/925-3840. www.hotellenado.com. 19 units. Winter $215–$540; summer $265–$325; spring and fall $90–$250. Rates include full breakfast. AE, DC, MC, V. **Amenities:** Bar; hot tub; concierge; limited room service; in-room massage; valet laundry service. *In room:* A/C, TV/VCR or TV/DVD, hair dryer, complimentary wireless Internet access.

Limelight Lodge *Value* We were distraught when we heard the old Limelight was falling to the bulldozer in 2006, but our spirits were immediately lifted when we heard about the plans for the new one that will go up in the same quiet spot near downtown Aspen. Due to reopen in early 2008, the property is trading its mom-and-pop looks for a slick, classic-meets-contemporary facade, sheathing larger rooms spread over four stories. Dale Paas, whose family has owned the motel since 1958, is committed to sustainable design, and the new project is a model of green architecture and design. While we'll have to wait until 2008 to see how it plays out completely, we've been so happy with the Limelight over the years that we expect the property to continue to offer one of the best values in town.

228 E. Cooper Ave. (at Monarch St.), Aspen, CO 81611. © **800/433-0832** or 970/925-3025. Fax 970/925-5120. www.limelightlodge.com. 126 units. $200–$350 double, $300–$450 suite. Rates include continental breakfast. AE, DC, DISC, MC, V. **Amenities:** Whirlpool; coin-op laundry. *In room:* A/C, cable TV, fridge, hair dryer, iron.

INEXPENSIVE

In addition to the property discussed below, those on a budget might want to consider the **St. Moritz Lodge & Condominiums,** 334 W. Hyman Ave., Aspen, CO 81611 (© **800/817-2069** or 970/925-3220; www.stmoritzlodge.com), which is one of the best deals in Aspen; small double rooms with shared bathrooms start at $68 in spring and fall, $89 in summer, and $90 in ski season. There are also hostel beds ($30–$52 per person), plus rooms with private bathrooms, units with kitchenettes, and one- and two-bedroom condominium units.

The Mountain Chalet You'll find a friendly, ski-lodge atmosphere here, just 1½ blocks from the lifts. There's a TV in the lobby (where complimentary wine and hors d'oeuvres are served on Mon nights in winter) and a piano and game room on the lower level. Rooms are light-colored, with wood furnishings and good-quality twin, double, queen, or king beds, plus a few trundle beds. There are even some bunk rooms with four beds, rented by the bed at greatly reduced rates in ski season. Most rooms have refrigerators; some have central air-conditioning. Ski lockers are available.

333 E. Durant Ave., Aspen, CO 81611. © **888/503-9355** or 970/925-7797. Fax 970/925-7811. 59 units. Winter $95–$365 double, $480 apt., rates higher during holidays; summer $90–$200 double, $250 apt.; spring and fall $55–$130 double, $160 apt. Children 3 and under stay free. Rates include full breakfast in winter, continental breakfast in summer. DC, DISC, MC, V. Underground parking. **Amenities:** Outdoor heated pool; exercise room; large indoor whirlpool; sauna and steam room; game room; massage; coin-op laundry. *In room:* TV, fridge, hair dryer.

WHERE TO DINE

Most restaurants in the Aspen-Snowmass area are open during the ski season (Thanksgiving to early Apr) and summer (mid-June to mid-Sept) seasons. Between seasons, however, some close their doors or limit hours. Call ahead if you're visiting at these times.

EXPENSIVE

Krabloonik ✦✦ (Moments) INTERNATIONAL There's something very wild, something that hearkens back to Jack London, perhaps, about sitting in a log cabin watching teams of sled dogs come and go as you bite into a tender caribou loin or wild-boar chop. That's part of the pleasure of Krabloonik. A venture of the largest dog kennel in America's lower 48 states, this rustic restaurant has huge picture windows with mountain views and seating around a sunken fireplace. Skiers drop into the restaurant from the Campground Lift for lunch, and visitors can dine before or after an excursion on a dog sled (see "Dog Sledding," earlier in this section). For dinner there's Krabloonik smoked trout with creamy horseradish for starters and a wide variety of game, beef tenderloin, lamb, and fish for the main course. Those with hearty appetites can choose between two combination game entrees: caribou, elk, and deer; or caribou, quail, and boar. Smoking is not permitted.

4250 Divide Rd., off Brush Creek Rd., Snowmass Village. ⓒ 970/923-3953. www.krabloonik.com. Reservations recommended at lunch, essential at dinner. Lunch main courses $14–$22; dinner main courses $29–$65. AE, DC, DISC, MC, V. Winter Mon–Fri 11am–1:30pm and 5:30–9:30pm; Sat–Sun 5:30–9:30pm (Sat–Sun also 11am–1:30pm during Christmas holidays). Closed from the end of ski season until Thanksgiving.

Piñons ✦✦✦ CONTEMPORARY REGIONAL The apex of the Aspen dining scene, Piñons has been one of Colorado's best restaurants since it opened its doors in 1988. The room, heavy on suede and lodgepole pine, is casually elegant, with picture windows providing the ideal lens to gaze at Aspen Mountain over a truly splendid splurge of a meal. With starters as delectable as this—lobster strudel, anyone?—it's hard to make it to the entrees, but they are works of inventive culinary art, letting the fresh flavors shine in simple but timeless preparations. You can't miss with herb-crusted ruby trout with spinach, crab, pancetta, and sweet corn puree; or pistachio-crusted rack of lamb with potato-rutabaga hash. The desserts include an unforgettable raspberry crème brûlée and homemade ice cream.

105 S. Mill St. ⓒ 970/920-2021. www.pinons.net. Reservations recommended. Main courses $40–$65. AE, DC, DISC, MC, V. Daily 5:30–10pm. Closed Apr to early June and Oct–Nov.

MODERATE & INEXPENSIVE

Gusto Ristorante ✦ ITALIAN Locals love this place, and we do, too. Open year-round, the spare, sleek eatery is lively and social, delivering great Italian specialties and assured service from an international staff. Chef Mateo Mangiarotti is a native of Italy, and he shows his skills with such knockout dishes as *tarozzi con pesto* (homemade pasta stuffed with ricotta cheese and sautéed with *haricot verts* [green string beans] and a pesto sauce) and *gnocchi masseria* (potato dumplings with sausage, mushrooms, and tomatoes in red wine sauce). There are also gourmet pizzas and a nice list of mostly Italian wines.

415 E. Main St. ⓒ 970/925-8222. www.gustoristorante.com. Reservations accepted. Main courses $9–$17 lunch, $12–$32 dinner. AE, DC, DISC, MC, V. Daily 11:30am–10:30pm. Bar open later.

Jimmy's ✦ SOUTHWESTERN Another local favorite, Jimmy's (subtitled "An American Restaurant & Bar") is known for its steaks and seafood, but loved for its luscious meatloaf. Proprietor Jimmy Yeager says it's "fierce American food," busting with flavor and prepared without fear. Other signature dishes include the crab cakes, Colorado rack of lamb, and the addictive homemade chocolate chip cookies. The BBQ sauce and salsas are also worth a taste. Jimmy's also prides itself upon its selection of tequilas and mescal: 67 in all!

205 S. Mill St. ⓒ 970/925-6048. www.jimmysaspen.com. Reservations accepted. Main courses $12–$38. MC, V. Daily 5:30–11pm. Bar open later.

Woody Creek Tavern 𝕴𝕴 *Finds* AMERICAN/MEXICAN   We love this place. A funky rustic tavern with personality to spare, Woody Creek is a true local hangout, and a favorite of late gonzo journalist (and one-time local) Hunter S. Thompson. Its walls are now covered with a variety of news clippings and other paraphernalia, much of it relating to Thompson. You'll find a good selection of well-prepared tavern food, including barbecued pork ribs, thick steaks, and burgers (made with low-fat Colorado limousine beef); plus fresh tilapia, organic salads, vegetarian (and organic when possible) soups, as well as excellent Mexican food, hot and spicy just like we like it, which goes well with the house-specialty drink—fresh-squeezed lime-juice margaritas made with 100% blue-agave tequila.

Upper River Rd., Woody Creek. ℭ 970/923-4585. Reservations not accepted. Main courses $8–$21. No credit cards. Daily 11:30am–10pm, bar stays open later. Drive west on Colo. 82, ¾ mile past the Snowmass Village turnoff, turn right on Smith Rd. into Woody Creek Canyon, turn left at the first fork, and continue 1¼ miles. This road can be icy in winter.

ASPEN AFTER DARK

Aspen's major performing arts venue is the 1889 **Wheeler Opera House,** 320 E. Hyman Ave., at Mill Street (ℭ **970/920-5770** box office; www.wheeleroperahouse.com). Built at the peak of the mining boom by silver baron Jerome B. Wheeler, this meticulously restored stage hosts a year-round program of music, theater, dance, film, and lectures. The building itself is worth a visit, with brass wall sconces, crystal chandeliers, gold trim and stencils on the dark-blue walls, rich wood, red carpeting, and red velvet seats. The box office is open daily from 10am to 6pm (until 5pm Sun).

Among Aspen's top nightspots, **Syzygy,** 520 E. Hyman Ave. (ℭ **970/925-3700**), ranks high with young, high-energy types who live for the "Aspen scene." Aspen's oldest bar is the **Red Onion,** 420 E. Cooper Ave. (ℭ **970/925-9043**), which opened in 1892 and today remains a noisy, popular hangout, with occasional live music. **Bentley's at the Wheeler,** 328 E. Hyman Ave. (ℭ **970/920-2240**), is an elegant English-style pub, good for the older crowd. The **Lobby Lounge** at the St. Regis, at the base of Aspen Mountain (ℭ **970/920-3300;** www.stregis.com), draws scores of après-skiers; and among our favorite Aspen bars is the quietly sophisticated and historic **J-Bar,** in the Hotel Jerome at Main and Mill streets (ℭ **970/920-1000**). The rich, hip, young, and wasted flock to **39 degrees,** in the Sky Hotel at 709 E. Durant Ave. (ℭ **970/925-6760**) for drinks like the Sex by the Pool Martini and the unbeatable slopeside pool, which you can use if you're a bar customer and not a guest. For the opposite side of the spectrum and the best burger deal in town, hit the casual, funky, and unpretentious **Cooper Street Pier,** 508 E. Cooper Ave. (ℭ **970/925-7758**). Live rock, folk, and country concerts are the hallmark of **Belly Up,** 405 S. Galena St. (ℭ **970/544-9800;** www.bellyupaspen.com). **Eric's Bar,** 408 E. Hyman Ave. (ℭ **970/920-6707**), is four bars in one, with a cigar bar, pool hall, a Mexican eatery, and the bustling main bar.

11

The Western Slope

Separated from Colorado's major cities by the mighty Rocky Mountains, the communities along the state's western edge are not only miles, but also years away from the hustle and bustle of Denver and the California-style sophistication of Boulder. Even Grand Junction, the region's largest city, remains a sprawling Western town, and the rugged canyons and stark rocky terrain make you feel like you've stepped into a John Ford Western. The lifeblood of this semidesert land is its rivers—the Colorado, Gunnison, and Yampa—for not only have they brought life-giving water, but over tens of thousands of years their ceaseless energy has also gouged out stunning canyons that lure visitors from around the world.

Colorado National Monument, west of Grand Junction, is remarkable for its land forms and prehistoric petroglyphs; Dinosaur National Monument, in the state's northwestern corner, preserves a wealth of dinosaur remains; and the Black Canyon of the Gunnison, a dark, narrow, and almost impenetrable chasm east of Montrose, challenges adventurous rock climbers and rafters.

But it's not all rocks and dinosaurs here. In the tiny community of Palisade, outside Grand Junction, some of the West's best wine is produced; and downtown Grand Junction boasts a continually changing and evolving outdoor art exhibit with its delightful Art on the Corner sculpture display.

1 Grand Junction, Colorado & Dinosaur National Monuments

251 miles W. of Denver, 169 miles N. of Durango

One of our favorite Colorado cities, Grand Junction is an excellent base camp for those who want to drive or hike through the awe-inspiring red-rock canyons and sandstone monoliths of Colorado National Monument, explore the canyons at Dinosaur National Monument, about 2 hours north, or get a close-up view of America's automotive heritage at a fantastic new automobile museum in the community of Gateway, about 1 hour to the southwest.

Grand Junction is also the eastern entrance to one of the West's most scenic and challenging mountain-biking treks, Kokopelli's Trail, which ends in Moab, Utah. For the less athletically inclined, Grand Junction has an active visual arts community, good museums, and a fine botanical garden. Nearby you'll find more than a dozen wineries.

Located at the confluence of the Gunnison and Colorado rivers at an elevation of 4,586 feet, the city was founded in 1882 where the spike was driven to connect Denver and Salt Lake City by rail. It quickly became the primary trade and distribution center between the two state capitals, and its mild climate, together with the fertile soil and irrigation potential of the river valleys, helped it grow into an important agricultural area. Soybeans, and later peaches and pears, were the most important crops.

Grand Junction

ATTRACTIONS ●
The Art Center **9**
Bananas Fun Park **10**
Cross Orchards Historic Farm **7**
Museum of the West /
   Smith Educational Tower **13**
Western Colorado
   Botanical Gardens **16**
Western Colorado Math &
   Science Center **17**

ACCOMMODATIONS ■
Best Western Sandman Motel **5**
Comfort Inn **2**
Doubletree Hotel **3**
The Gallery **8**
Grand Vista Hotel **1**
Mesa Inn **6**
Quality Inn **4**

DINING ◆
Crystal Cafe & Bake Shop **11**
Good Pastures **4**
Main Street Café **14**
Pablo's Pizza **12**
The Winery Restaurant **15**

The city was also a center of the western Colorado uranium boom in the 1950s and the oil-shale boom in the late 1970s, and today is a fast-growing trade center serving practically all of western Colorado and eastern Utah.

ESSENTIALS

GETTING THERE   By Car   Grand Junction is located on I-70. U.S. 50 is the main artery from the south, connecting with Montrose and Durango.

By Plane   On the north side of Grand Junction, **Walker Field,** 2828 Walker Field Dr. (© **970/244-9100;** fax 970/241-9103; www.walkerfield.com), is less than a mile off I-70's Horizon Drive exit. More than 20 commercial flights connect Grand Junction with the West's major cities.

Airlines serving Walker Field include **Allegiant Air** (© 800/432-3810), **America West Express/Mesa Airlines** (© **800/235-9292** or 970/728-4868), **The Delta Connection/SkyWest** (© 800/453-9417), **Frontier** (© 800/432-1359), **Great Lakes Aviation** (© 800/554-5111), and **United Express/SkyWest** (© 800/241-6522).

By Train   Amtrak (© **800/USA-RAIL** or 970/241-2733; www.amtrak.com) has a passenger station at 337 S. First St. The California Zephyr stops twice daily, once in each direction, on its main route from San Francisco and Salt Lake City to Denver and Chicago.

VISITOR INFORMATION   Contact the **Grand Junction Visitor & Convention Bureau,** 740 Horizon Dr., Grand Junction, CO 81506 (© **800/962-2547** or 970/ 244-1480; fax 970/243-7393; www.visitgrandjunction.com). There's a visitor center on Horizon Drive at I-70 exit 31 (open 8:30am–8pm in summer and 8:30am–5pm the rest of the year), and a Colorado Welcome Center at I-70 exit 19 (Fruita and Colorado National Monument), 12 miles west of Grand Junction, which is open daily from 8am to 5pm.

GETTING AROUND   Main Street and named avenues run east-west, and numbered streets and roads run north-south. Downtown Grand Junction lies south of I-70 and north of the Colorado River, encompassing 1 block on each side of Main Street between First and Seventh streets. There is metered street parking (free 2-hr. parking on Main Street between First and Seventh sts.), plus several public parking lots. Scheduled for completion in 2007 is a new multistory parking garage, very convenient for those going downtown, at Fourth Street and Rood Avenue.

Car rentals are available in the airport area from **Alamo** (© 970/243-3097), **Avis** (© 970/244-9170), **Budget** (© 970/244-9155), **Dollar** (© 970/255-9400), **Enterprise** (© 970/242-8103), **Hertz** (© 970/243-0747), **National** (© 970/243-6626), and **Thrifty** (© 970/243-7556). **Sunshine Taxi** (© 970/245-8294) offers 24-hour service, and **Grand Valley Transit** (© 970/256-7433) operates buses in the Grand Junction area, including a shuttle service to and from Walker Field.

FAST FACTS   There's a 24-hour emergency room at **St. Mary's Hospital,** Patterson Road and Seventh Street (© **970/244-2273**). The main **post office** is at 241 N. Fourth St.; contact the U.S. Postal Service (© **800/275-8777;** www.usps.com) for hours and other information. For **weather conditions,** call © **970/243-0914;** for **road conditions,** call © **877/315-7623.**

SPECIAL EVENTS   Cinco de Mayo, early May; Dinosaur Days, mid-June in Fruita; Art & Jazz Festival, mid-May; Junior College Baseball World Series, starting

Memorial Day weekend; Mesa County Fair, late July; Peach Festival, mid-August in Palisade; Colorado Mountain Wine Fest, late September.

COLORADO NATIONAL MONUMENT 🏛🏛

Just minutes west of Grand Junction, this relatively undiscovered national monument is a delight, offering a colorful maze of steep-walled canyons filled with an array of naturally sculpted spires, pinnacles, and other impressive sandstone rock formations. Easy to get to and easy to see, in many ways it's a miniature Grand Canyon, without the crowds. You can see much of the monument from your car on the 23-mile Rim Rock Drive, and there are ample opportunities for hiking, horseback riding, and cross-country skiing. Bighorn sheep, mountain lions, golden eagles, mule deer, and lizards are among the monument's residents. The monument ranges in elevation from 4,700 feet to 7,028 feet.

Carved by water and wind over millions of years, Colorado National Monument encompasses 32 square miles of red-rock canyons and sandstone monoliths, more than 1,000 feet above the Colorado River. A combination of upward lifts and erosion caused the chaos of formations here. Each layer visible in the striations of the canyon walls marks a time in the land's history. Fossils permit scientists to date these rocks back through the Mesozoic era of 225 million to 65 million years ago, and the Precambrian formation dates back 1.67 billion years.

The east entrance is only 5 miles west of Grand Junction, off Monument Road, but the best way to explore the monument is to follow the signs off I-70 from Fruita to the west entrance, 15 miles west of Grand Junction. It's here that **Rim Rock Drive,** built during the Great Depression, begins. Snaking up dramatic Fruita Canyon, it offers panoramic views of fanciful and bizarre natural stone monuments as well as the cliffs and mesas beyond. At 4 miles it reaches the national monument headquarters and **visitor center.** Exhibits on geology and history and an interactive video program introduce the park, and rangers can help you plan your visit. Guided walks and campfire programs are offered during the summer.

Rim Rock Drive—open to bicycles as well as motor vehicles—offers access to hiking trails varying in length from 400 yards to 8.5 miles. Many of the short, easy trails lead to spectacular canyon overlooks, while the longer backcountry trails head out across the mesas or down into the canyons. Strange formations such as Window Rock, the massive rounded Coke Ovens, the boulder-strewn Devils Kitchen, and the freestanding Independence Monument—all of which can be viewed from the road—are easily reached by foot.

If you're looking for an easy walk, try the 1-mile (round-trip) **Canyon Rim Trail,** which follows the edge of a cliff to spectacular views of the colorful rock formations in Wedding Canyon. Allow about an hour. An even shorter walk—the **Window Rock Trail**—also affords views of Wedding Canyon. Allow a half-hour for .3-mile loop.

Those who want to get down into the monument, rather than viewing it from above, should tackle one of the backcountry trails. The relatively difficult 12-mile round-trip **Monument Canyon Trail** drops 600 feet from the plateau into the canyon, among many of the monument's more dramatic rock formations, such as the aptly named Kissing Couple. The canyon is home to rattlesnakes and scorpions, so watch where you put your feet and hands. Also, it's hot and dry down there, so be sure to carry plenty of water. The **Black Ridge Trail,** the national monument's highest, offers panoramic views of the countryside that stretch to the canyons of Utah. Allow about 6 hours for the rugged, 11-mile round-trip hike, and again, carry plenty of water.

Winter visitors may want to take their skis along. Among your best choices here is **Liberty Cap Trail,** which meanders across gently sloping Monument Mesa through a piñon-juniper forest and sagebrush flatlands. The trail is 14 miles round-trip, but cross-country skiers may want to turn back before the last 1.5 miles, which drop sharply into the Grand Valley.

While the monument is worth visiting at any time of year, the best time to go is fall, when the air is crisp but not cold, the cottonwood trees turn a brilliant gold, and the summer crowds have departed. Those visiting in May and June should carry insect repellent to combat the clouds of gnats that invade at this time.

The monument's **Saddlehorn Campground,** located in a piñon-juniper forest near the visitor center, has 80 sites, some shady, and restrooms but no showers or RV hookups. Cost is $10 per night. Like most areas administered by the National Park Service, pets must be leashed and are not allowed on trails or in the backcountry.

The national monument is open year-round. The day-use fee is $7 per vehicle or $4 per person for cyclists and pedestrians. The visitor center is open daily from 8am to 6pm in summer and 9am to 5pm the rest of the year. To obtain a brochure and other information, contact **Colorado National Monument,** Fruita, CO 81521 (© **970/858-3617;** www.nps.gov/colm). Those who want more in-depth information can order topographic maps, books, and other materials from the nonprofit Colorado National Monument Association at the monument's address and phone number above, or online at www.coloradonma.org.

DINOSAUR NATIONAL MONUMENT 🐾

This national monument, about 2 hours north of Grand Junction, is really two separate parks divided by the Utah-Colorado border. One side takes a close-up look at the world of dinosaurs, while the other opens onto a wonderland of colorful rock, deep river canyons, and a forest of Douglas firs.

About 150 million years ago a river and sufficient vegetation made this region a suitable habitat for dinosaurs. Most of their skeletons decayed and disappeared, but in at least one spot they were preserved under a layer of sediment, when the river dried up and they died of thirst.

The **Dinosaur Quarry** and visitor center that provided access to it was closed in July 2006, and will remain closed indefinitely until much-needed structural repairs can be completed. In the meantime, there is an **outdoor visitor center** near the Jensen, Utah, entrance that has fossil displays, exhibits, films, and additional information. From Dinosaur, Colorado, head 20 miles west on U.S. 40 to Jensen, Utah, and then go 7 miles north into the park. This is the only place in the monument to see dinosaur bones.

However, even though exploration of the quarry area has been curtailed, there is still plenty to do here, especially on the Colorado side. Encompassing 325 square miles of stark canyons at the confluence of the Yampa and Green rivers in Colorado, the national monument also has hiking trails to explore, spectacular panoramic vistas, and the thrill of white-water rafting. Your first stop should be the **Canyon Area Visitor Center** located about 2 miles east of the town of Dinosaur, Colorado, at the intersection of U.S. 40 and Harpers Corner Drive.

Allow about 4 hours for the scenic **Harpers Corner Drive.** This paved 62-mile round-trip drive has several overlooks offering panoramic views of the gorges carved by the Yampa and Green rivers, the derby-shaped Plug Hat Butte, and a variety of other colorful rock formations. The drive also offers access to the easy .3-mile round-trip **Plug Hat Nature Trail,** and the moderately difficult 2-mile round-trip **Harpers Corner Trail,** highly recommended for a magnificent view of the deep river canyons. In addition to several developed trails, experienced hikers with the appropriate maps can explore miles of unspoiled canyons and rock benches.

A superlative way to see this rugged country is on the river, crashing through thrilling white water and gliding over the smooth, silent stretches. One of the best authorized companies running the Yampa and Green rivers through the monument is **Hatch River Expeditions** (ⓒ **800/342-8243** or 435/789-4316; www.hatchriver.com). Prices start at $69 for adults, $59 for kids ages 6 through 14 for a 1-day trip; multiday trips over longer stretches are also available. The season generally runs from mid-May through mid-September, depending on water levels. A complete list of authorized river-running companies is available from monument headquarters.

Rivers are not safe for swimming or wading; the water is cold, and the current is stronger than it may first appear.

Fishing in the Green and Yampa most often yields catfish, northern pike, and smallmouth bass, although there are also some trout. Several endangered species of fish—including the razorback sucker and humpback chub—must be returned unharmed to the water if caught. You'll need Utah and/or Colorado fishing licenses, depending on which side of the state line you're fishing.

There are **campgrounds** in both sections of the monument, but no showers or RV hookups, and camping fees range from $8 to $12 per night.

The national monument entrance near Dinosaur, Colorado, is about 110 miles north of Grand Junction. From Grand Junction, head west on I-70 about 12 miles to exit 15, turn right (north) onto Colo. 139 and go about 75 miles to Colo. 64, where you turn left, and follow it west for 20 miles to the town of Dinosaur. Then turn right onto U.S. 40 and go east about 2 miles to the monument entrance. The monument is open around the clock, and the outdoor visitor center in Utah is open daily year-round, except Thanksgiving, Christmas, and New Year's Day. Hours in summer are 9am to 6pm, with shorter hours in winter, The Canyon Area Visitor Center in Colorado is open daily in summer from 8am to 4pm but closed weekends in winter. The admission fee, charged only at the Utah entrance as of this writing, is $10 per vehicle, and $5 per person for those on foot, motorcycles, or bicycles.

For information contact **Dinosaur National Monument,** 4545 East U.S. 40, Dinosaur, CO 81610-9724 (ⓒ **970/374-3000;** www.nps.gov/dino). In addition, the nonprofit **Intermountain Natural History Association,** 1291 E. U.S. 40, Vernal, UT 84078-2830 (ⓒ **800/845-3466;** fax 801/781-1304; www.inhaweb.com), offers numerous publications, maps, posters, and videos on the park's geology, wildlife, history, and especially its dinosaur fossils.

SPORTS & OUTDOOR ACTIVITIES

In addition to activities in Colorado and Dinosaur national monuments, there are numerous opportunities for hiking, camping, mountain biking, off-roading, horseback riding, cross-country skiing, snowmobiling, and snowshoeing on other public lands administered by the federal government. Contact the **Bureau of Land Management,** 2815 H Rd., Grand Junction, CO 81506 (ⓒ **970/244-3000;** www.co.blm.gov), and the **Grand Valley Ranger District of Grand Mesa National Forest,** 2777 Crossroads Blvd., Ste. 1 (off Horizon Dr.), Grand Junction, CO 81506 (ⓒ **970/242-8211;** www.fs.fed.us/r2).

You'll also find plenty to do at **James M. Robb–Colorado River State Park** (© 970/434-3388; www.parks.state.co.us), which has two main sections, both with campgrounds (see "Camping" under "Where to Stay," later in this section). **Island Acres** (© 970/464-0548), on the east side of Grand Junction at I-70 exit 47, also offers hiking, picnicking, fishing, and just gazing out at the river. The **Fruita** section (© 970/858-9188), located in the community of Fruita about ½-mile south of I-70 exit 19, covers 81 acres and has all of the above, plus boating and a swimming lagoon. Day-use fee at both sections is $5 per vehicle.

The Grand Junction **Parks and Recreation Department** (© 970/254-3842; www.gjcity.org) manages more than 30 parks and other facilities, covering about 467 acres, which offer picnicking, hiking, tennis, playgrounds, swimming pools, softball, playing fields, horseshoe pits, and golf courses.

A busy local shop where you can get information on the best spots for outdoor recreation is **Summit Canyon Mountaineering,** 461 Main St. (© **800/254-6248** or 970/243-2847; www.summitcanyon.com). In addition to information, it stocks a wide variety of outdoor-sports equipment, plus travel and outdoor clothing.

GOLF   Our favorite course here, in large part because of the views—it's like golfing in the Grand Canyon—is the 18-hole **Golf Club at Redlands Mesa,** 2325 W. Ridges Blvd. (© **866/863-9270** or 970/263-9270; www.redlandsmesa.com), with greens fees of $39 for 9 holes and $76 for 18 holes. You'll also find great golfing and wonderful views at the 18-hole **Tiara Rado Golf Course,** 2057 S. Broadway (© **970/254-3830**), at the base of the Colorado National Monument canyons. Greens fees Monday through Thursday are $12 for 9 holes and $22 for 18 holes; Friday through Sunday $16 and $26, respectively. The **Chipeta Golf Course,** an 18-hole executive course at 222 29 Rd. (© **970/245-7177**), has weekday fees of $10 for 9 holes and $19 for 18 holes, with weekend rates of $13 and $23, respectively. The 27-hole **Adobe Creek National Golf Course,** 876 18½ Rd., Fruita (© **970/858-0521**), is 9 miles west of Grand Junction. On weekdays it charges $23 for 18 holes; on weekends the fee is $28.

HIKING   Hikers and walkers who want to stay close to town can explore the trails in the Colorado Riverfront Project. Collectively known as the **Colorado River Trails,** the system includes almost 20 miles of paved trails that meander along the Colorado and Gunnison rivers, offering the chance to see ducks, geese, blue heron, deer, and rabbits. They are open to walkers and hikers, runners, bikers, in-line skaters, and horseback riders, but are closed to all motorized vehicles (except wheelchairs). Dogs are permitted if leashed, but owners are asked to clean up after their dogs. Most of the trails are between .5 and 2 miles long, and they can be combined for longer hikes. Although all the trails tend to be busy on weekends, on weekdays you'll find they're very quiet. An excellent brochure with maps of the various river trails and directions to their trail heads is available free at the Grand Junction Visitor & Convention Bureau (see "Visitor Information," above).

You'll also find hiking trails at **Colorado River State Park** (see the introduction to this section, above).

HORSEBACK RIDING   Trail rides near the west entrance of Colorado National Monument are available through **Rimrock Adventures,** P.O. Box 608, Fruita, CO 81521 (© **888/712-9555** or 970/858-9555; www.rradventures.com). The stables are about a mile south of Fruita on Colo. 340. Rates for a 1-hour ride are $28 for adults and $20 for children 5 to 12, and a half-day ride into the wilderness of Devil's Canyon costs $60 for adults and $50 for children. Kids' pony rides, lasting about 15 minutes, cost $10. Those with their own horses will enjoy the 14-mile (round-trip) Liberty Cap Trail through Colorado National Monument, which winds through a scrub forest and over a sagebrush mesa before dropping steeply into a valley.

ICE SKATING   Bring your skates (or rent them for $2.50 a pair) and hit the ice at this new regulation NHL-size sheet of ice. **The Glacier Ice Arena,** 2515 River Rd. (© 970/242-7465; www.theglacier.net), which opened in 2006, offers public skating, learn-to-skate sessions, hockey games, and figure-skating programs. General admission costs $6 for those 13 and older, $5 for children 5 to 12 and seniors, and is free for kids under 5. Public skating times vary, so call ahead or check the website.

MOUNTAIN BIKING   Grand Junction has become important to mountain bikers as the eastern terminus of **Kokopelli's Trail** to Moab, Utah. Winding for 142 miles through sandstone and shale canyons, it has an elevation differential of about 4,200 feet. There are primitive campsites at intervals along the trail. The Colorado gateway is at the Loma Boat Launch, 15 miles west of Grand Junction off I-70.

For information on Kokopelli's Trail and several other area trails, contact the **Colorado Plateau Mountain-Bike Trail Association,** P.O. Box 4602, Grand Junction, CO 81502 (© 970/244-8877; www.copmoba.com). There's also a bike route through and around Colorado National Monument (see earlier in this chapter). Covering 33 miles, it follows Rim Rock Drive through the park and 10 additional miles on rural South Camp Road and South Broadway at the base of the canyons. Rim Rock Drive does not have a separate bike lane, or shoulders, so be alert for motor traffic. The national monument publishes a free brochure.

There are also several short mountain bike rides in the area. Inquire at the Visitor & Convention Bureau (see "Visitor Information," earlier in this chapter) for their brochures. You can also get information on area biking, plus rent mountain and road bikes, and see some antique and unique bikes at **Brown Cycles,** 549 Main St. (© 970/245-7939). Bikes rent for $25 to $35 per day, and the shop's bicycle museum includes an 1885 high-wheeler, Schwinns from the 1920s and 1930s, and a human-powered bicycle airplane.

RIVER RAFTING   For our money, one of the best ways to see this area's beautiful red sandstone canyons is from the river, in a big old rubber raft. Colorado river-rafting trips are provided by **Rimrock Adventures** (see "Horseback Riding," above). Cost for a 1½-hour trip about 5 miles down the Colorado is $25 for adults and $18 for children 12 and under; a 25-mile full-day float trip costs $100 per adult and $75 per child under 14. An exciting 17-mile white-water trip through Westwater Canyon costs $140 per person. The company also rents rafts ($60–$110 per day), canoes ($35 per day), and inflatable kayaks ($30–$40 per day) for those who want to explore the river on their own.

Adventure Bound River Expeditions, 2392 H Rd., Grand Junction, CO 81505 (© 800/423-4668 or 970/245-5428; www.raft-colorado.com), offers 1- to 7-day trips. Rates for a 1-day trip through Westwater Canyon are $150 per adult and $135 for youths under 18. Two-day trips cost $335 per adult and $310 for youths under 18; call for additional rate information.

SKIING & SNOWBOARDING   **Powderhorn Resort** ⚜, Colo. 65, 7 miles south of Mesa (© 970/268-5700; www.powderhorn.com), is located 35 miles east of Grand

Wine Tasting & More Amid the Canyons

Colorado may not be the first location that comes to mind when winemaking is mentioned, but the state does have a growing wine industry and the heart of it is here in the fertile Grand Valley. Area wineries welcome visitors for tastings and sometimes tours, and they all have picnic areas so bring your lunch. Organized tours by van or limousine are also available. Most of the wineries are located in the community of **Palisade,** about 12 miles east of Grand Junction, up the Grand Valley along U.S. 6 (or I-70 exit 42).

The state's oldest existing winery, **Colorado Cellars Winery,** 3553 E Rd., Palisade (🏕 **800/848-2812** or 970/464-7921; www.coloradocellars.com), produces an excellent selection of award-winning wines, including chardonnays, merlots, Rieslings, fruit wines, and port. In summer, tasting room hours are Monday through Friday from 9am to 5pm, and Saturday from 10am to 5pm; winter hours are Monday through Friday from 9am to 4pm, and Saturday from 11am to 4pm. **Carlson Vineyards,** 461 35 Rd., Palisade (🏕 **888/464-5554** or 970/464-5554; www.carlsonvineyards.com), produces a variety of easy-drinking wines from Colorado fruit. Visitors are welcome year-round, daily from 10am to 6pm.

Meadery of the Rockies, 3701 G Rd., Palisade (🏕 **800/720-2558**; 970/464-7899; www.meaderyoftherockies.com), produces honey wine—also known as mead. Popular in medieval times, mead was known as "the drink of the gods," and is often served at Shakespearean festivals. It contains no grapes, but is made from orange-blossom honey from citrus groves in Arizona, and ranges from very sweet to quite dry. Rocky Mountain Meadery also produces blends of honey wine and fruit, as well as hard apple and pear cider, and a port-style wine. The tasting room is open daily from 10am to 5pm.

Other local wineries include **Grande River Vineyards,** 787 Elberta Ave. (I-70 exit 42), Palisade (🏕 **800/264-7696** or 970/464-5867; www.granderiverwines.com), which produces a variety of wines including a merlot, a Bordeaux, and a chardonnay. The tasting room is open daily from 9am to 6pm from spring through fall, and daily from 9am to 5pm in winter. **Plum Creek Cellars,** 3708 G Rd., Palisade (🏕 **970/464-7586**; www.plumcreekwinery.com), produces a wide variety of wines, including chardonnays, cabernet sauvignons, merlots, Rieslings, and pinot noirs, using only Colorado grapes. The tasting room is open daily from 9:30am to 6pm April through November, and from 10am to 5pm the rest of the year. **Garfield Estates Winery,** located on a 100-year-old homestead at 3572 G Rd., Palisade (🏕 **970/464-0941**; www.garfieldestates.com), produces several fine wines made from Palisade-area grapes—merlot, cabernet sauvignon, sauvignon blanc, shiraz, and port. The tasting room is open daily from 11am to 5pm.

Canyon Wind Cellars, 3907 N. River Rd., Palisade (🏕 **970/464-0888**; www.canyonwindcellars.com), produces several big-bodied wines including a chardonnay, a merlot, and a cabernet sauvignon. Its tasting room is open daily from 10am to 5pm. **St. Kathryn Cellars,** 785 Elberta Ave., Palisade

(© **877/464-4888** or 970/464-9288; www.St-Kathryn-Cellars.com), produces a chardonnay, a merlot, blends, fruit wines, and port. Its tasting room is open daily from 10am to 5pm. **Confre Cellars,** 785 Elberta Ave., Palisade (© **970/ 464-1300**), offers a variety of grape, honey, and fruit wines, plus also produces fudge. The tasting room is open daily from 10am to 5pm.

The **Debeque Canyon Winery,** 3943 U.S. 6, Palisade (© **970/464-0550;** www. debequecanyonwinery.com), produces various oak-aged wines including a claret, chardonnays and cabernets, merlots and shiraz, and port. The tasting room is open daily from 10am to 6pm in summer and 10am to 5pm in winter. **Amber Ridge Vineyards,** 3820 G ¼ Rd., Palisade (© **970/464-5314;** www. amberridgevineyards.com), produces chardonnay, cabernet sauvignon, and merlot, and is open Thursday from 1 to 5pm, and Friday and Saturday from 11am to 5pm.

Wineries in Grand Junction include **Two Rivers Winery,** 2087 Broadway, Grand Junction (© **866/312-9463** or 970/255-1471; www.tworiverswinery. com), which has 11 acres of vineyards surrounding a French château–style winery and tasting room. Two Rivers' wines include a cabernet sauvignon, a chardonnay, and a shiraz. The tasting room is open from 10:30am to 6pm Monday through Saturday and from noon to 5pm Sunday. **Whitewater Hill Vineyards,** 220 32 Rd., Grand Junction (© **970/434-6868;** www.whitewater hill.com), produces a white merlot, chardonnay, and several other varieties, and also grows grapes used by other Colorado wineries. The winery and tasting room, which offer splendid views of the vineyards and surrounding valley, are open in summer daily from noon to 6pm and in winter the same hours but only Saturday and Sunday.

South of Grand Junction about 7 miles is **Reeder Mesa Vineyards,** 7799 Reeder Mesa Rd., Whitewater (© **970/242-7468;** www.reedermesawines. com) is known for its Riesling, and also produces cabernet sauvignon, merlot, and shiraz. They're open Friday and Saturday from 10am to 6pm, and Sunday from noon to 4pm. **Graystone Winery,** 3352 F Rd., Clifton (© **970/ 434-8610;** www.graystonewine.com), specializes is port, and also sells other Colorado wines in its tasting room in Clifton, just east of Grand Junction. It's open in summer daily from 10am to 6pm, and in winter Monday through Saturday from 10am to 5pm and Sunday from noon to 5pm.

The **Colorado Wine Room,** 455 Kokopelli Blvd., Fruita, (© **877/858-6330** or 970/858-6330; www.coloradowineroom.com), is located near the Colorado Welcome Center just off I-70 exit 19 in Fruita, west of Grand Junction. It offers tastings and sales of close to two dozen Colorado wines and also has exhibits on winemaking. It's open Tuesday through Saturday from 10:30am to 5:30pm and Sunday from noon to 5pm. Maps to the wineries and additional information can be obtained from the Grand Junction Visitor & Convention Bureau (p. 336) and online at **www.coloradowinecountry.com.**

Junction on the north face of the Grand Mesa. A favorite among local skiers and snowboarders of all ability levels, this pleasant resort offers 600 acres of skiable terrain with an average annual snowfall of 250 inches. Powderhorn has one quad lift and two doubles serving 27 trails, which are rated 20% beginner, 50% intermediate, 15% advanced, and 15% expert. Elevation at the top is 9,850 feet, and there's a vertical drop of 1,650 feet. Lift-ticket prices (highest Sat–Sun and holidays) are $43 to $48 for adults 26 to 59; $34 to $41 for young adults 19 to 25; $33 to $38 for students 7 to 18 and seniors 60 to 69; $20 for those 70 and older; and $12 for children 6 and younger. The resort has a ski school, a rental shop, and a repair center. It is usually open from early December through late March.

Located at Powderhorn is a slope-side lodge, the **Inn at Wildewood,** P.O. Box 370, Mesa, CO 81643 (© **970/268-5170**). It has 15 rooms with double rates in winter from $89 to $159 and a fully equipped condominium unit that can be rented with two or three bedrooms and sleeps from 8 to 10 people with winter rates of $319 to $399. Summer rates are roughly 15% less. The **Wildewood Restaurant** serves lunch and dinner in a casually elegant atmosphere, with an American/Continental cuisine of sandwiches, salads, exotic pizzas, and pasta dishes.

SNOWMOBILING   A trail connects Powderhorn Resort to Sunlight Mountain Resort, running 120 miles from Grand Junction's ski area to Glenwood Springs, the longest multiuse winter recreational trail in Colorado, traversing White River and Grand Mesa national forests. It is fully marked and continuously groomed. Other trails are accessed from parking areas along Colo. 65, between Mesa Lakes and Grand Mesa.

SWIMMING   Centrally located **Lincoln Park,** at 12th Street and North Avenue, has a 50m outdoor heated pool with a 351-foot water slide, along with lighted tennis courts, playgrounds, picnic areas, and a 9-hole golf course. The **Orchard Mesa Pool,** 2736 C Rd., has an indoor pool, open year-round, with a diving area and shallow-water section. For hours, fees, and other specifics, contact the Grand Junction Parks and Recreation Department (© **970/254-3842;** www.gjcity.org).

THE MUSEUM OF WESTERN COLORADO 🏛🏛

For a huge step through time—from 150 million years ago all the way up to the present—you'll want to visit the various facilities of the **Museum of Western Colorado** (© **888/488-3466** or 970/242-0971; www.wcmuseum.org). These include the **Museum of the West/Smith Educational Tower, Dinosaur Journey,** and **Cross Orchards Historic Farm** (each of which is discussed below).

In addition, the Museum of Western Colorado manages three **natural resource areas** (free admission, open 24 hr.), where you can get a firsthand look at the geology and paleontology of western Colorado. **Rabbit Valley Research Natural Area,** located at I-70 exit 2, about 30 miles west of Grand Junction, encompasses a working dinosaur quarry. The "Trail Through Time," a 1.5-mile self-guided walking tour, offers a close-up view of dinosaur fossils preserved in ancient stream channels. **Riggs Hill,** located off South Broadway in Grand Junction, is the site of the first official dinosaur excavation in western Colorado. It's named for paleontologist Elmer S. Riggs of Chicago's Field Museum of Natural History, who discovered huge fossilized bones of the previously unknown dinosaur *Brachiosaurus altithorax* here in 1900. The site has a .8-mile self-guided interpretive trail, as well as stupendous panoramic views from the top of Riggs Hill. **Dinosaur Hill,** south of Fruita, off Colo. 340 near Colorado National

Monument, is western Colorado's second excavated site, also dug by Riggs. It contains a 1-mile self-guided interpretative trail.

Combination admission tickets to the three facilities below, available at any of the sites, cost $12 adults, $10 seniors 60 and over, and $8 children 12 and under.

Cross Orchards Historic Farm   With over 22,000 apple trees covering 243 acres, Cross Orchards was one of the largest apple orchards in western Colorado during the first quarter of the 20th century. Today, the remaining 24 acres of the historic site preserve the feel of an old working farm and orchard, where blacksmiths and woodworkers continue to ply their trades, and visitors often smell ginger cookies baking in wood-burning stoves. Costumed guides lead tours through the original barn and packing house, workers' bunkhouse, and farm owner's gazebo. The site contains an extensive collection of vintage farm and road construction equipment, plus rail cars and a reconstructed depot. There's also a gift shop. Each year in mid-October visitors enjoy the **Apple Jubilee,** a harvest festival that includes plenty of fresh apple cider and other apple goodies. Allow 1½ to 2 hours.

3073 F Rd. © 970/434-9814. Admission $4 adults, $3 seniors 60 and over, $2.50 children 12 and under; immediate family rate $10. May–Oct Tues–Sat 9am–4pm. Closed Nov–Apr except for special events (© 970/242-0971 for schedule).

Dinosaur Journey *(Kids)*   Enter a virtual time machine to journey back to the age of dinosaurs, where you'll encounter the 18-foot forelimb of a brachiosaurus. There are cast skeletons of dinosaurs such as allosaurus and stegosaurus, as well as real bones and robotic reconstructions. The cleverly designed and constructed full-size models move, bellow, and occasionally spit water. Hands-on, interactive exhibits allow kids of all ages to learn about and experience the forces that created the lands around us, and to feel the earth shake on an earthquake simulator. There is also a working paleontology lab, where you can see scientists prepare dinosaur bones for study. Visitors can join in a real dinosaur dig at one of the museum's quarries with advance registration (© **888/488-3466**). Allow 1 to 3 hours.

550 Jurassic Ct., Fruita (just south of I-70 exit 19). © **970/858-7282.** Admission $7 adults, $6 seniors 60 and over, $4 children 12 and under; immediate family rate $20. May–Sept daily 9am–5pm; Oct–Apr Mon–Sat 10am–4pm, Sun noon–4pm.

Museum of the West/Smith Educational Tower   This extensive museum offers a step back into the history of the American West, with "immersive" exhibits that remove the glass between visitor and exhibit, allowing you to literally step into history. Listen to the antique siren as you inspect the 1921 LaFrance fire truck; or examine a superb collection of Southwestern pottery in an adobe villa. You can explore an 1890s schoolhouse and a 1930s post office, as well as venture inside a full-size uranium mine, where the sounds of blasting and drilling continue to echo, and even "fly" a computer-controlled 1950 Cessna and learn about Colorado aviation history. The museum also boasts one of the finest firearms collections in the region, and has a display on the life of Alferd Packer, Colorado's notorious cannibal. From the upper levels of the six-story Smith Tower you'll get impressive 360-degree views of Grand Junction and the surrounding countryside. Connect to a wealth of historical, genealogical, and natural history materials in the Loyd Files Research Library. Allow 1½ to 3 hours.

5th St. and Ute Ave. © 970/242-0971. Admission $5.50 adults, $4.50 seniors 60 and over, $3 children 12 and under; immediate family rate $16. Mon–Sat 9am–5pm, Sun noon–4pm. **Note:** The Museum of the West/Smith Educational Tower is expected to be closed from mid-Jan to mid-Apr, 2007 to update its exhibits.

MORE TO SEE & DO

In addition to the attractions discussed here, those with an artistic bent might check out the **pottery classes** offered at The Gallery bed-and-breakfast inn (see "Where to Stay," below).

The Art Center Formerly known as the Western Colorado Center for the Arts, this fine gallery and museum has hundreds of works of art, many with Western themes, as well as traveling exhibits. The collection includes lithographs by Western artist Paul Pletka and more than 50 Navajo weavings dating from the early 1900s. There's also a gift shop featuring unique handcrafted items. Classes, changing exhibitions, and other events are scheduled throughout the year (call for a schedule). Allow at least an hour.

1803 N. Seventh St. © 970/243-7337. Fax 970/243-2482. www.gjartcenter.org. Admission $3 adults, free for children under 12. Tues–Sat 9am–4pm.

Art on the Corner ☆ This outdoor sculpture exhibit, with more than 100 works, helps make Grand Junction's Downtown Shopping Park one of the most attractive and successful in the country. About half of the sculptures are on loan by the artists for 1 year, during which time they are for sale, while the rest are on permanent display. The sculptures were created in a variety of styles in bronze, chrome, iron, and other materials. We particularly like the whimsical frog called *Puffed Up Prince*, the large bronze pig named *Sir*, and *Greg La Rex*, a sculpture in steel that depicts a dinosaur skeleton atop a bicycle. The shopping park has art galleries, antiques shops, restaurants, and a variety of retail stores, with wide, tree-lined pedestrian walkways. Also see "Shopping," below. Allow at least an hour.

Main St., from Second to Seventh sts. © 970/245-2926. Free admission. Daily 24 hr., with shops and restaurants open usual business hours.

Bananas Fun Park *Kids* A fun place for kids of all ages (and the adults who are lucky enough to have their kids take them), this amusement park has a great miniature golf course—with waterfalls, fountains, and ponds—plus an arcade, go-carts, bumper boats in a small "bay," laser tag, batting cages, a playground, and a cafe. Allow 2 hours or more.

2469 River Rd. © 970/241-7529. www.bananasfunpark.com. Tickets for individual activities vary. Sun–Thurs 10am–10pm; Fri–Sat 10am–midnight.

Western Colorado Botanical Gardens ☆☆ *Kids* This botanical garden along the Colorado River offers a delightful escape into the natural world. Located on 15 acres, the facility includes a butterfly house, greenhouse with more than 600 exotic tropical plants, paved trails, and outdoor gardens and demonstration areas.

In the butterfly house, visitors stroll through a lush forest of flowering plants, ferns, and ponds. But don't let the butterflies land on your palms—oil from your hands will clog their taste buds, which are located on their feet, and prevent them from finding food. The adjacent greenhouse contains hundreds of plants, including orchids and other colorful tropical varieties. Also in the greenhouse are fishponds and several whimsical metal sculptures of animals, including one of the friendliest-looking snakes you've ever seen. The sculptures are for sale, along with numerous other botanically related items in the gift shop. Walkways connect the botanical gardens with the Colorado River Trails system, which is discussed under "Hiking" on p. 340. Allow 2 to 4 hours.

655 Struthers Ave. © 970/245-9030. Fax 970/245-9001. www.wcbotanic.org. Admission $3 adults, $2 students and seniors, $1.50 children 5–12, free for kids 4 and under. Feb–Oct Tues–Sun 10am–5pm; Nov–Jan Tues–Sun 10am–4:30pm. Located at the south end of Seventh St.

A Wonderful Auto Museum

One of the best antique and classic car museums in the American West opened in May of 2006 in a highly unlikely spot—the tiny community of Gateway, in the middle of nowhere, about an hour's drive southwest of Grand Junction. Part of the new and still-under-construction Gateway Canyons resort, the **Gateway Colorado Auto Museum** has some four dozen beautifully restored automobiles—many of them luxury models of the day—that trace the history of American automotive design. The cars on display are part of the collection of John Hendricks, the founder and chairman of cable TV's Discovery Channel, who considers the cars as much pieces of art as transportation.

The star of the collection is a one-of-a-kind 1954 Oldsmobile F-88 dream car, a fantastic piece of rolling sculpture that cost Hendricks $3.24 million when he bought it at auction specifically for the museum. Also on display are a 1906 Cadillac Model H Coupe, a 1913 Pierce Arrow, a 1939 Packard Darrin (a favorite of Hollywood stars), and a 1941 Lincoln V-12 Zephyr. There are also classics from the 1950s and 1960s, including muscle cars such as the 1967 Ford Mustang Shelby GT. There are also exhibits on the automobile's influence on American life, from the assembly line to roadside diners to Hollywood glitter. All the vehicles are complete, in perfect running condition, and authentic, and a six-minute video, narrated by Walter Cronkite, provides an excellent introduction to the museum.

Gateway Colorado Auto Museum is located in Gateway Canyons resort, in the community of Gateway, on Colo. 141 near the Colorado-Utah border. It's open daily from 10am to 7pm, with the last ticket sold at 5pm. Admission costs $9 for adults, $7 for seniors 65 and older, $5 for children 6 to 12, and free for kids 5 and younger. The resort includes a restaurant, deli, a store offering outdoor recreation gear and clothing, and lodging units. The address is 43200 Colo. 141, Gateway, CO 81522 (© **866/671-4733** or 970/931-2458; www.gatewaycanyons.com).

Western Colorado Math & Science Center 👧👧 (Kids   This incredible, hands-on facility is designed to "create enthusiasm and excitement for math and science" for kids of all ages—right on up to seniors. It's the brainchild of physicist John McConnell, who decided to turn from research to education and started a mentoring program in math and science for western Colorado K through 12 students. With sophisticated hands-on experiments and interactive presentations packed in the trunk of his car, McConnell traveled from school to school; eventually, the popular program outgrew the car's trunk and morphed into the Western Colorado Math & Science Center. Somewhere along the way it acquired the acronym SITHOK, or Science In The Hands Of Kids. And that's it in a nutshell: The basic elements of science and math are presented with explanations, and kids (and adults) are invited to "touch, turn, look, listen, feel, pull, adjust, try out, and question." The staff of volunteers are continually adding and changing exhibits. Be sure to schedule your visit around school hours, since schools from a 160-mile radius make field trips to the center. Allow 1 to 4 hours.

2660 Unaweep Ave. (©) **970/254-1626.** www.sithok.org. Admission $1. Wed–Sat 10am–4pm.

Western Slope Vietnam War Memorial Park   This outdoor memorial, located at the Colorado Welcome Center along I-70 in Fruita, is dedicated to the men and women who served in the U.S. armed forces during the Vietnam era, from 1959 through 1975. It's most prominent feature is a UH-1H "Huey" helicopter, which was used by all branches of the military and became a symbol of the Vietnam War. There is a memorial wall to honor Vietnam-era veterans, especially those from Colorado's western slope, plus displays of the Vietnam Service Ribbon, emblems of the five branches of the U.S. armed forces, a U.S. flag, and a Colorado flag. Allow a half hour.

I-70 exit 19, Fruita. www.field-of-dreams.org. Free admission. Open daily 24 hours.

SHOPPING

For Colorado's most artful shopping experience, head to Grand Junction's **Downtown Shopping Park,** where you'll find a variety of shops, art galleries, and restaurants set amid an outdoor sculpture garden that runs some 7 blocks along Main Street. (See "Art on the Corner," above.)

Our favorite gallery in the Downtown Shopping Park is **Working Artists Studio,** 520 Main St. (© **970/256-9952**), with a wonderful variety of hand-thrown pottery, delightful sculptures, weavings, wind chimes; large—and expensive—wondrous things and quite affordable smaller items. In addition, there is an area in the back where you can usually watch an artist at work. There's also a resident cat, though he doesn't always show himself. Another not-to-be-missed stop here is **Monument Art Glass,** 428 Main St. (© **970/245-6800**), a galley and studio specializing in hand-blown glass. You can often watch a glass blower at work, or browse the fascinating and colorful glass objects, ranging from Christmas ornaments to bowls to paperweights, lamps, and bottles.

The western slope's largest indoor shopping mall, **Mesa Mall,** is located at 2424 U.S. 6 and 50 (© **970/242-0009;** www.shopmesamall.com). It's anchored by Sears, Mervyn's, JCPenney, Target, and Herberger's, and contains more than 100 specialty shops, services, and eateries.

WHERE TO STAY

Major chains offering reasonably priced lodging in Grand Junction, are all conveniently lined up along Horizon Drive, include **Doubletree Hotel,** 743 Horizon Dr., Grand Junction, CO 81506 (© **800/222-8733** or 970/245-8198), with rates of $74 to $174; **Best Western Sandman Motel,** 708 Horizon Dr., Grand Junction, CO 81506 (© **800/937-8376** or 970/243-4150), with rates of $50 to $110; **Comfort Inn,** 750 Horizon Dr., Grand Junction, CO 81506 (© **800/228-5150** or 970/245-3335), with rates of $55 to $125; and **Quality Inn,** 733 Horizon Dr., Grand Junction, CO 81506 (© **800/329-7466** or 970/424-6423), with rates of $60 to $99. All rates listed above are for two people, with the highest rates during the summer. Room tax adds almost 11% to lodging bills.

The Gallery 🦋🦋   Are you the arty type? Then this small bed-and-breakfast inn might be just what you want. The Gallery is the home of local artist Damian Radice, who has made two comfortable bedrooms available for guests, along with two private bathrooms. Each room has a queen-size bed, plush robes, and a TV/VCR (videos are available). The attractive home also has a large living area with a fireplace for guests' use, and a ceramics studio where guests can often see local artists at work. Pottery lessons are offered at $40 per hour, with a minimum of 2 hours, for 1 to 4 people. The rate includes all materials plus domestic shipping charges for your finished work. The full breakfasts include a hot entree, in-season fruits, and coffee brewed from locally roasted beans; afternoon refreshments are also served. Also on the property is a separate house—called the Chicken Coop—with two bedrooms and one bathroom. It can be rented nightly and is ideal for a family or two couples traveling together.

547 30 Rd., Grand Junction, CO 81504. ⓒ **970/243-2501.** www.thegallerybb.com. 2 units in main house and a small separate house. Main house $75 double, $140 for both rooms; separate house $95 for one bedroom, $125 for both rooms. Rates include full breakfast for the main house and a continental breakfast for the separate house. MC, V. *In room:* A/C, TV/VCR, no phone.

Grand Vista Hotel ⟨ catch ⟩   The aptly named Grand Vista does indeed have grand views, especially from the upper floors of its six stories. On the south side of the building you'll be looking out over Colorado National Monument with its majestic canyons, while guests on the building's north side see the Book Cliffs and Grand Mesa. Units here are very quiet, with good lighting, comfortable seating, and solid wood furnishings. The minisuites are especially spacious, and come with a king bed, recliner, modem dataport, and whirlpool tub. All king rooms have pillow-top mattresses.

Oliver's Restaurant & Bakery serves buffets at every meal, and Bailey's Lounge is a handsome Old English–style pub with great deals on drinks and appetizers on weekday evenings. Golf and rafting packages are available. Four floors are designated completely nonsmoking.

2790 Crossroads Blvd., Grand Junction, CO 81506. ⓒ **800/800-7796** or 970/241-8411. Fax 970/241-1077. www. grandvistahotel.com. 158 units. Apr–Oct $59–$89 double, lower at other times. AE, DC, DISC, MC, V. Pets accepted for a $10/night fee. **Amenities:** Restaurant (American); bar; large 24-hr. heated indoor pool; use of a nearby full-service health club; 24-hr. hot tub; complimentary airport/train/bus shuttle; business center. *In room:* A/C, TV w/on-demand movies and video games, coffeemaker, hair dryer, iron, wireless Internet.

Mesa Inn   A comfortable and reasonably priced alternative to the numerous chain motels here, Mesa Inn offers everything you would expect in a modern American motel. Rooms have one or two queen-size beds, and the business units are especially nice, with well-lighted desks. Microwaves and refrigerators are available. Rates here include breakfast at Good Pastures (see "Where to Dine," below), attached to the nearby Quality Inn, which is owned by the same company.

704 Horizon Dr., Grand Junction, CO 81506. ⓒ **888/955-3080** or 970/245-3080. www.mesainngrandjunction.com. 123 units. $50–$80 double. Rates include full breakfast. AE, DC, DISC, MC, V. Pets accepted. **Amenities:** Heated indoor pool; exercise room; airport transportation; coin-op washers and dryers. *In room:* A/C, TV, coffeemaker, wireless Internet.

CAMPING

In addition to campgrounds at **Colorado National Monument** (see earlier in this chapter), **James M. Robb–Colorado River State Park** (www.parks.state.co.us) has two campgrounds. The **Island Acres** unit (ⓒ **970/464-0548**), 10 miles east of Grand Junction off I-70 exit 47, has 80 campsites, and the **Fruita** unit ⟨ catch ⟩ (ⓒ **970/858-9188**), off I-70 exit 19 and about 10 miles west of Grand Junction, has 57 campsites. Rates at both are $12 for tents, $16 for RV sites with electricity, and $20 for full RV hookups. These fees are in addition to the $5 per vehicle day-use fee. Reservations for both campgrounds are available from March through October for an $8 reservation fee; call ✆ **800/678-2267** or go to the park's website (see above). The Fruita campground is our top camping choice in the Grand Junction area—it's well laid out and very conveniently located just a few miles from the west entrance of Colorado National Monument. Both campgrounds have showers and laundry facilities, a playground, naturalist programs, picnicking, fishing, and hiking. The Fruita unit also boasts a swimming lagoon and boating.

There are also several commercial campgrounds in the Grand Junction area, complete with full RV hookups, hot showers, and all the usual niceties. We like **Junction West R.V. Park,** 793 22 Rd., Grand Junction (✆ **970/245-8531**), which not only has about the cleanest bathhouses we've seen anywhere, but is also quiet and conveniently located. There are 66 large, somewhat-shaded sites, a store, coin-operated laundry, a game room, propane, a dump station, and free wireless Internet. Our only complaint is that the park is open to RVs only—no tents or even tent trailers—which we find a bit elitist. Rates are $25 for two people. Registrations are not accepted after 9pm. To get there, take U.S. 6 and 50 to 22 Road (or I-70 exit 26), and go north half a mile.

WHERE TO DINE
MODERATE
The Winery Restaurant 🐟🐟 STEAK/SEAFOOD   Fine dining in an atmosphere of Western elegance is what you'll experience at the Winery, which we rate as one of the best restaurants in Grand Junction. The dining room, of redbrick and weathered barn wood, is decorated with lots of plants, stained glass, and wine barrels and bottles. It's hard to go wrong here. We especially enjoy the prime rib (get there early—it often sells out) and the grilled salmon with herb butter. The salmon and catch of the day are always fresh. Also recommended is the filet Oscar—filet mignon and asparagus, covered in a lobster/crab Newburg sauce. You can also get a variety of steaks, steak and seafood combos, rack of lamb, or pork chops. For dessert we suggest the homemade apple crisp with streusel topping, or the Palisade, the restaurant's signature dessert that is much too complicated for us to try to describe here.

642 Main St. ✆ **970/242-4100**. Reservations recommended. Main courses $14–$42. AE, DC, DISC, MC, V. Sun–Thurs 5–9pm, Fri–Sat 5–10pm; closed major holidays.

INEXPENSIVE
Crystal Cafe and Bake Shop *Finds* AMERICAN   You may have to wait for a table at this local favorite, especially for breakfast and lunch, but the food here is worth waiting for. The simple, modern decor includes hardwood tables and bentwood cafe-style chairs, with woven place mats and napkins. Selections are mostly innovative variations on standard American dishes, highlighted by the cafe's own fresh-baked breads, rolls, pastries, and desserts. For breakfast there's a variety of pancakes, as well as egg dishes that include a Greek omelet—a two-egg omelet with fresh tomatoes, black olives, red onions, oregano, and feta cheese. Lunch and dinner items include plenty of salads, hot and cold sandwiches, and a quiche of the day. Sandwiches often include uniquely seasoned mayonnaise. We particularly enjoy the smoked turkey with red onion and basil mayonnaise.

314 Main St. ✆ **970/242-8843**. Breakfast $3–$7.50; lunch and dinner main courses $6–$11. AE, DISC, MC, V. Mon 7am–2pm; Tues–Fri 7am–2pm and 5–9pm; Sat–Sun 8am–noon and 5–9pm.

Good Pastures AMERICAN   Much better than the average motel restaurant, this locals' favorite at the Grand Junction Quality Inn offers fast, friendly service and very good food at reasonable prices. All the traditional American selections are offered at breakfast, and lunch includes burgers, sandwiches, homemade soups, and our recommendations—quiche and real southern fried chicken. The dinner menu includes most of the lunch items plus some heartier fare such as charbroiled rib-eye or tuna, rainbow trout, and meatloaf. During lunch and dinner, diners are presented with bread baked fresh in a flower pot, and those who can remove the bread from the pot intact get a free dessert. The dining room is attractive but basic, open and spacious with lots of windows, and seating at tables and booths.

733 Horizon Dr. (at the Quality Inn) © 970/243-3058. Lunch main courses $4.50–$9.50, dinner main courses $4.50–$15. AE, DISC, MC, V. Daily 6am–9pm.

Main Street Café AMERICAN   The '50s are back at the Main Street Café, with an old-fashioned soda fountain (there's also seating at tables and booths), photos of Marilyn and Elvis, and 45-rpm records. In addition to the shot of nostalgia, you'll find good diner food at reasonable prices. Breakfasts include bacon and eggs, pancakes, and, for the more adventurous, several spicy combinations. For lunch there are several vegetarian items, numerous sandwiches and salads, excellent hand-packed cooked-to-order Black Angus burgers, and blue-plate specials including Italian-style meat loaf, brisket, and chicken-fried steak, all with real mashed potatoes and fresh vegetables. Leave room for the praiseworthy banana split or hot-fudge sundae.

504 Main St. © 970/242-7225. Breakfast $2.75–$6.95; lunch main courses $2.50–$11. AE, DISC, MC, V. Mon–Sat 7am–4pm; Sun 7am–3pm.

Pablo's Pizza ⓡ (Kids) PIZZA   Inspired by Pablo Picasso, who forever changed the art world with his revolutionary creations, Pablo's Pizza strives for the same sort of impact on our taste buds. And it succeeds. Being purists, we had a simple pepperoni pizza, which was delicious. But for the adventuresome spirit, there are specialty pizzas such as Dracula's Nemesis—garlic white sauce, roasted garlic, roasted red onion, chicken, green onions, and cheese; or Big Daddy's Rajun Cajun—spicy hot tomato sauce, andouille sausage, shrimp, red and green bell peppers, and cheese. Or you can build your own, beginning with one of their eight sauces, and adding cheese, meats, vegetables, and even fruits. You can watch them make your pizza from the tossing of the crust to when they take it from the oven on a wooden paddle. The redbrick-and-white walls are decorated with Picasso-style original artwork, and the ceiling is of pressed tin. All in all, the place has a 1960s Greenwich Village–coffeehouse atmosphere. Pablo's also offers panini sandwiches, soups, salads, and desserts; plus has take-out and delivery service.

319 Main St. © 970/255-8879. www.pablospizza.com. Pizza $7.75–$24; by the slice $1.90–$2.80. DISC, MC, V. Sun–Thurs 11am–8:30pm; Fri–Sat 11am–9pm.

2 Glenwood Springs

84 miles E. of Grand Junction, 41 miles NW of Aspen, 169 miles W. of Denver

Scenic beauty and hot mineral water are the lures here. Members of the Ute tribe visited the Yampah mineral springs on the banks of the Colorado River for centuries. Calling it "big medicine," they came from miles around to heal their wounds or use nearby vapor caves as a natural sauna. But it wasn't until the 1880s that the springs were commercially developed. The three Devereux brothers, who had made a small fortune in silver at Aspen, built what was at the time the largest hot-springs pool in the world, then added a red-sandstone bathhouse and built the Hotel Colorado. Soon everyone from European royalty to movie stars to President Theodore Roosevelt made their way to Glenwood Springs.

The springs supported the town until the Great Depression and World War II caused a decline in business. After the war, with the growth of the ski industry at nearby Aspen, Glenwood Springs began to reemerge as a resort town, but on a smaller scale. Today, this city of 8,200, at an elevation of 5,746 feet, is a popular recreational center. The hot-springs complex underwent a total renovation in the 1970s, and additional improvements were made in 1993, as it celebrated its centennial.

Also completed that year was a 12-year, $490-million project to build a four-lane interstate through the 18-mile Glenwood Canyon. One of the most expensive roadways ever built—as well as one of the most beautiful interstate highway drives in America—the road offers a number of trail heads and raft-launching areas as well as viewpoints from which travelers can safely gaze at the Colorado River and its spectacular canyon.

ESSENTIALS

GETTING THERE   **By Car**   I-70 follows the Colorado River through Glenwood Springs. Colo. 82 (the Aspen Hwy.) links the city with Aspen, 42 miles southeast.

By Bus   **Roaring Fork Transportation Agency** (© 970/925-8484; www.rfta.com) offers service between Glenwood Springs and Aspen, with numerous stops along the route, daily, at a cost of $6 each way, less for intermediate stops.

By Shuttle Van   Transportation from Denver to Glenwood Springs is provided by **Colorado Mountain Express** (© 800/525-6363 or 970/926-9800; www.cmex.com), at about $75 per person one way.

By Train   There's **Amtrak** service (© 800/USA-RAIL; www.amtrak.com) to Glenwood Springs daily aboard the California Zephyr, direct from Denver and Salt Lake City. The depot is at Seventh Street and Cooper Avenue.

VISITOR INFORMATION   The **Glenwood Springs Chamber Resort Association,** 1102 Grand Ave., Glenwood Springs, CO 81601 (© 970/945-6589; www.glenwoodchamber.com), maintains a visitor center on the south side of downtown, on the southeast corner of 11th and Grand. Brochures are available 24 hours a day.

GETTING AROUND   The confluence of the Roaring Fork and Colorado rivers forms a T in the heart of Glenwood Springs, and streets follow the valleys carved by the two streams. Downtown Glenwood is south of the Colorado and east of the Roaring Fork.

The city-run bus service, **Ride Glenwood Springs** (© 970/384-6400; www.ci.glenwood-springs.co.us/transpo/1a-1.htm) operates daily, providing free rides to and from hotels, motels, restaurants, shopping areas, and the Hot Springs Pool. Schedules are available at the Chamber Resort Association office (see above).

FAST FACTS   **Valley View Hospital,** providing 24-hour emergency care, is at 1906 Blake Ave. (© 970/945-6535; www.vvh.org), a block east of Colo. 82 at 19th Street. The **post office** is at 113 Ninth Street; contact the U.S. Postal Service (© 800/275-8777; www.usps.com) for hours and additional information.

SPECIAL EVENTS   Music on the Mountain, late May; Summer of Jazz, June and July; Strawberry Days Festival, mid-June; Vintage Baseball Game, late June; Fall Arts Festival, late September; Historic Ghost Walk, late October; and the Day of Infamy Snowshoe Race, early December.

Underground Fantasy and Above-Ground Thrills

Glenwood Caverns Adventure Park 🌟🌟 has something for everyone, from magnificent historic caves to a thrilling tram ride, plus horseback and mechanical bull rides, an alpine coaster (sort of like a rollercoaster ride through the mountains), a giant swing, climbing wall, and chuck wagon dinner shows. The centerpiece of this park is the historic **Fairy Caves,** which were a major tourist attraction in the late 1890s and early 1900s. The caves were a sight to see—numerous stalactites and stalagmites, needles, gypsum flowers, bacon, soda straws, and other delicate and colorful formations, illuminated by electric lights—all for the 1897 price of 50¢. Visitors would either walk to the caves' entrance or ride a burro.

Closed since the outbreak of World War I in 1917, the Fairy Caves were reopened to the public in 1999, along with a section of the caves that remained undiscovered until more recent times. The cave temperature remains a constant 52°F (11°C) year-round, so you'll probably want a light jacket even on the hottest summer day. Since you'll also be traversing some 127 stairs, be sure to wear comfortable walking shoes. New trails, hand rails, and lighting have been installed for the 1-hour guided **Cave Tour,** which covers a half-mile and costs $18 for adults, $16 for seniors 65 and older, and $13 for children 3 to 12.

Most of the caves have been left in as natural a state as possible for the guided 3- to 4-hour **Wild Tour,** which is for small groups of physically fit individuals who don't mind crawling on their stomachs through dirty narrow passages wearing knee pads and helmet lights. Participants must be at least 13 years old, and a parent or guardian must accompany each youth from 13 to 17. Reservations are required. Cost is $50 per person.

Eight six-person gondolas rise 1,400 feet from the valley floor up the side of Iron Mountain. The **tram ride** provides panoramic views all the way to the top, where there's a visitor center, gift shop, moderately difficult nature trail, good food, plus Discovery Rock (extra fee)—a place for kids to pan for jewels and unearth fossils. Tram rides cost $10 for adults, $9 for seniors 65 and up, and $7 for kids 3 to 12, and a tram ride is included in the cave tours.

Now a variety of other family activities have been added, including horseback riding (summer only), mechanical bull riding, various other rides, and rock climbing. There's a restaurant and gift shop, and chuck wagon dinner shows during the summer. For details, including the current schedule and all activity fees, contact Glenwood Caverns Adventure Park, 51000 Two Rivers Plaza Rd., Glenwood Springs, CO 81601 (ⓒ **800/530-1635** or 970/945-4228; www.glenwoodcaverns.com).

SPORTS & OUTDOOR ACTIVITIES

There are plenty of outdoor recreation opportunities in and around Glenwood Springs. Stop at the **chamber** office (see "Visitor Information," above), the **White River National Forest,** Ninth Street and Grand Avenue (ⓒ **970/945-2521;** www.fs. fed.us/r2/whiteriver), or the **Bureau of Land Management (BLM),** 50629 U.S. 6

and 24 (© **970/947-2800;** www.co.blm.gov), for maps, recreational suggestions, and other information.

A busy local shop where you can get information on the best spots for hiking, mountain climbing, rock climbing, kayaking, camping, and cross-country skiing is **Summit Canyon Mountaineering,** 732 Grand Ave. (© **800/360-6994** or 970/945-6994; www.summitcanyon.com). In addition to selling a wide variety of outdoor-sports equipment, it also sells travel and outdoor clothing, with an especially good selection of women's travel apparel. The shop also rents cross-country ski gear, tents, sleeping bags, and backpacks.

BICYCLING A paved bike trail runs from the Yampah Vapor Caves into Glenwood Canyon, and trails and four-wheel-drive roads in the adjacent White River National Forest are ideal for mountain bikers (see "Hiking," below). You'll find bike rentals ($5–$12 per hr. or $23–$36 per day) in town at **Canyon Bikes,** at the Hotel Colorado, 526 Pine St. (© **800/439-3043** or 970/945-8904; www.canyonbikes.com), which also offers a shuttle service ($13 per person), and **Sunlight Mountain Ski & Bike Shop,** 309 Ninth St. (© **970/945-9425;** www.sunlightmtn.com), which also offers repairs. Also offering bike rentals is **Rock Gardens Rafting,** 1308 C.R. 129 (© **800/958-6737** or 970/945-6737; www.rockgardens.com).

FISHING Brown and rainbow trout are caught in the Roaring Fork and Colorado rivers, and fishing for rainbow and brook trout is often good in the Crystal River above the community of Redstone. Get licenses, equipment, and advice from **Roaring Fork Anglers,** 2114 B Grand Ave. (© **970/945-0180;** www.rfanglers.com), who have offered guided fly-fishing trips since 1975. Rates for one or two people on a full-day float trip are $435, including lunch; a full-day wading trip, including lunch, is $295 for one and $360 for two. Half-day trips are available, and Roaring Fork also has 4 miles of private waters.

GOLF **Glenwood Springs Golf Club,** 193 Sunny Acres Rd. (© **970/945-7086**), is a 9-hole course, with fees of $22 for 9 holes and $37 for 18 holes. Some 27 miles west of Glenwood Springs, near Rifle, is the championship 18-hole **Rifle Creek Golf Club,** at 3004 Colo. 325, off I-70 exit 90 (© **888/247-0370** or 970/625-1093), which charges $18 for 9 holes and $35 for 18 holes.

Fans of miniature golf will discover two beautifully landscaped 18-hole water-obstacle courses at **Johnson Park Miniature Golf,** 51579 U.S. 6 and 24, in West Glenwood Springs (© **970/945-9608**). Open April through October, rates for 18 holes are $5 for adults and $4 for children under 12 and seniors over 60. The **Hot Springs Pool** (see "Taking the Waters," below) also has a miniature golf course, with rates of $5.25 for adults and $4.25 for kids under 12.

HIKING There are plenty of hiking opportunities in the area. Stop at the national forest office (see above) for free **Recreational Opportunity Guide (ROG)** sheets for many local trails. The office sells detailed forest maps and has other information, too. The BLM (see above) also has maps and information.

One convenient walk is the **Doc Holliday Trail** ⚲, which climbs about .5 mile from 13th Street and Bennett Street to an old cemetery that contains the grave of notorious gunslinger Doc Holliday (see "Exploring Glenwood Springs's Frontier Past," below).

Hikers will also find numerous trail heads along the **Glenwood Canyon Recreation Trail** ⚲ in Glenwood Canyon, with some of the best scenery in the area. Among them, **Hanging Lake Trail,** 9 miles east of Glenwood Springs off I-70, is especially popular. The trail head is accessible from eastbound I-70; westbound travelers must make a U-turn and backtrack a few miles to reach the parking area. The trail climbs 1,000 feet in 1 mile—allow several hours for the round-trip—and just beyond Hanging Lake is Spouting Rock, with an underground spring shooting out of a hole in the limestone cliff. Dogs, swimming, and fishing are forbidden. The **Grizzly Creek Trail** is in the Grizzly Creek Rest Area, along I-70 in Glenwood Canyon, where there is also a launching area for rafts and kayaks. The trail climbs along the creek, past wildflowers and dogwood trees.

The **Glenwood Springs Chamber Resort Association** offers a free map showing a variety of trails in the area with trail heads marked.

JEEP TOURS Explore the high country around Glenwood Springs in an open-air jeep. The knowledgeable and friendly guides at **Rock Gardens** (see above) will show you some breathtaking views—don't forget your camera—and share with you some of the natural history and wildlife of the area. Half-day trips cost $44 for adults, $39 for youths.

RIVER RAFTING Bouncing down the rapids through magnificent **Glenwood Canyon** 🐾🐾 is, to our way of thinking, one of the best ways to see this spectacular country. Companies offering raft trips include **Blue Sky Adventures,** with offices in the Hotel Colorado (*©* **877/945-6605** or 970/945-6605; www.blueskyadventure. com), which offers rafting on the Colorado and Roaring Fork rivers. The popular half-day Adventure Trip costs $43 for adults, $31 for youths 15 and under; the half-day Mild Trip costs $32 and $27 respectively. A popular full-day trip through the white water of Shoshone Rapids costs $69 and $53, respectively, including a hot barbecue lunch. Another good bet for a raft trip is **Rock Gardens Rafting,** 1308 C.R. 129, at I-70 exit 119 (*©* **800/958-6737** or 970/945-6737; www.rockgardens.com), which has similar rates.

SKIING & SNOWBOARDING **Sunlight Mountain Resort,** 10901 C.R. 117, Glenwood Springs, CO 81601 (*©* **800/445-7931** or 970/945-7491; www.sunlight mtn.com), is located 10 miles south of Glenwood Springs in the White River National Forest. Geared toward families, Sunlight has 470 skiable acres and a 2,010-foot vertical drop from its 9,895-foot summit; it's served by one triple and two double chairlifts and a ski-school surface lift. There are 67 runs, rated 20% beginner, 55% intermediate, 20% advanced, and 5% expert. There's also a special area for snowboarders. The ski area is usually open from early December to early April, daily from 9am to 4pm. A full-day lift ticket runs $45 for adults, $35 for children 6 to 12 and seniors 60 to 69, and $5 for kids under 6 and seniors 70 and over. For equipment rentals and repairs, see the **Sunlight Mountain Ski & Bike Shop,** 309 Ninth St., in downtown Glenwood Springs (*©* **970/945-9425**).

Sunlight's Cross-Country and Nordic Center has 10 miles of groomed Nordic trails, available free, with rentals and lessons available. Information and equipment are also available at **Summit Canyon Mountaineering,** 732 Grand Ave. (*©* **800/360-6994** or 970/945-6994; www.summitcanyon.com).

SNOWMOBILING The **Sunlight to Powderhorn Trail,** running 120 miles from Glenwood's local ski area to Grand Junction's, on the Grand Mesa, is the longest multiuse winter recreational trail in Colorado, traversing White River and Grand Mesa national forests. It is fully marked and continuously groomed. Other trails can be accessed from the end of C.R. 11, 2 miles beyond Sunlight Mountain Resort and 12 miles south of Glenwood Springs. For information and rentals, contact the resort.

TAKING THE WATERS

There may be no better or more luxurious way to rejuvenate the dusty, tired traveler than by soaking in a natural hot spring. In Glenwood Springs, there are two places to experience this ancient therapy.

Hot Springs Pool Named Yampah Springs—meaning "Big Medicine"—by the Utes, this pool was created in 1888 when enterprising developers diverted the course of the Colorado River and built a stone bathhouse. The springs flow at a rate of 3½-million gallons per day, and, with a temperature of 122°F (50°C), they're one of the world's hottest springs. The content is predominantly sodium chloride, but there are significant quantities of calcium sulfate, potassium sulfate, calcium bicarbonate, and magnesium bicarbonate, plus traces of other therapeutic minerals.

The two open-air pools together are nearly 2 city blocks in length. The larger pool, 405 feet by 100 feet, holds more than a million gallons of water, and is maintained at 90°F (32°C). The smaller pool, 100 feet long, is kept at 104°F (40°C). There's also a children's pool with water slides, plus a deli, sport shop, and miniature golf course. The red-sandstone administration building overlooking the pools was the Hot Springs Lodge until 1986, when the new Hot Springs Lodge and Pool (see "Where to Stay," below) and bathhouse complex were built, and an athletic club opened (day passes are $21).

Suit and towel rentals and coin-operated lockers are available, as are massages, starting at $76 for a full hour. Allow from 1 to 4 hours.

401 N. River Rd. Ⓒ **800/537-7946** or 970/945-6571. www.hotspringspool.com. Admission summer $15 adults, $9.25 children 3–12; rest of year $13 adults, $8.25 children 3–12; free for children 2 and under year-round. Reduced evening rates. Water slide summer $4.75 for 4 rides or $6.25 for 8 rides; rest of year $4 and $5.50 respectively. Summer daily 7:30am–10pm; rest of year daily 9am–10pm.

Yampah Spa and Vapor Caves The hot Yampah Spring water flows through the floor of nearby caves, creating natural underground steam baths. Once used by Utes for their curative powers, today the cave has an adjacent spa where such treatments as massages, facials, herbal wraps, body muds, and salt glow rubs are offered. There's also a full-service beauty salon on the premises. Allow at least 1 hour.

709 E. Sixth St. Ⓒ **970/945-0667**. www.yampahspa.com. Admission to caves $12²; spa treatments start at $38; a full body massage is $75. Daily 9am–9pm.

EXPLORING GLENWOOD SPRINGS'S FRONTIER PAST

Although most Colorado visitors tend to think of Telluride or Cripple Creek when the subject of the Wild West comes up, Glenwood Springs had its share of desperados and frontier justice. The Ute tribe first inhabited the area, using it as a base for hunting and fishing, and also making use of its mineral hot springs. When whites finally arrived in the mid- to late 1800s, the growing community—then called Defiance—was little more than a muddy street lined with saloons, brothels, and boardinghouses, where miners from nearby Aspen and Leadville could be relieved of their newfound wealth. The hot springs began to attract mine owners and other prominent businessmen to Defiance, and in 1885 the town's name was changed to the more refined Glenwood Springs. However, it wasn't until 1886 that civilization finally arrived, along with the railroad. The following year, notorious gunfighter Doc Holliday arrived, and although he is said to have practiced his card-playing skills (and even a bit of dentistry), there is no record that he was involved in any gunplay in the town. By 1888, the lavish Hot Springs Pool and Hotel Colorado opened, and Glenwood Springs—now dubbed the "Spa in the Rockies"—began to attract the rich and famous.

Much of the grandeur of Glenwood Springs in the late 19th and early 20th centuries remains, and can be seen on a walk through the downtown area. The self-guided **Historic Walking Tour** guide and map is available at the Chamber Resort Association's visitor center (see earlier in this chapter) and the Frontier Historical Museum (see below). The guide describes more than 40 historic buildings and sites, including the 1884 Mirror Saloon, the oldest existing building in downtown Glenwood Springs; the site of the 1884 Hotel Glenwood (only a small portion remains), where Doc Holliday died; the 1893 Hotel Colorado, which was used by President Theodore Roosevelt as his "Western White House" in the early 1900s; and the 1885 Kamm Building, where gangster Al Capone is said to have been a jewelry customer in the 1920s.

Doc Holliday's Grave   After the famous shootout at the OK Corral, Doc Holliday began a final search for relief from his advanced tuberculosis. But even the mineral-rich waters of Glenwood Springs could not dissipate the ravages of hard drinking and disease, and Doc died in 1887 at the Hotel Glenwood. Although the exact location of Doc's grave is not known, it is believed he was buried in or near the Linwood Cemetery, on Lookout Mountain overlooking the city. Also in the cemetery are the graves of other early citizens of Glenwood.

From the chamber office on Grand Avenue, walk or drive uphill on 11th to Bennett and turn right. Not far on the left is the sign marking the trail to the cemetery. The trail is a .5-mile uphill hike, and you'll have a grand view of the city along the way. In the cemetery, near the flagpole, is a tombstone with the inscription, "Doc Holliday 1852–1887 He Died in Bed," and in front of it is another monument that reads, "This Memorial Dedicated to Doc Holliday who is Buried Someplace in the Cemetery." Allow about a half-hour.

Linwood Cemetery.

Frontier Historical Museum   Highlights of this museum, which occupies a late Victorian home, include the original bedroom furniture of Colorado legends Horace and Baby Doe Tabor, brought here from Leadville. The collection also includes displays on famed dentist-turned-gunfighter Doc Holliday, plus other pioneer home furnishings, including a complete kitchen. There are also toys, historic photos and maps, American Indian artifacts, and a mining and minerals display. The museum contains an extensive archive of historic documents and photographs from the early days of Glenwood Springs. Allow an hour.

1001 Colorado Ave. (✆ **970/945-4448**. Fax 970/384-2477. www.glenwoodhistory.com. Admission $3 adults, $2 seniors 60 and older, free for children under 12. May–Sept Mon–Sat 11am–4pm; Oct–Apr Mon and Thurs–Sat 1–4pm.

WHERE TO STAY

Rates are usually highest in summer, although busy ski times, such as Christmas week, can also be high. You can get additional information from the **Glenwood Springs Central Chamber of Commerce Lodging Number** (✆ **888/445-3696;** www.glenwood chamber.com).

Among the reliable moderately priced chains and franchises are the **America's Best Value Inn,** 51871 U.S. 6 and 24, at I-25 exit 114 (✆ **888/315-2378** or 970/945-6279), with rates of $54 to $142; the **Best Western Antlers,** 171 W. Sixth Ave. (✆ **800/626-0609** or 970/945-8535), with rates from $75 to $229; the **Hampton**

Inn, 401 W. First St. (© **800/426-7866** or 970/947-9400), charging $79 to $200; the **Holiday Inn Express,** 501 W. First St. (© **800/465-4329** or 970/928-7800), charging from $79 to $99; and **Ramada Inn & Suites,** 124 W. Sixth St. (© **800/ 332-1472** or 970/945-2500), with rates from $59 to $129. All the above are in Glenwood Springs, zip 81601, and rates for all of hotels are for two people; taxes add close to 12% to lodging bills.

EXPENSIVE

Hot Springs Lodge & Pool ⚐ Heated by the springs that bubble through the hillside beneath it, this handsome modern hotel overlooks the Glenwood Hot Springs Pool complex. Three-quarters of the rooms have private balconies or patios. Rooms are spacious, with one king or two queen beds, cherry- or lightwood furnishings; some have hide-a-beds, refrigerators, and double vanities.

415 Sixth St. (P.O. Box 308), Glenwood Springs, CO 81602. © **800/537-7946** or 970/945-6571. Fax 970/947-2950. www.hotspringspool.com. 107 units. Mid-Mar to Sept and Christmas $162–$205 double; rest of year $120–$161 double. Rates include continental breakfast. AE, DC, DISC, MC, V. **Amenities:** Unlimited admission to the hot springs pool and discounts at the health club (see "Taking the Waters," above); whirlpool; basic business center; coin-op laundry. *In room:* A/C, TV, dataport, coffeemaker, hair dryer, safe.

MODERATE

Four Mile Creek Bed & Breakfast ⚐⚐ A lovely spot for a romantic getaway or a peaceful base from which to explore the area, this B&B has both antique charm and modern conveniences. The historic log home was the headquarters of the Four Mile Ranch, homesteaded in 1885 and listed on the National Registry of Historic Places, and the surrounding grounds boast aspen groves and gardens of herbs and flowers, a handsome red barn built in 1919, and a variety of animals, including llamas and goats.

In the main log house is a cozy living room with an imposing rock fireplace, a sunroom overlooking the creek, and a porch along the front. There are two rooms in the main house which share a bathroom: the Blackbird Room boasts wrought-iron blackbirds (what else?) perched on the queen bed, and its elegant furnishings are reminiscent of the mining boom era; the nearby Star Room sets a totally different mood, with whimsical folk art and celestial symbols. The B&B's two cabins, with kitchens and private bathrooms, can accommodate up to four persons each. The aptly named Garden Cabin offers the pleasant ambience of several nearby perennial gardens plus a gas fireplace. The charming Creekside Cabin—so named because Four Mile Creek gurgles its way along one side of the cabin—boasts log beams and barn-wood walls plus an unusual brightly colored bird chandelier. Smoking is not permitted.

6471 C.R. 117, Glenwood Springs, CO 81601. © **970/945-4004.** Fax 970/945-2820. www.fourmilecreek.com. 4 units, 2 with private bathroom. Room $85 double; cabin $130–$145 (up to 4 people). Rates include evening refreshments and full breakfast. AE, MC, V. *In room:* No phone.

Hotel Colorado ⚐ Want to step into the not-so-wild West of the late 19th century? This is the place. The stately Hotel Colorado, constructed of sandstone and Roman brick in 1893, was modeled after Italy's Villa de Medici. Among the most impressive hotels of the region in its day, the Hotel Colorado attracted all the VIPs of the era. Two American presidents—William Howard Taft and Theodore Roosevelt—spoke to crowds gathered beneath the orators' balcony in a lovely landscaped fountain piazza. There are claims (disputed by some) that this is the birthplace of the teddy bear: The story goes that when a disappointed Roosevelt returned to the hotel in May

1905 after an unsuccessful bear hunt, hotel maids made him a small bear from scraps of cloth and the president's daughter Alyce named it Teddy.

The attractive guest rooms are individually decorated, most with firm double beds and the usual hotel furnishings; suites are more spacious, with upgraded decor and period antiques. Fifth-floor penthouse suites also have wet bars and refrigerators, as well as outstanding views. Two bell-tower suites, reached by stairs only, have double Jacuzzis and private dining balconies. They also have private staircases into the ancient bell towers, where 19th-century graffiti can still be deciphered. There's a full bar and a large outdoor dining and cocktail area, with gardens and a fountain for summer use. There's also a specialty coffee and juice bar; a chiropractor; and seasonal rental shops for rafting, biking, or skiing.

526 Pine St., Glenwood Springs, CO 81601. © **800/544-3998** or 970/945-6511. Fax 970/945-7841. www.hotel colorado.com. 126 units. $149–$169 double; $189–$450 suite. Children under 18 stay free in parent's room. AE, DC, DISC, MC, V. Pets accepted with a $15 fee. **Amenities:** Restaurant; bar; exercise room and spa; massage. *In room:* TV, coffeemaker, hair dryer, iron, wireless Internet.

INEXPENSIVE

Glenwood Springs Hostel   Active travelers will find the bargain sports pack-ages this hostel offers a real plus. Featured activities include downhill and cross-coun-try skiing, rafting, kayaking, mountain biking, and caving. There's a large record library, free coffee or tea in the mornings, and two fully equipped kitchens for guests' use. Like most hostels, there are dormitory bunks, common toilets and showers, guest laundry, and other common areas. Linen is available ($2), and it's just a 5-minute walk from the train and bus. The individual rooms are great for couples and others who prefer more privacy, although they still share bathrooms.

1021 Grand Ave., Glenwood Springs, CO 81601. © **800/946-7835** or 970/945-8545. www.hostelcolorado.com. 42 beds including dorm and 5 private rooms. Dorms $14 per person per night (or $44 for 4 nights); private rooms $21 single; $29 double. No private bathrooms. Rates include tax. AE, MC, V. *In room:* No phone.

Red Mountain Inn *(Value)*   This bright, cheery, modern motel lives up to its adver-tising as "Glenwood's best value." Rooms are spacious, with better-than-average light-ing, firm mattresses, and comfortable seating. Most rooms have 10-foot ceilings. The dozen cabins are essentially larger motel units, with sleeping for two to eight, plus complete kitchens. Some cabins have fireplaces, while a few have private patios with picnic tables. There's a delightful shaded grassy picnic area away from the road; and several restaurants and a miniature golf course are within easy walking distance.

51637 U.S. 6 and 24, Glenwood Springs, CO 81601. © **800/748-2565** or 970/945-6353. Fax 970/928-9432. www.redmountaininn.com. 40 units. Summer $70–$100 motel units, $100–$216 cabins; winter $49–$71 motel units, $64–$165 cabins. Holiday rates higher. AE, DISC, MC, V. On I-70 north Frontage Rd. between exits 114 and 116. Pets accepted with a $10 fee. **Amenities:** Outdoor heated pool (seasonal); outdoor hot tub (year-round); coin-op laundry. *In room:* A/C, TV, wireless Internet.

WHERE TO STAY IN NEARBY REDSTONE

Crystal Dreams Bed & Breakfast and Spa   Located about 30 miles south of Glenwood Springs in the picturesque community of Redstone, this delightful B&B is the perfect spot for a romantic getaway or a base for exploring the mountains and streams in the surrounding White River National Forest—there's even fly-fishing right out the back door. The handsome house, built in country Victorian style in 1994, sits along the banks of the Crystal River, with splendid views of nearby red-rock cliffs and Elk Mountain.

The three guest rooms are decorated in Victorian style, with western touches such as the "twig" bed—the headboard and footboard are made of tree branches. The Mt. Casa Room, named for its fine mountain view, has a queen bed plus a separate twin bed, and a bathroom with a large shower. The Moon River Room has a king-size bed and a bathroom with a two-person claw-foot tub. In the Bighorn Room you'll find a pewter queen-size bed, rattan chairs, and a bathroom with a two-person claw-foot tub.

The facility includes a boutique spa—La Belle Femme—that offers skin and body care, including facials, eye contouring, skin exfoliating, and various types of massage. Smoking is not permitted.

0475 Redstone Blvd., Redstone, CO 81623. (℃ 970/963-8240. www.crystaldreamsgetaway.com. 3 units. May–Oct $130 double Fri–Sun and holidays, $120 double Mon–Thurs; Nov–Apr $110 double. Rates include full breakfast. Two-night minimum weekends June–Oct. No credit cards. Suitable for children over 12. *In room:* No phone.

WHERE TO DINE

To stock up for a camping trip or picnic, or to get food to take back to your room or RV, we recommend **City Market Food & Pharmacy,** 1410 S. Grand Ave. (℃ **970/ 945-8207;** www.citymarket.com), which is open daily from 6am to 11pm. The store not only has all the usual supermarket departments, including a deli and bakery with seating area, but it also has an excellent buy-by-the-pound salad bar.

The Bayou 🐸🐸 CAJUN/CREOLE   This delightful New Orleans–style eatery might not be the best choice for those who take themselves very seriously, but if you're looking for a good time along with excellent food, the Bayou is worth a trip. Located in a historic building in downtown Glenwood Springs, the decor is fun and funky, with harlequin masks on the walls. Come for down-home Cajun cuisine—such as seafood gumbo, shrimp Creole, chicken étouffée, or swamp and moo (redfish and rib-eye)—and stay for the staff-provided entertainment, including "dumb server tricks" and the Frog Leg Revue. The Bayou has the largest selection of hot sauces in the valley, rated from "spicy" to "hurt me." There are also a few vegetarian dishes.

919 Grand Ave. (℃ **970/945-1047.** Main courses $6.95–$16. AE, DC, DISC, MC, V. Sun–Thurs 4–10pm, Fri–Sat 4pm–midnight.

Daily Bread Cafe & Bakery 🐸 CAFE/BAKERY   Try not to be in a hurry when you go to the Daily Bread—the service isn't slow, but this is such a popular spot that you're likely to find yourself waiting behind a line of locals for your table or booth. Decor here is strictly American cafe: storefront windows with lace curtains, a high ceiling, oak floor, and local art on the walls. For breakfast you might try one of the many egg dishes, such as Terry's Delight—an English muffin topped with eggs, shaved ham, and melted cheese—or perhaps the healthful Fresh Fruit Special—a half cantaloupe stuffed with fresh fruit, covered with fat-free vanilla yogurt and granola. The lunch menu lists dozens of sandwiches, burgers, and salads, including a number of low-fat offerings. Favorites include the Grand Avenue Deli—roast beef, turkey breast, Swiss cheese, lettuce, tomato, sprouts, and Thousand Island dressing on your choice of the bakery's own bread.

729 Grand Ave. (℃ **970/945-6253.** $3.50–$9.95. MC, V. Mon–Sat 7am–2pm; Sun 7am–noon.

Glenwood Canyon Brewing Company BREWPUB   A varied and interesting menu along with some really good beer makes this a good spot for a hearty lunch or dinner. The decor is standard brewpub: brick walls, historic photos, wood tables, TVs with sporting events, and a view of the brewing equipment. The lunch menu, also available at dinner, includes a selection of half-pound burgers, sandwiches (such as a hot smoked-turkey Philly), salads, pasta, and bread bowls (filled with soup or stew). Dinner entrees are a bit more elaborate, and include a grilled salmon filet, shrimp tacos, and the steak and potato pie. There are usually eight handcrafted beers on tap—we suggest the Red Mountain ESB—and half-gallon growler jugs are available for takeout. The brewpub also has regulation-size billiard tables.

402 Seventh St. (in the Hotel Denver). © 970/945-1276. www.glenwoodcanyon.com. $5.95–$18. AE, MC, V. Sun–Thurs 11am–11pm; Fri–Sat 11am–midnight.

Italian Underground 🏵 (Value ITALIAN   A favorite of locals, the Italian Underground offers good Italian food at excellent prices. Get here early and expect to wait, especially on weekends. Located in a basement along busy Grand Avenue, the restaurant has stone walls, brick floors, red-and-white-checkered tablecloths, candlelight, and exceedingly generous portions of fine food. Try the lasagna, linguine with pesto, or spaghetti with tomato and basil sauce. All entrees come with salad, bread, and ice cream. There's an excellent selection of Italian wines by the glass and a full bar; espresso and cappuccino are also served.

715 Grand Ave. © 970/945-6422. Reservations not accepted. Main courses $8.95–$14; pizzas $8.95–$15. AE, DISC, MC, V. Daily 5–10pm.

Restaurant Sopris 🏵🏵 (Moments CONTINENTAL   This is the spot for those celebrating wedding anniversaries or other special events, or if you simply want to impress that someone special with your good taste. Swiss chef Kurt Wigger opened the Sopris in 1974, and it has been a favorite of locals ever since. Amid red-lit Victorian decor, accented by reproductions of classic oil paintings, Wigger serves generous portions of veal and seafood dishes, as well as steak, lamb, and vegetarian dishes. House specialties include the pepper steak flambé—New York strip with cracked pepper, shallots, and red-wine sauce; and Swiss veal—minced veal and mushrooms served in a cream sauce. There's an extensive wine list and a full bar.

7215 Colo. 82, 5 miles south of Glenwood Springs. © 970/945-7771. Reservations recommended. Main courses $10–$35. AE, DISC, MC, V. Daily 5–10pm.

3 Montrose: Gateway to Black Canyon of the Gunnison National Park

61 miles S. of Grand Junction, 108 miles N. of Durango

Although at first glance this quiet city of just over 12,000 is little more than a commercial center for area ranchers and farmers, Montrose is rapidly being discovered as an ideal base camp for hikers, mountain bikers, anglers, and others who want to explore western Colorado. Located at an elevation of 5,794 feet, Montrose is surrounded by the Uncompahgre, Gunnison, and Grand Mesa national forests, and it's within a short drive of Black Canyon of the Gunnison National Park and Curecanti National Recreation Area.

Ute Chief Ouray and his wife, Chipeta, ranched in the Uncompahgre Valley here until the government forced the tribe to migrate to Utah in 1881. Once the Utes were gone, settlers founded the town of Pomona, named for the Roman goddess of fruit. Later the town's name was changed to Montrose, for a character in a Sir Walter Scott novel. The railroad arrived in 1882, providing relatively reliable transportation and a means to ship out potatoes, beets, and other crops; and Montrose began in earnest its role as one of Colorado's major food producers, which continues today.

ESSENTIALS

GETTING THERE   By Car   Montrose is an hour's drive southeast of Grand Junction via U.S. 50, a 2½-hour drive north of Durango via U.S. 550, and a 5½-hour drive west of Colorado Springs via U.S. 50 through Salida and Gunnison.

By Plane   The **Montrose Regional Airport,** 2100 Airport Rd. (© **970/249-3203;** www.co.montrose.co.us/airport/airport.html), is off U.S. 50, 2 miles northwest of town. Regional airlines serving the town include **American** (© **800/433-7300**), **Continental** (© **800/525-0280**), **Delta** (© **800/221-1212**), **SkyWest** (© **800/241-6522**), and **United** (© **800/241-6522**).

GETTING AROUND   Montrose lies along the east bank of the Uncompahgre River. Townsend Avenue (U.S. 50 and U.S. 550) parallels the stream; Main Street (U.S. 50 and Colo. 90) crosses Townsend in the center of town. Numbered streets extend north and south from Main.

Montrose Taxi (© **970/275-8965**) provides local cab service. Car-rental agencies with outlets at the airport include **Dollar** (© 970/249-3770), **Hertz** (© 970/240-8464), **National** (© 970/252-8898), and **Thrifty** (© 970/249-8741).

VISITOR INFORMATION   Contact or stop at the **Montrose Visitors & Convention Bureau,** 1519 E. Main St. (P.O. Box 335), Montrose, CO 81402 (© **800/873-0244** or 970/240-1414; www.visitmontrose.net), or stop at the **visitor center** in the **Ute Indian Museum** (see "What to See & Do," below).

FAST FACTS   Montrose Memorial Hospital, with a 24-hour emergency room, is at 800 S. Third St. (© **970/249-2211;** www.montrosehospital.com). The **post office** is at 321 S. First St. Call the U.S. Postal Service (© **800/275-8777;** www.usps.com) for hours and other information. For **road conditions,** call © **970/249-6282.**

SPECIAL EVENTS   Chocolate Lovers Affaire, mid-February; Lighter Than Air Balloon Affaire, early July; Montrose County Fair, July; Parade of Lights, early December.

WHAT TO SEE & DO

Those wanting to step back into Montrose's past should ask at the visitor center, visitors & convention bureau, or city hall (433 S. First St.) for a free copy of the self-guided **Historic Montrose Downtown Walking Tour** brochure. It contains a map to help you locate numerous historic buildings and interpretative signs.

Montrose County Historical Museum   Pioneer life in western Colorado is highlighted at this museum, housed in a historic Denver & Rio Grande Railroad Western Depot. The museum features a furnished 1890s homesteader's cabin, log cowboy cabin, railroad memorabilia including a Union Pacific caboose, farm equipment, antique dolls and toys, old musical instruments, a country store, and American Indian artifacts. Historical photos and Montrose newspapers from 1896 to 1940 depict the town's history. Allow at least an hour.

W. Main St. and Rio Grande Ave. © **970/249-2085.** debbarr@rmi.net. Admission $4 adults, $3 seniors over 55, $1 students 12–21, 50¢ children 11 and younger. Mid-May through Sept Mon–Sat 9am–5pm.

Ute Indian Museum 🏇   Located on the site of the final residence of southern Ute Chief Ouray and his wife, Chipeta, the Ute Indian Museum offers one of Colorado's most complete exhibitions of Ute traditional and ceremonial artifacts, including clothing, baskets, and household items. Several dioramas depict mid-19th-century lifestyles, and historic photos are displayed. Also on the grounds are Chipeta's grave, bubbling Ouray Springs, a native plants garden, and an outdoor display on Spanish explorers who passed this way in 1776. The museum sponsors various festivals and programs throughout the year (call for details). It also has a store that specializes in Ute pottery and other handcrafted American Indian arts and crafts, and houses the Montrose Visitor Center. Allow about 1½ hours.

17253 Chipeta Dr. © **970/249-3098**. www.coloradohistory.org. Admission $3 adults, $2.50 seniors over 65, $1.50 children 6–16, free for children under 6. Mid-May to mid-Oct Mon–Sat 9am–4:30pm, Sun 11am–4:30pm; Mid-Oct to mid-May Mon–Sat 9am–4:30pm. Located 3 miles south of downtown at the intersection of U.S. 550 and Chipeta Dr.

SPORTS & OUTDOOR ACTIVITIES

In addition to boating and other outdoor recreational activities available in Black Canyon of the Gunnison National Park (discussed below) and nearby Curecanti National Recreation Area (see "Gunnison & Curecanti National Recreation Area," in chapter 13), there are plenty of opportunities for hiking, mountain biking, horseback riding, off-roading, fishing, camping, cross-country skiing, and snowmobiling on other federal lands in the area. Information is available at the **Public Lands Center,** 2505 S. Townsend Ave. (© **970/240-5300**). For camping and fishing gear, bike rentals and repairs, outdoor clothing, and other outdoor recreation items and sporting goods, stop at **Jeans Westerner,** 147 N. Townsend Ave. (© **970/249-3600;** www. jeanswesterner.com), with the entrance to its bike facilities around back at 120 N. Selig Ave.

BIKING There are more than 9 miles of paved off-street walking and biking trails in Montrose, plus numerous areas for mountain biking in nearby lands administered by the U.S. Forest Service and Bureau of Land Management. A free map of **city trails** is available at the visitor center, chamber of commerce, and city hall (433 S. First St.); stop at the Public Lands Center (see above) for information on where to ride on BLM and Forest Service lands. You can also obtain maps, information, bike repairs, and accessories at **Cascade Bicycles,** 21 N. Cascade Ave. (© **970/249-7375**), and **Jeans Westerner** (see intro to this section, above), which also rents basic mountain bikes at $29 per day.

The Tabeguache Trail—142 miles from Shavano Valley near Montrose, to No Thoroughfare Canyon near the Colorado National Monument west of Grand Junction—is a popular and challenging route for mountain bikers. For information, contact the **Colorado Plateau Mountain-Bike Trail Association,** P.O. Box 4602, Grand Junction, CO 81502 (© **970/244-8877;** www.copmoba.com). Bikers can also use the Uncompahgre Riverway; it's eventually scheduled to connect Montrose with Delta (21 miles north) and Ouray (37 miles south).

FISHING For starters, you can drop a line into the Uncompahgre River from Riverbottom Park, reached via Apollo Road off Rio Grande Avenue. Most anglers seek rainbow trout here and at Chipeta Lake, behind the Ute Indian Museum, south of Montrose. About 20 miles east via U.S. 50 is the Gunnison River, which produces trophy-class brown and rainbow trout.

GOLF The 18-hole **Black Canyon Golf Club,** 1350 Birch St. (© **970/249-4653**), is open year-round, weather permitting. Greens fees are $23 for 9 holes and $36 for 18 holes. The **Links at Cobble Creek,** 669 Cobble Dr., off Chipeta Dr. (© **970/240-9542**), is another 18-hole course with fees of $25 to $27 for 9 holes and $37 to $39 for 18 holes.

HIKING The best hiking in the area is in the Black Canyon of the Gunnison National Park (p. 365), but there are also paved paths in town (see "Biking," above) and plenty of trails on nearby national forest and BLM lands. These include the 4.5-mile Ute Trail along the Gunnison River, 20 miles northeast of Montrose; and the 17-mile Alpine Trail from Silver Jack Reservoir in Uncompahgre National Forest, 35 miles southeast of Montrose via Cimarron on U.S. 50. Contact the Public Lands Center (see above) for information.

WHERE TO STAY

In addition to the properties discussed below, Montrose (zip code 81401) has a **Best Western Red Arrow Motor Inn,** 1702 E. Main St. (© **800/468-9323** or 970/249-9641) with rates for two from $62 to $115, **Comfort Inn,** 2100 E. Main St. (© **800/424-6423** or 970/240-8000), with double rates from $59 to $99; **Holiday Inn Express Hotel & Suites,** 1391 S. Townsend Ave. (© **800/550-9252** or 970/240-1800), with rates for two from $89 to $159; and **Quality Inn & Suites,** 2751 Commercial Way (© **800/550424-6423** or 970/249-1011), with double rates from $54 to $119. Rates here are usually highest in July and August, and lowest November through April. Room tax is about 8.5%.

Canyon Trails Inn *Value* A well-kept mom-and-pop motel with reasonable rates and a much better than usual continental breakfast is what you'll find at Canyon Trails Inn. Rooms vary, from one double bed in a tiny room to a spacious king room with its own whirlpool tub, and several options in between, including family units that sleep five comfortably. The rooms are quiet—especially the ones along the back away from the road—and simply but attractively furnished in what we might call traditional American motel with a few Western touches.

1225 E. Main St., Montrose, CO 81401. © 800/858-5911 or 970/249-3426. Fax 970/240-4918. www.canyon trailsinn.com. 27 units. $50–$70 double. Rates include continental breakfast. AE, DC, DISC, MC, V. Pets accepted for $5 fee. **Amenities:** Outdoor year-round hot tub. *In room:* A/C, TV, fridge, coffeemaker, wireless Internet, microwave.

CAMPING

In addition to the campgrounds in Black Canyon of the Gunnison National Park discussed below, we recommend **The Hangin' Tree R.V. Park** at 17250 U.S. 550 S. (© **970/249-9966**), with rates from $18 to $26. Conveniently located within walking distance of Chipeta Lakes and open year-round, the Hangin' Tree has grassy tent sites, large pull-through RV sites, and very clean bathhouses.

DINING

A good bet for those seeking groceries, deli sandwiches, a bakery, or a pharmacy is one of the two **City Market** grocery stores in Montrose. There's one at 16400 S. Townsend Ave. (© **970/249-3236**), which is open daily from 5am to 11pm; and another at 128 S. Townsend Ave. (© **970/249-3405**), which is open daily from 6am to 11pm and also has a buy-by-the-pound salad bar.

La Cabaña at Sicily's *ζ* ITALIAN/MEXICAN This cozy restaurant, decorated with lots of wood and exuding a casual, friendly atmosphere, is a good place for hungry travelers to stop for authentic Italian and Mexican food at reasonable prices. There are booths and tables in both the dining room and the bar—the bar can be a bit noisy when there's live entertainment—and there is an attractive, tree-shaded outdoor patio. The lunch menu includes spaghetti, enchiladas, and a variety of sandwiches, including meatball and steak sandwiches. Dinner offerings include very tasty lasagna, fettuccine Alfredo, calzones, pizza, tamales, enchiladas, and the highly recommended fajitas—steak, chicken, or shrimp. Whatever you get, though, be sure to try the restaurant's house-made marinara sauce, which is among the best we've tasted in western Colorado. If you're not ordering Italian, you can get fresh-baked bread with marinara sauce as an appetizer.

1135 E. Main St. ℃ **970/240-9199.** Main lunch courses $5.95–$9.90; main dinner courses $5.95–$17. AE, DISC, MC, V. Daily 11am–10pm.

4 Black Canyon of the Gunnison National Park

The **Black Canyon of the Gunnison** ✾✾, which had been a national monument since 1933, became a national park on October 21, 1999. In a statement issued after the bill-signing ceremony, President Bill Clinton called the Black Canyon a "true natural treasure," and added, "Its nearly vertical walls, rising a half-mile high, harbor one of the most spectacular stretches of wild river in America."

The canyon was avoided by early American Indians and later Utes and Anglo explorers, who believed that no human could survive a trip to its depths. The entire canyon measures 48 miles long, and the 14 miles that are included in the national park (which at 30,385 acres is among America's smallest) range in depth from 1,730 to 2,700 feet. Its width at its narrowest point (cleverly called "The Narrows") is only 40 feet. This deep slash in the earth was created by 2 million years of erosion, a process that's still going on—albeit slowed by the damming of the Gunnison River above the park.

Most visitors view the canyon from the South Rim Road, site of the visitor center, or the lesser-used North Rim Road. Short paths branching off both roads lead to splendid viewpoints with signs explaining the canyon's unique geology.

The park also has hiking trails along both rims, backcountry-hiking routes down into the canyon, and excellent trout fishing for ambitious anglers willing to make the trek to the canyon floor. It also provides an abundance of thrills for the experienced rock climbers who challenge its sheer canyon walls. In winter, much of the park is closed to motor vehicles, but it's a delight for cross-country skiers and snowshoers.

The Black Canyon shares a portion of its south boundary with Curecanti National Recreation Area, which offers boating and fishing on three reservoirs, as well as hiking and camping.

JUST THE FACTS
ENTRY POINTS
The park is located northeast of Montrose. To reach the south rim, head east on U.S. 50 for 8 miles to the well-marked turnoff, where you will turn north (left) onto Colo. 347 for 6 miles. To reach the north rim from Montrose, drive north 21 miles on U.S. 50 to Delta, east 31 miles on Colo. 92 to Crawford, then south on an 11-mile access road.

FEES & REGULATIONS
Admission for up to 7 days costs $8 per vehicle. Required backcountry permits are free. Visitors are warned not to throw anything from the rim into the canyon, since even a single small stone thrown or kicked from the rim could be fatal to people

---

Impressions
No other canyon in North America combines the depth, narrowness, sheerness, and somber countenance of the Black Canyon.
            —Geologist Wallace Hansen, who mapped the canyon in the 1950s

below; and to supervise children very carefully because many sections of the rim have no guardrails or fences.

Unlike at many national parks, leashed pets are permitted on several trails (check with rangers), but they are specifically prohibited from wilderness areas.

VISITOR CENTERS & INFORMATION

The **South Rim Visitor Center** is open daily year-round, except winter federal holidays, with hours from 8am to 6pm in summer and from 8:30am to 4pm the rest of the year. For information on both the national park and the adjacent Curecanti National Recreation Area (discussed in chapter 13, "The Southern Rockies"), contact **Black Canyon of the Gunnison National Park/Curecanti National Recreation Area,** Park Headquarters, 102 Elk Creek, Gunnison, CO 81230 (© **970/641-2337**).

SEASONS

Temperatures and weather conditions often vary greatly between the canyon rim and the canyon floor, and it gets progressively hotter as you descend into the canyon. Average summer temperatures range from highs of 60° to 100°F (16°–38°C), with summer lows dropping to 30° to 50°F (–1° to –10°C). During winter, highs range from 20° to 40°F (–7°C to –4°C), with lows from –10° to 20°F (–23° to –7°C). Brief afternoon thunderstorms are fairly common in the summer. The South Rim Road usually remains open to the visitor center through the winter, but the North Rim Road is often closed by snow between December and March. The elevation at the South Rim Campground is 8,320 feet.

RANGER PROGRAMS

Ranger-conducted **nature walks, geology talks,** and **evening campfire programs** are presented daily from Memorial Day through late September on the South Rim (a schedule is posted at the visitor center). During the winter, guided **snowshoe walks** and **moonlight cross-country ski tours** are offered on the South Rim when snow conditions are right (stop at the visitor center or call ahead for information and reservations).

SEEING THE HIGHLIGHTS

It's fairly easy to see a great deal here in a short amount of time, especially if you stick to the South Rim. First stop at the visitor center to see the exhibits and get an understanding of how this phenomenal canyon was created. Then, drive the 7-mile (one-way) **South Rim Drive,** stopping at the overlooks. There are about a dozen overlooks along the drive, and in most cases you'll be walking from 140 feet to about 700 feet to reach the viewpoints from your vehicle. Among the not-to-be-missed overlooks are **Gunnison Point,** behind the visitor center, which offers stunning views of the seemingly endless walls of dark rock; and the **Pulpit Rock Overlook,** which provides a splendid view of the rock walls and about 1½ miles of the Gunnison River, some 1,770 feet down. Further along the drive is **Chasm View,** where you can see the incredible power of water, which here cuts through over 1,800 feet of solid rock. Near the end of the drive, be sure to stop at **Sunset View,** where there's a picnic area and a short (140 ft.) walk to a viewpoint, which offers distant views beyond the canyon as well as of the river, now 2,430 feet below your feet. And, if your timing is right, you might be treated to a classic Western sunset, in all its red and orange glory. Finally, take off on one of the **rim hiking trails,** such as the easy Cedar Point Nature Trail or the somewhat more challenging Warner Point Nature Trail (see "Hiking & Backpacking," below). If you'll be camping in the park or staying nearby, you might plan to attend the evening ranger program.

SPORTS & OUTDOOR ACTIVITIES

CLIMBING The sheer vertical walls and scenic beauty of the Black Canyon make it an ideal and popular destination for rock climbers, but, and we cannot emphasize this too strongly, this is no place for on-the-job training. These cliffs, known for crumbling rock, dizzying heights, and very few places to put protective gear, require a great deal of experience and the best equipment. Free permits are required, and prospective climbers should discuss their plans first with park rangers.

FISHING Dedicated anglers can make their way to the Gunnison River at the bottom of the canyon in a quest for brown and rainbow trout. The Gunnison within the park has been designated as Gold Medal Waters. Only artificial lures are permitted, and other special rules apply (check with park rangers). A Colorado fishing license is required.

HIKING & BACKPACKING Trails on the park's rims range from short, easy walks to moderate-to-strenuous hikes of several miles. Hiking below the rim is mostly difficult and not recommended for those with a fear of heights. Permits are not needed for hiking rim trails, but are required for all treks below the rim.

Trails along the **South Rim** include the easy **Cedar Point Nature Trail.** From the Cedar Point trail head, along South Rim Road, this .7-mile round-trip walk has signs along the way describing the plants you'll see, and provides breathtaking views of the Gunnison River, 2,000 feet down, at the end. The moderately rated **Rim Rock Nature Trail,** which is 1 mile round-trip, is accessed near the entrance to the campground's Loop C. Following the rim along a relatively flat path, this trail leads to an overlook, providing good views of the Gunnison River and the canyon's sheer rock walls. A pamphlet available at the trail head describes plant life and other points of interest.

The moderate **Warner Point Nature Trail** begins at High Point Overlook at the end of South Rim Road. It's 1.5 miles round-trip and offers a multitude of things to see, from flora such as mountain mahogany, piñon pine, and Utah juniper, to distant mountains and valleys, as well as the Black Canyon and its creator, the Gunnison River. A trail guide is available at the trail head. The trail head for the 2-mile round-trip **Oak Flat Loop Trail,** rated moderate to strenuous, is near the visitor center. Dropping slightly below the rim, this trail offers excellent views into the canyon, while also taking you through a grove of aspen, past Gambel oak, and finally through a forest of aspen, Gambel oak, and Douglas fir. Be aware that the trail is narrow in spots, and a bit close to steep drop-offs.

Trails along the **North Rim** include the moderate **Chasm View Nature Trail,** .3 miles round-trip, with a trail head at the end of the North Rim campground loop. Beginning in a piñon-juniper forest, this trail heads to the rim for good views of the canyon and the river; you'll also have a good chance of seeing swallows, swifts, and raptors here.

A longer North Rim trail is the 5-mile round-trip **Deadhorse Trail,** rated easy to moderate, which begins at the Kneeling Camel Overlook. Actually an old service road, this trail offers a good chance of seeing various birds, plus views of Deadhorse Gulch and the East Portal area at the southeast end of the park. The 7-mile **North Vista**

Trail, which begins at the North Rim Ranger Station, is moderate to strenuous. It offers some of the best views into the Black Canyon and also rewards hikers with a good chance of seeing red-tailed hawks, white-throated swifts, Clark's nutcrackers, and ravens.

Experienced **backcountry hikers** in excellent physical condition may want to hike down into the canyon. Although there are no maintained or marked trails, there are several routes that rangers can help you find. Free permits are required. There are also a limited number of campsites available for backpackers. The most popular inner canyon hike is the strenuous **Gunnison Route,** which branches off the South Rim's Oak Flat Trail and heads down to the river. Eighty feet of chain help keep you from falling on a stretch about a third of the way down. This hike has a vertical drop of 1,800 feet and takes 4 to 5 hours.

WATERSPORTS   Although the river may look tempting, our advice for watersports enthusiasts is **don't do it!** The Gunnison River through the park is **extremely dangerous,** for both swimmers and rafters (it's considered **unraftable**). There are sections of the river west of the park that are more suitable; information is available from the **Public Lands Center,** 2505 S. Townsend Ave., Montrose, CO 81401 (© **970/240-5300**). The only exception is for **experienced kayakers,** who find the river an exhilarating challenge. Free permits are required.

WILDLIFE VIEWING   The park is home to a variety of wildlife, and you're likely to see chipmunks, ground squirrels, badgers, marmots, and mule deer. Although not frequently seen, there are also black bear, cougars, and bobcats; and you'll probably hear the lonesome high-pitched call of coyotes at night. Peregrine falcons can sometimes be spotted along the cliffs, and you may also see red-tailed hawks, turkey vultures, golden eagles, and white-throated swifts.

WINTER SPORTS   When the South Rim Road is closed by winter snows, the park service plows only to the South Rim Visitor Center, leaving the road a perfect cross-country ski trail. There are also several areas in the park that are good for snowshoeing; get directions at the visitor center.

CAMPING

There are campgrounds on both rims, with pit toilets and no showers; but there are electric hookups available on Loop B of South Rim Campground. Cost per site is $12, $18 with electric hookups. The **South Rim Campground,** which is open year-round and is rarely full, has 88 sites, but the **North Rim Campground,** open from spring through fall and with only 13 sites, does occasionally fill up. Reservations can be made for some sites in the South Rim Campground from late May through early September through the park website or www.reserveusa.com, or by phone © **877/444-6777.**

12

Southwestern Colorado

A land apart from the rest of the state, southwestern Colorado is set off by the spectacular mountain wall of the San Juan Range. The Ancestral Puebloans (also called the Anasazi) who once lived here created cliff dwellings that more closely resemble structures found in New Mexico and Arizona than anything you might expect to see in Colorado. The ancient cliff dwellings of Mesa Verde National Park are a case in point, and there are similar but less well-known sites throughout the area, primarily around Cortez.

Durango is the area's major city. Its vintage main street (ca. 1880) and narrow-gauge railroad hearken back to the Old West days of the late 19th century, when it boomed as a transportation center for the region's silver and gold mines. Telluride, at the end of a box canyon surrounded by 14,000-foot peaks, has capitalized on its highly evident mining heritage in its evolution as a major ski and summer resort. And those who drive the Million Dollar Highway—down U.S. 550 from Ouray, over 11,008-foot Red Mountain Pass through Silverton, and on to Durango—can't miss the remains of turn-of-the-20th-century mines scattered over the mountainsides.

1 Durango

332 miles SW of Denver, 169 miles S. of Grand Junction, 50 miles N. of Farmington, New Mexico

Born as a railroad town more than a century ago, Durango remains a railroad town to this day, as thousands of visitors take a journey back in time aboard the Durango & Silverton Narrow Gauge Railroad. Durango was founded in 1880 when the Denver & Rio Grande Railroad line was extended to Silverton to haul precious metals from high-country mines. Within a year, 2,000 new residents had turned the town into a smelting and transportation center. Although more than $300 million worth of silver, gold, and other minerals rode along the route over the years, the unstable nature of the mining business gave the town many ups and downs. One of the "ups" occurred in 1915, when southern Colorado boy Jack Dempsey, then 20, won $50 in a 10-round boxing match. Dempsey went on to become the world heavyweight champion.

Durango remained a center for ranching and mining into the 1960s. In 1965, with the opening of the Purgatory ski resort (now Durango Mountain Resort), 25 miles north of Durango, a tourism boom began. When the railroad abandoned its tracks from Antonito, Colorado, to Durango in the late 1960s, leaving only the Durango-Silverton spur, the town panicked. But from that potential economic disaster blossomed a savior. The Durango & Silverton Narrow Gauge Railroad is now Durango's biggest attraction, hauling more than 200,000 passengers each summer. Durango also attracts mountain-biking enthusiasts from all over the country—in fact, opportunities abound for outdoor activities of all kinds, from river rafting to trout fishing.

Durango

ATTRACTIONS ●
Animas Museum **3**
Center of Southwest Studies **7**
Children's Museum of
 Durango **12**
Durango & Silverton Narrow
 Gauge Railroad Museum **17**
Durango Fish Hatchery &
 Wildlife Museum **6**

ACCOMMODATIONS ■
Best Western Mountain
 Shadows **2**
Comfort Inn **4**
Days Inn **1**
Econo Lodge **5**
The Leland House B&B Suites **14**
Quality Inn **18**
Rochester Hotel **13**
Strater Hotel **15**

DINING ◆
Cyprus Cafe **11**
Durango Diner **9**
Mahogany Grill **15**
Olde Tymer's Cafe **8**
The Palace Restaurant **16**
Steamworks Brewing Co. **10**

ESSENTIALS

GETTING THERE By Car Durango is located at the crossroads of east-west
U.S. 160 and north-south U.S. 550.

By Plane Durango/La Plata County Airport, 14 miles southeast of Durango off
Colo. 172 (℃ **970/247-8143;** www.durangoairport.com), has direct daily nonstop serv-
ice from Denver, Salt Lake City, and Phoenix, with connections to cities throughout
North America. The airport is served by **America West Express** (℃ 800/235-9292),
Delta (℃ 800/221-1212), **United Express** (℃ 800/241-6527), and **U.S. Airways**
(℃ 800/943-5436).

VISITOR INFORMATION   Contact the **Durango Area Tourism Office,** 111 S.
Camino del Rio, Durango, CO 81302 (℃ **800/463-8726;** www.durango.org). The
Durango Visitor Center is just south of downtown, on U.S. 160/550 opposite the

intersection of East Eighth Avenue. June through October, it's open Monday through Saturday from 8am to 5pm, and Sunday from 10am to 4pm; the rest of the year, hours are from 8am to 5pm Monday through Friday.

GETTING AROUND The city is on the banks of the Animas River. U.S. 160 lies along the southern edge, and is joined by U.S. 550 about 5 miles east of Durango. Just before U.S. 160 crosses the river, U.S. 550 branches north as Camino del Rio, and junctions with Main Avenue at 14th Street. Downtown Durango is built around Main Avenue from 14th Street south to Fifth Street. College Drive (Sixth St.) is the principal downtown cross street.

Transportation throughout Durango is provided by **The Durango Lift** (© 970/259-5438; www.durangogov.org/resident/services/transit.html). The **city bus** has three fixed-route loops that operate weekdays, from about 7am to 7pm, year-round (does not operate on major public holidays), and there are also some evening schedules, including late night transportation Friday and Saturday. The fare is $1 per ride one-way. Also part of the Durango Lift is the **Durango Trolley,** which runs along Main Avenue every 20 minutes, from 7am to 10:40pm daily. Cost is 50¢. Bus and trolley schedules and route maps are available at the visitor center (see above), and all are fully accessible for travelers with limited mobility.

Taxi service is provided 24 hours a day by **Durango Transportation** (© 970/259-4818). Car-rental agencies include **Avis** (© 970/247-9761), **Budget** (© 800/527-7000), **Dollar** (© 970/259-3012), **Enterprise** (© 970/385-6860), **Hertz** (© 970/247-5288), and **National** (© 970/382-8090).

FAST FACTS There's a 24-hour emergency room at **Mercy Regional Medical Center,** 1010 Three Springs Blvd. (© **800/345-2516** or 970/247-4311; www.mercy durango.org). The **post office** is at 3465 Main Ave.; contact the U.S. Postal Service (© **800/275-8777**; www.usps.com) for hours and additional information. For **road conditions,** call © **877/315-7623.**

SPECIAL EVENTS Iron Horse Bicycle Classic, Memorial Day weekend; Animas River Days, early June; Music in the Mountains, at Durango Mountain Resort, mid- to late July; La Plata County Fair, early August; the Main Avenue Arts Festival, mid-August; the Durango & Silverton Narrow Gauge Railroad Railfest, late August; the Durango Cowboy Gathering, late September or early October; and the Durango Christmas Tree Lighting Ceremony, November.

THE TOP ATTRACTION

The Durango & Silverton Narrow Gauge Railroad &&& Colorado's most famous train has been in continual operation since 1881. In all that time, its route has never varied: up the Río de las Animas Perdidas (River of Lost Souls), through 45 miles of mountain and San Juan National Forest wilderness to the historic mining town of Silverton, and back. The coal-fired steam locomotives pull strings of gold-colored Victorian coaches on the 3,000-foot climb, past relics of mining and railroad activity from the last century.

A summer trip takes 3¼ hours each way, with a 2-hour stopover in the picturesque town of Silverton before the return trip. You can also overnight in Silverton and return to Durango the following day. (For information on what to see and do during your layover, see "A Side Trip to Silverton," later in this chapter.) Stops are made for water, and also for hikers and fishermen at remote trail heads inaccessible by road. Refreshments and snacks are available on all trains. New in 2006 is Vista Class, the opportunity to

Southwestern Colorado on the Silver Screen

This is John Wayne country, where the Duke slugged it out, shot it out, and sometimes yelled it out as he tamed the American West on movie screens from the late 1920s through the 1970s. It was the location shoot for the multi-Oscar-winning 1969 hit *Butch Cassidy and the Sundance Kid,* starring Robert Redford and Paul Newman. It also hosted *City Slickers,* the 1991 comedy starring Billy Crystal as a hapless city dweller on an Old West–style cattle drive.

Movie critics may argue the point, but to many Americans, the king of them all was the Duke—this bigger-than-life symbol of American manhood made numerous films in and around Gunnison, Ridgway, Delta, Durango, and Pagosa Springs, where you can still find the exact spots certain scenes were filmed.

The classic, if bleak, 1956 John Ford film *The Searchers,* with Wayne, Jeffrey Hunter, Vera Miles, and Ward Bond, used a ranch near Gunnison as a military outpost. To reach the ranch, go north from Gunnison for 3 miles on Colo. 135, then turn left onto Ohio Creek Road and drive for about 8 miles, where you'll see a barn and several other buildings off to the left. Ford's later Western *How the West Was Won* (which, to the great disappointment of Wayne fans, didn't include the Duke) shows a wagon train crossing the Gunnison River west of Delta along 1800 Road, as well as scenes of the Durango & Silverton Narrow Gauge Railroad.

As real John Wayne aficionados know, in 1969 he teamed with Glen Campbell and Kim Darby to make one of his most famous films, *True Grit.*

ride in a replica of a historic glass-domed open-air gondola. The Parlor Car, another special car, has a bar, and the most luxurious car is the Cinco Animas, which oozes Victorian splendor. Several private cars are available for charter, including an 1886 caboose and the 1878 *Nomad*—believed to be the oldest operating private railroad car in the world, host of U.S. presidents from Taft to Ford.

The summer schedule runs from early May through October, making the full trip to Silverton and back to Durango, with several trains daily during the peak season, from early June through mid-August, and fewer trains at other times. From the last week in November through early May (except Christmas) there's a daily train to Cascade Canyon and back, 52 miles round-trip. Call or check the website for information on special excursions and events.

479 Main Ave., Durango, CO 81301. ⓒ **888/872-4607** or 970/247-2733. www.durangotrain.com. Advance reservations advised. Summer round-trip fare $62 adults, $31 children 5–11, $119 for the Vista Class car (minimum age 16), $109 for the parlor car (minimum age 21), $129 for the Cinco Animas (minimum age 21); winter round-trip fare $45 adults, $22 children 5–11. Parking $7 per day per car, $9 for RVs and buses.

OTHER DURANGO HIGHLIGHTS

While taking a steam-train trip on the Durango & Silverton Narrow Gauge Railroad is undeniably the area's top attraction, there are other things to do here. Those interested in a close-up view of the city's numerous historic buildings will want to pick up

The town of Ridgway becomes Fort Smith in the movie, and nearby is the ranch where Wayne jumps his horse over a river. *The Cowboys,* filmed in 1972 outside Pagosa Springs, finds Wayne as a cattleman who hires a group of schoolboys to drive his herd of 1,500 cattle after the gold rush lures away his crew. There are several location shoots from this film in the area; ask for directions at the Pagosa Springs Chamber of Commerce.

But Wayne wasn't the only one shooting up Colorado's southwest corner. Several movie companies have made use of the area, particularly the classic Durango & Silverton Narrow Gauge Railroad. The best train scene has to be the one in *Butch Cassidy and the Sundance Kid,* where Butch, Sundance, and their gang attempt to blow open the train's safe and instead blow up the entire mail car, sending money flying in all directions. Reportedly, the extent of this explosion was a surprise to everyone, even the special-effects technicians who apparently were a bit too liberal with their use of black powder. You can see the train at the depot at 479 Main Ave. in Durango, or in summer hop aboard for a ride to Silverton and back. There's a plaque commemorating the filming about 10 miles east of Durango; ask at the chamber of commerce for directions.

The **Colorado Film Commission,** 1625 Broadway, Suite 950, Denver, CO 80202 (© **800/726-8887** or 303/592-4065; www.coloradofilm.org), works to bring film makers to the state, and also has information for those who want to work in the film industry, possibly as extras, and others interested in movie production.

free copies of several **walking-tour** brochures from the visitor center (see above). Along Main Avenue you'll see the handsome **Strater Hotel,** the building that housed the region's first bank, and the sites of saloons and other businesses of the late 1800s and early 1900s; while walking down Third Avenue you'll pass several stone churches and some of the finest homes in Durango from the same period, including the house where silent movie star Harold Lloyd lived during part of his childhood.

Animas Museum   A 1904 stone schoolhouse in north Durango is the home of the La Plata County Historical Society museum, so it's appropriate that a turn-of-the-20th-century classroom is one of its central displays. The museum, which makes a good first stop for those interested in the history of the area, also contains a restored 1870s log cabin from the early days of Animas City, the town that predated Durango. There are also changing exhibits depicting local history, American Indians, and the American West. The museum shop has a good selection of new and used books on regional history and culture. Allow a minimum of 1 hour.

31st St. and W. Second Ave. © **970/259-2402.** www.animasmuseum.org. Admission $2.50 adults, free for children 12 and younger. May–Oct Mon–Sat 10am–6pm; Nov–Apr Tues–Sat 10am–4pm.

Center of Southwest Studies   This museum and research facility, located on the Fort Lewis College campus northeast of downtown Durango, contains a variety of

Southwestern artifacts, including excellent exhibits of textiles, woven over 800 years by Navajo, Puebloan, and Hispanic weavers. Allow 45 minutes.

1000 Rim Dr., Fort Lewis College. © **970/247-7494.** http://swcenter.fortlewis.edu. Free admission. Mon–Fri 1–4pm and by appointment.

Children's Museum of Durango *(Kids* Hands-on activities for children from pre-school through preteen make a nice break for vacationing kids who have seen a few too many Victorian homes. Parents stay with and supervise their children while the kids enjoy the changing exhibits, which might include a wood shop, minigrocery store, puppet theater, dress-up area, and a variety of physics demonstrations with items such as magnets and optical illusions. There are also computer games, arts and crafts, and an archaeology section. Allow 2 hours. *Note:* A move to a new location is scheduled for 2008, so call first.

802 E. Second Ave., upstairs at the Durango Arts Center. © **970/259-9234.** www.childsmuseum.org. Admission $5.50 adults, $4 children, free for seniors and children under 3. Wed–Sat 9:30am–4:30pm; Sun 1–5pm.

Durango Fish Hatchery and Wildlife Museum *(Kids* A pleasant change from the usual attractions, this fish hatchery offers an opportunity to see and feed trout and also see mounted birds and other wildlife native to Southwestern Colorado. The hatchery, operated by the Colorado Division of Wildlife, also has a short video presentation on fish hatchery operation. Allow 1 hour.

151 E. 16th St. © **970/375-6766** or 970/247-0855. Free admission. Open mid-May to mid-Sept Mon–Sat 10am–4:30pm; Sun 11am–3pm.

Durango & Silverton Narrow Gauge Railroad Museum The glory days of steam trains come alive here, where you can climb up into a full-size locomotive, a caboose, parlor car, and other rolling stock to get a close-up view. The large museum, located in the Durango & Silverton rail yard, also houses a vast amount of railroad memorabilia, from conductors' uniforms, watches, and belt buckles to lanterns, railroad art, and historic photos. Allow 1 hour.

479 Main Ave. © **888/872-4607** or 970/247-2733. Admission $5 adults, $2.50 children under 12; free with a train ticket. Summer daily 8am–6pm; call for off-season hours.

SPORTS & OUTDOOR ACTIVITIES

In addition to contacting the various companies listed below, you can get additional information and even book some activities through the **Durango Area Tourism Office** (see "Visitor Information," above).

Durango is surrounded by public land, with numerous opportunities for hiking, mountain biking, fishing, and winter sports. For information contact the **San Juan Public Lands Center** (© **970/247-4874**) at 15 Burnett Ct., off U.S. 160 west in the Durango Tech Center, which offers information on activities in the San Juan National Forest (www.fs.fed.us/r2/sanjuan) and on lands administered by the Bureau of Land Management (www.co.blm.gov). The center is open Monday through Friday from 8am to 5pm.

The **Durango Parks and Recreation Department** (© **970/375-7300;** www.durangogov.org/resident/parks_leisure/parks.html) operates about 20 parks throughout the city, where you'll find picnic areas, free tennis courts, and other facilities. The department operates (and has its administrative offices in) the **Durango Community Recreation Center,** 2700 Main Ave., which has an indoor swimming pool, climbing wall, weights and other workout equipment, an indoor track, and other facilities.

A recreation center day pass, which includes all the facilities at the center, costs $4.50 for adults 18 to 59, $3.50 for kids 4 to 17 and adults 60 and up, and is free with a paying adult for children under 4.

Durango Mountain Resort, some 25 miles north of Durango on U.S. 550 (© **800/982-6103** or 970/247-9000; www.durangomountainresort.com), doesn't close down—or even slow down—after the winter's snows are gone. Summer activities here include the popular Alpine Slide, scenic chairlift rides, a climbing wall, miniature golf, disc golf, and bungee trampolines. Individual activities cost from $3 for a chairlift ride to $8 for the alpine slide or the bungee trampoline, but the best deal is the Total Adventure Ticket—a 4-hour pass for $29 or a full-day pass for $49, providing a shot at everything including unlimited alpine slide and chairlift rides, and disc and miniature golf. Durango Mountain Resort also offers free guided naturalist hikes; call © 970/385-1210 for times and registration.

FISHING   Six-mile-long **Vallecito Lake,** 23 miles northeast of Durango via C.R. 240 and C.R. 501, is a prime spot for rainbow trout, brown trout, kokanee salmon, and northern pike; for information, contact the Vallecito Lake Chamber of Commerce, P.O. Box 804, Bayfield, CO 81122 (© **970/247-1573;** www.vallecitolakechamber.com). There are also numerous streams in the Durango area. To buy Colorado fishing licenses and supplies, get information on the best fishing holes, rent equipment, or arrange for a guided fly-fishing trip, stop in at **Duranglers,** 923 Main Ave. (© **888/347-4346** or 970/385-4081; www.duranglers.com). Full-day float trips for two people cost about $350; wading trips for two cost about $325. Lunch is included. Similar guide services are offered by **Anasazi Angler** (© **970/385-4665;** www.sanjuantrout.com).

GLIDER RIDES   For a quiet, airborne look at Durango and the San Juan Mountains, take a glider ride with **Durango Soaring Club** (© **970/247-9037;** www.soardurango.com), located 3 miles north of Durango on U.S. 550. Rides are conducted daily from 9am to 6pm from mid-May through mid-October; soaring is smoother in the morning but there is greater thermal activity, offering the opportunity for longer rides, in the afternoon. Rates for one person are about $95 for 10 to 15 minutes and $145 for 30 to 35 minutes, and individuals cannot weigh less than 50 pounds or more than 260 pounds.

GOLF   Two public 18-hole golf courses open in early spring, weather permitting, in Durango. There's **Hillcrest Golf Course,** 2300 Rim Dr., adjacent to Fort Lewis College (© **970/247-1499**), with fees of $25 for 18 holes; and **Dalton Ranch and Golf Club,** 589 Trimble Lane (C.R. 252), 6 miles north of Durango via U.S. 550 (© **970/247-8774;** www.daltonranch.com), charging $89 for 18 holes, including a cart.

HIKING & BACKPACKING   Durango is at the western end of the 500-mile Colorado Trail to Denver. The trail head is 3½ miles up Junction Creek Road, an extension of 25th Street west of Main Avenue. There are numerous other trails in the Durango area, including paths into the Weminuche Wilderness Area reached via the Durango & Silverton railroad. For information on area trails contact the **San Juan Public Lands Center** (see above).

HORSEBACK RIDING & CATTLE DRIVES   To see this spectacular country as the pioneers did, arrange for a short horseback ride or a 2- to 6-day expedition into the San Juan National Forest or Weminuche Wilderness. Our choice for a licensed outfitter here is **Rapp Corral,** located on the east side of U.S. 550 about 20 miles north of Durango at 51 Haviland Lake Road. (© **970/247-8454**; www.rappguides. net). Riders go into the San Juan National Forest, and rides start at $32 for a 1-hour ride. A 2-hour ride to a natural cave costs $60 and a 4-hour or longer trip into southern Colorado's high country costs $150. Reservations are required, and payment should be made with personal or travelers' checks or cash; credit cards are not accepted. During winter, Rapp Corral offers sleigh rides (call for details).

LLAMA TREKKING Guided llama trips, overnight pack trips, and llama leasing are the specialty of **Buckhorn Llama Co.** (© **970/667-7411**; www.llamapack.com). Guided pack trips for one to three people cost $350 per person per day and include all equipment, meals, and necessary supplies, except for sleeping bags.

MOUNTAIN BIKING The varied terrain and myriad trails of San Juan National Forest have made Durango a nationally known mountain-biking center. The Colorado Trail (see "Hiking & Backpacking," above), Hermosa Creek Trail (beginning 11 miles north of Durango off U.S. 550), and La Plata Canyon Road (beginning 11 miles west of Durango off U.S. 160) are among our favorites. For information contact the **Public Lands Center** (see above).

You can also get information and rent mountain bikes at **Hassle Free Sports,** 2615 Main Ave. (© **800/835-3800** or 970/259-3874; www.hasslefreesports.com), which rents full suspension mountain bikes for $30 per half-day or $40 for a full day. Guided tours and bike rentals are available from **Southwest Adventure Guides,** 12th and Camino del Rio (© **800/642-5389** or 970/259-0370; www.mtnguide.net), with similar rentals rates and guided tour prices starting at $60 for a half-day.

MOUNTAINEERING & ROCK CLIMBING A variety of terrain offers mountaineering and rock-climbing opportunities for beginners as well as advanced climbers. Guided tours and instruction are offered by **Southwest Adventures** (see "Mountain Biking," above), with rates starting at $70 for a group half-day rock-climbing course and $310 for two people for a 1-day mountaineering course.

RIVER RAFTING The three stages of the Animas River provide excitement for rafters of all experience and ability levels. The churning Class IV and V rapids of the upper Animas mark its rapid descent from the San Juan Range. The 6 miles from Trimble Hot Springs into downtown Durango are an easy, gently rolling rush. Downstream from Durango, the river is mainly Classes II and III, promising a few thrills but mostly relaxation.

Most of the many outfitters in Durango offer a wide variety of rafting excursions, such as 2- to 4-hour raft trips that cost $25 to $45 for adults and $20 to $35 for kids, and full-day river trips, which include lunch, costing about $75 for adults and $65 for kids. Trips in inflatable kayaks are also offered at slightly higher rates. Among our favorite companies here are **Durango Rivertrippers** (© **800/292-2885** or 970/259-0289; www.durangorivertrippers.com), **AAM's Mild to Wild Rafting** (© **800/567-6745** or 970/247-4789; www.mild2wildrafting.com), and **Mountain Waters Rafting** (© **800/585-8243** or 970/259-4191; www.durangorafting.com).

RODEO From late June through the third weekend in July, the **Durango Pro Rodeo** series takes place most Tuesday, Wednesday, Friday, and Saturday nights starting at 7:30pm at the La Plata County Fairgrounds, Main Avenue and 25th Street (© **602/237-3000**; www.durangoprorodeo.com). Admission costs $12 for adults and $5 for kids 12 and under. A Western barbecue ($7 per plate) is served from 6pm.

SWIMMING & MINERAL BATHS   Trimble Hot Springs ⟨⟩, 7 miles north of Durango just off U.S. 550 (© **970/247-0111**; www.trimblehotsprings.com), at the junction of C.R. 203 and Trimble Lane, is a National Historic Site more than 100 years old, where you'll often find Mom and Dad relaxing in the soothing mineral pools or getting a massage while the kids have fun in the adjacent swimming pool. Facilities include two natural hot-springs therapy pools, a separate Olympic-size swimming pool (heated by the hot springs but not containing hot-springs water), massage and therapy rooms, a snack bar, picnic area, and gardens. Water from the natural hot springs comes out of the ground at 118° to 120°F (48°–49°C), and the therapy pools are kept at a more comfortable temperature of 102° to 108°F (39°–42°C). The swimming pool is usually about 85°F (29°C). The complex is open daily from 8am to 11pm in summer, and in winter from 9am to 10pm Sunday through Thursday and until 11pm Friday and Saturday. From June through August day passes cost $11 for adults and $7.50 for children 12 and younger; the rest of the year the cost is $9 for adults and $6.50 for children 12 and younger. Day passes cover use of the therapy mineral pools and the swimming pool. The Trimble Hot Springs Spa (© **970/ 247-0212**) is open daily from 9am to 9pm year-round, providing expanded body treatments and a quiet relaxing atmosphere for therapeutic massage, herbal oil wraps, face and scalp treatments, dry body brush, and radiant salt glow. Massages start at about $50 for a half-hour. Reservations are recommended but walk-ins are welcome.

WINTER SPORTS   Some 25 miles north of Durango on U.S. 550, **Durango Mountain Resort** ⟨⟩⟨⟩, 1 Skier Place, Durango, CO 81301 (© **800/982-6103** or 970/247-9000; www.durangomountainresort.com), has bragging rights to more sunshine than any other Colorado resort. Surprisingly, the sun doesn't come at the expense of snow—average annual snowfall is 260 inches—so you really get the best of both snow and sun. The resort, which has a laid-back friendly atmosphere that we particularly enjoy, contains 1,200 acres of skiable terrain, with 85 trails rated 23% beginner, 51% intermediate, and 26% advanced, and 11 lifts (one high-speed six, one high-speed quad, four triples, three doubles, one surface lift, and one Magic Carpet). The mountain has a vertical drop of 2,029 feet from a summit elevation of 10,822 feet.

Snowboarders are welcome on all lifts and trails, and two snowboard parks offer jumps, slides, and a half-pipe. The Durango Nordic Center has 10 miles of trails for Nordic skiers for both classic and skate skiing, and charges $12 for a trail pass.

Three on-mountain restaurants complement the facilities, which include a hotel, condominiums, several restaurants and taverns, shops, and equipment rentals. All-day lift tickets are about $55 for adults, $30 for children 6 to 12, $45 for seniors 62 to 69 and students, $20 for seniors 70 and older, and free for kids 5 and younger. The resort is usually open from late November or early December to early April, daily from 9am to 4pm.

SHOPPING

You'll find some of your best shopping opportunities in southwest Colorado in downtown Durango, along Main Avenue from the Durango & Silverton Railroad Depot north to 10th Street. Here, interspersed among restaurants and historic hotels, are shops selling a wide variety of items—ranging from custom-made Western hats to kitchen gizmos to fine porcelain and imported gifts. And yes, there are plenty of tacky T-shirts, as well.

Those seeking the region's premier art gallery will have to leave Main Avenue, but it's not far to the **Toh-Atin Gallery,** 145 W. Ninth St. (© **800/525-0384** or 970/247-8277; www.toh-atin.com). Specializing in original Southwestern and American Indian art, the gallery stocks Navajo weavings, bronze and alabaster sculptures, original paintings, pueblo pottery, and handcrafted jewelry.

WHERE TO STAY

Durango has a definite lodging season. When the Durango & Silverton Narrow Gauge Railroad runs most of its trains in midsummer, expect to pay top dollar for your room, and expect higher rates during the Christmas holidays and in peak ski seasons as well. But go in the off-season—late spring and fall—and you'll find much more reasonable rates. An easy way to book accommodations is to contact the **Durango Central Reservations** (© **866/294-5187;** www.durangoreservations.org). Room taxes add 9.4% to lodging bills.

Among chain and franchise motels offering moderately priced rooms are the **Best Western Mountain Shadows,** 3255 N. Main Ave. (© **800/521-5218** or 970/247-5200), charging $64 to $159 double; the **Comfort Inn,** 2930 N. Main Ave. (© **800/424-6423** or 970/259-5373), with rates for two from $59 to $139; **Days Inn,** 1700 C.R. 203 (© **800/338-1116** or 970/259-1430), with double rates of $69 to $139; **Econo Lodge,** 2002 Main Ave. (© **877/883-2666** or 970/247-4242), charging $59 to $99 double; and **Quality Inn,** 455 S. Camino del Rio (© **800/424-6423** or 970/259-7900), with rates for two from $79 to $139. All are in Durango, CO 81301.

VERY EXPENSIVE

The Wit's End Guest Ranch & Resort 🐾🐾 *(Kids)*   A delightful dude ranch some 24 miles northeast of Durango at 8,000 feet elevation, the Wit's End is located on 550 acres in a narrow valley at the head of Vallecito Lake. Surrounded by the 12,000- to 14,000-foot peaks of the Weminuche Wilderness, the Wit's End offers a unique combination of rustic outdoors and sophisticated luxury, with numerous activities ranging from guided horseback rides and boating to a summer kids' program. The one- to four-bedroom log cabins, some dating from the 1870s, have retained their rustic outer appearance, but the knotty-pine interiors have been fully renovated. All have stone fireplaces, queen beds, full bathrooms with tub/shower combos, robes, porches (with porch swings), and striking views.

Most meals are served in the beautiful log lodge, dating from the 1870s, with a huge stone fireplace and walls mirrored with cut glass from London's 1853 Crystal Palace. Filet mignon, roast duckling, chicken Culbertson, and other hearty American dishes are served, with fine dining 3 evenings each week and outdoor Western cookouts the other nights. An on-site spa has four massage and treatment rooms, two multiple-head steam showers, a Swedish sauna, and hot tubs. The game room, on the second floor, has an antique billiards table.

254 C.R. 500, Bayfield, CO 81122. © **800/236-9483** or 970/884-4113. Fax 970/884-3261. www.witsendranch.com. 32 cabins. Memorial Day to Labor Day from $4,906 per week for 2 guests. Extra adult $2,973, extra child (4–12) $1,963, nannies $1,738. Rates include all meals and activities. Other plans also available. Off-season cabin-only rates available. AE, DISC, MC, V. **Amenities:** Restaurant (Western/American); bar; large outdoor pool (summer only); 2 outdoor tennis courts; exercise room; spa; mountain biking; extensive summer children's program for ages 4–17; game room; airport transportation; limited room service; horseback riding (private lessons available); fishing (Orvis-endorsed instruction available); hiking; boating; trap shooting; winter-sports equipment. *In room:* TV/VCR (videos available), kitchen.

EXPENSIVE

Strater Hotel 𝄐𝄐𝄐   Durango's most famous hotel is a wonderful place to relax and soak up the ambience of the real Old West (at least the real Old West for those who had money). An exceptional example of American Victorian architecture, the four-story redbrick Strater was built in 1887 by Henry H. Strater, a prominent druggist of the mining-boom era. It boasts the original ornamental brickwork and white-stone cornices, embossed ceiling designs, and intricately carved columns. Crystal chandeliers and a variety of ornate woodworking styles grace the public areas. The hotel has been in the Barker family (Rod Barker is the current CEO) since 1926.

Spread throughout the guest rooms is one of the world's largest collections of American Victorian walnut antiques, and even the wallpaper is authentic to the 1880s. One of the most popular units is no. 222, a corner room directly over the Diamond Belle Saloon, where prolific author Louis L'Amour gave life to many of his Western heroes. The bathrooms are modern, with tub/shower combos in most, but showers only in 16 of the 93 units. The hotel also boasts a Victorian-style hot tub, available by reservation only.

Employees—many of whom have been with the Strater for years—seem to take a personal interest in the happiness of each guest, and manage to be attentive and friendly without falling into the trap of becoming too chummy. Guests of the Strater from Thanksgiving through New Year's are treated to a display of Victorian Christmas decorations, plus complimentary homemade cookies. The Diamond Belle Saloon has live ragtime piano, the Office Spiritorium is a refined martini bar with exquisite charm, and the hotel's theater presents summer melodrama (see "Durango After Dark," below).

699 Main Ave., Durango, CO 81301. (**C**) **800/247-4431** or 970/247-4431. Fax 970/259-2208. www.strater.com. 93 units. Early May to mid-Oct and Christmas holidays $169–$249 double; mid-Oct to early May $99–$179 double. AE, DC, DISC, MC, V. **Amenities:** Restaurant (Mahogany Grillle, p. 380); 2 bars; hot tub; concierge; limited room service; valet laundry. *In room:* A/C, TV.

MODERATE

The Leland House Bed & Breakfast Suites 𝄐𝄐   Built as an apartment house in 1927 and handsomely restored in 1993, the Leland House offers an intriguing mix of lodging types in a comfortable inn with early-20th-century decor. Owned by the Komick family, who also own the historic Rochester Hotel across the street (see below), the Leland House contains six suites with sitting rooms and full kitchens, plus four studios with kitchenettes. All have private bathrooms with showers (no tubs), and are decorated with a compatible combination of good-quality beds, antiques, near-antiques, and contemporary furniture. The Pittman Suite is a large family suite with two full bedrooms, two bathrooms, a full kitchen, and a large living area. Rooms are named for historic figures associated with the Leland House and its neighbors, such as Max Baer, world heavyweight boxing champion in the 1930s. Throughout the house are photos, memorabilia, and framed biographies of these individuals, many of whom played significant roles in the development of early Durango.

In B&B style, you'll find the friendly staff to be service oriented. Breakfasts, which are served across the street at the Rochester, include a selection of fresh-baked goods, fruit, cereals, juice and coffee, plus a hot entree. Fresh-baked cookies and other refreshments are served in the evening, and like the Rochester, the Leland House has a great close-to-downtown location. Smoking is not permitted.

721 E. Second Ave., Durango, CO 81301. © **800/664-1920** or 970/385-1920. Fax 970/385-1967. www.leland
-house.com. 10 units. $109–$149 studio; $159–$199 1-bedroom suite; $299–$340 2-bedroom suite. Rates include
full breakfast. AE, DC, DISC, MC, V. *In room:* A/C, TV.

Rochester Hotel ★★ Among our favorite places to stay in Durango, the 1892
Rochester retains the feel of an Old West hotel with high ceilings, original trim and
hardware, antiques, historic photos and original Western art, and 1890s-style furnishings. Completely renovated in the mid-1990s the hotel offers 15 spacious rooms, each
with its own bathroom (two have whirlpool tubs with showers, and the rest have large
walk-in showers). Rooms have good, firm queen or king beds; one unit has a king bed
and a kitchen and another, a king and a separate living room. The hotel's hallways are
lined with posters and photos from many of the films shot in the area, including *City
Slickers, Butch Cassidy and the Sundance Kid, How the West Was Won,* and *The Cowboys.*
   Although technically a hotel, the Rochester is run more like a large bed-and-breakfast inn, with an innkeeper on hand to act as concierge. The wonderful breakfasts
include fresh-baked muffins, scones, or breads; a selection of fruit; oatmeal; cold cereals; yogurt; and beverages; plus a hot entree such as havarti-dill scrambled eggs with
potato-chive cake. Fresh-baked cookies and other refreshments are also provided in
the evening. Another plus is the location—within easy walking distance of Durango's
downtown restaurants and attractions. Smoking is not permitted.

726 E. Second Ave. (write to 721 E. Second Ave.), Durango, CO 81301. © **800/664-1920** or 970/385-1920. Fax 970/
385-1967. www.rochesterhotel.com. 15 units. $109–$199 double, $179–$229 suite (called King Deluxe). Rates include
full breakfast. AE, DC, DISC, MC, V. Pets accepted in 2 units with $20 per pet per night charge. *In room:* A/C, TV.

WHERE TO DINE
EXPENSIVE
Mahogany Grille ★★ NEW AMERICAN This fun upscale restaurant, attached
to the Strater Hotel, is a lively spot serving cutting-edge dishes to the sounds of jazz.
Serving only dinner, the Mahogany Grille serves primarily new American cuisine with
definite international influences. We suggest the pepper steak Herbert, a brandy-
flamed filet mignon with a mango-chutney sauce, and the oven-roasted pistachio-
crusted halibut with a lemon-and-garlic sauce. Save room for the decadent chocolate
avalanche—a huge homemade brownie loaded with other chocolate treats plus straw-
berries; or the strawberry rhubarb cobbler, served warm with cinnamon ice cream.
There's also an extensive menu of specialty martinis—the restaurant's signature
Mahogany Cheer contains vodka and a bunch of other stuff they won't talk about—
plus there's a good international wine list.

Adjacent to the Strater Hotel, 699 Main Ave. © **970/247-4433**. www.mahoganygrille.com. Main courses $15–$32.
AE, DISC, MC, V. Summer daily 5–10pm; rest of the year daily 5–9pm.

MODERATE
Cyprus Cafe ★★ MEDITERRANEAN This tiny restaurant a block from
Durango's busy Main Avenue offers a delightful alternative to the basic American and
Southwestern cuisine that dominates southwestern Colorado, and gets our vote as the
place to go when we feel adventurous. The dining room has a simple cafe atmosphere,
with 10 wood tables, a stained-glass window, and a few pieces of original art. In summer, there's also outdoor patio seating, which more than doubles the restaurant's
capacity. The emphasis is on freshness, with produce from local farms when available.
The menu changes seasonally, but dinner entrees might include spanakopita, spinach

and feta cheese wrapped in phyllo dough; Colorado beef and lamb; fresh seafood; and at least one vegetarian item. Those new to Mediterranean cuisine might try the combination appetizer plate that includes hummus, baba ganouj, olives, feta, spanakopita, and grilled pita, which can easily serve several people as an appetizer or one for dinner.

725 E. Second Ave. ✆ 970/385-6884. www.cypruscafe.com. Lunch $7.95–$13; dinner $14–$24. AE, DISC, MC, V. Mid-May to Sept daily 11:30am–3pm and 5–10pm; Oct to mid-May Mon–Sat 11:30am–2:30pm and 5–9pm.

The Palace Restaurant STEAK/SEAFOOD/PASTA   Adjacent to the Durango & Silverton Narrow Gauge Railroad terminal, the Palace Restaurant, which also contains the Quiet Lady Tavern, has a Victorian drawing-room atmosphere, with Tiffany lamps hanging over the tables, historical photos and classic oil paintings on the walls, and a large fireplace. House specialties at lunch include the lemon-thyme chicken sandwich with thinly sliced apples and grilled Rocky Mountain trout. At dinner, try the slow-roasted duck in a honey-almond sauce or the steak McMahon—a 12-ounce New York cut served on crisp hash browns with a roasted-garlic sauce. Available at lunch and dinner, and great at either meal, is the chicken and dumplings with cranberry compote. A variety of seafood and pasta dishes are also offered. The Quiet Lady Tavern, by the way, is named for the headless female sculpture at its entrance.

505 Main Ave. ✆ 970/247-2018. www.palacerestaurants.com. Main courses $6–$12 lunch, $13–$28 dinner. AE, MC, V. Mon–Sat 11am–10pm. Closed New Year's Day, Easter, and Christmas.

Steamworks Brewing Co. BREWPUB   Situated in a 1920s building, formerly a car dealership, this brewpub has made the most of the funky, warehouselike structure with huge wooden rafters and pipes of all sizes running in all directions. There's also patio dining. The food matches the decor: large, substantial portions to satisfy any appetite, and with an emphasis on spicy. Half-pound burgers come in a variety of choices, such as Southwestern, with green chile, pepper jack cheese, and a chipotle sauce. There's also a spicy Cajun chicken sandwich, and a grilled Reuben. Entrees include burritos, steak, chicken, and pasta selections such as the Cajun penne pasta—Cajun chicken with sausage, bell peppers, and onions in a spicy cream sauce with penne pasta. The tasty side salad with Italian vinaigrette dressing practically overflows the plate, and along with a pepperoni pizza is a perfect (and inexpensive) dinner for two. Close to a dozen of the brewer's beers are usually on tap, including a delightfully bitter pale ale.

801 E. Second Ave. at Eighth St. ✆ 970/259-9200. www.steamworksbrewing.com. Main courses $7.75–$17; pizza $7.95–$12 (serves 1 or 2). AE, DISC, MC, V. Daily 11am–10pm; bar open later.

INEXPENSIVE
Durango Diner AMERICAN   Locally famous for good basic grub at reasonable prices, the Durango Diner has been going strong since 1965. Serving breakfast and lunch only, the diner is a skinny storefront with a long counter and a table or two looking out on busy Main Avenue. Breakfasts include standard American egg choices, huge hotcakes, and a variety of specials such as excellent homemade green chili, chile rellenos, and breakfast burritos. Lunch here means sandwiches and burgers—the half-pound burger with Swiss cheese and green chili is great—plus turkey and roast beef dinners. The Durango Diner also does a booming business selling its green chile, salsa, and enchilada sauce by the pint, quart, and gallon.

957 Main Ave. ✆ 970/247-9889. www.durangodiner.com. Most items $3–$7. No credit cards. Mon–Sat 6am–2pm; Sun 6am–1pm.

Olde Tymer's Cafe AMERICAN   This popular local hangout is a busy, noisy place in a historic building, complete with the original tin ceiling and decorated with antique bottles and tins from the early-20th-century drugstore that was once located here. The food is primarily burgers, sandwiches, and finger food—the 8-ounce burger in an onion roll is especially good. The menu also features homemade chili, nachos, and hearty salads such as the chicken salad and Cobb salad, and there are daily specials. Service is fast, friendly, and efficient. The patio out back, open in warm weather, is especially pleasant (and quieter than inside).

1000 Main Ave. (at 10th St.) © **970/259-2990.** Reservations not accepted. Most items $3.50–$9. AE, DISC, MC, V. Daily 11am–10pm.

DURANGO AFTER DARK

During summer, the highly acclaimed **Diamond Circle Melodrama,** in the Strater Hotel, 699 Main Ave. (© **970/247-3400;** www.diamondcirclemelodrama.com), presents authentic late 1800s melodrama—hiss the evil villain and cheer the beautiful heroine—plus a vaudeville review of singing, dancing, and comedy from early June through late September on Wednesday through Monday evenings at 7:45pm, plus several Saturday matinees in midsummer. Tickets are $18 to $22 for adults, $13 to $17 for children 12 and under, $16 to $20 for students over 12, and $19 to $21 for seniors 62 and older.

You'll get a tasty meal and a live Western stage show at **Bar D Chuckwagon Suppers,** 8080 C.R. 250 (© **888/800-5753** or 970/247-5753; www.bardchuckwagon. com), 9 miles north of Durango via U.S. 550 and Trimble Lane (C.R. 252). Open from Memorial Day weekend through Labor Day weekend, Bar D offers a traditional chuck-wagon-style meal with a tasty choice of roast beef, barbecued chicken breast, or flame-broiled 12-ounce rib-eye steak, served with potato, beans, biscuits, applesauce, spice cake, and coffee or lemonade. There are usually seconds available, but most people get plenty the first time.

The ranch complex, which includes an Old West town of shops and a miniature train (5:30–7:15pm, $1 per person per ride), opens at 5:30pm. By 7:30pm you should be in the open-air dining area (yep, there's a portable roof in case of rain), to go through the chow line for your grub, piled onto big metal plates, before taking your seat at a long picnic table. After dinner comes the show—fine Western music with fiddle, flatpick guitar, mandolin, bass, and great singers; plus some really hokey comedy.

Reservations are required. Cost includes supper and show and is $17 for those 9 and older and $8 for children under 9 for the beef or chicken supper. The beef-chicken combination platter costs $20 per person and the rib-eye steak costs $26.

A SIDE TRIP TO SILVERTON

For a look at the real Old West, without the need for a time machine, head to the town of Silverton. At an elevation of 9,318 feet at the northern terminus of the Durango & Silverton Narrow Gauge Railroad, the town has a year-round population of about 500 and plenty of things to see and do for the more than 250,000 people who visit each year.

Founded on silver production in 1871, today the entire town is a National Historic Landmark District. In its heyday, Blair Street was such a notorious area of saloons and brothels that no less a character than Bat Masterson, fresh from taming Dodge City, Kansas, was imported to subdue the criminal elements. Today the original false-fronted buildings remain—some in better shape than others—but they now house restaurants and galleries, and are occasionally used as Old West movie sets. There are some fascinating shops and galleries here, along with plenty of places to buy tacky T-shirts, and we strongly recommend that you spend at least an hour just wandering around.

From Memorial Day through Labor Day the Silverton Gunfighters Association stages gunfights at the corner of 12th and Blair streets Thursday, Friday, Saturday, and holidays at 5:30pm. On Sunday from June through September the Silverton Brass Band performs at 6pm on one of Silverton's street corners—don't worry, you won't have any trouble finding them, just follow the music and the crowds.

You can get walking-tour maps of the historic downtown area; information on local shops, restaurants, and lodgings; plus details on the numerous outdoor activities in the surrounding mountains from the **Silverton Chamber of Commerce,** at the intersection of Colo. 110 and U.S. 550 (P.O. Box 565), Silverton, CO 81433 (✆ **800/752-4494** or 970/387-5654; www.silvertoncolorado.com). From July through September the chamber's visitor center is open daily 9am to 6pm; in May, June, and October it's open daily 9am to 5pm; and from November through April it's open daily from 10am to 4pm. Closed New Year's Day, Easter, Thanksgiving, and Christmas.

For a step back into Silverton's Wild West days, head for the **San Juan County Historical Society Museum,** in the 1902 county jail at Greene and 15th streets (✆ **970/387-5838**). Here you'll see memorabilia of Silverton's boom days, including lots of railroad stuff and a collection of Derringer handguns. Altogether, there are three floors of historic displays, including the most popular stop—the original jail cells, a good place to snap a photo of that would-be convict you're traveling with. From this building, a tunnel leads to the mining museum next door, which recreates the feeling of being deep in a mine with displays of mining machinery, ore cars, and other mining memorabilia. There's also a shop that sells books on area history. The museum is open daily, from Memorial Day weekend through September from 9am to 5pm; and from 10am to 3pm from October 1 to 15. Admission is $5 for adults and free for children 12 and under. The adjacent **San Juan County Courthouse** has a gold-domed clock tower, and the restoration of the **Town Hall,** at 14th and Greene streets, after a devastating 1993 fire, has won national recognition.

The **Old Hundred Gold Mine** (✆ **800/872-3009** or 970/387-5444; www.mine tour.com) is located about 5 miles east of Silverton via Colo. 110, offering an underground guided tour that takes 45 to 50 minutes and starts with a ride 1,500 feet underground in an electric mine train. The tour continues with a walk through lighted tunnels where you see drilling and mucking demonstrations. There's gold panning aboveground, plus a gift shop, snack bar, and picnic area. Cost is $17 for adults 13 to 59, $7.95 for children 5 to 12 (children under 5 held on a lap are free), and $15 for seniors 60 and older. Reservations are not necessary; the temperature in the mine is about 48°F (9°C), so a sweater or jacket is recommended. The mine is open from early May through mid-October, daily from 10am to 4pm, with tours on the hour.

The self-guided **Mayflower Gold Mill Tour** (✆ **970/387-0294**) takes place in the old Sunnyside Mill, about 2 miles northeast of Silverton via Colo. 110. Former miners are sometimes on hand to demonstrate the process of milling, and you can see the historic mill and its original milling equipment, much of it still operational. A video explains the mill's history. There's also gold panning and a gift shop. Cost for a self-guided tour is $8 for those 13 to 59, $7.50 for those 60 and older, and free for children 12 and younger. Guided tours for groups of eight or more are available with advance reservations for an additional $2.50 per adult and senior. The mill is open Memorial Day weekend through September daily from 10am to 5pm.

Expert and advanced skiers and snowboarders have discovered Silverton's newest attraction, **Silverton Mountain Ski Area,** which opened in early 2002 and has been booked solid ever since. Located almost 7 miles north of Silverton, the ski area has one double chairlift that accesses more powder than most skiers have ever seen. The base is at 10,400 feet, with a peak lift-served elevation of 12,300 feet and a fairly easy hike to 13,300 feet elevation. The area's steepest run is 55 degrees and its easiest runs are 25 to 30 degrees, what most other ski areas call a really steep run. In summer the area offers scenic chairlift rides Friday, Saturday, and Sunday. The area also has a difficult mountain bike trail for experienced riders. Both guided and unguided skiing are available (guided-only skiing from mid-January through March), and the season usually runs from Thanksgiving through April. Day rate for unguided skiing is $49, and rates for guided group skiing are $99 to $129. Private guided skiing is also available. For current hours, required equipment, and other details, contact **Silverton Mountain,** P.O. Box 654, Silverton, CO 81433 (© **970/387-5706;** www.silvertonmountain.com).

WHERE TO STAY

The Wyman Hotel & Inn 🏔🏔🏔 Our top choice for overnight lodging in Silverton, the Wyman fits in beautifully with the historic ambience of this Old West mining town, but then it ought to—the hotel's been here almost as long as the town. Built in 1902 and now listed on the National Register of Historic Places, this handsome red-sandstone building has arched windows, high ceilings, Victorian-style wallpaper, and rooms and common areas furnished with antiques dating from the 1870s to the early 1900s—mostly Renaissance and East Lake styles. Rooms are individually decorated and range in size. The hotel also offers a two-room suite, a three-room suite, and a very large family room. In addition to the rooms in the hotel, a Southern Pacific Railroad caboose has been converted into a honeymoon suite, with a hand-carved antique bed from Spain and a two-person whirlpool tub (four other units also have two-person whirlpool tubs). Ten rooms have showers only, and all have top-quality king- or queen-size feather beds with down pillows and down duvets. Telephones have dataports.

Although the rooms are wonderful, it would be well worth coming here simply for the food, which is truly a gourmet experience. Breakfasts include fresh-baked muffins, fresh fruit, beverages, and an entree such as quiche with rosemary potatoes; and those who opt for the dinner package enjoy a four-course candlelight meal. A wine-and-cheese social hour is included in the rates. The hotel also contains a small art gallery featuring the work of Colorado artists. Honeymoon packages are available, and the Wyman is popular for weddings and elopements. The entire hotel is nonsmoking.

1371 Greene St., Silverton, CO 81433. © **800/609-7845** or 970/387-5372. Fax 970/387-5745. www.thewyman. com. 17 units. B&B rates $145–$165 double, from $175 suite; B&B plus dinner $245–$265 double, from $275 suite. AE, DISC, MC, V. Rates include full breakfast and afternoon wine and cheese or tea and homemade cookies. **Amenities:** Guest computer. *In room:* TV/VCR, dataport, hair dryer.

2 A Spectacular Drive Along the San Juan Skyway

The **San Juan Skyway** 🏔🏔, a 233-mile circuit, crosses five mountain passes and takes in the magnificent San Juan Mountains, as well as the cities and towns of the region. It can be accomplished in a single all-day drive from Durango or divided into several days, incorporating stops in Cortez, Telluride, and Ouray—all of which are discussed later in this chapter. Check for closed passes in winter and early spring.

The route can be driven either clockwise (heading west from Durango on U.S. 160) or counterclockwise (heading north from Durango on U.S. 550). We'll describe the clockwise route.

Eleven miles west of Durango you'll pass through the village of Hesperus, from which a county road runs 10 miles north into **La Plata Canyon,** with its mining ruins and ghost towns.

Farther west, U.S. 160 passes the entrance road to **Mesa Verde National Park.** About 45 miles west of Durango, just before Cortez, turn north on Colo. 145, which traverses the historic town of Dolores, site of the **Anasazi Heritage Center** (see section 4 of this chapter), then proceeds up the **Dolores River Valley,** a favorite of trout fishermen.

Sixty miles from Cortez, the route crosses 10,222-foot **Lizard Head Pass,** named for a startling rock spire looming above the roadside alpine meadows. It then descends 13 miles to the resort town of **Telluride,** set in a beautiful box canyon 4 miles off the main road.

Follow Colo. 145 west from Telluride down the San Miguel River valley to **Placerville.** Then turn north on Colo. 62, across 8,970-foot Dallas Divide, to Ridgway, a historic railroad town and home of **Ridgway State Park (© 970/626-5822;** www. parks.state.co.us), with a sparkling mountain reservoir, trout fishing, boating (there's a full-service marina), swimming, hiking, mountain biking, horseback riding, and camping.

From Ridgway, turn south, and follow U.S. 550 to the scenic and historic town of **Ouray.** Here begins the remarkable **Million Dollar Highway,** so named for all the mineral wealth that passed over it.

The 23 miles from Ouray over 11,008-foot **Red Mountain Pass** to Silverton is an unforgettable drive. It shimmies up the sheer sides of the Uncompahgre Gorge, through tunnels and past cascading waterfalls, then follows a historic toll road built in the 19th century. Mining equipment and log cabins are in evidence on the slopes of the iron-colored mountains, many of them over 14,000 feet in elevation. Along this route you'll pass a monument to snowplow operators who died trying to keep the road open during winter storms.

From Silverton, U.S. 550 climbs over the Molas Divide (elevation 10,910 ft.), then more or less parallels the track of the Durango & Silverton Narrow Gauge Railroad as it follows the Animas River south to Durango, passing the **Durango Mountain Resort** (p. 375) en route.

3 Cortez

45 miles W. of Durango, 203 miles S. of Grand Junction

An important archaeological center, Cortez is surrounded by a vast complex of ancient villages that dominated the Four Corners region—where Colorado, New Mexico, Arizona, and Utah's borders meet—1,000 years ago. Mesa Verde National Park, 10 miles east, is certainly the most prominent nearby attraction, drawing hundreds of thousands of visitors annually (see section 4 of this chapter). In addition, archaeological sites such as those at Canyons of the Ancients and Hovenweep national monuments as well as Ute Mountain Tribal Park are an easy drive from the city. San Juan National Forest, just to the north, offers a wide variety of recreational opportunities. The community of Cortez provides lodging, food, and supplies, making it the best spot to use as a home base when visiting these sites. Elevation is 6,200 feet.

ESSENTIALS

GETTING THERE   By Car   Cortez is located at the junction of north-south U.S. 491 and east-west U.S. 160.

As it enters Cortez from the east, U.S. 160 crosses Dolores Road (Colo. 145, which goes north to Telluride and Grand Junction), then runs due west through town for about 2 miles as Main Street. The city's main thoroughfare, Main Street, intersects U.S. 491 (Broadway) at the west end of town.

By Plane   Cortez Airport, off U.S. 160 and 491, southwest of town (© **970/565-7458;** www.cityofcortez.com), is served by **Great Lakes Airlines** (© **800/554-5111** or 970/565-9510), with direct daily flights to Denver.

Budget (© **800/527-0700** or 970/564-9012) and **Enterprise** (© **800/325-8007** or 970/565-6824) provide car rentals at the airport.

VISITOR INFORMATION   Stop at the **Colorado Welcome Center at Cortez,** Cortez City Park, 928 E. Main St. (© **970/565-4048;** www.swcolo.org), open daily from 8am to 6pm in summer and from 8am to 5pm the rest of the year; or contact the **Mesa Verde Country Visitor Information Bureau,** P.O. Box HH, Cortez, CO 81321 (© **800/253-1616;** www.mesaverdecountry.com), or the **Cortez Area Chamber of Commerce,** P.O. Box 968, Cortez, CO 81321 (© **970/565-3414;** www.cortez chamber.org).

FAST FACTS   The local hospital is **Southwest Memorial Hospital,** 1311 N. Mildred Rd. (© **970/565-6666**), which has a 24-hour emergency room. The **post office** is at 35 S. Beech St.; contact the U.S. Postal Service (© **800/275-8777;** www.usps. com) for hours and additional information.

SPECIAL EVENTS   American Indian Dances and Cultural Programs, mid-May to late August; Indian Arts and Culture Festival, Memorial Day Weekend; Ute Mountain Round-Up and Rodeo, early June; Arts and Crafts Fiesta, mid-June; Wine & Art Festival, early October; Parade of Lights, early December.

WHAT TO SEE & DO

In addition to the area's excellent archaeological sites, discussed in section 4 of this chapter, attractions here include the **Four Corners Monument,** the only place in the United States where you can stand in four states at once. Operated by the Navajo Parks and Recreation Department (© **928/871-6647;** www.navajonationparks.org), there's a flat monument marking where Utah, Colorado, New Mexico, and Arizona meet, and visitors perch for photos. The official seals of the four states are displayed, along with the motto, "Four states here meet in freedom under God." Surrounding the monument are the states' flags, flags of the Navajo Nation and Ute tribe, and the U.S. flag.

A visitor center has crafts demonstrations by Navajo artisans, and jewelry, pottery, sand paintings, and other crafts are for sale. In addition, traditional Navajo food, such as fry bread, is available. The monument is located half a mile northwest of U.S. 160, about 40 miles southwest of Cortez. It's open daily from 7am to 8pm in summer, with shorter hours in winter. Admission costs $3 per person. Allow 30 minutes.

WHERE TO STAY

Summer is the busy season here, and that's when you'll pay the highest lodging rates. Among the major chains providing comfortable, reasonably priced lodging in Cortez (zip code 81321) are **Best Western Turquoise Inn & Suites,** 535 E. Main St. (📞 **800/547-3376** or 970/565-3778), with rates for two from $59 to $159; **Comfort Inn,** 2321 E. Main St. (📞 **800/424-6423** or 970/565-3400), which charges $49 to $139 double; **Econo Lodge,** 2020 E. Main St. (📞 **800/553-2666** or 970/565-3474), with double rates of $49 to $129; **Holiday Inn Express,** 2121 E. Main St. (📞 **888/465-4329** or 970/565-6000), with rates for two from $89 to $159; **Super 8,** 505 E. Main St. (📞 **800/800-8000** or 970/565-8888), with rates of $49 to $79 double; and **Travelodge,** 440 S. Broadway (📞 **800/578-7878** or 970/565-7778), with rates for two from $45 to $79. Room tax adds about 8% to lodging bills.

Anasazi Motor Inn This standard, well-kept motel offers spacious Southwest-decorated rooms with either one king-size bed or two queens; many of the ground-floor rooms have patios. There's also a sand volleyball court, horseshoe pits, a short walking trail, and free shuttle service to downtown.

640 S. Broadway, Cortez, CO 81321. 📞 800/972-6232 or 970/565-3773. Fax 970/565-1027. www.anasazimotorinn. com. 87 units. $55–$75 double. AE, DC, DISC, MC, V. Pets accepted. **Amenities:** Restaurant (American); bar; pool (outdoor heated); hot tub; airport shuttle. *In room:* A/C, TV.

WHERE TO DINE

Homesteaders Restaurant 𝒢 AMERICAN/MEXICAN A rustic, Old West atmosphere pervades this popular family restaurant, which is decorated with historic photos and pioneer memorabilia. The menu has a good selection of home-style American basics, with charbroiled beef, including burgers, T-bones, and top sirloins. Those wanting a bit more zip might try the Southwestern steak—top sirloin smothered with salsa, green chile, and cheese. We also suggest the barbecued baby back ribs and the old-fashioned dinners, such as thin-sliced roast beef or deep-fried catfish filet. Several Mexican standards are also offered, as well as salads and vegetarian items. Smoking is not permitted.

45 E. Main St. 📞 970/565-6253. www.thehomesteaders.com. Main courses $5–$9 lunch, $7–$19 dinner. AE, DISC, MC, V. Mon–Sat 11am–9:30pm; summer also Sun 4–9:30pm.

Main St. Brewery and Restaurant 𝒢 AMERICAN Fans slice the air under a stamped-tin ceiling, and fanciful murals splash color above subdued wood paneling. The pleasant contrasts found in the decor carry over to the menu. In addition to brewpub staples such as fish and chips, pizza, and bratwurst, this brewery and restaurant offers steaks and prime rib—dry-aged Angus beef from its own herd of Angus cattle, raised with no artificial growth stimulants or antibiotics—plus a vegetarian stir-fry plate and Rocky Mountain trout. The beers brewed here go well with everything. We especially recommend the hoppy, slightly bitter Pale Export and the Munich-style Pale Bock.

21 E. Main St. 📞 970/564-9112. Main courses $5.95–$23. AE, MC, V. Daily 3:30pm–close.

Nero's 𝒢𝒢 ITALIAN/AMERICAN Our top choice in this area when we're craving something a bit different. The innovative entrees, prepared by Culinary Institute of America chef Richard Gurd, include house specialties such as the Cowboy Steak (a charbroiled 12-ounce sirloin seasoned with a spicy rub and served with pasta or fries); our favorite, the mushroom ravioli served with an Alfredo sauce, sautéed spinach, sun-dried tomatoes, and pecans; and shrimp Alfredo—sautéed shrimp with spinach served over fettuccine with Alfredo sauce and Romano cheese. There's an excellent selection of beef, plus seafood, fowl, pork, veal, and lots of homemade pasta. A small, homey restaurant with a Southwestern art-gallery decor, Nero's also offers pleasant outdoor seating in warm weather.

303 W. Main St. ℭ **970/565-7366.** http://subee.com/neros/home.html. Reservations recommended. Entrees $8.95–$21. AE, MC, V. Daily 5–9:30pm. Closed Sun in winter.

Pippo's Cafe AMERICAN   This friendly down-home cafe is an easy place to like, especially if you like a casual atmosphere, good basic American cooking, and reasonable prices. Located along busy Main Street, Pippo's serves only breakfast and lunch, and the specialty is breakfast, served during all open hours. We especially like the omelets and the homemade hash browns, but then we wouldn't turn down the steak and eggs either. The lunch menu includes the usual burger and fries, along with homemade soups, Navajo tacos, and fried chicken with mashed potatoes and gravy.

100 W. Main St. ℭ **970/565-6039.** Main courses $1.90–$5.90. MC, V. Mon–Sat 6:30am–3pm; Sun 6:30am–2pm.

4 Mesa Verde National Park & Other Archaeological Sites of the Four Corners Region

MESA VERDE NATIONAL PARK

Mesa Verde is the largest archaeological preserve in the United States, with some 4,000 known sites dating from A.D. 600 to 1300, including the most impressive cliff dwellings in the Southwest.

The earliest known inhabitants of Mesa Verde (Spanish for "green table") built subterranean pit houses on the mesa tops. During the 13th century they moved into shallow caves and constructed complex cliff dwellings. Although a massive construction project, these homes were only occupied for about a century; their residents left in about 1300 for reasons as yet undetermined.

The area was little known until ranchers Charles and Richard Wetherill chanced upon it in 1888. Looting of artifacts followed their discovery until a Denver newspaper reporter's stories aroused national interest in protecting the site. The 52,000-acre site was declared a national park in 1906—it's the only U.S. national park devoted entirely to the works of humans.

Fires have plagued the park in recent years, and burned, dead trees and blackened ground are very evident today. Two lightning-induced fires blackened about 40% of the park during the summer of 2000, closing the park for about 3 weeks. Officials said that although the park's piñon-juniper forests were severely burned, none of the major archaeological sites were damaged, and in fact the fires revealed some sites that they were not aware existed. Then a lightning-induced fire struck again in the summer of 2002, closing the park for about 10 days. It destroyed several employees' homes, a sewage treatment plant, and phone and power lines, and also damaged a water storage tank. Officials said that the only damage to archaeological sites was the scorching of the wall of one ruin.

JUST THE FACTS

ENTRY   The park entrance is located on U.S. 160, 10 miles east of Cortez and 6 miles west of Mancos.

FEES & REGULATIONS   Admission to the park for up to 1 week costs $10 per vehicle. Tours of Cliff Palace, Balcony House, and Long House are $3; ranger-guided tours of other areas are free. To protect the many archaeological sites, the Park Service has outlawed backcountry camping and off-trail hiking. It's also illegal to enter cliff dwellings without a ranger present. The Wetherill Mesa Road cannot accommodate vehicles longer than 25 feet. Cyclists must have lights to pedal through the tunnel on the entrance road.

VISITOR CENTERS & INFORMATION   **Chapin Mesa,** site of the park headquarters, museum, and a post office, is 20 miles from the park entrance on U.S. 160. The **Far View Visitor Center,** site of Far View Lodge, a restaurant, gift shop, and other facilities, is 15 miles off U.S. 160. For a park brochure, contact Mesa Verde National Park, P.O. Box 8, Mesa Verde, CO 81330 (© **970/529-4465;** www.nps.gov/ meve).

HOURS & SEASONS   The park is open daily year-round, but full interpretive services are available only from mid-June to Labor Day. In winter, the Mesa Top Road and museum remain open, but many other facilities are closed. The **Far View Visitor Center** is open from mid-April through mid-October only, from 8am to 5pm daily. The **Chapin Mesa Archeological Museum** is open daily from 8am to 6:30pm from early April through early October, daily from 8am to 5pm the rest of the year.

AVOIDING THE CROWDS   With close to half a million visitors annually, Mesa Verde seems packed at times, but the numbers are much lower just before and after the summer rush, usually from June 15 to August 15. Another way to beat the crowds is to make the 12-mile drive to Wetherill Mesa, which attracts only a small percentage of park visitors.

RANGER PROGRAMS   In addition to guided tours to the cliff dwellings (see below), rangers give nightly campfire programs at Morefield Campground in summer.

SEEING THE HIGHLIGHTS IN A DAY

If you have only a day to spend at the park, stop first at the Far View Visitor Center to buy tickets for a late-afternoon tour of either Cliff House or Balcony House— visitors are not allowed to tour both on the same day. Then travel to the Chapin Mesa archeological museum for a look at the history behind the sites you're about to see. From here, walk down the trail behind the museum to Spruce Tree House. Then drive the Mesa Top Loop Road. Cap your day with the guided tour.

EXPLORING THE PARK

The **Cliff Palace,** the park's largest and best-known site, is a four-story apartment complex with stepped-back roofs forming porches for the dwellings above. Accessible by guided tour only, it is reached by a quarter-mile downhill path. Its towers, walls, and kivas (large circular rooms used for ceremonies) are all set back beneath the rim

---

Tips **Keeping Fido Safe & Happy**

While there's plenty to do for human visitors to Mesa Verde National Park, the U.S. Park Service is not very welcoming to our canine friends, and prohibits them on all trails (the only exceptions are for service dogs, such as Seeing Eye dogs). This means that if you want to explore the park you'll need to leave your dogs behind. Fortunately, there are several kennels in the area, including **The Dog Hotel,** 33350 Colo. 184, Mancos (© **970/882-5416**), which is a well-run facility, open 7 days a week, that also offers accommodations for cats. Appointments are necessary, and pet owners must have proof of current vaccinations.

of a cliff. Another ranger-led tour takes visitors up a 32-foot ladder to explore the interior of **Balcony House.** Each of these tours is given only in summer and into fall (call for exact dates). Guided tours are also offered by Far View Lodge (see "Where to Stay & Dine in the Park," below).

Two other important sites—**Step House** and **Long House,** both on Wetherill Mesa—can be visited in summer only. Rangers lead free tours to **Spruce Tree House,** another of the major cliff-dwelling complexes, only in winter, when other park facilities are closed. Visitors can also explore Spruce Tree House on their own at any time.

Although none of the trails to the Mesa Verde sites is strenuous, the 7,000-foot elevation can make the treks tiring for visitors who aren't used to the altitude. For those who want to avoid hiking and climbing, the 12-mile **Mesa Top Road** makes a number of pit houses and cliff-side overlooks easily accessible by car. **Chapin Mesa Archeological Museum** houses artifacts and specimens related to the history of the area, including other nearby sites.

OUTDOOR ACTIVITIES   Although this isn't an outdoor recreation park per se—the reason to come here is to see the cliff dwellings and other archaeological sites—you'll find yourself hiking and climbing to get to the sites. Several longer hikes into scenic Spruce Canyon let you stretch your legs and get away from the crowds. Hikers must register at the ranger's office before setting out.

CAMPING   Open from early May to early October, **Morefield Campground** (*(C)* **800/449-2288** or 970/529-4421; www.visitmesaverde.com), 4 miles south of the park entrance, has 435 sites, including 15 with full RV hookups. The campground is set in rolling hills in a grassy area with scrub oak and brush. The attractive sites are fairly well spaced, and are mostly separated by trees and other foliage. Facilities include modern restrooms, coin-operated showers (not within easy walking distance of most campsites), picnic tables, grills, and an RV dump station. Programs on the area's human and natural history and other subjects are presented nightly at the campground amphitheater from Memorial Day weekend through Labor Day weekend. Campsites cost $20, $25 with hookups. If you're hoping to snare one of the 15 full hookup sites, try getting to the park by late morning; there are almost always nonhookup sites available. There are also several commercial campgrounds along U.S. 160, just outside the park entrance.

WHERE TO STAY & DINE IN THE PARK

We like to be where the action is, and recommend staying overnight at either the Morefield Campground (see "Camping," above) or the Far View Lodge (see below); both are operated by park concessionaire Aramark, which also operates several restaurants in the park. There are numerous lodging and dining possibilities in Cortez, too (see "Cortez," above).

Far View Lodge *(★)*   Located in the heart of Mesa Verde National Park, Far View Lodge offers not only the most convenient location for visiting the park, but also the best views of any accommodations in the area. The facility lodges guests in 17 separate buildings spread across a hilltop. Rooms aren't fancy and they're a bit on the small side, but they are well maintained and more than adequate, with Southwestern decor. "Kiva" rooms have handcrafted furniture, one king- or two queen-size beds, bathrobes, CD players, and other upscale amenities. Most standard rooms have one queen-size bed or two doubles, although a variety of bed combinations is available. For a couple, we prefer the rooms with one bed—they seem less cramped than rooms with two

---

Fun Fact **What's in a Name?**

The prehistoric inhabitants of the ancient villages of the Four Corners region have long been known as the Anasazi. That word is being phased out, however, in favor of "Ancestral Puebloans" or "ancient Pueblo people," because modern American Indians who trace their roots to the Ancestral Puebloans consider the word Anasazi demeaning. "Anasazi" is a Navajo word meaning "enemy of my people," as the Navajos considered the Ancestral Puebloans their enemies.

---

beds. There are no TVs, but each unit has a private balcony, and the views are magnificent in all directions.

There's a 24-hour front desk, complimentary morning coffee and newspaper, and gift shop. Half- and full-day guided tours of the park embark from the lodge and campground daily during the warmer months. Rates for full-day tours to Cliff Palace and Spruce Tree House, including lunch, are $65 adults, $48 children 5 to 12, and free for children under 5. The cost for the half-day tours to Spruce Tree House or Balcony House is $39 adults, $28 children 5 to 12, and free for those under 5.

Mesa Verde National Park (P.O. Box 277), Mancos, CO 81328. (C) **800/449-2288** or 970/529-4421. www.visit mesaverde.com. 150 units. Open late Apr through late Oct only. $119–$149 double. AE, DC, DISC, MC, V. Pets accepted with a deposit. **Amenities:** 2 restaurants (Southwestern American). *In room:* Fridge (in some units), coffeemaker.

NEARBY ARCHAEOLOGICAL SITES
CORTEZ CULTURAL CENTER

The center, 25 N. Market St., Cortez ((C) **970/565-1151;** www.cortezculturalcenter. org), includes a museum with exhibits on both prehistoric and modern American Indians, an art gallery with displays of regional art, a good gift shop offering crafts by local tribal members, and a variety of programs including American Indian dances during the summer. From June through August the center is open Monday through Saturday from 10am to 10pm, and the rest of the year it is open Monday through Saturday from 10am to 5pm. Admission is free and you should plan to spend at least an hour. Call or check the website for the schedule of Indian dances and other programs, which are also free.

UTE MOUNTAIN TRIBAL PARK *ww*

If you liked Mesa Verde, but would have enjoyed it more without the company of so many fellow tourists, you'll *love* the Ute Mountain Tribal Park (P.O. Box 109, Towaoc, CO 81334; (C) **800/847-5485** or 970/565-3751 ext. 330; www.utemountainute. com/tribalpark.htm). Set aside by the Ute Mountain tribe to preserve its heritage, the 125,000-acre park—which abuts Mesa Verde National Park—includes ancient pictographs and petroglyphs as well as hundreds of surface sites and cliff dwellings that are similar in size and complexity to those in Mesa Verde.

Access to the park is strictly limited to guided tours. Full- and half-day tours begin at the Ute Mountain Museum and Visitor Center at the junction of U.S. 491 and U.S. 160, 20 miles south of Cortez. Mountain-biking and backpacking trips are also offered. No food, water, lodging, gasoline, or other services are available within the park. Some climbing of ladders is necessary on the full-day tour. There's one primitive **campground** ($12 per vehicle; reservations required).

Charges for tours in your vehicle start at $22 per person for a half-day, $42 for a full day; it's $8 per person extra to go in the tour guide's vehicle, and reservations are required.

ANASAZI HERITAGE CENTER

When the Dolores River was dammed and the McPhee Reservoir was created in 1985, some 1,600 ancient archaeological sites were threatened. Four percent of the project costs were set aside for archaeological work, and over two million artifacts and other prehistoric items were rescued. Most are displayed in this museum. Located 10 miles north of Cortez, it is set into a hillside near the remains of 12th-century sites.

Operated by the Bureau of Land Management, the center emphasizes visitor involvement. Children and adults are invited to examine corn-grinding implements, a loom and other weaving materials, and a re-created pit house. You can touch artifacts 1,000 to 2,000 years old, examine samples through microscopes, use interactive computer programs, and engage in video lessons in archaeological techniques.

A half-mile trail leads from the museum to the **Dominguez Pueblo Ruins,** atop a low hill, with a beautiful view across the Montezuma Valley.

The center also serves as the visitor center for Canyons of the Ancients National Monument (see below). It is located at 27501 Colo. 184, Dolores (© **970/882-5600;** www.co.blm.gov/ahc). It's open March through October, daily from 9am to 5pm; November through February, daily from 9am to 4pm; and is closed Thanksgiving, Christmas, and New Year's Day. An admission fee of $3 for adults is charged March through October only; admission is free for those 17 and under. Allow 2 hours.

CANYONS OF THE ANCIENTS NATIONAL MONUMENT

Among the country's newest national monuments, Canyons of the Ancients was created by presidential proclamation in June 2000. The 164,000-acre national monument, located west of Cortez, contains thousands of archaeological sites—what some claim is the highest density of archaeological sites in the United States—including the remains of villages, cliff dwellings, sweat lodges, and petroglyphs at least 700 years old, and possibly as much as 10,000 years old.

Canyons of the Ancients includes **Lowry Pueblo,** an excavated 12th-century village that is located 26 miles from Cortez via U.S. 491, on C.R. CC, 9 miles west of Pleasant View. This pueblo, which was likely abandoned by 1200, is believed to have housed about 100 people. It has standing walls from 40 rooms plus 9 kivas (circular underground ceremonial chambers). A short, self-guided interpretive trail leads past a kiva and continues to the remains of a great kiva, which, at 54 feet in diameter, is among the largest ever found. There are also a picnic area, drinking water, and toilets.

Canyons of the Ancients is managed by the Bureau of Land Management, and as yet has no on-site visitor center or even a contact station. Those wishing to explore the monument are strongly advised to contact or preferably stop first at the visitor center located at **Anasazi Heritage Center** (see above) for information, especially current road conditions and directions. Information is also available online at www.co.blm. gov/canm, and from the Welcome Center in Cortez (see the Cortez section, earlier). Allow at least 2 hours.

HOVENWEEP NATIONAL MONUMENT

Preserving some of the most striking and isolated archaeological sites in the Four Corners area, this national monument straddles the Colorado-Utah border, 40 miles west of Cortez.

Hovenweep is the Ute word for "deserted valley," appropriate because its inhabitants apparently left around 1300. The monument contains six separate sites, and is noted for mysterious, 20-foot-high sandstone towers, some square, others oval, circular, or D-shaped. Archaeologists have suggested their possible function as everything from guard or signal towers, celestial observatories, and ceremonial structures to water towers or granaries.

A ranger station, with exhibits, restrooms, and drinking water, is located at the **Square Tower Site,** in the Utah section of the monument, the most impressive and best preserved of the sites. The **Hovenweep Campground,** with 30 sites, is open year-round. Sites are fairly small—most appropriate for tents or small pickup truck campers—but a few sites can accommodate RVs up to 25 feet long. The campground has flush toilets, drinking water, picnic tables, and fire pits, but no showers or RV hookups. Cost is $10 per night; reservations are not accepted, but the campground rarely fills.

From Cortez, take U.S. 160 south to C.R. G (McElmo Canyon Rd.), and follow signs into Utah and the monument. The other five sites are difficult to find, and you'll need to obtain detailed driving directions and check on current road conditions before setting out. Summer temperatures can reach over 100°F (38°C), and water supplies are limited—so take your own and carry a canteen, even on short walks. Bug repellent is advised, as gnats can be a nuisance in late spring.

The visitor center/ranger station is open daily from 8am to 6pm from April through September and 8am to 5pm the rest of the year; it's closed New Year's Day, Thanksgiving, and Christmas. Trails are open from sunrise to sunset. Admission for up to a week costs $6 per vehicle or $3 per person on bike or foot. For advance information, contact Hovenweep National Monument, McElmo Route, Cortez, CO 81321 (© **970/562-4282;** www.nps.gov/hove).

5 Telluride

126 miles N. of Durango, 127 miles S. of Grand Junction

This was one seriously rowdy town a century ago—in fact, this is where Butch Cassidy robbed his first bank, in 1889. Incorporated with the boring name of Columbia in 1878, the mining town assumed its present name the following decade. Some say the name came from tellurium, a gold-bearing ore, while others insist the name really means "to hell you ride," referring to the town's boisterous nature.

Telluride became a National Historic District in 1964, and in 1968 entrepreneur Joe Zoline set to work on a "winter recreation area second to none." The Telluride Ski Company opened its first runs in 1972, and Telluride was a boomtown again. Telluride's first summer festivals (bluegrass in June, film in Sept) were celebrated the following year. Today, the resort, at 8,745 feet elevation, is a year-round destination for mountain bikers, skiers, anglers, and hikers.

ESSENTIALS
GETTING THERE   By Car   Telluride is located on Colo. 145. From Cortez, follow Colo. 145 northeast for 73 miles. From the north (Montrose), turn west off U.S. 550 at Ridgway, onto Colo. 62. Proceed 25 miles to Placerville, and turn left (southeast) onto Colo. 145. Thirteen miles ahead is a junction—a right turn will take you to Cortez, but for Telluride, continue straight ahead 4 miles to the end of a box canyon. From Durango, in summer take U.S. 550 north to Colo. 62, and follow the

directions above; in winter it's best to take the route through Cortez and avoid Red Mountain Pass above Silverton.

By Plane   **Telluride Regional Airport** (© **970/728-5313**), 5 miles west of Telluride atop a plateau at 9,078 feet, is served year-round by **Great Lakes Airline** (© 800/ 554-5111) from Denver and **America West** (© 800/235-9292) from Phoenix. During ski season, flights from various cities are available from **American Airlines** (© 800/433-7300), **Continental Airlines** (© 800/525-0280), and **United Airlines** (© 800/241-6522).

VISITOR INFORMATION   Contact **Telluride & Mountain Village Convention & Visitors Bureau,** 630 W. Colorado Ave. (P.O. Box 1009), Telluride, CO 81435 (© **888/605-2578;** www.visittelluride.com). The **Telluride Visitor Information Center,** open daily from 9am to 6pm, can be found at the corner of West Colorado Avenue and Davis Street, on the west side of town.

GETTING AROUND   The city is located on the San Miguel River, where it flows out of a box canyon formed by the 14,000-foot peaks of the San Juan Mountains. Colo. 145 enters town from the west and becomes Colorado Avenue, the main street.

With restaurants, shops, and attractions within easy walking distance of most lodging facilities, many visitors leave their cars parked and use their feet. However, if you do want to ride there's a free town shuttle in winter and summer. Telluride Mountain Village, at 9,500 feet, can be reached in winter and summer by a free gondola, operating daily from 7am to midnight. Motorists can take Mountain Village Boulevard off Colo. 145, a mile south of the Telluride junction.

Budget (© **800/527-0700** or 970/728-4642) and **National** (© **800/227-7368** or 970/728-9380) provide car rentals, including vans and four-wheel-drive vehicles, at the airport, and **Dollar** (© **800/800-4000** or 970/369-0020) has an outlet in Telluride.

FAST FACTS   The hospital, **Telluride Medical Center,** with a 24-hour emergency room, is at 500 W. Pacific Ave. (© **970/728-3848**). The **post office** is at 150 S. Willow St.; call the U.S. Postal Service (© **800/275-8777;** www.usps.com) for hours and other information. For **road conditions,** call © **877/315-7623.**

SPECIAL EVENTS   Telluride Wine Festival, late June; Chamber Music Festival, mid-August; Culinary and Art Festival, late August; Imogene Pass Run, early September; Oktoberfest, early October. See also "The Festival Scene," below.

DOWNHILL SKIING & SNOWBOARDING

The elegant European-style Mountain Village, built in 1987, offers a fascinating contrast to the laid-back community of artists, shopkeepers, and dropouts in the 1870s Victorian mining town of Telluride below. Located midmountain at an elevation of 9,450 feet, the Mountain Village offers ski-in/ski-out accommodations; a variety of slope-side restaurants; and great skiing.

The mountain's **South Face,** which drops sharply from the summit to the town of Telluride, is characterized by steep moguls, tree-and-glade skiing, and challenging groomed pitches for experts and advanced intermediates. **Lift 4,** which rises from the Mountain Village Resort, caters to intermediate skiers. The broad, gentle slopes of the **Meadows** stretch to the foot of Sunshine Peak. This part of the mountain, with trails over 2½ miles long devoted entirely to novice skiers, is served by a high-speed quad chair. Average annual snowfall is 300 inches (25 ft.). The gently rolling slopes of **Ute**

Park (Lift 11) serve as the beginner training area, while **Prospect** (Lift 12) accesses intermediate and expert terrain. **Gold Hill** (Lift 14) offers intermediate and expert skiers an expanse of steep terrain as well as breathtaking views.

In all, Telluride offers more than 1,700 acres of skiable terrain. The lift-served vertical drop is an impressive 3,530 feet from the 12,255-foot summit. The mountain has 84 trails served by 16 lifts (two high-speed gondolas, seven high-speed quads, two triples, two doubles, two surface lifts, and one Magic Carpet). Of the trails, 24% are rated for beginners, 38% for intermediates, and 38% for experts. The longest run here, at 4½ miles, is **Galloping Goose,** but for some of the most spectacular views in Colorado, ski the aptly-named run **See Forever.** Telluride also has one of the top **snowboarding parks** in Colorado, offering more than 13 acres of terrain.

Full-day lift tickets during the regular season cost about $76 for adults, $45 for children 6 to 12, $56 for seniors 65 and older, and are free for children under 6. Rates over the Christmas holidays are higher, and rates at the very beginning of the season are lower. Ski and snowboarding lessons are offered, as well as child-care. The resort is usually open daily from 9am to 4pm from Thanksgiving to early April.

For additional information, contact **Telluride Ski and Golf Company,** 565 Mountain Village Blvd., Telluride, CO 81435 (© **800/801-4832** or 970/728-6900; www. tellurideskiresort.com).

OTHER WINTER ACTIVITIES

In addition to skiing at Telluride Ski Resort, there are plenty of other opportunities for cold-weather adventures in the Telluride area. Much of it takes place at **Town Park,** at the east end of town (© **970/728-3071;** www.town.telluride.co.us), where there are groomed cross-country trails, daytime sledding and tubing at Firecracker Hill, and free ice skating. There's also free ice skating at the outdoor rink in the Mountain Village. Skate rentals are available at local sporting-goods stores. The **River Corridor Trail** follows the San Miguel River from Town Park to the valley floor. Popular with bikers and hikers in warm weather, it's perfect for cross-country skiing and skate-skiing after the snow falls. The Mountain Village at Telluride Ski Resort (see above) has 19 miles of **Nordic trails,** which connect with 12 miles of groomed trails at Town Park and River Corridor Trail, giving cross-country skiers a total of 31 miles.

Guided snowmobile tours ranging from 2 hours to all day, with rates starting at about $150 for one rider on one machine, are offered by several local companies including **Dave's Mountain Tours** (© **970/728-9749;** www.telluridetours.com). Those who want to (and can afford to) take a helicopter to some of the best powder skiing available should contact **Telluride Helitrax** (© **866/435-4754** or 970/728-8377; www.helitrax.net), with rates for a 5- or 6-run day of about $950 per person.

WARM-WEATHER & YEAR-ROUND ACTIVITIES

Telluride isn't just a ski town—there's a wide variety of year-round outdoor activities. **Town Park** (see above) is home to the community's various festivals. It also has a public outdoor pool, open in summer, plus tennis courts, sand volleyball courts, a small outdoor basketball court, a skateboarding ramp, playing fields, picnic area, and fishing pond (see "Fishing," below). A campground for tent and car campers, open from May 15 to October 15, has 34 sites, showers ($2) but no RV hookups, and costs $15 to $20 per night.

There are a number of outfitting companies in the Telluride area, including **Telluride Outside,** 121 W. Colorado Ave. (© **800/831-6230** or 970/728-3895;

www.tellurideoutside.com), which offers a wide range of guided adventures. Equipment rentals are available throughout Telluride and Mountain Village. You'll find mountain bikes, fishing gear, camping equipment, and inflatable kayaks at a number of locations operated by **Telluride Sports** (© **800/828-7547** or 970/728-4477; www.telluridesports.com).

FISHING   There's excellent fishing in the San Miguel River through Telluride, but it's even better in nearby alpine lakes, including Silver Lake, reached by foot in Bridal Veil Basin, and Trout and Priest lakes, about 12 miles south via Colo. 145. At Town Park there's the Kids Fishin' Pond for children 12 and under, which is stocked Memorial Day to Labor Day.

FOUR-WHEELING   To see old ghost towns, mining camps, and spectacular mountain scenery from the relative comfort of a bouncing four-wheel-drive vehicle, join **Telluride Outside** (see above) or **Dave's Mountain Tours** (see "Other Winter Activities," above). A variety of trips are offered, including rides over the 13,000-foot Imogene Pass jeep road, with prices for full-day trips about $115 for adults and $95 for children 12 and younger. Half-day trips are about $75 and $55, respectively.

GOLF   The 18-hole par-71 **Telluride Golf Course** is located at Telluride Mountain Village (© **970/728-6366** or 970/728-6157). Greens fees with the required cart are $160 from July through Labor Day, lower at other times.

HIKING & MOUNTAINEERING   The mountains around Telluride offer innumerable opportunities for hiking, mountaineering, and backpacking. Sporting-goods stores and the visitor center have maps of trails in the Telluride area. Especially popular are the easy 4-mile (round-trip) **Bear Creek Canyon Trail** ⭑, which starts at the end of South Pine Street and leads to a picturesque waterfall; the **Jud Wiebe Trail** that begins at the north end of Aspen Street and does a 2.7-mile loop above the town, offering views of Bridal Veil Falls, the town, and ski area; and the 1.8-mile (one-way) hike to the top of **Bridal Veil Falls,** which starts at the east end of Telluride Canyon.

HORSEBACK RIDING   One of the best ways to see this spectacular country is by horse. **Telluride Horseback Adventures** (© **970/728-9611;** www.ridewithroudy.com) has "gentle horses for gentle people and fast horses for fast people, and for people who don't like to ride, horses that don't like to be rode." Another good company is **Many Ponies Outfit** (© **970/728-6278;** www.manyponiesoutfit.com). Rates are about $80 for a 2-hour ride, $130 for a half-day ride, and $190 for a full day in the saddle.

MOUNTAIN BIKING   Telluride is a major mountain-biking center. The **San Juan Hut System** links Telluride with Moab, Utah, via a 206-mile-long network of backcountry dirt roads. Every 35 miles is a primitive cabin, with bunks, a wood stove, propane cooking stove, and cooking gear. The route, open to mountain bikers from June through September, is appropriate for intermediate level riders in good physical condition, and an advanced technical single track is found near the huts for more experienced cyclists. Cost for riders who plan to make the whole trip is about $550, which includes use of the six huts, three meals daily, sleeping bags at each hut, and maps and trail descriptions. Shorter trips, guide services, and vehicle shuttles are also available. For information contact San Juan Hut System, P.O. Box 773, Ridgeway, CO 81432 (© **970/626-3033;** www.sanjuanhuts.com).

SEEING THE SIGHTS

The best way to see the Telluride National Historic District, examine its hundreds of historic buildings, and get a feel for the West of the late 1800s is to take to the streets. Either follow the **walking tour** described in the *Telluride Visitor's Guide,* available at the Telluride Visitor Information Center (see "Visitor Information," above), or rent a minidisk player with a disk and accompanying map at the Telluride Historical Museum (see below) for one of the recorded **audio walking tours** of Telluride. Cost of the audio tour rental is $7, and there are five tours available, each concentrating on a different part of the community.

Among the buildings you'll see are the **San Miguel County Courthouse,** Colorado Avenue at Oak Street, built in 1887 and still in use today. A block north and west, at Columbia Avenue and Aspen Street, is the **L. L. Nunn House,** home of the late-19th-century mining engineer who created the first high-voltage alternating-current power plant in the world. Two blocks east of Fir Street, on Galena Avenue at Spruce Street, is **St. Patrick's Catholic Church,** built in 1895, whose wooden Stations of the Cross figures were carved in Austria's Tyrol region. Perhaps Telluride's most famous landmark is the **New Sheridan Hotel** and the **Sheridan Opera House,** opposite the county courthouse at Colorado and Oak. The hotel, built in 1895, rivaled Denver's famed Brown Palace Hotel in service and cuisine in its early days. The exquisite opera house, added in 1914, boasts a Venetian scene painted on its roll curtain.

Colorado's highest waterfall (365 ft.) can be seen from the east end of Colorado Avenue. **Bridal Veil Falls** freezes in winter, then slowly melts in early spring, creating a dramatic effect. Perched at the top edge of the falls is a National Historic Landmark, a hydroelectric power plant that served area mines in the late 1800s. Recently restored and once again supplying power to the community, it's accessible by hiking or driving a switchback, four-wheel-drive road.

Telluride Historical Museum 🏛🏛 This fine museum should be the first stop in Telluride for anyone interested in learning about the history of this Wild West town. Built in 1896 as the community hospital, this beautifully restored facility contains a collection of some 9,000 artifacts and 1,400 historic photos that show what Telluride was like when the likes of Butch Cassidy stalked the streets. Exhibits include hard rock mining, with displays of mining equipment and models of mines and mills; the narrow-gauge railroad; the area's Ute Indian heritage; the history of medical facilities and treatments in Telluride (this was the town hospital, after all); and the development of the town's AC electric power—the world's first AC-generating plant was built here in the 1890s. There is also a replica of a local mining family's cabin in the early 1900s, plus exhibits on the town's Victorian architecture and Telluride's emergence as a major outdoor recreation destination. You'll learn about train and bank robber Cassidy and other historic figures from Telluride's past, and see some of the fancy dresses worn by Big Billie, one of the community's leading madams during the town's red-light days. The museum store is a good source for books on the area's history—an especially good local read is *Tomboy Bride* by Harriet Backus—and you can rent equipment for a self-guided audio tour of Telluride (see above). Allow 1 to 2 hours.

201 W. Gregory Ave., at the top of Fir St. 🕿 **970/728-3344.** www.telluridemuseum.com. Admission $5 adults, $3 seniors and students 6–17, free for children under 5. Summer Tues–Sat 11am–5pm, Sun 1–5pm; the rest of the year Tues–Sat 11am–5pm.

THE FESTIVAL SCENE

Telluride must be the most festival-happy town in America, and visitors come from around the world to see the finest new films, hear the best musicians, and even pick the most exotic mushrooms. In addition to the phone numbers listed, you can get additional details and often tickets from **Telluride & Mountain Village Convention & Visitors Bureau** (see "Visitor Information," above).

The **Telluride Film Festival** 🐾🐾, an influential festival within the film industry that takes place over Labor Day weekend, has premiered some of the finest films produced in recent years (*The Crying Game, The Piano,* and *Sling Blade* are just a few examples). What truly sets it apart, however, is the casual interaction between stars and attendees. Open-air films and seminars are free to all. Call (© **970/728-4640**) for further information.

MountainFilm, which takes place every Memorial Day weekend, brings together filmmakers, writers, and outdoor enthusiasts to celebrate mountains, adventure, and the environment. Four days are filled with films, seminars, and presentations; recent guests have included Sir Edmund Hillary. Call © **970/728-4123** for tickets and information.

The **Telluride Bluegrass Festival** 🐾🐾 is one of the most intense and renowned bluegrass, folk, and country jam sessions in the United States. Held over 4 days during mid- to late June in conjunction with the Bluegrass Academy, recent lineups have featured Mary Chapin Carpenter, Mark O'Connor, Shawn Colvin, and James Taylor. Call © **800/624-2422** for details.

Telluride Jazz Celebration, a 2-day event in early August, is marked by day concerts in Town Park and evening happenings in downtown saloons. Recent performers have included Leon Russell, Marleena Shaw, Stanley Jordan, and Terence Blanchard. Call © **970/728-7009** for information.

Nothing Fest, a nonevent begun in the early 1990s, is just that—nothing special happens, and it doesn't happen all over town. It's usually scheduled in mid-July. When founder Dennis Wrestler was asked how long the festival would continue, he responded, "How can you cancel something that doesn't happen?" Admission is free, and you can get all the noninformation you need from Telluride & Mountain Village Convention & Visitors Bureau (see above, or don't).

WHERE TO STAY

Telluride's lodging rates probably have more different "seasons" than anywhere else in Colorado. Generally speaking, you'll pay top dollar for a room over the Christmas holidays, during the film and bluegrass festivals, and at certain other peak times. Non-holiday skiing is a bit cheaper, summertime lodging (except for festival times) is cheaper yet, and you may find some real bargains in spring and fall. The key to finding inexpensive lodging and avoiding crowds is timing; unless you particularly want to attend the Bluegrass Festival, plan your trip another time. You're also much more likely to find attractive package deals on skiing and other activities if you go during quieter times, and not on weekends.

Telluride has a wide variety of lodging options, including B&Bs, hotels, private homes, and in our opinion, far too many condominiums. Many are managed by **ResortQuest Telluride** (© **866/538-7731;** www.resortquesttelluride.com). Perhaps the best way to book lodging, however, is with the **Telluride & Mountain Village Convention & Visitors Bureau** (© **888/605-2578;** www.visittelluride.com). Room tax adds a bit over 12%.

EXPENSIVE

Camel's Garden Resort Hotel 🏜️🏜️ This luxury property, with 30 rooms and suites plus six condo units, has a perfect location—it's ski-in/ski-out, only steps from the town gondola, and also within 2 short blocks of the main shopping and dining section of historic Telluride. The hotel rooms—even the smallest, least expensive ones—are spacious, with the feel of upscale condo units, and all have high-speed Internet and two-line phones with voice mail. All units have cherry-oak furnishings, Italian marble bathrooms with oversized tubs, CD players, and gas fireplaces. All the condos and suites and all but four of the hotel rooms have balconies, with views of either the town or mountains. Rooms have quality beds (mostly kings) on pedestals (step stools are available on request). The simple but tasteful decor includes nature prints and black-and-white photos of the area. The one-, two-, three-, and four-bedroom condos are huge, with complete kitchens, washer/dryers, jetted tubs and showers, and heated towel racks.

The continental breakfast includes the usual fresh fruit, juices, coffee, tea, and cereals, plus excellent baked goods from an on-site bakery. Afternoon refreshments are served during ski season. Other amenities include a 25-foot outdoor jetted hot tub that offers great views of the nearby mountains, a sporting-goods store, and ski storage and ski valet services. The entire property is nonsmoking.

250 W. San Juan Ave. (P.O. Box 4145), Telluride, CO 81435. © 888/772-2635 or 970/728-9300. Fax 970/728-0433. www.camelsgarden.com. 36 units. Ski season and festivals $375–$675 double hotel room and suite, $725–$2,500 condo; other times $155–$395 double hotel room and suite, $460–$900 condo. Rates include continental breakfast. AE, DC, DISC, MC, V. Free underground heated parking (6-ft., 4-in. height limit); outside parking available for larger vehicles. **Amenities:** Restaurant (Continental); spa; Jacuzzi; steam room; laundry. *In room:* TV/VCR, dataport, safe deposit boxes available on request.

MODERATE

Ice House Lodge and Condominiums A full-service lodging just half a block from the Oak Street chairlift, the Ice House offers casual and comfortable accommodations in a European alpine style. Stairs and an elevator ascend from the ground-floor entrance to the lobby, which is furnished with simple Southwestern pieces. The decor carries to the guest rooms, which contain a king-size bed and sleeper sofa or two full-size beds, European comforters, custom-made light wood furniture, and great mountain views from private decks. Thirty-nine of the rooms have shower/tub combos with oversized tubs; three rooms have showers only. The one-, two-, and three-bedroom condominium units have full kitchens, washers and dryers, two bathrooms, and a large deck. Guests also have access to a nearby spa.

310 S. Fir St. (P.O. Box 2909), Telluride, CO 81435. © 800/544-3436 or 970/728-6300. Fax 970/728-6358. www.ice houselodge.com. 42 units. Ski season and festivals $245–$650 double lodge room and suite, $450–$1,149 condo; other times $155–$425 double lodge room and suite, $375–$875 condo. Rates include continental breakfast and afternoon refreshments. AE, DC, DISC, MC, V. **Amenities:** Pool (half indoors and half outdoors); hot tub; steam room; limited room service; massage; laundry service. *In room:* TV, minibar.

New Sheridan Hotel 🏜️ The pride of Telluride when it was built in 1895, the New Sheridan reached the peak of its fame in 1902 when presidential candidate William Jennings Bryan delivered a speech from a platform outside. Completely renovated in 1995, the decor of this delightful historic hotel, located a few blocks from the slopes, still proclaims its Victorian heritage while introducing the comforts of the modern age. Rollaways or day beds are available; some units have whirlpool tubs. The suites, in a separate building, are condominium-style units, with a full kitchen, living room, and bedrooms. The Sheridan lounge, with an Austrian-made cherrywood bar, is on the hotel's first floor. Smoking is not permitted.

231 W. Colorado Ave. (P.O. Box 980), Telluride, CO 81435. © 800/200-1891 or 970/728-4351. Fax 970/728-5024. www.newsheridan.com. 32 units (24 with private bathroom). $100–$300 double; $200–$425 suite. Rates include full breakfast. AE, DC, MC, V. **Amenities:** Restaurant (American), bar. *In room:* TV, dataport.

INEXPENSIVE

The Victorian Inn ✦ *Value*   Built in 1976, in keeping with the turn-of-the-20th-century flavor of the town, the well-maintained and service-oriented Victorian offers a pleasant alternative to the seemingly hundreds of condos that populate Telluride. The spacious rooms, decorated with Victorian-style furnishings, are fully carpeted and have individually controlled heating, one or two queen beds, and refrigerators. Two units have kitchenettes, and there is also a honeymoon suite and a cottage. The continental breakfast includes fresh-baked pastries, coffee, juice, assorted teas, and hot cocoa. The inn is located a half-block from Main Street, the free gondola, and ski lift no. 8. Smoking is not permitted.

401 W. Pacific Ave. (P.O. Box 217), Telluride, CO 81435. © 800/611-9893 or 970/728-6601. Fax 970/728-3233. www.tellurideinn.com. 32 units. $99–$249 double. Children 12 and under stay free in parent's room. Rates include continental breakfast. AE, DC, DISC, MC, V. **Amenities:** Hot tub; dry sauna; coin-op laundry. *In room:* TV, dataport, fridge, coffeemaker, hair dryer.

WHERE TO DINE

Telluride lives by its seasons, and some restaurants will close for a few weeks in the slow seasons, generally spring and fall.

EXPENSIVE

Cosmopolitan ✦✦ CREATIVE AMERICAN   An elegant fine-dining restaurant, the Cosmopolitan is also casual enough for a relaxing meal after a hard day on the slopes. The decor is modern and comfortable, and there's a delightful enclosed patio. The dinner menu includes a variety of dishes—beef, fish, lamb, duck, and vegetarian—all prepared with an innovative flair by chef-owner Chad Scothorn. Recommended dishes are the sesame grilled wild king salmon with shoestring sweet potatoes, sesame vegetables, and seaweed; and the all-natural Colorado lamb loin with polenta, grilled eggplant, and roasted red pepper rouille. The wine list—there are more than 200 wines—has received the "Award of Excellence" from *Wine Spectator* magazine.

300 W. San Juan Ave., in the Hotel Columbia © 970/728-1292. www.cosmotelluride.com. Reservations recommended. Main courses $15–$32. AE, MC, V. Daily 5–9:30pm.

MODERATE

Fat Alley *Value* BARBECUE/AMERICAN   A favorite of local ski bums with big appetites and near-empty wallets, Fat Alley offers a variety of hickory-smoked meats, sandwiches, burgers, and vegetarian items. In a small, simply decorated, cafe-style restaurant, it delivers spicy pork spare ribs or beef ribs by the rack or half rack, and whole, half, or quarter roast chicken. Sandwiches include smoked brisket, chicken, or pork shoulder; and vegetarian entrees include a ziti and black-bean plate. It's also worth a visit just for the peach cobbler.

122 S. Oak St. © 970/728-3985. Reservations not accepted. Main courses $5.95–$14. AE, MC, V. Daily 11am–10pm.

INEXPENSIVE

Maggie's Bakery & Cafe AMERICAN   The atmosphere here is simple, with oak tables and antique cookie jars, and the cuisine is geared toward those who appreciate home-baked breads and pastries, and hearty sandwiches. Breakfast dishes include traditional bacon and eggs with potatoes and fresh-baked bread, pancakes, biscuits with sausage gravy, and fresh fruit. Lunch possibilities include large burgers on home-baked buns, a variety of deli and vegetarian sandwiches, pizzas, and soups.

217 E. Colorado Ave. ✆ **970/728-3334.** Reservations not accepted. Breakfast and lunch $3.95–$7.95. No credit cards. Daily 7:30am–3pm.

6 Ouray

73 miles N. of Durango, 96 miles S. of Grand Junction

Named for the greatest chief of the southern Ute tribe, whose homeland was in this area, Ouray, at an elevation of 7,760 feet, got its start in 1876 as a gold- and silver-mining camp. Within 10 years it had 1,200 residents, a school, a hospital, dozens of saloons and brothels, and even a few churches. Today Ouray retains much of its 19th-century charm, with many of its original buildings still standing. It offers visitors a restful getaway while serving as home base for exploring the beautiful San Juan Mountains, with peaks rising to over 14,000 feet.

ESSENTIALS

GETTING THERE   By Car   U.S. 550 runs through the heart of Ouray, paralleling the Uncompahgre River, and connecting it with Durango to the south and Montrose to the north. As you enter town from the north, the highway becomes Main Street. Above Third Avenue, U.S. 550 begins its climb up switchbacks to the Million Dollar Highway.

VISITOR INFORMATION   Stop at the **Ouray Visitor Center** beside the Ouray Hot Springs Pool, on U.S. 550 at the north end of town, open from 9am to 5pm Monday through Saturday, 10am to 4pm Sunday; or contact the **Ouray Chamber Resort Association,** P.O. Box 145, Ouray, CO 81427 (✆ **800/228-1876** or 970/ 325-4746; www.ouraycolorado.com).

FAST FACTS   The **post office** is at 620 Main St.; contact the U.S. Postal Service (✆ **800/275-8777;** www.usps.com) for hours and additional information.

SPECIAL EVENTS   Ouray Ice Festival, mid-January; Evenings of History Lectures, June; the Artists' Alpine Holiday, August; Oktoberfest, early October.

WHAT TO SEE & DO

The main summertime outdoor activity here is exploring the spectacularly beautiful mountains and forests by foot, mountain bike, horse, or four-wheel-drive vehicle. Our favorite local outfitter, which can arrange for a variety of outdoor adventures, is **Switzerland of America,** 226 Seventh Ave. (✆ **800/432-5337** or 970/325-4484; www.soajeep.com), which also rents four-wheel-drive jeeps for about $135 per day. The company leads jeep tours into the high country ($60 for a half-day, $125 for a full day), and arranges horseback rides (starting at $60 per person for 2 hr.), raft rides ($65 for a half-day on the San Miguel River), and balloon rides ($225). Children 12 and under are charged about half. Another local company offering jeep rentals and tours at similar rates is **Colorado West,** 701 Main St., Ouray (✆ **800/648-5337** or 970/325-4014; www.coloradowesttours.com).

At the southwest corner of Ouray, at Oak Street above Third Avenue, the **Box Canyon Falls & Park** ✪✪ (✆ **970/325-4464**), which features among the most impressive waterfalls in the Rockies. The Uncompahgre River tumbles 285 feet through—not over, *through*—a cliff: It's easy to get a feeling of vertigo as you study the spectacle. The trail to the bottom of the falls is easy; to the top it is moderate to strenuous. Admission to the area is $3 for adults, $2.50 for seniors 65 and older, and $1.50 for children 5 to 12. It's open daily 8am to 8pm or dark, whichever comes first.

Winter visitors will likely be basing themselves in Ouray to ski at Telluride or head out into the mountains on cross-country skis or snowshoes, but Ouray's main claim to winter fame is the **Ouray Ice Park,** located in the southwest corner of town off U.S. 550 (© 800/432-4170 or 970/325-4061; www.ourayicepark.com), which Ouray folks claim is the world's first park devoted exclusively to the sport of ice climbing. Climbing in the park is free and it's open at any time during the winter. Ice-climbing courses are offered by **San Juan Mountain Guides** (© 970/325-4925; www.ourayclimbing. com); a 2-day basic ice-climbing course costs $315 and includes all equipment.

Bachelor-Syracuse Mine Tour 🎯🎯 For a fun time where you'll actually learn something, we heartily recommend this trip into the underworld. A mine train takes visitors 3,350 feet inside Gold Hill, to see where some $8 million in gold, $90 million in silver, and $5 million in other minerals have been mined since silver was discovered here in 1884. Guides, many of them former miners, explain the mining process and equipment and recount the various legends of the mine. Also on the property is an operating blacksmith shop, plus streams where you can learn the technique of gold panning ($6.95 extra). An outdoor cafe serves an all-you-can-eat breakfast until noon ($6 adults, $4 children under 12) and Texas-style barbecue all day ($4.50–$8). The mine temperature is a cool 50°F (10°C), so jackets are recommended, even in summer. Allow about 1½ hours.

2 miles from Ouray via C.R. 14. © 888/227-4585 or 970/325-0220. Admission $16 adults, $7.95 children 4–11, free for children under 3. Mid-May to mid-Sept 9am–5pm; shorter hours at the beginning and end of this period. Closed July 4th. Reservations recommended, especially July–Aug.

Ouray County Museum Lodged in the original Miners' Hospital, which was completed in 1887 and operated by the Sisters of Mercy, this large three-story museum is packed to the rafters with fascinating exhibits from Ouray's past. There are more than two dozen exhibit rooms, each having a different theme, plus many small displays and changing exhibits. You'll see pioneer and mining-era relics, items relating to railroad and other transportation modes of the 19th century, ranch artifacts, memorabilia of Chief Ouray and the Utes, early hospital equipment including some scary-looking medical devices, Victorian artifacts, and historic photos. Allow about an hour, and ask here for a walking-tour guide to the town's many historic buildings.

420 Sixth Ave. © 970/325-4576. www.ouraycountyhistoricalsociety.org. Admission $5 adults, $1 children 6–12, $3.50 seniors 60 and older. Summer Mon–Sat 10am–5pm, Sun 1–5pm; shorter hours the rest of the year.

Ouray Hot Springs Pool & Fitness Center This oval outdoor pool, 120 feet by 150 feet, holds nearly a million gallons of odorless mineral water. Spring water is cooled from 150°F (66°C) and there are three separate soaking sections, with temperatures ranging from 88° to 105°F (31°–41°C). Also on the property is a fitness center, with aerobic exercise equipment including treadmills, a stair climber, a stationary bicycle, free weights, leg-press machines, and an abdominal board. There's a picnic area and playground in an adjacent municipal park. Allow 1 to 2 hours.

U.S. 550, at the north end of Ouray. © 970/325-7073. Pool only $8 adults, $6 students 7–12 and seniors 62 and over, and $3 children 3–6, free children under 3; fitness center only $8 for everyone; both pool and fitness center $10 everyone. Memorial Day through Labor Day daily 10am–10pm; the rest of the year Mon–Fri noon–9pm, Sat–Sun 11am–9pm.

WHERE TO STAY

Rates here are usually highest during summer and at Christmastime. A good chain motel is the **Comfort Inn,** 191 Fifth Ave. (P.O. Box 771), Ouray, CO 81427 (© **800/424-6423** or 970/325-7203), with rates for two from $99 to $140 in summer and lower at other times. Room tax is 7% plus $2 per night.

Ouray Victorian Inn   Located in Ouray's National Historic District, this handsome Victorian-style inn offers spacious rooms with outstanding views and lots of historic charm, plus a sun deck and playground. There's a variety of choices, including rooms with one king-size bed, units with two queen beds, and lavish two-room suites. In addition, the management rents privately owned cabins, town houses, and apartment-type units with full kitchens (call for rates).

50 Third Ave. (P.O. Box 1812), Ouray, CO 81427. © **800/846-8729** or 970/325-7222. www.ouraylodging.com. 38 units. $65–$100 double; $80–$120 suite. Rates include buffet breakfast. AE, DC, MC, V. **Amenities:** 2 outdoor hot tubs; playground. *In room:* TV, coffeemaker, wireless Internet.

St. Elmo Hotel 🐾🐾   An 1898 town landmark restored to Victorian splendor, the St. Elmo has an old-fashioned lobby that's a meeting place for locals and guests alike. All the units here ooze historic charm, and contain many original furnishings. Each of the six standard rooms has one queen-size bed. They're average size for a historic hotel, which means they're a bit small compared to a modern chain; some have shower/tub combos and a few have showers only. The suites are larger, with separate sitting areas and stained glass, polished wood, and brass trim throughout; the Cascade Suite has a king-size bed plus a second bedroom with a double bed. There's a TV in the parlor and the well-regarded Bon Ton Restaurant (see "Where to Dine" below) is on the premises. Smoking is not permitted.

426 Main St. (P.O. Box 667), Ouray, CO 81427. © **866/243-1502** or 970/325-4951. www.stelmohotel.com. 9 units. $60–$145 double; $85–$155 suite. Rates include full breakfast buffet and afternoon wine-and-cheese social hour. AE, DC, DISC, MC, V. Not suitable for children under 10. **Amenities:** Restaurant (steak/Italian); hot tub; sauna. *In room:* No phone.

WHERE TO DINE

Bon Ton Restaurant 🐾🐾 STEAK/ITALIAN   A fixture in Ouray for more than a century—it was in another location before moving into the St. Elmo Hotel basement in 1898—the Bon Ton is one of Ouray's finest restaurants. With stone outer walls, hardwood floors, and reproduction antique furnishings, it carries a Western Victorian appeal. The menu includes a variety of pasta dishes, such as our choice, the lasagna Luciano—a classic seven-layer, four-cheese lasagna with spinach and either marinara or meat sauce. We also recommend the beef, including the charbroiled 8-ounce Colorado beef tenderloin, wrapped in bacon and served with a Bordelaise sauce and herb butter. There's an exceptionally good wine list, and an elaborate brunch is offered each Sunday.

In the St. Elmo Hotel, 426 Main St. © **970/325-4951.** www.stelmohotel.com. Reservations recommended. Main courses $12–$34. AE, DC, DISC, MC, V. Sun 9:30am–1pm and 5:30–9:30pm; Mon–Sat 5:30–9:30pm.

7 Wolf Creek Ski Area

75 miles E. of Durango, 65 miles W. of Alamosa

Wolf Creek is famous throughout Colorado as the area that consistently has the most natural snow in the state—an annual average of 465 inches (almost 39 ft.)!

One of the state's oldest ski areas, Wolf Creek has terrain for skiers of all ability levels, but especially intermediates. Expert skiers often leave the lift-served slopes to dive down the powder of the Water Fall Area. The Alberta Peak area offers extremely steep skiing and one of the most spectacular views of the peaks and pristine wilderness. Slopes are rated 20% beginner, 35% intermediate, 25% advanced, and 20% expert. Snowboarders are welcome in all areas of the resort.

In all, the area has 1,600 acres of terrain with 50 miles of trails, and a vertical drop of 1,604 feet from the 11,904-foot summit. The mountain has 50 trails served by six lifts—one quad, one detachable quad (new for the 2006–07 season), two triple chairs, one double, and a Magic Carpet. Wolf Creek Lodge is a day lodge with restaurant and bar service. The Sports Center offers ski sales, rentals, and lessons.

Contact **Wolf Creek Ski Area,** P.O. Box 2800, Pagosa Springs, CO 81147 (© **970/264-5639;** www.wolfcreekski.com). Lift tickets cost $46 for adults, $25 for children 12 and under and seniors 65 and over. The resort is usually open from early November through mid-April, daily from 8:30am to 4pm.

WHERE TO STAY   Among nearby communities with lodging, dining, and other services is Pagosa Springs, 25 miles southwest of the ski area via U.S. 160. For information, consult the **Pagosa Springs Area Chamber of Commerce,** P.O. Box 787, Pagosa Springs, CO 81147 (© **800/252-2204** or 970/264-2360; www.pagosasprings chamber.com).

13

The Southern Rockies

If Colorado is the rooftop of America, then the southern Rockies are the peak of that roof. Some 30 of Colorado's fourteeners—14,000-plus-foot peaks—ring the area, and from Monarch Pass, at 11,312 feet, rivers flow in three directions.

Isolated from the rest of Colorado by its high mountains and rugged canyons, this region has historically bred proud, independent-minded people. In the 18th century, settlers came from Taos, New Mexico, and built some of the region's striking Spanish architecture.

Today these mountain and river towns are renowned as recreational capitals:

Gunnison for fishing and hunting, Crested Butte for skiing and mountain biking, and Salida and Buena Vista for white-water rafting. Alamosa is within easy reach of numerous attractions, including the remarkable Great Sand Dunes National Park and Preserve. In the foothills of the San Juan Range are the historic mining towns of Creede and Lake City, and in the tiny community of Antonito you can hop a narrow-gauge steam train for a trip back to a simpler (though smokier) time. This is rugged and sparsely populated land, with numerous opportunities for seeing the wilds of mountain America at their best.

1 Gunnison & Curecanti National Recreation Area

196 miles SW of Denver, 161 miles W. of Pueblo, 65 miles E. of Montrose

A rough-and-ready Western town, Gunnison is where you go to get a hot shower and a good meal after a week of camping, hiking, boating, or hunting in the rugged mountains and canyons in the surrounding area.

Utes began hunting here about 1650, and although Spanish explorers probably never penetrated this isolated region, mountain men, who were pursuing pelts, arrived by the 1830s. First mapped by U.S. Army captain John Gunnison in 1853, the town was established in 1874, soon growing into a ranching center and transportation hub for nearby silver and gold mines. Established in 1911, Western State College now has an enrollment of 2,400, and was the first college in the United States with a certified technical-evacuation mountain-rescue team. Ninety percent of the all-volunteer team is made up of college students, with the remainder coming from the community. Gunnison sits at an elevation of 7,681 feet and its population is about 5,400.

ESSENTIALS

GETTING THERE **By Car** Gunnison is located on U.S. 50, midway between Montrose and Salida. From Denver, the most direct route is U.S. 285 southwest to Poncha Springs, then west on U.S. 50. From Grand Junction, follow U.S. 50 through Montrose.

By Plane   The **Gunnison–Crested Butte Airport,** 711 Rio Grande Ave. (© **970/ 641-2304**), is just off U.S. 50, a few blocks south of downtown Gunnison. **American Airlines** (© **800/433-7300**) provides air service during ski season and **United Express** (© **800/241-6522**) provides daily year-round service from Denver.

VISITOR INFORMATION   Contact the **Gunnison Country Chamber of Commerce,** 500 E. Tomichi Ave., Gunnison, CO 81230 (© **800/851-0482** or 970/641-1501; www.gunnisoncrestedbutte.com), which operates a visitor center at the same location, open Monday through Friday from 8am to 5pm.

GETTING AROUND   The town lies along the southeast bank of the west-flowing Gunnison River. Tomichi Avenue (U.S. 50) runs east-west through town. Main Street (Colo. 135) intersects Tomichi Avenue in the center of town and proceeds north to Crested Butte.

Car-rental agencies include **Avis** (© 970/641-0263), **Budget** (© 970/641-4403), **Dollar** (© 970/642-0199), and **Hertz** (© 970/641-2881).

FAST FACTS   **Gunnison Valley Hospital,** with a 24-hour emergency room, is at 711 N. Taylor St. (© **970/641-1456**), 2 blocks east of Main Street and 6 blocks north of U.S. 50. The **post office** is located at 200 N. Wisconsin St. at Virginia Avenue; for hours and other information contact the U.S. Postal Service (© **800/275-8777;** www.usps.com). For **road conditions** (winter only) call © **877/315-7623** (in-state only).

SPECIAL EVENTS   Winter Carnival, early February; Cattlemen's Days, Colorado's oldest continually held rodeo, late July; Art in the Park, mid-July; Classic and Custom Car Show, late August; and the Night of Lights, early December.

CURECANTI NATIONAL RECREATION AREA

Dams on the Gunnison River, just below Gunnison, have created a series of three very different reservoirs, extending 35 miles to the mouth of the Black Canyon of the Gunnison (see "Black Canyon of the Gunnison National Park," in chapter 11). **Blue Mesa Lake** (elevation 7,519 ft.), the easternmost (beginning 9 miles west of Gunnison) is the largest lake in Colorado when filled to capacity and a watersports paradise popular for fishing, motorboating, sailboating, board sailing, and other activities. Fjordlike **Morrow Point Lake** (elevation 7,160 ft.) and **Crystal Lake** (elevation 6,755 ft.) fill long, serpentine canyons accessible only by precipitous trails and thus are limited to use by hand-carried boats. These lakes offer some of Colorado's best boating (permits cost $4 for 2 days, $10 for 14).

There are two full-service marinas, both under the same management, offering fuel, supplies, boat rentals, a guided fishing trips. **Elk Creek Marina** is on Blue Mesa Lake, 16 miles west of Gunnison off U.S. 50 (© **970/641-0707;** www.bluemesalake.com); and **Lake Fork** (© **970/641-3048;** www.bluemesalake.com) is 25 miles west of Gunnison, at the reservoir's west end. Contact either marina for current boat rental and guide rates. There's also a restaurant, Pappy's, at Elk Creek Marina, serving three meals daily.

A boat tour, offered by the park service, leaves the Pine Creek Trail boat dock on Morrow Point Lake at 10am and 12:30pm daily except Tuesday, Memorial Day through Labor Day, to explore the Upper Black Canyon of the Gunnison. *Be forewarned:* There is a .8-mile hike followed by 232 steps down to get to the dock; all of which has to be repeated in reverse after the boat ride. Rates are $15 adults, $12 children 12 and under. Reservations are required; stop at the Elk Creek Visitor Center or call ((C) **970/641-2337,** ext. 205).

Hikers find a variety of trails, often with splendid views of the lakes. Those who want to see birds can't go wrong with the **Neversink Trail,** a 1-mile round-trip hike on the north shore of the Gunnison River, near a great blue heron rookery. Also watch for warblers, redwing blackbirds, and great horned owls, plus an occasional mule deer among the cottonwoods and willows that shade the river. The trail is flat and relatively easy, and also provides fishing access. A moderately strenuous hike where you might see a golden eagle or two, and possibly some bighorn sheep, is the 4-mile round-trip **Dillon Pinnacles Trail,** which is open to horseback riders as well as hikers. It provides spectacular views of the strangely eroded volcanic formations called the Dillon Pinnacles. The visitor center has a free brochure that describes these and several other hikes.

Anglers visit Curecanti year-round—there's ice fishing in winter—but the main season is May to October, when rainbow, brown, and Mackinaw trout and kokanee salmon are caught in large numbers. **Hunting,** especially for elk and deer, is popular in the adjacent West Elk Mountains.

The recreation area has 10 developed **campgrounds,** with about 350 sites. Showers are available for a small fee at Elk Creek (160 campsites) and Lake Fork (90 campsites). Elk Creek is open year-round, but water is turned off in winter. The other campgrounds are open spring through fall. Camping costs $12 per night, $18 with electric. Reservations are available from late May through early September through the recreation area's website or www.reserveusa.com, or by phone (C) **877/444-6777.** Several campgrounds have marinas, boat ramps, and RV dump stations; Loop D at Elk Creek has electric hookups. Backcountry and boat-in camping is also permitted, at no charge; check with rangers.

The **Elk Creek Visitor Center,** 16 miles west of Gunnison off U.S. 50, has exhibits and audiovisual programs, as well as maps and publications. It's open daily 8am to 6pm in summer, and Monday through Friday from 8:30am to 4pm the rest of the year, except for federal holidays in winter. Nature hikes and evening campground programs are presented throughout the summer. At **Cimarron,** 35 miles west of Gunnison, there's a visitor center open intermittently from mid-May through September, with a historic train exhibit, book sales, and a road to **Morrow Point Dam** power plant. The **Lake Fork Visitor Center,** 25 miles west of Gunnison off U.S. 50, near Blue Mesa Dam, is open daily from mid-May through September.

For a brochure and other information before your trip, contact Curecanti National Recreation Area, 102 Elk Creek, Gunnison, CO 81230 ((C) **970/641-2337;** www.nps. gov/cure).

OTHER SPORTS & OUTDOOR ACTIVITIES

In addition to activities in the recreation area, there are opportunities for hiking, mountain biking, hunting, fishing, camping, and four-wheeling on other nearby public lands under the jurisdiction of the U.S. Forest Service and Bureau of Land Management. For maps and other information, contact the offices of the **Gunnison Ranger District** and the **Bureau of Land Management Resource Area** at 216 N. Colorado St. ((C) **970/641-0471;** www.fs.fed.us/r2 or www.co.blm.gov).

A good base for exploring this area is **Three Rivers Resort and Outfitting,** 11 miles north of Gunnison at 130 C.R. 742 (P.O. Box 339), Almont, CO 81210 ((C) **888/761-3474** or 970/641-1303; www.3riversoutfitting.com). Located between

The Bizarre Tale of Alferd Packer

The winter of 1873 to 1874 was bad in southwest Colorado's San Juan Mountains—deep snow, staggeringly strong winds, and below-zero temperatures. But among the many miners who found themselves there, drawn by the hope of staking a claim among the region's newly discovered silver deposits, the temptation to change their fortunes in a day was just too powerful to resist. In February, six eager miners, led by Alferd Packer, set out from a Ute encampment near the present-day town of Delta, ignoring warnings from Ouray, chief of the Ute people. They took only 10 days' worth of food and weren't heard from for over 2 months, until Packer arrived alone at Los Piños Indian Agency, about 25 miles south of the present town of Gunnison.

Packer told Indian Agency officials that after he became ill, his companions abandoned him, and he survived on roots and bushes while making his way through the mountains. Curiously, he refused food upon his arrival. After resting, Packer traveled to the nearby community of Saguache, where he went on a drinking binge, paying with money from several wallets.

Since Packer had been penniless when the six men left the Ute encampment, and was the only one to return, Indian Agency officials became suspicious. When strips of what appeared to be human flesh were discovered along the path Packer had taken he changed his story, claiming that others in the party had killed their companions one by one, until only he and fellow miner Wilson Bell remained. Finally Packer was forced to kill Bell in self-defense. After admitting to eating the remains of his companions, Packer was arrested and jailed.

Packer escaped from jail that August, at just about the time that five partially decomposed bodies were discovered along the northeast side of Lake

Gunnison and Crested Butte, close to the national forest, Three Rivers offers fishing and rafting trips (see below), and also has fully equipped and furnished cabins ($65 and up) and a campground ($25 for tents and RVs, including hookups).

FISHING   The Gunnison River, both above and below town, and the tributary Taylor River, which joins the Gunnison at Almont, 11 miles north of town, are outstanding trout streams. In addition, the region's lakes are also rich in fish. **Willowfly Anglers,** located at Three Rivers Resort, Almont (© **970/641-1303**), offers fly-fishing instruction, rentals, and guide service. Full-day float fishing trips cost $265 for one person and $315 for two, and walking trips are also available, starting at $155 for one person, half-day.

GOLF   The 18-hole **Dos Rios Golf Club,** off U.S. 50 about 2 miles west of town (© **970/641-1482**), charges $65 for 18 holes, including a cart.

HORSEBACK RIDING   One of the best ways to see this beautiful area is from a saddle. **Ferro's Blue Mesa Lake Ranch,** P.O. Box 853, Gunnison, CO 81230 (© **800/617-4671** or 970/641-4671; www.coloradodirectory.com/ferrosbluemesa),

San Cristobal, a few miles south of the present town of Lake City. Four of the men had apparently been murdered in their sleep, their heads split open with an ax, while a fifth had been shot. Chunks of flesh had been cut from at least two of the men's chests and thighs, and one was decapitated.

The search was now on in earnest, but Packer was nowhere to be found. About 9 years later, he was discovered living in Wyoming, using the name John Schwartz. He was arrested, and in April 1883 was convicted of premeditated murder and sentenced to hang. That should have been the end of Packer, but the trial was declared unconstitutional on a technicality.

Retried in 1886, Packer was convicted on five counts of manslaughter, and sentenced to 45 years in prison. However, due to poor health, he was pardoned by Governor Charles Thomas after only 5 years behind bars. Packer died of natural causes in the Denver area in 1907, at the age of 64, and was buried in the Littleton Cemetery. As an interesting aside, all through his life, Packer's first name, Alferd, had been misspelled. Apparently, it was a problem that followed him into death, since today the name "Alfred" is prominently displayed on his tombstone.

Though many at the time considered it an open-and-shut case, some have questioned whether Packer was really guilty of murder, or if he was simply convicted because of the public's revulsion at his admission of cannibalism. In 1989, the bodies were exhumed, and it was determined that they had likely been victims of cannibalism—but no evidence has shown definitively that Packer killed them. The site where the bodies were found, near the town of Lake City (see "A Side Trip to Lake City," below), is now known as Cannibal Plateau.

offers horseback rides into remote areas of Curecanti National Recreation Area and to nearby national forests from late April through mid-November, weather permitting. Rates start at about $20 for 1 hour, and half- and full-day rates are also available. Also contact Ferro's about multiday pack trips. Ferro's is located on Soap Creek Road, about 26 miles west of Gunnison, overlooking Blue Mesa Reservoir. In addition to horseback rides, Ferro's has a general store with fishing licenses and supplies, plus six lodging units, including several historic cabins, with rates from $40 to $100. There are also 33 campsites, starting at $10.

RIVER RAFTING & KAYAKING   For trips on the Taylor and other rivers, check with **Three Rivers Resort and Outfitting** (see above). Rates for 3-hour raft trips over relatively calm stretches are $25 for adults and $20 for children under 12. Three Rivers also offers guided white-water trips with rates from $45 per person.

SKIING   The two major winter-sports centers in the area are **Crested Butte,** 32 miles north on Colo. 135 (see section 2 of this chapter), and **Monarch,** 44 miles east on U.S. 50 (see section 3 of this chapter).

DISCOVERING GUNNISON'S PAST

Founded in the 1870s, the town of Gunnison has a number of historic buildings, ranging from log cabins to fancy 1880s homes—many in Gothic revival and Italianate styles—plus the 1882 stone Episcopal Church. A free walking-tour brochure is available at the chamber of commerce visitor center (see above).

Gunnison Pioneer Museum   A Denver & Rio Grande narrow-gauge steam train and depot are highlights at this museum, which includes a dozen buildings from the area's past. There's an emphasis on ranching and homemaking equipment from the late 1800s and early 1900s, and exhibits include a rural schoolhouse (ca. 1905), a home with 19th-century furnishings, a dairy barn (ca. 1880), minerals and arrowheads, wagons, toys, and Gunnison's first post office (1876); plus over 50 antique and classic motor vehicles on display, from a Model A Ford tanker truck to an old Cadillac hearse. Allow 2 hours.

East U.S. 50 at the corner of S. Adams St. and Tomichi Ave. ✆ 970/641-4530. Admission $7 adults, $1 children 6–12, free for children under 6. Memorial Day to mid-Sept. Mon–Sat 9am–5pm; Sun 1–5pm.

WHERE TO STAY

Lodging rates are at their highest in Gunnison in summer and at Christmas. You'll usually find the lowest rates in late winter and early spring. Major chain and franchise motels that provide reasonably priced lodging in Gunnison include the **Best Western Tomichi Village Inn,** on U.S. 50, 1 mile east of Gunnison (✆ **800/641-1131** or 970/641-1131), charging double rates of $79 to $149 in summer and $59 to $85 the rest of the year; **Comfort Inn,** 911 N. Main St. (✆ **800/424-6423** or 970/642-1000), with rates of $90 to $100 double in summer and $70 to $90 at other times; and **Quality Inn,** 400 E. Tomichi Ave. (✆ **800/424-6423** or 970/641-1237), with double rates from $85 to $115 in summer and $55 to $85 at other times. Room tax adds just over 11% to lodging bills.

Wildwood Resort   Built in 1928 as a summer refuge for members of the Chicago underworld, the Wildwood is today a favorite hideaway for budget-conscious outdoor sports lovers. The rooms are quaint, quiet, and cozy, and all have a full kitchen. Units were recently remodeled with all new soft goods, upgraded plumbing, flooring, and kitchens. Five units have shower/tub combos and the rest have showers only. There are also two handsome cabins, both with two bedrooms, two bathrooms, a washer and dryer, and private deck.

The property boasts a playground, swings, horseshoe pits, shady picnic tables, a fish-cleaning station, and two duck ponds, where Tasmanian rainbow trout are raised for release into the Gunnison River.

1312 W. Tomichi Ave., Gunnison, CO 81230. ✆ **866/770-1663** or 970/641-1663. www.wildwoodmotel.net. 18 units. $75–$85 double, $175–$195 cabin. Fishing, hunting, and ski packages available. MC, V. From downtown, continue straight on Tomichi Ave. when U.S. 50 curves to the left and you see the motel's blue sign; from the west turn left on New York Ave. (1st traffic light), then right on 8th and left onto Tomichi. The motel is ahead on the right. **Amenities:** Outdoor hot tub, laundry. *In room:* TV, kitchen.

CAMPING

In addition to the campgrounds in Curecanti National Recreation Area (see above), you'll find dozens of sites scattered throughout the Gunnison National Forest and lands administered by the Bureau of Land Management (✆ **970/641-0471**). Wildwood Resort (see above) also offers RV sites.

Mesa RV Resort A good base camp for fishing, hunting, or sightseeing trips, this campground caters mostly to RVs but does accept tents. The campground has large pull-through sites to accommodate big RVs, and 50-amp electric service is available. Facilities include clean bathhouses with plenty of hot water, a dump station, self-service laundry, gas pumps, a playground, a recreation room, and a store with propane and a limited selection of groceries and RV supplies.

36128 W. U.S. 50, Gunnison, CO 81230. © 800/482-8384 or 970/641-3186. www.mesarvresort.com. 135 sites. $24–$32. MC, V. Closed mid-Oct through mid-Apr. Located 3 miles west of Gunnison.

WHERE TO DINE

Blue Iguana *Value* MEXICAN Homemade Sonoran-style Mexican food is the fare at the Blue Iguana, a better-than-average fast-food restaurant in the Elk Horn Building, 2 blocks east of Main Street—look for the big chrome sculpture of an elk out front. Inside, the decor is simple: picnic tables with red plastic coverings, and light-colored walls with bright red trim and red chile designs. Order at the counter and pick up your taco, burrito, enchilada, or combo plate when your name is called. We recommend either the burrito (it's huge) or the house specialty, a chimichanga—a deep-fried flour tortilla stuffed with your choice of five fillings (shredded beef, beans, chicken, rice, green chile, red chile, and on and on), and topped with sour cream and guacamole. Locals consistently declare the Blue Iguana the best place for Mexican food—and we agree!

303 E. Tomichi Ave. © 970/641-3403. Reservations not accepted. Most items $3–$8.95. MC, V. Summer Mon–Sat 11am–10pm; closes 9pm in winter.

Josef's Restaurant ** AMERICAN/EUROPEAN A European old-world atmosphere pervades this fine restaurant adjacent to the Best Western Tomichi Village Inn. The menu features a variety of steaks, poultry, pasta, and fresh seafood, but we recommend the house specialties, all true European favorites such as traditional Wiener schnitzel, Hungarian-style goulash (slowly braised beef tips with onions, mushrooms, paprika, and cabernet sauvignon demi-glace sauce), and hickory smoked rib-eye steak with a Gorgonzola cheese cream sauce. Try Josef's fresh-baked pastries for a special treat.

41883 E. U.S. 50, 1 mile east of Gunnison. © 970/641-5032. Main courses $9.95–$24. AE, DC, DISC, MC, V. Daily 5–9pm.

A SIDE TRIP TO LAKE CITY **

The historic mining town of Lake City is 55 miles southwest via Colo. 149 (turn south off U.S. 50, 9 miles west of Gunnison). Founded in 1874, this former silver and gold town is set at 8,671 feet elevation against a backdrop of 14,000-plus-foot peaks in three different national forests—the Gunnison, Uncompahgre, and Rio Grande. Although the year-round population is a bit under 400, that figure quintuples in summer.

One of Colorado's largest national historic districts, Lake City has more than 75 buildings that date from the 19th century. Visit the renovated **Hinsdale County Courthouse,** 317 N. Henson St., built in 1877 and still the home of county government. You'll see exhibits on the trial of the notorious Alferd Packer and the courtroom where his trial took place (see "The Bizarre Tale of Alferd Packer," above).

History buffs will also enjoy the **Hinsdale County Museum,** 130 N. Silver St., at the corner of Silver and Second streets (© 970/944-2050 in summer, or 970/944-2515 at other times; www.lakecitymuseum.com), with exhibits about the

Packer trial, of course, plus the area's silver-mining heritage and other aspects of Lake City's history. There's also a Denver & Rio Grande Western caboose and a delightful Victorian garden with a sitting area. Next door is the 1870s **Smith-Grantham House,** a small, furnished Victorian home where you can see how people here lived in the late 1800s. The museum and Smith-Grantham House are open from mid-June until Labor Day, Monday through Saturday from 10am to 5pm and Sunday from 1 to 4pm; and irregular hours the rest of the year. Admission, which includes both the museum and the Smith-Grantham House, costs $3 for adults, $1 for children 8 to 12, and is free for children 7 and younger. The museum leads historic walking tours, home tours, cemetery tours, and ghost tours; call for the current schedule and prices.

For those intrigued with mining, visit the **Hard Tack Mine Tours & Museum,** about 3 miles west of town, via C.R. 20 (© **970/944-2506;** www.hardtackmine.com). George and Beth Hurd of Lake City own the property and, with the help of their daughter Buffy, developed the tour and museum. The 40-minute tour through the state-inspected mine takes you back more than 100 years and show you how the miners lived and worked, and you'll also see all sorts of mining equipment and an excellent display of crystals in the museum. Be aware that the temperature underground is a constant 45°F (7°C), so take a jacket even on the hottest summer day. There's also a gift shop, and gold panning is also offered (call for times and rates). Open Monday through Saturday from 10am to 5pm and Sunday from noon to 5pm, from early June through early September. Cost is $10 for adults and $6 for youths 14 and under.

Surrounded by some 600,000 acres of public land, Lake City is an important recreational center, offering hiking, mountain biking, horseback riding, jeep rides, camping, and fishing in summer; and ice fishing, cross-country skiing, snowshoeing, and snowmobiling in winter. Lake San Cristobal, just south of town via C.R. 30, is Colorado's second-largest natural lake and is particularly popular with fishermen. Also nearby you'll find several ghost towns and historic sites, most of which will require a four-wheel-drive vehicle, horse, mountain bike, or a good pair of hiking boots.

For information, including lists of boat and jeep rentals, outfitters, stables, accommodations, and restaurants, contact the **Lake City/Hinsdale County Chamber of Commerce,** P.O. Box 430, Lake City, CO 81235 (© **800/569-1874** or 970/944-2527; www.lakecity.com). The chamber operates a visitor information center at 800 N. Gunnison Ave., on the north side of town, which is usually open from 9am to 5pm Monday through Saturday and from 11am to 3pm Sunday.

2 Crested Butte ⋆⋆

28 miles N. of Gunnison, 224 miles SW of Denver

A delightful little gem of a town, Crested Butte is a year-round destination resort, with wonderful skiing in winter, and hiking, mountain biking, and other outdoor recreational activities in warmer weather. In fact, Crested Butte has the best mountain biking in the state, and boasts of having some of the most colorful displays of wildflowers you'll see anywhere.

The town of Crested Butte was born in 1880 as the Denver & Rio Grande line laid a narrow-gauge rail track from Gunnison to serve the gold and silver mines in the area. But it was coal, not the more precious minerals, which sustained the town from the late 1880s until 1952, when the last of the mines closed. The economy then languished until Mt. Crested Butte ski area was developed in 1961.

An influx of newcomers began renovating the old buildings in the 1970s, and in 1974 the entire town was designated a National Historic District—one of the largest in Colorado. Crested Butte is as different from those other overcrowded interstate highway resorts as you can get. A guest really has a sense of having gotten away from it all with a vacation here.

ESSENTIALS

GETTING THERE   By Car   Crested Butte is 28 miles north of Gunnison on Colo. 135, the only year-round access. In summer, the gravel-surface Kebler Pass Road links Crested Butte with Colo. 133 at Paonia Reservoir, to the west.

By Plane   The **Gunnison–Crested Butte Airport,** 711 Rio Grande Ave. (© 970/641-2304), is just off U.S. 50, a few blocks south of downtown Gunnison. **American Airlines** (© 800/433-7300) provides air service during ski season and **United Express** (© 800/241-6522) provides daily year-round service from Denver.

Alpine Express (© 800/822-4844 or 970/641-5074; www.alpineexpressshuttle.com) provides shuttle service from the airport to Crested Butte, frequently in ski season; call to check on availability at other times. Reservations are required.

VISITOR INFORMATION   Consult the **Crested Butte–Mt. Crested Butte Chamber of Commerce,** P.O. Box 1288, Crested Butte, CO 81224 (© 800/545-4505 or 970/349-6438; www.crestedbuttechamber.com). Another good source is the **Gunnison–Crested Butte Tourism Association** (© 800/851-0482; www.gunnisoncrestedbutte.com); and an excellent website with numerous links is **www.visitcrestedbutte.com.** An **information center** is located downtown at the four-way stop at the corner of Elk Avenue and Sixth Street.

GETTING AROUND   There are actually two separate communities here: the old mining town of Crested Butte and the modern resort village of Mt. Crested Butte, 3 miles away. Colo. 135 enters Crested Butte from the south and is intersected by Elk Avenue, which runs east-west as the town's main street.

Free transportation throughout Crested Butte and the ski resort is provided by **Mountain Express** (© 970/349-7318; www.crestedbutte-co.gov).

FAST FACTS   The **Crested Butte Medical Center,** in the Ore Bucket Building in downtown Crested Butte (© 970/349-0321; www.cbmedicalcenter.com), can handle most health needs; the medical center also operates a clinic at the ski area during winter (© 970/349-4370). The **post office** is on the north side of Elk Avenue between Second and Third streets; contact the U.S. Postal Service (© 800/275-8777; www.usps.com) for hours and other information.

SPECIAL EVENTS   Fat Tire Bike Week, June; Crested Butte Music Festival, early July; Wildflower Festival, July; Festival of the Arts, early August; Wild Mushroom Festival, early August; Vinotok Slavic Fall Festival, September.

SKIING & OTHER WINTER SPORTS

Crested Butte may be Colorado's best-kept secret. Situated at the intersection of two overlapping winter storm tracks, it's guaranteed to have outstanding snow. Offering abundant opportunities for beginners and intermediate skiers, Crested Butte also has what many experts consider the most challenging runs in the Rockies.

The resort has 1,125 acres of skiable terrain. Altogether, trails are rated 23% beginner, 57% intermediate, and 20% advanced. The vertical drop is 3,062 feet from a summit of 12,162 feet. There are 121 trails served by 15 lifts (four high-speed quads, three triples, three doubles, three surface lifts, and two Magic Carpet rolling conveyors). Average annual snowfall is 240 inches, and there's snow making on trails served by all but two of the resort's lifts. The resort also has an easily accessible snowboard terrain park, half-pipe terrain, and offers snowboarding lessons.

Crested Butte offers both a ski and snowboard program (plus year-round recreation) for visitors with disabilities, with specially trained and certified instructors, at the Adaptive Sports Center, located at the base of the ski area in the Treasury Center Building. The resort's Kid's Ski & Snowboard World provides lessons, day care, and nursery services. Private and group lessons are available in half- or all-day packages. The resort offers rentals of skis, snowboards, helmets, snowshoes, ski boards, and telemark equipment, in single and multiday prices, with overnight storage included. A full-service repair shop is available also. All children 12 and under who participate in lessons are required to wear a helmet (included in the lesson price and available at the rental shop). Equipment rental is also available at several other shops in the base area and around town.

Don't forget to keep an eye out for Bubba and Betty Bear, the beloved mascots of Crested Butte Mountain Resort, who will gladly stop for a warm, fuzzy hug, and a picture.

For more information, contact **Crested Butte Mountain Resort,** 12 Snowmass Rd. (P.O. Box 5700), Mt. Crested Butte, CO 81225 (© **800/810-7669** or 970/349-2222; 888/442-8883 or 970/349-2323 for snow reports; www.skicb.com). Full-day regular season lift tickets are $74 for adults, $56 for seniors 65 and older, $56 for youths 13 to 17, and $37 for children 7 to 12. Early season lift tickets are less. The resort is usually open from mid-November to early April, daily from 9am to 4pm.

CROSS-COUNTRY SKIING, SNOWSHOEING, SLEDDING & ICE SKATING
The **Crested Butte Nordic Center,** based at Big Mine Park, Second Street and Whiterock Avenue in downtown Crested Butte (P.O. Box 1269), Crested Butte, CO 81224 (© **970/349-1707;** www.cbnordic.org), maintains 26 miles of marked and groomed trails and organizes backcountry tours over more than 100 miles of wilderness trails. It's open in winter daily from 9am to 4pm. A 1-day trail pass costs about $15, with discounts for children and seniors. Nordic ski rentals (skis, boots, and poles) cost $20 per day for adults and $12 for children. The center also maintains a free lighted ice-skating rink and a free sledding hill, plus skate and sled rentals. In addition, it offers snowshoe tours and rentals.

WARM-WEATHER SPORTS & OUTDOOR ACTIVITIES

This is rugged country, surrounded by **Gunnison National Forest,** three wilderness areas, and towering 12,000- to 14,000-foot peaks. For maps and tips on the many activities available, contact the Gunnison Ranger District office at 216 N. Colorado St. in Gunnison (© **970/641-0471;** www.fs.fed.us/r2). The lifts at Crested Butte Mountain Resort don't stop just because the snow's gone, but operate daily from late June through early September for hikers or those who simply want to enjoy the beautiful mountain scenery without effort. Single trips cost $15 for adults, $8 for children 7 to 17 and seniors 65 and older; all-day passes cost $17 and $10, respectively. Kids 6 and younger ride free.

There are numerous area outfitters and guide services that will help you with practically any outdoor activity. **Alpine Outside** (© 800/833-8052 or 970/349-5011; www.3riversoutfitting.com), located at the four-way stop in downtown Crested Butte, is open from late May through September and works with a number of local guides and can book a wide variety of warm-weather outdoor adventures.

GOLF   The 18-hole course at **The Club at Crested Butte,** 2 miles south of Crested Butte off Colo. 135 (© **970/349-6131**), is one of Colorado's best mountain courses. It's usually open from mid-May through October. The fee for 18 holes, including the mandatory cart, is $175 in summer, lower in the off-season.

HIKING   There are practically unlimited opportunities for hiking and backpacking in the Crested Butte area. Ask the chamber of commerce for trail suggestions, or contact the Gunnison National Forest office (see above).

HORSEBACK RIDING   Guided rides are offered year-round by **Fantasy Ranch Horseback Adventures,** P.O. Box 236, Crested Butte, CO 81224 (© **888/688-3488** or 970/349-5425; www.fantasyranchoutfitters.com), ranging from 1½ hours to week-long pack trips. Trips go into three different mountain wilderness areas, at elevations from 7,000 feet to 12,700 feet, including the incredibly beautiful Maroon Bells. Prices per person are $55 for the 1½-hour ride and $80 for a 3-hour ride. Call or check the website for other trips.

MOUNTAIN BIKING   **Crested Butte** has established a firm reputation as the place to mountain bike in Colorado. From single-track trails to jeep roads, there's something here to please every ability level. You can get information from the Crested Butte Visitor Center or the Forest Service (see above). Among local shops where you can get trail information, maps, and mountain-bike rentals (from about $30 per day), we recommend **Flatiron Sports** (© 800/821-4331 or 970/349-6656; www.flatiron sports.net) in the Treasury Center at Mt. Crested Butte, and **Crested Butte Sports** (© **800/301-9169** or 970/349-7516; www.crestedbuttesports.com) and **The Alpineer** (© **800/847-0244** or 970/349-5210; www.alpineer.com) in the town of Crested Butte.

Popular choices include the **Strand Hill** route, which runs for 18 miles and is considered intermediate. It climbs to 10,255 feet elevation, through wooded areas, and includes several miles on downhill single-track. Advanced mountain bikers will love **Trail no. 401,** one of the best trails in the area. This 26-mile round-trip route climbs to 11,500 feet and offers incredible mountain scenery, including views of the magnificent Maroon Bells (see the "Natural Attractions" box on p. 325) as it passes through aspen groves and meadows of wildflowers.

Guided mountain-bike tours are offered by **Crested Butte Mountain Guides,** 416 Sopris Ave. (© **877/455-2307** or 970/349-5430; www.crestedbutteguides.com), which charges $125 for a 6-hour guided ride, not including bike rental.

OTHER HIGHLIGHTS

The chamber of commerce provides a free brochure on a **self-guided walking tour** of more than three-dozen historic buildings in Crested Butte, including the picturesque 1883 Town Hall, 1881 railroad depot, numerous saloons and homes, and a unique two-story outhouse.

Downtown Crested Butte is home to a half-dozen or so **art galleries,** mostly along or just off Elk Avenue. The **Paragon Galley,** at the corner of Second Street and Elk

Avenue (© **970/349-6484**), is a cooperative, displaying the works of more than a dozen local artists and craftspersons.

Crested Butte Mountain Heritage Museum This museum, located in a historic building, concentrates on the area's mining, ranching, and skiing heritage, with interactive exhibits, historical photos, and a wide array of memorabilia from local settlers' cabins. There are also vintage mountain bikes and an exhibit on the local Ute tribe. You can pick up a free copy of the Crested Butte walking-tour map here, and borrow (also free) an audio tour with player. Allow about an hour.

331 Elk Ave. © **970/349-1880**. Admission $3, children under 12 free. Winter Tues–Sun 2–7pm; summer Tues–Sun 1–6pm; call for hours spring and fall.

WHERE TO STAY

Lodging properties listed below with Mt. Crested Butte addresses are at or near the ski slopes, while those in Crested Butte are about 3 miles away. However, free transportation from Crested Butte to the slopes is available with the Mountain Express (see "Getting Around," above).

Rates in Crested Butte are usually highest during ski season, and lowest in what locals call "mud season," after the ski area closes and before summer.

Crested Butte International Lodge & Hostel 𝒦 This handsome, three-story hostel is among the nicest you'll find in Colorado, and it's just 100 feet from the free ski shuttle. Dorm rooms have four, six, or eight single beds, so a family can have a private room by renting all its beds. Of course, in the hosteling tradition, they'll share the large bathrooms and other facilities. Each bunk has its own reading light and a lockable drawer, and all rooms have a desk. Sleeping bags, sheets, and towels can be rented. The large shared living room has a stone fireplace and comfortable sitting areas; and guests have use of a fully equipped kitchen. Ski and other outdoor recreation packages are available. There are three private rooms for two, a family room that sleeps five, and an apartment that sleeps six; linens are provided for these. They offer the use of copy and fax machines. Smoking and alcoholic beverages are not permitted.

615 Teocalli Ave. (P.O. Box 1332), Crested Butte, CO 81224. © **888/389-0588** or 970/349-0588. www.crestedbutte hostel.com. 50 total beds; 4 private rooms; 1 apt. All but one private room share bathrooms. Bunk rooms $22–$38 per bed; private rooms $60–$99 double; apt. $150–$250. MC, V. **Amenities:** Coin-op laundry. *In room:* No phone, wireless Internet.

Elk Mountain Lodge 𝒦 Built in 1919 as a miners' hotel, this historic three-story lodge has been beautifully renovated, and is a good choice for those seeking both a good night's sleep and a bit of historic ambience. Located near the center of town, it offers individually decorated, basic rooms with twin, queen, or king beds. Third-floor units have spectacular views of the town and surrounding mountains, and many have balconies. There's also ski storage.

Second St. and Gothic Ave. Crested Butte, CO 81224. © **800/374-6521** or 970/349-7533. Fax 970/349-5114. www.elkmountainlodge.net. 19 units. $120–$160 double. Rates include full breakfast. AE, DISC, MC, V. No children under 10 years of age. **Amenities:** Bar; indoor hot tub. *In room:* TV, dataport, hair dryer, wireless Internet.

The Historic Pioneer Guest Cabins Located 10 minutes from Crested Butte ski area, the Pioneer is a great escape for those seeking a rustic (but not too rustic) log cabin in the woods. Although these historic cabins lack TVs and in-room phones, they have modern bathrooms (showers only); fully furnished and equipped kitchens; handmade wood furniture; and cozy down comforters on the beds. In addition to propane heaters, the cabins have either fireplaces or antique wood-burning stoves, and outside each cabin is a fire pit and picnic table.

The four small cabins, each with two double beds, were built as part of a historic ski resort that closed in the early 1950s. The four larger cabins, built in the late 1960s and early 1970s, have three double beds, are more open, and have more of a modern feel than the historic cabins. Located in the Gunnison National Forest, the cabins provide easy access to fishing, hiking, mountain biking, cross-country skiing, and snow-shoeing. All units are nonsmoking.

Cement Creek Rd., Crested Butte, CO 81224. ℂ **970/349-5517.** Fax 970/349-9697. www.thepioneer.net. 8 units. $109–$179 double. Free for children 4 and under. MC, V. Most breeds of dogs accepted for $10 per dog per night fee (maximum 2 dogs per unit) at management discretion. From Crested Butte, take Colo. 135 south 7 miles to Cement Creek Rd., turn left and go 2 miles. *In room:* Kitchen, no phone.

The Nordic Inn *Kids*   Among the first lodges built at the foot of the Crested Butte ski slopes, this well-kept, family-owned inn is still going strong. The big fireplace in the lobby is the focus of attention at breakfast, and the whirlpool tub on the sun deck is open year-round. Guest rooms have Scandinavian decor; most have two double beds, although a few contain either one king- or two queen-size beds. Each also has a bathroom with a tub/shower combo and a separate vanity. Especially good for families are the kitchenette and full-kitchen units, which sleep from four to eight people. The entire inn is nonsmoking.

14 Treasury Rd. (P.O. Box 939, Crested Butte, CO 81224), Mt. Crested Butte, CO 81225. ℂ **800/542-7669** (reservations only) or 970/349-5542. Fax 970/349-6487. www.nordicinncb.com. 28 units. $82–$180 double. Rates include continental breakfast. AE, MC, V. Closed from the end of ski season through May. **Amenities:** Whirlpool tub. *In room:* TV, hair dryer, wireless Internet.

WHERE TO DINE

In addition to the restaurants recommended here, you'll find information on a number of dining choices, some with menus, on the Internet at **www.visitcrestedbutte.com**.

Le Bosquet COUNTRY FRENCH   Green plants peek through the lace curtains of this popular restaurant, which is our choice for a quiet, intimate dinner. Under the same ownership since 1978, the restaurant's menu changes seasonally, but always includes fresh seafood, beef, lamb, and vegetarian entrees. Typical entrees might include a roast rack of lamb in a red wine–and–garlic butter sauce; fresh tilapia in a sauce of tomatoes, spinach, feta cheese, Kalamata olives, fennel, and garlic; and the 10-ounce all-natural range-fed New York strip steak served with horseradish mashed new red potatoes. Available from 5:30 to 6:30pm only, the Twilight Menu offers, for $20, soup or salad, a choice of several entrees such as filet of ruby trout or grilled rack of pork, and a choice of desserts. There's also an excellent wine list.

Sixth St. at Belleview Ave. (in Majestic Plaza). ℂ **970/349-5808.** Reservations recommended. Entrees $18–$36. AE, DISC, MC, V. Daily 5:30–10pm. May be closed 1 month in spring and 2 weeks in fall.

The Slogar Bar & Restaurant AMERICAN   If you do something right, why mess around with anything else? That's the way the Slogar feels about its skillet-fried chicken and we couldn't agree more. The fixed-price menu offers chicken every night—the best in the region—accompanied by tangy coleslaw, mashed potatoes and gravy, biscuits with honey butter, creamed corn, and ice cream. Also available is a family-style steak dinner, which is fine, but we still prefer the chicken. The atmosphere here is 1880s Victorian, somewhat elegant but not so highbrow as to scare off families.

517 Second St., at Whiterock Ave. (© 970/349-5765. Reservations recommended. Fixed-price dinner $16–$24. AE, MC, V. Daily 5–9pm.

3 Salida: White-Water Rafting Center of the Rockies

138 miles SW of Denver, 96 miles W. of Pueblo, 82 miles N. of Alamosa

With a strategic location on the upper Arkansas River, it was natural that Salida (elevation 7,080 ft.) should become an important farming, ranching, and transportation center in its early days, and a major river-rafting and kayaking center today. Zebulon Pike opened the area for Americans in the early 19th century; he was followed by trappers, then miners after the discovery of gold in 1859. When Leadville boomed on silver in the late 1870s, the Denver & Rio Grande Railroad built a line up the Arkansas from Pueblo, and the town of Salida was founded at a key point on the line. The downtown core has kept its historic ambience alive, and now has a growing arts community while it serves as a base camp for outdoor recreation enthusiasts.

ESSENTIALS

GETTING THERE   By Car   U.S. 50 connects Salida with Gunnison, 66 miles west, and Pueblo, 96 miles east on I-25. Colo. 291 heads north from Salida, providing a vital 9-mile link between U.S. 50 and U.S. 285, which runs north-south 5 miles west of Salida (through Poncha Springs).

By Plane   The nearest airport with commercial service is at **Gunnison,** 65 miles west (see "Gunnison & Curecanti National Recreation Area," earlier in this chapter).

VISITOR INFORMATION   Consult the **Heart of the Rockies Chamber of Commerce,** 406 W. Rainbow Blvd. (U.S. 50), Salida, CO 81201 (© **877/772-5432** or 719/539-2068; www.salidachamber.org), which operates an information center Monday through Friday from 9am to 5pm.

GETTING AROUND   Salida sits on the southwestern bank of the Arkansas River, just above its confluence with the South Arkansas. U.S. 50 (Rainbow Blvd.), which follows the north bank of the South Arkansas, marks the southern edge of town. At the eastern city limit, Colo. 291 (Oak St.) turns north off U.S. 50, and 6 blocks later, turns northwest as First Street through the historic downtown area.

FAST FACTS   The **Medical Clinics,** 550 W. U.S. 50 (© **719/530-2000**), provides 24-hour emergency care. The **post office** is at 310 D St. Contact the U.S. Postal Service (© **800/275-8777;** www.usps.com) for hours and other information.

SPECIAL EVENTS   Continental Divide Auto Hill Climb, early June; FIBArk Whitewater Festival, mid-June; Art Walk, late June; Colorado Brewers Rendezvous, early July; Crest Crank Mountain Bike Ride, late August; Banana Belt Bicycle Weekend, mid-September; Lighting of Christmas Mountain USA, Thanksgiving weekend, late November.

RIVER RAFTING

Considered the white-water rafting center of the Rockies, Salida is the perfect base for enjoying the **Arkansas Headwaters Recreation Area,** a 148-mile stretch of river from Leadville to Pueblo Lake. With headquarters off Colo. 291 in downtown Salida at 307 W. Sackett Ave., Salida, CO 81201 (© **719/539-7289;** www.parks.state.co.us), the recreation area includes about 20 developed sites along the river, offering raft and kayak access, fishing, hiking, camping, and picnicking. There are also undeveloped areas that offer access to the river, but be careful to avoid trespassing on private property. User fees are $5 per vehicle per day, plus $12 per night for camping.

The busiest stretch of the river is Browns Canyon, a granite wilderness between Buena Vista and Salida, with Class III and IV rapids (moderately difficult to difficult) along a 10-mile stretch of river from Nathrop to Stone Bridge.

Most people explore Colorado's rivers with experienced rafting companies, which provide trips on stretches of river that range from practically calm and suitable for everyone to extremely difficult, with long, violent rapids that are recommended only for skilled white-water boaters. Leading outfitters include **Dvorak's Expeditions** ✿✿ (© **800/824-3795** or 719/539-6851; www.dvorakexpeditions.com); **Whitewater Encounters** (© **800/530-8362** or 719/530-0937; www.weraft.com); and **American Adventure Expeditions** (© **800/288-0675** or 719/395-2409; www.american adventure.com). Generally, adult rates for half-day raft trips are $40 to $60; full-day trips including lunch are in the $70 to $95 range, and multiday excursions start at about $200. Prices for children are about 20% less. For a full listing of dozens of rafting companies approved to run the Arkansas, contact the recreation area office (see above).

OTHER SPORTS & OUTDOOR ACTIVITIES

FISHING   The Arkansas River is considered by many to be the finest fishing river in Colorado. There's also trout fishing in numerous alpine lakes, including Cottonwood Lake, Twin Lakes, and O'Haver Lake. For tips on the best fishing spots, plus licenses, supplies, and equipment sales and rentals, stop at **Arkansas River Fly Shop,** 7500 W. U.S. 50, Salida (© **719/539-3474;** www.arkanglers.com), which also offers a guide service. Cost for a guided half-day wading trip for one person is $125, and a half-day float-fishing trip on the Arkansas River for two costs $225. The company also offers fly-fishing and fly-tying lessons.

GOLF   The **Salida Golf Club,** a municipal course that opened in 1926, is at Crestone Avenue and Grant Street (© **719/539-1060**). Greens fees are $23 for 18 holes.

HIKING   There are outstanding trails for all experience levels throughout the region, particularly in the San Isabel National Forest, along the eastern slope of the Continental Divide west of Salida. Of particular interest are hikes into the Collegiate Range (mts. Harvard, Columbia, Yale, Princeton, and Oxford) off Cottonwood Creek Road west of Buena Vista, and trips from the ghost town of St. Elmo up Chalk Creek Road from Mount Princeton Hot Springs.

For maps and other information, stop at the **Salida Ranger District** office, 325 W. Rainbow Blvd. (© **719/539-3591;** www.fs.fed.us/r2).

MOUNTAIN BIKING   There are numerous trails suitable for mountain biking throughout the area, and many provide stupendous views of the surrounding 14,000-plus-foot peaks. **Absolute Bikes,** 330 W. Sackett St. (© **888/539-9295** or 719/539-9295; www.absolutebikes.com), rents, sells, and services mountain bikes and can provide information on nearby trails. Rentals—from three-speed townies to full-suspension, plus kid bikes, tandems, and road bikes—are available. Prices start at $30 per day for mountain bikes; $10 for kid bikes and adult's town cruisers.

ROCKHOUNDING   The richest mineral and gem beds in Colorado are found in the upper Arkansas River valley and the eastern slope of the Continental Divide, just west of Salida. For a free brochure on rockhounding locations, stop at the chamber of commerce office. Those wanting hammers, eye protection, and other equipment will find it at **The Rock Doc** at Prospector's Village, 17897 U.S. 285, north of Salida (© **719/539-2019**).

SKIING & SNOWBOARDING   Among the finest of Colorado's small ski resorts, **Monarch Mountain** 🏔🏔, 20 miles west of Salida at Monarch Pass on U.S. 50, serves all levels of ability with 54 trails, with 14% rated beginner, 28% intermediate, 27% advanced, and 31% expert. The longest run is one mile.

Covering 800 acres, the mountain has a vertical drop of 1,170 feet from its summit of 11,961 feet. It gets about 350 inches of snow annually, and has no snow-making equipment. It has one fixed quad and four double chairs. All-day tickets are $49 for adults, $31 for youths 13 to 15, $19 for juniors 7 to 12, $26 for seniors 62 to 69, and free for those under 7 or over 69. The area is usually open from late November to early April, daily from 9am to 4pm. For information, contact the resort at 1 Powder Place, Monarch, CO 81227 (© **888/996-7669** or 719/539-3573; www.skimonarch.com). You'll find comfortable accommodations and dining at the 100-room **Monarch Mountain Lodge,** 22720 W. U.S. 50, Monarch, CO 81227 (© **888/996-7669** or 719/530-5000; www.skimonarch.com).

SEEING THE SIGHTS

Monarch Crest Tram   Climbing from 11,312-foot Monarch Pass to the Continental Divide at an altitude of 12,012 feet, this tram offers views of five mountain ranges—up to 150 miles away—when skies are clear. The tram includes six four-passenger gondolas. At the top is a large gift shop. Allow about 2 hours.

Monarch Pass, U.S. 50, 22 miles west of Salida. © **719/539-4091**. Admission $7 adults, $6 seniors over 55, $4 children 12 and under. Mid-May to mid-Sept, weather permitting, daily 8:30am–5:30pm.

Mt. Shavano Fish Hatchery   This state-run fish hatchery, about a half-mile northwest of town off Colo. 291, produces some 2 million trout each year, used to stock Colorado's numerous streams and lakes. Visitors can see how the hatchery operates, walk among the fish raceways and ponds, and feed the fish (food provided from coin-operated machines). Guided tours are provided daily 10am to 4pm from June until Labor Day, and self-guided tours are available at other times. Allow 30 minutes to an hour.

7725 C.R. 154. © **719/539-6877**. Free admission. Daily 7:30am–4pm.

Salida Hot Springs   Colorado's largest indoor hot springs have been in commercial operation since 1937, when the Works Progress Administration built the pools as a Depression-era project. Ute tribes considered the mineral waters, rich in bicarbonate, sodium, and sulfate, to be sacred and medicinal. Today, the main 25m (82-ft.) pool, with two lap lanes available at all times, is kept at a refreshing 82°F (28°C), and a 4-foot-deep leisure pool, with a ramp entrance, is kept at about 100°F (38°C). Also available are aquasize and arthritis classes, and swimming lessons for all ages. Adjacent Centennial Park has a picnic pavilion, playground, and tennis and volleyball courts. Allow 1 to 3 hours.

410 W. Rainbow Blvd. (U.S. 50). © **719/539-6738**. www.salidapool.com. Admission $6 adults, $5 seniors 60 and older, $4 students 6–17, $2 children 5 and under. Memorial Day to Labor Day daily 1–9pm; call or check website for winter hours.

Salida Museum   The Salida Museum provides a look at the history of this part of Colorado, with a wide selection of pioneer, mining, and railroad exhibits, plus displays on the lives of the American Indians who lived here. You'll see lots of arrowheads, plus exhibits that explain how baskets and pots were made. The museum also contains rocks, fossils, and shells from the area, plus petrified wood and dinosaur bones and teeth. You can learn about Laura Evans, a local madam who operated a brothel in Salida from the late 1800s until 1953, and see a replica of a lady's bedroom of the late 1800s, bizarre-looking medical equipment, and bone baskets—used to transport corpses in the late 1800s. Allow 30 minutes.

406½ W. Rainbow Blvd. (U.S. 50). ℭ 719/539-7483. www.salidachamber.org/museum. Admission $3 adults, $1 children 6–12, free for kids under 6. Memorial Day to Labor Day Mon–Sat 10am–4pm. Located just behind the chamber of commerce.

WHERE TO STAY

Rates are highest here during summer, and lowest in late winter and early spring (before rafting season begins). Among reliable chain motels in the area are the **Best Western Colorado Lodge,** 352 W. Rainbow Blvd./U.S. 50 (ℭ **800/777-7947** or 719/539-2514), with double rates from $64 to $92; **Comfort Inn,** 315 E. Rainbow Blvd./U.S. 50 (ℭ **800/424-6423** or 719/539-5000), with rates from $70 to $100 for two; **Days Inn,** 407 E. Rainbow Blvd./U.S. 50 (ℭ **800/329-7466** or 719/539-6651), with double rates from $50 to $99; **Econo Lodge,** 1310 E. Rainbow Blvd./U.S. 50 (ℭ **800/553-2666** or 719/539-2895), with rates for two from $49 to $119; and the **Travelodge,** 7310 U.S. 50 (ℭ **800/234-1077** or 719/539-2528), with double rates from $59 to $109. Room tax adds just under 9% to lodging bills.

Aspen Leaf Lodge *Value*   This small family-owned-and-operated motel has a friendly feel, from the forest of large evergreens and aspens surrounding the hot-tub pavilion to the coffeepot that's on in the office each morning. The one-story motel has simply but attractively decorated rooms with one king or two queen beds. Rollaways are available. Guests also have use of a secluded deck overlooking a peaceful horse pasture, and there are restaurants within walking distance.

7350 W. U.S. 50, Salida, CO 81201-9341. ℭ 800/759-0338 for reservations only, or 719/539-6733. Fax 719/539-6304. www.aspenleaflodge.com. 18 units. $50–$99 double. AE, DISC, MC, V. Small pets accepted with $5 fee. *In room:* A/C, TV, fridge, wireless Internet, microwave.

River Run Inn *★*   Built by Chaffee County in 1895 as a home for the indigent, this building—about 3 miles northwest of town—served that purpose for half a century. Since 1983, however, it has functioned as a charming bed-and-breakfast, and is listed on the National Register of Historic Places. A wide front porch leads into a large sitting room and library, and the back porch looks out over a small pond and to the rolling hills and mountains beyond. The lovely guest rooms, most with mountain views, are decorated with period furnishings, including brass or four-poster beds and have either all new showers or tubs (not both). The king room bathroom has its own whirlpool tub. The dormitory, available to parties of 5 to 13 people, who share a bathroom, covers the entire third floor. Full breakfasts include a hot entree, such as a specialty rolled oven omelet or stuffed French toast, fresh baked goods, and fresh fruit. The grounds include a section of the Arkansas River that provides private fishing access (a Colorado fishing license is required). Smoking is not allowed.

8495 C.R. 160, Salida, CO 81201. ℭ 800/385-6925 or 719/539-3818. Fax 801/659-1878. www.riverruninn.com. 7 units (6 with private bathroom). $100–$125 double with private bathroom; $30–$40 per person for dormitory. Rates include full breakfast. AE, MC, V. Children over 12 welcome. *In room:* Wireless Internet, no phone.

WHERE TO DINE

Country Bounty Restaurant & Gift Shoppe AMERICAN   This combination gift shop and restaurant gives diners plenty to look at while waiting for their meals. The gift shop seems to spill over into the restaurant with all manner of country-style crafts, Southwestern jewelry, and other items. The lunch menu (also served at dinner) offers cheeseburgers, sandwiches and wraps, and some great salads—try the spinach Cobb salad: fresh spinach, egg, crumbled bacon, red onion, fresh mushrooms, tomatoes, and avocado, topped with a grilled lemon chicken breast and crumbled Gorgonzola cheese. For dinner you might choose the traditional pot roast (slowly braised beef with carrots, onions, celery, and yellow and red potatoes, in a rich gravy) or opt for the fresh Atlantic salmon filet, seasoned with lemon, roasted garlic, virgin olive oil, capers, and dry white wine. The Country Bounty is also locally famous for its pies and cobblers.

413 W. U.S. 50. ⓒ **719/539-3546.** www.countrybounty.net. Lunch items $5.50–$11; dinner entrees $5.50–$17. AE, DISC, MC, V. Summer daily 7am–9pm; winter daily 7am–8pm.

First St. Café ⓖ AMERICAN/MEXICAN   In the heart of historic downtown Salida, First St. Café occupies an 1880 two-story brick building, with hardwood floors and regional paintings. Among the town's most popular restaurants, it's a focal point for artists, musicians, and other creative types. The kitchen turns out excellent homestyle cooking such as pepper steak, made with either a New York strip or filet mignon, plus fresh cracked pepper and a burgundy-mushroom sauce. Another plus: The steaks are hand cut in-house, and the hamburgers are prepared from fresh, extra-lean ground beef. The spicy Colorado burrito is cooked the proper way—with shredded beef (ground beef is acceptable only in cheap fast-food joints) plus beans, all smothered with red chile and cheese. The restaurant also serves vegetarian casseroles, fish and chips, burgers, a variety of sandwiches, a daily quiche, and fish. The soup and salad bar is included with all dinners.

137 E. First St. ⓒ **877/314-7145** or 719/539-4759. www.firststreetcafe.net. Lunch items $6.95–$9.95; dinner main courses $8.95–$21. AE, DISC, MC, V. May–Sept Sun–Thurs 11am–9pm; Fri–Sat 11am–10pm; closed Sun and closes 1 hour earlier the rest of the year.

4 Alamosa & Great Sand Dunes National Park & Preserve

212 miles SW of Denver, 149 miles E. of Durango, 173 miles N. of Santa Fe, New Mexico

If you're looking for Colorado's largest sandbox, here it is: Just 35 miles from Alamosa are the tallest sand dunes in North America.

Founded in 1878 with the extension of the Denver & Rio Grande Railroad into the San Luis Valley, the town was named for the cottonwood (*álamo* in Spanish) trees that lined the banks of the Rio Grande. Soon rails spread out in all directions from the community, and it became a thriving transportation center for farmers and a supply depot for miners. Farming remains important today, but Alamosa has also become an educational center with Adams State College, a 4-year institution founded in 1921. Elevation is 7,544 feet, and the population is a bit under 8,000.

ESSENTIALS

GETTING THERE   By Car   Alamosa is at the junction of U.S. 160, which runs east 73 miles to I-25 at Walsenburg and west to Durango; and U.S. 285, which extends south to Santa Fe, New Mexico, and north to Denver. Because of a jog in U.S. 285, however, a more direct route into the city from the north is to take Colo. 17 the last 50 miles.

By Plane   The **San Luis Valley Regional Airport** (© **719/589-9446**), 2500 State St., 3 miles off U.S. 285 South, has service to and from Denver with **United Express** (© **800/241-6522**).

VISITOR INFORMATION   The **Alamosa County Visitor Information Center,** Cole Park (Chamber Dr. at Third St.), Alamosa, CO 81101 (© **800/258-7597** or 719/589-4840; www.alamosa.org), operates a visitor information center, with summer hours from 8am to 6pm Monday through Friday and from 9am to 4pm Saturday and Sunday; and winter hours from 8am to 5pm Monday through Friday.

FAST FACTS   The **San Luis Valley Regional Medical Center,** with a 24-hour emergency room, is at 106 Blanca Ave. (© **719/589-2511**). The **post office** is at 505 Third St., off State Avenue. Contact the U.S. Postal Service (© **800/275-8777**; www.usps.com) for hours and other information.

SPECIAL EVENTS   Crane Festival, mid-March, in Monte Vista; Rodeo, late June; Farm and Ranch Heritage Days, early July, Monte Vista; Early Iron Festival (classic cars and hot rods), Labor Day weekend.

GREAT SAND DUNES NATIONAL PARK & PRESERVE 🐾🐾

Just 35 miles northeast of Alamosa, on Colo. 150, is Colorado's fourth—and newest—national park. Since 2000, when Congress passed the law approving park status pending the acquisition of "sufficient land having a sufficient diversity of resources," Coloradoans had been waiting for this moment. It came in 2004, when the U.S. secretary of the interior arrived at Great Sand Dunes to publicly announce the designation of Great Sand Dunes National Park and Preserve. The necessary property was acquired with the help of the Nature Conservancy.

Far from any sea or major desert, this 39-square-mile expanse of sand seems incongruous here. The dunes are the tallest on the continent, piled nearly 750 feet high against the western edge of the Sangre de Cristo Mountains—a startling sight. The dunes were created over thousands of years by southwesterly winds blowing across the valley. They formed when streams of water from melting glaciers carried rocks, gravel, and silt down from the mountains. In addition, as the Rio Grande changed its course, it left behind sand, silt, and debris.

Even today the winds are changing the face of the dunes. So-called "reversing winds" from the mountains pile the dunes back upon themselves, building them higher and higher. Though it's physically impossible for sand to be piled steeper than 34 degrees, the dunes often appear sheerer because of deceptive shadows and colors that change with the light: gold, pink, tan, sometimes even bluish. Climbing dunes is fun, but it can be tiring at this 8,200-foot altitude. *Beware:* The sand's surface can reach 140°F (60°C) in summer.

Among the specialized animals that survive in this weird environment are the Ord's kangaroo rat, a creature that never drinks water, plus four insects found nowhere else on earth: the Great Sand Dunes tiger beetle and three other beetle varieties. These animals and the flora of the adjacent mountain foothills are discussed in evening programs and guided walks during summer.

For orientation, walk the easy .5-mile self-guided nature trail that begins at the visitor center. If you want more of a challenge, hike the dunes—you can get to the top of a 750-foot dune and back in about 90 minutes. Those who make it all the way to the top are rewarded with spectacular views of the dunes and the surrounding mountains.

Pinyon Flats Campground, with 88 sites, is open year-round. It has picnic tables, fire grates, flush toilets, and drinking water, but no showers or RV hookups. Campsites are assigned on a first-come, first-served basis, and cost $14 per night. Admission to the monument for up to a week is $3 per person (free for those under 17). The **visitor center** (© 719/378-6399) is open daily year-round (closed on winter holidays). For further information, contact Great Sand Dunes National Park and Preserve, 11999 Colo. 150, Mosca, CO 81146 (© **719/378-6300;** www.nps.gov/grsa).

From Alamosa, there are two main routes to Great Sand Dunes: east 14 miles on U.S. 160, then north on Colo. 150; or north 14 miles on Colo. 17 to Mosca, then east on Six Mile Lane to the junction of Colo. 150.

SPORTS & OUTDOOR ACTIVITIES

Many of the best outdoor activities in this part of the state take place in the **Rio Grande National Forest,** with the Supervisor's Office at 1803 W. U.S. 160, Monte Vista, CO 81144 (© **719/852-5941;** www.fs.fed.us/r2). For equipment for a variety of outdoor activities (including mountain bike and ski rentals), visit **Kristi Mountain Sports,** Villa Mall, 3217 Main St., Alamosa (© **719/589-9759**).

FISHING   The Rio Grande is an outstanding stream for trout, walleye, and catfish; and there are numerous high mountain lakes and streams throughout the Rio Grande National Forest where you're apt to catch rainbow, brown, brook, cutthroat, and Rio Grande cutthroat trout. For information, contact the Forest Service office (see above). You can get licenses, tackle, and advice at **Wal-Mart,** 3333 Clark St., off U.S. 160 about 3 miles east of downtown Alamosa (© **719/589-9071**).

GOLF   The **Cattails Golf Club,** 6615 N. River Rd. (© **719/589-9515**), is an 18-hole course along the Rio Grande on the north side of Alamosa. Generally open March through November, the cost is $30 for 18 holes. The 9-hole **Monte Vista Country Club,** at 101 Country Club Dr. in the town of Monte Vista (© **719/852-4906**), 17 miles west of Alamosa, is a particularly challenging course due to its small greens. Open April through October, the course is on the migratory path of sandhill and whooping cranes. The fee is $22 for 18 holes.

HIKING   The best opportunities in the region are found in the surrounding **Rio Grande National Forest,** with nearly 2 million acres. One of the most popular hikes, with easy access, is **Zapata Falls,** reached off Colo. 150 about 20 miles northeast of Alamosa and south of Great Sand Dunes. This cavernous waterfall on the northwest flank of 14,345-foot Mount Blanca freezes in winter, turning its cave into a natural icebox that often remains frozen well into summer. More challenging hikes include trails into the **Wheeler Geologic Area,** known for its unique rock formations. Obtain directions from the Forest Service (see above).

MOUNTAIN BIKING   There are plenty of opportunities for mountain biking on local federal lands. Stop at the visitor center to pick up a copy of the *San Luis Valley Mountain Bike Guide.* Get additional information from the Forest Service (see above), or stop at **Kristi Mountain Sports** (see above) for tips on the best places to go, rentals (starting around $25 per day), repairs, and accessories.

SWIMMING   **Splashland Hot Springs,** 5895 S. Colo. 17 (© **719/589-6307**), 1 mile north of Alamosa via U.S. 160, has a geothermally heated outdoor pool (94°F/34°C average temperature) measuring 150 feet by 60 feet, with both high dive and low dive, and a popular mini–water slide. There's also an 18-inch-deep wading

Moments   The Cumbres & Toltec Scenic Railroad

This is our idea of the best way to see this country. Built in 1880 to serve remote mining camps, the **Cumbres & Toltec Scenic Railroad** ★★ follows a spectacular 64-mile path through the San Juan Mountains from Antonito, Colorado, to Chama, New Mexico. This narrow-gauge steam railroad weaves through groves of pine and aspen and past strange rock formations before ascending through the spectacular Toltec Gorge of the Los Piños River. At the rail-junction community of Osier, passengers picnic or enjoy a catered lunch while the *Colorado Limited* exchanges engines with the *New Mexico Express*. Round-trip passengers return to their starting point in Antonito, while onward passengers continue a climb through tunnels and trestles to the summit of 10,015-foot Cumbres Pass, then drop down a precipitous 4% grade to Chama. A joint venture by the states of Colorado and New Mexico, the train is a registered National Historic Site.

A through trip from Antonito to Chama (or vice versa), traveling one-way by train and return by bus, costs $72 for adults, $36 for children 11 and under. A regular round-trip to Osier is $59 for adults and $30 for children 11 and under, but this omits either the gorge or the pass. Either way, it's an all-day adventure, leaving between 8 and 10:30am, and returning between 4:30 and 6:30pm. All fares include a hot lunch at Osier. The train operates daily from Memorial Day weekend to mid-October. For reservations and information, contact the Cumbres & Toltec Scenic Railroad, P.O. Box 1057, Chama, NM 87520 (© **888/286-2737** or 719/376-5483 for the Antonito Depot; www.cumbrestoltec.com). The depot is 28 miles south of Alamosa, just off U.S. 285.

pool. Bathing suits, towels, and pool paraphernalia can be rented; there's a snack bar and public showers. It's open Memorial Day to Labor Day, Thursday through Tuesday. Weekday hours are from 10am to 6:30pm; Saturday and Sunday from noon to 9pm. Pool passes cost $3 to $6.

OTHER HIGHLIGHTS

Adams State College–Luther E. Bean Museum   Located on the second floor of Richardson Hall in room 256, this museum has an excellent fine-art gallery featuring works by local artists. Also on display is the Woodard Collection, a sampling of artifacts from around the world. Allow about an hour.

208 Edgemont Blvd. © **719/587-7151.** Free admission. Mon–Fri 1–4:30pm. Closed Dec 23–Jan 1 and other major holidays.

Colorado Gators ★ *Kids*   Alligators in Colorado? Yep, they're here! Geothermal wells keep the temperature a cozy 87°F (31°C) at this fish and alligator farm and wildlife habitat, located 17 miles north of Alamosa off Colo. 17. There are more than 400 alligators at the farm—some up to 11 feet long and weighing about 600 pounds. Kids should love watching the alligator feedings, which happen several times each day. The farm also raises fish, desert tortoises, turtles, and iguanas. Allow about an hour.

9162 C.R. 9 North, Mosca. (C) **719/378-2612.** www.gatorfarm.com. Admission $10 adults, $5 children 6–12 and seniors 65–79, free for those under 6 and over 80. Memorial Day through Labor Day daily 9am–7pm; rest of year daily 9am–5pm. Closed Thanksgiving and Christmas.

Rio Grande Scenic Railroad   New in 2006, this must-do experience for railroad fans isn't really new at all. Diesel locomotives haul classic Pullman passenger railroad through the mountains and valleys of southern Colorado, with several trips available, over routes more than a hundred years old. Typical is the half-day round-trip excursion between Alamosa and Antonito, but you can also go one-way, perhaps catching a train back in a day or two, or go round-trip between Alamosa and the mountain community of La Veta. The passenger cars are climate controlled with comfortable seating, and the trains have snack bars and open-air observation cars. Allow at least a half-day.

601 State St. (C) **877/726-7245.** www.alamosatrain.com. From $12 adult, $10 senior, $8 child round-trip. Call for current schedule.

NATURAL HIGHLIGHTS

The **Alamosa–Monte Vista National Wildlife Refuges** ((C) **719/589-4021;** http://alamosa.fws.gov) together have preserved nearly 25,000 acres of vital land for a variety of marsh birds and waterfowl, including many migrating and wintering species. Sandhill and whooping cranes visit in early to mid-October and early March; at other times of the year there may be egrets, herons, avocets, bitterns, and other avian species. A wide variety of ducks are year-round residents, and waterfowl numbers are at their peak March through May.

The refuges have self-guided driving tours with a number of viewpoints, and also several hiking trails. Bring binoculars, since they'll be useful. To get to the Alamosa refuge, which contains the visitor center ((C) **719/589-4705**) and refuge headquarters, go 4 miles east of Alamosa on U.S. 160 and then south 3 miles on El Rancho Lane. Monte Vista refuge is located 6 miles south of the community of Monte Vista on Colo. 15. Admission is free.

The refuges are open daily from sunrise to sunset; the visitor center is open from March through November, Monday through Friday from 7:30am to 4pm; and the rest of the year it is open Monday, Wednesday, and Friday from 11am to 4pm.

WHERE TO STAY & DINE

Your base camp for exploring this area will likely be Alamosa (zip code 81101), where there are a number of typical chain motels and a variety of restaurants.

Some reliable chain properties include the **Best Western Alamosa Inn,** 2005 Main St. ((C) **800/459-5123** or 719/589-2567), with a restaurant that serves three meals daily and double rates of $70 to $95; **Comfort Inn,** 6301 U.S. 160 ((C) **800/424-6423** or 719/587-9000), charging $55 to $100 double; and **Super 8,** 2505 W. Main St. ((C) **800/800-8000** or 719/589-6447), with double rates of $59 to $69.

You'll find a number of restaurants along Main Street. We especially like the Mexican food at **Mrs. Rivera's Kitchen,** 1019 Sixth St. ((C) **719/589-0277**), open from 11am to 9pm (closes 8pm in winter) Monday through Saturday, with prices from $4.95 to $12. We also recommend the restaurant at the **Best Western Alamosa Inn** (see above).

Room tax adds almost 11% to lodging bills.

The Cottonwood Bed & Breakfast and Gallery   This delightful bed-and-breakfast has a distinctly artsy orientation. Innkeeper Deborah Donaldson has decorated the common areas and bedrooms as a gallery of regional art, much of which is for sale. The Cottonwood is composed of two main buildings and a carriage house. The 1908 neocolonial two-story bungalow has five guest rooms, furnished largely in Arts and Crafts style. Each room is unique: The Rosa Room has a queen and single beds to accommodate small families, along with children's books and stuffed animals, while the Blanca Room weds a nice airy white decor with Art Deco motifs. Bathrooms in three of these units have showers only; the others have shower/tub combos. Adjacent to the bungalow is a 1920s fourplex with four apartment suites, each with a kitchen and claw-foot tub with shower conversion. These are perfect for families with children or pets. Located between the two main buildings is a cobblestone courtyard with a hot tub, and the carriage house, perfect for those who prefer being off by themselves. Full homemade breakfasts often feature regional specialties, such as fresh fruit crepes with Mexican chocolate and whipped cream. Smoking is not permitted.

123 San Juan Ave., Alamosa, CO 81101. ℂ 800/955-2623 or 719/589-3882. Fax 719/589-6437. www.cottonwood inn.com. 10 units. $55–$125 double; $15 per extra adult; $10 per child. Rates include full breakfast. AE, DC, DISC, MC, V. Located 3 blocks north of Main St. Pets accepted in 2 apt suites with $60 deposit. **Amenities:** Outdoor hot tub.

5 A Side Trip to Creede: A Slice of Colorado's Mining History

Among the best preserved of all 19th-century Colorado mining towns, Creede had a population of 10,000 in 1892 when a balladeer wrote, "It's day all day in the daytime, and there is no night in Creede." Over $1 million in silver was mined every day, but the Silver Panic of 1893 eclipsed Creede's rising star. For most of the next century, area mines produced just enough silver and other minerals to sustain the community until the 1960s, when tourism and outdoor recreation became paramount. Today this mountain town, at an elevation of 8,838 feet, has a population of about 400. It's fairly easy to see most of the town in a day, and be sure to include a stop at the Creede Museum, drive the Bachelor Historic Tour route, and if at all possible attend a show at the Creede Repertory Theatre.

To get to Creede from Alamosa, drive west on U.S. 160 about 48 miles to South Fork, and turn north on Colo. 149, which follows the Rio Grande about 23 miles to Creede.

You can obtain information on what to see and do, as well as lodging and dining options, from the **Creede/Mineral County Chamber of Commerce,** in the County Annex building at the north end of Main Street (P.O. Box 580), Creede, CO 81130 (ℂ **800/327-2102** or 719/658-2374; www.creede.com). The office is staffed Monday through Friday from 9am to 5pm, and brochures and other information are available on a self-serve basis 24 hours daily. There's also a visitor information booth on Main Street in the middle of town, open daily from 9am to 5pm from Memorial Day to mid-September. Another good source for information is the **Divide Ranger District office** of the U.S. Forest Service, located at the corner of 3rd Street and Creede Avenue (ℂ **719/658-2556;** www.fs.fed.us/r2), which can provide maps and information on hiking, mountain biking, horseback riding, four-wheeling, fishing, cross-country skiing, and all sorts of other outdoor activities in the nearby San Juan and Rio Grande national forests.

There's plenty to do in Creede, but for our money the absolutely best way to spend some here is to take in a production by the **Creede Repertory Theatre** ☆☆, P.O. Box 269, Creede, CO 81130 (© **866/658-2540** or 719/658-2540; www.creederep.org). Established in 1966 by a small troupe of young actors from the University of Kansas, this theater company is now nationally acclaimed, and offers matinee and evening performances from mid-June to late September in its 243-seat main theater and a separate 90-seat theater, both at 124 North Main St. The company usually presents four full-length productions, a family show, and sometimes shorter plays, in repertory. Productions vary, but might be musicals, comedies, contemporary or classic dramas. Recent productions have included Matthew Barber's romantic comedy *Enchanted April*, Noel Coward's *Hay Fever*, and a family show, *The Magic of Roald Dahl*, storytelling with puppets. Tickets for full-length productions run from $15 to $25, and family shows are $7 to $15. In addition to its repertory theater productions, the company presents a variety of concerts and other special events year-round. Advance reservations are strongly recommended.

Stop at the chamber office, visitor information booth, or the Divide Ranger District office (see above) for directions to the **Wheeler Geologic Area,** a region of volcanic rock formations accessible only by jeep, horseback, or a 5-hour hike; and **North Creede Canyon,** where remnants of the old town of Creede still stand near the **Commodore Mine,** whose workings seem to keep a ghostly vigil over the canyon.

The former Denver & Rio Grande Railroad depot is now the **Creede Museum,** behind City Park (© **719/658-2004**), which tells the story of the town's wild-and-woolly heyday. There were dozens of saloons and gambling tables, and shootouts were not uncommon. Bob Ford, the killer of Jesse James, was murdered in his own saloon, and Bat Masterson and "Poker Alice" Tubbs were other notorious residents. Photographs and exhibits on gambling and other activities are included in the museum's collection, as well as a horse-drawn hearse, and you can obtain a walking-tour map of the town here. It's usually open Monday through Saturday from 10am to 4pm in summer, with free admission.

The **Underground Mining Museum,** on the north edge of town (© **719/658-0811**), is contained in a series of rooms and tunnels blasted into a cliff face. Inside this subterranean world are exhibits that trace the history of mining, along with displays of mining memorabilia and gemstones. It's always 51°F (11°C) down here, so bring a jacket. Guided tours are offered ($10, reservations required), and there's also a gift shop. The museum is open daily from 10am to 4pm in summer, with shorter hours the rest of the year. Admission costs $6 for adults, $5 for seniors 60 and over, and $4 for children 12 and under.

The 17-mile **Bachelor Historic Tour** is described in a booklet available from the chamber of commerce ($1). The route follows a Forest Service road through the mountains, past abandoned mines, mining equipment, the original Creede cemetery, and 19th-century town sites. The road is fine for passenger cars in dry weather, but may be closed by winter snow. Allow 1 to 2 hours.

14

Southeastern Colorado

Colorado's southeastern quadrant owes its life to the Arkansas River, which forges one of the world's most spectacular canyons—the deep, narrow Royal Gorge. On the river's trek through Pueblo it not only supplies water for a major steel industry but also provides the reason-for-being for a delightful riverfront park, walkway, and shopping area. From Pueblo, the river rolls across the Great Plains, providing life-giving water to an arid but soil-rich region that produces a wide variety of vegetables and fruits. Bent's Old Fort, a national historic site that has re-created one of the West's most important frontier trading posts, also rests beside the river, east of the community of La Junta. South of Pueblo, the town of Trinidad is the center of a century-old coal-mining district, boasting a number of handsome old Victorian-style buildings.

1 Pueblo

111 miles S. of Denver, 42 miles S. of Colorado Springs, 317 miles N. of Albuquerque, New Mexico

Don't trust your first impressions. As you drive through Pueblo along the interstate, it might appear that this bland but industrious city—with its railroad tracks, warehouses, and factories—doesn't warrant a stop. But take the time to get off the superslab and discover the real Pueblo. You'll find handsome historic homes, fine Western art, a well-run zoo, a delightful riverfront park, and a number of outdoor recreational opportunities.

Although Zebulon Pike and his U.S. Army exploratory expedition camped at the future site of Pueblo in 1806, there were no white settlements here until 1842, when El Pueblo Fort was constructed as a fur-trading outpost. It was abandoned following a Ute massacre in late 1854, but when the Colorado gold rush began 5 years later, the town of Pueblo was born on the site of the former fort.

In the early 20th century, the city grew as a major center for coal mining and steel production. Job opportunities attracted large numbers of immigrants, especially from Mexico and eastern Europe. Pueblo today is home to high-tech industries as well as the University of Southern Colorado. As the largest city (pop. a bit over 100,000) in southeastern Colorado, it is the market center for a 15-county region extending to the borders of New Mexico, Oklahoma, and Kansas. Elevation is 4,695 feet.

ESSENTIALS

GETTING THERE   By Car   I-25 links Pueblo directly with Colorado Springs, Denver, and points north; and Santa Fe, Albuquerque, and other New Mexico cities to the south. U.S. 50 runs east to La Junta and west to Cañon City, Gunnison, and Montrose.

By Plane   Pueblo Memorial Airport, 31201 Bryan Circle, Keeler Parkway off U.S. 50 East (© **719/553-2760;** www.pueblo.us), is served by **Great Lakes Airlines** (© **800/554-5111;** www.greatlakesav.com) with daily flights to Denver and other locations. Agencies providing rental cars at the airport include **Avis** (© **800/831-2847** or 719/948-9665) and **Hertz** (© **800/654-3131** or 719/948-3345).

VISITOR INFORMATION   Contact the **Greater Pueblo Chamber of Commerce,** 302 N. Santa Fe Ave. (P.O. Box 697), Pueblo, CO 81003 (© **800/233-3446** or 719/542-1704; www.pueblochamber.org and www.destinationpueblo.com), for most travel-related needs. The **Visitor Information Center** is located at the chamber office, which is open year-round Monday through Friday from 8am to 5pm, and some Saturdays from 10am to 2pm.

GETTING AROUND   Pueblo lies on the eastward-flowing Arkansas River at its confluence with Fountain Creek. The downtown core is located north of the Arkansas and west of the Fountain, immediately west of I-25. Santa Fe Avenue and Main Street, 1 block west, are the principal north-south thoroughfares; the cross streets are numbered (counting northward), with Fourth and Eighth streets the most important. Pueblo Boulevard circles the city on the south and west, with spurs leading to the nature center and Lake Pueblo State Park.

Public transportation is provided by **Pueblo Transit** (© **719/553-2725;** www.pueblo.us). For taxi service, call **City Cab** (© **719/543-2525**). In addition to the rental-car agencies at the airport (see above), there is also an outlet for **Enterprise** in Pueblo (© **800/325-8007** or 719/542-6100).

FAST FACTS   Medical services, including emergency services, are provided by **Parkview Medical Center,** 400 W. 16th St. (© **719/584-4000;** www.parkviewmc.com), and **St. Mary-Corwin Medical Center,** 1008 Minnequa Ave. (© **719/560-4000;** www.stmarycorwin.org). The main **post office** is located at 1022 Fontino Blvd.; call the U.S. Postal Service (© **800/275-8777;** www.usps.com) for hours and locations of other post offices.

SPECIAL EVENTS   Bluegrass Festival, at the Greenway & Nature Center, early June; Boats, Blues & BBQ on the Historic Arkansas Riverwalk, mid-June; Rocky Mountain Street Rod Nationals, late June; National Little Britches Rodeo Finals, mid-July; Colorado State Fair, late August into early September; the Chile and Frijoles Festival, late September; Veterans Day Parade, early November; and the Christmas Art Show and Parade of Lights, late November.

WHAT TO SEE & DO

Historic Pueblo runs along Union Avenue north from the Arkansas River to First Street, a distance of about 5 blocks. More than 40 buildings in the **Union Avenue Historic District** (www.seepueblo.com) are listed on the National Register of Historic Places, including the **Vail Hotel** (217 S. Grand Ave.), headquarters of the **Pueblo County Historical Society** museum and library (© **719/543-6772;** www.pueblo history.org), with railroad memorabilia, locally made saddles, and some 8,000 books, historical maps, and photographs depicting Pueblo's history. **Union Depot,** with its mosaic-tile floors and beautiful stained-glass windows, houses retail stores and offices, yet still serves rail freight lines. **Walking-tour maps** can be obtained at the Visitor Information Center (see "Visitor Information," above), as well as from Union Avenue businesses.

ACCOMMODATIONS ■
Abriendo Inn **6**
Best Western Eagle Ridge
Inn & Suites **4**
Comfort Inn **4**
Hampton Inn **4**
Quality Inn & Suites **4**

DINING ◆
Ianne's Whiskey Ridge **2**
La Renaissance **7**
Patti's Restaurant **13**

ATTRACTIONS ●
CF&I Museum of Industry & Culture **17**
El Pueblo History Museum **12**
The Greenway & Nature Center **1**
Hose Company #3 **8**
Infozone News Museum **9**
Pueblo Weisbrod Aircraft Museum **15**
Pueblo Zoo **3**
Rosemount Museum **5**
Sangre de Cristo Arts & Conference Center **14**
Southeastern Colorado Heritage Center **10**
Steelworks Museum of Industry & Culture **16**
Vail Hotel **11**

Located in an historic fire station built in 1881 is **Hose Company #3—Pueblo's Fire Museum,** 116 Broadway Ave. (© **719/553-2830;** www.pueblofire.org). Open for guided tours by appointment only (free, donations encouraged), the museum contains antique fire engines, firefighting equipment, photographs, and other firefighting-related displays.

Steelworks Museum of Industry & Culture   Scheduled to open by early 2007, this facility focuses on the history and impact of the Colorado Fuel and Iron Corporation, which began in the 1870s to provide steel rails for the region's railroads and grew to include mining, steel and iron production, and then merged with a fuel company. At one time it operated mines and quarries throughout the West, and the company was the single largest private landowner in Colorado.

Housed in an historic medical dispensary building, the museum's exhibits examine the history of mining and steel production, including the company's sometimes violent labor relations, plus railroading and general history of the area. Among the displays are a one-of-a-kind mine rescue railcar and exhibits on industrial medicine. There is also a gift shop. Allow at least an hour and a half.

1612 E. Abriendo Ave. © **719/564-9086.** www.cfisteel.org. Admission $3 adults, $2 children 4–12, and free for children under 4. Mon–Sat 9am–4pm; Sun 1–4pm.

El Pueblo History Museum 🎨🎨 This beautiful museum is a splendid introduction to this region. Located at the intersection of West First Street, Union Avenue, and Grand Avenue, the museum also serves as the Scenic Byways Visitor Center and as a gateway to the Arkansas Riverwalk (see "Outdoor Activities," below) and the historic district.

Evocative of a mid-1800s trading post, the museum's design replicates a square adobe building with a central plaza, reminiscent of Bent's Old Fort. The museum showcases the traditions of the numerous cultural and ethnic groups in the area, utilizing maps and photos plus displays specific to each era. It begins with such items as beaded garments, pouches, American Indian baskets, and stonework; then, it moves into the Spanish, French, and American exploration of the area, highlighting the fur traders and Bent's Fort. The founding of the city through farming, ranching, and the early steel and mining industries comes next, followed by early-20th-century labor issues.

The museum also explores the area's continued industrial expansion, which brought a tremendous influx of immigrants, resulting in a rich cultural mix. Other exhibits explain how outdoor activities drew visitors to the area in the 20th century, and will likely tempt visitors outside to explore the Riverwalk. Allow at least an hour and a half.

301 N. Union Ave. ✆ **719/583-0453**. www.coloradohistory.org. Admission $4 adults, $3 seniors 65 and older, students with IDs, and children 6–12; free for children under 6; Saturdays 12 and under free. Tues–Sat 10am–4pm.

The Greenway & Nature Center 🎨 A major recreation and education center, this area provides access to more than 36 miles of paved biking and hiking trails along the Arkansas River and around Lake Pueblo. There's also a 150-foot fishing dock, volleyball courts, horseshoe pits, an amphitheater, nature trails, picnic areas, and a large children's playground. Boats and canoes can be put into the Arkansas River here. Bikes and recreational equipment are available for rent (call for rates). An interpretive center displays exhibits on the flora and fauna of the area, there are demonstration gardens along the river, and the Cafe del Rio serves American and Southwestern dishes. At the Raptor Center, injured eagles, owls, and other birds of prey are nursed back to health and released into the wild. The center also houses several resident birds of prey. Allow at least an hour.

5200 Nature Center Rd., via W. 11th St. ✆ **719/549-2414** main office, 719/549-2327 Raptor Center. www.gncp.org. Free admission, donations welcome. On-site parking $3. Grounds open daily sunrise–sunset; Raptor Center Tues–Sun 11am–4pm; Interpretive Center and gift shop Tues–Sat 9am–5pm.

Infozone News Museum *(Kids)* Say whatever you want about this museum—one of its primary goals is to increase our knowledge and understanding of Americans rights to freedom of speech and freedom of the press. Located on the fourth floor of the public library, this state-of-the-art facility also provides a look at the history of Pueblo and its newspapers, and has hands-on activities that youths will especially enjoy. There's a working Linotype typesetting machine to examine and a 100-seat movie theater where a variety of films are shown. Interactive touch-screen computer kiosks turn visitors into reporters as they go on assignment, interview those close to the action, and then see the story in print. Allow 45 minutes.

Robert Hoag Rawlings Public Library, 100 E Abriendo Ave. ✆ **719/562-5604**. www.infozonenewsmuseum.com. Free admission. Mon–Thurs 9am–9pm; Fri–Sat 9am–6pm; Sun 1–5pm. Closed major holidays.

Pueblo Weisbrod Aircraft Museum The place to come to see some fascinating old airplanes, this museum has more than two dozen historic aircraft—World War II and postwar—on display, as well as numerous exhibits and photographs depicting the

B-24 bomber and its role in World War II. It's hard to miss the restored Boeing B-29 Superfortress, with its 141-foot wingspan, which dominates a large hangar. Also on display are a Douglas A-26 Invader, a Grumman F-9 Cougar, a Douglas C-47 Sky-train (or, as the G. I.'s dubbed it, a Gooney Bird), a Boeing Stearman training plane, and a McDonnell Douglas F-101A Voodoo. There's a well-stocked souvenir shop, offering hard-to-find military and general aviation-related items. Allow 1 to 2 hours.

31001 Magnuson Ave. © 719/948-9219. www.pwam.org. Admission $6, free for children under 10. Mon–Fri 10am–4pm; Sat 10am–2pm; Sun 1–4pm. At Pueblo Memorial Airport, 6 miles east of downtown via U.S. 50.

Pueblo Zoo *Kids*   More than 300 animals representing over 100 species live in this 25-acre zoo, listed on the National Register of Historic Places for several buildings and other structures (including a moat) that were constructed of native sandstone during the Depression by WPA (Works Projects Administration) workers. Attractions include a Northern River Otter exhibit, a tropical rainforest, and a black-footed penguin underwater exhibit. You'll find all sorts of reptiles and insects in the herpetarium; kangaroos and emus in the Australia Station; an excellent African lion exhibit; and endangered species such as cottontop tamarins, prehensile tail skinks, and maned wolves. You'll also see zebras, Malayan sun bears, and Lar gibbons. Kids in a participatory mood should flock to Pioneer Farm, where they can feed a variety of rare domesticated animals, and to the Discovery Room, which features hands-on exhibits for all ages. Stop by the Watering Hole snack bar or the Wild Things gift shop, which boasts a better-than-average selection of animal-related items, if you need a rest between exhibits. Allow 2 to 4 hours.

City Park, 3455 Nuckolls Ave. © 719/561-1452. www.pueblozoo.org. Admission $6 adults, $5.25 seniors 65 and older, $3.50 children 3–12, free for children 2 and under. Memorial Day weekend through Labor Day daily 9am–5pm; rest of year Mon–Sat 9am–4pm and Sun noon–4pm. Closed from noon on the day before Thanksgiving, Christmas, and New Year's and all day on those three holidays.

Rosemount Museum *ℱ*   Were you a rich and sophisticated westerner in a previous life? Then you probably lived in an elegant home like this. Completed in 1893 for the pioneer Thatcher family, this 37-room mansion is one of the finest surviving examples of late-19th-century architecture and decoration in North America. The three-story, 24,000-square-foot home was built entirely of pink rhyolite stone. Inside you'll find handsome oak, maple, and mahogany woodwork; remarkable works of stained glass; hand-decorated ceilings; exquisite Tiffany lighting fixtures; period furniture; and 10 fireplaces. Allow 1 hour for the guided tour.

419 W. 14th St. (at Grand Ave.) © 719/545-5290. Fax 719/545-5291. www.rosemount.org. Admission $6 adults, $5 seniors 60 and over, $4 youths 6–18, free for children 5 and under. Tues–Sat 10am–4pm (last tour begins at 3:30pm). Closed major holidays and Jan. Take the I-25 exit for 13th St.

Sangre de Cristo Arts & Conference Center *ℱ* *Kids*   Pueblo's cultural hub is a three-building complex that houses a 500-seat theater, two dance studios, four art galleries (including one with a fine collection of Western art), a gift shop, restaurant, and the state-of-the-art Buell Children's Museum, which covers 12,000 square feet with a wide variety of hands-on arts and science exhibits. The high-tech, multisensory "Sensations" exhibit has some 50 sensors in the floors and walls, which activate lights, sound clips, or videos. The "Artrageous Studio" provides visitors with paper, ribbon, Mylar, and other wonderfully sparkly and gooey materials to use while creating their own masterpieces. The center also hosts concerts and other performing arts events, including a children's theater program (call for details). Allow 2 to 3 hours.

210 N. Santa Fe Ave. Ⓒ **719/295-7200**. www.sdc-arts.org. $4 adults, $3 children 15 and under. Galleries and children's museum Tues–Sat 11am–4pm; restaurant Tues–Sat 11am–2pm.

Southeastern Colorado Heritage Center Located across the street from the historic Union Depot train station, this facility includes exhibits on southeastern Colorado's pioneer days, including a mid-1800s store and early communications equipment. There are also railroad exhibits, presented in cooperation with the Pueblo Railway Museum, which also maintains the outdoor exhibits of locomotives, passenger cars, and freight cars just west of the depot at 132 W. B St. (www.pueblorailway.org). Allow at least one hour for the museum and rail yard.

201 W. B St. Ⓒ **719/295-1517**. www.theheritagecenter.us. Free admission. Tues–Sat 10am–4pm.

OUTDOOR ACTIVITIES

Pueblo's mild climate makes it a popular destination for boating, fishing, and other outdoor recreation, with several major stops for the region's outdoor enthusiasts.

Watersport aficionados are drawn to **Lake Pueblo State Park** 𝒻 (also called Pueblo Reservoir), which boasts some 4,500 surface acres of water and 60 miles of shoreline. The lake is popular among **anglers** trying for rainbow trout, brown trout, crappie, black bass, and channel catfish, and there's a free fish-cleaning station.

It's also a huge attraction for boaters, who come from all over southern Colorado, and the park offers swimming, hiking, and biking. The park's **North Marina** (Ⓒ **719/ 547-3880**) provides a gas dock, boating and fishing supplies, groceries, and a restaurant. The **South Marina** (Ⓒ **719/564-1043**; www.thesouthshoremarina.com) provides the same services and also rents pontoon boats ($120–$160 for 4 hr. and $240–$320 for 9 hr., plus fuel) and fishing boats ($80–$100 for 4 hr. and $160–$200 for 9 hr., plus fuel), April through October.

The **Rock Canyon Swim Beach** (Ⓒ **719/564-0065**) at the east end of the park is open daily from Memorial Day through Labor Day and has lifeguards on duty. There's a five-story, three-flume **water slide** ($1.75 per ride or $9.95 all day), plus rentals of bumper boats and paddle boats ($3.50–$6 per half hour), and a snack bar. Entrance to the beach only costs $1 and a pass for the beach, boat use, and the water slide costs $13. These fees are in addition to the general park admission fee (see below).

The park has about 400 **campsites**, some with electric and water hookups. A dump station and showers are available, and camping rates are $14 to $22 May 1 through Labor Day; $12 to $20 the rest of the year. Camping reservations are available for an extra charge of $8 by calling Ⓒ **800/678-2267**, or through the state parks website listed below. Day-use costs $5 per vehicle, and campers must pay this in addition to camping fees.

From Pueblo, take U.S. 50 west for 4 miles, turn south onto Pueblo Boulevard and go another 4 miles to Thatcher Avenue, then turn west and go 6 miles to the park. For information, contact the park office at Ⓒ **719/561-9320**, or go to **www.parks.state. co.us**.

One of the nicest urban renewal projects we've ever seen is the **Historic Arkansas Riverwalk of Pueblo** 𝒻𝒻, a beautifully landscaped waterfront park that covers some 26 acres and offers pedestrian and bike paths, benches, sculptures, gardens, and natural areas that provide good wildlife-viewing opportunities. Pedal-boat rentals are available from early April through late September on a small lake along the Riverwalk, weekends only in April and daily the rest of the season. Rates are $6 per half-hour for a one-person boat and $10 per half-hour for a two-to-four-seater boat. Excursion boat rides along the Arkansas take place on weekends in April, and operate daily from May through late September. Rates for the narrated 25-minute tours are $5 adults, $4 for seniors and members of the military, and $3 for children 3 to 12. Hours for both pedal-boat rentals and the excursion-boat rides vary throughout the season; call the boathouse (© **719/595-1589**) for the schedule. The Riverwalk is located near the south end of the Union Avenue Historic District (see "What to See & Do," above), and is easily accessed via Main Street. For information, contact Historic Arkansas Riverwalk of Pueblo Authority, 200 W. First St., Suite 303, Pueblo, CO 81003 (© **719/595-0242;** www.puebloharp.com).

Also in town, stop at **City Park,** northeast of the intersection of Pueblo Boulevard (Colo. 45) and Thatcher Avenue. The park, home to the Pueblo Zoo (see above), covers some 200 acres, and offers 2 fishing lakes, 17 tennis courts, a swimming pool (open in summer), and playgrounds. There's also a beautiful hand-carved antique carousel built in 1911, with music provided by a 1920 Wurlitzer Military Band Organ. The carousel is open evenings and Sunday afternoons in summer; the park is open daily year-round. For information, call the Pueblo Parks and Recreation Department (© **719/553-2790;** www.pueblo.us).

There are plenty of opportunities for hiking, backpacking, mountain biking, fishing, and camping nearby in lands under the jurisdiction of the U.S. Forest Service. For information, contact the headquarters of the **Pike and San Isabel National Forests and Comanche and Cimarron National Grasslands,** 2840 Kachina Dr., Pueblo, CO 81008 (© **719/553-1400;** www.fs.fed.us/r2).

Local **golf courses** open to the public include **Walking Stick,** 1301 Walking Stick Blvd. (© **719/553-1180**), at the northwest corner of the University of Southern Colorado. Rated among Colorado's best courses and best values, this 18-hole course has a driving range and charges $28 to $30 for 18 holes. Other local courses include **Elmwood** at City Park, 3900 Thatcher Ave. (© **719/561-4946**), with an 18-hole regulation course plus executive 9-hole course. Greens fees for 18 holes are $28 to $30. **Desert Hawk Golf Course at Pueblo West,** 251 S. McCulloch Blvd. (© **719/547-2280**), is an 18-hole regulation course with greens fees for 18 holes from $25 to $30.

SPECTATOR SPORTS

MOTOR SPORTS Stock-car races are held every Saturday evening from April through September on what is billed as "the fastest paved ¼-mile oval in the West," at **I-25 Speedway,** off I-25 at exit 108 (© **719/583-2277;** www.i25speedway.com). Nationally sanctioned drag racing, Sports Car Club of America road racing, and other motor sports take place at the **Pueblo Motorsports Park,** U.S. 50 and Pueblo Boulevard in Pueblo West (© **719/583-0907;** www.pueblomotorsportspark.com), April through September.

RODEO Those visiting Pueblo from mid-August to early September can take in the **Colorado State Fair** (© **800/876-4567** or 719/561-8484; www.coloradostate fair.com), which includes a professional rodeo, carnival rides, food booths, industrial displays, horse shows, animal exhibits, and top-name entertainers.

WHERE TO STAY

There are numerous lodging possibilities in Pueblo, with many of the national chains represented. Rates are highest in summer, and most motels in Pueblo also charge higher rates during the State Fair (mid-Aug to early Sept). Among the reliable major chains are the **Best Western Eagle Ridge Inn & Suites,** 4727 N. Elizabeth St.

(© **800/WESTERN** or 719/543-4644), with double rates of $55 to $120; **Comfort Inn,** 4645 N. Freeway (© **800/424-6423** or 719/542-6868), charging $55 to $90 double; **Hampton Inn,** 4703 N. Freeway, just west of I-25 exit 102 (© **800/972-0165** or 719/544-4700), with double rates from $79 to $109; and **Quality Inn & Suites,** 3910 Outlook Blvd. (© **800/424-6423** or 719/544-5500), with rates from $69 to $175 double. Room tax adds just under 12%.

Abriendo Inn 🦀🦀 This delightful B&B, built in 1906 as a mansion for brewing magnate Martin Walter, his wife, and their eight children, is the best place to stay for those who want to soak up some of the region's history without sacrificing modern comforts and conveniences. A traditional four-square-style house listed on the National Register of Historic Places, the Abriendo Inn has won a deserved number of awards. It's also very conveniently located in Pueblo's historic district, close to shops, the Riverwalk, and other attractions.

The comfortable guest rooms are decorated with antique furniture and period reproductions, plus king- or queen-size brass or four-poster beds. Four units have showers only; the rest have shower/tub combos or whirlpool tubs for two. Delicious homemade breakfasts, which might include egg-sausage soufflé or baked apricot French toast, are served in the oak-wainscoted dining room or on the outdoor patio. Smoking is permitted on the veranda only.

300 W. Abriendo Ave., Pueblo, CO 81004. © 719/544-2703. Fax 719/542-6544. www.abriendoinn.com. 10 units. Summer $84–$170 double, rest of the year $74–$150 double. Rates include full breakfast and 24-hr. refreshments. AE, DISC, MC, V. *In room:* A/C, TV/VCR, dataport, fridge (in some units), hair dryer, wireless Internet.

CAMPING

There are two Kampgrounds of America (KOA) campgrounds in the Pueblo area, both open year-round and with all the usual commercial campground amenities, including seasonal swimming pools. The **Pueblo KOA** is 5 miles north of the city at I-25 exit 108 (© **800/562-7453** for reservations, or 719/542-2273) and charges $18 to $21 for tent sites and $26 to $33 for RV hookup sites. The **Pueblo South KOA,** about 20 miles south of Pueblo at I-25 exit 74 (© **800/562-8646** for reservations, or 719/676-3376), charges $17 to $23 for tent sites and $25 to $34 for RV hookup sites. Both also have camping cabins (you share the bathhouse with other campers) with rates in the $36 to $48 range. There are also some 400 campsites at **Lake Pueblo State Park** (see "Outdoor Activities," above).

WHERE TO DINE

In addition to the dinner-only restaurants discussed below, we like the basic American and Italian food served for breakfast, lunch, and dinner at **Patti's Restaurant,** 241 S. Santa Fe Ave (© **719/543-2371**). Located on the Riverwalk, in the same location since 1936, Patti's offers American favorites, including sandwiches, burgers, steak, and seafood, plus Italian specialties, in a relaxed family-friendly atmosphere. Available at both breakfast and lunch, we recommend the Half Breed—a spicy Italian sausage wrapped in a tortilla and smothered with spaghetti and green chili sauce. Hours are 6:30am to 9pm Wednesday and Thursday, 6:30am to 10pm Friday and Saturday, and 7am to 8:30pm Sunday (closed Monday and Tuesday). Lunch and dinner prices run $6 to $15 and MasterCard, Visa, and Discover cards are accepted.

Ianne's Whiskey Ridge 🦀 ITALIAN/STEAK/SEAFOOD Serving Pueblo for well over 50 years, this family-owned-and-operated restaurant prepares made-from-scratch meals at reasonable prices, making it among our favorites in southern Colorado. Pasta dishes are the specialty here; we especially recommend the lasagna and ravioli. There's also a large selection of fresh seafood, chicken, veal, and certified Angus steaks. The early bird menu, served daily from 4 to 6pm, is an especially good value, with main courses averaging about $8. On Sunday a Champagne brunch buffet is featured from 11am to 2pm, at $13 for adults and $7.95 for children 12 and younger, offering all-you-can-eat breakfast specialties plus lunch and dinner items including fresh salmon, ribs, and pasta. Also Sunday, all day, an all-you-can-eat rigatoni or spaghetti dinner is served at $4.95 per person. The atmosphere here is casual but attractive, with dark-wood accents—what we think of as upscale family dining, and there is also an attractive year-round patio for outdoor dining.

4333 Thatcher Ave. © **719/564-8551.** Main courses $9–$26. AE, MC, V. Mon–Thurs 4–9pm; Fri–Sat 4–10pm; Sun 11am–9pm.

La Renaissance ✦✦ STEAK/SEAFOOD   Housed in a historic 1880s Presbyterian church, La Renaissance, a favorite of locals since it opened in 1974, offers casually elegant dining in a unique atmosphere. The decor includes stained-glass windows, high vaulted ceilings, and oak pews, which provide some of the seating. Dinners begin with a tureen of soup and finish with dessert, which might be the delightful cream puffs. Although the menu changes periodically, entrees might include the tender slow-roasted prime rib, steamed Alaskan king crab legs, rack of lamb in a rosemary glaze, baby back pork ribs, or breast of chicken with sautéed mushrooms. There's a wide variety of domestic and imported wine and beer, and service is attentive and friendly.

217 E. Routt Ave. © **719/543-6367.** Reservations recommended. 5-course dinner $12–$36. AE, DC, DISC, MC, V. Mon–Sat 5–9pm. From I-25 exit 97B, take Abriendo Ave. northwest for 4 blocks, turn left onto Michigan St., and go 2 blocks to the restaurant.

2 Royal Gorge & Cañon City

The Royal Gorge, one of the most impressive natural attractions in the state, lies 8 miles west of Cañon City off U.S. 50, at the head of the Arkansas River valley.

This narrow canyon, 1,053 feet deep, was cut through solid granite by 3 million years of water and wind erosion. When Zebulon Pike saw the gorge in 1806, he predicted that man would never conquer it. But by 1877, the Denver & Rio Grande Railroad had laid a route through the canyon and it soon became a major tourist attraction.

The gorge is spanned by what is said to be the world's highest suspension bridge and an aerial tramway, built for no other reason than to thrill tourists. The quarter-mile-long bridge was constructed in 1929, suspended from two 300-ton cables, and reinforced in 1983. An incline railway, believed to be the world's steepest, was completed in 1931; it plunges from the rim of the gorge 1,550 feet to the floor at a 45-degree angle, giving passengers a view from the bottom as well as the top. Added in 1968, the 35-passenger tram provides views of the gorge and the bridge from a height of 1,178 feet above the Arkansas River.

Owned by Cañon City, the park also includes a 260-seat multimedia theater (where visitors can see a video presentation on the area's history and construction of the bridge), miniature railway, trolley, old-fashioned carousel, various thrill rides and children's attractions, restaurants, gift shops, a petting zoo with free burro rides, and herds of tame mule deer. Live entertainment and a variety of special events are presented throughout the year.

The park is open year-round, daily from 10am with closing ranging from 4 to 7pm, and the bridge is open daily 8:30am to dusk. Admission—$21 for adults, $19 for seniors, $17 for children 4 to 11, free for children under 4—includes crossing the bridge and all park rides, attractions, and entertainment. For information, contact **Royal Gorge Bridge & Park,** P.O. Box 549, Cañon City, CO 81215 (© **888/333-5597** or 719/275-7507; www.royalgorgebridge.com).

An interesting way to view the canyon is from the **Royal Gorge Route Railroad,** in the Santa Fe Depot at 401 Water St. (south of U.S. 50 on Third St.), Cañon City, CO 81212 (© **888/724-5748** or 303/569-1000; www.royalgorgeroute.com). The train takes passengers on a 2-hour 24-mile trip through the canyon. From late May to early October, the train departs daily at 9:30am and 12:30pm, and during the height of the season there are also departures at 3:30pm; departures are less frequent the rest of the year. Coach tickets cost $30 for adults and $20 for children 3 to 12, and are free for children under 3 who sit on a guardian's lap. The more luxurious first-class parlor cars cost $40 for adults and $30 for children 12 and under. Observation dome car, lunch, dinner, murder mystery, and other specialty train rides are also offered; call or check the website for details. Reservations are recommended.

To see this beautiful gorge looking up from the river, while also enjoying some thrills, consider a **raft trip.** Rates for adults run $85 to $100 for a full-day trip, including lunch; a half-day trip is from $40 to $60. Most Royal Gorge raft trips include rough white-water stretches of the river, but those preferring calmer sections should inquire about such excursions with local rafting companies. Major outfitters include **Arkansas River Tours** (© **800/321-4352** or 719/942-4362; www.arkansasrivertours.com), **Echo Canyon River Expeditions** (© **800/755-3246;** www.raftecho.com), and **Wilderness Aware Rafting** (© **800/462-7238** or 719/395-2112; www.inaraft.com).

OTHER AREA ATTRACTIONS

Cañon City was a popular setting for filmmakers during the industry's early days, and it was a special favorite of silent screen actor Tom Mix, who reputedly worked as a cowboy in the area before becoming a film star. The drowning death of a prominent actress temporarily discouraged film companies from coming here, but the area's beautiful scenery and Old West heritage lured the industry back in the late 1950s with the creation of Buckskin Joe, a Western theme park and movie set where dozens of films have been shot, including *How the West Was Won, True Grit, Cat Ballou,* and *Lightning Jack.*

While movies are rarely shot here nowadays, **Buckskin Joe Frontier Town & Railway** (© **719/275-5149;** www.buckskinjoe.com), located about 8 miles west of Cañon City on U.S. 50, remains a popular tourist attraction and is a great place to take kids. The authentic-looking Old West town was created from genuine 19th-century buildings relocated from across the state. Visitors can watch gunfights, pan for gold, see a magic show, ride horseback (or a horse-drawn trolley), and wander through a Western maze. **The Scenic Railway** (© **719/275-5485**) offers a 30-minute trip through rugged Royal Gorge country, where you're likely to see deer and other wildlife, to the rim of the Royal Gorge for a panoramic view of the canyon and bridge.

Frontier Town is open May through September. Hours from Memorial Day to Labor Day are daily 9am to 6:30pm, and there are shorter hours at other times. The railway runs from March through December; call for current times. Combination admission tickets, which include the Scenic Railway, horse-drawn trolley, and all the Frontier Town attractions and entertainment, are $16 for adults, $14 for children 4 to 11, and free for children under 4. Railway-only tickets are $9 for adults and $8 for children, and Frontier Town–only tickets cost $12 and $10, respectively. Expect to spend 2 to 4 hours here.

Other Cañon City attractions include the **Museum of Colorado Prisons** ✪, 201 N. First St. (📞 **719/269-3015;** www.prisonmuseum.org), just the thing for those with an appreciation of the macabre. Housed in the state's former women's prison, just outside the walls of the original territorial prison that opened in 1871, this museum contains an actual gas chamber, historic photos of life behind bars, weapons confiscated from inmates, the last hangman's noose used legally in the state, a simulation of a lethal-injection system, a simulation of the "Old Gray Mare" (a cruel apparatus used to punish obstreperous prisoners), and other artifacts and exhibits showing what prison life was like in the Old West, and even in more modern times. There's even a gift shop selling arts and crafts made by inmates housed at a medium-security prison next door. The museum is open Memorial Day to Labor Day, daily from 8:30am to 6pm; May 1 to Memorial Day and Labor Day through mid-October daily from 10am to 5pm; and mid-October through April, Friday through Sunday from 10am to 5pm. Admission is $7 for adults, $6 for seniors 65 and older, $5 for ages 6 to 12, and free for those 5 and under. Allow about an hour.

Those interested in Colorado history might also enjoy stopping at the **Royal Gorge Regional Museum and History Center,** 612 Royal Gorge Blvd. (📞 **719/269-9036;** www.ccpl.lib.co.us), which has displays of American Indian artifacts, guns, gems, minerals, wild-game trophies, historic photos, old dolls, pioneer household items, and other memorabilia. There is an extensive collection of historic phonographs, and several impressive renovated and authentically furnished buildings out back. Here are the 1860 log cabin built by Anson Rudd, local blacksmith and first warden of the Colorado Territorial Prison, and the Rudd family's three-story stone house built in 1881. The museum also contains archives of local history. From Memorial Day to Labor Day, hours are 9:30am to 5pm Monday through Friday and 9:30am to 4pm Saturday; the rest of the year the museum is open Monday through Friday from 10am to 5pm. Closed on major holidays. Admission is free. Allow one hour.

Another local attraction, especially fascinating for young would-be dinosaur hunters, is **Dinosaur Depot** ✪, 330 Royal Gorge Blvd. (📞 **800/987-6379** or 719/ 269-7150; www.dinosaurdepot.com). The depot's main claim to fame is the dinosaur lab, where paleontologists are working to remove various dinosaur fossils from the rock that has encased them for the last 150 million years. There are also several interpretive dinosaur exhibits, including fossilized bones that visitors can hold in their hands, what is considered one of the world's most complete stegosaurus, a fossilized tree, a children's Discovery Room with plenty of hands-on exhibits, and a museum store well stocked with dinosaur-related items. Dinosaur Depot also arranges tours of the internationally renowned **Garden Park Fossil Area** just north of town, which is the source of many of the museum's exhibits, and to see some 90-million-year-old dinosaur tracks nearby. The museum is open daily from 9am to 5pm from Memorial Day to mid-August, with shorter hours the rest of the year. It's closed Thanksgiving, Christmas, and New Year's Day. Admission is $3 for adults, $1.50 for children 4 to 12, and free for children under 4. Allow 45 minutes at Dinosaur Depot, and another 1 to 2 hours at Garden Park Fossil Area.

There are several midpriced lodging options in Cañon City, including the **Best Western Royal Gorge Motel,** 1925 Fremont Dr., Cañon City, CO 81212 (📞 **800/ 231-7317** or 719/275-3377), with double rates ranging from $75 to $100 in summer and $50 to $90 the rest of the year; **Quality Inn & Suites,** 3075 E. U.S. 50, Cañon City, CO 81212 (© **800/424-6423** or 719/275-8676; www.qualityinncanoncity.com), which has six indoor hot tubs, with rooms priced from $99 to $109 double. The **Restaurant** at the Quality Inn features Mexican and American food, with most dinner entrees from $8 to $18. Another good dining option is **Merlino's Belvedere,** 1330 Elm Ave. (© **719/275-5558;** www.belvedererestaurant.com), specializing in gourmet Italian cuisine, steaks, and seafood at lunch and dinner daily. Dinner main courses run $8.40 to $33.

For more information on where to stay and eat, a walking tour of historic downtown Cañon City, and details on scenic drives and other attractions, contact the **Cañon City Chamber of Commerce,** 403 Royal Gorge Blvd., Cañon City, CO 81212 (© **800/876-7922** or 719/275-2331; www.canoncitychamber.com).

3 Trinidad

197 miles S. of Denver, 247 miles N. of Albuquerque, New Mexico

Western history and art are two good reasons to stop in Trinidad when traveling along I-25 through southern Colorado. Bat Masterson was sheriff in the 1880s, Wyatt Earp drove the stage, Kit Carson helped open the trade routes, and even Billy the Kid passed through. Many historic buildings—handsome structures of brick and sandstone—survive from this era. Plains tribes roamed the area for centuries before the 17th- and 18th-century forays by Spanish explorers and settlers. Later, traders and trappers made this an important stop on the northern branch of the Santa Fe Trail.

German, Irish, Italian, Jewish, Polish, and Slavic immigrants were drawn to the area starting in the late 1800s for jobs at area coal mines and cattle ranches, and agriculture and railroading were also important economic factors. Ranching remains a cornerstone of the economy today, and the tourism industry is growing. Today the population is slightly above 9,000; elevation is 6,019 feet.

ESSENTIALS

GETTING THERE   By Car   If you're traveling from north or south, take I-25: Trinidad straddles the interstate, halfway between Denver and Santa Fe, New Mexico. From the east, take U.S. 50 into La Junta, then turn southwest for 80 miles on U.S. 350; or from southern Kansas follow U.S. 160 to Trinidad. From Durango and points west, follow U.S. 160 to Walsenburg, then travel south 37 miles on I-25.

By Train   The **Amtrak** Southwest Chief passes through Trinidad twice daily—once eastbound, once westbound—on a run between Chicago and Los Angeles. The depot is on Pine Street just off North Commercial Street, next to Pizza Hut (© **800/872-7245;** www.amtrak.com).

VISITOR INFORMATION   The **Colorado Welcome Center,** 309 N. Nevada Ave. (I-25 exit 14A), Trinidad, CO 81082 (© **719/846-9512**), open daily from 8am to 5pm in winter and from 8am to 6pm in summer, has information not only on Trinidad and southeastern Colorado, but also on the entire state. Information before your trip can be obtained from the **Trinidad & Las Animas County Chamber of Commerce** (© **866/480-4750;** www.historictrinidad.com or www.trinidadco.com).

GETTING AROUND   Main Street (U.S. 160/350) parallels El Rio de Las Animas en Purgatorio (The River of Lost Souls in Purgatory), better known as the Purgatoire

Trinidad

ACCOMMODATIONS ■
Best Western Trinidad Inn **9**
Budget Host Derrick Motel **10**
Quality Inn **10**
The Stone Mansion B&B **8**
Super 8 **3**

DINING ◆
El Capitan Restaurant &
   Lounge **1**
Nana & Nano Monteleone's
   Deli & Pasta House **7**

ATTRACTIONS ●
A.R. Mitchell Memorial Museum
   of Western Art **5**
Louden-Henritze Archaeology
   Museum **2**
Old Firehouse No. 1 Children's
   Museum **4**
Trinidad History Museum **6**

River, which flows south to north through the center of town. The historic downtown area is focused around Main and Commercial streets on the south side of the river. Main Street joins I-25 on the west side of downtown.

   Car rentals are available from **J&J Motors** (⟨℃⟩ **719/846-3318**) and **Pioneer Motors** (⟨℃⟩ **719/846-4100**). Taxi service is provided by **The Taxi Company** (⟨℃⟩ **719/859-1558**).

   The **Trinidad Trolley,** operating Memorial Day to Labor Day, provides an excellent—and free—way to see this historic city. Running daily from 10am to 3pm, you can board the trolley at the Colorado Welcome Center (see above), and get on and off at the various museums and other attractions. Pick up a schedule at the Welcome Center.

FAST FACTS   Medical services, including a 24-hour emergency room, are provided at **Mt. San Rafael Hospital,** 410 S. Benedicta Ave. off Main Street (⟨℃⟩ **719/846-9213**). The **post office** is at 301 E. Main St. Contact the U.S. Postal Service (⟨℃⟩ **800/275-8777;** www.usps.com) for hours and other information.

SPECIAL EVENTS   Santa Fe Trail Days, in June; fireworks display over Trinidad Lake on the Fourth of July; Trinidaddio Blues Festival, late August; Las Animas County Fair and Rodeo, early September.

WHAT TO SEE & DO

Main Street was once part of the Mountain Route of the Santa Fe Trail, and many of the streets that cross it are paved with locally made redbrick. The Trinidad Historical Society distributes a booklet titled *A Walk Through the History of Trinidad,* available at local shops and museums. Among the buildings it singles out for special attention are the Trinidad Opera House (1883) and Columbian Hotel (1879), which are across from each other on Main Street, as well as the Trinidad Water Works (1879), on Cedar Street at the Purgatoire River.

A. R. Mitchell Memorial Museum of Western Art *ℱ*   The Old West is alive and well here, at least on canvas and photographic paper. More than 250 paintings and illustrations by Western artist Arthur Roy Mitchell (1889–1977) are displayed, along with works by other nationally recognized artists and a collection of early Hispanic folk art including bultos, retablos, and tinwork plus Penitente artifacts. The museum also contains a historic collection of photographs, taken by Oliver E. Aultman, Benjamin Wittick, and Almerod Newman from the late 1800s through much of the 20th century; plus early cameras, darkroom equipment, and studio props. The museum gift shop sells a wide variety of jewelry, pottery, prints, and some original works of art, at fairly reasonable prices. The huge building, originally a department store, is a 1906 Western-style structure with the original pressed-tin ceiling, wood floors, and a horseshoe-shaped mezzanine. Allow 1 to 1½ hours.

150 E. Main St. © **719/846-4224.** Admission $5 adults, $3 seniors and students, free for children under 12, free admission Sun. May–Sept Tues–Sat 10am–4pm; Sun noon–5pm; off-season by appointment.

Louden-Henritze Archaeology Museum   Millions of years of southern Colorado history are displayed here, including fossils, casts of dinosaur tracks, arrowheads, pottery, petroglyphs, and other prehistoric-man artifacts discovered during area excavations. Watch for the fossilized partial skeleton of a mosasaur (a sea reptile) that lived in the area some 80 million years ago. There's also a gift shop. Allow 1 to 2 hours.

Freudenthal Memorial Library, Trinidad State Junior College, near the intersection of Park and Prospect sts. © **719/846-5508.** www.trinidadstate.edu/museum. Free admission. May–Sept Mon–Fri 10am–3pm; call for off-season hours.

Old Firehouse No. 1 Children's Museum *Kids*   As you would expect, one of the key attractions here is a shiny red historic fire truck, but you'll also see Trinidad's original 1930s-era alarm system, a model train diorama where kids take turns blowing the whistle, and a restored turn-of-the-20th-century schoolroom. Kids especially enjoy the hands-on displays, including Grandma's trunk for dress-up and Trinidad's original jail cells (a good place to leave that pain-in-the-neck brother or sister). Allow 30 minutes to an hour.

314 N. Commercial St. © **719/846-8220** or 719/846-2024. Free admission. June–Aug Mon–Fri 11am–3pm. Closed Sept–May and July 4th.

Trinidad History Museum *ℱℱ*   Trinidad has a rich and interesting history, and this is the best place to find out about it. Together, the Baca House, Bloom Mansion, and Santa Fe Trail Museum, along with historic gardens, are known collectively as the Trinidad History Museum, and rank as Trinidad's principal attraction. The 1870 Baca House, along the Mountain Route of the Santa Fe Trail, is a two-story Greek Revival–style adobe. Originally owned by sheep rancher Felipe Baca, the house contains some of the Baca family's original furnishings. Nearby stands the 1882 Bloom

Mansion, a Second Empire–style Victorian manor embellished with fancy woodcarving and ornate ironwork. The Colorado Historical Society operates both homes as well as the Santa Fe Trail Museum, located behind the homes in a building that was originally living quarters for Baca's hired help. Both the Baca House and Santa Fe Trail Museum are certified sites on the Santa Fe National Historic Trail.

On the grounds are shade trees and gardens of hollyhocks, grapevines, and cacti. The museum bookstore offers a good selection of books on local history, the Santa Fe Trail, Hispanic culture, area recreation, and children's books. Allow 2 to 3 hours.

312 E. Main St. ℂ 719/846-7217. www.coloradohistory.org. Admission $5 adults, $4.50 seniors 65 and older, $2.50 children 6–16 and students, free for children under 6. May–Sept daily 10am–4pm; off-season Santa Fe Trail Museum Mon–Fri 9am–1pm; Baca House and Bloom Mansion by appointment only.

SPORTS & OUTDOOR ACTIVITIES

Located 3 miles west of town on Colo. 12, **Trinidad Lake State Park** (ℂ 719/846-6951; www.parks.state.co.us) is the place to go for all sorts of outdoor recreational possibilities, and it's also a good base for campers who want to explore southern Colorado and northern New Mexico. Its 800-acre reservoir on the Purgatoire River is popular for powerboating, water-skiing, sailboating, and sailboarding. Swimming is prohibited, however. There's a boat ramp and dock, but no boat rentals or supplies. Fishermen go after largemouth bass, rainbow and brown trout, channel catfish, walleye, crappie, and bluegills. Ten miles of hiking and mountain-biking trails here include the Levsa Canyon Nature Trail, a 1-mile self-guided loop that also branches off for another 4 miles to the historic town of Cokedale (see "A Drive Along the Scenic Highway of Legends," below). For those with their own horses, there are 4 miles of equestrian trails on the south side of the lake. The Long's Canyon Watchable Wildlife Area offers viewing blinds in a wetlands area. Commonly seen in the park are great blue herons, Canada geese, red-tailed hawks, great horned owls, hummingbirds, mule deer, cottontail rabbits, and ground squirrels. An attractive 62-unit campground, with fees of $12 to $16, has some electric hookups, a dump station, and coin-operated showers. Reservations are available through the state parks website (see above) or by calling ℂ 800/678-2267 for an extra charge of $8. Day-use admission costs $5 per vehicle, which is also tacked onto camping fees. During the winter there's cross-country skiing, ice skating, and ice fishing.

BICYCLING, ROLLERBLADING & SKATEBOARDING Rated as one of the top skate parks in the country since it opened in 2003, the **Trinidad Skate Park** covers 15,000 square feet and offers a terrific layout with the snake leading into the two bowls, offering long runs with plenty of speed and opportunity for tricks. Use of safety equipment (helmets, knee and elbow pads, wrist supports, proper shoes) is required at all times, and users are responsible for the proper maintenance of their gear. Summer hours are daily, 8am to 10pm, and admission is free. For additional information, contact the City of Trinidad (ℂ 719/846-9843 or the chamber of commerce (ℂ 719/846-9285). From I-25 take exit 13B onto Main Street east, turn right (south) onto Santa Fe Trail Drive, then left onto Jefferson Street. Take the second right (follow the community center sign) and continue straight to the park.

GOLF The 9-hole **Trinidad Golf Course,** off the Santa Fe Trail adjacent to I-25 at exit 13A (ℂ 719/846-4015), is considered among the best 9-hole courses in the state, with fees of $15 for 9 holes and $20 for 18 holes.

WHERE TO STAY

Several national chains provide most of the lodging in Trinidad (zip code 81082). Rates here are for two people in summer; rates at other times are usually 10% to 20% lower. Among your choices are the **Best Western Trinidad Inn,** 900 W. Adams St., I-25 exit 13A (© **800/955-2215** or 719/846-2215), charging $109 to $119 double; **Budget Host Derrick Motel,** just off I-25 exit 11 at 10301 Santa Fe Trail (© **800-BUD-HOST** or 719/846-3307), with double rates of $59 to $69; **Quality Inn,** 3125 Toupal Dr, I-25 exit 11 (© **800/424-6423** or 719/846-4491), charging $110 to $130 double; and **Super 8,** 1924 Freedom Rd., I-25 exit 15 (© **800/800-8000** or 719/846-8280), charging $65 to $90 double. Taxes totaling about 11% are added to lodging bills.

Those looking for lodging with more character, along with a bit of pampering and a really good full breakfast, should consider **The Stone Mansion Bed and Breakfast** ✸, 212 E. Second St., Trinidad, CO 81082 (© **877/264-4279** or 719/845-1625; www.stonemansionbb.com), an elegant home built in 1904 that combines Victorian and Arts and Crafts styles. Located 2 blocks from downtown, the inn has three rooms, decorated with mostly Victorian antiques. Summer rates for two, which include a full breakfast with entrees such as peach puff pancakes, are $99 to $110 with a private bathroom and $85 for a shared bathroom; November through April rates are lower. Smoking is not permitted inside, and children 8 and older are welcome.

WHERE TO DINE

El Capitan Restaurant & Lounge MEXICAN/ITALIAN/AMERICAN   This attractive but simply decorated restaurant, with a relaxing, comfortable atmosphere, serves some of the best margaritas in southern Colorado. It's known for its Mexican and Italian dishes, although you can also get steaks, seafood, barbecued ribs, burgers, and sandwiches. Mexican items include green or red chili, bean or beef burritos, and enchiladas. On the Italian side of the menu you'll find gnocchi, beef ravioli, and spaghetti with meatballs, meat sauce, or sausage. There are a number of vegetarian items, including vegetable fajitas and pasta with olive oil, garlic, and vegetables. Whatever entree you pick, be sure to top off your meal with the tasty fried ice cream for dessert.

321 State St. © **719/846-9903.** Sandwiches and a la carte Mexican items $2–$6.95; dinners $5–$14. AE, DISC, MC, V. Mon–Fri 11am–9pm; Sat 4:30–9pm.

Nana & Nano Monteleone's Deli & Pasta House ITALIAN   The Monteleone family takes pride in the Italian specialties served here, each cooked to order and served with salad, bread, and butter. Daily specials include rigatoni, spaghetti, and ravioli, and the regular menu offers a good selection of pasta, sandwiches, and fish. Many pasta selections are available with a choice of meatballs or Italian sausage, and there is also a "Smaller Appetite" menu for all ages. Monteleone's Deli, located in the restaurant, offers traditional deli sandwiches to eat in or takeout, plus deli meats and cheeses by the pound.

418 E. Main St. © **719/846-2696.** Main courses $5.50–$11; deli sandwiches $4.75–$5.75. AE, DISC, MC, V. Tues–Wed 10:30am–6pm; Thurs–Sat 10:30am–7pm.

4 A Drive Along the Scenic Highway of Legends

Unquestionably the most fascinating day trip from Trinidad is the appropriately named Scenic Highway of Legends, which runs some 80 miles west, north, then northeast, mostly on Colo. 12, from Trinidad to Walsenburg.

Traveling west about 7 miles from Trinidad, past Trinidad Lake State Park, the first site of special note is **Cokedale,** just north of the highway. The best existing example of a coal camp in Colorado, **Cokedale** was founded in 1907 by the American Smelting and Refining Co. as a self-contained company town, and by 1909 was a thriving community of 1,500. When the mine closed in 1947, residents were offered the company-owned homes at $100 per room and $50 per lot. Some stayed, incorporating in 1948, and in 1984 Cokedale was placed on the National Register of Historic Places. Many of today's 120 or so residents are descendants of those miners, or retired miners themselves. As you drive in, you'll see some of the 350 coke ovens, used to convert coal to hotter-burning coke, for which the town was named. Walking through the community, you'll see the icehouse, schoolhouse, mining office, Sacred Heart of Jesus and Mary Church, Gottlieb Mercantile Company, and other buildings, including a boardinghouse where bachelors could get room and board for $25 a month.

Proceeding west, you'll pass several old coal towns, including Segundo, Weston, and Vigil, and two coal mines—the Golden Eagle, where underground mining is still done, and New Elk Mine, now a processing plant—before entering **Stonewall Valley,** 33 miles west of Trinidad. Named for a striking rock formation—a vertical bed of lithified sandstone—Stonewall is both the site of a small timber industry and the location of many vacation homes.

From Stonewall, Colo. 12 turns north past **Monument Lake,** part of Trinidad's water-supply system, named for a rock formation in the middle of the lake that some say resembles two American Indian chiefs. Several miles past Monument Lake is **North Lake,** a state wildlife area and home to rainbow, cutthroat, kokanee, and brown trout.

The highway continues north across 9,941-foot **Cucharas Pass.** Overlooking the pass are the **Spanish Peaks,** eroded remnants of a 20-million-year-old volcano. The native Arapaho believed them to be the home of the gods, and they served as guideposts to early travelers. Legends persist about the existence of a treasure of gold in this area, but none has been found. Several miles north of Cucharas Pass is **Cucharas River Recreation Area,** home of Blue Lake, named for its spectacular color.

Numerous geologic features become prominent as the road descends toward Walsenburg. Among them are the **Devil's Stairsteps,** one of a series of erosion-resistant igneous dikes that radiate out like spokes from the Spanish Peaks; **Dakota Wall,** a layer of pressed sandstone thrust vertically from the earth; and **Goemmer Butte,** sometimes called "Sore Thumb Butte," a volcanic plug rising 500 feet from the valley floor. At this point, about 65 miles from Trinidad, is the foothills village of **La Veta** (pop. just over 900), founded in 1862 by Colonel John M. Francisco, who reportedly said after seeing the pretty valley, "This is paradise enough for me."

Continuing east, Colo. 12 joins U.S. 160, which goes by **Lathrop State Park** (© **719/738-2376;** www.parks.state.co.us), the state's oldest state park, with two lakes for boating (no rentals), swimming, and fishing (rainbow trout, channel catfish, tiger muskie, bass, walleye, bluegill, and crappie). There's also a 3-mile paved trail around the lake for hikers and bikers; plus the 2-mile Hogback Trail, a self-guided nature hike (free brochures available at the visitor center). Also available at the visitor center are a list of birds sighted in Lathrop, and the wildflowers found here, with descriptions and blooming times noted. In winter, there's cross-country skiing, ice skating, and ice fishing. There are 100 campsites, about 40 with electric hookups, plus showers and a dump station. Camping costs $12 to $16 per night, and reservations are available for an extra charge of $8 by calling © **800/678-2267** or through the state park website (see above). The park's day-use fee is $5 per vehicle, which is also added to camping fees. Located at the park but managed independently is the 9-hole **Walsenburg Golf Course** (© 719/738-2730; www.thewgc.com), with a fee of $12 for 9 holes and $18 weekdays and $19 weekends for 18 holes.

From the park it's about 2 miles to Walsenburg on U.S. 160, and then just under 40 miles south down I-25 to return to Trinidad.

5 La Junta

81 miles NE of Trinidad, 64 miles E. of Pueblo, 274 miles NW of Amarillo, Texas

Situated in one of Colorado's pockets of fruit growing, this busy little town has several surprises for visitors, including some of the best American Indian art in the country, and a nearby handsome reconstruction of a historic fort.

Once the hunting and fishing grounds of the Arapaho, Cheyenne, and Ute tribes, and visited briefly by Spanish soldiers in the 17th and 18th centuries, this area did not become known to white Americans until Zebulon Pike led his exploratory expedition into the Arkansas River valley in 1806. Trappers and traders followed, creating the Santa Fe Trail, and brothers William and Charles Bent built Bent's Fort in 1833 as a trading post and the first American settlement in the region.

La Junta was founded in 1875 as a railroad camp, and named La Junta—Spanish for "the junction"—on completion of rail links to Pueblo and Trinidad in 1877. The town flourished as a farming and ranching center. Today, it produces a wide variety of fruits, vegetables, and wheat. The population is a bit over 7,500, and the town sits at an elevation of 4,052 feet.

ESSENTIALS

GETTING THERE   By Car   La Junta is easily reached via U.S. 50, which comes into town from Kansas in the east, and continues west to I-25 at Pueblo. From New Mexico, exit I-25 at Trinidad and take U.S. 350; from Durango and southwestern Colorado, take U.S. 160 to Walsenburg, and continue on Colo. 10 to La Junta.

By Train   Passenger service is available aboard **Amtrak** (© 800/872-7245; www.amtrak.com), with a depot on First Street at Colorado Avenue. The Southwest Chief passes through twice daily (once in each direction) on the main line between Chicago and Los Angeles.

VISITOR INFORMATION   Contact the **La Junta Chamber of Commerce,** 110 Santa Fe Ave., La Junta, CO 81050 (© 719/384-7411; www.lajuntachamber.com).

GETTING AROUND   La Junta is located on the Arkansas River, and U.S. 50, which runs through town as First Street, follows the river's south bank. Highways from Trinidad and Walsenburg join it just west of town. The downtown core focuses on First, Second, and Third streets, crossed by north-south Colorado and Santa Fe avenues. At the east edge of town, Colo. 109 (Adams Ave.) crosses the Arkansas into north La Junta (where it becomes Main St.); 6 blocks past the river, Colo. 194 (Trail Rd.) forks to the right and leads 5 miles to Bent's Old Fort.

Auto rentals are available from **Enterprise** (© 800/261-7331 or 719/384-4888).

FAST FACTS   Health services are provided by the **Arkansas Valley Regional Medical Center,** 1100 Carson Ave. at 10th Street (© 719/384-5412), which has a 24-hour emergency room. The **post office** is located at 324 Colorado Ave. (at Fourth

St.); contact the U.S. Postal Service (© **800/275-8777;** www.usps.com) for hours and other information.

SPECIAL EVENTS   Santa Fe Trail Caravan, May; Kid's Rodeo, early August; Early Settlers Day, Saturday after Labor Day; Santa Fe Trail Encampment, at Bent's Old Fort, October; Traditional Holiday Celebration, at Bent's Old Fort, early December.

WHAT TO SEE & DO

To see a number of buildings from the late 1800s and early 1900s that are listed on the National Register of Historic Places, take the self-guided Historic Homes of La Junta walking/driving tour, described in a free packet available from the La Junta Chamber of Commerce (see "Visitor Information," above).

Bent's Old Fort National Historic Site ⟨⟨⟨   Once the most important settlement on the Santa Fe Trail between Missouri and New Mexico, Bent's Old Fort has been reconstructed as it was during its reign as a major trading post from 1833 to 1849. Located 7 miles east of modern La Junta, this adobe fort on the Arkansas River was built by brothers Charles and William Bent and partner Ceran St. Vrain. It was the hub of trade for eastern U.S. merchants, Rocky Mountain fur trappers, and plains tribes (mainly Cheyenne, but also Arapaho, Ute, Apache, Kiowa, and Comanche).

As American settlement increased, driving off the buffalo that were the lifeblood of the tribes, the Bents were caught between two cultures. Serious hostilities began in 1847, and trade rapidly declined during a cholera epidemic in 1849. Part of the fort burned that year, and was not rebuilt until modern times. Reproductions furnish the 33 rooms, which include a kitchen with adjoining pantry, a cook's room, and a dining room; a trade room with robes, pelts, and blankets; blacksmith and carpenter shops; William Bent's office and bedroom; quarters for Mexican laborers, trappers, and soldiers; a billiards room; and the quarters of a merchant's wife (who kept a meticulous diary).

It's a quarter-mile walk on a paved path from the historic site's entry station to the fort itself, where hosts in period costume greet visitors during the summer. You'll see demonstrations of frontier life, such as blacksmithing, adobe making, trapping, cooking, and medical and survival skills. You can tour the fort on your own or take a guided tour. Tours are offered twice daily from September through May and more frequently in summer; call for the current times. A 20-minute film on the fort is shown year-round. There's also a gift and bookshop. Allow 1 to 4 hours.

35110 Colo. 194 E. © **719/383-5010.** www.nps.gov/beol. Admission (including optional guided tour) $3 adults, $2 children 6–12, free for children under 6. June–Aug daily 8am–5:30pm; Sept–May daily 9am–4pm. Closed Thanksgiving, Christmas, and New Year's Day.

Koshare Indian Museum and Kiva ⟨⟨⟨   American Indian art—featuring Pueblo and plains tribal members both as artists and subjects—is the focus of this excellent museum, which gets our vote as a must-see for anyone even remotely interested in the arts and crafts of American Indians and art depicting the American West. On display are authentic American Indian clothing, jewelry, pottery, and baskets. There are also Western paintings and sculptures, including one of the finest collections of works by early Taos, New Mexico, artists we've seen—watch for the painting *Relics of His Ancestors,* considered one of the best works by Bert Phillips, one of the founding artists of the Taos art colony in 1898. In operation since 1949, the museum is housed in an adobe-style building resembling a northern New Mexico pueblo.

In Search of Dinosaur Tracks

Dinosaur tracks from the Jurassic period, about 150 million years ago, are a highlight of the **Comanche National Grassland,** and more than 1,300 prints in about 100 separate track ways makes this the largest known dinosaur track site in North America. The grassland, a 442,000-acre area south of La Junta, also draws bird-watchers, hunters, anglers, and hikers. Access to Picket Wire Canyonlands, where the dinosaur tracks are located, is limited to those hiking or on mountain bikes or horseback, and by taking a guided tour.

The tracks are believed to be from dinosaurs in the Sauropodmorpha "lizard feet" and Theropoda "beast feet" families, who lived here when the area was a savanna—a tropical grassland with a few scattered trees. There was plenty of food for the sauropods, who were plant eaters, making them all the more tempting to their enemies, the meat-eating theropods. The sauropods, particularly the brontosaurus, grew to about 14 feet tall and weighed up to 33 tons. Theropods grew up to 16 feet tall, but were not as long, and generally weighed much less. Still, with their sharp claws, they would attack the sauropods whenever given the chance.

You can see the dinosaur tracks on your own on a strenuous hike or ride by mountain bike or horse—gets maps and other details from the Comanche National Grassland office (see below)—but the best way to see the dinosaur tracks is on a U.S. Forest Service guided tour. The tours, which are scheduled by appointment Saturday in May, June, September, and October, cost $15 for adults and $7.50 for children, and those taking the tours need to provide their own high-clearance four-wheel-drive vehicle. Information is available from the **Comanche National Grassland office,** 1420 E. Third St., La Junta, CO 81050 (© **719/384-2181;** www.fs.fed.us/r2/psicc/coma). Also contact the office for information on other attractions in the grasslands, including its wildlife—such as the threatened lesser prairie chicken—and rock art that's hundreds of years old.

The Koshare Dancers, a nationally acclaimed troop of Boy Scouts, have been honing their dancing skills since 1933. They perform an average of 60 times a year, primarily in their own great kiva, a circular chamber traditionally used for religious rites by Southwestern tribes. Dances are held frequently in summer (call or check the website for the current schedule), and the Koshare Winter Ceremonials are a December tradition. Allow at least 2 hours for a museum visit, longer for a museum visit and to see the dances.

Otero Junior College, 115 W. 18th St. © **800/693-5482** or 719/384-4411. www.koshare.org. Museum admission $4 adults, $3 seniors 55 and older and students 7–17, free for children 6 and under; dance performance & museum admission $8 adults, $5 youths 17 and younger. Mon–Sat 10am–5pm; Sun noon–5pm (until 9pm on dance nights); extended hours during ceremonials. Located 1 block west of Colorado Ave.

Otero Museum One of the more interesting small town museums we've run across, this museum complex—there are several historic buildings—provides a look at what life was like in eastern Colorado between the 1870s and 1940s. Although lighting could be a bit better and exhibits tend to be a bit dusty, there's a good collection here, and anyone who likes old stuff is bound to find something of interest. There's a genuine 1865 Concord stagecoach, an 1880s-type reaper, a well-stocked grocery store from the early 20th century, a fully restored and working windmill, an early 1900s blacksmith shop, a replica of the community's first school, railroad equipment and memorabilia, and items from both world wars plus the Civil War. Being fans of classic cars, we especially like the 1905 Reo Sidewinder, and the 1954 fire engine, purchased by the Rural Fire Department after its formation in 1953. Allow 1½ to 2 hours.

Third and Anderson sts. ⓒ 719/384-7500. www.coloradoplains.com/otero/museum. Free admission, donations welcome. June–Sept Mon–Sat 1–5pm; off-season tours by appointment.

OUTDOOR ACTIVITIES

Among Colorado's newest state parks, **John Martin Reservoir** 🐾🐾🐾, is a delight, a welcome oasis in the plains of southeastern Colorado. The entrance is off C.R. 24 out of Hasty, about 35 miles east of La Junta, although the reservoir stretches along the south side of U.S. 50 for some 10 miles before you reach it. That's just to whet your appetite for the many recreational opportunities that await you.

The park's namesake reservoir is very popular with those who love to windsurf, water-ski, or zip around in personal watercraft. There are three boat ramps, some great fishing, picnic areas scattered about, two campgrounds, plus birding and a little swimming.

On the back side of the dam that forms John Martin Reservoir is the much smaller Lake Hasty, where only small watercraft with electric motors—no gas—are permitted. Lake Hasty also boasts a wheelchair-accessible fishing pier and small swimming area; plus there are several picnic areas and the developed Hasty Campground lies on its north side. This is where you'll find coin-op showers, laundry facilities, and a dump station; and all sites have electric hookups. The many cottonwood and Russian olive trees provide shade and shelter numerous birds—we saw about a dozen turkey vultures resting in a group of trees not far from our campsite—and you'll see cottontail and jack rabbits all over the place. Point Campground is on a peninsula on the north side of the reservoir, with vault toilets, no electricity or water, but stupendous views of the reservoir and surrounding plains. It's closed in winter.

Anglers try for walleye, wiper, large and small mouth bass, crappie, catfish, bluegill, and perch in the main reservoir. Lake Hasty has those plus rainbow and cutthroat trout, and nearby is a fish-cleaning station. A portion of the reservoir is usually closed to all public access from November through mid-March. That's the nesting and brooding season of the threatened piping plover and endangered interior least tern, and the shores of the reservoir are one of their few remaining nesting areas in Colo-rado. The bald eagle also likes to winter here, in the large trees in Hasty Campground, so some of the campsites there are closed from November through March.

A 4.5-mile graveled hiking trail circles Lake Hasty and leads to a Santa Fe Trail Marker overlooking the reservoir. In 2002 a beautiful new visitor center, several restrooms, plus numerous improvements to handicapped access points and camping facilities were completed.

There are 109 electric sites in Hasty Campground and 104 basic sites in the Point. Camping rates are $7 to $16; reservations are available for an extra charge of $8 by calling ⓒ **800/678-2267,** or through the state parks website listed below. Day use costs $5 per vehicle, and campers must pay this in addition to camping fees. From La Junta, take U.S. 50 east for 35 miles, then turn south on C.R. 24 to the park. For information, contact the park office at ℂ **719/829-1801,** or go to **www.parks.state. co.us**.

WHERE TO STAY

Among the national chain motels in La Junta is **Holiday Inn Express,** 27994 U.S. 50 Frontage Rd. La Junta, CO 81050 (ℂ **800/HOLIDAY** or 719/384-2900), with rates from $79 to $99 double. In Las Animas, about 20 miles east of La Junta, there is the **Best Western Bent's Fort Inn,** 10950 E. U.S. 50 (P.O. Box 108), Las Animas, CO 81054 (ℂ **877/236-8738** or 719/456-0011), with rates of $67 to $79 double. Room tax of just over 7% is added to lodging bills.

Mid-Town Motel ℛ *Value*   A great little mom-and-pop motel off the main highway, the Mid-Town offers clean, quiet, and comfortable rooms with good-quality beds and linens, and standard, well-kept bathrooms. Rooms have desks and one or two beds; several have couches or love seats, and the rooms with one bed also have recliners. The friendly staff is an invaluable source of information for area visitors. Free morning coffee is served in the lobby.

215 E. Third St., La Junta, CO 81050. ℂ **719/384-7741.** Fax 719/384-7323. 24 units. $40–$46 double. AE, DC, DISC, MC, V. Pets accepted ($10 per pet fee). *In room:* A/C, TV.

Appendix:
Colorado in Depth

The Rocky Mountains are the backbone of North America, and Colorado is their heart, with more than 50 peaks that soar above 14,000 feet. The Rockies—with their evergreen and aspen forests, racing streams and rivers, and wealth of wildlife—are perfect for recreation year-round, from summer hiking, mountain biking, and rafting, to winter skiing through deep powder snow.

But Colorado isn't just mountains. It's also the wheat and cornfields of the vast eastern prairies, the high plateau country of the west, numerous historic towns and American Indian communities, and the modern, sophisticated cities of the Front Range.

1 The Natural Environment

First-time visitors to Colorado are often awed by the looming wall of the Rocky Mountains, which come into sight from a good 100 miles away, soon after drivers cross the line from Kansas. East of the Rockies, a 5,000-foot peak is considered high—yet Colorado has 1,143 mountains above 10,000 feet, including 54 over 14,000 feet! Highest of all is Mount Elbert at 14,433 feet, southwest of Leadville.

The Rockies were formed some 65 million years ago by pressures that forced hard Precambrian rock to the earth's surface, breaking through and pushing layers of earlier rock up on end. Then millions of years of erosion eliminated the soft surface material, producing the magnificent Rockies of calendar fame.

An almost-perfect rectangle, Colorado measures some 385 miles east to west, and 275 miles north to south. The ridge of the Continental Divide zigzags more or less through the center of the 104,247-square-mile state, eighth largest in the nation.

2 Geography

Colorado's basic topography can be visualized by dividing the state into vertical thirds: The eastern part is plains; the midsection is high mountains; and the western third is mesa land.

That's a broad simplification, of course. The central Rockies, though they cover six times the mountain area of Switzerland, are a series of high ranges running roughly north-south. East of the Continental Divide, the primary river systems are the South Platte, Arkansas, and Rio Grande, all flowing toward the Gulf of Mexico. The westward-flowing Colorado River system dominates the western part of the state, with tributary networks including the Gunnison, Dolores, and Yampa-Green rivers. In most cases, these rivers are not broad bodies of water like the Ohio or Mississippi, but streams heavy with spring and summer snowmelt, which are reduced to mere trickles during much of the year by the demands of farm and ranch irrigation. Besides agricultural use, they provide life-giving water to wildlife and offer wonderful opportunities for rafting and fishing.

The forested mountains are essential to retaining precious water for the lowlands. Eleven national forests comprise 15 million acres, and there are 8 million acres controlled by the Bureau of Land

Management; these are also open for public recreation. Another half million acres are within national parks, monuments, and recreation areas managed by the National Park Service. In addition to all this, Colorado has more than 40 state parks.

Colorado's name, Spanish for "red," derives from the state's red soil and rocks. Some of the sandstone agglomerates have become attractions in their own right, such as Red Rocks Amphitheater west of Denver and the startling Garden of the Gods in Colorado Springs.

3 Colorado Today

Ask any Coloradan what makes the state unique, and the response most likely will be its mountains. It is almost impossible to exaggerate the spectacular beauty here, or the influence it has had on the development and present-day character of the state. Colorado has been a prime tourist destination practically since the day the first pioneers arrived. Particularly in the 19th century, those attracted to this rugged land tended to be independent types—sometimes downright ornery and antisocial—who sought wide-open spaces, untamed wilderness, and plenty of elbow room. Of course, the dream of riches from gold and silver mines helped, too.

These early transplants established the state's image as the domain of rugged individualists—solitary cowboys, prospectors, and others—who just wanted to be left alone. Much of that feeling still survives, and today's Coloradans have a deserved reputation as a feisty, independent lot. Colorado has the distinction of being home to some of the most politically active liberals and conservatives in the country. They don't follow trends; they make them. It's where some of the country's first municipal gay-rights ordinances were passed; yet it's also home to the vanguard of the family values movement: Focus on the Family, one of the most powerful lobbying organizations for the Christian right's political agenda, is based in Colorado Springs.

Somewhat understandably, such a diversity of political perspectives doesn't exactly engender accord. In the early 1990s, the rest of the country got a quick lesson in Colorado-style politics during the controversy surrounding Amendment 2, a state constitutional amendment aimed at prohibiting certain antidiscrimination laws.

Although the successful 1992 ballot measure was vaguely worded, its intent was clear: to eliminate local gay-rights ordinances that Aspen, Boulder, and Denver had passed.

A high-profile nationwide boycott of the state was launched in 1993, and although it scared off some convention business and kept a few tourists away, the end result was a bit of a wash, and the 1992–93 ski season was among the best in the state's history. The boycott was called off when the amendment was declared unconstitutional by the state Supreme Court later that year. The state appealed, but the ruling was upheld by the U.S. Supreme Court in the spring of 1996.

An issue on which almost all Coloradans agree, pretty much regardless of other differences, is the need to control tourism. While the industry's financial benefits to the state are well understood, it's generally acknowledged that if tourism is allowed to grow unchecked, the cost to the state's natural resources will be tremendous.

To that end, town officials in Vail reached an agreement with resort management in 1995 to limit the number of skiers on the mountain and alleviate other aspects of overcrowding in the village. The word from Vail and other high-profile Colorado tourist destinations is that visitors will be given incentives, such as discounts, to visit at off-peak times. Ski area officials also have not ruled out turning away skiers after a set number of passes are sold.

Conflicts between environmentalists and the ski industry came to a head in October 1998, when militant environmental activists set fires at a Vail resort that caused more than $12 million in damage. A group called Earth Liberation Front claimed credit for the arson, although investigators said they could not prove the group was responsible. The organization wanted to halt an expansion project at Vail that it said would harm a potential habitat for the lynx, a threatened member of the cat family that is similar to a bobcat.

Another issue that has wide support across the state is controlling growth. The rugged mountains and scenic beauty that lure tourists and outdoor recreation enthusiasts have also fueled an influx of transplants—a modern version of the gold seekers and pioneers who settled the state. Since 1990, Colorado has gained new residents at the staggering rate of three times the national average.

The challenge for Coloradans in the 21st century is to solve the twin riddles of tourism and growth that are plaguing much of the American West: How do we achieve a balance between preserving a state's unique character and spectacular natural resources for future generations, while still enjoying all it has to offer today?

4 History 101

To explore Colorado today is to step back into its history, from its dinosaur graveyards, impressive stone and mud cities of the Ancestral Puebloans, reminders of the Wild West of Doc Holliday, and elegant Victorian mansions, to today's science and technology. The history of Colorado is a testimony to the human ability to adapt and flourish in a difficult environment.

The earliest people in Colorado are believed to have been nomadic hunters, who arrived some 12,000 to 20,000 years

ago following the tracks of the now-extinct woolly mammoth and bison. Then, about 2,000 years ago, the ancestors of today's Pueblo people arrived, living in shallow caves in the Four Corners area, where the borders of Colorado, Utah, Arizona, and New Mexico meet.

Originally hunters, they gradually learned farming, basket making, pottery making, and the construction of pit houses. Eventually they built complex villages, such as can be seen at Mesa Verde National Park. For some unknown reason,

Dateline

- **12,000 B.C.** First inhabitants of Colorado include Folsom Man.
- **3000 B.C.** Prehistoric farming communities appear.
- **A.D. 1000** Ancestral Puebloan cliff-dweller culture peaks in Four Corners region.
- **Late 1500s** Spanish explore upper Rio Grande Valley, colonize Santa Fe and Taos, New Mexico, and make

forays into what is now southern Colorado.
- **1776** U.S. declares independence from England.
- **1803** The Louisiana Purchase includes most of modern Colorado.
- **1805** The Lewis and Clark expedition sights the Rocky Mountains.
- **1806–07** Captain Zebulon Pike leads first U.S. expedition into the Colorado Rockies.

- **1842–44** Lieutenant John C. Frémont and Kit Carson explore Colorado and the American West.
- **1848** Treaty of Guadalupe-Hidalgo ends the Mexican War, adds American Southwest to the United States.
- **1859** General William Larimer founds Denver. Major gold strikes in nearby Rockies.

continues

possibly drought, they had deserted the area by the end of the 13th century, probably moving southward into present-day New Mexico and Arizona.

EXPLORATION & SETTLEMENT

Spanish colonists, having established settlements at Santa Fe and Taos in the 16th and 17th centuries, didn't immediately find southern Colorado attractive for colonization. Not only was there a lack of financial and military support from the Spanish crown, but the freedom-loving, sometimes-fierce Comanche and Ute also made it clear that they would rather be left alone.

Nevertheless, Spain still held title to southern and western Colorado in 1803, when U.S. President Thomas Jefferson paid $15 million for the vast Louisiana Territory, which included the lion's share of modern Colorado. Two years later the Lewis and Clark expedition passed by, but the first official exploration by the U.S. government occurred when Jefferson sent Capt. Zebulon Pike to the territory. Pikes Peak, Colorado's landmark mountain and a top tourist attraction near Colorado Springs, was named for the explorer.

As the West began to open up in the 1820s, the Santa Fe Trail was established, cutting through Colorado's southeast corner. Bent's Fort was built on the Arkansas River between 1828 and 1832, and the reconstructed fort is a national historic site near La Junta.

Much of eastern Colorado, including what would become Denver and Colorado Springs, was then part of the Kansas Territory. It was populated almost exclusively by plains tribes until 1858, when gold seekers discovered flakes of the precious metal near the junction of Cherry Creek and the South Platte, and the city of Denver was established, named for Kansas governor James Denver.

The Cherry Creek strike was literally a flash in the gold-seeker's pan, but two strikes in the mountains just west of Denver in early 1859 were more significant: Clear Creek, near what would become Idaho Springs, and in a quartz vein at Gregory Gulch, which led to the founding of Central City.

THE TERRITORY

Abraham Lincoln was elected president of the United States in November 1860, and Congress created the Colorado Territory 3 months later. Lincoln's Homestead Act brought much of the public domain into private ownership, and led to the platting of Front Range townships, including Denver.

Controlling the American Indian peoples was a priority of the territorial government. A treaty negotiated in 1851 had guaranteed the entire Pikes Peak region to the nomadic plains tribes, but that was

- **1861** Colorado Territory proclaimed.
- **1863–68** Ute tribe obtains treaties guaranteeing 16 million acres of western Colorado land.
- **1864** Hundreds of Cheyenne and Arapaho killed in Sand Creek Massacre. University of Denver becomes Colorado's first institution of higher education.
- **1876** Colorado becomes 38th state.
- **1877** University of Colorado opens in Boulder.
- **1878** Little Pittsburg silver strike launches Leadville's mining boom, Colorado's greatest.
- **1879** Milk Creek Massacre by Ute warriors leads to tribe's removal to reservations.
- **1890** Sherman Silver Purchase Act boosts price of silver. Gold discovered at Cripple Creek, leading to state's biggest gold rush.
- **1901–07** President Theodore Roosevelt sets aside 16 million acres of national forestland in Colorado.
- **1906** U.S. Mint built in Denver.
- **1915** Rocky Mountain National Park established.
- **1941–45** World War II establishes Colorado as a military center.
- **1947** Aspen's first chairlift begins operation.

made moot by the arrival of settlers in the late 1850s. The Fort Wise Treaty of 1861 exchanged the Pikes Peak territory for 5 million fertile acres of Arkansas Valley land, north of modern La Junta. But when the Arapaho and Cheyenne continued to roam their old hunting grounds, conflict became inevitable. Frequent rumors and rare instances of hostility against settlers led the Colorado cavalry to attack a peaceful settlement of Indians—who were flying Old Glory and a white flag—on November 29, 1864. More than 150 Cheyenne and Arapaho, two-thirds of them women and children, were killed in what has become known as the Sand Creek Massacre.

Vowing revenge, the Cheyenne and Arapaho launched a campaign to drive whites from their ancient hunting grounds. Their biggest triumph was the destruction of the northeast Colorado town of Julesburg in 1865, but the cavalry, bolstered by returning Civil War veterans, managed to force the two tribes onto reservations in Indian Territory, in what is now Oklahoma—a barren area that whites thought they would never want.

STATEHOOD Colorado politicians began pressing for statehood during the Civil War, but it wasn't until August 1, 1876, that Colorado became the 38th state. Occurring less than a month after the United States' 100th birthday, it was natural that Colorado would become known as "the Centennial State."

The state's new constitution gave the vote to blacks, but not to women, despite the strong efforts of the Colorado Women's Suffrage Association. Women finally succeeded in winning the vote in 1893, 3 years after Wyoming became the first state to offer universal suffrage.

At the time of statehood, most of Colorado's vast western region was still occupied by some 3,500 members of a half-dozen Ute tribes. Unlike the plains tribes, their early relations with white explorers and settlers had been peaceful. Chief Ouray, leader of the Uncompahgre Utes, had negotiated treaties in 1863 and 1868 that guaranteed them 16 million acres—most of western Colorado. In 1873, Ouray agreed to sell the United States one-fourth of that acreage in the mineral-rich San Juan Mountains in exchange for hunting rights and $25,000 in annuities.

But a mining boom that began in 1878 led to a flurry of intrusions into Ute territory and stirred up a "Utes Must Go!" sentiment. Two years later the Utes were forced onto small reserves in southwestern Colorado and Utah, and their lands opened to white settlement in 1882.

- **1948–58** Uranium "rush" sweeps western slope.
- **1955** Environmentalists prevent construction of Echo Park Dam in Dinosaur National Monument.
- **1988** Senator Gary Hart, a front-runner for the Democratic presidential nomination, withdraws from the race after a scandal involving a Miami model.
- **1995** The $4.2-billion state-of-the-art Denver

International Airport and $2.16-million Coors Field baseball stadium open. Denver goes sports-crazy with its fourth major professional sports team, the Avalanche, a member of the National Hockey League.
- **1996** The Avalanche win the Stanley Cup, giving Colorado its first championship in any major league.
- **1998** The Denver Broncos win the Super Bowl, defeating

the Green Bay Packers (the defending champs) 31–24. The stunning victory saves the Broncos the indignity of becoming the first team to lose five Super Bowls.
- **1999** The worst school shooting in United States history takes place in suburban Denver when two students open fire inside Columbine High School, killing 13.

continues

THE MINING BOOM Colorado's real mining boom began on April 28, 1878, when August Rische and George Hook hit a vein of silver carbonate 27 feet deep on Fryer Hill in Leadville. Perhaps the strike wouldn't have caused such excitement had not Rische and Hook, 8 days earlier, traded one-third interest in whatever they found for a basket of groceries from storekeeper Horace Tabor, the mayor of Leadville and a sharp businessman. Tabor was well acquainted with the Colorado "law of apex," which said that if an ore-bearing vein surfaced on a man's claim, he could follow it wherever it led, even out of his claim and through the claims of others.

Today the town of Leadville is among the best places to relive the West's mining days.

Although the silver market collapsed in 1893, gold was there to take its place. In the fall of 1890, a cowboy named Bob Womack found gold in Cripple Creek, on the southwestern slope of Pikes Peak, west of Colorado Springs. He sold his claim to Winfield Scott Stratton, a carpenter and amateur geologist, and Stratton's mine earned a tidy profit of $6 million by 1899, when he sold it to an English company for another $11 million. Cripple Creek turned out to be the richest gold field ever discovered, ultimately producing $500 million in gold.

THE MODERN ERA Colorado continued its steady growth in the 1950s, aided by tourism and the federal government. The $200-million U.S. Air Force Academy, which opened to cadets in 1958, is Colorado Springs's top tourist attraction today. There was a brief oil boom in the 1970s, followed by increasing high-tech development and even more tourism.

Weapons plants, which seemed like a good idea when they were constructed during World War II, began to haunt Denver and the state in the 1970s and 1980s. Rocky Mountain Arsenal, originally built to produce chemical weapons, was found to be creating hazardous conditions at home by contaminating the land with deadly chemicals. A massive cleanup was begun in the early 1980s, and the arsenal is now well on its way to accomplishing its goal of converting the 27-square-mile site into a national wildlife refuge.

The story of Rocky Flats, a postwar nuclear-weapons facility spurred on by the Cold War, is not so happy. Massive efforts to find a solution to contamination caused by nuclear waste have been largely unsuccessful. Although state and federal officials announced early in 1996 that they had reached agreement on the means of removing some 14 tons of plutonium, their immediate plan calls for

- **2000** Colorado ski resorts report that the 1999–2000 season was the worst in history due to poor snowfall and potential skiers' fears about Y2K problems.
- **2001** The Avalanche win the Stanley Cup again, beating the New Jersey Devils 3–1.
- **2002** One of the worst wildfire seasons in history hits Colorado, with about 1,000 fires burning some 364,000 acres across the state.

- **2004** Colorado obtains its fourth national park when Great Sand Dunes gains national park status, after getting additional land with help from the Nature Conservancy.
- **2006** T-REX, the biggest road and light-rail project in Denver history, is completed.
- **2006** Despite objections from birders, officials approve a $480,000 project to build

Colorado's largest turbine wind farm in prime raptor habitat in southeast Colorado.

keeping it in Denver until at least the year 2010, and Department of Energy officials don't know what they'll do with it then. In the meantime, plans are under way to build storage containers that will safely hold the plutonium for up to 50 years.

As the state enters the 21st century, thoughts have turned to controlling population growth. With a growth rate of three times the national average—the state grew by 1 million people during the 1990s—residents and government leaders are questioning how this unabated influx of outsiders can continue without causing serious harm to the state's air, water, and general quality of life.

Index

FROMMER'S® CRUISE GUIDES

Alaska Cruises & Ports of Call

Cruises & Ports of Call

European Cruises & Ports of Call

FROMMER'S® NATIONAL PARK GUIDES

Algonquin Provincial Park
Banff & Jasper
Grand Canyon

National Parks of the American West
Rocky Mountain
Yellowstone & Grand Teton

Yosemite and Sequoia & Kings
  Canyon
Zion & Bryce Canyon

FROMMER'S® MEMORABLE WALKS

London
New York

Paris
Rome

San Francisco

FROMMER'S® WITH KIDS GUIDES

Chicago
Hawaii
Las Vegas
London

National Parks
New York City
San Francisco

Toronto
Walt Disney World® & Orlando
Washington, D.C.

SUZY GERSHMAN'S BORN TO SHOP GUIDES

France
Hong Kong, Shanghai & Beijing
Italy

London
New York

Paris
San Francisco

FROMMER'S® IRREVERENT GUIDES

Amsterdam
Boston
Chicago
Las Vegas

London
Los Angeles
Manhattan
Paris

Rome
San Francisco
Walt Disney World®
Washington, D.C.

FROMMER'S® BEST-LOVED DRIVING TOURS

Austria
Britain
California
France

Germany
Ireland
Italy
New England

Northern Italy
Scotland
Spain
Tuscany & Umbria

THE UNOFFICIAL GUIDES®

Adventure Travel in Alaska
Beyond Disney
California with Kids
Central Italy
Chicago
Cruises
Disneyland®
England
Florida
Florida with Kids

Hawaii
Ireland
Las Vegas
London
Maui
Mexico's Best Beach Resorts
Mini Mickey
New Orleans
New York City

Paris
San Francisco
South Florida including Miami &
  the Keys
Walt Disney World®
Walt Disney World® for
  Grown-ups
Walt Disney World® with Kids
Washington, D.C.

SPECIAL-INTEREST TITLES

Athens Past & Present
Best Places to Raise Your Family
Cities Ranked & Rated
500 Places to Take Your Kids Before They Grow Up
Frommer's Best Day Trips from London
Frommer's Best RV & Tent Campgrounds
  in the U.S.A.

Frommer's Exploring America by RV
Frommer's NYC Free & Dirt Cheap
Frommer's Road Atlas Europe
Frommer's Road Atlas Ireland
Great Escapes From NYC Without Wheels
Retirement Places Rated

FROMMER'S® PHRASEFINDER DICTIONARY GUIDES

French

Italian

Spanish

IF YOU BOOK IT, IT SHOULD BE THERE.

Only Travelocity guarantees it will be, or we'll work with our travel partners to make it right, right away. So if you're missing a balcony or anything else you booked, just call us 24/7 1-888-TRAVELOCITY

travelocity

You'll never roam alone